2

EDITION

COUNSELING AND DEVELOPMENT IN A MULTICULTURAL SOCIETY

John A. Axelson

Professor Emeritus
Northern Illinois University

BROOKS/COLE PUBLISHING COMPANY
Pacific Grove, California

 A CLAIREMONT BOOK

I(T)P ™
The trademark ITP is used under license.

Brooks/Cole Publishing Company
A Division of Wadsworth, Inc.

Printed in the United States of America
10   9   8   7   6   5   4   3

Library of Congress Cataloging in Publication Data

Axelson, John A., [date]
    Counseling and development in a multicultural society / John A.
Axelson.
      p.   cm.
    Includes bibliographical references and index.
    ISBN 0-534-19902-X
    1.   Cross-cultural counseling—United States.   2.   Minorities-
—United States—Counseling of.   3.   Counseling—United States.
I.   Title.
BF637.C6A94   1993
158′.3—dc20   92-26095
                                                         CIP

Sponsoring Editor: *Claire Verduin*
Editorial Assistant: *Gay C. Bond*
Production Editor: *Linda Loba*
Manuscript Editor: *Lorraine Anderson*
Permissions Editor: *Mary Kay Hancharick*
Interior Design: *Lisa Berman*
Cover Design and Illustration: *Lisa Berman*
Art Coordinator: *Susan Haberkorn*
Interior Illustration: *Susan Haberkorn*
Typesetting: *Graphic World Inc.*
Cover Printing: *Phoenix Color Corporation*
Printing and Binding: *Arcata Graphics-Fairfield*

TO MY STUDENTS, COLLEAGUES, AND FRIENDS WHO BELIEVE IT IS BETTER TO ASK *SOME* OF THE QUESTIONS THAN TO KNOW *ALL* OF THE ANSWERS.

The United States society has experienced tremendous change over the past three decades, and an approach for the delivery of counseling and human services is needed that moves in harmony with the new social direction. *Counseling and Development in a Multicultural Society* is organized around three basic themes—people, issues, and counseling practices. The interaction of these timeless themes is what constitutes the work of counselors and how they do it. The treatment of each theme is *interdisciplinary* and *intergrative* in order for the reader to gain better understanding of movements in our society and culture and the work of helping professionals. Relevant information is drawn from psychology, sociology, anthropology, education, economics, and other social sciences to form a comprehensive base of knowledge.

Counseling in today's ever-changing society must also be *inclusive:* it can no longer concern itself solely with one class of people or one cultural group. The study of various lifestyles and life experiences and the important issues that people face as they increasingly encounter the culture and changes in the culture is a major objective. The culture is well into a new phase of development, and trends indicate a process wherein various individuals and groups of individuals desire to take charge of their own lives. This movement toward inclusion and expression in the general society is known as cultural pluralism—both a giving and sharing process of all involved participants toward a new kind of unity through diversity.

Thus, this book emphasizes progress toward a better understanding of all clients whom counselors might encounter daily in a multicultural society. It is written in a clear and simple style so that students in various academic majors and at different program levels can readily comprehend the concepts. The content is realistic, factual, practical, and critical of what counselors should know and what they might do to assist individuals toward leading their lives with dignity and respect in the context of those groups and environments with which they identify and through which they can achieve self-actualization. The immediate objective for the reader is the assimilation of knowledge and the formation of attitudes that lead to a more complete view of today's people, today's issues, and today's counseling practices. The ultimate objective is the development of cultural consciousness and global understanding of the client in the helping process.

Counseling and Development in a Multicultural Society is intended as a comprehensive, broad-based text for those who are studying to become or who are human service counselors, elementary and secondary school counselors, college counselors, adult counselors, rehabilitation and mental health counselors, counseling psychologists, and social workers. Teachers will also benefit from the material by better understanding, counseling, and working with their students. Some of the specific courses for which the book may be used include

1. Multicultural and Cross-Cultural Counseling
2. Social and Cultural Foundations
3. Introduction to Counseling
4. Comprehensive Introduction/Orientation to Counseling and Human Services in Today's Society
5. Social and Cultural Issues in the Work of Counselors.

Part One begins by introducing the concepts of culture and multicultural counseling, examines the role of the counselor, and profiles various ethnocultural groups that make up the society. Part Two takes an organized and concrete approach to the presentation of major concerns and issues that most counselors typically encounter with their clients at some time. Part Three offers a concise summary of the major constructs of traditional counseling theories, an introduction to emergent approaches that might be termed *synergetic*, and representative excerpts of counseling sessions that illustrate issues and concerns confronting people today.

This new second edition retains the comprehensive three-part format that encompasses people, issues, and counseling practices. Chapter Two, *The Culture of the Counselor*, was shifted from Part Three to Part One because, like the Profiles of the American People in Part One, it presents a profile of the American counselor. Chapter Five (formerly *Group Relations*) is now titled *Sociopolitical Issues* in order to reflect more accurately the orientation of that chapter.

All chapters have been revised to some extent to stay abreast of today's fast-changing society and culture. Designations, terms, definitions, and concepts have been modified for clarity, meaning, appropriateness, or currentness. For example, many Black Americans now prefer use of the less color-based and more geopolitical "African American," and some North American Eskimos now call themselves "Inuit" (their word for people). And (going back in time), the American Personnel and Guidance Association (APGA)—that was formed in 1952—became the American Association for

Counseling and Development (AACD) in 1983, which in turn became the American Counseling Association (ACA) in 1992. Important demographic statistics throughout the book have also been completely updated and many new references are included so that the reader can be current in the multicultural field. A Name Index is an added feature so the reader can quickly and conveniently locate references to specific authors.

Events and changes in our diverse society and trends in the counseling profession are integrated into the second edition. For example, some of the areas updated, or new topics added, in Parts One and Two include: the resurgence of European values; Hispanic ethnic consciousness; African-American cultural identity; political correctness; new immigration laws; issues of gender gap, pay equity, and comparable worth; posttraumatic stress disorder; DSM III-R; adults living alone, unmarried couples, out-of-ethnic-group marriages; homelessness; concerns of the elderly; and age discrimination. In Part Three, transition toward greater wholeness and inclusiveness is observed in multicultural counseling paradigms; and an emphasis on accountability by counselors for their racial attitudes is noted in cross-cultural approaches.

A student manual designed to accompany this book has been developed in collaboration with Patrick R. McGrath. *Accessing Awareness* contains experiential activities, exercises, resources, and questions that stimulate insights related to the content of the book and that may be carried out individually or in small groups as class exercises.

The general viewpoint and direction for *Counseling and Development in a Multicultural Society* come from a variety of influences and experiences. Some personal influences and experiences have included growing up in a diverse ethnocultural community, living through the Depression and war years, witnessing counterculture and pro-culture movements, and being a part of the counseling profession for over thirty years. Directing a series of Vocational Guidance Institutes under the auspices of the National Alliance of Business, as well as many years of teaching courses and workshops in cross-cultural counseling, multicultural counseling, and basic theory and practice of counseling, brought specific content for the book into focus. The many students in my classes and the people of many different communities who have shared their cultural experiences with me, as I have with them, are the potent force behind this book.

So many people have directly or indirectly participated in the actual formation of the book that it is difficult to single out and list specific individuals. However, I extend special appreciation and gratitude to the following people, who so patiently and professionally gave their time in reviewing the Second Edition and who offered helpful and constructive criticism: Jesse Brinson, University of Nevada at Las Vegas; Anita Jackson, Kent State University; and Holly Stadler, University of Missouri at Kansas City.

Finally, I am very much appreciative of the humanistic working relationship that all the people at Brooks/Cole Publishing Company established with me. Claire Verduin helped give birth to the manuscript through her ongoing personal support, positive encouragement, and open willingness to offer excellent suggestions. I don't know how I could have polished the manuscript without the help of Lorraine Anderson and Linda Loba. My sincere thanks to all of you wonderful people!

John Axelson

CONTENTS

IX

Basic rules w/ culturally
Diverse clients
p. 292

elderly

PART THREE
TODAY'S COUNSELING PRACTICES
333

LIST OF SUMMARY TABLES

appendix A

Guidelines for Providers of Psychological Services to Ethnic, Linguistic, and Culturally Diverse Populations

XIII

TODAY'S SOCIETY

- Culture and Counseling

- The Culture of the Counselor

- Profiles of the American People: Native Americans, Anglo-Saxon Americans, White Ethnic Americans

- Profiles of the American People: Black Americans, Hispanic Americans, Asian Americans

CULTURE AND COUNSELING

The content of this book is oriented not toward any single group or specific groups of people but toward all the people who make up the multicultural society of the United States. It is also comprehensive, in the belief that ideas drawn from diverse social sciences can be integrated at some level with the psychology of counseling.

Chapter 1 introduces the reader to basic concepts and ideas that are relevant to counseling and development in a multicultural society. Culture and environment will be discussed as interactive experiences, and basic dimensions of culture will be specified. The evolution of North American culture will be described and stages of cultural development within U.S. society will be proposed. Counseling and development in a multicultural society will be described and the basic objectives and dimensions of multicultural counseling will be defined. A brief introduction to ethnocultural groups in the United States will be given.

■ CULTURAL DYNAMICS

A theme underlying this book is the role that culture plays in the lives of people and the implications of that role for the helping professions and the helping process. Culture is what has been learned from experiences in the environment and is reflected in the ways of people and their material and nonmaterial accumulations. Sensitivity to the cultural background and experiences of identifiable groups of people is especially important in our diverse U.S. society; and since culture is a product of learning, also important are the cultural impressions that both counselor and client bring to the counseling process.

This book uses a broad concept of culture: any group of people who identify or associate with one another on the basis of some common purpose, need, or similarity of background could constitute a cultural group. Although people often tend to live much as their neighbors do, modern media and mobility also encourage the formation of other kinds of group relatedness. Thus, though the elderly population located in Florida might share a cultural identity rooted in their geographic locale, they most likely also have much in common with other elderly populations in other parts of the nation. Other group identifications that are influenced by culture and environment and that might endure over time and space are likely to be found in ethnic populations, populations of a certain socioeconomic status, and members of the same sex. A group that can be characterized as having a culture base is seen not as a fixed or static entity but as one that is constantly changing in environmental interaction with other groups. However, members of a cultural group tend to reinforce certain attitudes and behaviors in one another, and those become identifiable features that are constant over time and space. Culture might thus be described as the *totality of learned, socially transmitted behavior* of a group that emerges from its members' interpersonal transactions. Since counseling is a process that enables the client to function more effectively as an individual and with other individuals, a major focus of counseling is the relationship that each client has with himself or herself and with others within the context of culture and environment.

▲ DIMENSIONS OF CULTURE

Counselors who are sensitive to cultural dynamics will be able to understand and respond better to the development of clients in counseling. For example, basic social expressions such as *language* (speech, writing, symbols, gestures), *norms* (appropriate/inappropriate behavior), *sanctions* (penalties/rewards), and *values* (collective conceptions of what is desirable/undesirable) tell a great deal about the cultural context of any group of people. Furthermore, culturally responsive counselors might also take into specific consideration where appropriate or important to members of distinct ethnic/racial groups: *family* composition and functions, *gender* identity and roles, *religious* and *spiritual* beliefs and practices, and degree of *ethnic/racial identity* and acculturation. The following discussion further explores and elaborates various cultural dimensions that shape the development of people in a multicultural society.

● CULTURE AS SOCIAL STRUCTURE

Terms such as *social structure, social system,* and *social organization* are often used interchangeably as core concepts to describe culture. Social structure implies the organized representation of culture. The institutions of government, education, religion, family unit, and the political and economic system exemplify and reflect basic culture and cultural patterns.

● CULTURE AS KINSHIP SYSTEMS

A kinship system is a natural, collective, social relationship pattern explaining group life. It especially implies an orderly system of formal and informal rules that govern or determine the relationships formed and the status of individuals within those relationships. Important kinship terminology includes *marriage, parenthood, patriarchal* and *matriarchal lineage, family unit, nuclear family, extended family,* and *blended family.* These and other kinship terms are interrelated, describing a system of people who live in relationship with one another. The commonly used expression *kith and kin*—acquaintances and relatives of common ancestry—sums up this world of intimate relationships.

● CULTURE AS PERSONALITY

Culture can be seen as the "total personality" of a people. This integrated pattern of human behavior includes thought, feeling, speech, and action; it depends on the human capacity for learning and transmitting knowledge to succeeding generations. What is learned is reflected in material objects, social structures, and traditional ideas and their attached values. The culture may be both a product of traditions and a conditioning element for future traditions. However, culture does not exist independently of people; people act to make their own culture, and the cultural environment thus created acts in turn upon people. Only the more obvious features of any group may be observable to outsiders as reflections of the culture. The deep inner layers of personal attitudes, beliefs, values, and feelings of the individuals who constitute a group are less subject to generalization.

Nevertheless, counselors must *cautiously avoid* equating culture and personality. Some social scientists have tended to stress one abstraction or the other. For example, White (1959a, 1959b) has emphasized that culture is the way things were at the start and that it can be observed in basic hierarchic levels of material objects, social structure, and ideology. However, Barnouw (1973) has stated that "personality must have existed before culture came into being" (p. 14). Hsu (1971, 1972) believes that treating culture and personality as separate entities is misleading and that theorizing is best accomplished within the unification found in the discipline of "psychological anthropology"; furthermore, he has suggested that the Chinese word *jen* (one's transactions with other human beings) could be substituted for the word "personality." The danger of treating either culture or personality as if it had concrete, independent reality is that this may tend to obscure the interactive processes that take place between culture and personality. It is best, therefore, for counselors to view "culture" and "personality" as the abstractions they are and ultimately to concentrate on the relationships and processes that might be discovered between them.

● CULTURE AS PSYCHOLOGICAL ADJUSTMENT

Psychological interpretation of culture emphasizes individual relations in the group. Such a conceptual dimension includes processes such as adjustment, coping, need meeting, learning, habit reinforcement, and support systems. Thus culture is seen primarily as a tool—or instrument—for satisfying collective individual needs, for solving problems, for relieving stress, and for adjusting to the external realities of life and to other individuals in the social environment. *Social environment* refers to the group or groups that the individual experiences in space and over time and that condition his or her psychological relationships. In the multiethnic society of the United States, an African American growing up in a predominantly Black community would most likely identify primarily with the Black group experience but would also identify with aspects of other groups as experienced in other social environments. A newly arrived Mexican immigrant would identify primarily with native Mexican culture and secondarily with United States culture. A White ethnic living in a Connecticut bedroom community might identify with both ethnic and mainstream group experiences. The dilution of primary group affiliation without forming other group ties can potentially lead to personal conflict and other psychological issues. Culture, from the psychological point of view, consists of traditional ways of solving problems within the social group, whose members have learned the accepted responses. But the traditional ways of adjusting to the social environment may not be acceptable to both the adult and the younger generations of a group, and conflict and disorientation may prevail until all learn new ways.

● CULTURE AS ETHNIC DIVERSITY

Ethnic group diversity occurs worldwide. Ethnicity derives from geographical places of origin where groups of people who live in close proximity to each other share similar ways of thinking, feeling, and acting that have been reinforced through group association over many generations. What is seen today as worldwide ethnocultural diversity evolved through a five-thousand-year cycle. Throughout most of prehistoric civilization, members of a tribe or clan were alike in race, religion, language, and other cultural components. The growth of cities as a result of stabilized food supplies in an agrarian economy brought specialization of human function and trade with other tribes and clans. Migration and conquest led in time to the development of larger governmental units and multigroup societies. Among the groups brought together, there were frequently one or more groups less powerful than others in the society, and these were often subject to capricious and discriminatory treatment at the hands of the larger and/or more powerful groups. The growth of nations and nationalism has especially spawned minority group situations, and creating unity out of cultural diversity is a major focus for the United States, as it is in many other areas of the world. Third World nations, as they move through a developmental cycle, are likely to encounter cultural conflict and competition with other technical/industrial nations in the transition from "minority" status to that of greater power.

● CULTURE AS SOCIOECONOMIC STATUS

The accumulation of wealth and material objects allows a person more options, opportunities, and freedom; greater leisure time; and eventually greater influence and power over others. A change of economic circumstances also influences a person's social expression, values, and ways of thinking and behaving; thus the interaction between economic advantage and social and personal conditioning can hardly be avoided.

Middle-class status. The language, values, behaviors, lifestyle, and social systems of U.S. society are generally oriented toward the middle-class majority, and it is presumed that the core or mainstream culture reflects that group. The people who constitute that cultural core are the ones who often bear the press for changes and shifts in the economic, political, and social life of the country to include other socioeconomic and culturally diverse groups. The large middle class, in real and practical terms, acts as a kind of buffer between the under classes and the upper classes. It also functions to educate the lower classes and other groups into the society's economic and social practices. It is consumption oriented, thus facilitating the economic system. The people included in the middle class do not want to lose their status to lower-class conditions, and most have little opportunity during their lifetimes to attain the security of upper-class socioeconomic position. Competition, hard work, moral living, certain codes of behavior, and an opportunity for self-expression are core values for most middle-class people. Their interest in these values ranges from ultraconservative to ultraliberal.

Major issues in socioeconomic class relations. Three major issues or problems are involved in the relations between under class and middle-class Americans. First, middle-class Americans may be fearful of losing their core values and will protect those values from what they might perceive to be the influence of homogeneous lower-class values. There is both truth and fallacy in this fear. The reality is that once one has attained a middle-class lifestyle and the opportunities that go with that status, one seldom wants to give it up or may not want to allow room for others. Though there are many weaknesses and problems involved in maintaining middle-class life, most people probably believe in being members of the U.S. mainstream and appreciate the fact that they are. The truth is that many lower-class members already possess, or desire to possess, middle-class values and opportunities.

Second, if the middle-class system does not educate or indoctrinate the lower-class system to middle-class ways, the core values of the middle class will be diluted or adulterated. Again, there is both truth and fallacy involved in this belief. Complete rejection of disadvantaged groups in order to protect core values simply reinforces alienation of a portion of the population. The ingenuity of both groups is necessary in order to determine how to develop valuable resources, both actual and potential, for the benefit of all—a desirable step toward a fusion that is mutually compatible and desirable.

A third issue involves the cultural stereotypes that nonmainstream groups are mostly of the lower socioeconomic level and that different culture-group ways offer nothing for the enrichment of mainstream America. Many members of minority groups do have low incomes and do face serious issues and dilemmas related to their environmental conditions. The fallacy is that they cannot, or should not, provide input to the total cultural experience. The fact is that when people of different groups come together they bring new ideas and new ways of doing things, and the infusion of cultural experiences can improve life for all.

Socioeconomic status and culture. Cutting across diverse groups is the influence of socioeconomic status (that is, power, prestige, and money). Some writers have even suggested that there is a "culture of the poor" that is a result of the characteristics of the poor themselves. Any social pattern, however, that might be attributed to any given group on the basis of lower socioeconomic class level can also be explained as simply a reaction to environmental conditions. It can be presumed that members of lower socioeconomic classes aspire to much of the dominant middle-class value system but cannot attain many of the elements and eventually become frustrated. One result of frustration is a stretched value system with a low degree of commitment to the values. (A stretched value system is one in which desired goals cannot be attained.) Thus expression of values varies among socioeconomic classes, but the differences are rooted in class and not in culture. They are not transmitted from generation to generation, as culture is; they are psychological reactions to oppression in the general society.

▲ SUBCULTURES

Some cultural groups, not necessarily related to socioeconomic level, that cut across diverse categories of major groups can be termed *subcultures.* Members of a subculture participate in the dominant culture, while at the same time engaging in distinctive forms of behavior. Such subcultures could include the drug culture, the gay culture, the college campus culture, and the adolescent culture. Even the environment found in the workplace could constitute a subculture. *Culture,* in this sense, may refer to many ways in which people associate with and are influenced by different groups that exist for a variety of reasons, including as a reaction to the general culture.

▲ THE MEANING OF GROUP LIFE

A cultural system is the process that a group of people have developed for satisfying needs, for solving problems, and for adjusting both to the external environment and to each other. Especially important for counselors is the notion that these responses have been accepted because they have met with success. Important motivational goals for most cultural systems include (1) social relationships: the customary manner of liking and relating with each other; (2) security: freedom from worry; and (3) status: the worth of a person in the eyes of others. The more culture is abstracted from the social system of the group, the more it is conceived as consisting of the ideas and beliefs that have guided traditional ways of solving problems. At whatever level culture is abstracted or defined, the parts of the system are unified by some kind and degree of interdependence, and these internal connections define the limits of and give character to the whole. Thus a cultural system is the gestalt of interrelated parts. It is impossible to define that gestalt comprehensively and precisely from the outside. Beliefs, ideas, and attitudes are often hidden or only implied rather than obvious or explicit. Broad cultural themes—the qualitative content versus quantitative content—may imply basic beliefs that consistently appear in the experiences of a group of people and that are often observable. They may also emerge as dynamic expressions that are integrated and internalized at different levels in the personality of the client as observed in counseling.

■ CULTURAL EVOLUTION

▲ NORTH AMERICAN CULTURE

The culture of North America is scarcely more than a dot on the map of the culture of humankind. The ancestors of the northern and western Europeans who settled North America were for thousands of years among the world's most isolated and backward people. Before the 15th century, these people lived on the bare margins of the civilized world and had little advantage when compared with other civilizations at the time. Of the basic discoveries of human civilization—such things as the wheel, the plough, the use of metals, the calendar, the alphabet, writing and numbering systems, paper, gunpowder, the compass, printing, and the domestication of plants and animals—none, it seems, can be credited to the northern and western Europeans, though earlier inventions and discoveries have been further utilized and developed by Europeans. The base for Western culture flows from Mesopotamia and Egypt through Crete, Greece, Rome, Byzantium, and Islam to Europe and North America. Contributions to human culture have come in the thousands of years past from Asia; and the sophisticated cultures in the New World—those of the Maya, the Aztec, and the Inca—that were superior in many ways to the European cultures of their day are too well known for discussion here.

Where have Europeans been in cultural development and where is the North American culture going? There is no single explanation for why cultures in different areas of the world have had or are having rapid development or why some cultures deteriorate. Race does not seem to correlate with cultural development, and civilizations of mixed ancestry have produced cultural innovations in a kind of "hybrid vigor." Proximity to centers of cultural activity where ideas and inventions spread, and perhaps geographical location, account for initial leadership in cultural development. The availability and use of the energy found in natural resources and sometimes an unusual creative activity that directs focus and interest toward certain ends can also be related to cultural advances. Northern Europe was at a disadvantage in these temporal and spatial factors but, according to some cultural anthropologists, the discovery of the New World and the development of its resources account for the cultural evolution and world leadership that have shifted to Europe and eventually to North America.

▲ EVOLUTIONARY STAGES

Cultural evolution implies some temporal process that is continuous and usually, but not always, accumulative and progressive. In this developmental process, cultural phenomena undergo change, with one form or stage succeeding another. Social scientists who have addressed the topic of cultural evolution include Durkheim (1933), Toonies (1957), Childe (1951), and Steward (1955), and the "neo-evolutionary" theorists, among them Redfield (1941), Service (1962), and White (1959a, 1959b). Another perspective—conflict theory in cultural evolution—has been formulated by Marx and Engels in their *Communist Manifesto* (1848) and by Marx in his *Das Kapital* (1867) and has led to social changes in cultures throughout the world and influenced the lives of millions of people.

The following hypothesis of the process of cultural development is especially pertinent to an industrial/technical society such as that of the United States. The stages proposed take into consideration the psychological and social movements that might occur in a culture and the effects they would have on the quality of life.

1. *Survival: subsistent level of existence.* Members of the culture attend to the need for bare survival; interpersonal cooperation and mutual dependence—especially among kith and kin—are necessary for life. People show fear and respect for the control that the environment and physical forces have over life. Spirit, mind, and body are interconnected with the environment in harmonious, cause-effect ways.

2. *Meeting basic needs: satisfaction of basic economic needs.* Availability of food, clothing, and shelter gives a greater sense of personal determinism. People continue to recognize and respect environmental and spiritual forces and the importance of family and group membership.

3. *Freedom from economic cares: satisfaction of basic economic needs and acquired wants.* (Acquired wants are ones that are learned through experiences.) Emphasis begins to shift in the balance among spirit, mind, and body within the environmental context when one's needs and wants are met. More emphasis is placed on the individual power of mind (brain) and will (motivation) over the environment; the power of natural and spiritual forces and dependence on a group are diminished in significance.

4. *Becoming a self-contained person: overindulgence and satiation of acquired wants.* People can meet their basic needs and acquired wants without having to give much in return to others or can meet them under conditions of detached, impersonal competition (radical individualism). Imbalance and fragmentation may occur in what was a harmonious balance among spirit, mind, and body in interaction with the environment. It is less possible to endure pain, and long-term psychological satisfaction is less likely or pleasure

is only short lived (Kinder, 1990). Preoccupation with accumulating new goods, hoarding capital, and seeking new growth experiences and lifestyles becomes contagious and spreads to others.

5. *Search for meaning and identity: antidote to despair and emptiness in life or life purpose.* The split from both larger culture-identity and immediate group relations drives the search for identity and ideals and the quest to find a group (family substitute?). Feelings of loneliness, mistrust, narcissism, selfishness, boredom, and depression occur and are experienced as problems in everyday living in the areas of family, work, and interpersonal relations (Lasch, 1983, 1984).

6. *Search for remedies: solutions and ways to break out of the condition.* The emergence of self-help groups and individual therapy as accepted agents of socialization to alleviate anxiety becomes legitimated by the society. Lowered national productivity, national purposelessness, and civic disinterest give alarm to political and economic interest groups. Government "crash" programs are instigated to force change and improvement. Even militancy and show of power have often been utilized by nations as means to express the will of the people and the culture. Short-term effects of institutional programs give renewed hope and interest in life until the program and resources run out or interest is diverted to other national needs. If fragmented components of humanness cannot be reconciled, deterioration in individuals and in the culture continues. If transformation takes place, a new balance of the total self in relation to the old self, others, and the environment can give motivation to individual development and stimulus for innovation in the culture (Kinder, 1990; Lasch, 1991; Oldenquist, 1986).

■ COUNSELING AND DEVELOPMENT IN A MULTICULTURAL SOCIETY

In view of the importance of culture in the life of the individual, it is critical for the helping professions to give due consideration to culture in the counseling process. The technical disciplines of counseling, psychotherapy, and other mental-health specialities have experienced great growth in theory building, technique construction, and procedural practices over the last 30 years. However, attention to the culture and environment in which these activities are carried out has lagged far behind. The helping institution is itself a social system that functions within the culture, and as such it is not immune to the same cultural-environmental dynamics that affect nearly all people and groups of people in the society.

▲ THE NEED FOR A MULTICULTURAL EMPHASIS

The United States is well on the way to becoming the first truly universalistic nation, but the psychology of counseling and other mental health disciplines have yet to address seriously the problems and issues involved in the counseling, guidance, and mental-health needs of culturally diverse populations and other emergent groups. Awareness of the complexities of the multicultural society is a key asset for the effective counselor.

There is evidence, however, that educators are responding to the need for greater attention to multicultural issues. Hollis and Wantz (1983, p. 81; 1990, p. 178) found that in 1983, 44 courses, and in 1990, 59 courses in multicultural counseling were added to counselor preparation programs throughout the United States. Ranked by number of new courses added, multicultural counseling courses ranked 1st out of 34 courses in 1990, 6th out of 20 in 1983, and 10th out of 20 in 1980. Other important courses that were added in 1990 and that reflect needs and concerns in today's society and in today's counseling profession included (in rank order)

substance abuse
marriage and family counseling
legal and ethical issues
internship
consultation
career and life planning
human sexuality
supervision
group practicum
women's studies
geriatric counseling

Another indicator of the emerging importance of an aspect of a field is the number of new professional groups formed in response to that felt need. The impact of cultural diversity on counseling and psychotherapy and on mental-health practices is reflected in the creation of organizations such as these:

Association for Multicultural Counseling and Development
Association for Women in Psychology
Association of Black Psychologists
Association of Psychologists for La Raza
Asian/American Psychological Association
Society of Indian Psychologists
National Coalition of Spanish Speaking Mental Health Organizations

▲ WHAT IS MULTICULTURAL COUNSELING?

In some respects all counseling is multicultural, or at least cross-cultural, taking into account infinite counselor-client combinations. Thus, in addition to distinctions of personality characteristics, the cultural similarity or dissimilarity of counselor and client, based on their backgrounds of cultural experiences, are factors in achieving a major goal in counseling: to create a cultural environment wherein two people can communicate with and relate to each other. Most people share some degree of culture in common with the general society. However, many also belong to groups that can be identified by their beliefs, feelings, values, and behaviors; conditioned, for example, by their experiences related to race, ethnicity, sex, generation, religion, socioeconomic status, lifestyle, sexual preference, or region of residence.

Multicultural counseling encompasses all the components of the many different cultural environments in a democratic society, together with the pertinent theories, techniques, and practices of counseling. In this regard, the approach takes into specific consideration the traditional and contemporary backgrounds and environmental experiences of diverse clients and how special needs might be identified and met through the resources of the helping professions.

▲ MULTICULTURAL COUNSELING AND DEVELOPMENT

Since lives and people change, attention is also given in multicultural counseling to developmental aspects. Development is what the human individual could become. The important role for the counselor in harmony with the client is to facilitate movement toward developmental goals. The developmental activity desired in most counseling experiences could be defined by any or all of the following:

· To help the person evolve the possibilities contained in his or her personality
· To help the person draw from his or her natural resources and strengths
· To help make something available or usable that the person needs
· To help the person move from a present position or situation to one providing more opportunity for effective use by the person
· To help something unfold gradually for the person
· To help the person grow and differentiate along lines natural to what the person is or wants to be
· To help the person acquire something that the person needs or wants
· To help the person expand by a process of growth

▲ GOALS AND APPLICATION OF MULTICULTURAL COUNSELING

Pertinent considerations for the role of multicultural counseling in personal and social development include (1) the study of issues that are faced by most of the people in the society and those that are faced by identified groups of people and (2) examination of counseling practices and services for diverse groups. It is important for the counselor to understand and respect useful modes of coping and treatment that are indigenous to specific groups and groups in different environments, the cultural relativity of the adjustment process and what is defined as normal and abnormal, and the world view of different population groups. It is also important for the counselor to carefully examine the appropriateness of counseling practices in cross-cultural situations and how to work more effectively in a multicultural society. To avoid professional encapsulation, it is essential for counselors to review their own cultural bases as well as the cultural bases of their clients; in this regard it is not so much what counselors do that counts, but who they are.

In terms of what counselors do, a culture-based approach requires that the appropriateness of existing counseling theories and practices be discovered in order to meet the personal needs of individuals and the demands placed on individuals by the society and culture. For example, diagnosis and treatment of a middle-class suburbanite who suffers from paranoia and depression, imagining being followed by gangs, may be different from the diagnosis and treatment of a poverty-stricken ghetto-urbanite who also suffers from paranoia and depression and the same fear of being followed by gangs. Though socioeconomic status and place of residence are only two of many categories of cultural influence, they account for many of the experiences that affect the social and personal adjustment or development of nearly all people. Fears that may be nonrational in a middle-class neighborhood might well be reality-based in a poverty-stricken neighborhood. Though the psychological pain and suffering of all people at all socioeconomic levels is similar, their sources may relate to socioeconomic class. For instance, pressures that surface in counseling middle-class populations often include worry about job promotion, perfectionism, feelings of inferiority due to overweight and the related eating disorders of anorexia and bulimia, depression at the thought of getting old, or a sense of meaninglessness in life. Life-threatening situations and daily survival problems are more often encountered in lower socioeconomic populations, among which depression may be a normal reaction to the environment and paranoia may be justified fear. The pains of meeting basic needs are often given attention before emotional pains, and the sufferer may postpone seeking counseling assistance for unattended psychological stress until the need is extreme, manifesting itself in feelings of rejection, anger, not being a part of society, and not having the freedom for options and choices.

▲ DIMENSIONS OF MULTICULTURAL COUNSELING

Multicultural counseling is defined as the interface between counselor and client that takes the personal dynamics of the counselor and client into consideration alongside the emerging, changing, and/or static configurations that might be identified in the cultures of counselor and client. Thus the emphasis for counseling theory and practice is equally placed on the impressions that are found in the *personal* and *social* experiences of both counselor and client.

● MAINSTREAM CULTURE

In U.S. society, counseling takes place in an environment having a basic, pervasive culture along with many adjunct cultures. The energy of mainstream culture comes from the dominant group of people, who give life and direction to the culture and who are in turn influenced and directed by it. The culture and the person interact to create the environmental and personal situations that surround the individual. A person who belongs primarily to the dominant culture may encounter any collection of problems, but the minority-group person will be affected by the special issues of his or her distinctive group situation in addition to the forces that are current in the dominant culture. However, nearly all people face in some way or at some level the issues related to sociopolitical climate, education and achievement, work and career development, and social and personal growth. Human development is also affected by the *quality* of these environments.

● CULTURAL PLURALISM

Multicultural counseling is most closely associated with the concept of cultural pluralism, toward which U.S. society is currently believed to be moving. The goal of a culturally pluralistic society is unity in diversity; the dominant culture benefits from coexistence and interaction with the cultures of adjunct groups. The key factor is the process whereby mainstream U.S. culture is developed through the equal cooperation and fusion of diverse groups. It should be noted that "groups" are defined as any current or future emergent people who are culturally distinguishable from the mainstream. Categories of individuals who collectively constitute groups of people and who may have special concerns and needs and/or seek respect, representation, and development in the society include racial, ethnic, and religious classifications, women, the elderly, single-parent families, the divorced, the handicapped, homosexuals, the poor, and young adults. *A major theme that characterizes these groups of people is the desire to live life in the way that they believe is the best or most natural for them. Whether a culturally pluralistic mode of existence can accommodate diverse groups and also sustain a national entity, of course, remains to be seen* (Schlesinger, 1991). Implicit in this discussion is the need for innovation in counseling theory and practice that is compatible with the pluralistic concept. Thus diversity in counseling is a key dimension. It may be somewhat analogous to dismantling a blueprint and starting over again. Some concepts and practices will be discarded, some modified and readapted, and new ways will be introduced and integrated into the old.

● THE CLIENT IN MULTICULTURAL COUNSELING

Theory in multicultural counseling and psychotherapy is based on cultural movements within an identified group of people. Cultural movements are the changes or shifts in attitudes and behaviors that are considered appropriate for the variety of situations in which the people find themselves. For example, although sexual openness and expression are generally accepted in today's society, persons identifying with certain groups might also adhere to the distinctive attitudes toward sexuality and sexual behaviors that are imposed by their groups. Human beings, beyond the most simple reflexes, are not born with a built-in response system to their daily existence. They adapt to life in the world through learning to organize and interpret experiences. Therefore, before any response to an experience can be made, meaning must be put into the situation. The acquired perceptual meanings become the patterns by which behavior is shaped and the culture is developed. The cultural meanings are passed to other people who are proximal or alike and, in most cases, to succeeding generations. The experience of each generation further modifies the perceptual meanings. What is real in a culture is the system of meanings and interrelationships developed by people concerning their perceptions of life and their experiences in the environment.

Objects of motivation. Basic motivations that might underlie behavior can often be observed in the expressions and attitudes of clients about life, other people, and themselves and their own situations. Important objects of motivation are identified in the following three categories:

1. Social relations: the person's relatedness to others
2. Status: the person's conditions in the eyes of others
3. Security: the person's freedom from worry and anxiety

Ultimately, cultural experiences and personality are linked to become one's identity, which affects one's behavior, and also to become one's sources of correction. Cultural norms, for example, represent a group's basic interpretation of life and hence can also influence an individual's outlook on life. Though observable expressions of these norms may have different direction and content for different groups, the basic objects of motivation address what is important to most human beings. A starting point in working with a client is an assessment of the client's placement with respect to objects of motivation. Table 1-1 gives dichotomous examples of the continua of life views or themes that could prevail for different groups and for individuals in different groups in relation to cultural-environmental conditions and experiences.

Any notion of a universal, static world view attributable to group identity, of course, runs the risk of perpetuating group stereotypes and disregards the infinite variations of views that might exist but that lean toward one of the extremes. However, it may be presumed, for example, that women, African Americans, and other repressed groups might be vulnerable to world views tending toward the left end of the continua. The tendency would be tempered by the person's environment and by the person's ability to choose one view over another. The more one differentiates one's own views from those of the group, the more one is conscious of one's own identity and aware of such differences in others. The person whose identity is based on the abstractions derived mostly from a single group might likely view social relations with other similar people as more important than those with dissimilar people. A statement of this person's views on social relations might sound like this:

"Those people who are similar to me are likely to understand me, like me, and move toward me; I understand, like, and move toward those most similar to myself."

TABLE 1-1	Objects of Motivation and Client Views in Multicultural Counseling.	
Levels of Motivation	*Objects of Motivation and Some Dichotomous Themes*	
	Social Relations	
World:	The world is a hostile, unsociable, closed place.	The world is a friendly, gregarious, open place.
Others:	Most people are un-friendly and avoid per-sonal relationships.	Most people are friendly and can form close per-sonal relationships.
Self:	I dislike and avoid close companionship with cer-tain others.	I like and seek close companionship with most others.
	Status	
World:	The world is a competi-tive place full of prejudice and discrimination, with little opportunity.	The world is a coopera-tive place of freedom, equality, and justice for all, with plenty of opportunity.
Others:	Most people are not treated with equal fairness and respect and their strengths and personal worth go unnoticed by others.	Most people are treated with equal fairness and respect and their strengths and personal worth are recognized by others.
Self:	I don't have much worth and my strengths are un-recognized by others.	I have as much worth as anyone else and my strengths are given recog-nition by others.
	Security	
World:	The world is a harmful place that is unpredictable and full of worry and in-certitude.	The world is a safe place that is predictable and free from worry and in-certitude.
Others:	Most people can't be trusted.	Most people can be trusted.
Self:	I mistrust and am suspi-cious of the motives of others.	I trust and accept the motives of others.

> "Those people who are dissimilar to me are likely to misunderstand me, dislike me, and/or avoid me; I do not understand, like, or seek out those most dissimilar to myself."

Of course, the more ideas one has about who one is, the more constructions one can make about the world and eventually the more accurate will be one's self-perceptions and one's perception of others (Anderson, 1990). Likewise, the more constructs a counselor has about diverse clients, the greater the opportunity for the counselor to sort out those that have valid meaning for the client from those that are inaccurate stereotypes.

Construction of world views. Kelly (1955) has formulated a theory of personality and devised an ingenious approach to determining the personal constructs that clients use in viewing life. These personal constructs determine what and how a person will perceive, learn, remember, think, and act in regard to elements that are encompassed by the construct. If an elderly person has the construct that groups of teenagers are dangerous, he or she will try to avoid them. People will generally tend to revise their constructs toward greater validity, although sometimes a person may cling to a construct despite evidence to the contrary. A personal construct is the way a person sees likenesses and differences from within a group of objects or persons (Powell-Hopson & Hopson, 1990). For example, an elderly person might think that all teenagers who wear black leather jackets are especially mean and inconsiderate, whereas "traditionally" dressed teenagers are kind and considerate. Constructs are also dichotomous and include some characteristics of a population but not others; the teenagers in the example were judged either mean and inconsiderate or kind and considerate based on their attire, whereas a great variety of other elements are, of course, included in the teenage population. Thus constructs include likenesses and differences, are dichotomous, and remain fairly constant unless altered by new experiences.

The goal of Kelly's *fixed-role therapy* is to change constructs that are invalid, too narrow, or too broad in scope and thus to help the client look at the world with a new perspective. His instrument/technique for revealing the personal constructs of an individual is the *Repertory* (or "Rep") test. Briefly, the technique consists of asking clients to name 12 significant people in their lives according to a predesignated listing of relationships such as mother, father, sister, brother, teacher, and boss. These people are then compared in combinations of three by asking, "Among the three people, which two are the most similar?" Identification of personal constructs comes next: the client is asked, "In what way are the two of them alike but different from the third?" and "How is the remaining person different?" For example, the client might perceive the two similar persons as being cold and distant. From the client's responses, the counselor derives a list of important motivational constructs for viewing the world, and this becomes material for exploration and possible reconstruction.

Application of Kelly's basic procedure has been made by Neimeyer and Fukuyama (1984) with counselor trainees to enable them to identify their cross-cultural attitudes. Their Cultural Attitudes Repertory Technique (CART) proposes a list of designated groups of people who might be perceived as likely to follow certain ethnocultural traditions or who are caught up in culturally imposed roles. The 12 identifiable groups are

Black male	International female
Latin female	Black female
White female	Latin male
Native American male	White male
Asian-American female	Native American female
International male	Asian-American male

The personal constructs that trainees are likely to identify could vary from valid cultural distinctions to stereotypes, depending on prior knowledge and contact. The result is a sampling of how they view various cultural groups.

● THE COUNSELOR IN MULTICULTURAL COUNSELING

Four general categories of questions for the counselor are threaded throughout this book as basic points of awareness for improving counseling in a multicultural society:

1. *Culture-total awareness:* What movements are taking place in the general society and in specific cultural environments?
2. *Self-awareness:* What are your own personal/professional strengths and points for improvement in multicultural counseling? Where are you now?
3. *Client awareness:* What is the internal/external frame of reference through which your client views his or her world?
4. *Counseling procedure awareness:* What goal and which process are most appropriate for your client in his or her situation at this time?

● FOCUSING ON THE CLIENT

A multicultural approach to counseling proposes that clients and their needs are best conceptualized starting with the broad base of human experiences and followed by more discrete distinctions, as illustrated in Figure 1-1. The approach consists of four steps:

1. Recognize the fact that all human beings possess the like capacity for thought, feeling, and behavior.
2. Be knowledgeable in several cultures; study about both differences and similarities among people of different groups and their special needs and problems.
3. Gain an understanding of how the individual relates to important objects of motivation, *what* his or her personal constructs are, and *how* they are constructed to form his or her world view.
4. Blend steps 1, 2, and 3 into an integrated picture of the distinctive person as experienced during the counseling process.

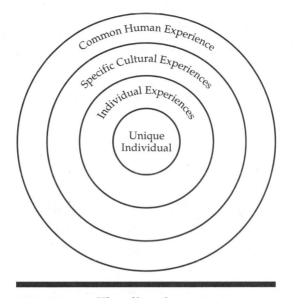

FIGURE 1-1 The client in context.

● THE COUNSELING PROCESS

A process is the means used to help a client reach goals. A bias toward any single theoretical approach will restrict a client to only the context represented in that theory, whereas a multicultural approach aims to generate as broad a base as possible for both counselor and client. A basic decision-making model provides the framework wherein other theoretical models can be used as appropriate. It can be assumed that the dimensions of mutual respect, responsibility and self-discipline, encouragement, appropriate verbal/nonverbal communication, and decision making are consistent with most approaches at some level or emphasis. The following questions are suggested as general guidelines for the counselor and client at various stages in the multicultural counseling process:

1. *Involvement stage* (trust and confidence building). How can I best relate to this client? How does the client want/seek to relate to me? What might she or he expect or want from/of me? What can I do to create a mutually cooperative relationship and a feeling of rapport?

2. *Exploration stage* (guided interaction with events, people, family; past, present, future). What experiences has the client had and what might have been learned from those experiences (self, others, the world)? What does the client need or want at this time in his or her life? Where is he or she now?

3. *Understanding/awareness stage* (working through, insight, struggling, resistance). Who or what works against what is needed or wanted (self, others, situation)? What strengths does the client have that can help get what he or

she needs or wants? What is standing in the way? Should/can it be confronted?

4. *Action/alternative stage* (doing something about self/others/situation). How can the client work to get what is needed or wanted? Does it involve self, others, and/or situation? Is a decision needed? Is an action needed? Can or should the client change/improve a perception, an expectation, attitude, feeling, behavior, skill? Can the client increase, decrease, strengthen, get rid of, get hold of, control, loosen control?

■ COMPOSITION OF OUR MULTICULTURAL SOCIETY

▲ MAJOR ETHNOCULTURAL GROUPS

All people in the United States, even though from different cultural groups, experience some things in common that provide points of reference for cross-cultural understanding: namely, the world, the self, and others. Within a cultural group, these shared dimensions of life make it possible for people to build their distinctive social relationships and group life. Across cultural lines, they also provide counselors with a source from which to develop understanding of and sensitivity toward the beliefs and viewpoints of diverse clients. Personal relationships, for example, are developed through family and kin, neighborhoods and friends, work, and use of spare time. The nature of these structural relationships is derived from basic beliefs about the world, the self, and others that have been developed over years. The cultural group with which one identifies influences one's living, working, and recreational activities; in combination or separately, all contribute to the shaping of group life and personal identity. Thus it is possible for counselors to identify with others on the basis of common social experiences, which provide them with the relationships, status, and security necessary to sustain life at some level.

The diversity of backgrounds represented in the multicultural society of the United States is shown in Table 1-2. The experiences of five major ethnocultural groups and selected other groups of people within those major categories will be described and discussed in Chapters 3 and 4. Knowledge of these groups will promote awareness of the many influences that impinge on the personal culture of the client in counseling.

It should be noted that there are no current *facts* about any population group, since facts are only what has already happened. What can be termed "factual reality" for any group or individual is only what has taken place in the past, whether measured in terms of years, months, days, minutes, or seconds. What is traditional for a group of people or what response an individual might give in counseling can only be determined by the consistency of past responses and expectations or desires for future responses.

▲ WHY STUDY GROUPS OF PEOPLE?

Identifying and understanding the various cultural groups of the United States is not meant to be an end in itself; it is an initial step that will provide counselors with an organized base from which to continue their study of the wide-ranging experiences that their clients bring with them to the counseling relationship. It is also meant as a way for counselors to learn about themselves. Continuing education in the changes, events, experiences, and problems that affect the lives of clients in their distinctive cultures and in the culture at large is emphasized as an ongoing activity.

To understand culturally diverse clients is really to become knowledgeable about all the people who make up U.S. society, because our perceptions are influenced by the actions of others, regardless of whether we are involved directly or indirectly. The decline in popularity of the "melting pot" theory of assimilation and the increase in the concept of American society as a conglomerate of racial and ethnic groups especially emphasize the need to determine crucial points of difference and similarity. It should be noted that in the United States, the term *racial group* is used to distinguish one group from another because of obvious physical differences; Whites, Blacks, and Asian Americans are considered racial groups. An *ethnic group* is identified in the United States by its national origin or distinctive cultural patterns, such as Italians, Puerto Ricans, and Polish Americans. The development of the unique individual and the development of the distinctive group are seen as units that are both interactive (that is, mutually influencing) and reciprocal (that is, mutually receiving). Thus, understanding clients in multicultural counseling is based on the understanding that we have of the uniqueness of each person in the context of that person's group experience. Time dimensions are also involved; thus the development of the ethnic group over historic periods and individual identity associated with these points of group development are also taken into consideration.

Counseling theories and approaches, in general, are based on the vast majority of White middle-class clients. Consequently, there are likely to be elements whose generalization to the experiences of other ethnic groups is inappropriate, distorting the uniqueness of the client and group experiences with which the client most readily identifies. Conceptually and practically, the "fit" may not be congruent with what is most familiar in the client's background of experiences. Basic assessment of the distinctive background of potential client populations is one of the standard first steps in counseling psychology.

TABLE 1-2 Ethnocultural groups in the United States (1990).

White	Black	Hispanic Origin[a]	Asian	Native American	Other	Total
199.6 m	30.0 m	(22.3 m)	7.3 m	2.0 m	9.8 m	= 248.7 m
80.3%	12.1%	(9.0%)	2.9%	0.8%	3.9%	= 100%
+6%[b]	+13%	+53%	+108%	+38%	+45%	+10%

Subgroups:

White	Black	Hispanic Origin	Asian	Native American
Anglo-Saxons		Mexicans	Chinese	American Indians (263 tribes and bands— Navajo Nation is largest)
English	African Americans	Puerto Ricans		
Celtics			Filipinos	
Welsh	West Indians	Cubans		
Scots			Japanese	
N. Ireland Irish	Haitians	Other Central & South Americans	Koreans	Eskimos
Swedes				
Norwegians				Aleuts
Danes		Spaniards	*Indochinese*	
Finns			Vietnamese	
Germans			Cambodians	
Dutch			Lao	
Appala-chians				
			Pacific Islanders	
White Ethnics			Native	
S. & E. Ireland Irish			Hawaiians	
Italians			Guamanians	
Sicilians			Samoans	
Poles			Fijians	
Austrians				
Hungarians				
Czechs			*Asia/Middle*	
Greeks			*East:*	
Portuguese			Indians	
Russians			Arabs	
Yugoslavs			Ethiopians	

(continued)

TABLE 1-2 *(continued)*

White	Black	Hispanic Origin[a]	Asian	Native American	Other	Total
Socioreligious Ethnics Jews, Amish, Mormons			Asia/Middle East: Iranians Egyptians Turks Pakistani			

SOURCES: Data from *Population Profile of the United States: 1980* by U.S. Bureau of the Census, June 1981, and Bureau of the Census *News*, March 11, 1991.

[a]Persons who identified their origin or ancestry as "Spanish/Hispanic" also reported their "race" category (that is, White, Black or Negro, Asian or Pacific Islander, American Indian or Eskimo or Aleut, or other). Thus the Hispanic Origin category represents 9% of the total population (248.7 million), or approximately 22.3 million people.

[b]Approximate increases from 1980 to 1990. Factors accounting for population increases, besides biological, are immigration (accounts for almost 40% of the increase, largely from Asia, Latin America, and the Caribbean), census definitions, and personal changes in racial/ethnic self-identification.

■ SUMMARY

1. Culture and environment were discussed as interactive group phenomena wherein people develop thoughts, actions, and ways of expressing feelings. In this regard, culture was described as the totality of learned behavior of a people that emerges from their interpersonal transactions.

2. Specific dimensions of culture were noted in the structure of a society, kinship/social relationship patterns, personality, modes of psychological adjustment, ethnic diversity, and socioeconomic class differences. Distinction was made between what might be class differences versus cultural differences. The fact that people may also associate or identify with other subcultural groups was pointed out. Culture-oriented counseling is responsive to clients' language, behavioral norms/sanctions, values, family and gender roles, religious/spiritual beliefs, and personal ethnic/racial identity.

3. Some aspects of the historic evolution of worldwide culture were discussed and the influence of cultural development on personal growth was pointed out. Six stages of cultural development were suggested, together with their implications for personality expression.

4. The need for a multicultural emphasis was noted in the increase of course offerings and in the formation of specific professional organizations.

5. The base for multicultural counseling was defined as encompassing concepts, ideas, information, research, and facts that are relevant to the many different cultural environments in a democratic society along with the pertinent theories, techniques, and practices of counseling.

6. The role of multicultural counseling in relation to personal development was indicated.

7. Basic objectives of multicultural counseling were defined as the study
of issues faced by groups of people and an examination of counseling practices
and services for different groups. Emphasis was placed on identification of
client strengths in balance with points for improvement. Awareness of
cultural-environmental experiences in relation to a presenting problem was
also stressed for appropriate diagnosis and treatment.

8. The process of multicultural counseling was further defined as the
ultimate interface between counselor and client that takes into consideration
the personal dynamics of the counselor and client alongside the emerging,
changing, and/or static configuration that might be identified in the cultures
of counselor and client. Important dimensions that were discussed included
the balance between mainstream culture and cultural pluralism, attributes of
clients, and role-awareness and functions of counselors. Basic objects of
motivation for clients were identified as centering on social relations, status,
and security. How both clients and counselors might construct their world
views was also described. A perceptual approach to assessing clients was
touched upon and stages in the counseling process were suggested as general
guidelines.

9. A brief introduction to ethnocultural groups in the United States was
presented. Major categories of groups were identified as White Americans,
Black Americans, Hispanic Americans, Asian Americans, and Native Americans.

CHAPTER

THE CULTURE
OF THE COUNSELOR

Every counselor and other helping professional has two cultures: one professional, the other personal. Experiences in the two dimensions influence the thoughts, feelings, and actions of counselors. Interaction between the two dimensions is what gives identity and focus to counselors and purpose and meaning to their work. Learned professional roles have evolved from the counselor's professional culture and thus may be assumed to represent the state of the counseling art and current counseling technology.

Four major topics are included in this chapter: (1) the background of helping professionals, (2) personal dimensions, (3) selected portions of codes of ethics that are especially related to culture, and (4) the interaction of the culture of the counselor and that of the client as a cultural episode.

■ BACKGROUND OF
HELPING PROFESSIONALS

This section examines the background of helping professionals from the standpoint of educational preparation, employment, counseling orientation, and cultural diversity.

▲ EDUCATIONAL PREPARATION AND EMPLOYMENT

Helping professionals constitute a complex and rapidly growing group of workers. Some of these workers have received graduate degrees in certain

TABLE 2-1 Master's degree graduates in counseling, by title of major and sex, 1990.

Title of Major	Male	Female	Total
Counseling psychology	276	507	783
Marriage and family counseling or therapy	107	207	314
Mental health counseling, agency counseling, community counseling	965	1,939	2,904
Rehabilitation counseling	292	607	899
School counseling	1,310	3,114	4,424
Substance abuse counseling	34	43	77
Total	2,984	6,417	9,401

SOURCE: From *Counselor Preparation 1990–92* by J. W. Hollis and R. A. Wantz, 1990, p. 50. Copyright © 1990 by Accelerated Development. Reprinted by permission.

fields of counseling; Tables 2-1 and 2-2 show 9,401 master's and 664 doctoral degree recipients for 1990. Not shown are the 8,680 bachelor's degrees and 9,391 master's degrees conferred in social work for the period of 1987 to 1988 (U.S. Department of Labor, April 1990).

The 1988 employment numbers and projected employment outlook for the year 2000 are shown for some workers in Table 2-3. The number of counselors employed, for example, is projected to increase by 33,000. The reason underlying this 26.9% increase is that the role of counselors is gradually expanding beyond academic counseling into such areas as family relations and substance abuse; thus, a moderate increase in counseling services, both public and private, can be expected. Human services workers and social workers can also foresee a moderate increase in employment by state and local governments due to the expected growth of public welfare and health agencies, which provide services to the elderly, mentally ill, and developmentally disabled. Table 2-3 also shows that the percentage of female employees exceeds that of male employees.

However, as shown in Tables 2-1 and 2-2, many more women than men also graduate from academic programs for the preparation of helping professionals (a trend that has been observed for a period of years). Women graduates with master's degrees outnumbered men two to one in 1990, while the ratio of female graduates with doctoral degrees to male graduates was approximately three to two. The possible long-term effects of a counseling and human services delivery system in which the diminishing number of male professionals is conspicuous needs the attention and study of the helping professions. We need to better understand why the ratio of men to women is decreasing and how men can be encouraged to enter the counseling

TABLE 2-2 Doctoral degree graduates in counseling, by title of major and sex, 1990.

Title of Major	Male	Female	Total
Agency counseling, correctional counseling, community counseling	8	11	19
Counseling psychology	116	180	296
Counselor education, counseling, guidance, school counseling	124	173	297
Marriage and family counseling or therapy	12	11	23
Rehabilitation counseling	16	13	29
Total	276	388	664

SOURCE: From *Counselor Preparation 1990–92* by J. W. Hollis and R. A. Wantz, 1990, p. 94. Copyright © 1990 by Accelerated Development. Reprinted by permission.

TABLE 2-3 Employment of helping professionals, 1988 and projected 2000 (numbers in thousands).

Occupation	1988	2000	Employment Change 1988 to 2000		Worker Characteristics, 1988 (Percentage of Employees)		
			Number	Percentage	Female	Black	Hispanic
Psychologists	104	132	+28	27.0	55.8	7.8	4.0
Counselors	124	157	+33	26.9	61.8	14.9	4.6
Human services workers	118	171	+53	44.9	NA	NA	NA
Social workers	385	495	+110	28.5	NA	NA	NA
Combined human services workers and social workers	503	666	+163	32.4	66.0	19.3	6.2

SOURCE: Data from *Occupational Projections and Training Data* by the U.S. Department of Labor, Bureau of Labor Statistics, April 1990.
NA = Not available.

profession. We also need to know how such an imbalance affects the aggregate character of the counseling profession and the effectiveness of the counseling process. An analogous concern, of course, is the importance of representation and participation by members of ethnic minority groups in the helping professions and in the counseling process.

▲ COUNSELING ORIENTATIONS

What counselors believe and how they might act on the basis of their world view can be influenced by the philosophical/theoretical orientation they are given in their preparation programs. With experience, many counselors become more eclectic in orientation.

● FACULTY AND STUDENTS

Hollis and Wantz (1983) surveyed the philosophical orientations of faculty members who teach or supervise in counseling preparation programs. An eclectic philosophical orientation far exceeded all other orientations in popularity, followed by Rogerian/client-centered, existential-humanistic, behavioral, and cognitive. The rankings are shown in Table 2-4.

Loesch and McDavis (1978) have developed a 35-item instrument, Counselor-Orientation Scale (COS), for assessing relative preferences for seven major counseling orientations. Field testing was conducted with 294 students enrolled in graduate-level counselor education programs at seven southern universities. The sample had a mean age of 28.4 and consisted of 37% men and 63% women; 86% were White, 13% Black, and 1% Hispanic. The total sample showed greatest preference for the client-centered orientation and least for the behavioral orientation; however, analyzed on the basis of cultural group membership, minority trainees (Black and Hispanic trainees combined) had

TABLE 2-4 Theoretical/philosophical orientations of faculty in counselor preparation programs.

Orientation	Rank
Eclectic	1
Rogerian/client-centered	2
Existential-humanistic	3
Behavioral	4
Cognitive	5
Systems oriented	6
Interpersonal relationship	7
Rational-emotive	8
Gestalt	9
Psychoanalytic	10
Social learning	11
Adlerian	12
Transactional analysis	13
Transpersonal	14
Art therapy	15

SOURCE: Adapted from *Counselor Preparation 1983–85* by J. W. Hollis and R. A. Wantz, p. 12. Copyright © 1983 by Accelerated Development. Adapted by permission.

significantly higher preferences for the rational-emotive, trait-factor, behavioral, and Freudian orientations than did the White trainees. The rankings for the total sample are shown in Table 2-5.

Khan and Cross (1980) also administered the COS to 157 students in counseling courses at 10 Australian universities and—though the means were generally lower for all the theoretical orientations—found the same rankings as did Loesch and McDavis. White (1983), who investigated the construct validity of the COS in his sample of 686 undergraduate students enrolled in human science classes at 11 institutions of higher education in the United States, also found similar rankings, the difference being that Freudian orientation ranked third and existential fourth. In addition, he concluded "that most respondents tended to agree more or less with most items" (p. 146). He suggests that most people may be eclectic in their personal orientations and that divisions among various theoretical/philosophical schools of counseling may not be as real as we believe, although exploration of the important constructs, such as are set forth in the COS, can be a valuable approach to learning.

● PRACTITIONERS

From the evidence showing that faculty in counselor preparation programs tend to favor eclectic, Rogerian/client-centered, and existential-humanistic orientations, and considering that faculty members possess more years of experience than students, one could hypothesize that experience tends to move faculty members toward an eclectic orientation. This tendency could also apply to practitioners of counseling. A tabulation of the theoretical orientations of Illinois registered psychologists who were members of the Illinois Psychological Association (Rosenthal, 1971, pp. 37–39) supports the hypothesis. The rankings for 13 theoretical orientations are shown in Table 2-6. Smith (1982), in his survey of clinical and counseling psychologists, found likewise that 41% of the respondents indicated "eclectic" as their primary theoretical orientation.

TABLE 2-5 Theoretical/philosophical orientations of graduate students enrolled in counselor education programs.

Orientation	Rank
Client-centered	1
Gestalt	2
Existential	3
Freudian	4
Trait-factor	5
Rational-emotive	6
Behavioral	7

SOURCE: From "A Scale for Assessing Counseling-Orientation Preferences" by L. C. Loesch and R. J. McDavis, *Counselor Education and Supervision*, 17 (1978), p. 267.

TABLE 2-6   Theoretical orientations of Illinois registered psychologists who were members of the Illinois Psychological Association.

Orientation	Number of Preferences	Percentage	Rank
Eclectic	193	43.0%	1
Client-centered	45	10.0%	2
Humanistic	41	9.0%	3
Existential	38	8.0%	4
Freudian	35	8.0%	4
Neo-Freudian	32	7.0%	5
Gestalt	20	4.0%	6
Sullivanian	16	3.5%	7
Rational-emotive	14	3.0%	8
Adlerian	11	2.0%	9
Behavioral	5	1.0%	10
Transactional	4	1.0%	10
Jungian	2	.5%	11
Total	456	100.0%	

SOURCE: From *Illinois Psychological Association Directory of Professional Services, 1971–1972*, edited by V. Rosenthal, 1971, pp. 37–39.

▲ CULTURAL DIVERSITY AND THE MENTAL HEALTH PROFESSIONS

Cannon and Locke (1977), citing a 1972 survey by the American Psychological Association, reported that only 396 (1.5%) of the 26,741 APA members and nonmembers who responded to a question on race/ethnicity were Black. According to Smith, Burlew, Mosley, and Whitney (1978), the Association of Black Psychologists has 500 Black psychologists in its contact file. Sue and Chin (1976) have estimated that there were approximately 170 Pacific/Asian-American psychologists in 1976. A survey by Dondero (1973) indicated that in 1971 the seven Los Angeles county mental health regions with 12 percent or more Mexican-American population had only 16 Spanish-surnamed professionals providing direct services to a Mexican-American population of approximately one million or more, and 11 of those professionals were in the East Los Angeles Region.

According to the American Association for Counseling and Development (now the American Counseling Association), out of approximately 58,000 members, 40,871 have reported their race/ethnicity: 90% are Caucasian, 5% are Black, 1.8% are Hispanic, 1% are Asian American, 0.7% are Native American, and 1.4% reported "other." Of the 42,740 members who have reported their gender, approximately two-thirds are female and one-third are male (American Association for Counseling and Development, 1991). Liu and Yu (1985) report that the 1984 ethnic distribution of the 42,460 psychiatrists in the United States was 84.7% White, 4.4% Asian Indian, 3.7% Spanish, 2.2% Filipino, 1.8% Black, 0.4% Puerto Rican, 0.3% Chinese and Japanese, 0.3% Mexican, and 0.2% Native American.

■ PERSONAL DIMENSIONS OF THE PROFESSIONAL COUNSELOR

This section examines the dimensions of self-identity, values, and stereotypes. It presumes that these dimensions are not necessarily static conditions but that they function in relation to the cultural background of counselor and client, and in relation to the environment created by the interaction of counselor and client in the counseling relationship and process.

▲ SELF-IDENTITY

It is often difficult for some White Americans to consider themselves as members of a cultural group. In fact, many are surprised by the realization of their "Whiteness" and a cultural heritage based on European traditions. Identification with the White Anglo-Saxon Protestant (WASP) culture is usually accepted by WASPs themselves as a matter of fact or quiet self-confidence, and without real awareness of the subtle influences on them or of how the culture might be viewed by non-WASPs (Brookhiser, 1991).

Informal classroom experiments by me reveal that White college students enrolled in counseling classes tend to classify themselves (in response to the question "Who, or what, are you?") as an American, a person, an adult, a man or woman, holder of a designated job title, or other general answers, while non-White or White ethnic students may tend to perceive themselves first as members of a race or ethnic group, such as Black, Chinese, Puerto Rican, or Italian. Thus racial/ethnic identity may be more acutely perceived and felt by non-Whites or ethnic Whites than by mainstream Whites. However, when students are asked to respond to what they are *not*, they all tend to respond by identifying ethnicity other than their own. Such open-ended questions asked of anyone often elicit self-evaluation that is indicative of self-concept or of self-esteem.

Self-evaluation in some form or another has been used by thousands of investigators to understand the single dimension of self-concept, but few have studied the dimensions that people actually use in viewing or thinking about themselves. McGuire, McGuire, Child, and Fujioka (1978) have studied self-perceived ethnic identity in what they call "spontaneous self-concept," which is seen as a function of one's ethnic distinctiveness in the social environment. They have found that people may, like an information-processing machine, selectively attend to and encode things that are most distinctive in their social milieu. Distinctive things that can affect our self-concept are (1) what we notice in our own distinctive features, (2) what others perceive in us and respond to, and (3) what views others have of us that we adopt. For example, a Black person in the presence of a group composed mostly of White members might be more aware of his or her Black ethnicity than in a group composed mostly of Black members. Intermixing of people of different ethnicity could thus be assumed to heighten ethnic awareness and feelings of differences. Yang and Bond (1980) have also noted heightened ethnic affirmation by bilingual Chinese students enrolled in psychology classes at Chinese University in Hong Kong: students' answers leaned in a more Chinese direction on a questionnaire printed in English than on the same questionnaire printed in Chinese. The investigators presumed that the Chinese students would have responded in a more Western fashion if they valued the non-Chinese elements in their environment more than the Chinese. The situation seemed to remind these Chinese students of their ethnicity.

The presumption that ethnicity gains or loses prominence in a person's self-concept according to the social context has important implications for the counselor, the client, and the counseling relationship and process. The degree of immersion in any one culture has its drawbacks and its benefits in a multicultural country. Overidentification with the background, traditions, and problems of any cultural group by its members could lead to monotony, narrow-minded ethnocentrism, or cultural encapsulation on the part of the group members. Avoidance of knowledge or recognition of cultural influences could inhibit the counselor's role in the counseling process. It implies unawareness, alienation, or even distrust of beliefs and values that are deeply ingrained in both counselor and client through their experiences in group living and group identification. Artificiality and incongruency on the part of *both* counselor and client are elements that work against the counseling process. From his experiences with the "ethnotherapy" approach to group counseling, Cobbs (1972) has pointed out the following aspects of the relationship between North American Blacks and Whites:

> *All* blacks store abundant memories of how their color negatively influences their life in America. These stored memories contain terrible pain, and as a matter of psychic economy, most blacks suppress them and hold them away from view. My findings also suggest that whites increasingly have their own memory bank about what it's like to be black. But while blacks acquire their memories in confrontations with a hostile, white-dominated society, whites gather their conclusions by observation and generally in the absence of any interaction. What the majority of white people do is to define and describe blacks as the opposite of whites in every way. Having so defined them, they unknowingly measure everything blacks say or do against a white standard rigged to make blacks appear inferior. This comparison is made universally by white Americans. Its universality and its importance belie the myths stating that racial prejudice is inversely related to education, social class, or emotional maturity. (p. 386)

▲ VALUES

The fast-changing technological society and the movement in the society toward a possible multicultural emphasis amplify the need for counselors to understand the role that values play in the motivation of counselor and client in counseling. Many of the issues related to counseling and values involve complex philosophical questions that can be answered only by each counselor according to his or her own awareness.

● THE FUNCTION OF VALUES

The abstract concept of values is a way to explain the purpose behind one's action. Thus values can be defined as the principles or standards that individuals and groups of people use in determining their behavior. Value is the degree of worth or excellence that human beings assign to an object or draw from an object. For example, on the material level, an individual might prefer tea over coffee or, on the psychological level, the person might desire autonomy over interdependence. Values determine for a person or a social group the relative worth of various goals or ends. People express their values when they do what they feel they ought to do according to their standards.

However, values are not merely a matter of subjective personal desires (the desired), but are also a matter of the objective quality of desire (the desirable). Objects of action that meet human needs acquire value or importance in the minds of people and thus the object itself (tea, coffee, autonomy, interdependence, and so forth) has value. Subjective values are relative to each individual and are more likely based on feelings, while objective values are authoritative and are more likely based on rational judgment. Objective values in the society at large are formally, or structurally, expressed through ethics, codes of morality, laws, and aesthetics. Because individual personalities exist within cultural groups, all members of a particular group do not share all values alike. The value experience for the person, then, is a dynamic relationship between subjective and objective elements. For example, the degree to which an individual values self-respect, love, truth, beauty, or honesty is determined by the interaction of the individual's desires and what is desired by the society or group.

● GROUP VALUES

Group values are the desirable standards that groups of people have developed over time. The experiencing of values and what is valued can be observed directly in the traditions, customs, and ways of the people. All groups have standards of values; otherwise, the world would be a chaotic place with each person doing what he or she desires. Some values are basic, or universal, in the sense that they have provided psychological and spiritual meaning for living in the world and they have probably existed in human groups over hundreds of years. Values also develop as a response to the situation in which a group finds itself. For example, a group that must constantly defend itself against other groups is likely to develop values oriented toward defense of its customs or its territory. The existence of a dominant group in the United States tends to submerge the values of other groups and even to exert pressure on the groups to accept the dominant group's ways. However, desirable values will be shared between groups when each group's values are found to be valuable, practical, or meaningful. Some values may be reinforced, modified, or even discarded during sudden urges of reformation, such as occurred in the 1960s and 1970s. For other values, a time lag may prevail between traditional group practices and environmental reality and some traditions may not be acceptable or useful in a fast-changing society. Under these conditions, values may continue to have potential for fulfillment of human needs and desires, but require new focus in the current society. It is especially important for counselors in the complex multicultural U.S. society to be aware of various group values and mainstream common values, how group values function to determine individual behavior, and the movements and changes taking place in the values of groups and the society. Likewise, the counselor should be aware of the values and the functioning of values in the counseling process itself.

● COUNSELING AND VALUES

The counseling process is an expression of values between counselor and client. It is critical that counselors be aware of and continuously examine their own values, the values of the society, and the value goals that they work toward in the counseling process. The complex interaction between counselor and client is influenced by the counselor's own values on two levels: the values that a counselor brings to the counseling relationship and the goals and means to the goals that the counselor believes are valuable for the client in the counseling process.

Although counselors aim for impartiality in working with all clients, they cannot avoid bringing their values to the counseling relationship. The values of a counselor are derived from both subjective and objective experiences in the environment. Subjective values are what the counselor feels personally are important and valuable (the desired) for meaningful behavior and a good life, while objective values are what the society, the work setting or bureaucracy, and the counseling profession believe are important and valuable (the desirable) for meaningful behavior and the right life. It is impossible to have a view of life that is not value oriented, and the effective counselor, like a social philosopher, questions what life is and what is important for life. This important endeavor ultimately leads to recognition of the interaction between one's subjective values and one's objective values and the eventual interplay between the counselor's values and the client's values in the counseling process. It is significant for counselors to realize that they, like other human beings, are not value-free or value-neutral. In this respect, it is especially important for a counselor to be sensitive to his or her tendency to make value judgments of clients. A value judgment by a counselor is a reaction to a client or the events and objects in the client's life in terms that imply an assessment of their worth (for example, good, bad, beautiful, or desirable) in relation to the counselor's own values or in relation to the values of others rather than in terms of their objective characteristics or in terms of the client's own value system. What is of value to the counselor is not necessarily of value to the client.

Goals in counseling are also determined by the counselor's values. A counselor who claims that he or she has no ultimate goals for the client, that it is the client's prerogative, will impose goals whether the counselor is aware of it or not. Counseling goals and the means (techniques) to reach the goals are implicit or explicit in the counseling theories that a counselor has learned. Thus counselors must be cognizant of the fact that all counseling theories and techniques are manipulative of human behavior. The theories or techniques are neither bad nor good; it is the goals for which they are intended that bring forth the question of values. The ultimate goal that a counselor accepts in counseling is what he or she must be most aware of. For example, at one extreme the counselor may value remediative (adjustive) goals or at the other extreme may value developmental (educative) goals. What the counselor values will shape the goals in counseling. The direction of the influence is what counselors should be most aware of and concerned about. Many counselors and theorists would be in fundamental agreement that the counselor should work for the dignity and worth of the client within the world of others and the client's right to freedom of choice in his or her own existence.

▲ STEREOTYPING AND STEREOTYPES

Stereotyping is the application to others of the *personality theories* that we all personally have about people whom we have met or have experienced in some way at some time. These personal theories of personality consist of our collected beliefs and preconceptions about classes of individuals, groups, or objects. For example, one might tend to believe that a person who wears a certain type of eyeglasses is intellectual and a social bore, or that the "bag ladies" sometimes observed in large cities are generally unintelligent and have no motivation. These stereotypes are the results of stereotyping and are our own implicit theories about personality. Stereotyping and stereotypes are circular and self-reinforcing phenomena: we may ascribe to a single individual the characteristics that we associate with a group of people, or we may extend to a group the characteristics that we attach to a single individual on the basis of a few contacts. A stereotype is not really a prejudice, since prejudice is a special category of belief based on stereotyping. However, a stereotype and a prejudice are the same in that they both contain elements that are false or inaccurate, evoke emotional feeling, and result from routinized habits of judgment and expectations. Stereotyping represents the lack of a fresh appraisal of each encountered phenomenon and essentially can be traced to inaccurate observations due to (1) faulty perceptual functioning involving part/whole relationships and/or (2) inadequate cognitive processes based on lack of knowledge and information.

Today, stereotypes are most generally associated with the group to which a person may state that he or she belongs or with which the person is visibly identified. The stereotype produces a fixed or overly general mental picture, usually representing a *negative* judgment of the group and consequently of the person. Stereotypes tend to be widely shared by members of a given society and must be confronted by any counselor working in a multicultural setting. All persons make use of stereotypes, and once the habit of stereotyping has been adopted, it is very resistant to change. Although a stereotype may contain kernels of truth—a circumstance that probably explains the self-reinforcing nature of the phenomenon—most psychologists tend to view all stereotypes as inaccurate and as usually accompanied by prejudice and dislike or disapproval of the group members. Social cognition theory, however, suggests that not all stereotypes are unfavorable and not all stereotypes are completely inaccurate. It has been implied that a bigot learns to observe and interpret expressive behavior and that people who are unprejudiced are less sensitive to their own identity and the identity of others with whom they deal. Archie Bunker, main character of the popular television series "All in the Family," seems to illustrate this phenomenon: both majority and minority group members were receptive to the frankness of Archie the bigot because of the nature of their conflictual relationships.

● MAJOR CHARACTERISTICS

Among the characteristics of stereotyping and stereotypes are these:

· They are *pervasive* in that most people have their own "pet" personality theories about the characteristics of others.
· They tend to emphasize *differences* when applied to individuals or groups different from oneself but to emphasize *similarities* when applied to individuals or groups similar to oneself.
· They tend to be *negative* when applied to characteristics of individuals and groups different from oneself or one's own group.
· They tend to become *habitual* and *routinized* unless challenged.
· *First impressions* are usually based on stereotypes.
· *New stereotypes* will supplement or supplant existent stereotypes as conditions and experiences in the culture change.
· Stereotyping and stereotypes *impair* the ability to assess others accurately and can readily lead to misinterpretations.

● IMPLICATIONS FOR COUNSELORS

Kluckhohn and Murray (1948) have observed that every person is in certain respects like all other people, like some other people, and like no other person. Thus we are alike as members of the human species, become similar in relation to the various groups with which we associate, and differ due to our distinctive personalities. Counselors are especially concerned with understanding the personality distinctions of their clients. However, "distinct" does not necessarily imply "unique." Approaching a client solely on the basis of his or her uniqueness prohibits any inferences regarding the individual. Counselors who seek to understand the psychological traits of their clients aim to differentiate among individuals when cultural group cues are reduced to a minimum. Becoming accurately sensitive to distinctive *individuals* requires differentiation among individuals in the same *group*. For sensitive understanding of differences, then, it could be said that the goal is to increase the *accuracy* of stereotypes and to decrease faulty stereotypes. A first step is to realize, as common sense and research seem to indicate, that stereotyping and stereotypes are pervasive, habitual, and based on minimal knowledge and facts, and usually single out groups by such traits as ethnicity, race, religion, age, or sex.

If a stereotype provides a means of communicating an image of the social role that members of a cultural group follow, then the more accurate is our stereotype of the social role, the more adequate is our knowledge of those roles. This is not to diminish the importance of understanding individual psychological distinctiveness, but only to concentrate on the "improvement" of stereotyping within the process of counseling individual clients. Accuracy of stereotype depends, in part, on the number of persons in any group we have known. Not infrequently the problem is that the number is often only one, or is so small that predictions are often made without any firsthand experience or knowledge. Such cases lead to the blind use of simplified and overgeneralized concepts. The best general rule to follow might be never to assume anything that is definite or that might seem to rigidly characterize a client's personality or situation. It is best to test out hypotheses rather than to risk the continued use of stereotypes. For example, in Chinese culture the younger generations are expected to treat older adults who have achieved status with passive and silent deference. Applied to specific Chinese clients, knowledge of this custom becomes a stereotype, but it also offers a tentative hypothesis that might be tested for its validity. The first four minutes of contact and the impressions that are received often influence the outcome of a counseling session (Zunin & Zunin, 1972). Learning about the cultural diversity of people means that the counselor must be open to new experiences, including a receptivity to new ideas about the people and the capability of looking at old facts about them in new ways. In the endeavor to build "accurate stereotypes," the counselor aims to test the accuracy of generalizations that he or she has acquired as a result of formal and informal experiences. To have competency in using stereotypes effectively means to realize when one is using biased impressions, to expand awareness, knowledge, and appreciation of the many different kinds of groups, and finally to concentrate on how the client is distinctive in his or her own way.

■ ETHICS OF THE PROFESSIONAL COUNSELOR

Ethics are rules of conduct or moral principles such as those that guide the practices of professional counselors. Most organized professional groups have statements of ethics that have been accepted by common consent and that bind the members together. Ethical standards are especially important in the counseling profession because of the intense involvement with people and the complexities that arise from those interpersonal interactions. Any profession continuously monitors its ethical standards according to conditions in the culture and the technical innovations and practices that are introduced within the speciality itself. Two major professional organizations to which the majority of counselors belong or with which they identify are the American Association for Counseling and Development (AACD), which is now called the American Counseling Association (ACA), and the American Psychological Association (APA). Both organizations have published statements of ethical standards that apply to the counseling profession. Although the majority of the statements have been developed out of the wisdom gained from practice within the dominant or common culture, or from what is relevant to mainstream customs, some apply explicitly to counseling in a multicultural society. The codes also have implications for the relationship between majority and minority groups.

▲ EMPHASIS ON INDIVIDUALITY

The introduction to most codes of ethics usually declares a basic premise underlying the existence of the professional speciality. The Preamble of the AACD's *Ethical Standards* (American Association for Counseling and Development, 1988) states:

> The Association is an educational, scientific, and professional organization whose members are dedicated to the enhancement of the worth, dignity, potential, and uniqueness of each individual and thus to the service of society.

The Preamble of the APA's *Ethical Principles of Psychologists* (American Psychological Association, 1981) states:

> Psychologists respect the dignity and worth of the individual and strive for the preservation and protection of fundamental human rights. They are committed to increasing knowledge of human behavior and of people's understanding of themselves and others and to the utilization of such knowledge for the promotion of human welfare.

Key in these statements is the recognition of and dedication to the development of individuals, which ultimately contributes to a strengthened society. The emphasis is on the importance of individuality and the obligation of counselors to direct their competencies toward that goal in order to ensure the general welfare of a healthy society. The concept of a healthy *multicultural* society is inconspicuous, and there is no reference to other important aspects or values, such as the role of the family, group identity, lifestyle, or religious beliefs, which are often viewed as having equal importance by many minority cultural groups and other groups.

▲ RESPONSIBILITY FOR THE RECOGNITION OF MINORITY/MAJORITY CULTURAL EXPERIENCES AND RELATIONS

Any helping profession that is aware of the diversity within American culture also recognizes the problems that exist. Under "Section A: General" of the AACD's *Ethical Standards* (1988), items 8 and 10 state:

> In the counseling relationship the counselor is aware of the intimacy of the relationship and maintains respect for the client and avoids engaging in activities that seek to meet the counselor's personal needs at the expense of the client. . . . Through awareness of the negative impact of both racial and sexual stereotyping and discrimination, the counselor guards the individual rights and personal dignity of the client in the counseling relationship.

In "Principle 3: Moral and Legal Standards" of the APA's *Ethical Principles of Psychologists* (1981), item b states:

> As employees or employers, psychologists do not engage in or condone practices that are inhumane or that result in illegal or unjustifiable actions. Such practices include, but are not limited to, those based on considerations of race, handicap, age, gender, sexual preference, religion, or national origin in hiring, promotion, or training.

Item c states:

> In their professional roles, psychologists avoid any action that will violate or diminish the legal and civil rights of clients or of others who may be affected by their actions.

The American School Counselor Association (ASCA), a division of the ACA, describes in its *Ethical Standards* (American School Counselor Association, 1984) the basic premises and basic tenets in the counseling process:

1. Each person has the right to respect and dignity as a human being and to counseling services without prejudice as to person, character, belief or practice.
2. Each person has the right to self-direction and self-development.
3. Each person has the right of choice and the responsibility for decisions reached.

Knowledge of the constitutional and civil rights of clients and respect for those rights are important in the work of multicultural counselors. Also explicit in the preceding statements is recognition by the profession of the power and influence that counselors wield in helping clients. Inherent in the counseling relationship is the possibility of meeting the counselor's needs rather than the client's. A counselor's unmet needs or deficiency-motivated needs, such as status, security, companionship, or love, could be satisfied through exploitation of the intimate relationship. Although all human beings have those basic psychological needs at varying levels of intensity, a trained and alert counselor is aware of his or her own personality dynamics and does not knowingly seek to use the relationship for personal aggrandizement. The following could be some symptoms of counselor self-aggrandizement in the counseling process:

· Superficial and trivial conversation by both counselor and client
· Lack of client progress
· Unnecessary or prolonged extension of the counseling
· Excessive and inappropriate counselor self-disclosure
· Domination of the client, creating a dependency relationship
· Unusual attraction or attachment to the client
· Social contact between counselor and client

● STEREOTYPING AND DISCRIMINATION

The ethical statements cited exhibit recognition by the profession of the dangers inherent in inaccurate or derogatory stereotypes and discriminatory behavior toward individuals and groups. The statements establish the fact that such conditions do exist in the minds and actions of the general society and potentially could also occur within the counseling process itself. In cross-cultural counseling situations, especially, symptoms could appear that are reflective of stereotyping and discrimination:

· *Patronizing the client.* Patronization in the counseling relationship is the attempt by the counselor to influence or give support to the client from a self-perceived position of superiority. It is based on an attitude of believed superiority and is shown through overt or covert condescension. The act of condescension often appears when a counselor intervenes for a client, or on behalf of a client, who has the capacity to do it alone. It may display itself when a counselor jumps to conclusions about a client's supposed competencies, problems, or personal attributes on the basis of exaggerated beliefs about the cultural group with which the client is identified (stereotyping). Patronization stems from an overconcentration on the client's weaknesses, or perceptual distortion of the client, with the resulting inattention to the strengths of the client. It is also evidenced when the counselor is too ready to give information, answer questions, or solve problems that clients, with encouragement and assistance, could find out or could analyze for themselves. The dividing line between genuinely wanting to help clients and acting on inaccurate stereotypical beliefs that clients are unable, unmotivated, "can't understand," or are otherwise subordinated, is often thin. The most extreme patronization is pitying or dominating the client. The deceptive reward of playing the patronizing role is the subtle feeling in oneself of power, superiority, status, and control. Concentrated focus on the client's undesirable situation and helping the client to develop personal resources in coping with it will lessen behavioral tendencies toward patronization and ultimately diminish the need for a superior-inferior relationship.

· *Insensitivity to the client's individuality.* Overgeneralization (inaccurate stereotyping) of the client's cultural background can lead to misperception of the client's distinctive personality dynamics and characteristics. Forming an opinion, or prejudging *(prejudice)*, of a client based on sight or on the client's membership in a particular group can result from false or mistaken beliefs about the group as a whole. Sincere exploration in an accepting and mutually shared relationship is necessary before the interaction between the client's individual personality and cultural forces can be fully comprehended.

· *Incomprehension of the client's verbal content.* Inability to relate to, or "feel for," the content of the client's story can often be attributed to lack of knowledge of the cultural conditions within which the client lives. Disbelief, amazement, shock, or intense reactive feelings by the counselor are behavioral symptoms often indicative of limited cross-cultural experiences or understanding. Preoccupation with one's own cultural universe distracts a counselor from giving full attention and care to the client. Psychological resistance to understanding is also often due to defensive denial by a counselor because the counseling content touches sensitive issues in the counselor's own life or experiences. When a counselor identifies such internal resistance, it is best to accept the feeling and, outside the counseling interview, discover the basis for the transference through introspection in order to comprehend the attitude or belief that is stimulating the feeling. Inappropriate feelings that interfere with or block full understanding within the counseling process can be partially controlled by striving for open-mindedness and accurate empathy toward the client's situation. Lack of comprehension based on incomplete knowledge of the lifestyle of culturally diverse clients can be overcome in the *immediacy* of the counseling session through honestly inviting the client further to describe or explain life as he or she sees it. One's transparency and willingness to admit ignorance and also one's desire to learn about the client's situation in order to be helpful will further the counseling process. Also helpful is the appropriate sharing of perceptions of common events, such as parenting, sibling relations, schooling, and work. Common events are issues we all face in life, and discussing them will help to increase the awareness of human similarities between counselors and clients who are culturally different.

· *Testing by the client.* Testing of the counselor by the client is another reaction that may emerge if the client perceives the counselor to be condescending, insensitive to the client's individuality, or naive or uninformed about the nature of the client's cultural experiences. It is literally a protest by the client in seeking competent treatment. It is sometimes used to check a counselor out, to see how the counselor handles the testing, and especially to see if the counselor's competence can be trusted. Of course, as in any other counseling situation, many clients could potentially generalize, or act out, their personal difficulties within the counseling relationship. A common psychological defense against personal pain or trouble is to deny its existence, and evasive action by a client will circumvent the pain. Testing is generally uncooperative behavior by the client, as witnessed by the counselor in the counseling process. It may be demonstrated through intellectualization, the telling of farfetched stories, unmeaningful silences, hostility, playing dumb, appearing late for appointments or missing appointments, excuse making, physically pacing around, embarrassing the counselor, or any number of other acts that can discourage or throw the counselor off. The patient counselor who recognizes testing by the client will confront it in an honest, open manner. One useful technique, when nonproductive testing prevails, is to ask clients to summarize how they see the counseling experience and the role of the counselor thus far. *Feedback* between counselor and client in cross-cultural counseling situations is most important to ensure open communication and to resolve "hidden agendas," or misunderstood feelings and thoughts.

Clients, of course, also possess stereotypical beliefs and attitudes toward counselors, especially in a culturally dissimilar relationship. The role of the competent multicultural counselor is to disprove the need or justification for the client to rely on these perceptual defense mechanisms. The excuse of "cultural barriers" should not deter competent counselors from their work. Clients who have had bad experiences in the mainstream culture will especially show distrust and suspicion of professionals, who are often seen as just another authority of the "majority system." Clients whose culture does not emphasize the role of formal helpers or who are reluctant to participate in what may seem like a strange process will benefit from structuring and clarification of the role that counselors perform and the ways that the client can assist in working for a successful counseling outcome.

With all the civil rights laws that prohibit discrimination and with the prevailing attitude of society that discrimination is distasteful and unwanted, it seems difficult to comprehend how discriminatory behavior could exist in counseling or in the counseling profession. However, preferential treatment, based on skin color, ethnic group, sex, age, or religion, has gone "underground" and operates as a subtle, often unconscious, mechanism. Slips of the tongue occur in public conversations and openly discriminatory statements are made in private. Hiring, career advancement and mobility, assignment to school classes, admission to college programs, public facilities, and services, and even choice of which clients to see first, are a few of many instances in which counselors may unknowingly or knowingly influence or give differential treatment based on group membership.

● OTHER FORMS OF DISCRIMINATION

Ironically, attitudes and differential or preferential treatment toward individuals according to their perceived status, roles, titles, or social and economic background are not so subtle. Granting differential treatment according to socioeconomic class rank or prestige of role appears to be generally condoned in American society and to even greater degrees in other societies. Thus, counselors should also be alert to the occurrence of such phenomena in their work with clients in the counseling process.

● PSYCHOSOCIAL ADJUSTMENT PROBLEMS AND COUNSELING

Value objects such as titles and socioeconomic standing are symbolic of the individualistic, competitive, achievement-oriented, and upwardly mobile mainstream people who live within a highly developed and complex technological society that is production-centered. "Success" in the general society is often associated with these value objects. Narrowly confining one's definition of success to possession of such value objects can lead to psychological problems in which one may even question one's personal worth. Feelings of hate, anger, hurt, or depression that are associated with impressions of rejection or worthlessness are often encountered in multicultural counseling. In a multicultural society, minority group members often have to face and overcome the complexities of dealing with perceived lower status, as based on cultural traits or inaccurate stereotypes, in addition to working toward "success" within the established and accepted patterns of the mainstream society in interaction with their own need for personal affirmation. The psychosocial conflicts provoked by perceived or real situations of discrimination and other social pressures need resolution in some way. Coping with psychosocial conflict can take on many forms. These various strategies, all of which could potentially engender or be accompanied by other conflicts, include any of the following, or combinations of the following:

· *Accepting* mainstream conditions, including values, practices, language, and customs, causing suppression or reduction of primary group identity and even personal psychological needs in order to gain success, is one form of coping. It demands adjustment to social conditions, including the existence of prejudice as well as cultural differences, and a sincere trust in the prevailing wisdom of the total society. It calls primarily for a self-seeking and individualistically oriented perspective or attitude that eventually could produce assimilation into the dominant culture, resulting in psychological harmony for the person. Minority groups and the majority group often reject those who succeed through becoming linguistically anglicized or culturally "Americanized." An attitude of ridicule is sometimes epitomized in the derogatory use of verbal labels, such as:

"Oreo Cookie" (assimilated Black, implying White on the inside and Black on the outside)
"Red apple" (assimilated Native American)
"Lemon," "banana" (assimilated Asian)
"Tio Tomas" (Mexican Uncle Tom) or "vendido" (sell-out)
"WASH" (White Anglo-Saxon Hebrew)

· *Compromising with* mainstream "standards" and conditions through harmoniously balancing or blending one's own distinctive culture and one's personal standards with the demands of the society, which may run contrary in varying degrees to one's individual needs or one's primary group identity, is a complex feat. Monitoring one's *personal* self in harmony with one's *social* self, which may include many social roles, is potentially stress-producing. Separating the two selves is often necessary, and maintaining cultural group ties and a personal identity apart from the everyday working world can be a source of psychological support and confirmation of self. The expression "Thank God, it's Friday" is symptomatic of a dichotomous existence for most people; it implies relief from the social behavior required by demands in the mainstream society and an increase in the social behavior that they actually desire. A Black social worker once stated that periodically she had to return to the urban ghetto for a rest from mainstream society. If the compromise can be adequately worked out, it represents taking the best of both worlds.

· *Revolting against* mainstream conditions and seeking to change the standards for acceptable behavior are other coping alternatives. The psychological reaction pattern of resistance and revolt was especially evidenced in the 1960s and 1970s throughout a large segment of the American population, both minority and nonminority, and many social changes came about as a result of this counterculture movement. When a client uses the coping strategy of revolt in reaction to frustration, it is likely to contain feelings of anger, hostility, resentment, and self-righteousness. Counselors are likely to be perceived as "representatives" of the established system that the client opposes, and they should anticipate a heavy transference of emotions. In such situations, the client's high energy level can be used constructively for his or her self-development, as well as for improvement of the undesirable conditions under which the client exists. The client's trust of the counselor and the counselor's acceptance of the client's true feelings are necessary in order to dissipate the emotions directed toward the counselor before a cooperative working relationship can be established. The counselor must guard against susceptibility to reacting with frustration and anger when faced with a frustrated and angry client. A counselor should not allow the client's negative outward behavior to serve as an excuse for reinforcement of the counselor's own hidden cultural prejudices. *Retaliatory hostility* sometimes takes the form of remarks such as these, overheard in both public and private conversations in the general society:

"She's just another angry woman."

"Give them an inch and they'll take a mile."

"If they don't like it here, why don't they go back to Africa?"

"If they stayed in their neighborhood (or barrio), we wouldn't be having these troubles."

· *Withdrawing* into the security of familiar cultural group patterns with which the person most clearly identifies and from which the person can readily gain self-respect is an adaptive mechanism that is often used in minority-majority relationship situations. It is one of the most difficult responses for multicultural counselors to deal with due to the self-reinforcing nature of the situation. What can't be found outside the group can be found inside the group. This principle will apply to membership in any group that satisfies personal needs for security, status, and social relationships, but it is especially evident in gang membership. Overidentification with any one group normally leads to self-development only within the context of that particular group and at the level of human development that the group has attained. *Life apathy,* another form of withdrawal, is giving up on life. It is the feeling in the person that there is nothing in any aspect or level of existence. The symptoms may be grieving or depression due to loss of self-esteem and meaning in life, and the accompanying feeling of nonbeing. Another version of this psychological response expresses the attitude: "If there is no meaning in life except imprisonment and suffering, why respect yourself or others?"

The ethical role of the multicultural counselor in working with culture-conflict problems is to assist the client in finding some suitable place in the society and life according to *where* the client is and *what* the client needs, not where the counselor is or what the counselor conceives is best for the client's "success." It is also important for the counselor to help the client to differentiate *psychodynamic* conflicts from *sociodynamic* conflicts. Psychodynamic conflicts are personal issues that have become internalized within the personality, whereas sociodynamic conflicts are the result of frustration in living in the society. Of course, the two aspects of the person interact and each influences the other, but *all* problems cannot be attributed solely to personality weaknesses, nor can *all* problems be attributed solely to an unfair society.

▲ RESPONSIBLE USE OF ASSESSMENT, MEASUREMENT, AND EVALUATION TECHNIQUES AND DEVICES

Thousands of psychological tests are administered daily in the United States. The decisions and interpretations that are made on the basis of test results are numerous and carry profound implications for those who are tested. Objective fairness and scientific exactness are gained from the *proper* use of appraisal devices. Level of intelligence, aptitude ratings, and achievement scores are of special concern to educators for many reasons, such as placement in special classes, promotion, admission to college, and diagnosis of learning difficulties. Industry and business personnel are also interested in whether or not individuals have special skills that may qualify them for job openings and whether employees can profit from further training or would be good potential candidates for advancement. Personality assessment is engaged in by just about everyone, whether informally or through psychological instruments. Knowledge of individual personality differences is both exciting and provoking in a multicultural society. Again, the implications are grave, for daily decisions are made about others on the basis of assessments: will a worker do a job if requested, can you trust others, do you possess undesirable habits, are you too rigid or too loose, do you complain about physical ailments, do you believe in spirits that communicate to you? The list could go on into infinity.

Because decisions based on individual assessment affect the lives of individuals, and institutional policies based on assessment also affect large groups of people, professional counselors' organizations have developed codes of ethical responsibility related to testing. Testing and test interpretation are an important function in the work of most counselors in one way or another. The ethical use of any measurement device that could potentially affect the personal mobility and development of clients is of utmost importance.

The AACD's *Ethical Standards* (1988), "Section C: Measurement and Evaluation," item 1, states:

> The member must provide specific orientation or information to the examinee(s) prior to and following the test administration so that the results of testing may be placed in proper perspective with other relevant factors. In

so doing, the member must recognize the effects of socioeconomic, ethnic, and cultural factors on test scores. It is the member's professional responsibility to use additional unvalidated information carefully in modifying interpretation of the test results.

The APA's *Ethical Principles of Psychologists* (1981), "Principle 8: Assessment Techniques," item a, states:

In using assessment techniques, psychologists respect the right of clients to have full explanations of the nature and purpose of the techniques in language the client can understand, unless an explicit exception to this right has been agreed upon in advance.

Item c declares:

In reporting assessment results, psychologists indicate any reservations that exist regarding validity or reliability because of the circumstances of the assessment or the inappropriateness of the norms for the person tested. Psychologists strive to ensure that the results of assessments and their interpretations are not misused by others.

Research is often conducted by counselors and psychologists on populations that include culturally diverse or minority subjects. When psychological tests are used in data collection procedures and when attempts are made to interpret or generalize the findings, care is necessary in order to guard against unfounded, incorrect, or misleading conclusions. "Principle 1: Responsibility," item a, in the APA's *Ethical Principles of Psychologists* (1981) states:

As scientists, psychologists accept responsibility for the selection of their research topics and the methods used in investigation, analysis, and reporting. They plan their research in ways to minimize the possibility that their findings will be misleading. They provide thorough discussion of the limitations of their data, especially where their work touches on social policy or might be construed to the detriment of persons in specific age, sex, ethnic, socioeconomic, or other social groups. In publishing reports of their work, they never suppress disconfirming data, and they acknowledge the existence of alternative hypotheses and explanations of their findings. Psychologists take credit only for work they have actually done.

The construction and use of tests and other assessment or measurement devices is a complex problem in a multicultural society: Sundberg (1977) points out that "the measurement of personal characteristics and the interplay between individuals and society—the study of lives—is inevitably intertwined with consequences for the person and his or her environment" (p. 28). There was little understanding of cultural differences when tests and measurements were first established in the early part of the century. Most tests, if not all, are biased toward the culture within which they were developed. If they were culture-free, they would not exist, since a test is an expression of aspects of a culture. Abel (1973) says: "In interpreting a test, the administrator needs to have some awareness of what the test may mean to the subject and how his cultural background may influence his perceptions and his attitudes" (p. 30). Although some objective tests, such as the Stanford-Binet and the Wechsler

Scales for intelligence, have been modified for language or have been standardized for various countries, the equivalence of meaning across cultures cannot be controlled, and it is best to assume that tests are not culture-free and need not be if they truly measure what they scientifically purport to measure. Certain activities and ways of thinking are rewarded and others are punished by cultural groups, and no assessment procedure can be used across cultures with the assumption that it is culture-free or is equally applicable and fair to persons of different cultures (Brislin, Lonner, & Thorndike, 1973).

▲ RESPONSIBILITY FOR MULTICULTURAL KNOWLEDGE AND COMPETENCE IN COUNSELOR TRAINING

The social reforms of the 1960s and 1970s provided the base for a society that would be more open to and inclusive of culturally diverse groups in political, economic, educational, and social areas. However, many of the psychological and sociological forces of oppression continue to function, and this fact is evident as an issue in the training and continuing education of professional counselors as well: "Few counselor education programs currently employ counselor selection and training practices that reflect a human rights orientation to counseling" (Atkinson, 1981, p. 102). The APA's *Ethical Principles of Psychologists* (1981) declares in "Principle 2: Competence" that differences among people should be taken into consideration by informed and competent psychologists:

> Psychologists recognize the need for continuing education and are open to new procedures and changes in expectations and values over time. They recognize differences among people, such as those that may be associated with age, sex, socioeconomic, and ethnic backgrounds. When necessary, they obtain training, experience, or counsel to assure competent service or research relating to such persons.

That it is unethical for those not competent in understanding persons of culturally diverse backgrounds to provide services to such groups was "officially" declared by the Conference Follow-Up Commission of the APA's Vail, Colorado, conference in 1973. It was also declared at that conference that it is unethical to deny such services because the staff is inadequately prepared and that it is the obligation of professional psychologists to gain continuing education to be better prepared to service culturally diverse populations. In 1980, the Education and Training Committee of APA's Division 17, Counseling Psychology, specifically recommended nine competencies that should be included in all training programs. They recommended that the culturally competent counselor have the following competencies:

1. Awareness of his or her own cultural characteristics
2. Awareness of how his or her cultural values and biases may affect minority clients

3. Understanding of the American sociopolitical system in relation to minorities
4. The ability to resolve differences of race and beliefs between the counselor and his or her client
5. The ability to know when a culturally different client should be referred to a counselor of the client's own race or culture
6. Knowledge and information about the particular group of clients with whom the counselor is working
7. Clear and explicit knowledge and understanding of counseling and therapy
8. A wide range of verbal and nonverbal response skills
9. The skill to send and receive both accurate and appropriate verbal and nonverbal messages

The Association for Counselor Education and Supervision, a division of ACA, has prepared "Standards for the Preparation of Counselors and Other Personnel Service Specialists," which contains specific recommendations for counselors working in a multicultural society. "Section 1: Objectives" states that a training program should "reflect the needs in society that are represented by different ethnic and cultural groups served by counselors and other personnel service specialists." Under "Section 2: Curriculum—Program of Studies and Supervised Experiences," a common core of studies is recommended; one of the core topics is social and cultural foundations, which includes "studies of change, ethnic groups, subcultures, changing roles of women, sexism, urban and rural societies, population patterns, cultural mores, use of leisure time, and differing life patterns." The standards also emphasize that ethnic, cultural, and sex factors should be considered when individual appraisal methods are studied, and that the supervised counseling practicum should include individuals and groups from the environments in which the student in counselor education is preparing to work. In a multicultural society, the requirement for counseling practicum would necessitate experiences with the many diverse types of people who make up the nation. The publication further states that faculty in a training institution should make an effort "to select individuals who represent a variety of subcultures and subgroups within our society."

Copeland (1982) has proposed four basic counselor education alternatives that could be introduced into traditional programs to upgrade the competencies of counselors who expect to work in pluralistic settings. Because nearly all counselors in today's society will encounter clients whose backgrounds are different from their own, the suggested alternatives are worthy of consideration for any counselor training program. The four approaches, summarized in Table 2-7, can be used alone or in combination, with each option having certain advantages and disadvantages.

Arredondo (1984) has also emphasized the importance of graduate programs to prepare counselors and other helping professionals in diverse settings to work with language minority populations and populations with

TABLE 2-7 Summary of Approaches to Incorporating Minority Counseling into Counselor Training Programs

	Advantages	*Disadvantages*
Separate course model	1. Assures coverage of topic. 2. Does not require total program evaluation. 3. Is easy to employ individuals with expertise in the area. Adjunct or visiting faculty may be hired if there is no one on the faculty to serve as instructor.	1. Does not require total faculty involvement or commitment. 2. May be viewed as ancillary. 3. May not be required of all students.
Area of concentration model	1. Provides more in-depth study. 2. Offers opportunity for practice with the designated population. 3. Provides experience with diverse groups and allows for the study of similarities and differences in approaches.	1. While this method provides training for those students with an interest in the area, it may not reach some students who will be working with minorities.
Interdisciplinary model	1. Encourages students to take courses in other related disciplines. 2. Provides for broad experiences. 3. Discourages redundancy of course offerings, which allows for total utilization of university resources.	1. May not be utilized by all students in the program.
Integration model	1. Involves evaluation of total program. 2. Involves faculty, students, and practicing professionals.	1. Will not work without faculty commitment. 2. Requires considerable time.

SOURCE: From "Minority Populations and Traditional Counseling Programs: Some Alternatives" by E. J. Copeland, *Counselor Education and Supervision,* 21 (1982), p. 192. Copyright © 1982 by American Association for Counseling and Development. Reprinted by permission.

limited proficiency in English. Major objectives of bilingual counselor training would be as follows:

1. To provide specific knowledge, skills, and competencies relative to the bilingual counseling role
2. To incorporate both English and a second language as media in the clinical practicum
3. To provide extensive field experiences

The basic categories of competencies, skills, and knowledge, as outlined by Arredondo, would include (1) cross-cultural awareness, (2) counseling theory and techniques, (3) assessment and diagnosis, and (4) research skills.

Without question, any counselor working in a multicultural nation is professionally and ethically obligated to be competent with all clients. Paradis (1981) believes that

> ethnicity and culture are important aspects of personal development and that it is the responsibility of all psychotherapists and counselors to develop an awareness of our ethnicity, our cultural biases, and stereotypes of our own and other cultural groups. Without a raised consciousness of and a system for managing our own cultural baggage, we cannot deal effectively with clients of varying cultures. (p. 137)

■ THE CULTURAL EPISODE

This book seeks to describe (1) American society and the experiences and ways of the people in our society; (2) the problems, needs, and issues encountered by people; and finally, (3) the theories and practices of counselors and other human services professionals who seek to help diverse clients. The formal or logical elements of various topics that will be presented and discussed often constitute what could be termed *structural reality.* A structural reality does not always or necessarily coincide with the client's perception. The objective in any one-to-one counseling relationship is to discover what the client conceptualizes, which is *psychological reality.* Both counselor and client bring to counseling their backgrounds of cultural experiences, and, to the extent that everyone possesses a distinct *personal* culture, any counseling relationship may be considered a cultural episode. One priority for the counselor is to have a clear understanding of his or her own personal culture, and a second priority is for the counselor to relate to the personal culture of the client. However, the client's personal culture becomes significant beyond a generalized description of ethnic or other group variations. The counselor is not an ethnographer conducting an ethnographic interview, but directs his or her attention to the client's selected perceptions of experiences in the culture. Though general knowledge of the client's background and group identity may provide clues to the identification of appropriate interventions, it is more productive to use the client as the "informant" of his or her personal culture. Making simple connec-

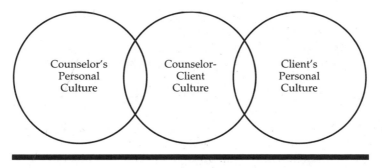

FIGURE 2-1   The cultural episode in multicultural counseling.

tions between generalizations based on the vast resources of cultural information that might be found in the literature of structural reality and client cognition can potentially reduce the client to only a caricature of ethnicity or other group identity.

Personal culture, defined as the knowledge that individuals have learned, cannot be observed directly. It is what clients think, feel, and experience in counseling that will describe their personal experiences in the culture. Both counselor and client make inferences about each other, and each learns to appreciate something about the psychological reality of the other. The existence of alternative realities becomes apparent during the process of counseling and urgent topics can be discovered that indicate the need for change, improvement, or development. The ultimate insights, interpretations, and concerns of clients themselves constitute what is significant. In the interface between counselor and client, the counselor might ask: "*Why* is the client in counseling and *what* happened?" The interaction of personal cultures with particular environments, which results in particular behaviors, is also the major focus of a cultural episode in the counseling process itself. The cultural episode thus defined is the interaction of two personal cultures in which a third cultural environment is momentarily created and shared during the counseling experience, as illustrated in Figure 2-1.

■ SUMMARY

1. This chapter identified some of the important dimensions that constitute the culture of counselors and other helping professionals.

2. Special career categories for helping professionals in which master's and doctoral degrees are being awarded include counseling psychology, marriage and family counseling, mental health counseling, rehabilitation counseling, school counseling, substance abuse counseling, social work, and human services.

3. The faculty in institutions of higher education who prepare helping

professionals appear to favor an eclectic orientation most, followed in popularity by Rogerian/client-centered, existential-humanistic, behavioral, and cognitive orientations. Students tend to favor client-centered, existential-humanistic, and Gestalt. It was noted that an eclectic orientation seems to characterize more experienced professionals. The great need for ethnic group members trained as helping professionals at all educational levels was indicated.

4. Personal dimensions that influence the professional counselor were discussed under the topics of self-identity, values, and stereotyping and stereotypes. These dimensions were defined not as static conditions but as influences operating in the context of the environment that is created with others.

5. Self-identity is the concept that one has of oneself when in the presence of others. For example, one's ethnicity may be felt more when in the presence of others who are different from oneself than when in the presence of others who are similar to oneself.

6. Values are defined as the standards that individuals and groups of people use in determining their behavior. One's values are based on what one desires and what the group defines as desirable. It is important for counselors to be aware of mainstream values and the values of the various groups in the multicultural society. A group's values may be shared with other groups, and group values change over time. Values influence the judgments that counselors make about their clients and the goals that are selected for clients. The implication for the counselor is the danger of imposing his or her values on individual clients.

7. Stereotyping is the process of formulating and applying the pet personality theories that each of us has acquired about the characteristics of other people, and stereotypes are the oversimplified mental pictures that we have of others. They tend to emphasize negative differences when applied to individuals and groups different from ourselves. Stereotypes change or are reinforced with changes in the society. Since stereotypes are based only on partial facts and on first impressions, they impair the ability to assess others accurately. The influence of stereotyping and stereotypes in the counseling relationship and process can be controlled through increasing the accuracy of stereotypes and differentiation of the distinctive characteristics of a client from the characteristics of his or her group.

8. Ethics were defined as rules of conduct or moral principles such as those that guide the practices of professional counselors. Specific passages, primarily those explicitly aimed at counseling in a multicultural society, were selected from the codes of several professional groups. The codes emphasize the importance of individuality and understanding one another. They also consider the following issues:

a. Responsibility for the recognition of minority-majority cultural experiences and relations. Implicit in this code is the belief that helping professionals need to be alert to the practices of stereotyping and discrimination. These practices could be occurring within the counseling session itself when the counselor patronizes the client, is insensitive to the client's individuality, or does not comprehend the client's verbal content, or when the client exhibits unusual testing of the counselor. It was also indicated that psychosocial adjustment problems could be misinterpreted. Various modes of reaction to discrimination could be manifested, such as accepting the conditions, compromising, revolting, and/or withdrawing.

b. Responsible use of assessment, measurement, and evaluation techniques and devices. Important decisions based on tests are made in the lives of clients. In using any testing device or in conducting research using tests, counselors must recognize the effects of socioeconomic, ethnic, and cultural factors on test scores.

c. Responsibility for multicultural knowledge and competence in training programs. It is important to take into consideration the special environmental experiences of clients and the acquiring of cultural competencies. Counselor education programs lag behind in this respect, and upgrading of specific competencies and instituting program alternatives were suggested.

9. Finally, the idea of the cultural episode was presented. The knowledge that can be found in structural reality or in group variations gives important clues to client identity and problem interventions; however, the interaction of counselor and client is composed of the distinct personal cultures of two individuals wherein a third cultural environment is momentarily created, which is psychological reality.

CHAPTER

PROFILES OF THE AMERICAN PEOPLE: NATIVE AMERICANS, ANGLO-SAXON AMERICANS, WHITE ETHNIC AMERICANS

The purpose of Chapters 3 and 4 is to introduce the complex mosaic of cultural groups in the United States. These chapters are not intended to be conclusive nor inclusive of what might be the experience of so many diverse people. Such an endeavor, if it were possible, would necessitate volumes of books written by many different people of different cultural backgrounds. The general objective is a broad survey that provokes a feeling for the United States as a multicultural country and the extension of that impression into the work of the counselor. It is based on the concept of cultural pluralism, which, for most purposes, has yet to be incorporated in any meaningful way into the profession of counseling. Cultural pluralism in counseling, thus, is a concept that *aims* toward a heightened sense of being and wholeness of the entire society. From this, we hope, will come greater comprehension of clients in general.

The many ethnic groups that constitute the pluralistic culture complicate the question of which groups to include in a survey. This chapter and the next discuss the following:

- Groups that constitute the major ethnic minorities in U.S. society
- Subgroups within the major ethnic minorities that differ from each other and from the mainstream culture group
- Groups that constitute mainstream culture or that have been assimilated into the social, political, and economic life of the country at different levels
- Groups that are known by their historic presence in the country
- Groups of people who have been ignored or inaccurately portrayed

Profiles are presented in this chapter for Native Americans, Anglo-Saxon Americans, and White Ethnic Americans; Chapter 4 presents profiles of Black

Americans, Hispanic Americans, and Asian Americans. Assignment of groups to Chapters 3 and 4 was arbitrary, but consideration was given to two variables: (1) time of arrival in North America and (2) assimilation patterns. Chronologically, Black Americans have had numerical presence in American society since precolonial days, but as a historically subjugated group they have experienced less freedom and movement. The same subjugation is true of Native Americans and Hispanic Americans. Hispanic Americans, and Asian Americans in smaller numbers, have also had historic presence in North America for many years.

The profiles presented in Chapters 3 and 4 generally include, where possible, the following information:

· A survey of historic background and origins
· Immigration and settling-in patterns
· Social, political, and economic influences and considerations
· Cultural patterns and influences, including traditional family life, values and beliefs, and interpersonal relationship behavior
· Current transitional experiences in the society

Providing such a broad spectrum of information for so many diverse groups has its limitations. *First*, a profile precludes extensive or in-depth examination of any single group of people. Further exploration through reading and experiential activities is recommended when more awareness is needed. *Second*, individual group members will see their own group and themselves according to their unique perceptions, acquired through their own personal experiences; the same holds true for the perceptions of other groups by nonmembers. *Third*, the study of cultural pluralism is not only complicated by the diversity of groups but also controversial in nature, thus leading to many viewpoints, beliefs, conclusions, and stereotypes. Perhaps it should be noted at this point that "stereotypic perception" is a major avenue through which understanding is communicated. Movement toward the goal of improving understanding and communication in counseling is furthered by conscientiously refining stereotypes of others until they are most congruent with how others (and ultimately each person) see themselves.

■ NATIVE AMERICANS

The first people to settle in the geographical region that we now call North America provided the initial culture base. Thus it is appropriate to begin the story of who the American people are with the original Americans.

"Original Americans," "Native People," "American Indians," "Amerindians," and "Native Americans" are all names applied to the people who first settled in large numbers about 12,000 years ago in what is now North America. Evidence suggests that the first few arrived at least 20,000 years earlier. The name "Indian" is a label mistakenly given to the native people by the early European explorers, who believed that they had arrived in India. What became known as the "Indian problem" in American history basically centered on one issue: land that the European settlers wanted and that the native people had. The problem of land rights continues today, but the most important underlying issue is the right to self-determination.

Most Americans are scarcely aware of who the Native Americans are and the significance of their many tribes. Even the use of the term *Indian* implies the idea that Native Americans are all one people, a grievous insult to the many diverse ethnic groups. There are about 263 distinct nations, tribes, bands, clans, or communities of Native Americans living in the United States today. Although tribalism is diminishing, many tribes are ethnically distinct, some belong to the same family of languages, some speak different dialects, and some are strangers to each other. However, the feeling for loss of their land is common to all Native Americans, and over the years they have made efforts to unite and resist infringement, whether it came from the early White settlers, the United States government and the military, or exploitation by private business enterprise. About 840,000 Native Americans, who spoke about 300 different languages or dialects, were living in what is now the United States at the time of the discovery of America by Europeans, and it is estimated that between 15 and 20 million were living in Latin America. By 1900, four hundred years later, only about 243,000 remained in the United States (Marquis, 1974; Price, 1976). Today, according to the Bureau of the Census (1991b), 2 million Native Americans live in the United States. Price (1976) reports: "In Canada there are some 275,000 'registered' Indians and about an equal number of persons who are not 'registered' but still identify themselves as Indians" (p. 253). Approximately 38% of the Native Americans in the United States live inside reservations and other federally identified areas. According to the 1990 census, about 46% live in the West, 29.7% in the South, 17.8% in the Midwest, and only 6.5% in the Northeast. Four states have more than 100,000 Native Americans: Oklahoma, California, Arizona, and New Mexico. About 50 to 100 different tribal tongues survive today, although the most widely spoken are the Athapascan (spoken by the Navajo) and the Siouan (spoken by the Sioux).

The largest of the 275 reservations is the Navajo Nation Reservation, which extends from northern Arizona into New Mexico and Utah. Four other reservations in Arizona, and two in Washington, two in South Dakota, one in Wyoming, and one in Montana each comprise more than a million acres. In California, some consist of only a few acres. Wisconsin has seven Native American reservations and four Native American communities; however, none of these is as large as the ones in the West. The federal government's policy of reserving land for exclusive use by Native Americans was established in 1787, although reservation dwellers are free to leave whenever they choose. Typically, depending on the region, they farm, raise livestock, fish, hunt, or engage in timber production. Many work outside the reservation in factories, mines, and farms, or as skilled craftsmen; others earn a living by selling their arts and crafts. The reservation system today, after more than two centuries, symbolizes in many ways a profound failure of government policy, despite annual federal expenditure exceeding $1 billion. The social, educational, and economic well-being of those living there remains significantly substandard.

Unemployment on reservations in 1985, for example, averaged 34%; poverty affected 45% of reservation residents; and only 43% of those over 25 on the ten largest reservations were high school graduates. Native Americans have begun to recognize the economic and political potential of their approximately 53 million acres of property and to translate this raw wealth into better lives for themselves. In recent years, through money received from land claims settlements and government grants, some enterprising native groups have started, for example, resort motels, fishing businesses, auto parts assembly plants, oil and gas ventures, sawmills, and a hydroelectric plant. Bingo and lottery games and gambling halls for the general public have also provided employment and alternative sources of income for tribal people.

The government has historically attempted to integrate and assimilate Native Americans into the mainstream culture, especially through reservation schools. Catholic missionary schools have also been influential in the lives of many Native Americans; however, the schools have decreased in number in the last 20 years. The use of education as a means of assimilation has diminished since the late 1960s, and the natural inheritance of Native Americans has assumed more importance. It is often difficult to determine who is a Native American. The Bureau of the Census counts as Native Americans only those who so declare themselves. Since 1924, all Native Americans born within the United States have been considered citizens.

▲ PREHISTORIC MIGRATIONS

The first people who migrated to North America more than 30,000 years ago were hunters. They emigrated from northeastern Asia in search of food and furs for clothing. When the Pleistocene ice age that had covered northern Europe ended, the game animals moved eastward and northward through the then-existing Bering isthmus and into North America. The first settlers who moved across the Bering bridge of land were small family groups on hunting expeditions. They eventually formed bands, tribes, and nations. Over thousands of years this migration continued eastward from the Rocky Mountains into the Great Plains and on to the Atlantic coast. Great migrations also extended far into Mexico and Central and South America. The land was full of game, and edible plants were abundant. The movement and settlement over extensive land areas in search of food is evidenced by the wide distribution of languages.

The term *Amerind* or *Amerindian* is often used to designate these nomadic people who lived in the Americas before the arrival of the Europeans. The great migration was still in progress at the time of the first European settlements along the East Coast (Price, 1976). Since the Native Americans had no written records at the time of the European settlement in North America, the voluminous flood of historical, sociological, anthropological, and other documents concerning them has been written primarily by others. Although much of the early history was written through the biased eyes of missionaries, who often perceived the Native Americans as "uncivilized heathens," many of the writers lived with Native American tribes and took on their culture, thus bringing a certain authenticity to their writings. Native American culture shows an amazingly diverse range of human activity. Its history is a story of exploitation and suppression of a group of human beings by the European immigrants in their great desire to conquer the land. The infusion of Native American culture into the society of North America is often taken for granted and without acknowledgment. More than half the states have names drawn from Native American languages, as have thousands of cities, towns, streets, rivers, and mountains. Infusion, or borrowing, of Native American culture has not always been positive; for example, the use of Native American symbols for the names of sport teams or as mascots and the archeological display of Indian bones in museums are regarded by many Indian groups as insensitive, ignorant, degrading, and/or offensive.

▲ EARLY NATIVE AMERICAN CULTURE AND EXPERIENCES

Native American tribal cultures have historically been identified by the way they gathered their food (hunting and farming) and the areas in which they pursued their livelihood. Figure 3-1 shows the major cultural areas of early Native American life in North America.

The various tribes have also been classified by the languages they spoke, and other studies have extensively explored Native American thought as expressed through philosophical belief systems, mythology, legends, ceremonies, and art. The basic theme that threads through historic Native American ideology is respect and reverence for the earth and nature, from which comes not only survival—fulfillment of basic physical needs—but also the comprehension of life and one's relations with a separate, higher spiritual being and with other human beings.

● PEOPLES OF THE FAR NORTH

The people. The ethnogeographic region known as the Far North is the home of the Cree and other Canadian tribes and the Eskimos, who inhabit an area from Siberia through Alaska, Northern Canada, and Greenland. It has always been sparsely populated on account of the extreme cold and heavy snows. The word *Eskimo*, as used by Northern Indians, means "eaters of raw meat." North American Eskimos call themselves Inuit and Siberian Eskimos call themselves Yuit. Both names mean "men." In Canada, the Eskimos prefer to be known as the Inuit people. Alaskan Eskimos, according to the 1990 census, number about 60,000, and the Aleuts, who live mostly in Alaska and the Aleutian Islands, number about 20,000. The Aleuts are considered Eskimos but have developed a different culture and language system. Although many continue their cultural traditions and customs, including hunting and fishing the sea and living in underground houses, most have been acculturated to the White person's way of life. Throughout their history, the Aleuts have been

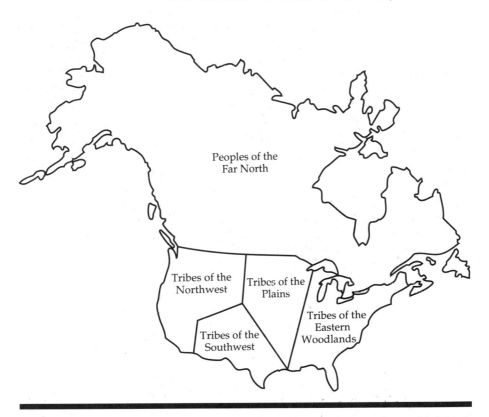

Peoples of the
Far North

Tribes of the
Northwest

Tribes of the
Plains

Tribes of the
Southwest

Tribes of the
Eastern
Woodlands

FIGURE 3-1 Ethnogeographic areas of early Native Americans in North America.

exploited by Russian traders, and during World War II many were sent to prison camps by the Japanese who invaded portions of the Aleutian Islands.

The Eskimos in Alaska, who are believed to have migrated to the area about 6,000 years ago, have not formed tribes, but rely on the family structure, and several families may temporarily group together to hunt and fish. The families are child-centered, and the male is considered dominant due to his important role as food seeker. Undesirable personal behavior, especially if it threatens the gathering of food, is controlled by laughter, which shames the offender. The struggle with the harsh environment often creates painful situations in which the band has to leave a child or old parent behind while searching for enough food to eat. Burland (1965) writes, "Nevertheless, every story in which events of this kind happen, refers to the sorrow of the people, the pain they felt at this sacrifice, and this has led to stories of a romantic cast in which the old people remain under the ground, and find means of attracting their descendants and giving them useful information" (p. 20).*

The relationship between Eskimo people and White people has been antagonistic throughout much of history. Whites have exploited valuable food resources (seals, fish, whales), Whites have transmitted diseases to the Eskimos, and racial discrimination is prevalent. The development of the Alaskan frontier has encroached upon the natives, resulting in cultural conflict and hardship, although many have also become acculturated to the manner of life and work found in North American White civilization (Richards & Oxereok, 1978).

Belief system. The philosophical beliefs of Eskimos center in nature and the availability of food. Dependence on the natural world can be observed in the traditional belief in a relationship between the inner personality and everything else in nature. All animals and objects in nature are seen as having spirits that are respected for their life-giving qualities. Bears, for example, have been believed to possess a spirit that can be called upon when needed to help in the search for food. Other spirits, such as the "Old Woman" who lives in the sea and provides fish, guard their well-being (Burland, 1965, p. 18). Returning unused portions of meat to the earth and water is believed to ensure future supplies.

Old beliefs hold that the human being possesses three spirits: the soul of the future, the present soul that gives life to the body, and an evil soul that stays with the body after death. As in other Native American groups, specially talented individuals, the *shamans* ("medicine men"), are traditionally believed to possess the psychic ability to heal and to accurately predict future weather conditions and the movements of local animals. The Eskimos would sit and listen quietly while their *angakok* (Eskimo shaman), in a trance, uttered prophecies to help the people deal with domestic matters or received words from the spirits informing them of forthcoming movements of animals and fish (Burland, 1965, p. 17). The shaman's talent rests in the ability to transcend and dissociate from conscious reality and to reach deeper unconscious memories and experiences. It is believed that through these visions spirits can be contacted for help and advice.

● TRIBES OF THE EASTERN WOODLANDS

The people. The first contacts that settlers from northern Europe had with Native Americans occurred in the eastern part of what is now the United States. The Eastern Woodlands region extends along the eastern coast from the Canadian boundary to the Gulf of Mexico and west to the Mississippi River. The Iroquois Nation, a cluster formed by five tribes in the late 1500s, inhabited the northern area, while major tribes in the Southeast were the Cherokee, Chickasaw, Choctaw, Creek, Natchez, and Seminole. The Great Lakes region included the Fox, Illinois, Menominee, Miami, Potawatomi, Sauk, Shawnee, and Winnebago tribes. The people who settled in the Mississippi and Ohio Valleys two thousand years ago became known as the Mound Builders because of the temple hills and burial grounds that they constructed.

The Eastern Woodlands was a rich geographic region, abundant in plant and animal life. Hunting, fishing, and the cultivation of corn, beans, and squash provided the people with their major source of food. By the time of the discovery of America by Europeans, many functions and customs had been developed by the tribal society, including the use of bowls and utensils, clothing made from deerskin and woven plant fibers, pottery, and the art of wicker basketry. Bark-covered wigwams, originally called *wetu* or *witu* and spelled as *wetuom* or *wekuwomut*, provided shelter for the Algonquians. The Iroquois constructed dwellings called longhouses, sectioned for occupancy by related families. The Creeks, in what is now the state of Georgia, organized their villages with a central plaza that included a council building and a place for ceremonies. Warfare was also a part of the relatively advanced civilization in the southeastern area, and slaves and scalps were taken in battles among various tribes. The Iroquois political practice was to carry on their tribal wars far away from their villages in order to protect their people.

The encroachment of White settlers on tribal land created fights and battles. During the conflict between France and Great Britain over control of the New World, various tribes took sides and often fought one another as well. By the time White settlers had pushed through to the Mississippi River in the early 1800s, many treaties had been broken with the Native Americans over land rights. In 1830, Congress passed the Indian Removal Act, which removed all but a few tribes to west of the river.

Belief system. The religious and philosophical beliefs of the tribes of the Eastern Woodlands traditionally consisted of shamanistic practices and songs and ritual to make contact with the gods. Warrior spirits were thought to inhabit the sky, with ancestral spirits to watch over them, and a land could be visited in dreams and through visions that brought forth the supernatural beings. The theology was highly organized and was expressed as a struggle between light and dark, a conflict between good and ill fortune in securing satisfaction of material needs. According to Burland (1965), "As among all American Indians the four directions, north, south, east, and west, were important to their beliefs. In many of the legends spirits behave in different ways according to which of the four regions their activities take place in. The universe was believed to be directed by spiritual powers of a mysterious nature to whom men must constantly pray for assistance and guidance" (p. 58). The growing seasons and special ceremonies in which offerings of corn and food were made and in which masked dancers impersonated the spirits of nature provided the people with a sense of time vital for planting and harvesting and for survival.

● TRIBES OF THE PLAINS

The people. The area known as the Plains, an endless expanse of grass, stretched west from the Mississippi River to the Rocky Mountains and from the Canadian border to Mexico. It is the story of the native inhabitants of the Plains that has been so overgeneralized and appears in so much literature and so many motion pictures. The inaccurate stereotype of *all* Native Americans riding horses, chasing buffalo, and fighting pioneers and the U. S. Army has been accepted by most Americans, and even by some Native Americans.

The region of the country was sparsely populated before the Spaniards introduced the use of horses and guns in the 1600s. Some of the major tribes included the Arapaho, Blackfoot, Cheyenne, Comanche, Crow, Pawnee, and various subgroups of the Sioux tribe. When they were discovered by the Europeans, the Plains people were engaged in agriculture, growing maize, beans, squash, and fruit, and hunting. The men, in their role of food provider, hunted buffalo and deer, and "as the buffalo were the main source of their meat supplies, many of the legends naturally related to Buffalo Spirits and the Earth Mother who gave shelter to the archetypal spirits of buffalo in her under-the-world-home. In times of famine the Indians would pray to her to send out more souls to inhabit the bodies of buffaloes and so bring food to the hungry people" (Burland, 1965, p. 66).

Small groups of buffalo hunters continually followed the herds and lived in tepees (skin-covered tents) while on the move and returned in the winter to their villages, where they lived in earth lodges that consisted of large structures made of timbers and covered with brush and sods of earth. During the winter, the men chipped and flaked flints for arrowheads and spear blades and the women worked at sewing and fine embroidery. The men typically wore deerskin breechcloths, leggings, and a simple loose jacket and the women wore skirts or loose shifts. In the cold winter, they wore buffalo-skin robes and moccasins.

The ways of the early Native Americans of the Plains were adopted by other tribes as they were forced westward by the advancing White civilization. To facilitate communication among the tribes, each having its own spoken tongue, an intertribal sign language was developed. The Dakota Sioux and the Pawnee were among the most distinguished tribes. The Pawnees lived in the Southwest at one time and over many years migrated to what is now Nebraska. By 1860, after the arrival of the White settlers, smallpox and cholera had almost destroyed the tribe. Placed on a reservation, they were further confronted by Sioux Indians who attacked and killed many of them. They also faced failure of their crops and the demands of Whites who desired their land. Later, they gave up their homeland in Nebraska and moved to the "Indian Territory" in Oklahoma. The Navajos and Apaches had migrated from Canada and Alaska and the Sioux from the eastern coastal area of North Carolina. Other late arrivals to the Plains included the Apache, Arapaho, Blackfoot, Cheyenne, and Comanche.

The mass killing of the buffalo for food, and often for sport, by White hunters led to the disappearance of the herds by 1890. The way of life in the Plains became cattle ranching, and the U.S. government moved the Native Americans to reservations in the belief that they would turn to farming. As "woman's work," farming was unacceptable to the Plains warriors. After a number of uprisings the United States Army trapped and annihilated a band of Sioux, including women and children, at Wounded Knee, South Dakota, in 1890, ending the will and ability of the people to resist.

Belief system. Great festivals and ceremonies were often held where magical functions were performed and offerings were made to ancestors and spirits of the sky and earth. The men grouped together into secret organizations at times and the dignified warriors elaborately painted themselves and wore animal disguises. These religious ceremonies—the Ghost Dance to bring back the buffalo is one example—often created fear and anger in the White settlers, who did not comprehend their meaning and who often misinterpreted them as hostile or warlike acts against them. In the great Sun Dance ceremonies, warriors inflicted pain upon themselves so that the spirits of the sky might intervene in human affairs of life.

● TRIBES OF THE PACIFIC NORTHWEST AND THE GREAT BASIN AREA

The people. The Cascade Mountains bisect the states of Washington and Oregon. On the east side, the Native American people were influenced by the Plains tribes and, due to this influence, may be called "horse people," while those in the northwest coastal region may be termed "water people." Survival on the humid West Coast was much easier, and over thousands of years the people developed a society characterized by layers of status-classes, ranging from royal chiefs and privileged nobility to common workers and slaves. Wealth and social rank were measured by material possessions such as hides, blankets, elaborately carved chests, immense canoes, tools, copper shields, and slaves. At the *potlatch* ("giving away") ceremony and feast, which took place at certain times of the year, groups would give away all their possessions, expecting others to do the same. By this practice they gained social prestige through the display of wealth, as well as an exchange of useful goods. Participants in the following potlatch festival were expected to exceed the value of the wealth exchanged in the preceding potlatch. Military victories over rival tribes and the kidnapping of slaves also brought prestige. A clan-type system was established that classified the important families, and ancestral totems were placed in front of houses to identify the occupants.

The Pacific Northwest tribes were basically a self-contained, isolated group, and except for military ventures, they seldom left their region for exploration or trade with other tribes. Although they were considered a preagricultural stone-age people at the time of discovery by European and Japanese sailors, they lived comfortably, due to an environment prolific in plant and animal life and heavily wooded. They did not have to farm, but obtained food by fishing, hunting, and gathering readily available plants and berries.

The Native Americans in what is now California and east of California were often called Diggers (first applied to the Paiutes) because they used roots as a main part of their diet. The Pomos were known for their excellent decorated baskets. The scarcity of food in the Great Basin area created a life of wandering and hardship for most of the tribes. Spanish Catholic missionaries were influential in the life of the people, and by 1800 many tribes had been converted to Christianity and had become dependent on the

Spaniards for their livelihood. Smallpox, starvation, and war with the U.S. government eliminated many of the California tribes.

The first contact with Europeans, through fur trading, was peaceful in comparison with what occurred in other regions of the country, and adjustment to the new White civilization was also less traumatic for the tribes of the Northwest.

Belief system. The philosophical/religious beliefs of the people, as demonstrated in their mythology and folklore, were based on the world of nature. Humans and animals were interchangeable in form and, as spirits, could be seen in visions by the shaman. A central power, above the spirits, was conceived as the "chief of the Sky People" and as the "Old Woman" who lived under the sea; other deities included the "Sky Being," Sun, Moon, and a trickster-creator known as the "Raven" (Burland, 1965, p. 28). A single God as understood in Western civilization is seldom found in any primitive culture and, according to scientists, the myths and folklore do not constitute a traditional religious system.

● TRIBES OF THE SOUTHWEST

The major tribes of the semidesert region, which is now Arizona, Colorado, New Mexico, Utah, and northern Mexico, included the Apache, Cochimi, Navajo, Papago, Pima, Pueblo (Hopi, Taos, Zuñi), Yaqui, Yuma, and others. They were basically farmers.

The Pueblos. The most highly organized communities were developed by the Pueblos, a peaceful people of mixed tribal origins. The Pueblos built their adobe and stone homes on the mesas (high, rocky tableland). For hundreds of years prior to settlement on the mesas, Pueblos had used cliff dwellings as a means of defense against raiding Apaches and Navajos, who were warlike tribes. From those high cliffs, they could watch and guard their fields. The gathering of food was an affair of the total community, and each family group was required to maintain a reserve of food in case of drought or crop failure. The Pueblos faced the hardships of drought many times. Living in the clustered pueblos required complex social organization; various clans were headed by chiefs or religious leaders.

Pueblo belief system. Ceremonies and festivals were held to bring rain. Enacted time and again, they portrayed the relationships between human and natural forces and between animals and plant environment. Because of the relative isolation of the Pueblos throughout history, much of their ancient culture has been preserved in the literature, and their story of creation, as told by the Zuñi, contains impressions of love, peace, and blessing beginning with the life-giving force, *Awonawilona.* The Pueblo people have preserved their highly developed religion and mythology system and continue today to practice traditional religious beliefs and customs. The spirits, *Kachinas,* are represented in Kachina dolls through which the young and old alike can learn about their religion.

The Navajos. The Navajo people were largely hunters and the gatherers of edible seeds, although they engaged in some farming, as did the Pueblos. They lived in hogans, eight-sided structures made from sod, clay, or adobe bricks. Because of harsh living conditions, they often formed small hunting groups, and their tribal government was only a loosely organized structure.

Navajo belief system. Shamans, believed to be selected by the spirit world, played an important role in Navajo life. Shamans today continue to receive respect for their power by Native Americans who adhere to traditional ways. According to custom, a young boy or girl entered the wilderness to remain alone for days without food, praying for protection from the spirits and hoping at the end to receive a vision. If received, the vision would be described to family and relatives, and if it was found to be significant, the boy or girl would start training and ritual to become a shaman. As a shaman, the person would heal and give inspiration to others of the tribe. The Navajo shaman was a special person whose behavior, however extreme, was seldom questioned. Says Burland (1965): "Many Navajo medicine men had a tendency to think of themselves as magically changed into women, and would often do women's work such as cooking and even wear women's clothing. They were beings set apart and regarded as rather strange, but also as people blessed by the spirits" (p. 87). Spiritual tribal ceremonies for healing and predicting have been used by Navajos for centuries. Sand paintings, beautiful works of art sketched in sand, are accompanied by sacred chants that recall the mystical experience of first receiving the painting rituals from the spirits, and they continue to be observed today in special ceremonies for curing afflictions. The influence of the Aztecs is also found in the culture of the southwestern tribes, and the name "Montezuma" is often used in Papago legend. Montezuma, or First Man, taught the people how to hunt and grow maize before leaving for a home farther south.

▲ RECENT NATIVE AMERICAN CULTURE AND EXPERIENCES

The arrival of Europeans on the American continent destroyed or in some manner influenced the diverse cultures and lives of the Native American people. Over a period of 300 years, most of the eastern tribes lost their native lands and were pushed far into the western part of the country to face different tribes and cultures. Diseases and social problems never before known in the Native American world befell them all, countless numbers were killed in fights and wars, and tribes in all parts of the country were subjected to many broken treaties and promises. The majority were moved to government-designated land areas under the supervision of the Bureau of Indian Affairs (BIA), which was first organized in 1824 under the War Department and later in 1849 under the Department of the Interior. Through defeat, demoralization, and displacement, the Native American culture and means of earning a living were eroded.

The historic conflict of cultures continues to create social and personal problems in the country today (Boyer, 1981; Tyler, 1973).

The French explorers and traders in Canada never intended to settle the land and usually were more cooperative in their treatment of the native inhabitants. Many of the French men intermarried with Native American women. The Canadian government's policy of allowing most tribes to remain on their land has generally resulted in a greater retention of native language and culture. The nonnative population that settled in Canada was numerically smaller than in the United States and conflict between the two groups was not as great. Nonetheless, ignorance of the status of Native Americans in Canada is as prevalent as in other parts of North America, and "political appointees design government policies which govern the lives of a people they have never seen. They relish the thought that they, and they alone, know what is good for the Indian and have all the answers to the Indian's problems" (Pratson, 1970, pp. 11–12).

● GOVERNMENTAL INTERVENTIONS

In the United States, the federal Indian Removal Act of 1830 forced eastern tribes to move beyond the Mississippi River to what, at the time, was considered worthless land. By 1840, of those who had been moved, more than 70,000 survived the long trips. The Cherokee and Choctaw were removed far from their sacred lands in the Southeast to Oklahoma, termed "Indian Territory" at the time, over what they called the Trail of Tears. The eastern tribe of Cherokees in western North Carolina and some of the Seminole in the Florida Everglades eluded capture and today remain on reservation lands in those states. The present-day Cherokee Tribe, numbering over 90,000 members, living mostly in Oklahoma, is the second largest tribe after the Navajo. The Oneidas were forced from New York to Wisconsin along with the Munsees and the Stockbridges. Most of the Winnebagos, more than 2,000, were moved several times, to Iowa, Minnesota, and South Dakota (next to their worst enemy, the Sioux). Finally, in the winter of 1863, they were made to settle in Nebraska. Eight hundred died on the trip. Today, only a small number remain in their native Wisconsin (Marquis, 1974, p. 13).

Various solutions to the so-called Indian problem were sought through governmental action and policies. Congress, in 1871, eliminated the need to make treaties by ruling that the tribes were no longer independent governments and making them wards of the government. The Dawes Act (the General Allotment Act) was passed by Congress in 1887 in an attempt to further break up the tribal groups and to encourage farming as a way of life by giving land to *individual* tribe members. However, much of the land could not be farmed, and many Native Americans had no knowledge of nor desire for farming. Marquis (1974) writes: "About thirty million acres were allotted to individual Indians. The land remaining, after the allotments were made, was opened to white settlement. Today little more than one million acres remains in the hands of individual Indians" (p. 13). Tribal ownership of land had dropped from 138 million acres in 1887 to 48 million in 1934. Living conditions on the reservations were deplorable by outside standards, and poor health, poverty, alcoholism, and suicide were major social and personal problems, as they continue to be today. In 1934, the Native American population in the country was about 250,000.

A more enlightened governmental policy was established in 1934 with the passage of the Wheeler-Howard Indian Reorganization Act, which provided for tribal ownership of reservation land and encouragement of self-government. The policy has been successful in that many reservation dwellers have formed tribal councils and take an active role in their own affairs. The Indian Self-Determination and Education Assistance Act of 1975 provided additional programs for advancement of managerial capabilities and development of businesses on the reservations. Another redress was made in 1946, when the Indian Claims Commission was established to settle Indian claims for loss of land resources and broken treaties.

After 1887 many reservations had been phased out, and during the 1950s a few were "terminated." During the termination phase, tribes were offered sums of money to give up their land and protection by the federal government. No provision or preparation for independence was provided, and the termination policy was halted as a failure. The Employment Assistance Program of the BIA, starting in 1951, was an endeavor to assist Native Americans with movement into urban areas through job training, education, and housing. Approximately 60% of those who participated in the program have remained in the cities, but many continue to be employed in semiskilled or unskilled work, and conflict between city life and land-centered cultural traditions has disrupted the lives and sense of status of many others. For the many who remain on the reservations or who return from the urban areas, status, group security, and personal identity are found in the reservation life. According to Price (1976), many urban Indians "miss the social contacts and activities of the reservation and, when possible, spend weekends or vacations back visiting on their reservation. As the years in the city go by, they tend to withdraw from reservation social contacts, idealize traditional reservation life, and perhaps talk of retiring or otherwise returning to their reservations, in which as members of the tribe, they have a right to reside" (p. 264).

● NATIVE AMERICAN TRADITION

Before the arrival of Europeans, the Americas were a land of hundreds of culturally diverse tribes and many small nations, each with identified political boundaries and cultural areas. Different social organizations and means of living distinguished the sea-hunters in the Far North; the hunters, fishermen, and farmers of the Eastern Woodlands; the buffalo hunters of the Plains; the fishermen of the Northwest; and the farmers of the Southwest. The advanced civilization of the Aztecs and Mayas flourished in Mexico and the Incas lived in South America. Although the tribes had their own social organization, cultural and religious beliefs, family structures, and art forms, common elements gave and continue to give a feeling of wholeness and identity shared by most Native American people. Today, the ancient traditions of most tribes are transmitted only through occasional ceremonies and existing legends, folklore, and art. Exceptions are the Eskimos, Pueblos (Hopi), Navajos, Sioux, and Iroquois, who have carried on strong tradition in many ways. Shamans, as prophets and healers, perpetuate in a few tribes some of the ancestral traditions and thought.

The universalistic laws of the mainstream society have reduced Native American diversity to common practices found throughout the country. For example, polygyny (having more than one wife or female mate at one time), common in some tribal societies, has been eliminated. Schooling is required, and traditional Native American education is thus weakened. However, isolation on the reservations and some grouping together in urban areas have meant resistance to acculturation, and even racial discrimination has para-doxically strengthened cultural continuity. Cultural continuity, to outsiders and for many Native Americans, may only be experienced in such things as stereotypical personal attributes, religious practices, music, food, dancing at powwows, and art forms. More important for many Native Americans, however, is that incorporation of self-identity with traditional ideology may give psychological strength for coping in an often hostile mainstream environment. What the majority society has derived from the native culture is mostly material in nature, but the social or ideological culture of Native American people also has potential worth for the majority society. As developed over thousands of years, it contains significant values from which much can be gained.

▲ NATIVE AMERICAN VALUES

Writings on the ideological culture of Native Americans are varied and wide-ranging. Some approach the topic from the scientific standpoint of social psychology, sociology, anthropology, or ethnology; some are historical; some probe Native American mythology; and some are candid and personal. The insight and outlook gained from these approaches range from extreme pessimism for the survival of Native American culture and its eventual assimilation into the dominant culture to the expression of optimism and the belief that infusion of "ideal" Native American values into mainstream society will provide vitality and direction for the life of our nation. Even though different writers approach the topic of Native American values from different viewpoints (Boyd, 1974; Bryde, 1971; Burland, 1965; Deloria, 1969, 1973; Lewis & Ho, 1975; Pratson, 1970; Price, 1976; Richardson, 1981; Trimble, 1981; Zychowicz, 1975), they generally agree on what they believe to be traditional in the Native American experience.

Bryde (1971, p. 10) lists four valued objects in the Native American conceptualization of the cosmos (universe) that have been important in the culture for thousands of years: God, self, others, and world. All values and value-oriented actions relate to these four objects, and from this value system comes a way of life that encompasses ideas, beliefs, views, behaviors, and traditions and customs of the people. It is reciprocal and reinforcing as long as most needs, attitudes, and desires continue to be defined and met within the system.

● GOD

God is the great power above everything. It is "the force which is responsible for action, and which can actually have control over man's destiny" (Zychowicz, 1975, p. 15). Humankind, nature, and the universe were created by God and instructions were given on how to live on the land. The inner spiritual power, or God, was called *orenda* by the Iroquois, *manitou* by the Algonkian tribes, *ahone* by the Powhatans, and *wakan* or *wakonda* by the Sioux. The Sioux also used the expression *wakan tanka,* meaning all of the *wakan* beings. The spiritual God of the Native Americans is positive, benevolent, and part of daily living. God's knowledge and advice are transmitted through traditional Native American wisdom. Ideal action toward God is accomplished through helping others understand and get along with people and through comprehending the natural world, of which everything (living and nonliving) is a part (Bryde, 1971). All of nature's objects are equally respected as both physical and spiritual entities.

One belief held by many Americans is that without productive and moral living the person falls out of favor with God and is subject to guilt and punishment by God; thus, the person is viewed as much lower than God and apart from God. Human fault, in the Native American experience, "was not in offending God, but in causing an imbalance in nature that resulted in his own destruction" (Zychowicz, 1975, p. 24). Ignorance of one's relation to nature and life is more likely to cause destruction than is moral sin, according to Native American values. Religion in the mainstream society is formal and worship generally occurs in a church on Sunday, whereas in the Native American experience religion is an integral part of the culture and praying is a part of daily life.

As does any other culture, the Native American culture contains norms and standards for behavior, but Native Americans are inclined to judge each person as a separate individual, taking into consideration the reasons for actions ahead of the norms of the society. The dominant majority society judges behavior as right or wrong, good or bad, and considers how things *should* be and not necessarily how they are. The practice of judging the behaviors of others is an important value in the mainstream society.

● THE SELF

The self is viewed as an integral part of nature, woven into life, the universe, and the total scheme of the world. Rolling Thunder, a medicine man, explained it by stating: "Man's inner nature is identical with the nature of the universe, and thus man learns about his own nature from nature itself" (Boyd, 1974, p. 81). One's true personality is what nature shows. Bravery and acceptance of life without fear, endurance of natural pain and suffering with patience and silence, self-containment and controlled emotions, honesty and strength, self-respect and individual worth, freedom of individuality, and respect for others were valued personality attributes (Deloria, 1969, 1973). In the old Native American world, and in modern times, these attributes were especially necessary for survival once one left the security of the village. Only the individual, himself or herself, could decide to do the right thing in certain moments when dependence on others was not possible. Individual survival was one's own responsibility in order for the family and tribe to continue.

Individualism is also prized in the majority society, but individual needs and rights often take precedence over the welfare of the group. Individual freedom is usually defined as doing what one wants to do within the law, whereas in the Native American culture individual freedom is defined as doing what one wants to do as long as it is in harmony with nature. In contrast, the emphasis in the mainstream culture on the accumulation of material possessions for one's own pleasure and for social status tends to create a loss of individuality, since the goal-object is often to conform with others or to exceed others. Material achievement and accumulation of money are taken as symbols of success in the dominant group, but Native American values tend to emphasize what a person is and to attach secondary importance to what the person has.

Practical skills and competency are valued in the majority society and increased efficiency and organization in work and technology are major goals. Knowing how to make a living and support a family are important in both cultures, but knowledge of relationships with others and nature takes precedence in Native American values over knowledge of how to earn money.

● RELATIONSHIPS WITH OTHERS

Interpersonal relationships are an integral part of Native American life. Attitudes toward others and mutual expectations define the important roles each person plays. Bryde (1971) writes: "The great Indian value of sharing and generosity, for instance, is seen most clearly in the two areas in which they shared: food and shelter, and praise and shame" (p. 264). Living in a group is helpful and often necessary in meeting the demands of life, and one gains respect by one's generosity in sharing materials, knowledge, and one's own personality with others. Helping others who are less fortunate is also a feature of the American society at large. Some psychoanalytic interpretations lead one to believe it is a means of "guilt reduction," but other views hold that American generosity is simply a cultural tradition. The American democratic system of equality, although not ideally universal in application and under all conditions in the society, has similarities to the Native American system of equality, except that according to Native American values, equality of position is based on what the person is *inside*, not by the person's social position or titles.

Native American child-rearing practices are characterized by early training in self-sufficiency, and physical development and psychological learning are in harmony with knowledge gained from the natural world. The aged are respected and protected because in "the days of their strength they also contributed to the common weal" (Seton, 1936, p. 19). Wisdom of life is received from the old people, whose task it is to acquaint the young with the traditions, customs, legends, and myths of the tribe. All members of a tribe care for the old. Death in the Native American experience is an accepted fact of natural life. The soul is believed to be immortal, but there is no concept of heaven and hell. Chief Seattle of the Suquamish tribe of the Puget Sound area of Washington, born approximately 1790, described death as "merely a changing of worlds" (Deloria, 1973, p. 184).

● THE WORLD

According to Native American belief, the world is interconnected, and everything, including human beings, lives according to the same process. Each being has its power, function, and place in the universe. Every part of nature has a spirit, which many tribes believe to possess intelligence, emotion, and free will. Praying, in fact, is praying to one's own power. Because the Great Spirit is everything, in all of nature, there is no need to question the existence of a God. Since nature is the essence of God, nature would stop if God no longer lived. Zychowicz (1975) states, "This concept also relates to the way people treat each other. If our relationship with all of creation is symbolic of our relationship with God, we are on good terms with God whenever we are on good terms with nature. Then, if we are on good terms with God and nature, we will be on good terms with ourselves because our spirit is the same. If we are living in harmony with nature, then our life is harmonious and we can live free of anxiety, appreciating life" (pp. 26–27).

The dominant society has attempted to master nature and to make material comfort an end goal in life. Any human group needs and enjoys comfortable shelter, adequate food, and clothing, but traditional Native American values do not place importance on those as ends in themselves. Lack of respect and reverence for nature and overuse of natural resources lead to imbalance and disharmony in the world, dysfunction in human relationships, and a softening of personal stamina.

Time-consciousness does not go by the clock in traditional Native American culture. Their system is difficult to understand or accept in modern society because everything is based on linear concepts. The orderly movement of seconds, minutes, and hours inform us of the passing of time. The emphasis on the single dimension of time has influenced such values as punctuality, eating schedules, age for entering school, and even "putting in time" to earn advanced degrees. The entire industrial and business complex is geared to the time dimension, and from this come many of the values that control our lives and determine the expression of our individual personalities. In mainstream society, for example, a person's reliability is often judged by his attentiveness to punctuality and a person's worth may be measured by the dollar value attached to his or her time. In Native American society, time is measured according to natural phenomena such as the cycle of day and night, the waxing and waning of the moon, and the turn of the seasons, which are part of a continuity and with which one coexists. The "right time" occurs when one is ready. *When* something happened is not as important as *what* happened. The dominant society is future-oriented, believing that better things are yet to come, instead of fully engaged in the present existence. Says Rolling Thunder, "These days people want everything in a hurry and they want it without effort. They miss a lot of understanding because they don't want to work for it" (Boyd, 1974, p. 49).

▲ MAINSTREAM CULTURE AND THE NATIVE AMERICAN

Contemporary Native Americans maintain cultural and tribal identities that are different from those of most other Americans, who do not understand many of the rituals, beliefs, and kinship differences. Traditional Native American values do conflict in many ways with those of the mainstream. When cross-cultural differences are not explored or their real meanings and implications understood, there is the danger of inaccurate, overgeneralized, or derogatory stereotypes. Thus misrepresentations of Native Americans and the Native American experience appear in the news media, in motion pictures and television, in misguided statements made in everyday conversations, and finally in the counseling process.

In any cultural group, a value system is the source from which people derive intimate social relationships, a feeling of status, and a sense of safety and security. No social system is perfect, yet within the United States are representations of almost every system known. If movement toward cooperation among diverse groups occurs, the best attributes of all the cultures could be exchanged for the betterment of life in each group. The general American society has renewed its interest in the culture of the native people. Whether the interest encourages compatibility with Native American philosophy and ideology or whether the effort continues toward assimilation of Native Americans into a value system that is more oriented toward materialism, ostentatious consumption, and self-interest remains to be seen. According to Price (1976), the current experience of the country shows movement in a "search for individual freedom within a socially tolerant community that is in ecological harmony with its environment" (p. 260).

Alliances of Native Americans, beginning with the early Iroquois Confederacy, continue to occur; the Chicago Indian Conference in 1961 is considered a significant event in Native American movement toward tribal cooperation and group identity. However, tribal loyalties also present hindrances to a single political group identity. Hundreds of different tribal publications and periodic newsletters are printed, and although these are dispersed as a general news network among the groups, each retains its autonomy. Many social and political organizations exist, but diversity and fractionalization rather than unity seem to characterize Native American life.

■ ANGLO-SAXON AMERICANS

The designation "Anglo-Saxon Americans" refers to Euroamericans of Anglo-Saxon descent and Americans who have been acculturated to Anglo-Saxon traditions at various levels. The first Americans who migrated from northern Europe played an important role in the United States, laying the foundation for the basic social structure that has prevailed for nearly 300 years. They did so with little thought that they were creating a way of life to serve the needs of what was to become the power group. The most visible group in

America for the first 200 years was mainly British, although 9% of the population in 1790 was German (Anderson, 1970, p. 80). If a member of another ethnic group was not or could not become like the original group, socially and culturally, that person did not qualify for the society. With acceptance into American society came social acceptance and material rewards. The first White Americans were also of the Protestant faith, which strongly influenced their group identity and self-image according to their way of believing and their way of living. The way in which family and kinship relations are structured and the moral/ethical standards and norms for acceptable behavior in group living all constitute important means by which *any* group of humans seeks to create an orderly and meaningful existence for themselves; such was the case for the first White North Americans.

For more than 200 years, U.S. culture has been dominated by a mixture of the cultures of northern and western Europe with the North American environment. Since the middle of the 19th century, many other cultural groups have immigrated and have questioned the belief that the institutions and interests of the nation belong only to the descendants of the original founders. A starting point for comprehension of what "mainstream America" is and some of the issues related to current cultural diversity lies in understanding the White Anglo-Saxon Protestant (WASP) experience in the United States.

▲ ANGLO-SAXON AMERICAN ORIGINS

The Anglo-Saxon nation was created by diverse Germanic tribes that settled in England in the A.D. 400s and 500s. The Germanic tribes drove out the natives of the area, who called themselves Britons. *England* is taken from the old English words *Engla* and *land,* meaning "land of the Angles." The English language is derived from that of the Anglo-Saxons and half the words used in English today can be traced back to the dialect developed in northern England. Nearly two-thirds (three million) of the population of North America in 1790 was English and lived primarily in the original colonies of England and on the Appalachian frontier.

● RACIAL/ETHNIC IDENTITY AND THE EARLY WHITE SETTLERS

The original White settlers in North America often called themselves English and identified with Britain and the Old World. The descendants of those original Americans called themselves "old Americans," combining assertion of their British background with pride in the new American traditions. Ethnic identification with the term *Yankee* has roots in colonial days and implies rural lifestyles, religious fervor, and the Revolutionary War experience (Solomon, 1965). Anderson (1938) believed "the old Americans, more than any other group, emphasized their ethnic origins or expressed race-consciousness" (p. 246). Recently, the term *Anglo American* has come into usage, but few Whites attach special meanings to it. Except for the outburst of strong feelings attached to the label "White honky," applied to all Whites in general in the late 1960s and early 1970s by Blacks, the Anglo-Saxon group has avoided being subjected to negative stereotyping. The stereotypical labels "John Bull," "lime-juicer," and "limey," all given to the early settlers of British descent, hardly generate the negative emotions triggered by so many labels applied to other racial/ethnic groups. English sailors were called "lime-juicers" because they sucked the juice from limes to prevent scurvy.

English settlers, according to Anderson (1970), often referred to new arrivals as emigrants (that is, coming *from* a place of origin), whereas in present-day American society, natives usually refer to newly arrived people as immigrants (that is, coming *to* a new country from another nation). The former usage implied acceptance and understanding of the origins of the new arrivals, while the latter tends to imply an intrusion. Attitudes toward new arrivals in the United States have also been influenced by immigration laws passed with the intent to limit the entry of the less skilled or "undesirable." "Undesirable," at the time (1805 to 1920), focused especially on emigrants from southern and eastern Europe and Asia, who were viewed as racially, mentally, or morally inferior in comparison with other Americans.

As is true of most immigrations to America, the Anglo-Saxons' incentives for leaving their place of origin were freedom of religion and ideological thought, socioeconomic mobility, and power in political life. The Anglo-Saxons successfully accomplished these purposes. As described by Anderson (1970), English people established the industrial centers of the North and stimulated a flow of workers and supervisors from Great Britain to the mills and factories. In 1950, 65% of the top executives of the largest American corporations were of British descent (Keller, 1953). Almost two-thirds of American presidents have been of English background, and through 1957, 78% of the Supreme Court justices were of British origin (Schmidhauser, 1959). Many millionaires and centimillionaires possess British surnames. These statistics are not meant to encourage the assumption that *all* English were extraordinarily successful, but only to emphasize the fact that the power and economic base of the country has been influenced by people of Anglo-Saxon descent. Although the only truly native Americans had established a culture in North America thousands of years earlier, the English developed the cultural base that was destined to become American society. The foundation of life for the American nation was hammered out through creative and industrious efforts and through force and usurpation of land.

● OTHER RELATED OR ASSIMILATED ANGLO-SAXON GROUPS

Following the English, other northern and western European groups immigrated to America. Most closely related to the English, both geographically and culturally, were the Welsh, the Scots, and the Protestant Irish from northern Ireland, who readily settled into the life of the new country. The great influx of Catholic Irish from southern and western Ireland did not occur until 1847, and over an eight-year period, about 1.4 million came in order to escape famine caused by the potato blight. They were poor peasants, mostly young single males. Between 1847 and 1920, nearly 4 million migrated to the United

TABLE 3-1 Subgroups of European immigrants arriving before and after 1880.

Date of Arrival	Immigrants from Northern and Western Europe		Immigrants from Southern and Eastern Europe	
	Number	Percentage	Number	Percentage
1820–1880	8,718,271	47.8%	271,618	2.0%
1881–1929	9,516,503	52.2%	13,622,516	98.0%
	18,234,774	100.0%	13,894,134	100.0%

SOURCE: From *Annual Report of the Commissioner General of Immigration*, 1929, table 82, p. 184.

States. They often experienced conflict, violence, and opposition in Protestant-English America.

The immigration of large numbers of Swedes, Norwegians, Danes, Finns, Germans, Dutch, and other northern and western Europeans occurred during the period from 1820 to 1929. The German migration has far exceeded all others. From 1820 to 1979, approximately 7 million Germans immigrated to the United States, the nearest competitor being Italians, who numbered 5.3 million for the same period. Even as recently as the period from 1961 to 1970, nearly 200,000 Germans arrived in the United States. Nearly half of the northern and western Europeans arrived prior to 1880, whereas 98% of the southern and eastern Europeans (White ethnic Americans) arrived after 1881. Table 3-1 compares the numbers and percentages of these two subgroups of European immigrants.

The reasons for leaving the native country varied, but usually had to do with specific conditions in specific countries. Typically, immigrants left to escape religious and political repression, military conscription, rigid class systems, and poverty. Coming to the United States meant new freedoms, an open class system, plentiful fertile land, and the dream of riches. Transportation across the ocean was cheap in today's dollars, even as reasonable as $12.50 in steerage class.

The original British Americans became the owners of business and industry, and the English people they brought from Great Britain became the supervisors and managers; others became clerks, government officials, and military officers. Some were sent from the old country as political and military prisoners and settled in the Appalachian area. As groups of other national origins arrived, they became the skilled craftspeople, the industrial factory workers, the store owners; there were also many who worked as common unskilled laborers, agricultural workers, and domestic help.

▲ THE MELTING POT

Although not all the other groups that immediately followed the English were Anglo-Saxon and not all spoke English, they were granted status on the basis of their successful adaptation to the Anglo-American society. Cultural assimilation was fairly painless, although not without conflict. The duration of their "hyphenated status" (such as from "German-American" to "American") was brief in comparison to that of later groups. The traditional pattern of successful adaptation for members of most newly arrived groups was to cluster together for psychological security before moving into the larger community. Of course, "ghetto-like" living may also be imposed on newcomers by the earlier-arrived or dominant group. This pattern of isolation or segregation has persisted much longer for African Americans and Native Americans than for any other group and because of historical events, is much more complex.

Many of the members of the earliest immigrant groups continue to associate, at least socially, and it is still relatively easy to locate in many towns and cities a club or community organization for Germans or Swedes or other ethnic groups. Many seek to perpetuate in a small way the Old World customs, traditions, and history. Hundreds of ethnic journals, newsletters, and newspapers serve to promote loyalty and ties to old cultures, and visits to ancestral homelands are becoming more frequent. As groups of greater cultural diversity have migrated to the United States, the melting pot concept, which envisions diverse cultures merging into a single U.S. culture, has given way to the currently popular concept of cultural pluralism, or diversity within unity.

▲ HISTORICAL PHASES IN GROUP RELATIONS

The relationship between the majority Anglo-Saxons and other groups has evolved through different epochs in the history of the nation. Each epoch has brought psychological and social adjustment problems for the members of both groups. Although there are overlaps and no clear-cut beginning and ending points for each epoch, three chronological themes, as illustrated in Table 3-2, can be identified.

The process of coexistence is potentially conflict producing in a multicultural society where minority group members experience difficulty in functioning with, or relating to, mainstream ways or where majority group members cannot relate to minority ways. Conflict is especially likely when the dominant group exerts its influence on minority groups for conformity or when misconceptions are perpetuated by both groups.

▲ CULTURAL PLURALISM AND THE PROCESS OF INCLUSION

Although cultural pluralism may become the concept that could give new democratic direction to the American people, it is not new in the country. Various groups that have either voluntarily or involuntarily immigrated (White ethnics, Blacks, Hispanics, Asians) or were in the country prior to

TABLE 3-2	Historical Phases in Cultural Group Relations	
Time Period	Concept	Major Theme
1750–1880	The melting pot	The melting pot theme (elaborated by Zangwill, 1910) conceived that the inhabitants of the United States would eventually melt into a new race of people. All the contributions of each new group would be gratefully received and fused with the dominant culture to create a superior biological and social culture that the world had never before experienced. Although the concept was idealistic and noble, domination by the Anglo-Saxon cultural group and rejection of non-White groups, as well as the reluctance of many ethnic minority groups to give up their cultural heritage and identity, led to collapse of the concept. Many Black Americans and other ethnic Americans also saw grave implications for racial and cultural genocide contained in the misuse of the melting pot doctrine.
1880–1950	Americanization	As a cultural theme (Cubberley, 1909; Fairchild, 1926), "Americanization" became especially prevalent after the mass immigration of eastern European people. It demanded assimilation into the dominant Anglo-Saxon culture by the ethnic Whites through desertion of their own values and mores. Shunted off and segregated from the benefits of the organized society were the non-White groups. After World War II, the trend toward Americanization moved away from the rigid imposition of Anglo-Saxon standards toward the infusion of many cultures into what could be called an "American" culture.
1950–present	Cultural pluralism	Cultural pluralism, or "unity in diversity" (Krug, 1976, p. 14), is a goal based on the belief that the dominant culture will benefit from coexistence and interaction with the cultures of minority groups. It basically features the process of developing mainstream American culture through the equal cooperation and fusion of separate minority groups (Kallen, 1956).

settlement by Europeans (Polynesians, Native Americans, Mexicans) have maintained cultural and social diversity apart from the dominant majority group. Some of the separation has been forced through noninclusion and some has been through choice. One explanation for cultural diversity and the continuance of ethnicity that characterizes many groups rests on the process of assimilation. Gordon (1964) has theorized that assimilation (inclusion of "new" groups) involves a number of subprocesses. Gordon's theory, as described and adapted by McLemore (1980, pp. 38–39), includes the following general components:

1. *Secondary structural assimilation* is defined as sharing by the dominant group and subordinate groups in educational, occupational, political, and public recreational settings, in residential living areas, and in income attainment. Generally, the settings and areas are characterized by formality and social relationships that are impersonal, cold, and distant. The psycho-social climate that is often found in schools that have been desegregated or in business establishments that have included equal opportunity practices, especially during the initial stages, exemplifies this level of assimilation.

2. *Primary structural assimilation* is defined as the entrance of subordinate groups into social cliques, social events, churches, clubs, fraternal and trade organizations, and other institutions of the dominant society. It is less formal, or informal, and characterized by social relationships ("friendships") that are personal, warm, and close.

3. *Cultural assimilation,* for the groups being assimilated by the larger and more dominant group, involves the loss of ethnic identity, personal expectations (beliefs, values), religion, native language, traditional family practices (child-rearing patterns, member relationships), and general interest in heritage. Americanization of assimilated groups may be permanent, or resurgence in ethnicity may occur from time to time. Resurgence can take place within individuals or entire groups, as noted, for example, in Novak's (1971) description of the rise of the "unmeltable ethnics" and Hansen's (1938) account of the phenomenon where many third-generation children (grandchildren) seek to revive their lost cultural roots. According to Glazer and Moynihan (1970), who were referring primarily to immigrants from southern and eastern Europe, most old country traditions do not last significantly beyond the third generation. McLemore (1980) has further pointed out that the conditions surrounding the initial contact between groups subsequently affect the course of their relations: "a conquered minority is likely to be hostile for a long period of time and to have separatist and secessionist tendencies," while "an immigrant minority is likely to exhibit hostility for a shorter period of time and to prefer assimilation" (p. 333).

4. *Marital assimilation* is viewed as the last step in the process toward cultural and national homogeneity: intermarriage occurs between members of the assimilated group and members of the majority.

Assuming that the preceding theoretical propositions are valid, individuals in a group may be at different stages of the inclusion process. Past a certain point, assimilation becomes inevitable, and thus the implications of Americanization may cause personal and social conflict for members of various groups. One way to cope with the uncertainty is to maintain one's ethnic and racial loyalties for the security they provide.

▲ THE PROTESTANT TRADITION

Views of life that stem from religious beliefs also influence social reality. Protestantism is as much a cultural trait as it is a religious faith. Hudson (1961, p. 4) states that although only 5% of the population of colonial America were church members, 98% of all colonial churches were Protestant. Organized churches were usually unavailable in the vast frontier and the religious life of the people was directed within the family through prayer and reading the Bible. Churchgoing for the colonists was not easy. It was a rigid, demanding, and hard duty in the eyes of the "God-fearing" Puritan people. Protestantism was the single belief system interwoven into the culture and customs of the society before the great influx of southern and eastern European immigrants. Association with Protestantism as a means of psychological security was evidenced in the 1840s when fear of Catholic strength became especially strong and anti-Catholic sentiment was rampant.

● THE PROTESTANT WORK ETHIC

The effects of Protestant reformers in 16th-century Europe have had long-range consequences reaching far into the American society today. Presbyterianism, inspired by the French Protestant reformer John Calvin, is one example. The Presbyterians were the strongest faction when Puritans took power in England in the 17th century, and large numbers of Scots immigrants spread the faith throughout the American colonies. The influence of Protestant beliefs as evolved over many years in Europe, and as transmitted through Calvinistic doctrines and other Protestant denominational beliefs to America, is especially felt in the *work ethic* (Weber, 1904–1905/1930). According to the ethic, work and productive activity in the society are an expression of one's spiritual being and one's eventual self-worth. It is one's "calling" in predestined service to a higher being. Tawney (1926) believed that the Calvinist attitude toward work and wealth was basically motivated by economic and political pressures arising from the social position and interests of the Calvinists. Although it was not foreseen by the Protestant reformers, and historically unintended (Birnbaum, 1959; Fischoff, 1944; Trevor-Roper, 1963), the concept of morality through hard work was very compatible with the concept of the capitalistic free-enterprise system. Work, thus defined and carried out in earnest, led to rapid economic growth for the country. The ethic has remained especially strong among older persons in rural populations and in the upper middle class, although modified expressions of it are present throughout all classes of the American population.

Generally, most Protestants accept the Bible as the source of information about a supreme Being. The Bible is preferred to secular interpretations of life because it is most representative of the life of Jesus Christ. God, through the

Bible, addresses individuals directly. Each person has a sacred "calling" in life that is work assigned by God. Protestants also believe that all persons are born in sin but that souls are saved by the grace of God. Faith is an act by which a sinner is saved from the penalty of sin. The Puritans strongly believed in moral living in order to gain redemption by God.

● THE PSYCHOLOGICAL COMPLEX

The idea of an intricate psychological complex associated with the Protestant ethic was first proposed by Weber (1930), who believed that the ethic "had become detached from its historical base, to spread throughout the industrial world ('The Puritan wanted to work at his calling but we are forced to do so')" (Gould & Kolb, 1964, p. 554). The phenomenon has also been noted in Riesman's "other-directed personality" (1950) and Whyte's "social conformist pattern" (1956). Although most of the extreme orthodoxy of Calvinism has not persisted in pure form to this day and the academic debate over the Protestant ethic as a sole vehicle to success has diminished, the importance of hard work, *productive* leisure, and the avoidance of personal pleasure (self-denial) is interwoven in much of the social and economic fabric of the core culture. Suppression of the physical self, or expression of the sexual self with concurrent feelings of guilt and anxiety, is often related to problems of sexual dysfunction, especially among middle-class Americans. Activities engaged in simply for personal pleasure are often taken only as a "special reward" for hard work, and even then the reward is often accompanied by feelings of guilt. Punctuality and time-centeredness, conscientious individuality, perfection and accomplishment, overwork and dedication to work, and conformity to the needs of bureaucratic structures continue to be important value objects in North America today, carrying with them the related psychological symptoms of stress, anxiety, guilt, and depression. As the society becomes ever more technical and complex, achievement and success, so defined by the social and individual work ethic, become harder and harder to attain. However, Lasch (1983, 1991) believes that the Puritan work ethic, which praised work as good for the human psyche, has gradually decayed until today it consists only of the idea of success that one gets from a marketable image and the ability to manipulate others.

Yankelovich (1981), May (1981), and Weingarten (1982) have described how social status, at least for the Anglo-Saxon majority, was homogeneous, clear, uniform, and rigid until the onset of social changes in the 1960s and 1970s. Perhaps much of the current shift in social values is a "shock wave" in the core culture leading to a reformulation of social ethics and personal behavior that will be more conducive to psychological and physical health. The pattern of inclusion of minority group culture in relation to value shifts within the dominant culture in future years is unknown. Psychological "worthwhileness" and social status are difficult to attain, and in many cases impossible, if unfair discrimination continues to be imposed, whether it be according to race, ethnic origins, religion, sex, or age. One of the greatest issues that faces the United States today may be how to reaffirm honorable work as a basis for self-respect within a complex, culturally diverse society.

● PROTESTANT AMERICANS TODAY

Those people who have joined Protestant churches number about 94 million in North America and approximately 351 million worldwide, according to the 1989 Encyclopaedia Britannica Book of the Year. There are hundreds of denominations and sects that may differ either slightly or greatly from one another. White Protestant men and women are found throughout every level of the socioeconomic class structure, and Protestant men have traditionally commanded the top positions in occupations. In particular, Protestants have maintained control of national leadership positions and influence in upper-class social institutions. Thus far all the presidents of the United States, with the exception of Jefferson, Lincoln, Andrew Johnson (all of who claimed no religious affiliation), and John Kennedy (who was Catholic), have been Protestants. Although non-White minority groups have achieved positions in local government and business, they have done so through the development of their own upper-class social institutions. Socioeconomic advantages for White Protestants due to higher educational attainment are especially evident. Greater socioeconomic mobility for White Anglo-Saxon Americans has also been evidenced but can be attributed to the smaller number of children in their families and the correspondingly greater availability of financial resources for educational expenses.

▲ APPALACHIAN AMERICANS

Who are the Appalachian Americans? Folklore conjures an image of "mountain people." This popular term for a group of people who may possess certain characteristics in common suggests a stereotype of a romantic, carefree, adventuresome, but hard life. In its negative or derogatory use, however, it implies a stereotype of a lazy, immoral, backward way of life. The offensive term "white trash" is still found in use at times, and the "hillbilly" label continues to connote a negative image. If a label has to be given, "Southern hill people" is probably the least offensive. Regardless of the name or the label, stereotypes continue to linger in the minds and actions of many Americans. Because Appalachian Americans are a group of people who have been segregated and isolated from mainstream U.S. society since the earliest history of the country, their background warrants description.

● WHAT IS APPALACHIA?

"Appalachia" is the name given to an economically deprived region in the Appalachian Mountains that includes portions of Alabama, Georgia, Kentucky, Maryland, Mississippi, New York, North Carolina, Ohio, Pennsylvania, South Carolina, Tennessee, and Virginia, and all of West Virginia. It is mountainous, rural, beautiful, and possessed of much natural wealth. Over

90% of the approximately 18 million people of Appalachia are White. Work in the coal mines has been the major source of economic livelihood for many of the people for many years; along with this has come health problems and physical disability or death from accidents and poor working conditions. During the 1950s, the increase in the use of oil and gas and the advancement in mining technology caused mass unemployment, resulting in much human despair and the need for the people to adapt to other sources of income. Many of the areas of Appalachia are accessible only by crude roads, and attempts to attract other types of industry continue to be only slightly successful. In 1965, Congress passed the Appalachian Regional Redevelopment Act, which was designed to create more jobs by attracting tourists and industry to the area.

Like so many other groups of people in search of a livelihood, Appalachian Americans (especially the men) have characteristically adjusted to the realities of life by migration to urban areas. Today, many of the migrants, for psychological and physical security, form Appalachian communities within these urban areas, although some tend to merge into existing neighborhood communities. Dependence on public assistance has contributed to feelings of personal conflict, and the lower quality of schools in Appalachia has produced a high rate of adult illiteracy. Differences in socioeconomic class standing are especially observable when the masses of poor Appalachians are contrasted with the smaller group of people in the area who are wealthier and more powerful. Of course, as in any other region of the country, there are a middle-class core and a professional class in Appalachia. West Virginia, where two-thirds of the population live in rural areas, is one of the poorest states in Appalachia. Between 1980 and 1990, the population of the state decreased by 8%, with many people leaving to find jobs in northern and western states. Nearly all the residents of West Virginia were born in the United States; many of the original settlers were Scotch-Irish. Methodists and Baptists constitute the largest religious groups in the state.

● APPALACHIAN AMERICAN ORIGINS

It is believed that much of the area of Appalachia was originally settled by debtors, orphans, and criminals who were sent by Great Britain to work the tobacco plantations and to provide a buffer against attacks from the French and the Native Americans (Caudill, 1963). The particular regional dialect of Southern hill people at times seems reminiscent of the inflections, vocabulary, and pronunciation of Old World, or Elizabethan, England. Vontress (1976) has noted that "mountain people tend to use simple Anglo-Saxon words as opposed to long Latinate words. Their speech is characterized by a reduction in qualifiers, adjectives, and adverbs, especially those which qualify feelings" (pp. 283–284). Their cultural system has persisted as a means of living a life that they know best. They are highly individualistic people with a strong sense of primary loyalty to family relations. Governmental authority and the science of medicine, for example, have lower priority than the wisdom, direction, and security that are derived from family life. The solution to civil matters and interpersonal relations is often best decided by the individual within the context of the family structure. My personal interviews with Appalachians reveal a minority-group perspective on the world; the majority group, or the mainstream society, is viewed as hostile to their way of life. The majority group is often represented by the Internal Revenue Service officers, who, like an enemy, seek to disrupt their social and economic life.

● VALUES AND BELIEFS OF APPALACHIAN AMERICANS

Southern hill people are interested in the preservation of their cultural individualism and a strong belief in the family as the primary structure for socialization. Dependence on kin is seen as vital to their existence. These forms of expression have been reinforced through many years as adaptive modes of living in a geographically isolated region with coal and lumber industries that are exploitive of both nature and individual, and as personal security against the hardships imposed by periods of low income.

Lewis (1979) has described some basic attitudes toward life that create conflict when Southern hill people relate to medical professionals; Table 3-3 summarizes the main points. These potential cultural barriers also function in relations with other types of professionals.

Professional training creates disciplined specialists. The content of the discipline often takes precedence over the person it seeks to assist. It is to be hoped that "professionals will learn to talk to people, not patients. They must unlearn a degree of their training and learn to be more human" (Lewis, 1979).

▲ THE U.S. MAINSTREAM AND THE ANGLO-SAXON HERITAGE

Core culture, dominant culture, majority culture, majority society, and *common culture* are all terms used interchangeably in reference to the social, economic, and political way of life that currently prevails in the United States. It does not mean the White Anglo-Saxon Protestant (WASP) culture in the strict or literal sense of the concept. The native WASP cultural system, through interaction with the environment of the New World, has been modified and changed. Some aspects were lost or weakened and some were strengthened and amplified in diverse ways during the historical evolution of the nation. The basic patterns of beliefs in the WASP cultural system provided the early settlers with a means by which social relations, security, and status needs could be met in adapting to the new environment. Thus, physical and psychological fulfillment and survival were defined according to the meanings that these people attached to life as they saw it and as they experienced it. The cultural system, as identified through their basic patterns of belief, became the reference point for the only possible way to comprehend and deal with life that they knew at the time. Cultural conflict, commencing with the Native Americans, was inevitable. As each succeeding wave of immigrants entered the country, the established system attempted to adapt to the newcomers according to a characteristic pattern of relationship phases:

TABLE 3-3 Attitudinal contrasts between trained professionals and mountaineers.

Trained Professionals	Mountaineers
Taught to relate impersonally and to deal with others on an objective basis. The trained professional learns how to act as a "doctor," "lawyer," or other role.	For mountaineers, impersonality is odd. They are brought up to act person-to-person; to be treated as a role is a dehumanizing and demoralizing thing.
A professional's aloof, objective approach could precipitate a suspicious reaction from mountaineers, which in response can prompt the doctor (or other professional) to think the mountaineer is just stupid or uncooperative.	If a mountaineer cannot penetrate the aloof "shell" of the professional, he or she tends to become suspicious.
Status roles may play a part in the professional/mountaineer relationship. One's sense of being is concerned with status in the predominant society.	In the old mountain society, there is no class structure or struggle. Underground in a coal mine, everybody is the same.
Professional people have organized lifestyles. Professionals are trained for order and punctuality. They think things can be arranged. Planning is essential and foremost.	Mountaineers have less ordered lifestyles. For them, life flows more naturally. They're not planners. They keep things "loose."
Professionals optimistically compete with life through striving to master and control imperfections in others and in life conditions.	Mountaineers have a more relaxed attitude toward life. They approach life with contentment and take it as it comes. Some might call this "fatalism." However, given a situation in which advancement and the opportunity to change things were nonexistent, it would not be fatalism, but realism.

SOURCE: Adapted from *"Trained professionals and mountaineers: Cross-cultural contrasts"* by H. Lewis. Presentation given at Northern Illinois University, September 24, 1979. Adapted by permission.

1. *Segregation:* isolation of the new group
2. *Accommodation:* furnishing what is needed by the new group as a settlement to "keep peace" or ensure their survival
3. *Adaptation:* modification or adjustment of differences so that the group is "more fit" for existence in the social environment
4. *Assimilation:* absorption of the group into the existing culture

The melting-pot idea of the formation of a new national culture out of an amalgamation of the cultures of new immigrants has not materialized. The initial political, economic, and social systems continue, while the country at large is characterized by the incipient heterogeneousness of many diverse cultural groups. Yet, Schlesinger (1991) believes that "to deny the essentially European origins of American culture is to falsify history" (p. 81). Whatever influence the Anglo-Saxon cultural base might have had, "it is no longer an exercise in Anglo-Saxon domination" (p. 67). Furthermore, Brookhiser (1991) says: "If the only living and healthy values to which the whole country has access are WASP values, then anything restorative or profitable we try to accomplish has to draw on them" (p. 16). Thus, according to Brookhiser, drawing on values and behaviors such as respect for democratic principles, individuals making their own choices, civic-mindedness, and following one's conscience will promote a common culture, a single society, a bond of union.

■ WHITE ETHNIC AMERICANS

Eighty-five percent of the immigrants who settled in the United States before 1880 were from northern or western Europe. These "old immigrants" brought with them the Anglo-Saxon culture or, through the process of acculturation, acquired major aspects of the culture. In the hundred years from 1820 to 1920, 33 million old immigrants entered the country. However, by the 1890s, "new immigrants" from southern and eastern Europe had altered the balance. These new people were predominantly from Austria, Hungary, Czechoslovakia, Greece, southern Italy, Sicily, Poland, Portugal, Spain, Russia, and Yugoslavia. The term *new White ethnic Americans* is applied because the immigrants from southern and eastern Europe constituted new groups of people who were culturally different from the old Anglo-Saxon immigrants. Jews from Russia, Poland, Lithuania, and Hungary also constituted a large mass immigration during the same period, but their socioreligious culture and historical pattern of settlement in the United States were different from those of both the old Americans and the other new ethnics. Although White ethnic Americans have moved into the economic mainstream of the United States, social assimilation into the WASP culture did not occur as it did for the many other people who immediately followed the English and who were more like the English people in religious and cultural life.

▲ THE CATHOLIC EXPERIENCE

One major difference between the old and new White immigrants occurs in their socioreligious world views. Catholicism functions as an influence in the adaptive process for many of the new White ethnic groups, and perpetuation of spiritual and ideological ties with Catholicism in one form or another is an important characteristic of many of the southern and eastern European people who migrated in great masses to the United States between 1880 and 1920 (Greeley, 1974, 1977; Novak, 1971).

● HISTORICAL RELATIONSHIP OF CHURCH AND SOCIETY

The Catholic church, which had bound Western culture into one Christian community for hundreds of years, became fragmented as a result of the

Protestant Reformation movement in the 1500s. The Reformation sought to reform the abuses of the established church as well as to restructure the image of the relationship between humankind and God. The great power of the Catholic church influenced all parts of living, and in order to maintain this influence, the church often made concessions to governments and kingdoms as a means of continuing to serve and reach the spiritual needs of the masses of people. The failure of its structural function to control materialistic impulses led to inconsistencies between the expressed Christian values and actual corruption of church officials. It is not unusual for any religious system to adapt to the secular order in the process of cultural evolution—both dominating and being dominated by it—and the balance between religious beliefs and social beliefs can be unpredictable at any time in history. The situation is especially complex in the multicultural society of the United States, where diverse religions are present within a predominantly Protestant-based society.

● CATHOLICISM AND THE NEW IMMIGRANTS

Some people believe that Catholicism is a religion of the heart and that Protestantism is a religion of the rational mind. The pervasive influence of Catholicism in the lives of the new immigrants can be found in their conscientious fulfillment of duty, awe of higher powers, deep reflection, inner sacred preoccupation, and a close and lasting relationship with the supernatural (that is, the ultimate structure of the universe, its center of power, and human destiny). Belief in the supernatural is emotionally charged—heartfelt—and personal direction is guided by the supernatural or deduced from its existence.

▲ PERSISTENCE OF WHITE ETHNIC CULTURES

The prevailing thought during much of American history has been that the United States was becoming a monocultural society and that the large numbers of immigrants who followed the British would be assimilated into one homogeneous cultural group. Even as recently as the 1940s and 1950s, this was a predominant theme in much of the writing of sociologists, and it was predicted that the ghetto-like living of the diverse ethnic groups would disappear by the second and third generations. The Americanization, or movement into Anglo-Saxon culture, of close-knit clusters of European ethnic groups living in proximity and maintaining Old World ways, at least in urban areas, has not occurred as expected (Abramson, 1970; Greeley, 1974, 1977; Novak, 1971).

Congress in 1973 passed the Ethnic Heritage Studies Bill, which provided for recognizing and encouraging the study of ethnic groups in the curriculum of the schools. However, the miniscule amount of financial assistance provided by the bill was considered ineffectual for the purpose. Inherent in the dual emphases of monoculturalism (or assimilation) and multiculturalism (or pluralism) within the nation is the influence of cultural diversity on opportunity for socioeconomic achievement (Greeley, 1969; Kantrowitz, 1973). Maintaining ties and identity with one's ethnic group can provide the means to achieve success and affluence, through what Greeley (1969) calls "mobility pyramids," but emphasis solely on ethnic advantages can hinder socioeconomic success in the larger society, and mobility pyramids can become "mobility traps." According to Gans (1962), Gordon (1964), and Lopreato (1970), rigid class factors in the larger society, more than ethnicity, may be linked to socioeconomic mobility. The State of Illinois passed House Bill 76, effective in 1982, which amended that state's Human Rights Act by adding the category "national origin" as a consideration in the hiring of state employees. Under the proposed rules, any ethnic group with 2% or more of the Illinois population is eligible to petition for consideration if less than 80% of its available work force is represented among the state's jobs. Though the Illinois act may be, in part, politically inspired as an enhancement of political group power, it also symbolizes and reflects the honest desire of White American ethnic groups to be recognized as Blacks have been in other governmental legislation. Krug (1976) has identified two events that he believes have given renewed vitality to White ethnic life: (1) the civil rights revolution in the Black community in the 1960s and 1970s, which generalized to White ethnic group demands for equal political and economic rights and a recognition of their aspirational needs, and (2) unprecedented changes in the social, political, and economic life of the country, which contributed to a return to former traditions and customs as a source of strength and security.

Although there is variation among individuals within a group and between groups, some ethnic groups continue to have some ties to old cultural values, language, nationality, or religion (Fast, 1977, 1978). Many prefer to live with members of the same group; for example, many large cities have Italian-American, Greek-American, or Polish-American communities. But in some areas such segregation has been historically forced by the majority group rather than voluntary. Ethnic groups provide their members with a feeling of belonging and can bring variety and vitality to a society by the introduction of their ideas and ways of life. Whether Old World heritages will persist in different ethnic groups is, of course, open only to speculation. Studies of second and third generations of immigrants are needed to determine the prevalence of cultural traditions and values beyond mere interest in the language, occasional celebration of special days, or preparation of traditional foods. Gans (1962), in reference to Italian Americans, has suggested that these small ethnic flourishes in lifestyle could be labeled "symbolic ethnicity." Three ethnic groups will serve here as examples of those whose members continue to identify in some way with aspects of traditional ways, while remaining aware of the interactive influence of mainstream culture with their values and world views.

● ITALIAN AMERICANS

In 30 years, from 1880 to 1910, a wave of 4.5 million emigrants from southern Italy and Sicily settled in America. Throughout Old World history, the Italian and Sicilian peasants experienced cruelty and repression in their native countries from many invading foreign nations, as well as from their own autocratic governments. The most important and most trusted structures were the family and other village residents. Most of the immigrants identified themselves in terms of their town or village of origin rather than country. Security was to be found only in the solidarity and affection of the immediate family and blood relatives (extended family). Sicily and southern Italy were the poorest areas of Italy, and these peasant people came to America to escape poverty and repression. However, they loved the small villages they had left, and many desired only to save money and return as wealthy Americans.

Settled-in Americans expressed strong attitudes of prejudice and ridicule toward "foreigners" who seemed to want only to exploit their new country for financial gain. The majority of Italians were illiterate and unskilled workers who worked hard and were subjected to exploitation by employers. Strength for survival in a hostile land was found in maintaining their old family life and settling in closely knit neighborhoods. The strong system of family loyalty, social relationships, and church preserved them from disintegration and absorption into the Anglo-Saxon culture. However, Italians who left that structure and eventually moved to other areas of the country, such as San Francisco and Chicago, assimilated many of the customs of the dominant society (Schiavo, 1975).

The historic suspicion of and hostility toward governmental authorities stimulated the development of the Italian crime syndicate, which to some Italians brought self-respect, security, and economic livelihood (Krug, 1976, pp. 23–28; Lopreato, 1970, p. 128). Corruption in some urban municipal governments during this period also reinforced the acceptability of organized crime as a means of economic accomplishment in the Italian immigrant society (Lopreato, 1970, p. 134). Although it was risky, gaining success in this manner was more expedient than achievement through education and hard work, which were so traditional, and readily available, to members of the mainstream culture. The old problem of the small number of Italian Americans who are members of organized crime, estimated at less than 6,000, continues to perpetuate a negative stereotype that is often generalized to all Italian Americans. The millions of law-abiding Italians and others who are offended by this distortion routinely confront the news media, government officials, and others who, intentionally or unintentionally, reinforce this stereotypic image. A "godfather," or "godparent," in Italian tradition is an honored individual who is given love and respect and has the welfare of a child at heart. It is a way of protecting the young and passing on wisdom and tradition. The *padrone* system also worked toward assistance in economic assimilation: "The padrone, or boss, was someone who spoke their language and who could contact American employers. . . . In America the padrone recruited mining, railroading, and agricultural labor, negotiating contracts for the laborers he herded around in gangs" (Rolle, 1972, p. 54).

Few second-generation Italian children went to college. The pressure to leave school and work to add to the family income was great. Many carved niches for themselves in certain occupational areas, such as city fire and police departments, and others took employment with utility companies and post offices. Subsequent generations of Italian Americans have attained income levels approximately the same as other ethnic groups. Population data for 1979 (U.S. Bureau of the Census, 1982a) show that respondents who identified their single ancestral origin as Italian had a median family income of $16,993. Although not as high as that reported by Scots ($20,018) and Germans ($17,531), the Italian median family income slightly exceeded the income reported by the Polish ($16,977), English ($16,891), and Irish ($16,092).

The Italians who immigrated to the United States were among the most illiterate of the ethnic groups, and conflict between the traditional Italian definition of achievement and that of the mainstream culture was inevitable (Lopreato, 1970, pp. 141–165). Before 1945, Italian Americans sent fewer children to college than did most other White ethnic groups (Abramson, 1970; Rolle, 1972, 1980). According to population data collected in 1979 (U.S. Bureau of the Census, 1982a) college attendance for males in this group is approximately on a level with that average among some other White ethnic groups, such as the Irish and Polish (28.6% of the male respondents and 16.5% of the female respondents who identified their single ancestral origin as Italian had attended college for one or more years). "Success," according to mainstream values, however, is only one way to compare the life and values of a minority culture. "Making it," according to Italian Americans, is more complex and involves attitudes and feelings about family relationships and personal identity. The mainstream culture emphasizes individuality and material achievement, often at the cost of breaking away from family, old friends, and the culture of parents and grandparents. For young Americans of ethnic Italian background, then, intergenerational cultural conflict follows from opposing messages: "move ahead" and "be successful" versus "don't change" and "remain close to us."

● POLISH AMERICANS

Although there have been Polish people in North America since colonial days, the large mass of three million Poles came to the United States between 1880 and 1920. They came from a country that had staunchly defended Catholic beliefs and Western civilization from the Russians, Turks, and Mongols. Throughout history, the stubborn and proud Poles had been faced with attack and division by other nations; finally, in 1918, a free Poland was created. To this day, Poles are characterized as strongly independent, freedom-loving, patriotic, and solidly united in ethnic spirit. To a Pole, church and country are the same; that is, it is the *Polish* Catholic church. Like the Italians who migrated to America, they were overwhelmingly poor, illiterate, powerless people from rural areas.

The Polish immigrants were mostly unskilled and came from the least advanced southern and eastern parts of Poland, areas that still practiced a feudal economy. They were not equipped to move into an industrialized country, and thus many willingly volunteered to perform hard, menial labor in the steel mills and coal mines of Pennsylvania, Ohio, and Indiana, in the automobile factories and foundries of Detroit, and in the stockyards of Chicago. The Poles were among the eastern Europeans who literally built the basic industry of America through their sweat and hard work. Even today, many work at two jobs. They value frugality, careful saving, and the wise use of financial resources. For them, culture shock was great, and because so many were illiterate, the few existing Polish-language newspapers could not help them much in the process of adaptation to their new country. Polish names, to the established Americans, were unpronounceable, so many Poles, sensitive and chagrined, "Anglo-Saxonized" their names to survive and to hide their true ethnic identity. A feeling of ethnic inferiority has been reinforced, even in many second- and third-generation Poles. Negative stereotypes of the Polish people linger today, despite the efforts of Polish Americans and others to eliminate offensive, distasteful, and unwarranted "Polish jokes" and other ethnic slurs.

Women in the Polish family were traditionally the managers of domestic affairs; the authority of the male parent over his offspring has been understood by long tradition in Polish culture. Children were always expected to obey without question and to contribute to the family welfare. In the United States, therefore, intergenerational conflict has often followed the children's movement toward economic independence if it seemed to threaten the family status. Uncooperative action or shaming the family in any way was punished by exclusion by both the immediate family and the extended family. Older parents also expected their children to fulfill economic obligations. Psychologically and financially, many parents are not prepared to maintain themselves independently of their adult children.

The crime rate, beyond the adolescent years, is lower than that of other groups. The divorce rate among Polish Americans is also relatively low for various reasons: one is adherence to Polish Catholicism and a second is the Poles' moral concept of human nature. Human nature is seen as impetuous and having potential for impulsive disturbance unless controlled. The family is a means of controlling basic human nature. Shame and ridicule will be brought on a man, and most certainly on a woman, who resorts to divorce. Open conflict is best handled, or balanced, by the mutual need for cooperative action (Lopata, 1976). Entering into marriage is a serious venture and not to be taken lightly.

● JEWISH AMERICANS

Whereas the Italians and Poles were illiterate peasants from villages or rural areas in their native countries, many of the three million Jews who came to America from Russia, Poland, Lithuania, and Hungary had been forced by governmental restrictions in those countries "to make their livelihood as small merchants, peddlers, and artisans" (Krug, 1976, p. 28). Doctors, teachers, writers, engineers, and other professionals were also represented in the migration of 1880 to 1914 and in the exodus from Germany in later periods. In their countries of origin they typically lived in city and town ghettos, and in those segregated areas they created the social structure they needed to survive. Ghetto living in the United States also provided a type of protective structure in their early settlement pattern (Wirth, 1928). The Jews were literate. They spoke Yiddish and read Hebrew. Like other immigrant groups, they sought economic improvement of their lives, but they also fled from religious and political persecution. During World War II, six million European Jews were murdered by the Nazis in the "Great Holocaust."

Culture shock was not as great for the Jews as for other ethnic groups because they were literate and because the United States represented a "permanent" home, away from political oppression and wandering, and a wonderful land of opportunity. Unlike other ethnic groups, they had no intention of ever returning to their place of origin, simply because there was no place to which to return. They were readily adaptable to the new culture and many were already accustomed to urban living. They were also experienced with the conditions and trauma of minority status in hostile surroundings. Jewish devotion to family life was, and is, highly valued, and loyalty to kin, along with a strong spirit of ethnocentrism, offered strength in confronting many environmental obstacles.

The Jews faced prejudice and discrimination, as did other groups, but they also made steady progress in their adaptation. Success and advancement through education have always been major goals, encouraged by generations of study of the Torah and Talmud. Characteristic Jewish "liberalism" and a desire for betterment of the world extend back "to the early history of the Jewish people and are the consequences of the long experience of almost 2,000 years of sojourns. . . . Responsibility for the plight of the poor, the widows, and the orphans has been a part of the Jewish religion which stresses *this* worldliness" (Krug, 1976, p. 46). The strong desire for formal learning and respect for the scholar are generally accepted cultural values for many Jews. Vocational movement into the clothing industry in New York and Chicago and into other businesses and factories elsewhere, and upward mobility away from blue-collar jobs, was yet another pattern of general movement for Jewish immigrants.

■ SUMMARY

1. This chapter has presented profiles of three cultural groups in the United States: Native Americans, Anglo-Saxon Americans, and White ethnic Americans.

2. Native Americans, the first people to immigrate to North America approximately 20,000 years ago, established separate nations and tribes, hundreds of which continue to exist today. About 840,000 of these original Americans were in North America at the time of discovery of the continent by Europeans, and it is estimated that between 15 and 20 million were living in Latin America. By 1900, only about 243,000 were recorded in the United States. Today, approximately 2 million Native Americans live in the United States, with the Navajo Nation being the largest group (approximately 148,000). Although the original Americans moved throughout the country, the interaction of cultural heritage with various geographical environments influenced the emergence of diverse tribal cultures.

3. Five general ethnogeographic native cultures are identified in North America:

a. Peoples of the Far North
b. Tribes of the Eastern Woodlands
c. Tribes of the Plains
d. Tribes of the Northwest
e. Tribes of the Southwest

4. Today, approximately 38% of Native Americans live inside reservations and other federally identified areas. The reservation system has encountered social, educational, and economic adversities; however, enterprising Native American groups have started various economic ventures that provide employment and alternative sources of income for tribal people.

5. Although Native Americans comprise approximately 263 distinct tribes having many languages and dialects, they share a value ideology and socioreligious culture. The basic theme is respect for the earth and nature, from which comes not only survival in meeting basic needs but also the comprehension of life and one's relations with a separate, higher spiritual being and with other human beings. A belief system manifested in four values is related to the Native American experience:

a. God is a benevolent force.
b. The self is understood by observing nature.
c. Relationships with others emphasize interdependence and sharing.
d. The world is interconnected according to the same process and relationships that can be observed in nature.

6. Although each tribe has its own distinct problems, all face certain issues in common: the feeling for loss of land, domination, desire for self-determination, value conflict with mainstream culture, and inaccurate stereotypes of Native Americans in mainstream society.

7. Anglo-Saxon Americans, beginning with the English, established the base that was to become the mainstream culture in the United States. Protestant ethics have especially influenced mainstream values that have become incorporated into the economic, political, and social life of the country. Some features of traditional Protestant values are as follows:

a. Individual direction, determination, independence, and autonomy, along with equality among individuals
b. Self-fulfillment and self-worth gained through hard work and signs of achievement
c. Assistance extended to others when needed for their own self-fulfillment or self-direction
d. Mastery over one's nature and one's environment
e. Dedication to God and moral living according to biblical scriptures

8. The early Anglo-Saxon immigrants established themselves in power positions and desired that the established Native Americans and other emigrants from northern and western Europe blend into a new culture. The pattern that characterized the settlement of newcomers seemed to be a process

of segregation, accommodation, adaptation, assimilation. As other groups that were more ethnically different from the early settlers emigrated from southern and eastern Europe, pressure for Americanization increased. Most newcomers embraced conformity in order to achieve economic success and mobility, but neither melting into a common pot (infusion of all cultures) nor forced Americanization was completely achieved. More recently, cultural pluralism—coexistence and interaction of the dominant culture with the cultures of other groups—has become more accepted as a concept that might afford new directions and unity to the nation. Resurgent WASP values may offer purposeful centrality to the multicultural blending.

9. Appalachian Americans were also discussed in this chapter as an Anglo-Saxon group that has experienced poverty and isolation from many aspects of mainstream culture. There are distinctive and identifiable values, beliefs, and experiences in the culture of the Southern hill people: a strong loyalty to family and kin, person-to-person informality, a realistic acceptance of life, and the necessity of flowing and coping with life's problems.

10. Like other immigrants, White ethnic Americans came to North America primarily for socioeconomic improvement, but freedom of religion and ideological thought as well as power in political life were also motivations. White ethnic Americans are defined as those people who emigrated in great masses from southern and eastern Europe to the United States between 1880 and 1920. The backgrounds and immigration experiences of three of the ethnic groups, Italian Americans, Polish Americans, and Jewish Americans, were described.

11. Catholicism and cultural ways related to national or ethnogeographic origins have played an important role in the experiences of White ethnic groups in America. Despite differences in ethnic languages and traditions, the bond of Catholicism has probably created some similarities. Socioreligious values appear in the following ways:

a. Conscientious fulfillment of duty
b. Awe of higher powers
c. Inner sacred preoccupations
d. Feeling-inspired closeness to the supernatural

12. A strong system of family loyalty and closely knit social relationships involving definite expectations and obligations are also often emphasized in the White ethnic groups. Expectations of marital and parental roles are usually clearly defined and authority of the father is customarily respected. Adult children are often obligated to protect and provide for the welfare of their parents.

13. The Jewish ethnic group in America was described as liberal-oriented, striving for fairness and equality, and concerned for the plight of less-fortunate others. Jews have sought to pursue those values in their own way through the improvement of their surroundings and living conditions, devotion to the family, self-improvement and learning, and respect for education. The degree to which any particular aspect of cultural ethnicity persists in the future for White ethnic groups can only be speculation. Ongoing research and study of second and third generations is needed.

CHAPTER

PROFILES OF THE AMERICAN PEOPLE: BLACK AMERICANS, HISPANIC AMERICANS, ASIAN AMERICANS

Like Chapter 3, this chapter presents profiles of three groups of people who belong to our multicultural society. Prior to the arrival of most other immigrants, African Americans were a group of people taken involuntarily from their African countries, transported to the American continent, and without choice subjugated into slavery early in the settlement of the country. Haitians are recent arrivals, and various groups of Asians and Hispanics constitute both early and recent arrivals. Because of the experience of enslavement for the Black people and because all three of these major groups—Blacks, Asians, Hispanics—originate in cultures that are traditionally different from Western culture, they can also be considered as subjugated minority groups who have experienced differential extremes of prejudice, segregation, and discrimination in the history of the nation. In this respect, Native Americans can also be considered a historically subjugated minority group.

■ BLACK AMERICANS

Although some early African immigrants arrived as indentured servants, the vast majority of African Americans came as slaves. The Portuguese and Spanish first brought African slaves, who were more immune than they to malaria and yellow fever, to work the sugar plantations in Brazil and the Caribbean area in the 1500s. The purchase and sale of slaves was a common practice at the time for many nations of the world. Africans, Moslems, and Christians all practiced the enslavement of prisoners of war in the Mediterranean Sea area. Up to 1885, the British, Dutch, and French brought approximately 10 million slaves to the Americas from West African countries. The international trade in slaves was outlawed by the United States and England in 1808, although some smuggling of slaves continued. A total of approximately 500,000 slaves came to the United States and Canada. A greater number were imported into Brazil, Haiti, Jamaica, and Cuba, but death rates were higher and birthrates were lower there than in the United States.

▲ PHASES OF BLACK HISTORY IN THE UNITED STATES

The social, political, and economic life of Blacks in the United States has passed through historical phases that can be categorized according to the characteristics of the relationship between Black Americans and the majority group. Pettigrew (1980), drawing from Turner and Singleton (1978), outlines the prevailing attitudes of White Americans toward Black Americans in nine chronological periods. These attitudes have generally emphasized notions of White racial superiority or patronage. Pettigrew points out that many White Americans have held more liberal and less abasing views of Blacks, but only the most predominant beliefs in the general society are summarized in Table 4-1.

▲ THREE BLACK SUBGROUPS

Sowell (1978) proposes that the history of Black people in the United States can be comprehended by understanding the contrasting patterns of three distinct Black subgroups: (1) "free persons of color," (2) emancipated slaves and their descendants, and (3) those Blacks who migrated from the West Indies. The fact that members of two of the groups, the free Blacks and those who came from the West Indies, experienced greater socioeconomic mobility sensitizes one to the impact that the slavery system has had on the third group, the freed slaves. Sowell's use of the label "free persons of color" is intended to distinguish those Blacks who did not experience the conditions of slavery from those who did; "freed" Blacks were those who were brought to the United States as slaves and continued so until they were freed after the Civil War.

● FREE BLACKS

Fourteen percent of the African American population in 1830, or about 320,000, were legally free or "quasi-free" people. This vanguard group, even since the 17th century, was economically self-sufficient. The origins of members of the free group are traced back to their status as indentured servants who worked off their bondage over a number of years. Historically, they have been prominent in the Black middle class. Their offspring, from birth, were also free. It was also common in the slaveholding system of the Western world for the slave owner to free a female slave by whom he had fathered children, as well as the children themselves. *Mulattoes*, in the strict

TABLE 4-1 Attitudes Toward Black Americans in American History	
Period of American History	Predominant Beliefs in the Mainstream Culture
Slavery and Racial Oppression	
–1650 (English heritage)	Blackness is evil in the eyes of God.
1650–1760 (colonial America)	Black "animalistic" nature needs control.
1760–1820 (Revolutionary era)	Slavery is necessary because Blacks cannot manage their own freedom.
1820–1860 (pre–Civil War)	Slavery is good for the development of the nation and is a means to "protect" uncivilized and dependent Blacks.
Racial Oppression	
1860–1914 (Civil War and Reconstruction)	The "failure" of Blacks to achieve positive advancement in the mainstream culture confirms their basic inferiority. Their inability to use available opportunities necessitates supervision and control to prevent degeneration to a primitive state.
1914–1941 (World War I to World War II)	The inferiority of Blacks is confirmed by scientific research, for example, in the areas of evolutionary theory and psychological testing. Continued racial segregation is necessary.

definition of the term, "have still been overrepresented to some extent among the Negro middle class, as they were among the 'free persons of color'" (Sowell, 1978, p. 13). Quasi-free Blacks also included slaves who were owned by plantation employers or by other Blacks but were free to hire themselves out. A large proportion of the free group lived in urban areas as skilled workers. Others were slaves who supervised other slaves or were house servants who enjoyed higher status relationships with the family members of the slave owners. According to Sowell (1978), this smaller group of quasi-free Blacks also added to the "more acculturated, educated (or education-minded) Negro middle class or leadership group in the later post–Civil War Period" (p. 9). Frazier (1932) believed that the early Black middle class was essentially formed from among this group of free Blacks.

Free persons were predominantly urban people who had moved to cities in the North or to the more liberal regions of the South. New Orleans, Louisiana, and Charleston, South Carolina, are two places where they established wealthy and respected communities. Many free Blacks also settled in Washington, D.C., and by 1830, half of the city's Black population were free

TABLE 4-1 (*continued*)	
Period of American History	Predominant Beliefs in the Mainstream Culture
Civil Rights "Promises"	
1941–1948 (World War II)	Segregation is rejected as national survival needs take precedence and public revulsion is felt toward the German Nazi ideas of a "pure race."
1948–1968 (postwar, civil rights years)	Blacks are not genetically inferior to Whites and can "change." Equal opportunities are necessary to counteract past discrimination and to maintain domestic tranquillity.
Moderation and "Readjustment"	
1968–present	Inferiority of Blacks is due to themselves and their motivational level. "Change" has been too sudden and some adjustments are necessary in the previously granted concession areas of housing, jobs, education, desegregation, and welfare and financial assistance. Many believe the social programs have failed and see them as creating a state of dependency for Blacks.

SOURCE: Adapted from *Social Forces, 56* (June 1978), 1001–1018. "A Theory of ethnic oppression: Toward a reintegration of cultural and structural concepts in ethnic relations theory," by J. H. Turner and R. Singleton, Jr., Copyright © 1978 the University of North Carolina Press.

persons. Washington, D.C., was the home of the first Black school, which was established in 1807, and the first public high school for Blacks, which was formed there in 1870. The high school became an institution of excellence, with three-quarters of its graduates going on to college (Sowell, 1974). Included among its graduates were "the first black general, the first black cabinet member, the first federal judge, the discoverer of blood plasma [Charles Drew], and the first black Senator since Reconstruction" (Sowell, 1978, p. 12). The founders of the National Association for the Advancement of Colored People in 1909 were free Blacks. Economically and socially, descendants of free Blacks continue to have prominence in the United States today. Although it may largely be a matter of conjecture, a concentration of Black physicians, dentists, lawyers, educators, and holders of academic doctorates have their origins in this group (Sowell, 1978, pp. 22–23).

The man was typically the head of the free Black family. Stability of family life was based on moral and social values rather than on material possessions or income and occupational class distinctions. Today, conscious identification by descendants of free Blacks as a separate class probably does not exist within the general Black community. However, their distinct historical background of freedom and independence provided them with the means by which they were able to achieve success in the society.

● FREED SLAVES

The elite group of free Blacks was often used historically by the White majority in questioning why other Blacks could not be successful, but the social, economic, and political situation of freed slaves was much different from that of free Blacks.

The act of bringing West Africans to the United States as slaves created a psychological paradox for a nation that was founded on principles of freedom and democracy. Suppression, violence, prejudice, and discrimination were overt symptoms of the dilemma. Even more complex were the rationalizations that evolved to defend individual egos and the cultural base of the nation. Economic, political, social, scientific, biological, moral, psychological, and religious justifications were all given, at one time or another, to explain away the dilemma. Today, the emotional residue continues to contribute to controversy and discussion in the United States, and the persistence of *regimented dependence* (governmental policies and cultural practices that work against self-reliance and personal development) continues to undermine the development of some groups of African Americans.

The slavery system. The slavery system was, by its very nature, restrictive to the development of the potential of African Americans. The most effective and profitable operation of the plantations necessitated "vocational retraining" of the slave-workers to fit the work pattern. For example, competence at reading and writing was unnecessarily counterproductive. Suppression and restriction of educational endeavors was so common by slave owners that only 1 or 2% of the slaves were literate, according to one estimate (Woodson, 1919). More recent data by Cornelius (1991) supports a much higher level of literacy that grew out of the epicenter of religion, the most powerful institution in the young nation.

Manual skills were valued, however, and the number of Black craftsmen during the period of slavery was large. Later, under discriminatory practices by labor unions, the resources and incentive to continue the training were lost. In some respects, slave life was better than that of many African and White Americans in today's society: "Nutritionally, the slave's diet exceeded today's recommended allowances . . . life expectancy of slaves in 1850 was four years less than the life expectancy of the white population of the United States at that time . . . and infant mortality was higher than for the United States as a whole, but not very different from that of southern whites" (Sowell, 1978, p. 27).

The effects of slavery on the African-American family have been controversial (Staples, 1976). Most recent research indicates that the family was a stable two-parent structure with the father as the head (Blassingame, 1972;

Fogel & Engerman, 1974). Only 1 to 2% of the children born to plantation slave women were fathered by White men (Fogel & Engerman, 1974); however, in the cities of the South, where only about 6% of all slaves lived, this proportion approached 50% (Wade, 1967). The high incidence of broken or matriarchal homes—often reported in current statistics for American Blacks living in urban ghettos—most likely originated following the period of mass migration to find employment in northern cities after 1910 (Grossman, 1989). In 1989, 43.5% of Black families had a female householder with no spouse present, as compared with 16% of all families (U.S. Bureau of the Census, 1990a). The divorce rate for African Americans in 1990 was 282 per 1,000 married persons, as compared with 142 per 1,000 married persons of all races (U.S. Bureau of the Census, 1990b).

Emancipation. The first ten amendments to the Constitution (the Bill of Rights) forbid federal encroachment on individual rights. But the Black person was not accorded any significant constitutional safeguards until after the Civil War, when the 13th Amendment (1865) abolished slavery; the 14th Amendment (1868) guaranteed all persons against abrogation of their "privileges and immunities," against deprivation of life, liberty, or property without due process of law, and against denial of equal protection of the law; and the 15th Amendment (1870) assured the right to vote. From 1866 to 1975 Congress passed a series of civil rights acts implementing those amendments.

Following emancipation, thousands of unskilled and undereducated African Americans wandered the country in search of a new existence. Northern White missionaries sought to help in this confused situation, as did established members of the free Black group. Many northern cities absorbed the freed slaves, but by 1900 the Black communities were crowded and efforts to help often turned to anger and antagonism among Blacks and between Whites and Blacks. The discriminatory system known as Jim Crow became firmly established in the South by 1900; the term *Jim Crow* refers to an offensive Black stereotype in a 19th-century song-and-dance act. The United States Supreme Court's "separate but equal" doctrine in *Plessy* v. *Ferguson* (1896) only further strengthened the double standards for Whites and Blacks. The *Plessy* decision was a landmark segregation case in which "the Court held constitutional a Louisiana statute requiring segregation on railroad facilities, saying that so long as 'separate but equal' accommodations were extended Negroes there was no denial of equal protection. Taking their cue from the Plessy decision, Southern states were able to endorse the separation of the races by providing segregated facilities for Negroes which excluded them from the use of white facilities" (*Civil Rights Progress Report 1970,* 1970, p. 13). Unfair voting regulations, unequal educational standards, and discriminatory economic opportunities were especially buttressed by the Jim Crow system. Violence and terror resulted in the lynching of approximately 160 Blacks per year in the South during the 1890s.

In the North, where integrated neighborhoods had been common before 1920 and where peaceful Black neighborhoods existed, race riots and the revival of the Ku Klux Klan were tragic events in the history of the nation. The beginnings of the modern ghetto were first seen in Chicago, Detroit, Cleveland, New York, St. Louis, Philadelphia, and other large urban areas, and numerous high-rise, segregated public housing projects began to appear in the 1950s (Lemann, 1991). One most infamous incident of ill-conceived architecture in public housing was the St. Louis Pruitt-Igoe Project, which was finally demolished in 1972 as "an irremediable mistake" (Gapp, 1982).

Governmental intervention. The experience of World War II helped to discredit racism, and Americans began to question themselves and the structure of their country. The postwar period was an era of much governmental action to remedy past injustices. The 1954 Supreme Court decision in *Brown v. Board of Education of Topeka, Kansas,* declared that segregated school facilities were inherently unequal and unconstitutional. However, changes in law often precede changes in attitude, and much evasion and tokenism continued. Seven major civil rights bills to strengthen the rights of various groups of Americans were passed by Congress in the period from 1957 to 1991:

- 1957—The Civil Rights Act of 1957 was the first civil rights legislation Congress had passed since the post–Civil War Reconstruction period. It prohibited action to prevent persons from voting in federal elections and authorized the Attorney General to bring suit when a person was deprived of his or her voting rights. It also created a Civil Rights Commission and set up a Civil Rights Division in the Department of Justice.
- 1960—The Civil Rights Act of 1960 strengthened provisions of the 1957 act for court enforcement of voting rights and required preservation of voting records. It also contained limited criminal penalty provisions relating to bombing and to obstruction of federal court orders. The act was aimed primarily at school desegregation orders.
- 1964—The Civil Rights Act of 1964 prohibited discrimination in public accommodations and in programs receiving federal assistance. It also prohibited discrimination by employers and unions and set up the Equal Employment Opportunity Commission. Enforcement of voting laws and desegregation of school and public facilities was strengthened.
- 1965—The Voting Rights Act of 1965 authorized the Attorney General to appoint federal examiners to register voters in areas of marked discrimination and strengthened penalties for interference with voters' rights.
- 1968—A civil rights bill prohibited discrimination in the sale or rental of about 80% of all housing. It also protected persons exercising specified rights, such as attending school or working, and civil rights workers urging others to exercise their rights. Anti-riot provisions also were included.
- 1990—The Americans with Disabilities Act of 1990 established civil rights protection for the estimated 43 million Americans having one or more physical or mental disabilities. The four-part law covers *employ-*

ment (discrimination in hiring or on the job); *public services* (exclusion from benefits of public entities, including transportation); *public accommodations* (access to hotels, restaurants, offices, and such); and *telecommunications* (interstate and intrastate phone services).

· 1991—The Civil Rights Act of 1991 was designed to reverse a series of Supreme Court decisions limiting the ability of workers to win job discrimination suits. It addresses four categories: it enables workers to challenge *unintentional discrimination* (neutral business practices, such as height-weight requirements, that an employer believes are justified for effective job performance); it prohibits *intentional discrimination* in hiring and on-the-job experiences as based on race, religion, sex, national origin, or disability; it removes the requirement of *quotas* for hiring or promoting minority workers; and it prohibits adjustment of *test scores* to increase hiring of minorities.

Programs to implement true equality remained slow in coming, and in the 1960s summer riots occurred in urban Black ghettos as a result of frustration and rising militant feelings among Blacks, along with a growing awareness of new Black identity and pride. Resistance to Black assertiveness by the White majority, although less overt, continued to be strong and often resulted in White *backlash,* or sudden violent reactions. Black people have historically resisted their externally imposed status in American society. Their protest has taken on many different expressions and adaptive modes throughout history:

1. Rebellion against slavery
2. Pretensions of incompetence and subservient actions
3. Peaceful sit-ins, marches, voter registration drives
4. Riots and destruction of their own communities
5. Back-to-Africa movements
6. Militancy through Black power and Black nationalism
7. Black consciousness-arousal and self-pride
8. Political power movements

The 1990s. Although both Blacks and Whites seem to have assumed a moderate position within the general society, the unsettled nature of their relationship is apparent. Localized angry reactions by Black citizens continue to occur sporadically over unfair treatment or perceived injustices; there were, for example, riots and destruction in the Liberty City section of Miami in 1980, the Overtown section of Miami in 1982 and 1989, and the South-Central section of Los Angeles in 1992. Many of the civil rights needed to bring a fairer balance to the relationship between Blacks and Whites were won in the 1960s and 1970s. African Americans have been accepted in the society to a degree that reduces the reason for protest, and unless injustices or setbacks occur, the tenuous state of the relationship between Black Americans and White Americans may continue for many years.

Though concern for the major issues of civil rights and race relations may have receded in comparison with that of the 1960s and the 1970s, the fulfillment of economic and political rights has taken on more importance in the 1980s and 1990s. Unrealistic government policies, such as extreme cutbacks in social programs, could pose a threat to the future of Black people. An equal concern that influences the status of Black people, and the resulting relationship between Blacks and Whites, is the lack of knowledge and sensitivity that both Black and non-Black Americans have toward how the civil rights movement evolved (Ashmore, 1982; Branch, 1988; Farmer, 1985; Powledge, 1991; Rowan, 1990). The great thrust of the traditional freedom movement has seemingly lost momentum, and many of the outstanding leaders, such as Dr. Martin Luther King, Jr., Whitney Young, Roy Wilkins, Malcolm X, and the Reverend Ralph Abernathy, are gone. However, the emergence of a new era in Black political leadership has been observed in the national prominence of the Reverend Jesse Jackson and in the election of Blacks to a number of mayoral positions, and L. Douglas Wilder, the nation's first Black elected governor, as governor of Virginia in 1990.

A large number of Blacks have been assimilated into the middle-class society at large, and those who possess the stability of middle-class background and who are able to attain an education are capable of mobility. But two other classes are also evident: poor Blacks and a Black underclass. Poor Blacks have potential for socioeconomic mobility; generally, members of this group possess stable family structure and a degree of acceptance in the society. However, a third group, those who constitute the Black underclass, have been left without role models as the more highly achieving Blacks have moved up and out. This group, according to Ashmore (1982), has less motivation for life, unstable family structure, and weak or no job skills, and many are the third generation of families on welfare. The Black underclass, especially young Black males, constitutes a major social problem in the United States today for which there is yet no solution in sight. Other significant and persistent problems are: the 30% of African Americans living below poverty, high infant mortality, high homicide rates, high unemployment rates, and missing fathers who cannot serve as role models for a youthful population of which 33% are under 18 years.

Religion in Black life. African Americans throughout the history of the United States have participated in American Protestantism, often merging tribal traditions of African religion with Christianity. According to Jones (1972, p. 150), some of the cultural components of African religion emphasized a belief system that enabled the people to cope with environmental conditions. These beliefs were pragmatic, magical and mysterious, secular, and family oriented. Today, many African Americans are members of various Black-oriented religious denominations, including

> African Methodist Episcopal Church
> African Methodist Episcopal Zion Church
> Black Muslims
> National Baptist Convention of America
> National Baptist Convention, USA, Inc.

National Primitive Baptist Convention in the USA
Progressive National Baptist Convention, Inc.

The Black nationalist movement, the Black Muslims, is a completely American brand of Islam that has grown to encompass more than 500,000 members. Founded in Detroit in 1930 by Wali Farad, known by his followers as "the Savior" or "the Great Mahdi," it embodies both religious and anti-integrationist beliefs. The members identify themselves with the ancient lost tribe of Shabazz. Mohammedan norms replace Western ones, and the members "are required to give up vices such as overeating, drinking, using narcotics, and fornication, which their leaders say were foisted on blacks by their white masters. Women are taught homemaking and are expected to obey their husbands" (Wallechinsky & Wallace, 1975, p. 1269). *Islam* means "submission" (that is, to the will of God) in Arabic, and the followers of Islam are known as Muslims ("those who submit"). Farad was replaced as the spiritual leader in 1934 by Elijah Muhammad, who served until his death in 1975. Malcolm X (born Malcolm Little) was Elijah Muhammad's assistant and a Muslim minister from 1953 until his suspension in 1963; an outstanding preacher, albeit with strong anti-White opinions, Malcolm X believed the time had come for peaceful Black and White coexistence (Malcolm X, 1964). He was assassinated in 1965. Today, the American Muslim Mission seeks to merge with worldwide Islamic traditions and end ideas of Black nationalism. Another Islamic mission, the Nation of Islam, headed by minister Louis Farrakhan in Chicago, was formed out of a breach created by the 1975 death of patriarch Elijah Muhammad.

Kwanzaa, although not considered a religion, is a movement that seeks to establish, express, and celebrate aspects of African-American cultural identity. Some of the ritualistic aspects were first created in 1966 by activist Dr. Maulana Karenga. *Kwanzaa* is derived from the Swahili word *kwanza*, which means "first"; it is part of the phrase *matunda ya kwanza*, meaning "first fruits" (that is, the African celebration of bringing in the harvests of a season). The principles celebrated during the annual seven-day festival participated in by the Kwanzaa followers in the United States, and upon which one should live one's life, are unity, self-determination, collective work and responsibility, collective sharing, purpose, creativity, and faith.

● WEST INDIAN IMMIGRANTS

The West Indies, a 2,000-mile stretch of islands near the southern tip of Florida and the eastern tip of Mexico, comprise the independent countries of Barbados, Cuba, the Dominican Republic, Haiti, Jamaica, and Trinidad and Tobago. Other islands are governed by England, the Netherlands, France, and the United States (the Virgin Islands are territorial possessions and Puerto Rico is a commonwealth of the United States).

Although few in number (1% of the total American Black population), some of the best-known Blacks are of West Indian origin. Historically, the majority of West Indians migrated to the United States at the turn of the century. The early immigrants were relatively poor and uneducated; most settled in Harlem or the surrounding New York City area, where they took menial jobs. The socioeconomic success of the second generation may be attributed to the "settling-in" pattern of the first generation, which seemed to follow the upward movement that characterized many European ethnic groups: hard work, vocational upgrading, conscientious thrift, and education. The initial advantage for the West Indian immigrants over African Americans may rest on the West Indians' avoidance of a dependent relationship with the dominant group in their native country. Sowell (1978, p. 49) explains that the West Indians escaped the trauma of devastation and disorganization that the Civil War and the period of Reconstruction brought to African Americans and the need to depend on the dominant group that was inherent in those conditions. Although the places that the West Indians left had also practiced racism, the nonslave group—the White and mulatto population—was numerically smaller and was in no position to wage war or exert restraint on Black slaves. The "avoidance" theory may in part explain their relative success in the United States, but another important factor was the opportunity they had to strengthen *group independence,* which promoted their upward experience in the economic life of the country. The West Indian group is characterized by a distinct social self-identity, mutual interaction, group solidarity, and intragroup marriage (Maynard, 1972; Reid, 1939; Sowell, 1978). Some partial carry-over of social self-identity, at least in the early years, was seen in the Anglophilic sentiments manifested in their admiration for England and things English (Sowell, 1978, p. 47).

Haitian Americans. The historical experiences of the first West Indian immigrants were described. The most recent arrivals of West Indians to the United States are Haitian Americans. The history of Haiti is one of violence (Rey, 1970), beginning with an uprising among a slave population of 500,000 against French rule in the period of 1791 to 1804. The Republic of Haiti that was subsequently formed has decreased its prosperity due to internal strife and disputes with neighboring Santo Domingo. A series of dictatorships, most recently the Duvalier family regime from 1957 until its downfall in 1986, has repressed the freedom of the people in this nation. Since 1986, social revolution and political instability have contributed to economic chaos, government disruption, and public fear and intimidation. Haiti has had five interim governments from 1986 to 1991; in 1991, the Reverend Jean-Betrand Aristide, a champion of the poor, won the first free presidential election in 187 years of Haitian independence, only to be forced out by the army a short time later. The population of Haiti is 95% Black, and is the poorest and most densely populated in the Western Hemisphere.

According to census reports for the period from 1950 to 1960, 4,000 Haitians came to the United States; from 1970 to 1979, the number was 50,000. Many came illegally. In one month alone (October 1980), 2,280 Haitian refugees came by boat to southern Florida to escape political repression or economic depression in their native country. The great influx started in late 1979 and ended in 1981 when the U.S. government imposed restrictions after 25,000 had fled their native country. Many of the refugees were granted political asylum. Others were detained for long periods of time in refugee detention centers ranging from upstate New York to Puerto Rico. Earlier Haitian immigrants have concentrated in the state of New York, but the most recent refugees have settled in "Little Haiti" in Miami or in isolated Haitian sections of other Florida cities such as Fort Lauderdale, Pompano Beach, Belle Glade, and Immokalee. Haitian refugees who entered the United States are, like Cubans, eligible for permanent resident status after five years, according to federal government decree. Again in 1991, boatloads of Haitians fled Haiti; however, the U.S. government intercepted more than 14,000 Haitians and detained them at the U.S. Naval Base in Guantanamo Bay, Cuba. The Refugee Act of 1980 authorizes asylum only to a person who demonstrates fear of persecution on account of race, religion, nationality, membership in a particular social group, or political opinion; it does not allow asylum for economic suffering. At least two-thirds of those who fled were not allowed asylum and were returned to Haiti.

These newest Black immigrants are poor, rural people who are darker skinned and less cosmopolitan than other Black Americans, and often the least welcome by both White and African Americans. Although African Americans and Haitians share a common heritage and a history of enslavement, there is little evidence of social mixture or mutual trust (Lowenthal, 1972). Haitians are seen as a most gentle people, according to police, anthropologists, social workers, teachers, priests, Haitians, and non-Haitians. The tradition of racism is not as severe in Haiti as it is in the United States, and hostility and tension are not visible in the Haitian American communities. According to Seligman (1977), "At least half of the Haitians now living in the U.S. have immigrated illegally. Accordingly, they not only do not show up in official immigration statistics but also choose to keep a low profile and avoid contact with governmental agencies for fear of being returned to Haiti" (p. 410). Of all the ethnic groups in Miami, the Haitians have the lowest crime rate (Winerip, 1981). Haitians are often the victims, not the aggressors. According to a source interviewed by Winerip (1981), aggression in Haiti is defused through conversation that provides an outlet before violence can break out. Arguing out disagreements is a common characteristic of Haitians. Worship in Haiti (Catholic, Protestant, or voodoo) is vigorous, physical, and energy-consuming. The appearance of gentleness may also be attributed to fear instilled by the 30 years of political control in Haiti, where protest has been futile.

French is the official language of Haiti but is spoken almost exclusively by the upper classes. Most Haitians in the United States speak Creole, creating complex problems in the public schools that serve them. Creole is a fusion of French vocabulary and African grammar and is primarily spoken, not written. Haitians are family oriented, with the mother as the stabilizing influence. The control of the parents over the children extends into adulthood, their selection of a marriage mate, and even the choice of an occupation that may enhance the family status. Parental authority is respected and usually accepted without question (Rey, 1970).

■ HISPANIC AMERICANS

Hispanic is a term of convenience for U.S. residents whose ethnic roots are in countries in Latin, Central, or South America. *Latin* customarily denotes those people using languages derived from Latin, such as Spanish; *Latino* customarily denotes U.S. residents of Latin American descent. However, according to Padilla (1985), there is a collectively generated Hispanic (Hispanismo) or Latino (Latinismo) ethnic consciousness that transcends individual nationality groups. This broader Hispanic/Latino ethnic identity is most salient when two or more Spanish-speaking ethnic groups unite to further mutual interests or to resolve a problem, such as in education, employment, or social inequality. Thus, ethnicity, as so described, is more than a static set of cultural attributes, but represents a political, contextual, and situational ethnic identity that functions according to the needs of the group.

▲ INCREASE IN NUMBER AND SIGNIFICANCE

The U.S. Bureau of the Census (U.S. Department of Commerce, 1991) reported 22.3 million Hispanics in the United States in 1990, up from 14.6 million in 1980, a 53% increase. Most of the difference between 1980 and 1990 figures is due to immigration and a higher fertility rate. Immigration contributed about one-half of the growth. According to geographic place of origin, approximately 64% were from Mexico, 14% from Central and South America, 10% from Puerto Rico, 5% from Cuba, and 7% from other Spanish-origin groups. The presence of Hispanics, more than any other ethnic group, demonstrates that many regions of the country are becoming increasingly bilingual. Sixty-four percent of the Hispanic-American population lived in California, New York, and Texas in 1990. The states having the largest numbers of Americans of Hispanic origins or descent are shown in Table 4-2.

According to Census Bureau forecasts, within the next 25 years the Hispanic population will become the largest minority group in the United States (over 32 million), and estimates place the Hispanic population at 39 million by 2025. American Hispanics come from different countries and social backgrounds; thus, they do not compose a uniform, cohesive population group. They are also not culturally homogeneous but varied and complex, incorporating Spanish and other European influences as well as Indian and African traits. There is little question in the writings of many authors that already the burgeoning Hispanic population is altering mainstream American culture in a way that touches almost all areas of life, including economics, education, politics, the arts, and religion. Hispanic communities are found in all parts of the country, from migrant labor camps to the tenements of New

TABLE 4-2   States with Hispanic populations of more than 100,000 in 1980 and 1990.

	1980	1990
California	4,543,770	7,687,938
Texas	2,985,643	4,339,905
New York	1,659,245	2,214,026
Florida	857,898	1,574,143
Illinois	635,525	904,446
New Jersey	491,867	739,861
New Mexico	476,089	579,224
Arizona	440,915	688,338
Colorado	339,300	424,302
Michigan	162,388	201,596
Pennsylvania	154,004	232,262
Massachusetts	141,043	287,549
Connecticut	124,499	213,116
Washington	119,986	214,570
Ohio	119,880	139,696

SOURCES: Data from *Supplementary Reports,* U.S. Bureau of the Census, May 1981, and Bureau of the Census *News*, March 11, 1991.

York's Spanish Harlem, Chicago's West 26th Street and Humboldt Park areas, and Dade County, Florida.

▲ URBAN INFLUX AND HISPANIC UNITY

The majority of Hispanic Americans live in metropolitan areas of the country. Between 1980 and 1990, the consolidated metropolitan Los Angeles area has experienced a 73.4% increase in the Hispanic population, adding more than 2 million Hispanics, and has become the center of Chicano life in America. It is one of at least a half dozen major American cities undergoing profound cultural transformation. During the same time period, Dallas–Fort Worth more than doubled its Hispanic population, with an increase of 271,000. Since 1980, the Hispanic population in the Boston area has doubled, with an increase of 100,736; in San Diego it has increased by 85.6%, in the Phoenix area by 73.6%, in Houston-Galveston by 72.2%, in Miami–Fort Lauderdale by 70.9%, and in the Chicago area by 41.3%. Nearly 3 million Hispanics live in metropolitan New York City; there the majority of Hispanics are Puerto Rican and are concentrated in the South Bronx and Spanish Harlem areas. In addition, an estimated 300,000 other Hispanic immigrants, many illegal, from the Dominican Republic and other South and Central American countries, are living in New York City. The Hispanic population in Chicago is estimated at 600,000 or more and is roughly divided between Mexicans and Puerto Ricans. There is also a large community of Cubans in Chicago, along with smaller numbers from a dozen other Latin American countries.

Despite their cultural and ethnic diversity, the Hispanic people are united by factors such as language, religion, customs, and attitudes toward self, family, and community. These factors vary in importance according to the degree to which an individual has been assimilated into the mainstream U.S. society (Chavez, 1991). Spanish language, for example, has traditionally been an important unifying factor; however, about 85% of second-generation Hispanics speak English as their dominant language, and to what extent Spanish will remain as a unifying emotional force among future generations is difficult to guess.

▲ YOUTHFULNESS AND FAMILY CHARACTERISTICS

Hispanic Americans are a young group; in 1989, 35% were under 18 years old and only 5% were 65 years or older, while of the U.S. population in general, only 25.6% were under 18 years old and about 12.6% were 65 years or older. The median age of Hispanics is 26 years, compared with a median age of 33 years for the total population; Cuban Americans are an exception, with the median age in 1989 being 41.4 years. Hispanic Americans have larger-than-average families; about 50% in 1989 had families of 4 or more persons, with a mean number of 3.75 persons, as against a national average of 35% having families of 4 or more with an average of 3.16 persons. Cuban-American families, again, are an exception, with only 34% having 4 or more persons and an average of only 2.91 persons per family. Mexican-American families have an average of 4.10 members. To a large degree (+80%), Hispanics tend to marry Hispanics. They also tend to have lower divorce rates than other races, as measured by the ratio of divorced persons per 1,000 married persons; in 1990, the ratio was 129 divorced Hispanic persons per 1,000 married persons as against 142 divorced persons of all races per 1,000 married persons.

▲ HISPANIC CULTURE IN THE NEW WORLD

The presence of Hispanics in the Americas is not new. The Spanish conquistadores had moved through Mexico and Florida and far into what is now the southwestern United States by 1528. These early Spanish explorer-soldiers brought with them their language, values, and Catholic religious traditions. They intermarried with the Native Americans in Mexico, and from the resulting genetic merger evolved a new mixed European-Indian (or Spanish-Indian) culture. The offspring of the intermarriages are called *mestizo*. The great majority of the Mexican people today are mestizos and think of themselves as mestizos as a matter of national pride. About 55% of the population in Mexico is mestizo, 30% Indian, and 15% White. Many of the Spaniards and mestizos settled in northern New Mexico and, due to isolation from Mexico and Spain, became known as Spanish Americans, or Hispaños.

The era of exploration took Spaniards into many other areas throughout the world, and over hundreds of years the process of intermarriage and cultural fusion took place. In Puerto Rico and Cuba, where African slaves were imported, fusion took place over many years among the cultures of the European Spaniards, the natives of the New World, and Blacks from West Africa. Merging of the Spanish culture with the native culture of Central America, South America, and the Philippine Islands also occurred. According to Ruiz and Padilla (1977), the *balance* between the values and traditions of the European Spanish culture and those of the native cultures often determines the nature and characteristics of various Hispanic subgroups; this point is important to understand when counseling clients of diverse Hispanic backgrounds.

▲ HISPANICS IN THE UNITED STATES

The term *Hispanic* may be currently popular in the United States because it simplifies the identification of a collection of different ethnic groups of people who are similar in language. Whereas the evolutionary fusion of Spanish culture with the cultures of other groups creates a kind of cultural unity, it would be a mistake to assume that the groups are all the same, just as it would have been erroneous to treat diverse ethnic groups from southern and eastern Europe as members of a single category. Each group has its own distinctive presence, movement, and origin. Three of the most numerous Hispanic groups—Mexican Americans, Puerto Rican Americans, and Cuban Americans—are described in the following sections.

In the early history of the United States, Mexicans as a people were repressed or ignored. Though their presence predates that of Europeans, their assimilation was an unlikely consideration until after California and most of the Southwest had been acquired from Mexico in 1848. Mexicans who lived in that part of the country were expected to conform to the dominant culture. Antagonism and violence toward Mexicans were especially prevalent in Texas.

Puerto Ricans began to migrate to the industrial northeastern United States after the passage of the Jones Act in 1917, which established Puerto Rico as a commonwealth territory of the United States. During the late 1950s and early 1960s thousands of middle- and upper-class Cubans fled Fidel Castro's revolution to settle in Florida. By 1967, more than 317,000 Cubans had been admitted to the United States. Again in 1980, thousands of additional Cuban political refugees came to this country. Like the ethnic groups before them—the Irish, the Poles, the Italians, and others—the Hispanics were expected to blend into the U.S. mainstream.

However, acculturation and assimilation have not occurred in the same way as they did for preceding ethnic groups. One reason is the difference in the immigration pattern for some of the Hispanic ethnic groups as compared with that of the Europeans, who immigrated knowing that most likely they would never return: Mexicans have always had presence in the southwestern United States, but less so as a perceived immigrant group; Puerto Ricans have a quasi-dependent relationship as a result of commonwealth status; many Cubans, who came as political refugees, have always intended to return someday to Cuba (Chavez, 1991). Another reason is that the great immigration of Europeans coincided with the economic opportunities and freedom for upward mobility that were made possible by the industrial and social revolution in Western society. The shift to a service economy and the ending of thousands of industrial production jobs are resulting in a different pattern of socioeconomic movement for today's immigrants. A third reason is the close proximity of Hispanic native countries, facilitating periodic returns and the resulting reinforcement of spoken language and valued traditions. The enormous influx of undocumented immigrants, a culture within a culture, is another factor related to the prevalence and perpetuation of Hispanic culture.

One can only speculate on the perpetuation of Hispanic culture into future years, but today's reality is that Hispanics represent a major segment of the population. The experience of European immigrant groups shows that traditional ethnic language and ways tend not to persist much beyond the third generation, except for small flourishes of "symbolic ethnicity." However, some ethnic practices and traditions in the United States today (for example, linguistic nuances, customs, celebrations, food, dress) have historical (frozen-in-time) authenticity, while the same traditions in the Old World have long since been forgotten or are no longer practiced.

▲ MEXICAN AMERICANS

More than 14 million persons of Mexican origin or descent live in the United States today. The vast majority (85%) live in five states: California, Texas, New Mexico, Arizona, and Colorado. The current social position of Mexican Americans has been shaped largely by their historical experience in the Southwest (Moore, 1970; Tyler, 1975).

● MEXICAN-AMERICAN ORIGINS

The Spanish, and Native Americans from what is now Mexico and Central America, were the primary explorers and settlers of the Southwest during the period from the 16th century until the Mexican War of Independence with Spain in 1821. Before 1821, the Spanish established colonies and Catholic missions in New Mexico and California, and to a lesser extent in Texas and Arizona, which served to convert the Native Americans to Christianity. Spanish, Mexican, and native contributions to the culture in the Southwest during this period included language, ethnic foods, names of places, irrigation systems, methods of cattle raising, and other customs and practices.

Relations between Mexico and the United States. In the period from 1821 to 1848, the relationship between Mexico and the United States in Texas was one of growing conflict. Mexico desired to colonize Texas and encouraged settlement in the area by Europeans. By 1834 the great mass of settlers had outnumbered the *Tejanos* (native Mexicans of Texas) by six to one. Attempts by the Mexican government to stem the migration culminated in the Texas War for Independence, 1846 to 1848. Nearly 30 years of cultural conflict were further provoked by the annexation of Texas to the United States in 1845. The residual hostility from the war continued into the early 1900s. During this time, many Mexican Americans lost their lands, and "in the Southwest, this was a period of the birth (or reaffirmation) of the stereotype that Mexican Americans, as a conquered people, were inferior. Since they were subordinate, they were readily exploited, and it is not surprising to find that signs of withdrawal, defeatism, and fatalism developed among them" (Alvirez & Bean, 1976, p. 274).

After 1900, mass migrations from Mexico tended to follow economic trends and seasonal periods in the United States. As did other immigrants, many Mexicans primarily sought to escape from poverty and political instability and also to look for progress and adventure. The lure of jobs in agriculture, mining, railroads, and other industry was a strong incentive but also resulted in much exploitation of the poor and largely illiterate immigrants. Gamio (1930/1971) notes that an estimated 890,746 Mexicans were legally in residence in the United States in 1926 and 228,449 were in residence illegally. The experience of illegal aliens in the United States in 1920 was strikingly similar to that of their present-day counterparts: "The real forces which move illegal immigration are, first of all, the smugglers, or 'coyotes,' who facilitate illegal entrance to Mexican immigrants, and the contractors, or *enganchistas*, who provide them with jobs. The smuggler and the contractor are an intimate and powerful alliance from Calexico to Brownsville. Second, indirectly, but logically and fundamentally, the origin of illegal immigration is to be found in the farmers and ranchers, and railroad, mining, and other enterprises to which Mexican labor is indispensable" (Gamio, 1930/1971, p. 11).

Immigrants in the United States. The movement to the United States by Mexicans was rapid; as a result, much of the commerce and industry in the border cities and states developed by using Mexican labor. Today, many of the agricultural, business, and manufacturing enterprises in parts of the country are so dependent on Mexican labor that they would have difficulty continuing without it. The political and financial influence of these employers, along with the proximity of the two countries and the enormous length of the border, makes it difficult, if not impossible, to prevent immigration. The governments of both Mexico and the United States cooperate in attempting to control the illegal flow of Mexicans into the United States. The *bracero* (contract labor) program, in which cheap Mexican labor was imported to meet manpower emergencies, was initiated in 1942 and again during the Korean conflict in 1951 (Public Law 78). Most of the *braceros* returned home to Mexico when the agricultural season was finished, but the program did nothing to stem the flow of undocumented immigrants. In 1954 the United States Immigration and Naturalization Service (INS) conducted a sweep through the Spanish-speaking barrios of Texas and California and even cities as far away from the border as Spokane, Chicago, Kansas City, and St. Louis. As many as 1,035,282 undocumented immigrants were apprehended in "Operation Wetback." Those raids were bitterly resented in the Mexican-American community, and there were complaints that agents simply rounded up anyone who looked Mexican and deported them without all the legal proceedings. An operation of basically the same type, labeled "Project Jobs," was conducted in 1982 by the INS in the hope of selectively catching aliens working in high-paying positions in construction and manufacturing industries and freeing the jobs for unemployed citizens ("Futile Raids on Illegal Aliens," 1982).

The complex problem of the legal rights of illegal immigrants within the democratic structure of the United States Constitution was further highlighted with the landmark Supreme Court ruling in 1982 giving illegal alien children the right to free public education. The case struck down a 1975 Texas law enacted to conserve school funds. The Texas law cut off funds for the education of children who could not prove their legal residence. The Supreme Court decision also raised the question of whether states would be forced to extend social services such as health care, housing, food stamps, unemployment compensation, and other welfare benefits to illegal immigrants (Elsasser, 1982). A newspaper editorial comments: "In the Texas schools case, the court had reasons to avoid saying either that unlawful immigrant status is a suspect category or that education is a fundamental right. It recognized that the federal government must put special, heavy burdens upon unlawful immigrants if it is to have any hope of enforcing its immigration laws. And it also knew that if it called education a constitutional right, it would be driven to reviewing every state and local school policy that someone could show treats some children differently from the way it treats others" ("The Schooling of Illegal Immigrants," 1982, p. 8).

Military service during World War II provided many of the 300,000 to 500,000 Mexican-American servicemen with their first opportunity to interact with members of the majority culture on an equal basis. Arousal of pride in being an American of Mexican ancestry was initiated in the mid-1960s through the excitement created by the Chicano (Americans of Mexican ancestry) movement in the Southwest. The organization of farm workers through the efforts of Cesar Chavez and his United Farm Workers also gave impetus to a new identity, although it may have fostered the myth that Hispanics in the United States are likely to be migrant workers (Alvirez & Bean, 1976, p. 275).

● MEXICAN FAMILY LIFE

Although many stereotypes of traditional Mexican-American families may reflect cultural traits, some also derive from the poverty that is present among Mexican Americans. The Mexican-American family places great emphasis on interpersonal relationships and, in comparison with family relations typical of the dominant culture, may be considered person oriented rather than goal oriented. Thus, "the roles played therein appear to make Mexican Americans more warm and emotional than Anglos, whom the former often see as cold and unfeeling" (Alvirez & Bean, 1976, p. 276). Emphasis on interpersonal relations over materialism and competitiveness may also promote emotional security.

The deep feeling for the family, *familism,* often includes members of the extended family as well. While the female role is often viewed in traditional families as nurturing and emotionally supportive, the male role is often viewed as dominant *(machismo)* and gives strength, honor, and protection to the female in her role. The father is seen as the authority in the family, and younger persons are subordinate to and respectful of older persons. Children early in life are assigned responsibilities for the welfare of the family. The older children are expected to have authority over and to take care of the younger ones, and brothers are expected to protect sisters. It has been argued that these roles may be related more to a rural life or a life whose environmental conditions have necessitated such definitions in order to get the work done rather than to cultural norms of behavior. As Mexican-American families participate more in middle-class lifestyles, the traditional dominant role of the man and subservient role of the woman may well move toward a relationship of egalitarianism. If so, role stress can be anticipated for the participants in more traditional families (Gomez, 1972).

▲ PUERTO RICAN AMERICANS

Puerto Rico was a Spanish colony from 1493 until 1898. The native Borinquen people, later called "Twainos," disappeared soon after the Spanish conquest, and in 1511 the first African slaves in the New World were brought to Puerto Rico. The population of Puerto Rico is a mixture of many colors in the complete range from Black to White. As was the case in Mexico, the Spanish colonial culture became a pervasive influence, fusing with that of the natives and Blacks.

When the Spanish-American War ended in 1898, Puerto Rico became an occupied territory of the United States. A civil government was established in which the governor and all governmental officials of the island were appointed by the president of the United States. Puerto Ricans were made citizens of the United States at the onset of World War I in 1917. In 1948, free elections were held and the first governor was elected under the commonwealth status. As citizens of an associated free state, Puerto Ricans are able to migrate to other parts of the United States without restriction. Although they enjoy the rights of American citizens, they do not vote for the president or have elected representatives in Congress. They also pay no federal taxes. In the 1990s, Puerto Ricans remain divided between those who favor statehood in the United States and those who favor maintaining commonwealth status; those seeking independence are a small minority.

● MIGRATION TO THE UNITED STATES

In the 1930s, there were fewer than 55,000 Puerto Ricans in the mainland United States. After World War II and the development of air travel, large-scale migration began. Today, there are more than 2 million Puerto Ricans living on the mainland, the great mass of them concentrated in New York City. Many come only as temporary contract labor. Because of the poverty and limited economic base of the island, many Puerto Ricans migrate to the mainland with the hope of bettering their economic standing and eventually returning to the island. The cultural orientation of second- and third-generation Puerto Ricans who have remained on the mainland is different from that of island Puerto Ricans (LeVine & Padilla, 1980, p. 25). The flow of Puerto Ricans to United States cities has been reversed in recent years, and now more Puerto Ricans are emigrating from the mainland to the island.

● PUERTO RICAN SOCIORELIGIOUS LIFE

Aspects of traditional Puerto Rican socioreligious life that are described in this section can also be found in other Hispanic groups. The Spanish deliberately organized the culture around community life (the pueblo) with the plaza in the center, the main building being the church. Celebration and public interaction always occur conspicuously in the plaza. People participate in Catholic religious sacraments, however, not as members of the organized church but rather as members of a pueblo (community) that is Catholic. To the people, religious practice implies a pattern of intimate personal relationships, *personalismo*. As in other Hispanic groups, the pattern is characterized by a network of personal relationships with the saints and the Blessed Virgin or other manifestations of God as espoused by Catholicism. The network also includes personal and intimate friends, *compadres*, who are needed for favors, help, or protection. For example, a *compadre* (man) and a *comadre* (woman) may at times serve as informal parents along with one's natural parents. Other intimate friends also become sponsors of the children, or godparents *(padrinos)*. This ritualistic kinship network is as important as natural kinship. There is a deep feeling of obligation to help one another, whether through economic assistance, encouragement, or personal advice and correction of social behavior. These beliefs would probably continue in the culture even if the formal church structure were to disappear. Like representatives of the Catholic church serving Mexicans in the early Southwest, most priests and nuns working among the Puerto Ricans were from ethnic groups other than Puerto Rican. A few native priests and a large number of priests from Spain provided religious leadership before 1898, and from then the function was performed by American bishops until 1961, when the first native-born Puerto Rican bishop was appointed.

African religious rites, brought by Black slaves, were often intermingled with the folk practices of Catholicism. Today, widespread subscription to *espiritismo* (a folk system to explain illness) and folk medicine continues. It is believed that people can contact the spirit world and can influence the spirits, controlling unfavorable actions of evil spirits or gaining favorable action of good spirits. The *medium*, the person who claims the power to contact the spiritual world, is often sought for assistance with interpersonal problems. There is also a belief in the power of a "healer." The *curandero* (man) or *curandera* (woman) practices the folk art of medicine through the use of herbs, potions, and other remedies. Almost every Puerto Rican or Mexican *barrio* (neighborhood) has a *botanica,* or drugstore, that sells herbs, potions, rituals, prayers, and other instruments or devices for remedying psychological and physical afflictions.

● PUERTO RICAN FAMILY LIFE

To understand Puerto Rican family life it is important to understand the Puerto Ricans' historical view of marriage and married life. Traditional Roman law, which prevailed in Puerto Rico, only recognized a marriage union that had been "regularized," or made formal, but it also *accepted* the situation in which two people lived together without formally getting married. A man and woman's act of living together in Puerto Rico is not the equivalent of the English common-law marriage, in which after some time the union is recognized as legal. Regardless of how outsiders might define it, Puerto Ricans who "refer to themselves as *amancebados*" are those living together without marriage (Fitzpatrick, 1971, p. 84). The Christian view notwithstanding, it is not seen as an immoral relationship. It is simply an expression of the need for a man and woman by mutual consent and love to live together and to raise children from their union or other unions that either one may have had. There are no "illegitimate" children in the Puerto Rican culture. In Roman-law tradition the term was never used. A child of a regularized marriage was a "legitimate" child. All others were termed *natural.* In Puerto Rico the term *hijo reconocido,* the recognized child, has come into usage. It implies certain legal rights for children, including those of stable consensual unions or casual unions (Fitzpatrick, 1971, p. 87).

According to Fitzpatrick (1971, p. 83), four family structures—though not unique to Puerto Ricans—can be found among Puerto Ricans living on the mainland:

1. The *extended family* includes the natural kin and ritual kin (the intimate friends from the social network). Grandparents, parents, children, compadres, and comadres associate together for group support and identification, regardless of whether the marriage is consensual or regularized. As more Puerto Ricans move into the socioeconomic middle class, the number of consensual unions is rapidly declining. Many Puerto Ricans enter initially into a consensual marriage not because they do not respect religious marriage but because they understand its permanent characteristics and do not wish to commit themselves until they feel confident that it will work.

2. The *nuclear family,* consisting of the father, mother, and children, is becoming more common with the rise of the middle class. The bonds of the extended family are weakened as permanent migration to the mainland increases.

3. The *mixed family* includes the father, mother, their children, and children of another union or unions of husband or wife. Children in the same household may have different last names.

4. The *single-parent family* is usually mother-based, with children of one or more men but with no man residing permanently in the home.

▲ CUBAN AMERICANS

Cuba, consisting of one large island and about 1,600 uninhabited smaller ones, is in the West Indies and only about 90 miles south of Florida. It is a very beautiful place, sometimes referred to as "the Pearl of the Antilles." The Cubans struggled for independence during most of the 400 years of Spanish rule. In fact, through much of Cuban history the people have been exploited by various ruling groups and by wealthy owners of sugar and tobacco plantations. After discovery of Cuba by Columbus in 1492, Cuba became one of the richest of Spanish colonies in the West Indies. Its history then followed the usual pattern in the West Indies: settlement by the Spanish, search for valuable minerals and wealth, decline of the native population, and importation of Black slaves—the first arriving in 1517. It is estimated that one million Ciboney tribespeople were living on Cuba at the time of Columbus's arrival. By 1600 virtually none had survived the diseases, harsh treatment, and exploitation of the Spanish. Slave uprisings occurred in many periods of Cuban history until the practice of slavery ended in 1886. The struggle of the Cuban people against domination by Spain culminated in 1895, when a Cuban rebel group-in-exile in New York declared Cuba a republic. The Spanish-American War followed, and Spain was forced to withdraw from Cuba in 1898. A United States military government ruled the island until 1902, when a constitutional government was elected; however, the United States remained as a trustee and continued to be involved in Cuban affairs for 20 more years. In 1934, dictator Fulgencio Batista took control. During the period from the Spanish defeat to the beginning of the Castro regime in 1959, very little was done to help the masses of lower-class people.

● 26TH OF JULY MOVEMENT

The most recent history of Cuba begins with a young Cuban lawyer, Fidel Castro, who initiated a revolution on July 26, 1956, against the Cuban government of Fulgencio Batista. The revolutionary group, named the 26th of July Movement, took control of Cuba in 1959. Although the United States government lent its support, its influence was seen as undesirable to the cultural and revolutionary movement. American-owned sugar plantations, cattle ranches, oil refineries, and other businesses were seized.

The Castro government has inaugurated much reform for the common people. Although the economy has developed slowly, medical care and education are free. Literacy has increased and many adult education programs have been established; one example is the recruitment of high school and college students to teach uneducated Cubans to read and write. A large number of adults have completed elementary school, and there is much emphasis on job training. Political and social equality is a major aim of the government.

● RELATIONS BETWEEN THE UNITED STATES AND CUBA

Intertwined throughout much of the last 75 years of Cuba's revolutionary struggles against exploitation have been the extensive interests and influence of American business and investments on the island. Relations between the two nations have deteriorated since 1959, and about 500,000 middle- and upper-class Cubans opposed to Castro's revolution have left Cuba. The majority settled in Miami, Florida, and in Mexico, Puerto Rico, and Spain. The Cubans exiled in America agitated against the Castro revolution and in 1961 attempted to invade Cuba in the ill-fated Bay of Pigs expedition. All of the 1,500 Cuban refugees who sought to "liberate" Cuba were either killed or captured in a few days by Cuban armed forces. The refugee expedition had been trained and armed in Guatemala by the United States Central Intelligence Agency (CIA), and later testimony revealed that all U.S. agencies involved had unanimously recommended the attack. Eighteen months later, Cuba released more than 1,000 of the invaders, along with many of their Cuban relatives, in exchange for medical supplies and baby food. In 1964, with the strong persuasion of the United States, the Organization of American States (OAS) voted political and economic sanctions against Cuba, barring hemispheric countries from conducting trade or other relations with Cuba. Prior to the blockade, the United States had provided 90% of Cuba's imports; Cuba was thus forced to turn to the Soviet Union and other Eastern European countries to buy goods. However, with the demise of the political structures of the Union of Soviet Socialist Republics and other European nations in the 1990s and the instituting of democratic reform and free markets, Cuba was left on its own.

Strained relations continue today, and at various times Castro has attempted to spread revolution throughout other Latin American countries and even into Africa, particularly in Angola and Ethiopia in 1979. As a goodwill gesture to the Cuban-American community, Castro released 3,600 political prisoners in 1979, half of whom went to the United States under a special parole program. In return, he encouraged Cuban Americans to return as tourists and to renew relationships with relatives and friends still living in Cuba.

● RECENT CUBAN IMMIGRATION

In 1980 an extraordinary event occurred when a group of Cuban refugees, sailing in a "freedom flotilla," arrived in Key West, Florida. With the permission and encouragement of Castro, an estimated 125,000 Cubans migrated to Florida from April through August 1980. Although welcomed by Americans at first, the masses of refugees soon alarmed the United States government, which attempted to stem the fleets of small boats. Prior to that influx of Cubans, an estimated 25,000 Haitians had sailed to Florida in 1979, and the United States began to question whether it could handle the deluges of political refugees. Although many Cubans were detained for long periods of time at refugee camps throughout the nation, most were eventually resettled once sponsors had been found who were willing to assist in their economic adjustment.

The high cost of resettlement angered many Americans, and others were concerned about how to cope with the Cubans who were hard-core criminals or who suffered from psychological and social problems. Toward the end of the Cuban exodus, Castro released inmates from prisons and mental institutions. Many homosexuals were included among the "social misfits" that Castro desired to purge from Cuba. Some of the problems that surfaced in this nation, at least as reflected by the United States news media, may indicate some of the complexities of behavioral and cultural conflicts experienced by the more alienated—and numerically small—group of "social misfits." Some incidents of crime (armed theft and homicide) in New York City and Miami were attributed to this group, but whether their numbers were out of proportion to the population is unknown. Newly arrived Cubans tend to shun any organized crime structure, although devotion to a religious type of sect, which sprang up in Cuba during the 1960s, has appeared in New York: "This particular sect, which venerates various saints of the Roman Catholic Church while also featuring elements of voodoo, apparently thrives in Cuban prisons" (Coakley, 1982, p. 5). A system of body tattoos often indicates their criminal specialty. Coakley (1982) cites examples: "Executioners use a pierced heart over a wreath; enforcers favor a devil's pitchfork; and drug dealers, a distinctive five-lined symbol" (p. 5).

● CUBANS IN THE UNITED STATES

The first Cubans to leave Cuba following the revolution in 1959 were mostly middle-class and wealthy upper-class business people, political officials, and professionals. The most recent migration, which occurred during 1980, brought semiskilled and skilled workers, many of whom are handicapped by their lack of ability in speaking, writing, and reading English. The majority of Cubans in the United States live in Miami, although many are scattered throughout the country in large cities such as New York and Chicago. Among the earlier arrivals, many wealthy Cubans joined established Cuban enclaves or formed new enclaves in "Little Havana" sections of Miami and Tampa, Florida. Whereas those arriving in 1980 were encouraged to disperse throughout the country, many also migrated to the Cuban enclaves. All Cuban Americans in one way or another have experienced the effects of revolution and the disjointing of relations with family members, relatives, and friends in Cuba. Like other immigrants, they have also come for political freedom and economic improvement.

Further generalization of the background and pattern of the Cuban group in the United States would be difficult without additional research. The extent to which other characteristics of Cuban nationals are represented in Cuban Americans can only be assumed. In Cuba, about 75% of the people are listed as White and of Spanish descent. The rest are Black, mulatto, Native American, or of other mixed ancestry. The majority speak Spanish; in the cities many also speak English. Some of the Blacks speak the African language Yoruba. Historically, the majority of Cubans have identified with Catholicism. Some practice Santeria, a Black folk religion that combines African tribal and Catholic ceremonies and includes the belief that Catholic saints represent African gods. LeVine and Padilla (1980, pp. 143–146) have discussed Santeria as a form of folk medicine and faith healing.

■ ASIAN AMERICANS

The 7,273,662 Asian Americans, Polynesians, and Pacific Islanders in the United States in 1990, according to the Bureau of the Census, included Chinese, Filipino, Japanese, Asian Indian, Korean, Indochinese (Vietnamese, Laotian, and Cambodian), Hawaiian, Samoan, and Guamanian peoples. Figures are shown in Table 4-3. Other nationalities also included Pakistanis, Indonesians, and Fiji Islanders.

The Census Bureau counted about 1.5 million Asians and Pacific Islanders living in the United States in 1970 (U.S. Bureau of the Census, 1981). By the 1980 census, that figure had more than doubled to 3.5 million (U.S. Bureau of the Census, June 1981), due in large part to increases in immigration as a result of the lifting of restrictive quotas on Asians after the passage of the Immigration and Naturalization Act of 1965 and to the more than 400,000 Indochinese refugees who came during 1975–80 under the Refugee Resettlement Program. The result, according to Kim (1978), is that "most of the publicly held stereotypes about the social conditions and composition of Asian-American minorities have lost whatever limited validity they may have once possessed. Over the years the American public has most often based its conceptions of Asian-Americans on the perceived conditions of the West Coast Japanese and Chinese populations" (p. 1).

Between 1980 and 1990, 2.4 million more Asian immigrants entered the United States, resulting in a 1990 census count of nearly 7.3 million Asian Americans, an increase of 3.8 million or 108% (U.S. Bureau of the Census, 1991b). The great majority of Chinese, Japanese, Korean, and Filipino immigrants have migrated to urban population centers, while the Vietnamese have settled in scattered parts of the country. Fifty-eight percent of the total

TABLE 4-3   Composition of the Asian-American population of the United States in 1980 and 1990.

	1980	1990
Chinese	806,027	1,645,472
Filipino	774,640	1,406,770
Japanese	700,747	847,562
Asian Indian	361,544	815,447
Korean	354,529	798,849
Vietnamese	261,714	614,547
Hawaiian	167,253	211,014
Samoan	42,050	62,964
Guamanian	32,132	49,345

SOURCES: Data from *Supplementary Reports,* U.S. Bureau of the Census, May 1981, and Bureau of the Census *News,* March 11, 1991.

Asian-American population is located in the states of California (39.1%), New York (9.5%), and Hawaii (9.4%).

▲ EARLY EXPLOITATION AND RESTRICTION IN THE UNITED STATES

According to Kim (1978, p. 2), the *earlier* groups of Asian immigrants arrived in the greatest numbers during certain time periods: the Chinese, from the 1850s to 1882; the Japanese, from 1890 to 1908; and the Filipinos, from 1900 to 1930. The pattern of immigration for the "old" Asian groups (pre-1924) and the "new" Asian groups (post-1965) has been influenced by economic needs in the United States, world political conditions, and legal restrictions imposed by the United States. Hostility to Chinese and other Asian immigrants is especially seen in various acts passed by Congress and in the laws of some Western states and cities. The Chinese Exclusion Act of 1882 suspended Chinese immigration and made Chinese born in China ineligible for American citizenship. Eventually the need for cheap agricultural labor created by the halting of Chinese immigration led to the importation in the 1890s of Japanese, first to Hawaii and later to the West Coast. Many of those Japanese moved from working as field laborers to achieving success in small truck farming. Immigration from Japan continued until 1908, when it was halted according to conditions of the "Gentlemen's Agreement." Other harassment was evident in the laws of some states that made citizenship a prerequisite to land ownership, for which the Japanese were therefore not eligible. Koreans were also imported as laborers to Hawaii and some eventually migrated to the West Coast before emigration was forbidden by the Korean government in 1905. After 1902 Filipinos migrated to work as field hands in California, but they too were not allowed to become citizens. The Filipino Exclusion Act of 1934 limited immigration to 150 persons a year, and when independence was granted to the Philippines in 1946, Filipinos became subject to the same restrictions that prevailed for other Asian groups.

The Immigration Exclusion Act of 1924 essentially ended most immigration from China, Japan, Korea, and other Asian countries, since it denied admission to the United States of all persons ineligible for citizenship. During World War II, the combination of anti-Japanese feeling and the alliance with China led to the granting of token immigration quotas for Chinese and Koreans, but it was not until 1965 that the American attitude toward national origins and citizenship eligibility departed from previous policies. The following section reviews the historic nature and details of United States policy toward settlement in this country by various nationality groups.

▲ LEGAL RESTRICTIONS ON IMMIGRATION AND CITIZENSHIP

There were virtually no restrictions of any type on the earliest settlement of the country. Later, policies and legislation were aimed at the exclusion of certain ethnic groups. Congressional acts have historically determined both citizenship eligibility and immigration quotas for various groups of Asians and—either directly or through implication—the immigration quotas for southern and eastern Europeans. The systematic harassment of Asians in California and other Western states and cities has also been evident in discriminatory laws that sought to limit their economic movement and ownership of land. Fear of "racial deterioration" and weakening of American institutions by "masses" of European and Oriental immigrants led to a number of acts that sought to exclude non-Anglo-Saxons. The following are chronological examples of some of the most apparent Congressional acts, "agreements," or other governmental laws that have affected immigration numbers, patterns of settlement, and citizenship eligibility in the United States over the last hundred years:

· 1882—*Chinese Exclusion Act.* This congressional act expanded restrictions on all immigrants to include convicts, lunatics, and idiots. Most significant was the fact that it suspended immigration of Chinese laborers and made Chinese born in China ineligible for American citizenship. Anti-Asian emotions were stirred up each time the act faced a ten-year renewal, and following a series of conflicting court decisions, the exclusion was further extended to apply to other Asians. Thus, beginning with the Chinese, "for the first time, American policy accepted the idea that an entire group may be undesirable because of its race or nationality" (McLemore, 1980, p. 71). This policy lasted until 1943, at which time a limited, or token, Chinese and Korean immigration was permitted. When the Philippines received independence in 1946 a small Filipino quota was established.

· 1908—*Gentlemen's Agreement.* The San Francisco school board in 1906 segregated all Asian children into a single inadequate school. That act touched off a complaint to President Theodore Roosevelt by Japan, a powerful and respected nation, that could not be ignored. The eventual outcome of the "gentlemen's agreement"—a series of diplomatic exchanges between the United States and Japan—was that the school board rescinded its order and Japan began restricting immigration to nonlaborers or members of prior residents' families, thus stemming the flow of Japanese immigrants.

· 1917—*Literacy Test Requirement.* With the advance of the intelligence-testing movement, an immigration act was passed that included a literacy test as a requirement for entering immigrants.

· 1918—*California Alien Land Law (Webb-Heney Bill).* This and other California laws prevented persons ineligible for citizenship from owning or leasing land for more than three years. It was directed at the many Japanese who were gradually becoming successful in small truck farming. Soon other Western states followed the precedent set by California to contain the estimated 6,000 Japanese farmers throughout the West. Court decisions and/or legislative repeal eventually determined that American-born children of Asian parents could not be denied their citizenship or have their economic activities restricted. However, the right of citizenship through naturalization of foreign-born Asians was not gained until 1952.

· 1921—*Emergency Quota Act.* This act "restricted immigrants from all European countries to 3 percent of the number of each nationality present in the United States in 1910. This legislation was intended not only to reduce the total number of immigrants but also to reduce the number originating in southern and eastern Europe" (McLemore, 1980, p. 81).

· 1924—*Immigration Act.* According to Kim (1978), the 1924 "Exclusion Act" for non-Whites for all essential purposes "ended immigration from China, Japan, and Korea since it denied admission to the United States of all persons ineligible for citizenship, a category which at that time included Asians and other 'non-whites'" (p. 4). The same act also reduced quotas for all nations from 3% to 2%, changed the base year from 1910 to 1890, and included a national origins provision that went into effect in 1929. As noted in Chapter 3, 98% of the immigrants from southern and eastern Europe arrived after 1880. The fact that the law was designed to prevent any major change in the basic composition of the American population "clearly showed America's official preference for people from the countries represented by the old immigration" (McLemore, 1980, p. 81). The emphasis on an immigrant's country of origin rather than the country of citizenship was notably aimed at the exclusion of Asians; thus, for example, a Pole who had acquired French citizenship was considered eligible whereas a Chinese from Hong Kong who was a British subject would have come under the Chinese quota.

· 1948 and 1950—*Displaced Persons Acts.* This legislation permitted more than 400,000 persons from Europe to enter the United States. In 1952 Japan was allowed the same privileges of sending immigrants that China had been granted in 1943.

· 1965—*Immigration and Nationality Act.* Actually an amendment to the Immigration and Nationality Act of 1952 (McCarran-Walter Act), this current law represents an end to the discriminatory provisions of citizenship eligibility based on national origins. Individual national quotas have been replaced by an annual limit of 170,000 visas for persons from countries *outside* the Western Hemisphere, with a limit of 20,000 persons allowed from any one country in any one year; 120,000 persons are allowed from *inside* the Western Hemisphere, but no limits are placed on individual countries within the Western Hemisphere. Priorities are established for visas, beginning with relatives of current U.S. citizens, then professionals, skilled laborers, refugees, unskilled laborers, and so on. Thirty-one reasons, such as illness, a criminal record, and activities harmful to the United States, are given for barring an alien from entering.

· 1986—*Immigration Reform and Control Act.* There are three major provisions to this law: *legalization* (amnesty for various categories of aliens), *employer sanctions* (severe fines for hiring, recruiting, or referring aliens), and *temporary agricultural worker status* (permission to hire aliens when and where there are insufficient legal workers available). In addition, there are many other provisions, including protection from discrimination for legal job applicants who appear foreign. Although the act was proposed to curb illegal immigration, there is little indication that the flow has slowed.

· 1990—*Revision of the nation's existing immigration law.* Overall immigration to be allowed was increased to 700,000 each year from 1992 to 1994 and stabilized at 675,000 after that. The revamping also reduced the severity and scope of restrictions on new citizens and other immigrants. For example, the existing system gave priority to recent immigrants, largely Asians and Hispanics, who were allowed to bring in family relatives at the expense of those wishing to come independently. The new law has increased the limit on the number of immigrants sponsored by family members to 520,000 a year through 1994 and at least 480,000 thereafter; in addition, it allows 40,000 visas a year for independent persons from Italy, Poland, Ireland, and other countries virtually shut off from immigration in the last 20 years. It also allows more people (140,000 a year) to enter with desirable employment skills, sets aside 10,000 visas for investors who create new jobs, and eliminates the automatic exclusion of people with acquired immune deficiency syndrome (AIDS).

Since the United States admits many *more* immigrants than what the laws specify, there are clearly exceptions to the specified limitations. The immigration rate is much higher today than in the recent past; however, with the dramatic decline in the American birthrate and total fertility rate, the United States may need *more* immigrants just to maintain current population levels. *Birthrate* is the average annual number of births during a year per 1,000 population; it was 16.7 in 1990, 18.4 in 1970, and 24.1 in 1950 (Universal Almanac, 1991). *Total fertility rate* is defined as the average number of births one woman will likely have in her lifetime; the rate was 2.09 in 1990, 2.48 in 1970, and 3.09 in 1950 (Universal Almanac, 1991). The level necessary for natural replacement of the population is generally regarded as 2.1.

On the other hand, the influx of large numbers of ethnically different immigrants raises the risk of animosities until economic, political, and social accommodation occurs. A related condition is the real pain of disillusionment and discouragement felt by many unemployed American workers who must compete with large numbers of both legal and illegal immigrants.

▲ ASIAN-AMERICAN ORIGINS

Asian Americans come from the world's largest continent in both size and population. Asia extends from Africa and Europe in the west to the Pacific Ocean in the east. It is extremely varied in geographical features and the population is diverse in ancestry, language, customs, religious beliefs, and lifestyles. All the original Eastern religions were founded in Asia, including Buddhism, Confucianism, Hinduism, Islam, Judaism, Shintoism, Taoism, and Christianity.

● SOUTH ASIA

India, Pakistan, and Bangladesh are major nations making up South Asia. It is the world's most populous area, with about a fifth of all people living there. Sharp lines of religion, language, and social class divide the people of South Asia. The differences between Hindus and Muslims led to the creation of Pakistan in 1947, which divided India into two nations: India for Hindus and Pakistan for Muslims. Unlike Christianity, Islam, and Judaism, Hinduism is not based on the belief in a single, personal god. Hindus worship many gods and believe that all living creatures have a spirit whose goal is to become united with Brahman, the Supreme World Soul or Spirit. After death a soul in one body passes on to another body. Passing from body to body continues until the soul becomes perfect enough for union with Brahman.

● SOUTHEAST ASIA

Burma, Cambodia, Laos, Vietnam, Thailand, Malaysia, Indonesia, and the Philippines are major nations making up Southeast Asia today; also included are thousands of islands south and east of China. An area rich in natural resources, much of the region was controlled by various outside nations from 1500 to the late 1800s. Not only the Portuguese, Spanish, British, Dutch, and French but also the Chinese and the United States practiced conquest and control during that period of history. The presence of many ethnic, unassimilated Chinese is still felt in several Southeast Asian countries and in some cases has led to considerable internal political problems. Colonialism has always been resented by the people, and in 1945 after World War II many independent free nations emerged. The Communists gained a strong hold in many cases during the independence movement. The most wasteful struggle took place in the former French colony of Indochina, comprising what is now Cambodia, Laos, and Vietnam (Buttinger, 1977).

Buddhism is the dominant religion of much of Southeast Asia. A major belief of Buddhism is that peace, harmony, and happiness can be gained by ridding oneself of personal desires; for example, Buddhists may have little or no desire to accumulate wealth or material possessions. Partly because of their religious beliefs, many Southeast Asians seem to people of the West to have a noncompetitive, easygoing manner. Western anthropologists and sociologists often interpret this relaxed characteristic as an example of "fatalism"; that is, the outlook that much of life is uncontrollable. To the Buddhist, acceptance of basic natural forces leads to greater harmony within the person. The Buddhists' calm attitude is also attributable to their well-defined family and generational system of beliefs. Many Southeast Asians, especially rural people, mix the religious beliefs and practices of Buddhism with animism, the belief that everything in nature has a spirit and that good and bad spirits cause good and bad experiences. Sacrifices such as food, incense, and cloth are offered to the spirits in the hope that they will bring good fortune and not harm.

Islam is most prevalent in Malaysia and Indonesia and some parts of the Philippines. Due to Spanish influence or rule in the Philippines from 1565 to 1898, Roman Catholicism is the major religion in that country. Over one million Vietnamese are also Catholic as a result of the influence of the French.

The large migration of Southeast Asian refugees from Cambodia, Laos, and Vietnam to the United States following the Vietnam War included a broad spectrum of people. The early arrivals were mainly businesspeople, professionals, government officials, and military personnel, whereas the later arrivals included agricultural and industrial workers (Montero, 1979). Most rural Southeast Asians have kept the extended family system, although, except in the Philippines, relationships between older and younger generations are generally not as strict as in other parts of Asia.

● EAST ASIA

China, Japan, North and South Korea, and Taiwan are major countries in East Asia. China alone covers 90% of East Asia, and 80% of East Asians live in China. Throughout much of history the Chinese have ruled all or portions of East Asia, and China has the longest tradition of national identity in its 4,000 or more years of history. The present People's Republic of China was established in 1949, when Chinese Communists drove out the Nationalist Chinese, who then established their own (Nationalist) Republic of China on Taiwan. Although the mainland Chinese—who make up only 15% of the population of Taiwan—have held most of the power, local Taiwanese have increased their political role, land reform has taken place, the economy has prospered, and Taiwanese peasants have generally fared better than peasants in other Third World capitalist countries. The recent large-scale migrations to the United States from Taiwan have consisted mostly of wealthy and professional persons.

The historical background of Chinese from Hong Kong is different from that of other Chinese. The British Crown Colony of Hong Kong consists of the island of Hong Kong, a number of nearby islands, and an area on the mainland. The area was seized from the Chinese by England in 1841, and in 1898 the Chinese imperial government ceded Hong Kong to the British for 99 years. The deed lasts until 1997 and, with time running out, the question of the future status of Hong Kong is often raised. When the Nationalist Chinese were driven from mainland China in 1949, many groups from Canton and Shanghai moved their business investments to Hong Kong. The power is held by this wealthier group, and many of their children attend the Chinese University in Hong Kong or Hong Kong University. Others come to the United States for further education and sometimes settle here. Other individuals and families arriving in the United States from Hong Kong—at times reaching the rate of 600 immigrants per month, according to Huang (1976, p. 144)—have experienced many adjustment problems, at least in the estimation of outsiders: family and cultural dislocation, unemployment and limited occupational opportunities, language difficulties, clashes among gangs of youths, and crowded living conditions in American Chinatowns.

The influence of Chinese religious and philosophical beliefs in East Asia prevailed throughout early history. The most important philosophical contribution is Confucianism, which teaches ethical standards of behavior, especially the mutual duties of rulers and subjects, of family members, and of friends. Polite and respectful behavior and obedience to authority are stressed. The traditional religion of Buddhism is combined with the Confucian system of ethics in China and Taiwan, although in China today the government seeks to discourage the practice of any religious belief.

Japan has one of the highest standards of living in the world. The literacy rate is 99%. Buddhism and Shintoism are the two major religions in Japan today, and Confucianism also influences Japanese codes of personal conduct. Shintoism, as influenced by Confucianism, developed moral standards of honesty, kindness, and respect for elders and superiors. State Shintoism, beginning in the 1880s, emphasized patriotism and the divinity of the Japanese emperor; however, after World War II it was abolished as a state religion. *Shinto* literally means "the way of the gods." Early Shintoists worshiped many gods, or *Kami*; Kami are the basic forces in life processes, such as growth, disease, healing, and creativity. There is no emphasis on life after death; however, the traditional Japanese worship of ancestors is included in Shintoism.

The Koreans are an ancient people who have a distinct culture but who have been controlled by the Chinese throughout most of their history. Japan annexed the country in 1910 and ruled it as a dependency until the end of World War II. At that time, under the Potsdam Agreement, the Soviet Union occupied the northern half and the United States the southern half. The emergence of a Soviet-supported Democratic People's Republic of Korea and concomitant independence demonstrations were counteracted by the establishment of the American-supported anticommunist Republic of Korea. United States military advisers supervised resistance to the guerrilla campaign that was conducted in South Korea by North Korea, and when conventional warfare broke out in 1950, lasting until 1953, American troops were heavily involved. The Korean conflict caused the loss of 54,246 American lives; billions of dollars were spent, and virtually every major building in North Korea was bombed. Today, both North and South Korea claim themselves as rightful rulers of all Korea. Except for a few Chinese and others, the population in South Korea is all Korean. The people follow a strong Confucian tradition; other groups participate in Buddhism and folk religion, and there is a vigorous Christian minority comprising 28% of the total population.

This section has presented a basic demography and sketched other features of the areas of South, Southeast, and East Asia. Tables 4-4 and 4-5 compare the world's major religions or belief forms and show their key points. The next sections will treat in greater detail the origins, migration experiences, and cultural characteristics of Chinese Americans, Japanese Americans, Korean Americans, Filipino Americans, and Indochinese Americans.

▲ CHINESE AMERICANS

Between 1850 and 1882 more than 300,000 Chinese left China for the United States because of floods, food shortages, and political revolution in their native country. Religious beliefs in both Chinese and Japanese cultures at the time considered one of the greatest of Confucian sins to be leaving one's province and forsaking the spirits of deceased kin. Many Chinese migrated as contract laborers to the United States and other countries.

In 1865, 500 workers were transported to Hawaii on five-year contracts to work the sugar plantations. Local officials often extended these contracts without the consent or choice of the workers. Many other workers were abducted from China and forced into labor in distant parts of the world.

TABLE 4-4 Major Religions or Belief Forms of the World

Religion or Belief	Founded	Founder	Number of Followers	Concentration
Christianity	26	Jesus Christ (Messiah or teacher)	1 billion	Europe, North and South America, and scattered world-wide[a]
Roman Catholicism	300		580 million	
Protestantism	1500		342 million	
Eastern Orthodoxy	1054		77 million	
Islam	600	Mohammed (Prophet or messenger)	590 million	Africa, Middle East, Indonesia
Hinduism	2500 B.C.	Unknown; developed out of the culture	478 million	India
Buddhism	400 B.C.	Guatama Buddha (Enlightened One or Awakened One)	255 million	East Asia, Southeast Asia
Confucianism	500 B.C.	Confucius (Great Master or First Teacher)	156 million	East Asia (Japan, Korea), China (up to 1900s), Vietnam
Shintoism	2500 B.C.	Unknown; developed out of the culture	57 million	Japan
Taoism	500 B.C.	Lao-tze (Old Master or Old Philosopher)	31 million	China
Judaism	1200 B.C.	Abraham and Moses	14 million	Israel, United States, and scattered world-wide

(continued)

TABLE 4-4 *(continued)*

Religion or Belief	Founded	Founder	Number of Followers	Concentration
Sacred tribal beliefs				
Native Americans	15000 B.C.?	Developed out of the culture	1.5 million (U.S.)	North and South America
African and other native groups	—	Developed out of the culture	?	Africa and scattered world-wide
Animism	—	"Original" religion of humankind	?	Africa, South America, and scattered worldwide
Polytheism	—	—	?	Scattered worldwide
Other belief forms				
Atheism	—	—	?	Scattered worldwide
Agnosticism	—	—	?	Scattered worldwide
Scientism	1840 (Europe)	Early Greeks	3 million	Scattered world-wide; taught worldwide
Maoism	1920	Mao Tse-tung ("thought," as developed from Marxism-Leninism)	?	China

ªAlthough two-thirds of the world's Christians lived in Europe and Russia in 1900, by the year 2000 three-fifths are expected to be living in Africa, Asia, and Latin America. Africans are converting to Christianity by at least 4,000 a day through conversions and the birthrate (Barrett, 1982).

Petersen (1978) writes: "Of the total 40,413 Chinese coolies shipped to Cuba by 1876, 80 percent had been decoyed or kidnapped, 10 percent had died in passage. . . . Sold to the highest bidder, most went to sugar plantations, the rest to tobacco and coffee estates or other menial tasks" (p. 68).

TABLE 4-5   Key Points of the World's Major Religions or Belief Forms

Source of Power or Force (Deity)	Historical Sacred Texts or Source of Beliefs	Key Beliefs or Ethical Life Philosophy
Christianity		
God, a unity in tripersonality: Father, Son, Holy Ghost	Bible Teachings of Jesus through the Apostles and the Church Fathers	God's love for all creatures is a basic belief. Salvation (saving from sin or resurrection from death) is gained by those who have faith and show humility toward God. Brotherly love is emphasized in acts of charity, kindness, and forgiveness. Jesus' teachings insist on justice and mercy toward all people.
Islam[a]		
Allah (the only God)	Koran (the words of God delivered to Mohammed by the angel Gabriel) Hadith (commentaries by Mohammed) Five Pillars of Islam (religious conduct) Islam was built on Christianity and Judaism.	God is just and merciful; humans are limited and sinful. God rewards the good and punishes the sinful. Mohammed, through the Koran, guides and teaches people truth. Peace is gained through submission to Allah. The sinless go to Paradise and the evil go to Hell. A "good" Muslim obeys the Five Pillars of Islam: 1. Confess faith daily. 2. Pray five times a day. 3. Give charitable donations. 4. Fast and observe sexual abstinence during the ninth month of the Islamic calendar. 5. Visit Mecca at least once during a lifetime if possible.

(continued)

TABLE 4-5 *(continued)*

Source of Power or Force (Deity)	Historical Sacred Texts or Source of Beliefs	Key Beliefs or Ethical Life Philosophy

Hinduism

Brahma (the Infinite Being and Creator that pervades all reality)

Other gods:
Vishnu (preserver)
Siva (destroyer)
Krishna (love)

Vedas (doctrine and commentaries)

All people are assigned to castes (permanent hereditary orders, each having different privileges in the society; each was created from different parts of Brahma):

1. *Brahmans*: created from Brahma's face; includes priests and intellectuals.
2. *Kshatriyas*: created from Brahma's arms; includes rulers and soldiers.
3. *Vaisyas*: created from Brahma's thighs; includes farmers, skilled workers, and merchants.
4. *Sudras*: created from Brahma's feet; includes those who serve the other three castes (servants, laborers, peasants).
5. *Untouchables*: the outcasts, those not included in the other castes. They fill the most menial occupations (street sweepers, latrine cleaners, scavengers). Mahatma Gandhi desired to change their identities to *Harijans*, or "Children of God."

TABLE 4-5 *(continued)*

Source of Power or Force (Deity)	*Historical Sacred Texts or Source of Beliefs*	*Key Beliefs or Ethical Life Philosophy*
Buddhism[b]		
Buddha	Tripitaka (scripture)	Buddhism attempts to deal with problems of human existence such as suffering and death.
Individual responsibility and logical or intuitive thinking	Middle Path (way of life)	Life is misery, unhappiness, and suffering with no ultimate reality in the world or behind it. An endless cycle of existence (birth and rebirth) continues because of personal desires and attachments to the unreal self.
	Eightfold Plan (guides for life)	
	sutras (Buddhist commentaries)	Understanding the cause of all human suffering and misery as due to desire, and the ultimate transcendence of all desires, leads to nirvana ("blowing-out"), a state of happiness, peace, and love.
	sangha (monastic or ideal living)	
		The "middle path" of life avoids the personal extremes of self-denial and self-indulgence.
		Visions can be gained through personal meditation and contemplation; good deeds and compassion also facilitate the process toward nirvana, or enlightenment.
		The end of suffering is in the extinction of desire and emotion, and ultimately the unreal self. Present behavior is a result of past deeds; overcoming attachment to personal desires and worldly things leads to nirvana.

(continued)

TABLE 4-5 *(continued)*

Source of Power or Force (Deity)	Historical Sacred Texts or Source of Beliefs	Key Beliefs or Ethical Life Philosophy
Confucianism		
No doctrine of a god or gods or life after death Individual responsibility and logical and intuitive thinking	Five Classics (Confucian thought) Analects (conversations and sayings of Confucius)	Considered a philosophy or a system of ethics for living, rather than a religion that teaches how people should act toward one another. People are born "good." Moral character is stressed through sincerity in personal and public behavior. Respect is shown for parents and figures of authority. Improvement is gained through self-responsibility, introspection, and compassion for others. Early phases of Confucianism dealt with the problems of living by looking to the past exemplary society. Later phases of Confucianism stress personal enlightenment through meditation, introspection, and study.
Shintoism		
Gods of nature, ancestor worship, national heroes	Tradition and custom ("the way of the gods") Beliefs were influenced by Confucianism and Buddhism	Reverence for ancestors and traditional Japanese way of life are emphasized. Loyalty to places and locations where one lives or works and purity and balance in physical and mental life are major motivators of personal conduct.

TABLE 4-5   *(continued)*

Source of Power or Force (Deity)	*Historical Sacred Texts or Source of Beliefs*	*Key Beliefs or Ethical Life Philosophy*
Taoism		
All the forces in nature	Tao-te-Ching ("The Way and the Power")	Quiet and happy harmony with nature is the key belief. Peace and contentment are found in the personal behaviors of optimism, passivity, humility, and internal calmness. Humility is an especially valued virtue. Conformity to the rhythm of nature and the universe leads to a simple, natural, and ideal life.
Judaism		
God	Hebrew Bible (Old Testament) Torah (first five books of Hebrew Bible) Talmud (commentaries on the Torah)	Judaists have a special relationship with God; obeying God's law through ethical behavior and ritual obedience earns the mercy and justice of God.
		God is worshiped through love, not out of fear. Personal satisfaction is gained through love of learning. Heartfelt good deeds without concern about rewards are stressed. Justice for all and morality in living are major goals in life. Coexistence with enemies is sought.
		Belief-practices range from orthodox-conservative to ultraliberal. The distinction depends on the level of adherence to codes of daily living and the amount of Hebrew spoken in services.

(continued)

TABLE 4-5 (continued)

Source of Power or Force (Deity)	Historical Sacred Texts or Source of Beliefs	Key Beliefs or Ethical Life Philosophy
Tribal Beliefs[c]		
Animism Souls, or spirits, embodied in all beings and everything in nature (trees, rivers, mountains) Polytheism Many gods, in the basic powers of nature (sun, moon, earth, water)	Passed on through ceremonies, rituals, myths, and legends. Oral history, rather than written literature, is the common medium.	All living things are related. Respect for powers of nature and pleasing the spirits are fundamental beliefs in order to meet basic and practical needs for food, fertility, health, and interpersonal relationships and individual development. Harmonious living is comprehension and respect of natural forces.

Summary of Other Belief Forms

Atheism: the belief that no God exists, as "God" is defined in any current existing culture or society.

Agnosticism: the belief that whether there is a God and a spiritual world or any ultimate reality is unknown and probably unknowable.

Scientism: the belief that values and guidance for living come from scientific knowledge, principles, and practices; systematic study and analysis of life, rather than superstition, lead to true understanding and practice of life.

Maoism: the faith that is centered in the leadership of the Communist Party and all the people. The major belief goal is to move away from individual personal desires and ambitions toward viewing and serving each other and all people as a whole.

[a]Islam has two major sects: (1) *Sunni* (orthodox): traditional and simple practices are followed; human will is determined by outside forces; (2) *Shiite*: practices are rapturous and trancelike; human beings have free will.

[b]Buddhist subsects include (1) *Lamaism* (Tibet): Buddhism is blended with spirit worship; (2) *Mantrayana* ("sacred recitation") (Himalayan area, Mongolia, Japan): intimate relationship with a *guru* and reciting secret *mantras* are emphasized; the belief in sexual symbolism and demons is also practiced; (3) *Zen* (Japan, China): self-reliance and awareness through intuitive understanding are stressed; *Satori* ("enlightenment") may come from sudden insight or through self-discipline, meditation, and instruction.

[c]Although the need for self-sufficiency with a spiritual foundation is a major goal of Native North American identity, Christianity and other nonnative beliefs have influenced or been incorporated in aspects of some Native American tribes. The Creeks, for example, handled new experiences by the process of gradual assimilation: "They absorbed many folk-tales from the European settlers into their mythology, and many from the negro slaves from West Africa. The Creeks in turn had a considerable influence on the Trickster Spirit, personified as the Rabbit, on to the cycle of Ashanti stories abut Anansi, the Trickster. In Jamaica Anansi suffers a spelling change and is often called Nancy, but in the south-eastern United States he took over the name of his Creek Indian archetype and has since charmed the world as Brer Rabbit" (Burland, 1965, p. 110).

The discovery of gold in California in 1848 intensified the migrations, although Chinese were not always welcomed and White miners feared unfair competition from the cheap Chinese labor. Hundreds of Chinese contributed their labor in the construction of the first transcontinental railroad; however, when that was completed in 1869, and with the drying up of many gold mines, the presence of the Chinese aroused hostility. They frequently faced mob violence. Special miner's and fisherman's taxes were imposed on the Chinese. In the Territory of Hawaii at the time, citizenship was denied contract laborers. Strikes, boycotts, and riots pushed the Chinese from many occupations and communities and forced them into Chinatowns (Huang, 1976; Petersen, 1978). It was at that time that many Chinese entered into laundry and restaurant businesses to gain a livelihood. The oppression also extended into and affected their cultural traditions and customs; for example, they began to cut their distinctive braids, or *queues.* The tradition of burying the ashes of dead kin in their Chinese native villages was restricted by actions of coroners in California, who often used the prescribed ordinance in a discriminatory manner. Anti-Chinese sentiment and prejudice were prevalent by the time they began to migrate to the Midwest and East (Lyman, 1974).

● INTERPERSONAL RELATIONS AND SOCIALIZATION

Most of the Chinese who migrated to North America were men who intended to bring wives or families later, but the exclusion acts made that impossible. Most of the western states at the time also prohibited interracial marriages. Compounding the problem was the traditional viewpoint in China (and Japan) that discouraged children's marrying out of their native village or province and certainly out of the country or race. Chinese men in Hawaii, however, have intermarried with women of other groups.

Between 1930 and 1946, the sex ratio of Chinese in the United States was 80% male to 20% female. Because there were few American-born Chinese before 1930, the Chinese were essentially a community of men (Schwartz, 1951). Huang (1976) believes that "Chinese women born in China or in America have for many years been in great demand, especially among Chinatown-based men" (p. 129). However, she also believes that in social relationships, dissonance may occur between Chinatown bachelors and educated Chinese women who are American citizens, due to their dissimilar backgrounds and the need to speak English because of their different dialects: "Differential degrees of acculturation on either side of the Pacific Ocean thus creates difficulties in heterosexual associations, either before or after marriage" (p. 130). In the 1940s and 1950s marriage outside the Chinese group was viewed by the Chinese as unconventional or considered as a social inconvenience wherein potential communication difficulties among relatives and in-laws would have to be faced. The desire to avoid situations that would engender hostility or feelings of marginality and the propensity of native-born Chinese to maintain group traditions also discouraged intermarriages. In the

1970s and 1980s, with increased assimilation and acculturation, out-of-group marriages for both male and female Chinese Americans became more common. Today, approximately 40% of Chinese Americans marry outside of their ethnic group (Sung, 1990).

Chinese Americans whose early socialization in the Chinese household has taught them to be relatively inhibited tend to be less socially aggressive than White Americans. Thus it may be especially difficult for them to initiate emotional expression with non-Chinese (Sue, 1980, pp. 186–189). But it has also been speculated (Huang, 1976) that a complementary relationship might potentially exist between the generally more aggressive or emotionally expressive White Americans and their generally more reserved, conservative, or quiet Chinese-American counterparts. If so, the socially more subtle behavior of Chinese Americans may allow for conservation of emotional energy. Recognition of this characteristic is important in the counseling process so that social reserve is not mistaken for the absence of emotions. The acquired restraint of emotions should be respected and emotional expression allowed in accordance with the person's ability and willingness.

● TRADITIONAL CHINESE FAMILY PROCESS

Hsu (1961) has described traditional Chinese families, and also Japanese and Korean families, as basically *patrilineal*, emphasizing and placing importance on descent or kinship through the male line. The most important relationship in Chinese families is that of the father and son. All other relationships in the family are extensions of or subordinated to or modified by this central relationship. There is only one father, but parents always desire many sons. The mutual dependency between father and son(s) is continuous and includes deceased male kin from the past, present kin, and kin yet to be born. The son owes his father services, obedience, and respect, and the father is expected to assist the son in his education, to arrange his marriage, and to grant the inheritance of possessions. The kinship obligation between mother and son is derived by virtue of her marriage to the father, assumption of his family group, and her biological relationship with the son. Thus the son owes her the same obligations that he owes the father. Her duties are to her husband's parents and her sons. Similarly, the married man's duties are to his parents and to his sons.

Although such a structure may restrict the freedom to assume other personal roles within the family, it also provides a strong feeling of security, belonging, identity, and duty to have roles that are so well defined and understood. Romantic love, as defined in the Western world, is not expressed, and negative emotional impulses that may endanger or stress family solidarity are repressed. Furthermore, divorce is considered a shame and is generally disapproved of. Chinese children grow up under the umbrella of an extended family and take part in its social life. Hsu (1970, p. 10) describes the American family as individual-centered, while members of the Chinese family are more dependent on each other and are more other-centered.

▲ JAPANESE AMERICANS

Although Japan was opened to trade in 1854, the Japanese did not migrate to the United States in great numbers until after 1890. Most of the early immigrants were poor males from rural areas, minimally educated and speaking little English. They hoped to gain a fortune and return to their native country in as short a time as possible. They entered Hawaii and California, where the majority of Japanese Americans remain clustered today. Daniels (1962) believes that they faced more obstacles and prejudice than did other immigrants. They were non-White, were considered an "enemy" group, and had a culture that Americans viewed as incomprehensible. During World War II, 110,000 persons of Japanese ancestry were evacuated from their homes in California and interned in relocation camps. The confinement was imposed without due process of law, and the disposal of homes and possessions caused great financial loss. Payment and retribution for the unprecedented act continue to be an emotional issue in the United States today, even after a 1988 federal law acknowledging the fundamental injustice and the payment of $20,000 to each of those who were restricted. Although there were no recorded acts of sabotage, American sentiment was highly anti-Japanese and acts of prejudice and discrimination were not uncommon (Kitagawa, 1967).

The early arrivals worked as farm hands, in canneries, lumber mills, and mines, and for railroads. As was the case with the early Chinese immigrants, the first Japanese to migrate to the United States came primarily from the same areas of Japan; for example, many of the Japanese settlers in Hawaii came from Okinawa. Although the Japanese faced the same exclusion restrictions as the Chinese, they imported women from Japan under the "Gentlemen's Agreement," which allowed Japanese wives of men in the United States to migrate. Often a marriage broker in Japan stood in for a prospective husband in the United States and couples were sometimes matched on various characteristics to ensure a proper union. Considering the obstacles to "overseas" marriages, the divorce rate for the early immigrant group was low (1.6%) compared to that of other ethnic groups (Kitano, 1969, p. 156).

● SOCIOECONOMIC MOBILITY OF JAPANESE AMERICANS

In the years following World War II, Japanese Americans have moved toward educational, occupational, and social assimilation into American society. Although members of both the Japanese-American and Chinese-American groups have experienced occupational success, a higher proportion of Chinese are in service occupations. One view holds that Chinese Americans may be under greater continuing pressure than Japanese Americans to remain in traditional settings, such as Chinatowns, wherein these service occupations are often likely to be performed (Petersen, 1978, p. 85). Other explanations of the success of Japanese Americans, especially in terms of education and occupation, have mentioned *value compatibility* and *community cohesion* (McLemore, 1980, pp. 191–197).

Value compatibility. This viewpoint proposes that there is a "good fit" between the value system of Japanese culture and the value system in mainstream American middle-class culture. Much of the support for this explanation rests on studies of some 20,000 Japanese who were released from relocation centers and resettled in Chicago. Within a few years this group had accomplished rapid movement into higher occupational levels, achieved educational advancement, and moved into more desirable residential areas. Although prejudice and discrimination toward some ethnic groups prevailed in Chicago, it did not encumber the Japanese at the level of intensity that was found on the West Coast. In addition, the availability of job opportunities during World War II enhanced their pattern of success. It is also believed that the experience of disruption during internment gave the American-born Japanese—who most often were included in the resettlement groups— encouragement to break away from the confinement of a traditional monocultural lifestyle and to relate to mainstream American society. Their ease of relating is explained on the basis of a compatibility that can be found between some Japanese values and some American middle-class values. According to McLemore (1980, p. 192), key shared values include politeness, respect for authority and parental wishes, duty to the community, hard work, cleanliness, neatness, education, occupational success, the pursuit of long-range goals, and building a good reputation.

Community cohesion. McLemore (1980) furthermore suggests that generational transmission of those "traditional success values" may rest most on the pattern of ethnic unity that "was a continuation of the traditional solidarity in Japan" (p. 194). The historic pattern of group conformity, with its approved set of ethnic values, has provided interpersonal connectedness that binds individuals, families, religion, and other social institutions in mutual responsibility and obligation for the behavior of each other. The merging of individual and group as one unity, or "community," thus gives strength to the individual, and in return the individual takes pride in belonging, is loyal, and is careful not to bring dishonor to the group.

McLemore expresses concern about some Asian Americans' criticism of the ways that Japanese-American success might be misused or misinterpreted:

1. The emphasis only on success may perpetuate a stereotype of all Asian Americans.
2. The success of one group may serve as a convenient excuse for expression of racial prejudice against other minorities.
3. Success as equated with material wealth may not really be success, but may simply conform to a culture-bound definition of success. When success is defined on the basis of other value sources—such as spiritual or humanistic—it has not been achieved.

● TRADITIONAL JAPANESE FAMILY LIFE

The *Issei*, or those Japanese born in Japan, brought with them their native Japanese culture. Traditional *Issei* families emphasized the old-country culture, including language, ceremonies, religion, arts, and the morals and ethics of proper social and interpersonal behavior. The father-son relationship is important, and in Japan inheritance rules were governed by primogeniture, the exclusive right of inheritance belonging to the eldest son.

In Japan, the *ie*, the family or household unit, provides the basic reference group for socialization. Loyalty to the *ie* is important, and from it come group unity, cohesion, and control. Conservatism and self-control, especially of emotions, are taught as a means of showing maturity. The "ideal" character is one that is correct, careful, clean, and composed (Kitano & Kikumura, 1976). In an interview by Webster, Stanford Lyman stated, "Issei parents used a considerable amount of ridicule and teasing in bringing up their children. There's very little physical or corporal punishment used by Japanese parents; it is almost never used. . . . Parents ridiculed and teased their children into conformity, and at the time when peer groups take over social controls from parents, at adolescence, the teasing was continued by friends" (Webster, 1972, p. 387).

Parents have positions of authority and privilege along with responsibility and obligation to the children. The concept of *enryo*, or the expression of deference toward those in a superior position, guides proper conduct in moments of social ambiguity that might arouse emotional feelings of embarrassment or confusion (Kitano & Kikumura, 1976, pp. 48–49). Nakane (1970) also describes the effect that the "group-ideal" has on its members in different situations. Japanese, according to Nakane, identify with the situation where they are. Group identity may also refer to the company that employs them or the school or university that they attend. Status in these situations is determined primarily by age, sex, order of entrance, or period of service.

Nisei are the American-born children of the *Issei*. The concept of cultural family solidarity and ethnic identification continues in this group in spite of a high rate of out-of-group relationships for both male and female Japanese. The rate of out-of-group marriages for the *Issei* in 1973 was about 5% and for the *Nisei* about 15%, whereas intermarriages for the *Sansei* (children of the *Nisei*) were about at the 50% level—at least in areas such as San Francisco, Fresno, Los Angeles, and Honolulu (Kikumura & Kitano, 1973). Today, more than 60% of all Japanese Americans marry outside of their ethnic group (Sung, 1990).

While the *Issei* are motivated by strong ties with their native Japan, the *Nisei* are eager to become Americanized. Many parents have resigned themselves to this circumstance and give their children the best they can in accordance with traditional custom. Education as a means to accultura-tion in the American situation is highly emphasized. In many *Issei* and *Nisei* families, the parents and children remain Buddhist, but traditional religious principles carried from Japan have undergone modification in the United States. As is true for members of other ethnic groups, the effects of cultural assimilation on individual Japanese Americans are diverse. It would be a mistake to generalize about the acculturation of any particular Japanese Americans by simply placing them into one of the three generational categories.

▲ KOREAN AMERICANS

The immigrants from Korea can be considered recent arrivals by comparison to the other Asian Americans. They have little history of early migration to the United States, although some were employed as contract laborers in Hawaii and on the West Coast in the very early 1900s. Since 1965, immigration of Koreans has been heavy. Americans in the United States probably know less about Koreans than they do about any of the other Asian-American groups.

● KOREAN ORIGINS

The earliest Korean ancestors settled in what is now Korea more than 30,000 years ago. The Korean people are a homogeneous group, and the only large noticeable minority group in Korea is the Chinese, who are few in number. Traditional Korean society, before the early 1900s, was primarily agricultural and built on strong extended-family ties and loyalties. The oldest male traditionally served as head, and all persons were expected to obey their elders. Japan seized the country in 1910 and brought industry to the city areas. Since World War II, the Korean way of life has changed drastically. In the North, the government has taught and encouraged placing the interests of the nation above those of the family and structured the country into an industrial society. In the South, Western nations have greatly influenced Korean life and customs, although the traditional culture and family ties remain stronger than in the North. The philosophy of Confucianism has been the most widely followed set of beliefs, and Buddhism is the major religion. There are also many Protestant and Roman Catholic Koreans.

● KOREANS IN THE UNITED STATES

Few Koreans—approximately 7,000, and most of them male, according to Kitano and Matsushima (1981)—were included in the early migrations of Asian groups to the United States. The decennial census of the United States did not separate Koreans as a population group until 1970, at which time 70,598 were reported. Although South Korean refugees migrated following the Korean conflict, the majority of the immigrants have arrived since 1965. Characteristics of the recent immigrants reflect the current immigration laws in that they tend to be more educated and possess professional skills. One survey (Kim, 1978) indicates that Korean Americans living in Chicago are young (early to mid-30s) and probably came to the United States fewer than six years ago. They are most likely to be married and have one or two children. They attend church regularly and are usually Protestant. They speak English, but it is a second language; Korean is used in the home and when conversing with other Koreans. They tend to come from families living in Korean cities and to have fathers who are in managerial positions, own businesses, or are professional persons. Higher education and economic improvement were major aims of the survey respondents. Many have attained these goals; however, many are also underemployed and probably hold a job below what they had in Korea. Kim (1981) has conducted a similar study of the Korean community in New York. Today, more than 30% of Korean Americans marry outside of their ethnic group (Sung, 1990).

▲ FILIPINO AMERICANS

The Chinese and Japanese were the first Asians to arrive in North America. As a result of amendments to the immigration act in 1965, the Filipino American population increased 36% between 1965 and 1974. Other Asian American populations also increased dramatically. Like the Koreans, the Filipino people in the United States are misunderstood or not understood: "The average American, if he thinks of the Filipino at all, is likely to picture him as someone rescued in 1898 from deprivation and perhaps from depravities both indigenous and induced, and nourished sacrificially ever since, until he has become indistinguishable from the creditor whose goods he imports so lavishly" (Chin, Chan, Inada, & Wong, 1974, p. liv). Writing by Filipino authors about the Filipino-American experience is not widely available. Much of the background of the people of the Philippine Islands is a picture of historical domination by three different world powers and its influence on the development of the Filipino national culture and personal self-identity.

● FILIPINO ORIGINS

The Negritos are believed to have been the first people to live in what is now the Philippines. After 3000 B.C., Asians from Indonesia and Malaysia entered the islands, followed by Japanese and Chinese traders and Muslim Arab missionaries. The first permanent Spanish settlers arrived in 1565, in search of gold and other valuable resources, and gradually converted the people to the Roman Catholic faith and other traditions of Spanish culture. The Philippines, or *Las Felipinas*, were named in honor of King Philip II of Spain. The Spanish priests were powerful and ruled the people harshly, along with the *caciques*, chiefs of the villages. The *caciques*, of Spanish-Filipino or Filipino ancestry, became the wealthy landowners. Revolution and demands for reform were attempted against the Spaniards throughout history. In 1898, at the conclusion of the Spanish-American War, Spain ceded the Philippines to the United States. The leader of the Filipino revolutionary movement, Emilio Aquinaldo, had expected independence from Spain; faced with yet another foreign domination, he struggled against American control. The fighting ended in 1901 and the United States extended its rule until 1946, when the nation was granted independence. During the period of 1901 to 1946, the Americans trained the Filipinos in the American style of idealism, self-government (the Commonwealth of the Philippines was established in 1935), public education methods, and the system of free business enterprise.

The American influence marked the historic beginning of a new philosophy of life for the inhabitants. According to Corpus (1938), "The introduction of popular education was to some degree instrumental in stimulating the latent potentialities of the masses. Through the public schools they became socially near to each other . . . new attitudes were developed, to be sure. This new social psychology, therefore, foreshadowed somewhat social progress in the Philippines" (p. 1). The Japanese invaded the Philippines in 1941 and occupied the country until 1945. The aftermath of the Japanese-American War brought the Huk rebellion, or revolution of Communist-led poor farmers, lasting until 1954. Throughout much of their history the people have experienced foreign domination, conflict, war, and little opportunity to freely develop their own national psyche. Today, great numbers of powerless and poor Filipinos continue to be politically oppressed and economically exploited by a small, affluent ruling class.

The majority of native Filipinos are classified by anthropologists as Filipino-Malaysian and are further classified according to religion, as either Christian, Muslim, Protestant, or Buddhist. About 83% of the Filipino people are Roman Catholic, and the culture is heavily characterized by Spanish tradition, although North American beliefs and customs have recently influenced Filipino life. The country also feels the presence of other minority groups in addition to the Muslims, who live chiefly in Mindanao and the Sulu Archipelago. Chinese form the second-largest racial group, and others include Indonesians and Negritos. Negritos, a scattered tribal people, are pygmies who are descendants of the original inhabitants of the country. Although English and Filipino (Tagalog) are the official languages, many local or tribal dialects are also spoken. The family structure has become similar to that of North American families, in which parental responsibility is equally shared.

● FILIPINOS IN THE UNITED STATES

Filipino youth migrated to Hawaii and to North America by the thousands in the early years of this century. In 1930, according to the *Fifteenth Census of the United States*, 47,699 Filipinos were living on the mainland. The majority—35,334—were located in the Pacific coast states (in California, 30,640). There were 2,505 in the New York City area, 2,085 in the Chicago area, and the remainder scattered throughout all parts of the country in small numbers. Seasonal jobs were available all the year 'round along the Pacific coast. About 4,000 Filipinos made their home in Los Angeles in 1935 (Corpus, 1938, p. 3).

The earliest Filipino immigrants became laborers on sugar plantations in Hawaii. When labor shortages occurred in California in 1923, thousands migrated to the mainland, where they engaged in work under conditions others would not accept. They became servants, houseboys, cooks, dishwashers, janitors, "stoop" laborers in the lettuce, carrot, and asparagus fields, and workers in the fish canneries and sawmills. Many of the immigrants were also students sent by the Philippine government to complete their training for professional careers. They were expected to study hard to achieve high scholarship and to display fine manners as "ambassadors of good will." Lasker (1969, p. 63) notes that in 1930 "the astonishingly large number of Filipinos in the Chicago Post Office is partly explained by their preference for night work which does not interfere with their studies at the local colleges." He also points out that whereas 300 Filipinos were employed in the Chicago Post Office at the time, only 18 were employed in San Francisco, 7 in Los

Angeles, and none in Seattle: "Apparently the intentions of the civil service law do not altogether prevail against the traditions of racial relations in different parts of the United States" (p. 63).

Most of the early immigrants remained in agricultural work. According to Kitano and Matsushima (1981), "They were known as hard workers and their elderly years have been characterized by isolation, loneliness, and poverty" (p. 174). They have also been subjected to discrimination and stereotyping based on their brown skin color. Current adaptation of Filipinos living in Hawaii has been studied by Alcántara (1981) and in Los Angeles by Tiger (1978).

Recent immigrants to the United States have included doctors, nurses, and other highly educated professionals. Kim's 1978 survey of Filipinos residing in urban Chicago reveals a young group of males and females, usually married, better educated and paid than those residing in other areas of the country, and with two or three young children. Like the Korean sample in Chicago, they probably emigrated fewer than six years ago and also have experienced underemployment. Most are professional, skilled, or white-collar workers. Although many have had trouble with the English language, they have not had as hard a time adjusting to their new culture as have other Asian Americans. The historical connection of the Philippines with the United States has probably helped in the adjustment. The Filipino cultural community in North America, in comparison with those of the Chinese and Japanese, is less visible and cohesive, and group identification and support are not as readily available.

Although the Filipino group in the United States has been geographically identified as originating in Asia, it is different from the other Asian groups. Colonization by Spain and the United States and the experience of Japanese occupation during World War II have created a series of influences that seem to both blend into and impinge on ethnic group consciousness and personal identity awareness. Unlike members of the Chinese-American and Japanese-American communities, whose culture is economically and geographically visible, Filipino Americans may find it difficult to distinguish their Filipino uniqueness from their Americanization. For one thing, the Filipino culture was initially borrowed from regional cultures, and during the last four hundred years the people have been influenced by the European and American presence. The effect of foreign domination is not meant to be ethnic rejection, but the opportunity to develop and maintain an ethnic psyche and spirit has been erratic. In 1964, McWilliams perceived the Filipino experience in California as a "blood brotherhood, a free masonry of the ostracized" which through out-of-group marriages "seemed destined to disappear or vanish into larger minority clusters. Here, again, the lack of an integrated native culture facilitates the adoption of the ways and customs of other groups" (p. 141). Peñaranda, Syquia, and Tagatac (1974, p. viii) wrote: "The Filipino still asks, What is love? What is liberty? Who am I? What am I doing here? He asked the same questions in 1921, and only now he blushes with the answer he is often forced to give." And, in 1981, Kitano and Matsushima stated: "There is great diversity among the Filipinos and they have not developed the cohesive communities that were a part of the Chinese and Japanese experience.

Filipinos are constantly mistaken for Japanese, Chinese, American Indians, and Mexicans, especially since many of them have Spanish surnames" (p. 174).

▲ INDOCHINESE AMERICANS

The Vietnamese are the most numerous subgroup of Indochinese recently arriving in North America. The 1990 census reports 614,547 Vietnamese living in the United States, an increase of nearly 135% since 1980. The literature available on their migration and adjustment to the United States is scanty, and many of the official governmental records and documents remain in files and storage, many of them perhaps never to be printed or made accessible to researchers (Montero, 1979).

● VIETNAMESE ORIGINS

The Indochinese countries of Vietnam, Cambodia, and Laos have histories that extend far into the past. Vietnam was formed during the third century by migrations of people from southern China. It is believed that Cambodia—one of the oldest kingdoms of Southeast Asia—was created prior to the first century A.D., and the kingdom of Laos ("Land of a Million Elephants") in the 14th century. During its history Laos has faced altercations with and control by Thailand—called the Kingdom of Siam at the time—and Cambodia was subject to intense pressure and boundary disputes at various times with Thailand and Vietnam. In the 1890s the French took control and grouped the three countries together, forming the Indochinese Union and establishing the present national boundaries. The Japanese invaded and occupied Vietnam during World War II. Upon conclusion of the war the French attempted to regain control but faced opposition by the *Vietminh*—adherents of the Vietnamese Communist independence movement—that eventually led to the Vietnam War.

The French colonial influence brought Western ideology and industry and established a class of wealthy landowners. Before French rule, Vietnam was essentially a traditional agricultural society, but during the colonization period many Vietnamese left their rural villages to work in the cities and factories. Buddhism is the most general religious belief system in South Vietnam; in rural areas many also worship the spirits of animals and nature, such as "guardian" spirits, which are thought to protect villages. As in many other Southeast Asian countries, the people also believe in the teachings of Confucianism and Taoism; thus the synthesis of Buddhism, Taoism, Confucianism, and individual characteristics make up their personalities. Due to the influence of the French, about 10% of the people in Vietnam have been reported to be Roman Catholic.

● MIGRATION OF AN UPROOTED PEOPLE

The war in Vietnam ended on April 30, 1975, and one year later North and South Vietnam were reunified. As the Communist demolition units entered

South Vietnam in 1975, thousands of terrified refugees poured into Saigon, and on April 29 and 30 more than 1,300 Americans and 5,600 Vietnamese were removed by helicopters to waiting United States Navy ships in the South China Sea. In a short period of time, more than 140,000 refugees left on planes, ships, and fishing boats. Soon after, about 132,000 had settled in North America and a few other countries. In 1978, Vietnam invaded Cambodia and, again, thousands of both Cambodians and Vietnamese voluntarily fled their countries; many were driven out by the government, including ethnic Chinese. More than 170,000 Indochinese refugees had entered North America by 1978, and three years later the number had swelled to nearly one-half million (Baker, 1981).

During the 1978 exodus, an estimated 30,000 per month arrived in neighboring nations, but many drowned at sea or were attacked by pirates. The wandering refugees endured appalling conditions in refugee camps. The world had never been so moved as it was by the tragedy of Indochina's refugees. They were Vietnam's "boat people" forced from their homes by government action. They were Cambodians fleeing from harsh rule, war, famine, and disease. They were Lao pushed from their homeland by war. Some estimates of the boat people run as high as 500,000.

● VIETNAMESE IN THE UNITED STATES

Vietnamese Americans "have grown up under wartime conditions and many of them may bring with them memories of bombings, guerrilla attacks, loss of family and loved ones" (Intercultural Development Research Association, 1976, p. 1). In addition, they have been torn from their homes and way of life and must cope with a new language and new culture in a strange land. The initial policy of the United States government in the settlement of the refugees has been to disperse them systematically in small groups throughout the country under the care of private sponsors. Tran (1976) believes this separation from their ethnic group has caused a loss of emotional support when it is most needed in the crucial period of adjustment. Whether or not this is true will only be known in future years of social and psychological development, but the immediate emotional pain of separation and alienation is a reality. Census data for 1990 show that Vietnamese are largely located in California (45%, or more than 275,000).

The Vietnamese have encountered problems of cultural conflict, culture shock, and personal adjustments that are similar in some ways to those of other immigrants, but they also have had to cope with experiences that no other group has faced. The trauma of uprooting in some respects perhaps has similarities to the trauma felt by African slaves in being torn from their homelands.

Background of the refugees. According to Montero's report (1979, pp. 22–24), the Vietnamese are a young group almost equally divided between males and females. Forty-three percent of the arrivals were 18 years and under and 37% were between 18 and 34 years of age. Also included in the earlier arrivals were nearly 4,000 unaccompanied minors under the age of 18 (Baker, 1981). The group possesses relatively high education standards, with nearly 50% of the adults having at least a secondary school education and more than 25% being college graduates. Their occupational background is broadly based, with 24% being professional, technical, and managerial, 16.9% transportation, and 11.7% clerical and sales. Only 4.9% are listed as farmers or fishermen. Evidence also indicates that the great majority have urban rather than rural backgrounds. Their typical extended-family structure centers on strong kinship ties and loyalty. More than 50% are Roman Catholic and 27% are Buddhists (Rahe, Looney, Ward, Tran, & Liu, 1978).

Some of the resentment and ethnic myths directed toward the earlier arrivals by longtime American residents have subsided as the emigrés have become established in their communities. More recent arrivals tend to be rural and unskilled people; in some areas with large Vietnamese populations, more than half of the Vietnamese live in poverty. Adjusting to American ways, trying to raise their children in a new culture, and not losing sight of the old culture are other issues faced by the Vietnamese. Butler (1992) and Matthews (1982) reveal the inner lives of Vietnamese Americans and also show, through their eyes, how the rest of Americans appear.

Confucian ethics. The great importance of the family and the respect given to learning and age are grounded in the Confucian ethic. Vietnamese who come from rural areas, and many urban Vietnamese, continue to observe the ceremonies honoring their ancestors. The relationship between father and sons is especially emphasized. The father is expected to be the teacher and role model. Love is shown through respect to the father, and the traditional ancestral worship is thus upheld. With the overrepresentation of Catholics among the refugees, it might be expected that Confucian ethics are integrated into traditional Roman Catholic beliefs, as is often the case in the native Vietnamese culture. Most traditional Vietnamese follow a mixture of Taoism and Buddhism and animistic practice.

Interpersonal behavior. The people have been brought up to respect and accept opinions of elders and not to disagree openly. If an opinion of another person turns out to be wrong, it is important to overlook it in order to save face. This custom helps to maintain family harmony and relationships among friends. Accepting orders and directions from superiors is valued rather than taking the initiative. Westerners often misinterpret Vietnamese as being passive and shy, whereas the actual behavior being displayed is motivated by their valuing of respect. Vietnamese customs emphasize modesty and restraint in revealing what one knows. Modesty and sincerity are highly valued social behaviors and polite praise is given only when it is truly deserved. "This behavior stems from the fact that they have been taught not to be demonstrative in public, especially not to express personal emotion which might be considered immodest or boastful" (Intercultural Development Research Association, 1976, pp. 9–10).

■ SUMMARY

1. This chapter has presented profiles of three ethnic groups in the United States: Black Americans, Hispanic Americans, and Asian Americans.

2. The nature of the relationship between European Americans and Black Americans during various historic phases in the life of the country was described. A major thread throughout the phases was the perpetuation of control over Black Americans as observed in prejudicial attitudes and beliefs and as practiced by discrimination in social, political, and economic areas.

3. The historic presence of three groups of Blacks in the United States was described: free Blacks, freed Blacks (emancipated slaves and their descendants), and Blacks who migrated from the West Indies. The free Blacks and those from the West Indies were fewer in number than the freed Blacks, and evidence suggests that they achieved greater economic self-sufficiency and status. The opportunity for progress that came with independence and freedom was not available to freed Blacks until very recent times. The destructive effects of slavery, the chaos and disruption following emancipation, and restrictions imposed by prejudice and discrimination all hindered the development of Black Americans. Governmental intervention on behalf of Black Americans was invoked soon after the Civil War, but real social, economic, and political freedom did not occur until the 1954 Supreme Court decision that segregated school facilities were inherently unequal and unconstitutional. Other important legislation for the benefit of Americans, such as the Civil Rights acts, followed.

4. Many Black Americans have made social, economic, and political gains due to the intervention of governmental and legislative action, but the progress of poor Blacks and a Black underclass continues to constitute a major problem for the country. Current relationships between Black and White Americans seem to be characterized by a position of moderation and cooperation; however, incidents of racial violence and antagonism continue to occur sporadically.

5. The recent migration of Haitian refugees to the United States was also noted. These immigrants are primarily poor and rural people who have left Haiti to escape political oppression and the lack of economic opportunities. Their low profile and appearance of gentleness have been attributed to years of fear instilled by experiences in their native country, culturally rooted methods of defusing aggression, and/or the desire to avoid U.S. government agencies out of fear of being returned to Haiti. Interpersonal relationships and roles emphasize the importance of family membership, with the mother often being the stabilizing influence and parental authority extending into adulthood to enhance the family status.

6. Hispanic Americans constitute a rapidly growing group in the United States, of which 64% are from Mexico, 10% from Puerto Rico, and 5% from Cuba. Although Hispanic communities are found in all parts of the country, the majority tend to migrate to urban areas. They are also a youthful group with larger-than-average families and lower-than-average divorce rates.

7. The Hispanic culture developed as a result of the fusion of Spanish culture—as brought by the early explorer-soldiers from Spain—with the Native American cultures in Mexico, Latin America, and other areas of the hemisphere. The term *Hispanic* is a generic term that connotes a culture shared by several nationality groups. Commonality is found most in the use of the Spanish language, the influence of Catholic traditions in the culture (spiritualism), respect for the traditional family (familism), and the bonds of affective interpersonal relationships (personalism). The three ethnic groups discussed in this chapter—Mexicans, Puerto Ricans, and Cubans—are distinctive in their presence, movement, and origins.

8. Mexicans predate Anglo-Europeans in North America by many years, and their evolving relations with the dominant culture have been largely shaped by their historical experience in the Southwest. The migration of Mexicans after 1900 in search of economic improvement was described and the problem of exploitation and treatment that is faced by illegal immigrants from Mexico was discussed. Traditional Mexican family life was described as emphasizing affective relationships and defined roles for parents and children. However, it was also noted that as Mexican-American families participate in middle-class lifestyles, traditional role relationships may well move toward egalitarianism, potentially causing stress in more traditional families and creating intergenerational conflicts.

9. Puerto Ricans began to migrate to the United States after 1917, when Puerto Rico was established as a commonwealth of the United States. Since the development of air travel, migration between the island and the mainland has become characteristic in the lives of many Puerto Ricans. Family/marriage relationships and roles that have been traditional in Puerto Rico were discussed, and it was noted that for those who settled on the mainland, the cultural orientation of second and third generations is different from that of island Puerto Ricans. Four family structures of mainland Puerto Ricans were noted: extended family, nuclear family, mixed family, and single-parent family.

10. The historic exploitation and influence in Cuba by Spain and the United States was discussed. Two groups of Cubans who migrated to the United States were noted: those who migrated following the establishment of the Castro regime in 1956 and those who migrated as political refugees during 1980. The earlier group consisted primarily of persons from the middle and upper socioeconomic classes, and the recent group consists of many semiskilled and skilled workers.

11. Though Chinese migrated to the United States beginning in the 1850s, Japanese in 1890, and Filipinos in 1900, the largest migration of Asians has occurred since the passage of the Immigration and Naturalization Act of 1965, which lifted restrictive quotas based on national origins. Other major laws and legal actions governing immigration and naturalization (citizenship) over the last hundred years were outlined. The effects of these actions on the patterns of ethnic immigration to the United States were noted, as was the effect on the American population rate. Today, Chinese Americans constitute the largest group of Asian origin, Filipinos the second, and Japanese the third. Asian

Indians and recent Korean, and Vietnamese immigrants also constitute large numbers.

12. The historic origins and some aspects of traditional culture for the many diverse Asian Americans were described according to three geographic locations: South Asia (Asian Indians), Southeast Asia (Indochinese, Filipinos), and East Asia (Chinese, Taiwanese, Hong Kong residents, Japanese, Koreans). Major religious belief forms existing in the world and key points for each were also outlined in this section.

13. The early Chinese immigrants in Hawaii and the United States were primarily laborers seeking economic opportunity. During periods of economic recession and depression, anti-Chinese sentiments and prejudice and discrimination contributed to Chinese withdrawal into Chinatowns and the initiation of their own business enterprises. Some examples of problems of interpersonal relations and the socialization process were described. Social dissonance between Chinatown bachelors and educated Chinese girls who were American citizens was noted, as was the reluctance of traditional Chinese families to relate outside their group. Chinese Americans who have been socialized early in the Chinese household to be less socially aggressive may find it especially difficult to initiate emotional expression with non-Chinese. "Conservation of emotional energy" was suggested as a concept that needs further understanding in its operation as a dimension in the cross-cultural counseling process. Traditional Chinese family structure was described as basically patrilineal and other-centered (group-centered), in contrast with the individual-centered family of the mainstream American culture.

14. Some historic aspects of the culture in Korea were noted; like other Asian groups, the Koreans have a long history of cultural integration. More recently, traditional life and customs in South Korea have been influenced by Western nations. Findings from one survey of Koreans living in Chicago noted that current immigrants include those who tend to be well educated and possess professional skills.

15. Japanese immigrants to the United States faced prejudice and discrimination as did the Chinese; in addition, they experienced dislocation from their homes and confinement during World War II. The earlier arrivals worked as laborers and many eventually started truck farms, arousing resentment in White Americans and leading to various restrictions on the ownership of land by Japanese noncitizens. The relative success of Japanese Americans in educational and economic assimilation was described and explained through two theories: value compatibility and community cohesion. Changing patterns of Japanese family life and member roles were shown for the *Issei, Nisei,* and *Sansei* groups.

16. Filipino Americans—although geographically identified as Asians— were described as a group of people whose native culture has been historically dominated or influenced by Spain, the United States, and Japan. The majority are Roman Catholic, and Western ways have pervaded many aspects of the lives of the people. The first group of Filipinos who immigrated in the early 1900s took work as agricultural laborers and faced discrimination similar to

that confronting other Asians; their elderly years have been characterized by isolation, loneliness, and poverty. The more recent group includes highly educated professionals and, according to one survey of Filipinos living in Chicago, they have not experienced the hard time adjusting to American culture that has hampered other recent groups of Asian Americans. However, issues for the development of a Filipino and a Filipino-American ethnic identity were discussed in relation to the experience of many years of foreign domination in the indigenous culture and the lack of a visible or cohesive community in the United States.

17. Indochinese immigrants include Vietnamese, Cambodians, and Lao; Vietnamese constitute the most numerous group. All three groups experienced uprooting from their native cultures and resettlement in the United States and other countries. The French colonial influence in Indochina was described and events leading up to the Vietnam War were noted, as was the traumatic exodus of thousands of refugees from Vietnam and other Indochinese countries. Vietnamese refugees in the United States were described as a young group, with 43% under 18 years and 37% between 18 and 34 years old. Coming primarily from urban areas in Vietnam, they tend to possess relatively high educational levels. More recent arrivals tend to be rural and unskilled. The important role of Confucian ethics in family and personal relationships was discussed. Respect for and acceptance of opinions of elders, avoidance of open disagreement, accepting orders and direction rather than taking the initiative, and modesty and sincerity have been observed in the behavior of Vietnamese Americans.

TODAY'S ISSUES

- ■ Sociopolitical Issues
- ■ Education and Achievement
- ■ Work and Career Development
- ■ Social and Personal Growth

CHAPTER

SOCIOPOLITICAL ISSUES

The purpose of this chapter is to identify factors and major issues that can influence intergroup relations and affect the quality of interpersonal communication among members of various groups in the multicultural society. The topics include a definition of minority groups, the influence of differences, prejudice, psychological variables related to prejudice, social variables related to prejudice, and political and economic variables related to prejudice. The ramifications of prejudice are related to racism, issues of cultural differences, and color conflict. Finally, movement toward authentic interpersonal relations is discussed.

■ WHAT IS A MINORITY?

▲ RACIAL MINORITY

The term *racial minority* is often used in reference to members of those groups who are readily identified by distinctive physical characteristics that are perceived as different from those of members of the dominant group in a society. Skin color, hair type, body structure, shape of head or nose or eyes, and color of eyes are often singled out as "different." The scientific subdivision of the species *Homo sapiens* into races has perpetuated barriers among people and influenced the operation of psychological mechanisms that contribute to racism (the belief in the superiority of one race over another). It is not unusual for any established society to use its own inventions, under any name, to maintain itself. For many years, it has been claimed that the races of the world are black (Negroid), white (Caucasoid), Archaic white (Australoid), and yellow (Mongoloid). Some writers disagree: "The myth of human races constitutes one of man's most damnable masses of misinformation, and . . . has led to wars, strife, murder, and waste of natural resources" (Calloway & Harris, 1977, p. 7). The idea that racial classifications correspond to a reality or collection of characteristics has not been demonstrated. According to the viewpoint of some geneticists, the concept of ethnic group differences is more accurate and appropriate for present-day usage than is a classification of races. Montagu (1974) states his belief: "It is preferable to speak of these four large groups of mankind as *major groups* rather than as *races,* and to speak of the varieties of men which enter into the formation of these major groups as *ethnic groups.* The use of the term 'major group' is purely arbitrary and is merely calculated to indicate that the likeness in certain characters exhibited by some populations appear to link them more closely than to other populations. Nothing more is implied in the term than that" (p. 9).

▲ ETHNIC MINORITY

Ethnic minorities are usually identified by cultural practices, such as language, accent, religion, customs, beliefs, and styles of living. Ethnic characteristics, essentially, can be traced to national origins or geographic regions. The misuse of racial classifications and the tendency to treat the ideas of race and ethnicity as if they were interchangeable are undesirable practices that can lead to illogical conclusions. When physical characteristics (race) and cultural ways (ethnicity) are taken to be synonymous, the attitudes prevailing toward either one may be associated with the other. Thus, if the racial category of a group of people is viewed as inferior or superior, by implication their cultural ways may also be viewed in the same manner. Prejudice and discrimination shown toward Chinese by Americans of European background in California in the middle of the 19th century, for example, singled out their yellow-brown skin color and eyefolds as well as their language, queue (a tail of braided hair), manner of dress, food preferences, and other cultural characteristics.

▲ NUMERICAL MINORITY

Although the term *minority* literally means numbering less than half, it does not customarily refer to numerical size when it is used to describe groups of people. For example, when women are described as a minority, the term refers to their political, economic, and social status and freedom in relation to men in the society. In the South and in many urban areas of the North and Southwest, Blacks and/or Hispanics form the majority of the population, but they are still a minority people if the politically and economically more powerful group perceives and treats them as inferiors.

■ THE INFLUENCE OF DIFFERENCES

Minority groups may differ from the majority group and also from each other in their native spoken language, values, beliefs, behavior, customs, and/or experiences. Exclusion of others who are different is a phenomenon that can be found in any group of people because change in the status quo, or inclusion of others who are different, may be perceived as a threat to established group patterns. A group's established pattern is felt and perceived as bringing status, security, and a coherent means for social relationships to those who are included.

Cultural bias, or adherence to what is familiar, is an especially complex and vexing phenomenon in the multicultural U.S. society. Mainstream culture in the United States seems to move toward what is *similar* to itself and away from what is *different*. Valuing similarity has influenced American life throughout history and is shown through uniformity of language, conformity in social relations, agreement on proper psychological distance, economic order, stress on equality, and other forms of cultural homogeneity. According to Stewart (1981), "Although research may modify the significance of similarity, the principle continues to influence values in American society. Its importance perhaps is great enough to qualify, for Americans, as an assumption in thought, in social life, and in communication. Thus, the more similar two persons are, the better they should be able to communicate, whereas differences impede communication. In some other cultures, however, differences may be assumed to be necessary for communication to take place, and the degree of success is not measured by agreement and conformity as it tends to be in American life" (p. 65). The assumption that people in the United States tend to favor similarity over differences may be related to the sense of security that people derive from familiar patterns. Movement toward close relations with different others arouses the fear that one's values may be changed or lost, while movement toward similar others reinforces one's values. However, taking risks in everyday interpersonal contacts can also provide the opportunity for increased personal development for all parties concerned.

The implications for the counseling relationship are, of course, critical if either counselor or client tends to look only for what is familiar and avoid what is unfamiliar. According to Rogers (1961), a counselor and client who come from different backgrounds and have different values may experience dissonance in their counseling relationship. However, Rogers also believes: "I learn from these experiences in ways that change me, that make me a different and, I think, a more responsive person" (p. 19). Rogers's assumption about the role of the counselor in the counseling process is that when the counselor's perception becomes more open and accurate toward both himself or herself and the client, the client has more opportunity for change.

■ PREJUDICE

In the literal sense, *prejudice* is defined as a preconceived judgment or opinion without just grounds or sufficient knowledge. Prejudices can be positive or negative. As used in this book, *prejudice* is negative. It is an irrational attitude or behavior directed against an individual or a group, or their supposed characteristics. Groups that become targets of prejudice are most often categorized by racial, geographic, or ethnic background, religious beliefs, socioeconomic class, sex, or age. Some of these prejudices are so intense that they are considered "isms" or doctrinaire (racism, classism, ageism, sexism). Racial prejudice is one of the most serious psychological and social problems existing in U.S. society today. One example of such prejudiced thinking is the sentiments expressed during a newspaper interview by an individual who had just been acquitted in the shooting of a Black civil rights leader. The following are excerpts from the interview: "Our real enemies are the Jews. White people are the chosen people of God. . . . Whites are better looking than blacks, Mexicans, or other races. . . . That is a sign that whites are God's chosen people" ("Racist May Escape Charges," 1982, p. 26).

Hayakawa (1979) believes that the words we use directly convey how we think and *evaluate*, not only to others but also to ourselves: "Don't all prejudices—racial, ideological, religious, occupational—work in just this way? 'I don't like Russians.' 'You know how taxi drivers are!' 'I can't stand women's clubs.' . . . Hence the unexamined key words in our thought processes, whether 'fish' or 'free enterprise' or 'radicalism' or the 'Establishment,' can hinder and misdirect our thought by creating the illusion of meaning where no clear-cut meaning exists" (p. 81).

The faulty reasoning behind the attitude of prejudice may even mistakenly lead to lumping diverse groups into a single category based on a single trait. The German Nazis, for example, regarded Jews, Poles, and Gypsies as inferior races and sought to exterminate them, even though their ethnic cultures were quite dissimilar. The segregation of people, especially according to racial categories, and the idea of racial and ethnic superiority have existed in the U.S. culture for generations, despite a democratic political system and the Christian tradition. Says Barnouw (1973), "We thus have a long heritage of prejudice behind us from which it may be difficult to extricate ourselves, especially since much of it is on a more or less unconscious level" (p. 73).

The adaptation of the cultural system in the United States to the modern ideology of cultural pluralism is a major developmental stage in the life of the people today. The members of the society are mutually interdependent and the survival of each member depends to a large degree on the behavior of the other members. Understanding the causes or variables related to prejudice and comprehending how prejudice functions as a self-defeating mechanism will be helpful to counselors in their work in the culturally diverse society. Both counselor and client are susceptible to the forces of prejudice within their own psychodynamics, as well as having to face the effects of prejudice as a sociocultural problem in the context of the collective society. Some social scientists are reluctant to accept the notion of prejudice as a scientific concept since its use opens the door to value judgments of the user. However, the term is in common usage in the general culture, and understanding its ramifications and implications is part of one's background of technical knowledge.

Prejudice is analyzed in the following sections according to psychological, social, and political and economic variables. The ramifications of prejudicial attitudes are discussed in relation to racism, cultural differences, and color conflict.

▲ PSYCHOLOGICAL VARIABLES

The manner in which one's personality is *integrated* is often related to prejudicial attitudes that are directed against an object, person, or group. The notion central to a theory of personality integration is that the basic units of personality (emotions, thoughts, motivations, and needs) are functionally dependent on one another, or, at times, competing with one another for expression. The common expression "Your emotions are getting in the way of your understanding" points to an overemphasis on emotions at the expense of intellectual comprehension founded on fact. By some means, these personality units must be sorted and priorities assigned to those demanding expression at any particular moment. A personality is integrated to the extent that such sorting and assignment are possible. However, if an individual's personality is too highly integrated, variation and speed in sorting and assignment among the components are less possible. Highly integrated personalities are sometimes called *rigid personalities*. Individuals with rigid personalities tend to choose the same response consistently over several situations. The choice that was considered appropriate by the individual in one situation—for example, the way to discipline a child or how to view a feminist activist—may not be appropriate for all situations involving children or activists.

● AUTHORITARIAN PERSONALITY

An authoritarian personality is motivated by biased, inappropriate, or too hasty conclusions that are based on inadequate *reality testing*. According to psychoanalytic researchers (Ackerman & Jahoda, 1950; Adorno, Frenkel-Brunswik, Levinson, & Sanford, 1950), inadequate reality testing, or inaccurate stereotypical beliefs about an ethnic group, serves an irrational function in the personality. The outward manifestations are seen in personality traits of inflexibility, contempt for weakness, aggressive tendencies, and a lack of self-awareness. The inflexibility of children raised in authoritarian families is shown in their inability to tolerate *ambiguity* (Frenkel-Brunswik, 1949). Children who experience strict authoritarianism and obedience tend to be less spontaneous, less flexible in perception, more submissive, and more prejudiced. Fear of self-expression and gaining of safety in conformity often lead to restriction in the individual's range of perception and in the normal expression of emotions.

Prejudice can also be attributed to a dysfunction in the cognitive processes (perception, judgment, reasoning and remembering, thinking and imagining). Rokeach (1960) has demonstrated how generalized mental rigidity is related to higher rates of *ethnocentrism.* Personality rigidity, or "mental rigidity," is experienced as difficulty in restructuring one's perception in a given situation, with the predisposition being to stick to the same, or familiar, approach to a problem in spite of other possibilities or solutions. The inability to consider new, or different, approaches and solutions when coping with a situation or problem has also been described by Allport (1954), who emphasizes that prejudice is a function of faulty and inflexible generalizations within the cognitive process itself.

● **PSYCHOLOGICAL DEFENSE MECHANISMS**

Psychological defense mechanisms play an important part in maintaining a self-image that is based on beliefs and fears acquired early in life; they also restrict a person's ability to accurately perceive both self and others. The functioning of defense mechanisms as a component of personality, or at least as so conceptualized and defined, seems to be present in many cultures, and especially in Western cultures. The function of most defense mechanisms is (1) to provide some psychological gain, (2) to express an impulse, or (3) to reduce anxiety temporarily. In working with problems of prejudicial attitudes that are attributed to dysfunction *within* the personality, counselors should be alert to the mechanisms of *projection* and *displacement.*

Projection. Projection is the process of perceiving in others motives or traits that are actually within the perceiver, and not necessarily in the personality of the other. According to psychoanalytic theory, the motives that are projected are "bad," or disliked, and are conflict-producing for the person. Thus, a shift occurs between self and other in which a trait or motive belonging to the self is imputed to the other. Projection reduces intrapsychic conflict and anxiety through deflecting onto others those unwanted or disliked parts of one's own personality. In its most extreme forms, it may be epitomized in paranoia (suspiciousness) and reaction formation (forming conscious behavior that is opposite and in reaction to how a person actually feels; thus, a person who feels weak and insecure may place high value on toughness and despise the excluded "out groups").

Projection is also seen as a means to distort or hide unacceptable impulses, which if recognized in the self might cause discomfort. There is, for instance, a myth in the White culture that Blacks, especially Black males, possess unusual sexual prowess and activity. The combination of projection and fantasy "safely" fulfills sexual impulses for the believer, and Blacks become typified as sexual machines. Such myths are carry-overs from old beliefs within the White culture that Blacks are primitive and animalistic. It was also expedient in the old society to encourage fertility in order to perpetuate the slave-centered economy. Such myths continue in the human psyche as convenient means for denying one's own weaknesses or for fulfilling one's own repressed impulses.

Actual sexual aggression, as in rape, however, involves a deep sense of impotency on the part of the perpetrator, whether White or non-White. Sexual aggression can also serve as an outlet for hatred, anger, and hostility, and can thus be considered as a form of psychological displacement.

Displacement. Displacement is discussed by both psychoanalytic theorists and learning theorists. In the psychoanalytic conceptualization it refers to a feeling that is related to one object but that is expressed toward another, which is remote from or only superficially connected to the original object. A second meaning of *displacement* denotes the process in which an impulse shifts from one object to another because the first object is simply not available in the environment.

The displacement of emotional feelings to objects or others not directly connected with the cause of the feeling is analogous to kicking the family dog in anger because you didn't get a raise in pay. It creates interpersonal havoc for both the recipient of the displaced emotion and the "displacer." Studies have shown that when individuals are raised in an overly strict or authoritarian environment, they learn not to express feelings or opinions for fear of reprisal. Expression of anger by the children of authoritarian parents may result in a withdrawal of love and affection by the parents. The unacceptable emotion is therefore not directed toward the parents but displaced onto other objects or people. According to psychoanalytic theory, for example, individuals who express sudden outbursts of resentment and hostility toward minority groups possess residual, or repressed, anger within their personalities, and they have also been conditioned, or are vulnerable, to using displacement as a defense mechanism. There are two counseling problems involved here. One problem is the *dissociation,* or fragmenting, of the personality caused by the separation of the anger from its true source, and the second is the *distortion of reality,* or overgeneralization, caused by the operation of the displacement mechanism.

Displacement of hostility, as a result of frustration from discriminatory treatment in the economic, educational, political, and social life of the society, was witnessed when urban ghetto Blacks in the late 1960s burned down their own neighborhoods in moments of angry and hostile *collective behavior.* Many White business establishments were specifically targeted for looting and destruction, and the theme was "Burn, baby, burn." In 1977, Puerto Ricans in Chicago's Humboldt Park area set fire to many stores and buildings in their community, and police cars were especially subjected to attack. Similarly, rioting and uprising by Blacks and Hispanics occurred in South-Central Los Angeles in 1992 as a result of frustration over police brutality and perceived racial injustice; at least 50 deaths were attributed to the disturbance and many Korean-owned businesses were looted and burned in fits of displaced anger.

Learning theory conforms with psychoanalytic views in the belief that prejudice is a function of cognitive processes. According to learning theory, displacement is the diverting of affect from one object to another because of the fear of punishment. Striking out at minorities, or any others who are seen as inferior and incapable of retaliation, will be *less* likely to produce consequential punishment, while anger directed toward parents, an employer, other members of a close group, or any object that provides rewarding conditions would normally be avoided. Withdrawal of affection is a form of punishment. However, the behavioral concept of avoidance of external punishment does not adequately correspond to the psychoanalytic concept of internal personality components that compete with each other, according to which displacement is seen as a means of personal defense that hides the unwanted part of the self from the person.

Another interpretation of learning theory holds that displacement is only a form of stimulus overgeneralization, rather than a defense mechanism. In this case, displacement is produced by similarity of stimuli when the original object for the direction of emotion is unavailable, whereas in the case of punishment that functions as an instrument of approach-avoidance behavior there is environmental frustration that leads to displacement in order to avoid punishment. The learning theory of overgeneralization based on similarities implies that the condition is not adjustive and that the aggression or other emotion is not depleted but broadens to additional objects.

● IMPLICATIONS FOR GROUP RELATIONS

Prejudice is an undesirable condition that leads to disrupted relationships for both the individual and the society. It is especially deplorable when it is directed against vulnerable minority group members. Prejudice has been described as a psychological phenomenon in which a person's consciousness of reality is altered in order to exclude unwanted ideas, feelings, or impulses. Prejudice and related defense mechanisms have been learned as a solution to internal psychological conflicts. It is also presumed that degrees of prejudicial attitudes and culturally related bias are basic human imperfections present in all people. In today's society, admission of prejudicial attitudes is usually not condoned. But awareness of hidden prejudices is the first step in the development of rational open-mindedness in any interpersonal relationship, including relationships between counselors and clients and those between groups of people.

The psychological viewpoint emphasizes authoritarian personality traits, inner personality conflicts, and the functioning of defense mechanisms as causes of prejudice. But "this is certainly not the whole explanation, since people in other cultures who have the very same personality traits do not always reveal an inclination toward prejudice" (Farb, 1978, p. 286).[1] Another explanation rests in the sociology of group relations.

[1]From *Humankind,* by Peter Farb. Copyright © 1978 by Peter Farb. This and all other quotations from this source are reprinted by permission of Houghton Mifflin Company and Jonathan Cape Ltd.

▲ SOCIAL VARIABLES

People live in groups and through groups, and their interaction within them creates our social reality, or at least an illusion of some kind of meaning. This social interaction is the province of sociology: "The *psychological* position, which emphasizes feelings and attitudes, is in contrast to the *sociological* position, which emphasizes the primacy of 'groupness' " (Jones, 1972, p. 3). Identification with a group has both positive and negative ramifications. Group life and group membership bring a sense of security and belonging, a fulfilling of human gregariousness. In some cases, such as in newly arrived immigrant groups or ethnic groups that have had to face subjugation throughout history, cooperation and loyalty in group relations may even be necessary for basic survival.

Group identification begins with the family unit and later extends to childhood and adolescent peers, schools attended, and religious, occupational, socioeconomic, sex, and age groups. Our relationships in various social and categorical groups provide the reference points for development of individual self-identity in the culture and society. According to Festinger's (1954) *social comparison* theory, group identification is basic to the formation of individual perceptions and beliefs. What we think of ourselves and others is derived through comparing our position in a group with that of others in the group. Thus, association with a "winning team" is highly regarded, and to be a "winner" on a winning team is even more desirable.

In a culture that emphasizes competition and achievement as a source of self-esteem, cross-group comparisons are also inevitable in the search for validation of one's self. "The problem of prejudice follows from using the standards of one's own group when comparing the self to someone in another group. Moreover, this standard is unfairly used if one's own-group identification is always seen as the *positive pole* in the comparison process" (Jones, 1972, p. 3).[2] Social reality is collectively constructed and is an ongoing process, with the more powerful groups swaying the direction in proportion to their power.

● ETHNOCENTRISM

Ethnocentrism is a term used by anthropologists and sociologists to denote a belief that one's own group is the center of everything, the standard by which all others are rated. The individual identifies with his or her group's culture and assumes that the group's cultural patterns are the best and right ways of acting. Social psychologists generalize the term to *in-group* attitudes exhibited by religious, racial, and socioeconomic class groups. Ethnocentrism is sometimes evidenced in attachment to Old World (European) ways. When the beliefs and customs acquired in one place and time by older members of a group differ from those experienced by the younger members in a new culture, intergenerational conflict often follows. The older group members find

---

[2]From *Prejudice and Racism,* by J. M. Jones, pp. 3 & 6. Copyright © 1972 by Addison Wesley. This and all other quotations from this source are reprinted by permission.

security in the ways that are most familiar and best known. What is *unknown* arouses a sense of insecurity and can lead to hostility and suspicion toward other cultures. Since the concept of ethnocentrism implies a value bias, or an assumption about what is desirable, social scientists have tended to move toward the concept of cultural relativity in their research investigations.

● CULTURAL RELATIVITY

Cultural relativity is the idea that any behavior must be judged first in relation to the *context* of the culture in which it occurs (Hall, 1976). This concept makes any comparative appraisal or cross-cultural analysis more difficult, if not impossible. The possible benefit of this theoretical approach is that studies or practice based on this theory should be free of inherent cultural biases. In the multicultural counseling process it is crucial that the counselor relate first to the interpretations of experiences that the client gives in terms of the client's own background, frame of reference, and norms of social behavior, since those are what influence perceptions and values.

An application of cultural relativity is useful in understanding cases such as those of the Southeast Asian refugees in the early 1980s who failed to appear in court because they thought money posted for bond actually served as bribes. In many Southeast Asian countries gifts are exchanged for services; they would not be considered gifts in U.S. culture. Money offered to the clerk in the driver's license office for helping with issuance of a license would be considered a gift for services rendered, not a bribe. When the principle of *contextualism* is applied to comprehending clients from the standpoint of their distinctive cultural structure and the value system it entails, cultural differences can be identified that may cause misunderstanding or conflict within the general society and that need to be overcome or resolved in some way. Understanding clients from the perspective of their own situation, however different from the counselor's culture it may seem, is also necessary in helping them deal with problems *within* their own cultural environment.

● CULTURAL UNIVERSALS

In addition to considering the context of the client's own cultural experiences, counseling must adapt to a broadened perspective of existence within the majority-minority pluralistic American society. The idea of *cultural universals* implies that there is a fundamental uniformity behind the seemingly endless diversity of cultural patterns. In the most general form, for example, the following structures or functions are found in every extended culture: a family unit, marriage, parental roles, education, medicine, forms of work or endeavors to meet basic physiological needs, and forms of self-expression that meet psychological and spiritual needs. These themes are universal, or common, in the sense that every culture has them, although there may be multiple expressions of the same theme. When *differences* in expressions are emphasized, instead of the *commonality* of themes, the tendency toward prejudice and bias is increased. In a culturally pluralistic society, with one dominant cultural group and many minority cultural groups, the pressure toward conformity to the dominant standards of expression is great. Insight into culturally diverse clients can be enhanced when basic life themes and life content are perceived as being the same for all clients.

● HUMAN NATURE AS A UNIVERSAL EMERGENT

The ability to accept and accurately perceive commonalities in diverse cultures is subject to the influence of prejudice, which emphasizes that one culture is better than another and that the people in the "inferior" culture are therefore inferior. Psychologists have endeavored to show that *all* people develop, learn, and function according to the same basic principles of human nature, though there is hardly conclusive agreement on what those general principles are. If counselors take the attitude that there are basic personality components that can be identified in all people across cultures, they are more likely to comprehend the totality of client motivation within cultural context. All human beings possess basic emotions and feelings, but learned ways of expression may vary from culture to culture. Basic emotions are stimulated in different ways by particular cultural environments. The group norm tends to set the type and pace of allowable expression. Thus, traditional Asian culture emphasizes the restraint of negative emotions in the interests of group harmony, whereas traditional Italian culture is more likely to encourage the open expression of feelings. A culture that overemphasizes competition, perfection, and success as measures of self-value and self-esteem can also potentially stimulate negative emotions of hate and hostility toward others or, when directed inward, feelings of self-depreciation and depression. When this condition exists in a multicultural society, racism often appears as a symptom.

▲ POLITICAL AND ECONOMIC VARIABLES

Politics and economic conditions in the society are interrelated and inter-twined. The political structure, through legislation and governmental insti-tutions and agencies, seeks to work out agreements for all the various groups, and politicians attempt to solve conflicts that might otherwise have to be solved by aggression and force. Hundreds of books have been written on the "minority problem" in the political and economic life of the country, but they neglect the fact that the overall issue is a concern not solely for minorities but for all Americans. The problem is basically the application to all Americans of the American creed of equality and fairness. The problem is to make universal the concept of cooperative freedom to participate in the formation of the laws and regulations that control our movements and the concept of freedom of access to fair participation in the economic system. Much of the resistance to change in the general society is based on preconceived attitudes that something has to be *given up* rather than that there is something *to be gained*. Myrdal (1944) called it the "American dilemma." Genuine cooperation and successful racial dialogue have been hindered historically by paternalistic attitudes on the part of the White majority (van den Berghe, 1958) and recently by lack of common purpose, such as the mutual goal of racial and moral equality that characterized the early civil rights movement and that gave the participants a feeling of cohesion and a common sense of direction. Steele (1990) asserts that racial groups have become competing power groups who use the distinction of race to sanction each other's pursuit of power in relation to the other. As a result, this choreographed behavior is likely to have angry Black Americans on one side speaking for racial entitlement and White Americans on the other showing deference to Black authority on the subject.

● POLITICAL VARIABLES

Preconceived attitudes about what is correct and proper, attitudes that may limit the expression of others, function through the interaction of *power, authority,* and *influence.* In the most general sense these variables can be found operating at all interpersonal levels, ranging from the relationship between a third-grade classroom teacher and his or her students to the relationship within highly organized governmental structures. Gunnings and Simpkins (1972), following a systemic approach, believe that counseling involving members of minority groups should take into consideration the environmental factors that impinge on the movement and development of individuals. Thus, counseling of the "system" is often just as appropriate as counseling the individual, and possibly more feasible. Yet, Steele (1990) believes the time for blaming the system is over, simply because racial barriers have fallen and individuals now must take the courage to succeed on their own merits, not out of consideration for race.

Power. Power is the capacity and skill to get what one wants or to get one's way. The opposite of power is impotence. The ability of individuals or groups to exercise their will, despite resistance by others, defines what could be termed the relationship between the *oppressor* and the *oppressed.* Oppression is a nasty aspect of social reality and the study of it arouses unpleasant or negative emotions: "It is much safer to study the psychodynamics of racism rather than its economics, or to study the culture of poverty as distinguished from the politics of oppression" (van den Berghe, 1972, p. 235). Power can be defined, and used in interpersonal relations, as *energy* or as *force.* As an energy, it provides the holder with authority, status, prestige, and influence that give a sense of significance. According to May (1972), "sense of significance" refers to "a person's conviction that he counts for something, that he has an effect on others, and that he can get recognition from his fellows" (p. 100). Powerlessness is the inability to express or to be oneself. When power is used as force, or as coercion and compulsion, it tends to destroy the spontaneity of the person. May (1972, pp. 81-97) describes his counseling with a young Black woman who felt impotent and unable to experience self-esteem or to assert her own capacities. Clark (1965), through his analysis of the social dynamics of northern ghettos and the psychological effects on the inhabitants, and in his study of prejudice (1963), believes that one historic and tragic problem for *all* of society has been that Blacks have not taken themselves seriously because no one else has.

Authority and influence. Power, whether used as energy to develop or as force to control, is intimately related to authority. Authority can be defined as legal power, or power that is perceived as right and proper. The authority of the president and the Congress is legitimate power, as is that of other governmental agencies, and commands influence in the minds of people. Other wielders of influence are political groups, lobbyists, and special interest groups. The authority of the legitimate government and the influence of other groups make up the *political institution* of the country. Being represented in the political institution, or having the capacity to change existing conditions or the possible outcome of an event or process, is crucial for the life of the many groups that exist in a multicultural society. The political institution basically protects the country from outside threat, maintains internal order, and promotes the general welfare. How the authority and influence are being used and for whose benefit has historically taken on different shapes. The force of the dominant political group has always been instrumental in the process. Either the Left or the Right may prevail in setting the trend of sociopolitical beliefs and actions at any one time. Table 5-1 compares the views of the Left and the Right on some major issues.

The terms *left* and *right* were first applied to politics in France during the Revolution. It is believed that, at the first meeting of the States-General in 1789, the nobility took the place of honor on the right hand of the king and the Third Estate (landowners and others who were considered third in order of power and influence) went to the king's left. It also happened that the more revolutionary representatives sat on the left of the French National Assembly and the more conservative on the right. The newer political structures of socialism and communism also became identified with the Left because of their call for governmental intervention in economic life. The political institution in the United States has moved through a range of historical phases: the New Deal of Franklin Roosevelt in the 1930s and the liberalism of the Great Society of Kennedy and Johnson in the 1960s, the conservatism of Nixon in the early 1970s, the "mixed" liberalism of Carter in the late 1970s, a return to conservatism in Reagan's federalism in the 1980s, and Bush's focus on creating a "new world order" and strengthening traditional American core values in the 1990s.

The greatest movement toward liberal political thought after World War II occurred during the 1960s, a time of gaining civil rights and creating many social reform programs to assist the poor and to include minorities in the society. It was not unusual at the time to observe the picture of John F. Kennedy hanging in the homes of minority group members alongside pictures of minority group leaders or other symbols of hope. Many Hispanics displayed Kennedy's picture along with the Cross and pictures of Christ. During Richard Nixon's first administration, political catch phrases like "law and order" became almost synonymous with racial and political oppression. Ronald Reagan's federalism stimulated fundamental ideas from the Right; for example, a push toward less government intervention, a reemphasis on religious values (prayer in the schools and antiabortion sentiment) and a return to majority traditions ("Some Radical Ideas from the Right," 1982). Thus

TABLE 5-1   Historic Tendencies in Sociopolitical Thought

Sociopolitical Issue	Left (Liberalism)	Right (Conservatism)
Human potential	Belief in a greater degree of educability in human beings	Acceptance of the value of established authorities in controlling irrational and limitedly educable human beings
Social rights versus individual rights	Recognition of many social rights and needs, either as essential to the preservation of individual rights and needs or as superior to those of the individual when conflict occurs	Emphasis on individual rights rather than social rights and needs, except where individual needs appear to be more fully satisfied within those of traditionally valued and overriding authorities, such as church and state
Social institutions	A greater faith in the power of institutions to influence or determine human conduct	Acceptance of evolved institutions only
Degree of change	Desire for much rapid change in government and society	Minimum of change, or cautious change, or return to past forms of government and society
Method of change	Acceptance of or belief in the inevitability of violence, as compared with evolution or with governmental action	Belief in the limitation of governmental activities in the maintenance of law and order, internal and external, or only in such extensions of it as are suggested by current experiences

(continued)

TABLE 5-1 (*continued*)		

Sociopolitical Issue	Left (Liberalism)	Right (Conservatism)
Church and state	Objection to church participation in political action and decision and, in particular, in control of education	Belief in religion, or in church influence, as stabilizing and moralizing factors in political life, and especially in education
Economics	Belief in the necessity or desirability of governmental intervention in, or partial or total control of, the process of production, distribution, and exchange	Belief in governmental intervention in economic life largely or exclusively when overall national interest appears to justify such intervention
The individual	Belief in the individual liberty and in the equality of all in political rights and before the law; frequent reliance on emotions, such as desire to help the weak, or trust in the people	Belief in individual freedom; distrust of free individuals; acceptance of human inequalities as natural and capable of modification only within narrow limits

SOURCE: Adapted from *A Dictionary of the Social Sciences,* by Julius Gould and William L. Kolb, Eds., pp. 381–384. Copyright (©) 1964 by The United Nations Educational, Scientific, and Cultural Organization. Used with the permission of The Free Press.

the authority and influence commanded by the political system affect not only politics but all of society.

The colonial model within the United States. On a broader sociological scale, the potential for conflict in minority-majority and minority-minority relations, within the country or among countries of the world, has been misused as a means of gaining influence and perpetuating authority and power to the benefit of some individuals and groups, following the old notion of "divide and conquer." Blauner (1969) has proposed a modified model of colonialism in Black-White relations in the United States. "Internal colonialism," according to Blauner, is a process of White colonization of Blacks that has resulted in a dispersed minority who are completely isolated in ghettos. No nation, group, or individual appreciates being called "poor." Low-income nations have received various labels designating their status. "Undeveloped" was used first. Later, "the name 'developing nations' was tried but dropped. Too many of the nations in question were not actually developing" (Barkley,

1977, p. 373). Inherent in the use of these value-loaded, categorical labels is always the question: Less developed than what? *Colonialism*, in the usual ideological sense, refers to a state of inferiority or of servitude by a group that is dominated politically, economically, or culturally by another more developed group. It is especially applied when the dominant nation is European or North American and the less developed is non-European: African, Asian, or South American. Related terms are *less developed countries* (LDC) and *Third World* nations; *First* and *Second World* basically signify the older industrialized Western European nations and the United States. Moore (1970) adopts the colonial model to describe the relationship between some identified regional groups of Mexican Americans and the majority group. She sees "classic colonialism" in the unique historical situation of New Mexico, "conflict colonialism" in Texas, and "economic colonialism" in California.

Political correctness (PC) within the United States. "Political correctness" is a political/ideological movement on college campuses and elsewhere in the 1990s that seeks expanded pluralistic diversity in American society, often by government mandate and often by pervading educational curricula, on behalf of disadvantaged groups. The term *political correctness* is used to refer to a liberal orthodoxy that includes, for example:

- Supporting affirmative action programs and quota systems
- Outlawing hate speech
- Viewing Black crime solely as a by-product of a racist system
- Favoring minority persons over majority persons
- Requiring multicultural education
- Requiring instruction in feminist beliefs as part of general education
- Downplaying European and male influence on Western civilization
- Teaching students to think critically about European culture, but not about non-European culture

D'Souza (1991) believes that intolerance in the form of political correctness has institutionalized resentment toward minorities by alienating and even making conditions unfair for the majority student in schools and colleges. If politically correct thinking does stifle intellectual freedom, it seems most counselors and other professional caregivers would want to assist their clients to become more tolerant and rational and to make reasonable judgments based on evidence and free expression, *not* on what is politically correct. Finally, multicultural counseling embraces all of America's cultures, but includes the freedom to deal with *both* the positive points and negative points of each.

● ECONOMIC INEQUITIES

Access to food, shelter, clothing, and other necessities of life is a basic need of all people living in any socioeconomic system. The availability of these necessities, at any level, is susceptible to control so that some groups or individuals receive more at the expense of other groups or individuals. The creation of unfair or unjust competition through discriminatory practices occurs when categories of people are differentially treated on arbitrary grounds without reference to their actual behavior.

Discrimination is a process of social control that serves to perpetuate or maintain social distance; it is often institutionalized and rationalized. The practice of discrimination may include isolation and *segregation* or may include personal acts growing out of prejudice. During the 1950s, 1960s, and early 1970s, it was widely believed that intergroup and minority relations could be improved through changing prejudicial attitudes of one group toward another. The prevailing viewpoints emphasized that racial prejudice was deeply ingrained and motivated by ignorance and irrationality. The "social pathology" theory placed heavy emphasis on therapeutic and educational approaches in attempts to resolve the situation. According to this viewpoint, the elements of threat, frustration, and status are related to prejudice and bigotry. It is from this base that the human relations training movement has sought to increase social and psychological interactions among different peoples and to foster understanding of situations in which prejudice might be manifested. However, it has also been determined that larger *social group norms* heavily influence individual behavior, regardless of individual personality characteristics or individual life experiences. Thus, even a strongly prejudiced person would alter his or her behavior if it ran contrary to group norms. The civil rights movement has emphasized understanding intergroup relations as a conflict over possession of power and has sought to resolve the conflict through changes in the political and economic structure (van den Berghe, 1972, pp. 163–165). Table 5-2 gives examples of situations in which discrimination is a behavioral manifestation of prejudicial attitudes in the economic system.

■ RAMIFICATIONS OF RACISM

Racism is the belief that some races are *inherently* superior to others; prejudice is the emotional aspect of racism. Even though intergroup differences formerly thought to be racial are now attributed to cultural biases, the doctrine of racism persists in maintaining a connection between racial and cultural traits in the minds and emotions of many people. Racial prejudices have probably always existed in the world. How people see themselves sometimes betrays prejudices:

> The names American Indian tribes gave themselves, for example, usually translate as "Human Being" or "The People," thereby implying that other tribes must belong to a subhuman race. The people who live around the Arctic Circle are usually called "Eskimos"—a contemptuous name, meaning "eaters of raw meat," given them by neighboring Indians—but their own name for themselves is *Inuit* or *Inupik,* which translates roughly as "The Real People." The Eskimos thereby separated themselves from the rest of humankind, which might qualify as "people" but not as "real" ones. Citizens of the United States of America do much the same thing when they identify themselves as "Americans"—thereby effectively ignoring Canadians, Mexicans, Guatema-

TABLE 5-2 Discrimination and Economic Issues

Area of Discrimination	Underlying Attitudes and Economic Issues
Neighborhoods and housing	It is believed than when Blacks or other non-Whites move into a White neighborhood, property values will decline. According to economic concepts of supply and demand, property values will be driven down in relation to the intensity of the discrimination by White sellers and buyers, not as a result of integration.
	It is believed that minority group members do not take care of their houses, property, and neighborhoods and let them run down. The mass of Black people and other minorities are at the bottom of the economic ladder and consequently cannot afford to live in the type of housing they would like. Because there is a lack of affordable housing, two or three families or generations are forced to live in one-family units. The property becomes run down because more people live in the unit than can be accommodated, and city government often does not adjust to accommodate the overcrowding in the ghetto. As minorities move up the economic ladder, there is generally less discrimination. Blacks are less inhibited about moving into other neighborhoods when they are integrated and when they are middle class.
Employment	Certain categories of people (women, non-Whites, aged, handicapped, homosexuals) are believed to be unfit to perform wage-producing labor, or to be fit for only certain types of jobs or for the more menial jobs. According to economists, discrimination exists when the general marketplace is sorted into collective employment submarkets. For example, when the price (wages) for labor is determined primarily by what is valued and preconceived as a "male" occupation, the demand for women is smaller and the number of women who might prepare or look for jobs in that occupation is also smaller. However, when the individual abilities of people are recognized and valued and when equal pay for equal work is demanded, the exclusion of any minority group is less likely.[a]

(continued)

TABLE 5-2 *(continued)*

Area of Discrimination	Underlying Attitudes and Economic Issues
Income	Minorities, as an economically and politically oppressed group, are paid lower wages. There is a seemingly permanent supply of minority workers, generation after generation, that fills the lower-paid menial service occupations. The discriminatory association of minorities with cheap labor is both an economic and a social problem when employers unfairly use it to their advantage for profit and when the government can do nothing to alleviate it. Some of the income differential, however, is also due to complex cultural variables and demographic factors and not discrimination.[b]

[a]According to economists (Spencer, 1980, pp. 296–297), eliminating discrimination in the open marketplace will permit fair competition and more equitable distribution of wages and, depending on the relative productivity of different categories of oppressed minorities, should lead to greater economic growth (production of goods and the ability to purchase the goods) in the whole society.

[b]According to Sowell (1982), what may appear to be a difference in income due to discrimination may actually be due to differences in cultural attitudes toward education, age of marriage, and number of children. For example, the median income of Puerto Rican families in 1970 was 37% below the national average, while Jewish families were 72% above the national average. However, the median age of Puerto Ricans on the mainland was 18 and the median age of Jews was 46. The income-earning heads of Jewish families were 14 years older than the heads of Puerto Rican families, with an average of six more years of education. Although women, as a group, earn about 68 cents for every dollar that men earn, many women have also structured part-time work around their children or have entered the labor market later in life, after their children are raised.

lans, Peruvians, Brazilians, and other inhabitants of the Americas, all of whom are equally worthy to be so identified. [Farb, 1978, p. 284]

The study of biological differences, or genetic qualities and heredity, as well as sociological and anthropological differences, has been pursued for many generations. The findings from the investigations of these scientific disciplines have often been misused as a justification and perpetuation of prejudice, hence the term *scientific racism.* (Race as a subdivision of a species simply implies a degree of inbreeding among the ancestors of the group during their evolution within a specified region of the world.) It also implies the ability to adapt to the surrounding physical environment. Research, for example, has led to the belief that darker skin color, or pigmentation, provides better protection than does a light complexion against the harmful effects of ultraviolet radiation from the sun. Similarly, a light-skinned person presumably makes more Vitamin D in the winter than does a more deeply pigmented one (Calloway & Harris, 1977, p. 20). Racial prejudice, as a psychosocial process, is used to gain a feeling of superiority through making incorrect or inappropriate assumptions based on racial group characteristics. Farb (1978) states, "When analyzed statistically, the genetic difference *between* two geographical populations is very much the same as the difference *within* a single population. In other words, Europeans differ genetically from one another almost as much as a European differs from an Asiatic or an African. The misery caused by racism therefore turns out to hinge on only a few percentage points of genetic differences" (p. 276). The popular use of the term *race* is practically universal in its emotional attachment to the idea that certain groups possess inherited superiority, a belief that inevitably produces conflicts among groups. As long as racial preconceptions exist in the culture, the development of higher levels of personality functioning will be hindered, both for the perceiver and for the perceived. The conflict is essentially a problem of social relationships as influenced by racial preconceptions. When referring to group differences or group relations, it is more accurate for counselors to use the term *social race, social group, geographic group, ethnic group,* or *cultural group.* "Cultural group" is more accurate and acceptable language than "race" in our society today.

▲ THE INFLUENCE OF RACISM IN OUR CULTURE

The attitude of racism surfaces at times in disturbing and overt ways and at other times is subtly used by some groups to subjugate and control other groups. The effects of racism in our society can be shown in the following two formulas:

racial prejudice + power = control
racial prejudice + power + control = interpersonal and intergroup conflict

Only a most restricted viewpoint could conceive that racism in the United States is a contemplated and intended plan of some identified group powerful enough to control the destinies of more than 248 million individuals. The perpetuation of racial superiority, of course, confers benefits on many members of the dominant group because it maintains the status quo of power and any advantages that might accrue from that position. "Benefits" are defined as whatever gains are manifested in personal psychological feelings, social privilege, economic position, or political power.

When the country has experienced cultural trauma from the angry demands of minority groups for fair treatment, a kind of mass hysteria has followed. The police and military authorities are especially susceptible to involvement in this interplay of social forces. Stories about the so-called "King Alfred" plan, whether fact or fantasy, surfaced in parts of the society during the 1960s. This "secret" government plan allegedly outlined procedures for participating agencies to follow in the event of mass disturbances by the Black minority. Dossiers on the leaders of Black organizations were compiled, areas of greatest concentration of Blacks (deep South, eastern seaboard, Great Lakes region, West Coast) were identified, minority members of the armed forces were to be deployed on dangerous missions with the aim of eliminating them, and a timetable was established to activate the plan. During the same fearful period of the 1960s, some people even believed that the interstate highway system was being specially designed and oriented so that heavy military equipment could be rushed to inner-city areas where large concentrations of Blacks lived.

Other views see racism as simply an outmoded, purposeless element in the social development of the culture. Culture is an ongoing process, and optimistic viewpoints hold that a fair society will continue to evolve. Opponents to this position point out the more than three hundred years of unfair treatment that African Americans have received in the society. *Cultural lag* refers to the period of time it takes a culture to approximate a goal that is valued by the society. Although African Americans and other minority groups have seen some gain in their social, economic, educational, and political positions, elements of racism continue to exist between majorities and minorities and among minorities.

▲ FORMS OF RACISM

Racism can be classified into three categorical forms (Jones, 1972): individual, institutional, and cultural. The expression of and interaction among the three forms are often subtle and at other times overt.

● INDIVIDUAL RACISM

Individual thoughts, feelings, and behaviors are often motivated by attitudes of generic superiority assumed by a person in relation to others, who are consequently viewed as inferior. In a reciprocal and circular process, the person with a self-perception of superiority fulfills deficiency-based needs at the expense of the perceived-inferior person. The perceived-inferior person may, in turn, internalize the other's perception and behave accordingly. Until the cycle is broken, the perceived-inferior person, or group, is vulnerable to a *self-fulfilling prophecy* in relation to the power possessed by the "superior" person or "superior" group.

Some examples of individual racism, as expressed either consciously or unconsciously through personal attitudes and behaviors, are as follows:

· Belief in White supremacy
· Belief that Blacks, or other minority groups, are genetically inferior
· Belief that Native Americans are primitive and savage, or that most are alcoholic
· Belief that all people are treated equally and fairly, that all can pull themselves up by their "bootstraps," and that those who don't improve must be inferior people
· Denial of the existence of racism in any form
· Laughing at racist jokes
· Use of slang racial language labels, among them "black boy," "nigger," "wop," "dago," "wetback," "redskin," "kike," "jap," "chink," "kraut,"

"polak," "bohunk," "canucken," "scandihoovian," and "beadrattler"—the list could go on forever.

Lowered self-esteem and inadequate self-concept are major problems often encountered in the status relationship of Blacks to Whites and in the sex-role relationship of women to men (Bagley, Vernia, Mallick, & Young, 1979; Banks & Grambs, 1972; Huber, 1973; Seward & Williamson, 1970). The *Pygmalion effect* (Rosenthal & Jacobson, 1968), a self-fulfilling prophecy in which people conform to the expectations that others hold for them regardless of their actual or true abilities, is familiar to sociologists and educators. For example, when students are believed by their teacher to be slow learners, they tend to act slow or dull. Most counselors are well aware of self-fulfilling prophecies in which clients themselves create the conditions that lead to their own unwanted experiences. Their own expectations of others generate the response that they receive. If a person expects that others are unfriendly or untrustworthy, the person will probably be treated that way by others. Acting in response to the expectations of others, whether positive or negative, confirms their expectations and permits them to continue to act as they have done before, and so the process becomes circular and self-confirming.

Thus, for a given individual, racism is a state of mind, a set of values and emotions, and a constellation of behaviors. Individual modes of racism range from hostile domination (acting out bigoted beliefs and hatreds) to passive acceptance (ignoring, avoiding, or pretending to be polite and correct). Through the societal upheavals of the past 20 years, progress has been made and outward hostility has been reduced to something more like acceptance, or at least passive tolerance, in individual relationships between minority and majority group members. But greater understanding is needed before goodwill and equal acceptance can be achieved (Lindsey & Lindsey, 1974). Katz (1978) has devised a White-awareness format that counselors will find useful in working toward the improvement of minority-majority relations. Her training procedures emphasize the responsibility of Whites for their own thoughts, feelings, and behaviors. Various minority group movements have also emphasized pride in self-identity as a means of positive personality development and self-acceptance. Positive personal expectations and attitudes, for example, that are acquired from the belief structure underlying such themes as "Black is beautiful" (King, 1974) and "Chicano identity" (Ruiz, 1975) can be helpful catalysts in deterring psychological effects of racial prejudice.

Power movements, as epitomized in Black Power, Red Power, and Brown Power, have sought to equalize the balance of power in the economic, political, and social structure of the society. The approaches that have been used range from peaceful sit-ins, voter registration drives, and boycotts of company products to militant demonstrations and even endeavors to establish separate minority-group nations (Carmichael & Hamilton, 1967).

● **INSTITUTIONAL RACISM**

The structure of a society, which is based on the blueprint provided by the culture, can be identified by the educational, economic, social, and political institutions that have been established in the country. The function, form, and practices followed by many of these institutions or structures intentionally or unintentionally perpetuate inequality based on racial preconceptions (Fernandaz, 1981; Knowles & Prewitt, 1969; Kovel, 1970). The report of the United States Commission on Civil Disorders (1968)—known as the Kerner Report, after the chairman of the commission—gathered data on 24 disorders in 23 cities. The commission found that although specific grievances varied from city to city, at least 12 deeply held grievances could be identified and ranked into three levels of relative intensity:

First Level of Intensity
  1. Police practices
  2. Unemployment and underemployment
  3. Inadequate housing

Second Level of Intensity
  4. Inadequate education
  5. Poor recreational facilities and programs
  6. Ineffectiveness of the political structure and grievance mechanisms

Third Level of Intensity
  7. Disrespectful White attitudes
  8. Discriminatory administration of justice
  9. Inadequacy of federal programs
  10. Inadequacy of municipal services
  11. Discriminatory consumer and credit practices
  12. Inadequate welfare programs

Social, economic, educational, and political institutional forces or policies are impersonal and ingrained in ways that operate to foster discriminatory outcomes or to give preferential treatment to members of one group over the members of another. Some historical or current examples in our society are the following:

  · Exclusion from craft unions, professional organizations, and social clubs
  · Seniority systems that result in "last hired, first fired"
  · Income differentials
  · Role casting in media productions and advertising according to racial stereotypes
  · Discriminatory pricing practices in real estate sales and rentals
  · Neglect in the maintenance and repair of housing owned by absentee slum landlords
  · Inferior municipal services (trash pick-up, police protection, maintenance of streets) in minority group neighborhoods
  · Gerrymandering of legislative voting districts
  · Admission to college based on culturally biased tests
  · Differential educational treatment based on preconceived beliefs about educational potential or intellectual ability
  · Teaching of United States history that neglects the history of ethnic minorities

● CULTURAL RACISM

Cultural racism is defined as the beliefs, feelings, and behaviors of the members of a cultural group that assert the superiority of their group's accomplishments, achievements, and creativity over those of other groups because of the differences in the racial composition of the groups. The functioning of *in-group/out-group* attitudes can be found at many levels of intergroup relations, ranging from the rivalry between two high schools to the long-standing differences among the professions of psychiatry, psychology, social work, and counseling to the ethnocentrism that exists among the nations of the world and among the subcultures within those nations. Cultural racism, however, is based on the belief that one culture is superior to another because of the racial background of the members of the groups. As the nation moves toward cultural pluralism, it could be imagined that a new mainstream culture will emerge that blends and integrates the accomplishments of the many existing subcultures. This possibility has already been demonstrated by some trends in art and music. However, the forces behind majority-group dominance generally lead to preconceptions of what is valuable, and the reference point for standards of accomplishment becomes based on single-group expressions. Our value assumptions are influenced by what is most accepted and prevalent in the society, and we tend to take as reality what is most familiar to us. Racially prejudiced attitudes can be found in the following cultural elements:

language
education
medicine
science
religion, philosophy, standards and norms of morality
law, politics
economics
aesthetics, art, music, architecture

Culture is the way that a society lives. The U.S. cultural pattern is based on Western European culture and considered by the majority of citizens to be the best in the world. It is psychologically important for any national group to have confidence and belief in its own culture; otherwise, the means for satisfying human expression and development would deteriorate and ultimately would end in self-destruction of the people. The basic issue behind cultural racism is the suppressive effect that a strong majority culture exerts on the diverse cultural minority groups in the nation and the difficulty for many minorities to function in and relate to the structure of the culture. The mental and emotional association of the majority group with cultural superiority and the association of minority groups with cultural inferiority is what produces cultural racism. And it is also the hardest type of racism to recognize: "It is cultural racism that has been most transparent to the eyes of American race-relations analysts. It is a matter of cultural racism when the achievements of a race of people are fully ignored in education. It is a matter of cultural racism when the expression of cultural differences is unrewarded or is interpreted negatively. It is not just black people who have been victimized by the cultural melting pot myth, but all ethnic minorities. White Western-European religion, music, philosophy, law, politics, economics, morality, science, and medicine are all without question considered to be the best in the world" (Jones, 1972, p. 6).

Cultural racism or cultural bias? The semantic denotation and connotation of *racism* and *racist* tend to evoke negative emotional responses, and the usage of these terms accomplishes little toward the improvement of intergroup relations. Whether the charge is based on fact or emotion, to be labeled a racist stirs up anger and hostility and in today's society is degrading of actual human potential in the movement toward equality. The traditional concept of racism has been applied most often to explain the imbalance in the relationship between Whites and Blacks. A similar situation is noted in the use of the terms *sexism* and *sexist* in the relationship between males and females. Because the use of these terms is inflammatory, it is proposed that the term *bias* is more appropriate when referring to the prejudicial attitudes on the part of individuals toward other individuals or on the part of one group toward another group. The expression *cultural bias*, rather than *cultural racism* or *cultural sexism*, may accurately reflect the actual conditions existing in most parts of our society today. *Racism* and *sexism* are also slanted in that they represent only extreme conditions.

Attitudinal change. The idea of bias indicates a point in the movement toward more compatible relationships and is thus based on some degree of optimism and hope for improvement. The use of the term *bias* also places more emphasis on education and understanding than on innate personality predispositions or weaknesses. Table 5-3 shows the degrees of movement that are possible in the society from an "ism"-centered orientation to a rational orientation. Though bias is often equated with prejudice, in Table 5-3 *bias* refers to systematic distortion in the collection and/or analysis of observations leading to an inaccurate estimate of cultural phenomena. Using *bias* in this sense, a biased definition of a person or situation may lead to a prejudiced attitude toward the person or situation, but the attitude itself is *not* biased.

TABLE 5-3 Potential movement and change in prejudicial attitudes.

	Level of Human Functioning	
"Ism" ⟶	*Bias* ⟶	*Rational Orientation*
Extreme prejudice and discrimination based on deeply rooted beliefs of superiority (racism, sexism, ageism, classism, scientism)	Unreasoned distortion of judgment leading to a slanted viewpoint or simple inclination of outlook due to ignorance and lack of accurate information	Prejudice-free outlook based on who, what, and where each individual is in relation to cultural background of experiences

■ RAMIFICATIONS OF CULTURAL DIFFERENCES

There are many complex issues in cross-cultural group relations; no single listing can be considered inclusive. Cultural practices are taken for granted, and deeply embedded cultural differences are often difficult to discern or to accept.

▲ SCIENTISM

Scientism is an exaggerated trust in the efficacy of the methods of modern science to explain social phenomena, to solve pressing human problems, or to provide a comprehensive picture of the cosmos. Modern science and technology as practiced in the Western world have in some ways led to a closed system of thought, although other world views contain valuable ideas that have also contributed to human life. For example, acupuncture or acupressure—long practiced in the culture of China to cure diseases or relieve pain—is beginning to be examined by Western medical scientists, although it does not exactly fit into medical practice and cannot be precisely explained by modern medical science.

Modern science has also divided mind (awareness) and matter. Mind is scientifically conceived as simply a portion of the brain that dies when the brain dies, and thus that has no history nor past. However, mind is more than physical matter. It is the complex of memories, ideas, knowledge, and feelings that continues on through succeeding generations. Science emphasizes rational, intellectual, and deductive explanations based on cause-and-effect relationships, in contrast to other explanations based on spiritual or psychic-sensory forces that are contained in unconscious, intuitive, affective, and collective human memory traces (Astor, 1975; Grof, 1976; Grof & Halifax, 1977; Jung, 1933a, 1933b, 1964; Kübler-Ross, 1975, 1981; Lang, 1975; Moody, 1976).

▲ HUMAN POTENTIAL

What might be the actual potential for different individuals or different groups of people is never really known. Some writers (Buzan, 1976; Garrett, 1976; Mintzberg, 1967; Ornstein, 1972; Pribram, 1969; Samples, 1975; Sperry, 1975) have proposed differential specialties and posited their development in the functioning of either the *right* brain hemisphere (for example, unconscious and fantasy processes encompassing intuition, imagery, and aesthetic specialties, and the holistic processing of information) or the *left* brain hemisphere (for example, conscious and methodical processes encompassing logical, analytical, and intellectual specialties, and the linear processing of information). Scientific comparison of human potential is often susceptible in a multicultural society to misinterpretation that is knowingly or unknowingly applied to further the superior/inferior relationship dichotomy. Williams (1972) points out the dangers of intelligence testing in which Blacks are intentionally compared with Whites and labeled as mentally deficient and the notion is perpetuated "that this deficiency is due to genetic or cultural factors, or both" (p. 10). Voci (1982) believes that the concept of human potentials should not be viewed according to preconceived attitudes of preference for one specialty over another, but that all human attributes contribute in some way to human existence and understanding of life. According to Voci (1982), the sight of a brilliant rainbow would be experienced, for example, by Mexicans and Native Americans primarily through their perception of wholeness and their feeling for the beauty, power, and marvel of nature; by North Americans of European background, primarily through their perception of details and their empirical factual knowledge and analysis of its marvelous scientific cause. And many would have little or no reaction. The fact that hearing the sound of rain is a right-brain function for the Japanese and a left-brain function for Americans has been cited on a 1984 Public Broadcasting Service series entitled *The Brain*. If the concept of right/left brain functioning is applied, the implication is that the North American cultural group, of European heritage, emphasizes left-brain specialties over right-brain specialties. Or, to put it another way, development of right-brain capacity has been neglected for the sake of left-brain specialties.

Table 5-4 gives general examples of cultural preconceptions of what is superior and what is inferior.

■ RAMIFICATIONS OF COLOR DIFFERENCES

Color conflict, or the potential for hostile confrontation between people who possess different skin pigmentations, is based on deeply ingrained attitudes derived from painful past experiences. Intergroup animosities can be both rational and irrational. Color conflict is also circular, for hostility and aggression can stimulate defensive hostility and aggression in return. The insulation of majority group members from the experiences of minority group members further confounds the movement toward better understanding between both groups. Fantasy, rumors, misunderstanding, and selective reporting by the media are often the only available substitutes for real information.

The fact that skin color is visible simply reinforces the predisposition for behavioral demonstrations of personal and group attitudes. The historic segregation of public facilities, such as rest rooms, transportation, restaurants, and theaters, was always based on color. When the distinction of skin color has not been available for labeling groups, other means have often been used to further discriminatory systems. During the Nazi era in Germany, Jews were forced to wear the star of David (historic hexagram for David, the sec-

TABLE 5-4 Cultural Preconceptions in Mainstream Society	
Cultural Element	*Attitudes Reflecting Belief in Cultural Superiority*
Language	Lack of respect for the spoken native language or dialect of others, or the belief that it is inferior to standard English. Language also structures perception and can imply what is preferred or valued.[a]
Education	Formal learning that is acquired through structured school systems, professional teachers, and the attainment of degrees is superior to the informal, interpersonal learning that is acquired through family, peers, and group. The acquisition and communication of knowledge through the *oral tradition*, for example, is primitive and inferior to the *written tradition*.[b] Racial stereotypes that evaluate minority group members according to only mainstream literacy standards do not take into account the thoughts, information, and human values and standards that are contained in their traditional legends, folklore, and ways.
Medicine	The belief that curing of physical and mental diseases is best accomplished only through scientific medicine and, for example, that Native American tribal ceremonies for healing or Hispanic botanical remedies are merely superstitious nonsense or novelties. Scientific medicine has indeed produced major achievements in the prevention of many life-threatening diseases and in the correction of physical afflictions. Health and psychological conditions (nutrition and stress) related to the sociophysical environment of the dominant group have also been alleviated through medical and scientific approaches. Prejudice occurs when traditional minority group cultural practices are ignored or collectively viewed as inferior or subhuman, or when the mutual cross-cultural sharing of healing knowledge is felt to be valueless. Racial discrimination occurs when unethical, substandard, or overpriced scientific medical treatment is offered to minority group members.

(continued)

ond King of Israel, and the symbol of Judaism) to reveal their ethnic background.

Racial labels have usually had a "for colored only" application. Whites seldom refer to their own color, except when describing racial encounters. It

TABLE 5-4	*(continued)*
Cultural Element	*Attitudes Reflecting Belief in Cultural Superiority*
Science	Perceptions of the universe, since the development of Isaac Newton's theory of gravity three hundred years ago, have emphasized mathematical configurations and physical mechanics of life as based on the ideas of time, space, mass, motion, and gravitation. The relation, or relativity, of these ideas forms a unified framework that embraces all laws of nature and has changed the philosophical and physical notions of space and time.[c] The whole mode of the world has been remodeled and from modern innovation have come scientific and technical progress, and also the means for mass destruction of natural life. The scientific paradigm of nature and the universe is an invention of the human mind and is believed to be correct and superior to other views. The belief in another realm of interrelated consciousness, or a transpersonal reality that is be-

is unusual to note media articles that specifically state the skin pigmentation of a White person, whereas mention of color frequently accompanies references to non-Whites; for example, "Mr. Jones, a Black, was appointed to the president's cabinet."

▲ WHITE AWARENESS

The avoidance of "whiteness" by White people, according to Terry (1970), indicates a lack of self-acceptance and psychic wholeness. He proposes that White persons overcome color defensiveness through becoming more White-conscious and that they define "whiteness" with its full meaning. Thus, an aware White person

- *moves beyond guilt* through acknowledging color prejudice and lives out of commitment to the future, not guilt for the past;
- *values self-worth* as good in itself and does not seek to prove it at the expense of others;
- *understands power* and how to use it for constructive change for all people, realizing that in reality there are only a few who really possess the power in the total society;
- *is proactive, not reactive,* in using political power to change unfair situations (power has to be sought, it is not given);
- *accepts self-interest as valuable* for *all* to live by;
- *takes risks* in working for change and in relaxing the "hoarding" attitude that endorses ever-higher levels of consumption in living;

TABLE 5-4 (continued)	
Cultural Element	Attitudes Reflecting Belief in Cultural Superiority
Science (continued)	lieved to encompass all human beings and nature, is demonstrated through spiritual, magical, and mystical experiences that are found across cultural groups. When these physical phenomena or human experiences cannot be explained by science, or conflict with the majority cultural ways, they are often labeled psychotic, delusional, fanatic, superstitious, illogical, or stupid.
Religion	Mainstream religion is moralistic and values the adherence to absolutes, or "right" and "wrong" behavior, while other cultural groups generally perceive behavior in relation to the person-in-the-situation. Monotheism is also adhered to, rather than polytheistic conceptions of religion. Mainstream religious holidays are generally recognized and celebrated, while others are ignored or perceived as unimportant.

[a]One example of linguistic perception is demonstrated through standard-English dictionary definitions of the meanings associated with various colors. The underlying value assumptions are explicit, if taken literally:

White. Free from color or having the color of pure snow or milk; free from moral impurity; innocent and pure; upright and fair; free from spot or blemish (according to scientific discovery, ordinary "white light" is actually a mixture of all the colors of the rainbow).

Black. Opposite to white, of the color of coal and darkness; without light; dirty, soiled; sinister or evil, wicked; sad, sullen, heavy, serious; "black with rage."

Yellow. The color of ripe lemons; sensational or scandalous, as in "yellow journalism"; mean, cowardly.

Red. The color of blood; inciting or endorsing political or social radicalism by force; failing to show a profit, or showing a loss, "to go into the red"; flushed with anger or embarrassment.

Brown. Having the color of chocolate, a mixture of red, black, and yellow; or a group of colors between red and yellow; a brown-skinned person.

[b]The oral communication of life's experiences, meanings, and knowledge from person to person has been traditional, for example, to the African-American and Native American cultures for thousands of years, and thus has value in and of itself as a cultural tradition. Literacy, according to standard mainstream dictionary definition, means being "well-read" and emphasizes reading and writing as the sole means of communicating truth and knowledge. Basic communication skills are, of course, important for survival in any technical society. However, the formal educational system has generally failed to promote literacy within many minority groups and in addition has underestimated the wisdom that might be contained in oral traditions as a legitimate form of "literacy."

[c]Time and order in the scientific sense are linear and sequential, and importance is given to evaluation of progress between the past and present and to what can be changed or manipulated for the future. The viewpoint of other groups conceives of tradition as more important, and the past and present are seen as the continuations of the same.

- *is open to new lifestyles* that emerge in a more open society;
- *is committed to pluralism* and to appreciating many different cultures and persons and the potential that they represent;
- *needs support groups* composed of other aware Whites to maintain and stimulate movement toward new consciousness.[3]

▲ COLOR PREFERENCE AND SOCIAL LEARNING

Drawing the line of intergroup relations on the basis of skin color pigmentation has historic antecedents (Jones, 1972, pp. 149–154) that have continued into the cultural practices of present-day U.S. society. Hall (1968) comments:

> Do you think that a Negro child and a white child born on the same day have an equal opportunity to achieve any aspirational level that they might have? What happens to these kids between the time they are born and when they're five or six years of age? Do you think kids are born prejudiced? For example, one day, two Negro boys were walking along holding their arms out and comparing them. One boy said to the other, "Yah man, but you're blacker than I am." What does this mean? It means that at that early age they have discovered that when you're black there is something wrong with you and the blacker you are, the worse off you are. This is something that should have meaning to you as counselors, because very seldom do we touch upon this color aspect. (p. 5)

Early research through the late 1960s concluded that self-hatred existed in much of the Black community. Later research (McAdoo, 1977; Williams & Moreland, 1976) continues to show that children prefer the color white over black (in choice of objects such as dolls, toys, animals) and that the preference is related to self-concept. Color preference has also been shown to be related to social class as well as to the amount of interracial contact. Porter (1971) has interpreted her finding by hypothesizing that preference for white dolls does not *always* mean rejection of brown dolls or of the self. She found that middle-class White families were more likely to prefer white figures, while Black children from working-class families and living in Black communities showed greater preference for brown dolls. Banks (1976) believes that the question of white preference in Blacks may rest in a type of scientific illusion, or a "paradigm in search of a phenomenon." Steele (1990), drawing on the conviction that the content of our character is more important than the color of our skin, speaks of psychological impediments such as the "Black antiself," a self-destructive inclination fed by the realization that race is no longer a competitive advantage and that one must rely on one's own merits; and "race-holding," a self-protective defense mechanism, in which the individual refuses to recognize the decline of racism and insists that it is worse than ever.

[3]List adapted from *For Whites Only,* by R. W. Terry. Copyright © 1970 by W. B. Eerdmans Publishing Company. Adapted by permission of the publisher.

▲ DISCREPANCIES IN INTERGROUP PERCEPTIONS AND INTERPERSONAL RELATIONS

In the early 1940s, the Swedish social scientist Gunnar Myrdal was invited to the United States to conduct one of the most thorough studies of race relations ever performed. One of his important findings was that what southern Whites believed to be most important to or desired by southern Blacks was actually the *reverse* of what Blacks said was important to them (Myrdal, 1944, Vol. 1, pp. 60-61). Whites perceived the following, in rank order, to be most wanted by Blacks or most important to Blacks:

1. Intermarriage and sexual intercourse with Whites
2. Social equality and the manners, etiquette, and customs of White society
3. Desegregation of public facilities
4. Political rights
5. Fair treatment in courts and the right to serve on juries
6. Economic opportunities

Intimate social relations between the two groups are what may be most feared by both Whites and Blacks. In Malamud's (1963) novel *Idiots First* and also in Hernton's (1965) work, some of the agony of intimate Black-White relationships is portrayed. A southern White, in candor, expressed his perception that southern Whites "love the Black individual but hate the race, and that Northern Whites love the race but hate the individual." Of course, the personal beliefs and feelings of individual Whites and Blacks may be exceptions to these generalities.

▲ PSYCHOGENETIC ASPECTS OF COLOR DIFFERENCES

Cress's theory of color confrontation (Cress Welsing, 1974) has proposed that conflict based on skin color is derived from the evolutionary struggle of the numerically smaller (worldwide) White group against perceived domination by the numerically larger (worldwide) non-White population. According to Cress, the function of racism as based on White superiority is a symptom of White inferiority motivated by fear of inadequacy. Her thesis suggests that the lack of distinctive skin color and numerical inferiority has led to dependency on compensatory defense mechanisms characterized by hostility and aggression "throughout the entire historic epoch of the mass confrontations of the whites with people of color. Only after long periods of great abuse have the 'nonwhites' responded defensively with any form of counter-attack" (p. 34). Since Blacks have the greatest color potential, they are "the most envied and the most feared in genetic color competition" (p. 35). Phenomena that she cites in support of her thesis include the following:

· The desire of Whites to get good feelings by attaining suntans
· The reaction of Blacks to social conditioning by attempting to change their skin color
· The prevailing myth of White genetic superiority
· Projection of hostility toward non-Whites
· Use of the negative term "non-White," resulting in a positive statement for the White person
· Projected desire by Whites for sexual relations with Blacks in order to produce color, which is desired by White women
· Fantasized identification by White men with the Black man's capacity to give a color product to White women, as the White man cannot
· The attack on the genital areas of Black men during lynchings
· The degrading of sexual acts in the general White society, which is not found in most societies

Discussion with several Black Americans seems to indicate some agreement with Cress's theory; others offer no reaction beyond the impression that it is an interesting idea. It generally arouses strong feelings and argumentation in Whites. A related fear that is sometimes expressed is that if Whites relax their control and domination, they will be treated the same as they have treated Blacks. Cress's theory seeks to explain confrontation between two groups of people, but it places the major responsibility on one group—Whites—and may thus tend to create White reactionary attitudes and behaviors. Except for circumstantial evidence, there is little scientific data to support the concept. Its main importance may rest in drawing attention to what intergroup dishar-mony based on unconscious reaction to skin color may do. If alienation of the White self is part of the motive related to alienation of others who are different, it must be faced by Whites themselves. And if numerical inferiority and fear are part of the motive, they must be faced through cooperative harmony and compromise.

■ TOWARD AUTHENTIC INTERPERSONAL RELATIONS

Attitudes can be modified by individuals, and counselors can improve the quality of cross-cultural relations in the counseling process and also provide leadership in helping diverse groups develop better understanding of each other. The reservation of superior status for any one group is not acceptable in today's democratic society. Any individual of any group identity is first human. The initial step in moving toward open and honest relations is self-examination. Lindsey and Lindsey (1974) suggest that you begin by asking yourself three questions: Who, what, and where am I? Introspection also means taking on the role of others since "we are ourselves only in relation to others, their activities and our feelings toward others" (p. 86). Ask yourself: Compared with whom am I either superior or different? When, or in what ways, are these differences demonstrated? Whose equal am I? Who am I the same as? When, or in what ways, is this similarity demonstrated?

▲ OVERCOMING MISUNDERSTANDING

The segregation and distancing of people, according to either skin color or assumed personality traits or personal values, lead to greater chances for misunderstandings. A Hispanic counselor candidly remarked that it had taken him many years to understand fully the functioning of dominant cultural ways. His mobility in the larger society as he grew up often created internal value conflicts, as well as showing him that he simply did not understand the "ins and outs" of acceptable mainstream behavior. He also expressed the view that many of his professional colleagues and other non-Hispanic people lacked basic understanding of his Hispanic culture and really didn't know him or where he was coming from. Lack of language proficiency is often related to serious misunderstanding that can lead to disrupted interpersonal relations. Some verbal communication is necessary to counseling, but not indispensable. Heavy reliance on nonverbal signals, including facial messages, body posture, arm and hand movement, and even statements or diagrams put on paper, can often compensate for missing verbal exchange. Overcoming linguistic barriers to communication was historically demonstrated when Native American tribes, driven into the West by advancing European settlements, developed an intertribal sign language in order to communicate with tribes who spoke different languages. A Mexican from a rural area in Mexico who had little command of standard English was counseled about his serious auto accident through high levels of empathy and active verbal and nonverbal listening and responding. In this case, it was essential to relate to the seriousness of his physical condition and his legal situation. Providing psychological reassurance and support, as well as helpful information and backing on how he could obtain legal compensation in the structure of the society, were the major counseling goals. The use of bilingual interpreters, when available, is helpful in some situations and essential in others; however, there are potential hazards for counselor-client miscommunication and for relation-distancing and role conflict between the two helping persons.

▲ WHITE-BLACK INTERPERSONAL RELATIONS

Simple human error can occur in any cross-cultural exchange and without tolerance, open-minded understanding, and helpfulness on the part of both parties, can lead to incomplete relationships. During a human relations encounter group session, a Black participant spoke up to the White participants, "Why is it you Whites can't be up front with us?" Out of the intense communication and confrontation on Black-White issues in the late 1960s and early 1970s, Lee and Schmidt (1969, pp. 4–5) developed the following listing of assumptions and behaviors on the part of both Blacks and Whites that can either block or facilitate authentic relations. Many, if not all, points in the list continue to be applicable in light of many of today's social realities.[4]

Assumptions That Whites Make Which Block Authentic Relations
1. Color is unimportant in interpersonal relations.
2. Blacks will always welcome and appreciate inclusion in White society.
3. Open recognition of color may embarrass Blacks.
4. Blacks are trying to use Whites.
5. Blacks can be stereotyped.
6. White society is superior to Black society.
7. "Liberal" Whites are free of racism.
8. All Blacks are alike in their attitudes and behavior.
9. Blacks are oversensitive.
10. Blacks must be controlled.

Assumptions That Blacks Make Which Block Authentic Relations
1. All Whites are alike.
2. There are no "soul brothers and sisters" among Whites.
3. Honkies have all the power.
4. Whites are always trying to use Blacks.
5. Whites are united in their attitude toward Blacks.
6. All Whites are racists.
7. Whites are not really trying to understand the situation of the Blacks.
8. Whitey's got to deal on Black terms.
9. Silence is the sign of hostility.
10. Whites cannot and will not change except by force.
11. The only way to gain attention is through confrontation.
12. All Whites are deceptive.
13. All Whites will let you down in the "crunch."

Assumptions That Whites Can Make Which Will Facilitate Authentic Relations
1. People count as individuals.
2. Blacks are human—with individual feelings, aspirations, and attitudes.
3. Blacks have a heritage of which they are proud.
4. Interdependence is needed between Whites and Blacks.
5. Blacks are angry.
6. Whites cannot fully understand what it means to be Black.
7. Whiteness/Blackness is a real difference but not the basis on which to determine behavior.
8. Most Blacks can handle Whites' authentic behavior and feelings.
9. Blacks want a responsible society.
10. Blacks are capable of managerial maturity.
11. I may be part of the problem.

[4]Reproduced by special permission from B. M. Lee and W. H. Schmidt, "Toward More Authentic Interpersonal Relations Between Blacks and Whites," *Human Relations Training News*, 1969, 13 (4), 4–5. Copyright © 1969 by NTL Institute.

Assumptions That Blacks Can Make Which Will Facilitate Authentic Relations
1. Openness is healthy.
2. Interdependence is needed between Blacks and Whites.
3. People count as individuals.
4. Negotiation and collaboration are possible strategies.
5. Whites are human beings and, whether they should or not, do have their own hang-ups.
6. Some Whites can help and "do their own thing."
7. Some Whites have "soul."

Behaviors of Whites Which Block Authentic Relations
1. Interruptions.
2. Condescending behavior.
3. Offering help where not needed or wanted.
4. Avoidance of contact (eye-to-eye and physical).
5. Verbal focus on Black behavior rather than White behavior.
6. Insisting on playing games according to White rules.
7. Showing annoyance at Black behavior which differs from their own.
8. Expressions of too-easy acceptance and friendship.
9. Talking about, rather than to, Blacks who are present.

Behaviors of Blacks Which Block Authentic Relations
1. Confrontation too early and too harshly.
2. Rejection of honest expressions of acceptance and friendship.
3. Pushing Whites into such a defensive posture that learning and reexamination are impossible.
4. Failure to keep a commitment and then offering no explanation.
5. "In-group" joking, laughing at Whites—in Black culture language.
6. Giving answers Blacks think Whites want to hear.
7. Using confrontation as the primary relationship style.
8. Isolationism.

Behaviors of Whites Which Facilitate Authentic Relations
1. Directness and openness in expressing feelings.
2. Assisting other White brothers and sisters to understand and confront feelings.
3. Supporting self-initiated moves of Black people.
4. Listening without interrupting.
5. Demonstration of interest in learning about Black perceptions, culture, etc.
6. Staying with and working through difficult confrontations.
7. Taking a risk (being first to confront the differences).
8. Assuming responsibility for examining own motives—and where they are.

Behaviors of Blacks Which Facilitate Authentic Relations
1. Showing interest in understanding Whites' point of view.
2. Acknowledging that there are some committed Whites.
3. Acting as if "we have some power"—and don't need to prove it.

4. Allowing Whites to experience unaware areas of racism.
5. Openness.
6. Expression of real feelings.
7. Dealing with Whites where they are.
8. Meeting Whites halfway.
9. Treating Whites on one-to-one basis.
10. Telling it like it is.
11. Realistic goal sharing.
12. Showing pride in their heritage.

■ SUMMARY

1. Counselors, whether their background is minority or majority, need to be aware that sociopolitical issues in the general society will also condition the counseling process.

2. Distinctions in usage of the term *minority* were made. A racial minority, according to scientific definition, is identified by physical characteristics; ethnic minorities are usually identified by place of origin and cultural practices. The scientific concept of "race" has contributed to intergroup conflict. The use of the terms *ethnic group* and *cultural group* are more acceptable in today's society.

3. U.S. culture has traditionally emphasized conformity among people over the acceptance of differences. Implications for the role of the counselor were suggested.

4. *Prejudice* was defined as negative or unfavorable opinion, judgment, or view of a person or a group that ignores contrary evidence that might alter that evaluation. The patterns of prejudice were analyzed in reference to psychological, social, and political and economic variables.

5. Psychological variables that precipitate prejudice include (1) authoritarian personality traits, (2) psychological defense mechanisms, and (3) distorted cognitive learning processes. Counselors can work toward better intergroup relations and more effective counseling sessions by understanding the operation of psychological variables both in themselves and in their clients.

6. Social variables that influence prejudice begin with family and primary-group interactions. Ethnocentrism (in-group attitudes) was also noted as contributing to prejudice. Underlying concepts of which counselors should be aware in counteracting prejudice include (1) cultural relativity (judging behavior in the context of the culture in which it occurs), (2) cultural universals (behaviors and practices that are found in common across cultures), and (3) human nature as a universal emergent (basic personality motivations that are found in common across cultures).

7. Politics and economic conditions are intertwined. The importance of cooperative participation in the political structure and fair participation in the economic system was noted. Barriers that work against full participation and/or that foment prejudicial conditions have been, or are: domination, lack

of common purpose, resistance to change, colonialism, and the misuse and abuse of power, authority, and influence. The ways of liberal and conservative sociopolitical thought were outlined and the ideology of "political correctness" was discussed. Economic prejudice is the preferential treatment given to some groups at the expense of others in the distribution of national resources. It is exhibited in the practice of discrimination and segregation in neighborhoods, housing, employment, and income.

8. The ramifications of prejudicial attitudes were discussed in relation to racism, culture differences, and color differences.

9. *Racism* was defined as the belief that some races are inherently superior to others; prejudice is the emotional aspect of racism. White supremacy is a most virulent form of ethnocentrism. There are three forms of racism: (1) individual, in which thoughts, feelings, and behaviors are motivated by attitudes of generic superiority in relation to others, who are consequently viewed as inferior; (2) institutional, in which the society is organized to take into consideration only one group; (3) cultural, in which the beliefs, feelings, and practices of one group are deeply rooted in the life of the country and are thought to be the best or only way of life. It was proposed that the concept of cultural bias rather than the concept of "isms" (racism, sexism, and so forth) is more appropriate, useful, and accurate in explaining group relations in today's society.

10. Cultural difference issues that influence prejudice are deeply embedded in cultural traditions and practices. The differences impede full relations and can lead to potential conflict. The overemphasis on traditional science and its extension into all aspects of mainstream culture have contributed to the devaluation of other possible concepts of humanness that might be found in other diverse cultures. Other areas in which monocultural practices tend to subordinate pluralistic cultural expression include language, education, medicine, and religion.

11. Conflicts that are related to color differences are based on deeply ingrained attitudes derived from painful past experiences. It was proposed that such conflicts are perpetuated by lack of self-acceptance and awareness, social learning, miscommunication, and/or deeply rooted psychogenetic predispositions. It was noted that with the decline of racism, the content of character becomes ever more important than the color of skin.

12. Movement toward more authentic interpersonal relations in counseling and in general can be assisted by introspection, overcoming simple misunderstandings, more accurate identification of potential blocks in relationships, and the learning of behavior that facilitates communication.

CHAPTER

EDUCATION AND ACHIEVEMENT

The intent of this chapter is to examine (1) the status of education today, (2) the nature of the formal system of education, (3) basic issues in education, (4) concern for educational equality, (5) concern for economically and educationally disadvantaged students, (6) issues related to cultural diversity, (7) pressures on teachers and counselors, (8) special issues in the education of Native Americans, and (9) functional roles of counselors in a multicultural educational setting. The main purpose is to articulate some of the multitude of forces that impinge on the lives of students in an imperfect system. The discussion stresses neither individual causation nor social causation alone, but assumes that both factors interact and must be taken into consideration when counselors assist students with educational and achievement goals and when they provide teachers with consultative services.

■ THE STATUS OF EDUCATION TODAY

The education and achievement of the members of a society are crucial if the society is to survive. Biological, cultural, social, political, and economic realities are all bound up as issues in the educational experiences of the American people, from childhood to adulthood. Probably the largest single enterprise in the country is education, which involves 15,000 school districts, approximately 3,500 colleges and universities, and thousands of formal and informal adult education experiences that occur daily in the community and in business and industry. Within that immense structure is the human dimension, seeking to shape the process of instruction to accommodate individuality. Whenever "mass production" of learning occurs there is usually only minimal consideration for the wide range of individual differences, and the opportunity for intellectual and personal growth is usually limited to a hypothetical "middle-class average." Education in a pluralistic society involves the modification of the educational process to accommodate each person, one by one, since learning is unique by virtue of each person's experiences. If there is to be opportunity for intellectual growth and self-fulfillment, a major task of the educational process is to take what material is available and make it accessible and meaningful to individuals whose lives are very different. What is the picture for individuals who are most likely to be involved in education at all levels in today's society? Here are some facts about the American people that have implications for education and for counselors:

· The youthfulness of the general population is declining (see Table 6-1). In 1990, the over-65 population totaled 12.6% of all Americans and numbered 31.5 million, while 40 years ago, in 1950, it totaled 8% of all Americans and numbered 12 million. The Baby Boom generation (those born in the wake of World War II, between 1946 and 1964) will be over the age of 35 by the year 2000 and thus will contribute to the sharp increase in the median age during the rest of this century.

· Cultural minority populations are substantially younger (see Table 6-2). Much of the difference is attributed to higher immigration numbers after 1965

TABLE 6-1   Youthfulness of the general population of the United States.

	1970	1980	1990	2000[a]
Proportion of people under the age of 18	34.0%	28.0%	25.6%	24.5%
Proportion of people under the age of 25	46.2%	41.4%	36.0%	33.9%
Proportion of people age 65 and over	9.8%	11.3%	12.6%	13.0%
Median age of all people	27.9	30.0	33.0	36.4

SOURCE: Data from *Population Profile of the United States: 1991* by U.S. Bureau of the Census, 1991.
[a]Projected.

TABLE 6-2   Youthfulness of four cultural minority populations in the United States.

	White	Asian	Black	Hispanic	Native American
Median age in years	31.3	28.6	24.9	23.2	23.0
Under the age of 15 years	21.3%	25.0%	28.7%	32.0%	31.8%
Under the age of 25 years	39.5%	42.3%	50.3%	53.9%	54.3%
Age 65 and over	12.2%	6.1%	7.9%	7.9%	5.3%

SOURCE: Data from *Population Profile of the United States: 1980* by U.S. Bureau of the Census, 1981.

TABLE 6-3 Comparative school enrollments of three population groups.

		White	Black	Hispanic
High school graduates	1989	82%	76%	56%
(percentage of those aged 18 to 24)	1970	81%	60%	52%
High school graduates enrolled in college[a] (percentage of those 18 to 24)	1989	39%	31%	29%
Annual high school dropout rate[b]	1987–89	4.1%	6.8%	7.9%
	1977–79	6.2%	9.4%	10.0%

SOURCE: Data from *Population Profile of the United States: 1991* by U.S. Bureau of the Census, 1991.
[a] In 1989, 38% of *all* high school graduates aged 18 to 24 were enrolled in college; for young men and women, the proportions were nearly identical (38% for each).
[b] The dropout rate is the proportion of 14- to 24-year-olds enrolled in the 10th to 12th grades in October of one year who were no longer enrolled and had not graduated by October of the following year.

from Asian and Hispanic countries and higher fertility rates among Blacks, Hispanics, and Native Americans.

· Some cultural group populations receive less formal education than others and there is variation in the school holding power and enrollment patterns (see Table 6-3).

· There are differences in the levels of educational attainment among cultural group populations and between men and women (see Table 6-4). Not shown in Table 6-4 is the 80% of all Asian Americans aged 25 years and over who had completed four or more years of high school in 1990. In the same year (1990), 40% had completed four or more years of college, almost twice the rate for White Americans (22%), more than three times that of Black Americans (11%), and four times that of Hispanic Americans (9%).

· Few U.S. citizens (8.8%) are bilingual. In 1975, nine out of every ten persons in the country reported having no second language. Spanish is the second most widely used language (see Table 6-5). Approximately 60% (5 million in 1975) of all the population age 4 or over for whom English is not the usual language have difficulty in speaking or understanding English (see Table 6-6).

■ THE FORMALIZATION OF EDUCATION IN THE UNITED STATES

All social interaction contains the element of learning, or education. However, the methodical and systematic socialization of the young, and its extension into adulthood, seeks specifically to bring about a degree of homogeneity sufficient for life in the collective society. Formal education in the United States is the assimilation into a cultural tradition and is nonvoluntary up to a certain age. The implications for a multicultural society are, of course, both complex and immense. The question of what changes are desirable to make in children is often viewed differently by different groups, and all seek to exert their influence, including professional educators, boards of education, governmental agencies, politicians, producers of educational materials, the media, and many community interest groups. In less developed or less technical societies, the socialization process is conducted informally between the generations wherever their interaction occurs, but especially in the family. An intimate relationship between the generations in the United States, where youth and adults were once accustomed to working, learning, and socializing together, has diminished as a vital source for passing on cultural knowledge. Thus, the *formal* provision for instruction through specialized agencies and personnel has tended to supersede what was at one time an informal, or "natural," person-to-person socialization process. Social institutions, such as the family, business, industry, and the judicial system, have been separated from playing an important role in teaching the young, and now the people in them are basically spectators of the educational game. Religion, which also has the function of bringing about change, has likewise been disassociated from education through the historic separation of church and state.

TABLE 6-4 **Years of school completed, ages 25 and over, by sex.**

		White		Black		Hispanic	
	Year	*Male*	*Female*	*Male*	*Female*	*Male*	*Female*
Percent complet-	1989	78.6%	78.2%	64.2%	65.0%	51.0%	50.7%
ing 4 years of	1980	71.0%	70.2%	51.0%	51.4%	44.9%	44.1%
high school or	1970	57.2%	57.6%	32.4%	34.8%	33.4%	31.0%
more							
Percent complet-	1989	43.0%	35.9%	27.9%	28.3%	(NA)	(NA)
ing 1 year of	1980	37.8%	28.4%	21.0%	19.9%	22.0%	14.9%
college or more	1970	26.2%	18.6%	10.2%	10.4%	13.5%	8.7%
Percent complet-	1989	25.4%	18.5%	11.7%	11.9%	11.0%	8.8%
ing 4 years of	1980	22.0%	14.0%	7.6%	8.1%	9.2%	6.2%
college or more	1970	15.0%	8.6%	4.6%	4.4%	5.9%	3.2%

SOURCE: Data from *Population Profile of the United States: 1980* by U.S. Bureau of the Census, 1981; *Educational Attainment in the United States: March 1989 and 1988* by U.S. Bureau of the Census, 1991. NA = Not available.

TABLE 6-5 Languages used in the United States.

Usual Language	Percentage of All Persons in the U.S.[a]
English	95.9%
Spanish	2.0%
Chinese	0.1%
Filipino	0.1%
French	0.1%
German	0.1%
Greek	0.1%
Italian	0.2%
Japanese	0.1%
Portuguese	0.1%
Other	0.4%
Not reported	0.8%
Second Language	
English	2.5%
Spanish	2.2%
Chinese	0.1%
Filipino	0.1%
French	0.6%
German	0.6%
Greek	0.1%
Italian	0.7%
Japanese	0.1%
Portuguese	0.1%
Other	1.5%
Not reported	0.7%
No second language	90.4%
With second language	8.8%

SOURCE: Data from *Language Usage in the United States: July 1975* by U.S. Bureau of the Census, 1975.
[a]Includes only groups of 100,000 persons or more, ages 4 years and over.

▲ STRUCTURAL CHARACTERISTICS

Preindustrial societies have little difficulty with structural problems of education. Problems emerge when education becomes a formal institution that functions independently of the wider, changing society. In the United States the educational system has come to occupy a strategic position for determining the economic, political, and social characteristics of the society, and, conversely, most aspects that are found in the general society are also found in the system of education. For example, bureaucratization as it has evolved in industry and government is also found in educational systems. "Bureaucratization" is essentially the formalization of a social process and has distinctive system-management characteristics, some of the more obvious of which are

- administrative groups that make policy;
- specialization of functions;
- adherence to fixed rules and a hierarchy of authority;
- an official administrative order that tends to increase its own work load and personnel through a proliferation of red tape and through increasing its own additional functions, duties, and roles.

▲ MAJOR FEATURES

The general features of the public education system in today's North American society emphasize (1) the systematic changing of children for life in the culture, (2) a nonvoluntary process, (3) relative isolation from other socialization groups and institutions, (4) a tacit link to other subsystems in the society, which exert pressures or constraints on the system, (5) perennial questions and issues that seemingly are perpetuated by the system itself, and (6) a complex maze of specialized roles and functions that emerge from what is thought to be an orderly and organized procedure.

TABLE 6-6 Persons in the United States who have difficulty with English.

Usual Language of Person with Difficulty	Percentage Having Difficulty with English[a]	Percentage Unable to Speak English at All, or Well[b]
Spanish	54.0%	28.2%
Chinese	52.5%	28.0%
Filipino	20.5%	14.1%
French	30.7%	5.6%
German	0.3%	3.9%
Greek	60.0%	23.0%
Italian	67.1%	16.1%
Japanese	76.5%	23.4%
Korean	63.3%	45.1%
Portuguese	72.7%	29.0%
Other	49.1%	16.2%

[a]Ages 4 years and over. SOURCE: Data from *Language Usage in the United States: July 1975* by U.S. Bureau of the Census, 1975.
[b]Ages 5 years and over. SOURCE: Data from *Ancestry and Language in the United States: November 1979* by U.S. Bureau of the Census, 1982.

■ BASIC ISSUES IN EDUCATION

The issues of the society at large are also experienced in the school system, which is a microcosmic representation of the society. The pressure on the educational system to solve societal dilemmas, or to become a scapegoat for them, has persisted for decades.

▲ PERENNIAL ISSUES AND CONCERNS

Many questions are raised by those who are concerned with *what* changes are to be made in children and *how* they are to be changed. Other issues and problems arise as a result of a systematized, formal educational process that is often remote from direct communication with people in the society, or even with those who are the recipients of its service. These are some of the questions, issues, or problems that seem to be ever present:

· Where do educational ideas, theories, and policies originate? Who determines them? What are the implications?

· What is the relation of the educational system to the total social structure? What work force is needed in the economy? What are the size and potential of the population to be educated? How does the system contribute to the political leadership pool of the nation, and who becomes a part of that pool? How does the system assist in the upward mobility of the citizens?

· How do the structure and function of the system relate to the transmission and inculcation of social values? What values should be transmitted?

· What social relations arise out of the application of scientific principles and techniques in the educational system? Many questions and issues have also arisen in relation to modes of authority, the nature of discipline, and the social distance between instructional personnel and students.

· How does the wider social environment influence the system? How do the socioeconomic situation, size, and characteristics of the family promote or hinder the educational process? What effect do attitudes and values of social class, ethnic, religious, or other cultural subgroups have on the system?

▲ CURRENT ISSUES AND CONCERNS

Whether and how the usual educational system can confront the needs and demands for competence in a complex, technical society and also continue to reach the diversity of youth in ways that are functional and appropriate for them are major issues for the nation. It is through education that most Americans hope to fulfill their aspirations for social and economic advancement, but many young Americans seem to have been left behind or alienated from many aspects of that educational process. The provision of equal educational opportunities, or the development of unrecognized potential, continues to be a need unmet for many groups within the population, such as economically and educationally disadvantaged students, handicapped students, students with learning disabilities, culturally diverse students, preelementary children, urban youth, and women. Seemingly lost in the shuffle is the large array of average students whose problems, needs, and potential also go unrecognized as the focus of energy is often concentrated on those who need compensatory education or those who need accelerated education. Although the United States prides itself on offering public education to everyone, there is virtually no connection between what students do in school and what they do later in life; for example, distinction is made between standards for youth entering the work force and youth going to college, when in reality youth who enter the work force need to be as well educated as youth going to college.

Whenever alternative educational structures or approaches are proposed for students who have special needs or for those youth who prematurely leave the usual educational system, they are overwhelmingly characterized by the attention that is given to *individual* differences and individual styles and rates of learning. The personal caring and individual attention provided in many alternative educational programs seem to emphasize the inability of the usual mass system to promote achievement and to facilitate interpersonal relations among youth, and between youth and adults, as a medium for learning. For the many youth who leave the educational system prior to completion, there appears to have been less opportunity for personal achievement and participation in scholarship, athletics, music, clubs, leadership, and other important school activities, which are often only available to those who excel. The stigma attached to tracking students into set programs, placement in "slow" or "below average" classes, or in special education classes, often further accentuates personal beliefs of inadequacy or can contribute to feelings of not belonging or not relating to the mainstream of the school. Mainstreaming laws (Public Law 94-142) have helped to reduce some of the social relationship problems resulting from confinement of movement, as well as alleviating some of the disparaging stereotypes associated with those who have different learning styles and rates or who possess certain learning disabilities.

According to the panel gathered under the President's Commission for the Eighties (Hooks, 1981), some of the major dichotomous issues that exist in the multicultural American society, and in education, are as follows:

· Equality of opportunity in parallel with the chance for individual excellence
· Homogeneity in parallel with pluralism
· Cooperation in parallel with competition
· Community in parallel with individuality
· Investment in parallel with consumption

The panel also believed that three major commitments were especially essential for improvement of the educational process:

1. Equality of educational opportunity
2. Competence of instruction within an appropriate system
3. Individual excellence, or the chance for students to develop their talents to the full

▲ GOALS FOR COUNSELORS

Counselors can work toward improvements within educational settings if they apply the same commitments to the counseling and guidance process with students and to their consultative services to teachers. Counseling is essentially the individualization of the educational process through making more apparent the distinctiveness of each person. All three of the goals listed are compatible with what counselors seek to accomplish, and the following methods can further them:

· Help to personalize education through matching counselees with experiences that are most important for their stage of development, and actively seek to effect changes or additions when those experiences are not available.

· Provide helpful counseling communication, insight, and human relations principles in interaction with counselees and between counselees and school personnel within the instructional/educational process.

· Identify the resources and strengths possessed by counselees and help to resolve problems that might hinder them from fully using those resources and strengths. Provide developmental guidance activities for those aspects of self-learning and growth that are not available in the usual academic curriculum and that instructional personnel are not available, prepared, or ready to furnish.

■ CONCERN FOR EDUCATIONAL EQUALITY

Many national, state, and local laws have been promulgated to regulate and promote equal educational opportunities and procedures, but the relevance, appropriateness, and implementation of the laws continue to be controversial. The general sentiment in the nation is for state and local retention of control of the structure and content of education; thus, attitudes toward educational equality vary in different regions. The responsibility for financing education is an especially critical variable in the interplay between national, state, and local control. In 1988, state governments carried approximately 50% of total school costs, local governments carried 44%, and the federal government approximately 6% (U.S. Department of Education, 1990). The federal share has always been relatively small. How all schools can continue to be adequately and fairly financed will be a problem for many years to come.

▲ DESEGREGATION ISSUES

The "separate but equal" doctrine has not been appropriate or acceptable in the American educational system since the *Brown v. Board of Education* (1954) decision. The efforts at school desegregation were initially concentrated in the southern states during the 1950s and 1960s. Since the 1970s, school systems in the northern and western states that had become segregated through the establishment of private educational endeavors or through circumstance have received the attention of the United States Supreme Court. The role of the justice system in education and the relationship of education to Congress and laws passed by Congress is controversial. Urban areas, where "White flight" and racial imbalance have occurred, present an especially complex situation for the equitable remedy of segregation and racial isolation. Federal courts currently oversee desegregation plans in 500 school districts. Many of the plans include high quality schools that attract students, voluntary transfers by students, schools that share special programs, and transportation of students in attempts to create a balanced representation of various groups. (However, many districts, especially in urban areas, have few predominantly White schools to which non-Whites can be bused.) From the very first, federal supervision of local schools was intended only as a temporary measure to remedy past discrimination. In 1991, the U.S. Supreme Court declared that public school districts that have taken all practical steps to eliminate vestiges of past racially discriminatory systems can end court-ordered busing, even if it means a return to some one-race schools. In order to end court supervision of their desegregation efforts, a district must follow guidelines of a trial court to show it is protecting the rights of all students and that it is unlikely to return to former discriminatory practices. Desegregation action has resulted in much hostility, conflict, and stress for many of the participants. In the midst of these social dynamics is, for counselors, the very real task of helping to interpret and properly facilitate the same civil rights for students in the school situation that apply in any other aspect of the society (DeCecco & Richards, 1974, pp. 63–86).

▲ INTEGRATION ISSUES AND STUDENT RELATIONSHIPS

The interplay of psychosocial dynamics is assumed to be inherent in situations in which integration is occurring or where the presence of multicultural groups is accentuated by their numbers. Understanding the basic dynamics and determining ways to deal with their ramifications are important aspects of the work of counselors.

The tendency for students to cluster themselves into networks of social groups is normal in any school setting. The groups can be based on personal interests, abilities, friendship ties, extracurricular activities and sports, neighborhood of residence, and other motivational and relational factors. However, in culturally diverse settings, additional groupings based on ethnic and racial background can also occur. Petroni, Hirsch, and Petroni (1970), through personal group interviews with students in a high school that had been formally integrated since 1954, subjectively categorized the students according to their various cultural backgrounds and attitudinal orientations. Though the number of students who were interviewed was relatively small, the researchers felt that the diverse types of students were candid in expressing their viewpoints toward their integrated school environment at that time in their lives. Some of the characteristics and viewpoints that were identified in the Petroni, Hirsch, and Petroni study have also been described in research by DeCecco and Richards (1974); they are represented in the following list of student groups.

· *Black "elite" 1.* These students were considered by both Blacks and Whites to be at the top of the Black social ladder. They mixed easily with Whites, were high achievers, highly competitive and motivated, engaged in many school activities, and were often in better financial circumstances than other Blacks. Among the elites, it was felt that the lighter the skin color, the better. Since they seemed to identify with values of the White community, they were often resented by other Blacks and considered "Uncle Toms" or "White Negroes."

· *Black "elite" 2.* This group was more concerned with "self" as members of a group against which prejudice was shown. They united against the injustices of White attitudes toward Blacks and actively demonstrated their concern about racial justice.

· *Black militants.* Those who advocated Black Power were primarily interested in economic and political fairness and being represented in the system. They tended not to participate in organized school activities and were not high achievers, but they were considered by others to be "cool" moderators at times in potential intergroup conflicts. They were also sensitive to the inadequacies and rigidity of the educational system and perceived the school to be exploitive of Blacks in sports. The educational, economic, and political issues that are involved in the lives of Black athletes have also been comprehensively reported by Ashe (1988) and Green, Smith, Gunnings, and McMillan (1974).

· *White racists.* These students, as identified by other students, were males who were openly prejudiced. They were also "low academic achievers, not involved in extracurricular activities, and constantly in fights" (Petroni, Hirsch, & Petroni, 1970, p. 66). Since their prejudices were overtly expressed, they were often subjected to physical retaliation by Blacks; and the retaliatory action by Blacks, to many perceivers, offered a convenient self-perpetuating stereotype that all Blacks are aggressive and hostile.

· *White conservatives.* This group tended to respond according to socially desirable attitudes but also revealed more subtle and perceptually distorted prejudices. These students tended to see the relationships among various groups as falling within certain predetermined limitations that worked against perception of distinct individuals. Some of their expressed thoughts included: (1) Blacks were different because they tended to hang around in large groups, (2) Blacks were all alike, (3) Whites and Blacks *never* dated, (4) "cool" Blacks had more fun, (5) school personnel showed preference for White students, (6)

Black students discriminated against teachers, (7) integration was formal but not emotional, (8) Blacks did not engage in middle-class sports, and (9) students rarely discussed racial matters in class, nor was it necessarily appropriate for discussion.

· *Hippies.* Hippies tended to be the liberal White element in the school. They were usually a "bright, intellectual, rebellious, indignant group of young people" (Petroni, Hirsch, & Petroni, 1970, p. 101). Although they generally rebelled against the establishment, they did not have many Black friends. They also seemed to have inner problems that were projected onto others or displaced to their immediate environment. They rejected "White Negroes," "Lily Whites," and special treatment for Blacks, but they also tended to express helpful points of view and to take action when necessary. They were often disappointed that their parents were not more liberal and that the school personnel did not take action when acts of racial prejudice occurred or when the system did not respond with more adequate educational methods. They also expressed "sympathy" for and interest in Blacks.

· *Peaceniks.* This group generally consisted of White students who seemed to fully accept other cultural groups as equal and declared that they (peaceniks) were against any type of prejudice or discrimination. However, they were generally less involved in racial matters, nor did they have any strong feelings for civil rights. Their main preoccupation in 1970 was with the antiwar movement and their strong political feelings against violence. Though they seemed, in general, to mix readily with different fellow students, they didn't appear to have a great deal of feeling for racial equality. In fact, at times they expressed the conservative point of view toward racial matters.

· *The "successful" mixed group, Black and White.* This group of students seemed to take the integrated situation in their stride but also had to cope with the emotional stress that resulted from rejection by their group, peer pressure for conformity, personal desire for achievement, interference with self-expressed goals, generation gaps, stereotypes, racial tension, experiences of discrimination, superficial relations among different groups, internalized feelings toward self and others, conflicts in moral standards, impressions of being exploited, and feelings of impotence in a complex intergroup situation. Though taking the path of "neutrality" in race relations may appear to be a wise coping strategy for students who desire to move through the established system, it is also obvious that it can bring psychological and social problems.

· *Mexican Americans.* The "in-between" group, the "middle" group, the "left-out" group, and the "neglected" group were all generalized self-perceptions presented by these students in the integrated situation. The major impression was that sticking together would prevent being hurt or being rejected. Some members of this group felt that exclusive group relations, or superficial intergroup relations, were self-imposed and resulted in a type of defensive segregation. They also felt at times that they were being used by White students, who had their own interpersonal relationship problems with Blacks. They showed some vacillation between identifying with Whites and identifying with Blacks, but tended to distance themselves from Blacks by the use of "us" and "them" language. Association outside their cultural group on an intimate level, such as in dating, was generally not received positively. The "successful" Mexican Americans who had accepted mainstream values experienced rejection by their own group and were thought to be acting "better" than the rest.

· *The Agringado ("Angloized Mexican Americans")*. Carter and Segura (1979, p. 151) have described middle-class Mexican-American students who usually mix well with their Anglo peers. These students tend to achieve and demonstrate behavior that is similar to that of other middle-class youth. The degree of identity conflict that might exist for this group is not really known, but most likely it depends on how each person has integrated his or her personality components. *Most* Mexican Americans are statistically classified as holding lower socioeconomic class status and are not acculturated, according to the usual definition. It is presumed that within this broad group there are three subgroups: those who practice traditional Mexican cultural ways, those who have a barrio orientation, and those who are in transition.

The topic that produced the most intense feelings by the interviewees in the Petroni, Hirsch, and Petroni study was interracial dating. The strong pressures on students to adhere to certain lines or codes of conduct originated in the community, school, and from parents and friends: "While young black men dated white young women, white young men never dated black young women. This 'fact' always remained the same, even though its interpretation might differ from one person, or one sub-group, to another. Thus, black young men might evaluate the dating situation somewhat differently from white young men, and both might again interpret it differently from white or black young women. Still, all agreed on the major factual outlines of the dating patterns" (Petroni, Hirsch, & Petroni, 1970, p. 2).

The abstraction of themes that represent the dynamics of intergroup relations must be treated cautiously, for there are relatively few absolutes or homogeneous perceptions that might be commonly held by *all* youth or by selected subgroup categories. The influence of individual variables that affect the attitudes and perceptions of youth toward themselves and others in the school environment include family background, status needs and expectations, individual abilities, recreational interests, darkness of skin, attitudes toward school, peer relations, individual personality, and male-female relations. The fact remains that although schools may be *formally* integrated, the students are not necessarily *informally* integrated. Desegregation is, as it should be, a matter of law. Integration is inevitably a matter of personal option.

▲ THE SCHOOL AS MICROCOSM

The educational system is in many ways a microcosmic replay of the larger society, with its economic problems, social conflicts, current fads, and current events. Reactions to the death of Dr. Martin Luther King, Jr., illustrate how occurrences in the society often have a direct ripple effect that generalizes into the environment of the school itself. His tragic death aroused both Black and

White students and resulted in much conflict and hostility. Violent, dramatic, or emotional circumstances in the society will also influence students' feelings in the school environment; King's death, for example, affected many Black students personally. Traumatic interracial events, in general, evoke the behavior that is most consistent with individuals' existing sentiments or past attitudes. Dramatic changes in both positive and negative attitudes can result from the pouring out of emotion, or the strength of existing attitudes can be increased (Nevas, 1977, p. 2).

● INTERPERSONAL REALITIES

The immediate reality for school-age youth, however, is most anchored and defined in their school experiences, which occupy a major portion of their lives. For them, school is a real world. Since the school experience mirrors many of the events and conditions of the external society, and since adults serve as models, adults shouldn't be amazed that so much emphasis is given to the election of a Black cheerleader, homecoming queen or king, or class officer, or that students often demand that soul food, or other ethnic foods, be served in the lunchroom. They should not be surprised that students of similar group identity tend to segregate themselves, that many students are preoccupied with matters related to interracial relations but rarely are willing to discuss it, or that many Hispanics and other cultural group members often see themselves as caught between the problems of Whites and Blacks. Integration is really viewed only in a superficial manner; mixed groups attend the same school but informal patterns of social separation continue. As in the larger society, aspiring, achievement-oriented cultural group members are often discriminated against by some members of their own cultural group. Accomplishment in the system seems to be most necessary for adequate employment and socioeconomic mobility, yet is often rejected as "playing the White game." Many group members prefer to build positive identity through loyalty to their group, often at the expense of losing their motivation for school achievement. And because there is great diversity in each cultural group and in youth in general, why should anyone wonder when *most* youth accomplish their purposes in the educational system and move out into the society in self-actualizing ways?

● WHAT IS STOPPING GENUINE INTERPERSONAL RELATIONS?

As neoconservatism increasingly seems to be a major focus in the 1980s and 1990s, the momentum for school integration, formal or informal, faces greater resistance and stalling. If adult groups pull away from each other or establish power blocs to compete with one another, the possibility for the development of more open and cooperative relations among generations of youth will also be hindered. Although youth of diverse backgrounds do face many complex interpersonal relationship problems of their own making in the integrated school situation, it is not the integration that causes problems but the resistance to integration or the efforts to maintain or reestablish segregation. The striving for educational and economic betterment is a common goal for *all* people, and it seems difficult to understand why anyone would want to oppose equal opportunity for all. Lindsey and Lindsey (1974) believe that "if children get together, learn the same things together and about each other, are taught that we are all the same and equal human beings, then we, all of us, would be saved from the problems of worrying about who is or who is not 'equal' on the basis of such irrelevant characteristics as skin color. It is sad to remark that the parents of our children, who themselves were supposed to have been taught better, continue to teach their children the ways of hate and discrimination rather than the ways of love and acceptance" (p. 134).

● WHAT CAN TEACHERS AND COUNSELORS DO TO FACILITATE SCHOOL AND CLASSROOM INTEGRATION?

Helping youth during their impressionable years to form perceptual and rational alertness is especially important in overcoming the tendency toward prejudicial attitudes and thinking. The school, as a social institution, shares in the socialization process along with family, church, neighborhood, and peer groups. *Socialization* promotes the child to membership in the society by teaching behaviors, roles, personality characteristics, and interpersonal relations. *Enculturation* of the child provides the values, knowledge, and skills of the prevailing culture. The important question is whether the school can adequately identify children with different potentials and characteristics and prepare them differentially so that they are able to enter society with full use of their distinctive qualities, "or whether it merely perpetuates the status inherited from the parents" (Carter & Segura, 1979, p. 31).

Application of counseling skills. Counselors can assist in the identification of individual potential through applying their knowledge of patterns of human potential and their sensitivity toward the uniqueness of each person. Second, they can help determine the blocks that might prevent students from making full use of their individual resources. Third, they can enhance the mutual collaboration between individual students and school personnel through their training in human dynamics and communications skills, and fourth, they can facilitate intercultural understanding and awareness using their ability to lead student groups. From their experiences in living, different cultural groups have acquired different values and behaviors, and until they have an opportunity to confront, discuss, and if possible work out those differences, mutual acceptance will be unlikely, except on a superficial level.

Promoting positive intergroup relations. The interaction of students based on mutual respect and equal status is the major goal of integration (Nevas, 1977). It is a process that takes time, energy and caring by students, school personnel, and parents. The result of such a process helps promote academic achievement and individual self-esteem. Any plan to improve the school climate should be developed by the participants themselves, but the following approaches and techniques have been used by schools.

· Start a new classroom group with structured exercises to develop interpersonal communication skills, such as observing others, expressing oneself to others, listening to others, respecting others, and caring for each other. Arranging seats in a circle will encourage the flow of interpersonal exchange and give a sense of group identity. The increase in quantity and quality of interactions, through improved communication skills, will provide opportunities for students to learn more about each other. The ultimate long-range goal is the development of perceptions and attitudes that recognize each person as a unique and valued human being.

· Take the strengthening of self-esteem as a specific key goal for integration activities. The development of positive self-image requires thought, consideration, and action by students in facing such questions as Why am I a good person? How do I treat others? How do I interact with others? How do I assist others? Active mutual assistance in solving problems will also help build acceptance and cooperation.

· Rotate opportunities for group-related experience so that all students can practice small-group leadership skills as well as followership skills. The feeling of support and self-confidence can also be gained through coleading group discussions.

· Provide group discussions in which students can talk about the integration experience. What does it mean to them? What are their feelings about it?

· Conduct a workshop for students on differences. The aim is to help develop pride in ethnic heritage, to understand the backgrounds of others, and to accept and respect what they are and what others are.

· Keep children mixed in as many activities as possible.

· When children are segregated into bilingual or other programs, allow for activities in which different children can mix, work, or interact together.

· Introduce new norms of intelligence and achievement by emphasizing multiple intellectual abilities in addition to reading, writing, and computing skills. Logic, problem solving, creativity, expression of ideas, leadership, and cooperation are other areas in which students can take pride.

· Since children pick up adult attitudes, arrange small, informal group meetings of parents and teachers to discuss learning, the development of children, the schooling experience, and other topics important to the group.

· Work against the self-fulfilling prophecy that minority children will fail. Work for the success of all children. Be patient and take the positive attitude that your hard efforts will pay off.

■ CONCERN FOR DISADVANTAGED STUDENTS

The reality of human experiences and conditions is immediately confronted once the surface of the "system" is penetrated and the basic facts of existence emerge. The school is a system, but it is one that contains individuals who face certain economic and educational obstacles in getting the most out of the system. Some of the obstacles are within the person and some are within the system.

▲ ECONOMIC DISADVANTAGES

Poverty and the absence of power are crucial interrelated variables for families in many areas of the country but are especially visible in urban areas. Though the poor are very familiar with money because they live in a cash world, the lack of money itself is not as crucial as the lack of power that money can bring. Power, as energy, gives the feeling of control over one's own life. Feelings of frustration, anger, apathy, and meaninglessness in life are likely to result when self-determination is thwarted, when there is no hope for personal security, or when the collective security that others possess is viewed as desirable but unobtainable. Social conditions and psychological states of mind that might be related to economic deprivation, however, exist only when certain persons regard the situations as a problem. The divergence between what a situation actually is and what is preferred depends on the values held by the person viewing the situation. *Participants* in the situation and *spectators* of the situation will not necessarily have the same perceptions. No one appreciates being called poor by others, and the same variations of self-respect and levels of self-esteem exist among low-income people as can be found within any other socioeconomic class. Counselors who approach their clients with an attitude that there is individual diversity within groups of people will be more successful than counselors who tend to lump individuals into labeled categories that have been defined by outside spectators. When counselors take this holistic approach they will be more open to seeing the total person, with strengths and resources in balance with individual shortcomings and problems.

● IMPLICATIONS

Most low-income families do not have access to the power instruments of money, and their lack often determines the degree and kind of environmental stimulation available. Much of reality for these families is tied to here-and-now needs, with gross psychological potential often expended in meeting present situations. In middle-class homes, where the children's welfare generally has high priority, the children's development is usually encouraged by a linear flow of experiences that can be planned in orderly sequential phases and that harmonizes with the established schooling system. In many low-income families, the needs of parents generally must take precedence. All parents throughout all socioeconomic levels face emotional and real-life pressures, but the burden on mothers and fathers of low-income families often produces reactions to a reality they are powerless to confront. Educators often make certain assumptions about life-coping reactions of many low-income families.

Some assumptions that pertain to potential school conflicts or problems include the following:

- The necessity of older children to care for younger children, with less time and energy left to devote to their studies
- A raw, or limited, maturity of attitude toward life that is acquired by children who have faced harsh living and uncertainty
- The reinforcement of restricted communication modes
- Behavioral acting out of inner impulses that often work against school-task requirements and the efforts of school personnel
- Lack of proper nutrition resulting from unpredictable meals
- An established link between adult alcoholism and wife and child abuse, which most likely cuts across socioeconomic levels but is more easily concealed from public scrutiny in middle- and upper-class families

● HOW TO HELP

First, the term *cultural deprivation* should not unilaterally be applied to the manner of living for low-income families. It is not that they lack culture but that the culture they acquire is often far different from what schools expect, desire, or presume. Equally wide is the gap between the lifestyle of low-income children and the lifestyle of most school personnel. The challenge to school personnel is to produce a situation in which compatibility of differences can be reached and in which optimal learning can occur. The fact that many adults, as well as children, are economically disadvantaged is a major issue for social agencies and institutions. Adult educators, personnel counselors in business and industry, churches, welfare agencies, family agencies, and employment agencies are all involved either directly or indirectly in helping low-income members of the society. They are able to assist only so far as they have *understanding* of poverty conditions in the country and the *skills* necessary to relate to both the situation and the individuals in the situation.

Second, interpreting the needs of children whose cultural experiences are different from what is expected in the educational environment, or what is desired, is a significant task for school personnel and one that requires thought, planning, care, and interest. Many students face limitations imposed by the inability of their families to afford educational materials that stimulate learning in the home, and many students have not had the opportunity for broad cultural experiences. Children growing up in poverty often have a kind of maturity that has been developed through experiencing crime, disease, abuse, violence, and the absence of basic necessities. The maturity born of these harsh experiences needs to be funneled or associated in ways that can lead to achievement within the school environment. Early interventions such as Head Start programs and other preschool compensatory experiences have been especially designed with this purpose in mind. The primary goal is comprehensive child development that includes a classroom routine, health, nutrition, social service, parent education, and counseling. The most important aspect of these programs is establishing communication with the children through simply talking to them and getting a response. Talking with students in the formal school system and encouraging them to evaluate and question their own thoughts and actions will also broaden their perceptions. Acquiring the ability to see that life is bigger and more than one's immediate surroundings helps develop optimistic attitudes and expectation of something to aim for personally.

Third, students can feel more secure and learn better when teachers and counselors provide relationships that contain certain well-defined limits and that are consistent and fair, rather than vacillating between extremes of permissiveness and authoritarianism. Security in knowing what to expect will afford concreteness and clarity of behavior, which is less possible when expectations are either ambiguous, unknown, or dogmatic (Hayakawa, 1979, pp. 3–36). Security is also gained from a sense of self-worth through being valued by teachers and counselors. Students are more prone to like school, and to learn better, when they believe and feel that school personnel are fair, consistent, and interested in them and prize their presence.

▲ EDUCATIONAL DISADVANTAGES

When a preschool child does not generally exhibit the values and behaviors of a middle-class orientation, or does not use standard language, or otherwise has not had the opportunity to experience the ways that are customarily practiced and rewarded in the school system, he or she is considered at a disadvantage in that middle-class culture. A person with a middle-class background, or a mainstream cultural background, would likewise be at a disadvantage if he or she were expected to learn and function in an upper-class or underclass environment, or a minority cultural environment, in comparison with the members of those groups, who would be more experienced in the language, customs, and ways of their group. The concept of *culture shock* is found in the literature about cross-culture issues and is generally accepted as a real phenomenon. Anxiety as a result of being in unfamiliar surroundings is often felt by individuals who leave their native land for employment in foreign countries, by foreign students coming to the United States for study, by refugees, and, in documented studies, by Peace Corps volunteers and tourists. According to one definition, "culture shock is a series of experiences in which the person is unable to use formerly effective coping skills in a new environment and consequently loses self-confidence" (Higginbotham & Tanaka-Matsumi, 1981, p. 266).

● IMPLICATIONS

Educationally disadvantaged denotes a lack of background experiences that contribute to success in the educational process. The fact that many adults, as well as children, are educationally disadvantaged also has implications for adult learners within formal or informal educational systems and for adults who are involved in training and development activities within industry and business. Probably the most crucial need for adequate instruction and opportunity occurs when children first enter school. Many come unprepared or unready for what they find. Children at an early age will find the school experience frustrating, difficult, or conflicting if, for example, they do not know how to handle a pencil between thumb and finger, or are not aware of some of the gross differences in time (months, days, hours), or communicate in a language and behavior different from what is standard or expected in the school, or expect to relate to teachers only in the ways that are most customarily used in their family or neighborhood social interactions. Other problems appear for children when they do not yet possess memorization habits, give little attention to direction, punctuality, or cleanliness, are not quiet enough to hear the teacher, or in other ways are unfamiliar, suspicious, or fearful of what appears to be a strange, demanding, and perhaps even hostile environment.

● HOW TO HELP

First, accepting children according to their cultural background of experiences and helping them to move from their point of developmental readiness into tasks that they can successfully master is crucial at an early age. Fostering a sense of confidence through accomplishment and a liking for school and the learning process are among the most important early developmental tasks.

Second, the culture content of the real-world society is converted into a school curriculum, and how teachers pass on that *content* (knowledge, skills, values, and formal and informal codes of behavior) is critically involved in the *method* they use. It is also important that they present the content in an effective, sequential manner according to the varying needs and degree of readiness of each student.

Third, the content of any curriculum can be broken down into *formal* and *informal* components. Formal content includes materials, such as texts, films, and instructional units. Informal content includes the social atmosphere, or tone, that is created in the school environment, such as expectations for children, the reward system, standards for behavior, communication styles, and relations with parents. The curricular content, in most schools, focuses on what is most traditional and needed in mainstream society. The acquisition of basic skills (reading, writing, speaking, computing), so necessary for survival in the culture, is possible only insofar as teachers and their methods make contact with learners in ways that they understand.

▲ ISSUES OF CULTURAL DIVERSITY IN THE EDUCATIONAL SYSTEM

Because most teachers and other school personnel are trained in traditional, mainstream, middle-class cultural ways, incongruity often exists between what the teacher is accustomed to, or expects, and what may be the actual background of the students in a culturally diverse setting. Neither the teacher or counselor or the educational system, on the one hand, nor the background of the students, on the other, alone constitutes the "problem" for potential cultural conflict, disharmony, or miscommunication. Rather, it is the complexity of the multicultural situation, in which understanding of those who must be educated is sought, along with ways to do it that afford equitable treatment for all. The situation faced by educational systems and by diverse students in the situation encompasses many issues, differences, or problems that are often presumed to exist. The following concerns are often encountered in the educational situation and in the society at large.

There will be problems for the educational system:
· *When formal segregation, isolation, and alienation are present.* De facto segregation, or the actual practice of overt and covert segregation, still prevails throughout areas of the country. Racial imbalance in metropolitan areas, smaller urban areas, and rural areas, and in housing patterns and school attendance all influence the isolation of cultural groups. The assignment of school personnel can also contribute to cultural isolation when only minority teachers, counselors, and administrators are assigned to minority student populations, or where minority personnel are not available to provide role models for minority students or to serve as intercultural facilitators for students of the majority group culture. There is also the possibility that acculturated, upwardly mobile minority group members can become alienated from their original group, resulting in a "leadership drain." But where more individuals have developed intercultural competence along with social interest, isolation is less likely, and all groups will benefit from their contributions, leadership, skills, and modeling. The more groups (students, teachers, parents, community) are prevented from experiencing one another, the fewer opportunities there will be for sharing understandings and the greater the likelihood of communication gaps, misunderstanding, and potential conflict.
· *When there is informal segregation in schools.* Although formal integration is the law of the land, informal segregation or castelike social separation continues to create situations that hinder cross-cultural understanding and communication. The ethnic and social cleavage is often intensified by the atmosphere and policies embodied in the structure of the school. Students tend to cling together in ethnic and cultural groups, and parental involvement, especially in urban schools, is often gained only through special strategies for pulling them into closer cooperation. One such strategy in the Chicago public school system increased parental involvement in the children's schooling by asking the parents to pick up their children's report cards. In 1982, parents of 87% of Chicago's elementary school students and 61% of high school students came to the schools for the cards.

A psychosocial phenomenon also emerges as culturally diverse children learn stereotypes and develop differentiated perceptions of social groups. For example, "after the second grade, Anglo and Mexican-American children increasingly restrict their social choices to members of their own ethnic group. By the time they reach the upper elementary grades, there is virtually complete social separation between the two groups. That the children are aware of Anglo dominance is reflected in their leadership and prestige choice" (Carter & Segura, 1979, p. 151). The formation of social friendships in racially desegregated schools and classrooms is a complex interplay of personal and group dynamics and is related to variables such as racial proportions and control of turf, threat to socioeconomic status, geographical and regional traditions, and development of subnetworks due to size of the school (Longshore, 1982). Hallinan (1982) has indicated that "if white children realize that their black peers perceive them as friends, they are more likely to reciprocate with friendliness, leading to improved interracial interaction" (p. 70). She also believes that "in a society in which blacks are in a distinct minority, merely desegregating classrooms without direct intervention in the social dynamics of the classroom is likely to be most effective in improving race relations if the classrooms are majority white. On the other hand, if teachers and school officials design programs aimed at reducing status differences between blacks and whites, they may be able to modify negative effects of classroom racial composition on children's interracial friendships" (Hallinan, 1982, p. 70).

"Special" programs at all educational levels, from preschool through college, also compound the separation of members of diverse groups. The educational solution to individual differences and to the matter of assisting "nontraditional" students often includes compensatory and remedial procedures, bilingual/bicultural education, and other activities that tend to separate individuals of culturally and socially different backgrounds. All the approaches seek correction of learning and developmental disabilities or deficiencies and all contain philosophical assumptions for the enhancement of individual roles and status. Differential treatment is sometimes seen as perpetuating lower-class status and the separation of groups, although many programs have also been successful according to stated criteria.

· *When cultural diversity goes unrecognized.* The modification of the curriculum in schools to encompass cultural diversity is rare. Stereotypes based on inaccurate knowledge and beliefs tend to be perpetuated, and perceptions of other cultures tend to be distorted and go unchallenged. It is questionable whether the disadvantaged person, the person in transition, the ghetto dweller, the culturally different, or the "nontraditional" student can be brought into mainstream American ways, values, norms of behavior, and language without some psychological and social damage. Impediments to psychological and social development for members of the majority group can also be created when they are isolated from knowledge of or contact with other cultural groups. Most effective systems of teaching will take into consideration the content and learning approaches that might be most appropriate and useful for diverse individuals.

There will be communication problems for school personnel and learning problems for students:
· *When cultural differences are viewed only as deficiencies.* The lack of success in school of some minority children has been attributed to the absence of

important influences that are not provided in certain subcultures; or, to state it another way, such children are regarded by some as socially deficient and unable to function in *middle-class* culture and therefore needing "reeducation." Thus, whether due to deprivation or disadvantage, differences in cultural background are often perceived by school personnel in terms of deficiency or pathology. This approach leads to limited solutions, restricted educational strategies, and the labeling of children according to presumptive weaknesses based on their cultural group identity. If children are prejudged by cultural group, the group's successful attributes or strengths should at least get the same amount of recognition as is given to shortcomings (Shade, 1978).

· *When subcultures are viewed as monolithic and static entities.* Subcultural groups in the United States are in many respects highly distinguishable from one another. However, minority cultural groups are often lumped together and depicted as having all the same attributes and facing all the same problems in the educational system. The unique personalities that can be found in any cultural group are often lost when the homogeneity of any group is reflected in monolithic, stereotypical fashion. Oversimplification of individuals according to generalizations derived from folklore, fact, anthropological comparative studies, stereotypes, and real experiences can be best controlled through in-depth understanding of each person in contemporary times. Culture is not static, nor is any cultural group homogeneous. Roles for men and women, lifestyles, and life orientations do change. Continuous reinterpretation of individual ways in interaction with current life and current situations is basic for effective and most realistic multicultural counseling (Maldonado & Cross, 1977).

· *When language differences are viewed only as deficits.* The interaction between people who speak different languages or dialects is often assumed to be a cause of learning difficulties in the school situation. One issue is whether vernacular languages other than "school English" are suitable for learning and coping with life, but a more basic problem involves the attitude of superiority that educators might take toward nonstandard dialects or languages. The obstruction to learning is usually a result of conveying to the speaker or reader that the way that he or she speaks or reads is verbally destitute, inferior, or otherwise substandard (Carter & Segura, 1979, p. 91; Cooper, 1974; Dillard, 1972). At the same time, educators would be derelict if they did not assist youth to develop intercultural linguistic systems that enable them to move in larger areas of the society. There's nothing wrong or inferior about speaking in the manner one has learned or is accustomed to. For example, speaking only in the local vernacular, or slang, or dialect among persons in the barrio, inner-city ghetto, mountain area, or rural farm area would usually be considered appropriate, but wouldn't be acceptable on a job that required high fluency in standard English (*Dialect of the Black American,* 1970); nor would the vernacular used in Ivy League colleges be acceptable in conducting interviews with *most* urban Black children. One executive of a large manufacturing firm used highly polished and carefully expressed standard English during his working hours. In his off-hours, at home, he often used Black dialect or a mixture of the two speech forms. His fluency in two languages did not hinder his achievement and enhanced his ability in different groups.

· *When presumptions of intellectual inferiority are based on cultural group identity or membership.* The belief that certain cultural populations are intellectually inferior due to biogenetic background continues to be held by some educators and others. Writing and research by Arthur Jensen (1969, 1972, 1973) in particular have sought to demonstrate that intervention programs for disadvantaged Black children will not succeed and that the retardation pattern in ability or school achievement will become progressively worse. The issue of "race" and IQ continues to arouse controversy in scientific groups and the general public. It is trivial and nonresearchable in contemporary society. Single-score IQ, as based on the ratio between mental age and chronological age, more accurately measures the degree and kind of environmental stimulation the test taker has encountered, as represented by the content included in a particular intelligence test, than it does native intelligence. Or, to state it another way, it measures the degree of middle-class cultural assimilation.

Culture-fair tests are only possible when there is a culture-fair society. The average difference, for example, between IQ scores for Whites and Blacks is usually between 10 and 20 points. The disparity is attributable not to differences in hereditary background but to the degree of exposure to White, middle-class culture. Williams (1975) has demonstrated the effects of cultural influence on test scores through his BITCH test (Black Intelligence Test of Cultural Homogeneity; or, as some would have it, Black Intelligence Test Counterbalanced for Honkies). The test contains items derived from Black American folklore, history, life experience, and dialect that the author contends are more relevant and thus more fair for Black people. His point is that each group does have its own ways, slang, beliefs, values, and experiences. The problem of assumed intellectual ability based on cultural group identity encompasses prejudicial attitudes and the lack of intercultural exchange. It becomes a major problem for students to be treated according to prejudicial attitudes based on preconceptions of innate group intellectual inferiority and taken as fact.

· *When individual potential goes unrecognized.* When single-measurement systems for determining ability patterns are used, individual variations often go unrecognized. The closer the relation among genetically related individuals, the more alike they are in IQ, but the similarity is lessened if they have been raised in different environments. The extent and quality of parent-child relations during the child's early years affect mental development regardless of cultural group identity; that is to say, stimulation-deficient environments can vitiate mental growth. Highly intelligent individuals may come from any socioeconomic group. Personal traits that lead to adaptation in life situations, such as assertiveness, also tend to be related to level of mental abilities. Providing the opportunity and means by which to fully develop and express intellectual potential is the value-goal of society and the educational process.

· *When individual personality traits are distorted or overgeneralized according to cultural group identity or membership.* The notion that groups of people can be classified into distinct value types has been included in numerous theoretical paradigms and cross-cultural studies. The basic assumption holds that each cultural group has an integrated and homogeneous philosophy of life, or world view, that shapes the entire personality of the group members, and that through deductive reasoning we can understand individuals who are members of a certain group. However, when we see a person *only* as a member of a group, we tend to be influenced by what we believe about his or her group. Thus, a single White person might be assumed to possess the characteristics that the non-White perceiver ascribes to the White group in general. Group personalities, like common group stereotypes, are either incorporated into the beliefs of a perceiver or contrasted with the beliefs of the perceiver. For example, a person may believe that children from traditional Spanish-speaking families have a present-time orientation and take each day at a time, and that they are more than usually attuned to affective and emotional relationships with friends; the person might then be likely to see these traits or values in a single Spanish-speaking child. This is an instance in which the perceived attributes of an individual are affected by his or her group membership. To illustrate the opposite effect, the fact that some Americans believe that Blacks are unintelligent or that Native Americans do not have management knowledge or ability can lead to overestimation of an individual, such as a Black college professor or a Native American business entrepreneur. The perceived individual stands in contrast to beliefs held by the perceiver, who tends to see the Black professor as an exceptionally bright person or the Native American as an unusually capable businessperson. We often fail to see persons as possessing unique personalities but usually perceive them as members of some kind of group and view them in terms of what we believe about the group (Krech, Crutchfield, & Livson, 1974, pp. 783–784). As the saying goes, you can't judge a book by its cover, whether it is white, black, brown, yellow, or red.

· *When negative self-concept is simplistically related to feelings of success and failure.* Feelings of satisfaction and success follow accomplishment of a task only when students perceive the task as worthy of achievement according to their level of aspiration. Thus, success and failure are defined in terms of personal perceptions of standards of behavior. What is internalized by each person as success or failure is adjusted by external social factors relative to each person. Self-concept as developed through the process of self-appraisal is dependent on each person's world view across cultures and is not imposed solely by the school or society. Only a most restricted ethnocentric attitude would take the view that the school and dominant society, alone, influence self-concept. All social living plays a role in shaping inner ideas of what is success and what is failure. Carter and Segura (1979) point out that "despite the disagreeable school experience of many Chicano children, the projected negative stereotype, the low achievement, and the early dropout, there is no evidence of generalized negative self-concept. Chicanos seem to be maintaining the self as well as other groups do or better. This phenomenon, if true, can best be explained by pointing out that the group's significant others are found among peers and within the family and community—not within the dominant group or its schools" (p. 112).

The reality of economic conditions, more than self-concept, is linked to nonmotivation and withdrawal from school activities and achievement. Lifestyles that encourage work to supplement family income take priority over school achievement for many high school students, and for many college students the availability of financial stipends plays a more dominant role in potential achievement than does the influence of self-concept. The degree of generalization of the effects of the self-fulfilling prophecy on negative self-concept is controversial and is not conclusive for *all* persons of any one specific cultural group. McCarthy and Yancey (1971) have concluded that "to the degree that Negroes do not use biased white evaluators in developing a self-evaluation, the process of development of self-identity within the Black community will parallel the developmental process in the White community, and to that degree, when social class is controlled, Negroes and Whites should not differ in levels of self-esteem" (p. 663).

Individual problems of low self-esteem stem from multiple causes and can be found in the composition of any cultural group. Individual psychological characteristics result from infinite numbers of social interactions and are dependent on the combination of individual personality, others, and the conditions in the setting. The issue for counselors and other school personnel is how, and to what degree, specific individuals evaluate themselves in relation to situational conditions: "Students who see themselves as disadvantaged—as opposed to those who may be disadvantaged but do not believe it—operate from a negative frame of reference. These students must be understood and worked with as total individuals within the institutional environment. Only within this context can educational institutions and those trained as counselors or student development specialists have a positive impact" (Ellison, 1978, p. 75).

■ PRESSURES ON TEACHERS AND COUNSELORS

The situation faced by teachers and counselors in a multicultural society and in a multicultural educational system adds up to continual stress in their work, and adaptation to the stress often leads them to adjust the various pressures in order to protect their personalities. The usual ideology of the system tends to state that successful teachers and counselors do not have problems. When educational personnel cannot incorporate the reality of the social structure of the school and cannot express their anxieties about that reality, they are prevented from seeing issues that are often a consequence of the situation. For example, Ms. Smith, who came from a working-class background, was regarded by her students and colleagues as a knowledgeable teacher who had high performance expectations. She was generally considered by students to be fair and reasonable in her grading, but upper- and middle-class students thought she was unfair because she did not condone class-related favoritism. Lower-class students thought she was very fair because she often practiced a form of underdog empathy. Mr. Jones, on the other hand, took an approach of rigid universalism, or a belief that all students should be treated in the same manner, and lower-class students tended to perceive him as unfair and think that he favored students who exhibited certain socially acceptable behavior. The fact that the informal social reward system functions for teachers as well as students seems to be a reality in educational systems. One role for school counselors is that of assisting both students and teachers to give less emphasis to the personal implications of behavior and more to its educational outcomes.

▲ COPING WITH FEELINGS ABOUT POOR STUDENT PERFORMANCE

Most teachers are alike in wanting to see the school's role and their role as helping all students become productive citizens, but many teachers also succumb to attitudes or beliefs that work against their best efforts. Psychological defense mechanisms operate in teachers as in all others, and susceptive teachers are especially vulnerable to three types of psychological self-preservation. The same also holds true for counselors.

1. *Blame the culture.* Since it is difficult to understand the actual influence of the home and the social culture on personality and school performance, many teachers react to rejection of their teaching approaches by blaming the family or cultural background of the student. The teacher's feeling of personal failure can quickly lead to disliking, contempt, or the fostering of disparaging stereotypes of the student and his or her cultural group; thus self-exoneration is gained in exchange for failure of the culture.

2. *Blame the student.* The work of teachers can be distorted when they take for granted the status of minority cultural group students, viewing them as something like the "happy slave." That attitude produces tunnel vision and seems to say: "It is just the way they are, and they are happy and content doing their own thing, so why make a big fuss over it?" Stereotyping like this dampens the optimism of teachers and could lead to ignoring the potential inherent in students. Scapegoatism is another form of blaming the student. As one Texas school counselor interviewed a decade ago said, "Only a few days ago a teacher told me that these Mexican American children don't know their place: 'Why they are just the rowdiest people I've ever seen—they don't act typically Mexican. Since you got all these federal programs and all these aides, they think they own this school' " (Carter & Segura, 1979, p. 205).

3. *Blame oneself.* When conscientious teachers fail to teach a child, they often tend to internalize the feeling of responsibility and take it as personal failure, particularly in the upper grades and high school. The pessimism and hopelessness of some upper-level teachers mirrors the feelings of some of their

students, many of whom drop out or are finally pushed out. Teachers are also pushed out. Teacher *burnout*, characterized by excessive symptoms of headaches, insomnia, restlessness, fatigue, and feelings of apathy and depression, is a reaction to stress. A short period of stress raises the blood pressure and increases heart rate, breathing, and blood flow. These changes help energize a person to cope with a situation, but at the same time they may produce that harried, "end-of-the-rope" feeling. Generally, these physical changes go away as swiftly as they appear. However, more prolonged doses of stress, as occasioned by feelings of failure, can cause depression or nervous tension and the physical complaints of insomnia, fatigue, and headaches. Excellent teachers have left their profession to escape the sense of failure and the pain of burnout, an unfortunate condition that counselors should address in their work (Moracco & McFadden, 1982). Many people need to unwind after a long and trying day, whether the day was spent at school, at home, or in an office or factory. Few school systems have dealt with the burnout problem in a systematic way, although the Chicago teachers' union has introduced stress-coping workshops to help teachers. It is helpful in general for teachers to plan a break every day, even if for just a few moments, to ignore the clock briefly and to make no demands on themselves. Self-taught progressive relaxation techniques will also calm a person down and improve physical and mental well-being (McGuigan, 1981). Resting in a quiet, comfortable, dimly lit place while forcing oneself to adopt a passive attitude about one's problems for about 20 minutes each day will help relax both mind and body and reduce the stress. Exercise also helps reduce the effects of stress and prepares the body physically for the sudden appearance of stress. If these things don't work, it is best to seek additional assistance from friends, family, or a health professional.

It is necessary to create, or revive, a positive image of schools, youth, and teachers as resources, not as problems. Before a school can establish a climate that is both positive and conducive to learning, it must differentiate among what it "can accomplish alone, that which it cannot accomplish, and that which it can accomplish only with collaboration from one or more outside organizations" (Hooks, 1981, p. 102). School administrators must also be more than routine managers of systems. They should be people who can lead and who can act on their perceptions to resolve structural problems and encourage optimism.

▲ WHITE TEACHERS AND BLACK STUDENTS

Schools and teachers cannot "solve" the dilemma of Black and White separation in this country, but they can be helpful in its solution within the classroom. To this end, teachers need a better knowledge and understanding of their own attitudes, the students, and the community and culture in which they work. They need to apply themselves systematically and patiently to the specific task of teaching certain students at given levels in a given type of community. They also need to search for improvement of the educational environment and examine the content of subject matter for appropriateness and inclusiveness of diverse personalities and backgrounds. According to Paley (1979), "The black child is Every Child. There is no activity useful only for the black child. There is no manner of speaking or unique approach or special environment required only for black children. There are only certain words and actions that cause all of us to cover up, and there are other words and actions that help us reveal ourselves to one another. The challenge in teaching is to find a way of communicating to each child the idea that his or her special quality is understood, is valued, and can be talked about. It is not easy, because we are influenced by the fears and prejudices, apprehensions and expectations, which have become a carefully hidden part of every one of us" (pp. xv–xvi).

White teachers and counselors can do the following to cope with the multicultural classroom:

· *Let the outside world in* and accept it for what it is; flow with the experiences and feelings that are there. Don't block out what you don't like or don't want to hear and see. Later, when you feel confident that you have separated fact from fallacy, it is best to stop negative thoughts that arouse negative emotions.

· *Listen to your own body signals* and confusion, or conflict, of mental messages. Do you tense up and blurt out emotional statements? What are you feeling and telling yourself when Black faces look up at you, or when children seem to make jokes about skin color? Is it funny? Is it improper? Is it tasteful? Are you trying to "mind-read" what others are thinking but not disclosing to you? Do you overreact when a Black child speaks perfect English, or gives a correct answer, or provides a different way of looking at something?

· *Ask yourself if you feel hurt,* misunderstood, or angry when a Black child rejects your overture of friendship or tells you that no White person can teach him or her anything. What are you telling yourself that causes you that feeling? How does it interfere with your seeing the child as an individual? Do you accept your own color? Do dark skin colors turn you off? turn you on? Do you ever think about it or discuss it with anyone? Blacks know they're Black and they want it recognized. Identification with "soul brothers" and "soul sisters" by Blacks often makes White children and teachers feel like outsiders. But the need to be seen as they are and to be accepted and valued as they are is important for any individual or group of individuals.

· *Ask yourself if you ever discuss* White, Black, or mixed skin color, and other physical characteristics that make people different and special, with children in the classroom. If not, why not? Try it—it might improve a rocky relationship between you and the children and among the children in a racially mixed room. Frank discussion of color differences is often avoided by adults because it might change the way things are. Power positions held by some Blacks and Whites in their respective communities depend on the separation between Blacks and Whites. Without this condition, their power and leadership base would disappear.

· *Ask yourself if you can rationally and clearly apply a sensible system of discipline* for Black children the same as for White children. If not, what's stopping you? Are you trying to imitate what you believe is Black dialect in order to be accepted by Black children? Do you want to be "pals" with children in order to get class cooperation? Do you have friendship needs? Is this your way of trying to get it? Can you be an objective participant-observer of the group dynamics of your class? Black students, for example, are sometimes observed by teachers to engage in noisier conversations than White students. According to Kochman (1981) and Paley (1979), Blacks have had more experience in separating real communication from noise. Loud talking to the White observer may sound like meaningless noise, but in the Black community loud talking may be used to get an individual to do something or to draw attention to something that others would be disinclined to notice. Are you distracted by loud talking? Can you separate real messages from noise?

■ NATIVE AMERICANS IN THE EDUCATIONAL SYSTEM

▲ ISSUES

The education of Native Americans has always been controversial in the history of North America. The issues basically revolve around the pressures of domination, value conflict, and self-determination. The U.S. government has never developed a realistic policy for the education of Native Americans that seems to be harmonious and effective for both the mainstream society and the various Native American tribes. The legal relationship between the U.S. government and the Native American nations further confounds the situation. Historically, few of the treaties have been upheld. But Native American tribal law has developed that accepts the notion of *legal* responsibility of the larger society. When Native Americans were placed on reservations, they lost their self-determination and control of their own education. Since the 1970s, various governmental and educational programs have increased self-determination. Native American people have had encouraging results. Increasing involvement by parents and Native American community groups in the curriculum is especially important, and freedom for innovation appears possible in many areas of the country. But, according to Antell (1978), there continues to be dissatisfaction at the state and local level: "Control is still the dominant issue, but curriculum, certification, achievement levels, dropout rates, allocation of resources, civil rights laws, affirmative action programs, Indian preference, and the lack of an overall state policy on Indian education are other areas of concern" (p. 61).

What Native Americans learn and how they learn is related in varying degrees to the following factors, according to Fuchs and Havighurst (1973):

· Geographic location
· Type of school (70% of the school-age Native American population is in

public schools and the remainder is scattered in Bureau of Indian Affairs day schools, Bureau of Indian Affairs boarding schools, and mission schools)
· Degree of contact between the Native American community and the surrounding community
· Distance from urban employment centers
· Degree of Native American ancestry
· Educational level of parents
· Language spoken in the home
· Proportion of non–Native Americans in the schools attended

▲ VERBAL AND NONVERBAL COMMUNICATION STYLES

Philips (1983) and Mahan and Criger (1977) have argued that understanding the communication style that is characteristic of individuals of a given culture and managing appropriate classroom communication patterns are essential for educators who want to become more effective with minority students. Philips's study of White and Native American children in first- and sixth-grade classrooms reinforces the concept that communicative competence is best defined according to how individuals have been socialized. Depending upon the ratio of enculturation in mainstream society to enculturation in traditional Native American culture, Native American children will experience communication difficulties. These were some of Philips's general conclusions:

· All children are *similar* in their developmental sequence of growth on account of their common membership in the human species.
· Though all share the influence of mainstream culture, children are also *different* because of the early childhood socialization experienced in their specific cultural environment. Differences are related to general and specific cultural knowledge, dialect, and codes for appropriate response to the talk of others.
· Native American students may experience *communicative interference* that is related to deferential attention given by the teacher to other children or when the teacher regulates the talk flow of Native American students.
· *Both* students and teachers often *fail to comprehend* each other's talk style. Evidence is students' reluctance to engage in classroom discussions or willingness to participate only with other students of similar background. Likewise, the teacher shows, by repeating what he or she has just said or by differentially indicating to minority students that what they have said is not acceptable or not understandable, that he or she does not hear the students speaking.

The desire for reward and recognition is basic to all human beings and the opportunity for reinforcement plays a major role in any classroom interaction. Both teacher and students, through careful listening and verbal and nonverbal recognition of *all* others in the classroom, can increase the likelihood of participation in the learning experience.

■ FUNCTIONAL ROLES OF COUNSELORS IN A MULTICULTURAL EDUCATIONAL ENVIRONMENT

The work of trained counselors is most appropriate, meaningful, and effective when it applies and generalizes the counselors' understandings of the fundamentals of the counseling process to all aspects of the personal, intellectual, and social development of students within the total school or college environment. Although counseling is traditionally viewed within the confines of the one-to-one or group relationship, the principles underlying the counseling process have very real application for all aspects of the counselor's job. Thus, counselors who seek to integrate counseling principles in their total work endeavor will find greater clarity and meaning in what they do and more effective results in helping students. They may function in any or all of the following roles:

· *Intercultural communicator.* Shows and shares cultural awareness. Fosters intergroup understanding. Facilitates cross-cultural communication and works against alienation.

· *Student advocate.* Understands and interprets the needs, experiences, and situations of students in order to protect them from unresponsive, unrealistic, unreasonable, or harmful aspects of the educational environment.

· *Crisis intervenor.* Takes thoughtful risks in doing what is necessary and best for student development outside the educational environment.

· *Developmental facilitator.* Creates and applies experiences and activities that will help students with issues that most share in common. Some concerns that many students confront are starting school and college, peer relations and pressures, parent and family relations, male-female relations, parenting, generational conflicts, and self-concept. Some concerns faced by youth are also reflective of current issues in the society at large, such as the responsible use of drugs and issues related to abortion.

· *Information processor.* Screens, interprets, and uses subjective information and objective standardized data about students in ways that emphasize their motivations, strengths, and resources in balance with their weaknesses, problems, and points for improvement.

· *Career guide.* Uses and applies reality testing, appropriate role models, and nonbiased information with an optimistic attitude toward assisting students in expanding their possibilities of attaining career goals that best fulfill their personalities and potentials.

· *Interpreter of the bureaucratic system.* Assists in decoding the social, political, and class factors embedded both in the educational system and in the society at large. Functions as a type of intermediary who emphasizes the needs of individuals and cultural groups in an impersonal system. At times, he or she will seek to effect change in the system when administrative needs take precedence over individual needs.

· *In-service staff consultant.* Interprets immediate and long-range needs and experiences of students in interaction with staff goals through consultative counseling with individual staff members and staff groups.

■ SUMMARY

1. The mass production of education in the United States has led to specialized agencies that have become separated from the rest of society.

2. The general school- and college-age population is declining, but Asian, Black, Hispanic, and Native-American populations are increasing. Members of minority groups receive less formal education at both the school and college levels. Over 8% of the general population is bilingual; those citizens whose usual language is Japanese, Portuguese, Italian, Korean, Greek, Spanish, or Chinese report difficulty with English.

3. What should be included in formal schooling and how it should be taught have been perennial issues facing the educational system in the United States.

4. Current issues of education center on meeting individual and group needs of culturally diverse populations in an ever-changing society and economy.

5. The basic goals of counselors are to help personalize the learning process to meet individual needs, to facilitate human relations principles within cultural diversity, to identify student resources, and to help remove barriers to learning.

6. Desegregation of student populations continues to be an issue, especially in urban areas. Busing of students as a remedy has been deemphasized.

7. Formal integration has not resulted in informal (social) integration of students. Mutual respect, equal status, and self-esteem among students are educational goals toward which counselors and teachers can work in the educational environment.

8. Economic disadvantages limit the learning resources available to individual students and their accommodation to the middle-class learning environment. Understanding the extent of poverty conditions, interpreting special needs, providing a consistent environment, and valuing students are basic goals for effective counselors, administrators, and teachers.

9. Educational disadvantages limit the learning resources available to individual students and their accommodation to the middle-class learning environment. Understanding the students' cultural background of experiences, using teaching methods that take into consideration individual readiness, and providing an authentic and relevant curriculum that ensures basic skills are major goals for effective counselors, administrators, and teachers.

10. The educational system will have problems when formal segregation, isolation, and alienation are present in the general society, when there is

informal segregation in schools, and when cultural diversity goes unrecognized.

11. There will be communication problems for school personnel and learning problems for students when cultural differences are viewed only as deficiencies, when language differences are viewed only as deficits, when presumptions of intellectual inferiority are based on cultural group identity or membership, when individual potential goes unrecognized, when individual personality traits are distorted or overgeneralized according to cultural group identity or membership, and when negative self-concept is simplistically related to feelings of success and failure.

12. Teachers are especially susceptible to three types of defense mechanisms: blaming the culture, blaming the student, or blaming themselves. White teachers often face the national dilemma of Black and White separation within the classroom; getting in touch with and understanding their own attitudes, the student, the community, and the culture are ways to improve the situation.

13. Special issues in the education of Native Americans revolve around the pressures of domination, value conflict, and self-determination. Verbal and nonverbal communication styles are culture-bound and both students and teachers are often seen as not comprehending each other.

14. Counselors who work in multicultural education settings perform eight functional roles: (1) intercultural communicator, (2) student advocate, (3) crisis intervenor, (4) developmental facilitator, (5) information processor, (6) career guide, (7) interpreter of the bureaucratic system, and (8) in-service staff consultant.

CHAPTER

WORK AND CAREER DEVELOPMENT

The range of topics covered in this chapter includes (1) the nature of the work ethic and quality of life in the United States, (2) functions of the economic system and current changes in the economy, (3) how economic trends and conditions affect work and career development, (4) the variation in employment and career patterns among culturally diverse populations and factors that affect variation, (5) techniques used in relational counseling, (6) the need for theories and practices that are relevant to the psychological development process of minorities, and (7) equal opportunity/affirmative action practices in the culturally diverse workplace.

The goal for vocational counselors for many decades has been to help people find occupational and educational opportunities that would bring satisfaction and security. The counseling process was fairly uniform and adequate, and its aim was to guide clients by these principles:

· Know yourself.
· Learn about occupations.
· Compare your self-knowledge with knowledge about occupations; make a choice according to the "best match."
· Expect to spend a lifetime of employment in your chosen occupation.

Since the end of World War II, however, and as a result of the social and economic changes over the last 30 years, the conventional one-life/one-career imperative is viewed as less possible than it once was—and not necessarily desirable (Sarason, 1977, pp. 123–164). The conditions of work and of society have also led to the formulation of new outlooks, concepts, and approaches that can be used by counselors to help people find satisfaction and security during their span of life. *Career development* in today's society is more appropriately seen as a complex personal process in interaction with cultural, political, and economic forces over a lifetime of experiences. It is an ongoing process of using self-knowledge in harmony with the *self-in-the-situation* and in relation to others. *Career* is best understood as the expression of personality through the total pattern of jobs held during a worker's lifetime. Planning a career that allows for personal expression and making decisions that might facilitate personal expression require continuing experiences with the occupational life of a changing society. Self-expression is also possible through activities and experiences outside formal employment; for many Americans, these are as important as the job itself and provide as much satisfaction.

■ THE STATUS OF WORK AND THE WORK ETHIC IN TODAY'S SOCIETY

People in all cultures have worked, but the valuing of and motives for work also reflect the nature of a culture at particular times in history. Biological survival has always been a primary motive, but social, economic, and religious beliefs, values, and practices have also influenced the attitudes that people have toward work.

▲ HISTORICAL ATTITUDES TOWARD WORK

Is work painful drudgery, or is work self-fulfilling and satisfying? Philosophical differences on the question have existed for centuries. Ancient Hebrew tradition viewed labor as punishment for moral transgressions, but work was also seen as a positive act of redemption that restored one's relationship with God and from which came personal fulfillment and satisfaction. The Greeks and Romans believed that work was labor and not meant for intellectuals or citizens, but fit only for slaves who toiled from sunrise to sunset. Some occupations were also accorded higher status than others because they were valued for their life-sustaining qualities; thus, farming was not viewed as a "curse" by ancient Greeks (Borow, 1973, p. 28).

The beginnings of the early Christian church and the Reformation gave renewed emphasis to the Judean tradition of self-fulfillment through work as a moral obligation. The moral, or ethical, Christian principle of work was part of a spiritual pattern of life: "honest labor" was seen as an opportunity and a challenge to use the bountiful resources provided by God. Work thus conceived was a privilege, and each person would be guided, or called, to use his or her creative abilities for the good of all people. Work was not thought of as drudgery, boredom, or obligation. If work was viewed in this manner, it was taken to be an indication of human imperfection in striving to express the Christian commitment.

▲ THE PROTESTANT ETHIC TODAY

The Christian value that is placed on work has become secularized since its transition from the religious and social Reformation movement started by Martin Luther in Europe during the 1500s. Through the Protestant teachings of the Calvinists and Puritans in the New World, it continues to influence the North American culture in complex ways. Slocum (1974) notes that the work imperative has also been called *the Puritan ethic*, "probably because of the influence of the Puritans on the development of industries in New England" (pp. 19–20). The Protestant ethic, or the Protestant work ethic, has shaped the basic framework of thought for our economic, political, educational, and social systems. It exerts so much influence on the totality of the culture that, on the one hand, it is rarely thought about and its values seldom questioned. On the other hand, some people believe that the work ethic no longer offers adequate explanation of contemporary motives for work, or that it has lost the moral importance and usefulness that it once had (Severinsen, 1979). Borrow (1973) states that "its former universality has diminished in a pluralistic society whose divergent ethnic and social class groupings attach differential values to institutional roles" (p. 28). Other viewpoints hold that the mainstream work ethic has not basically changed but is simply expressed and refocused in new ways more conducive to harmony with what is still believed to be an ideal pattern of life, both for the individual and for the group standard of living (Fredrickson, 1982, pp. 9–10).

For Americans, World War II was in many ways a great leveler of people because of their common stake in national survival. People of diverse cultural backgrounds for the first time had an opportunity to see and share real problems and purposes. The great changes that occurred in American society, and in the culture, following World War II have led to speculation about the actual influence that values have on work. In the mid-1950s, Spindler (1963, pp. 136–147), for example, described *traditional* values in contrast with what he saw as *emergent* values. Table 7-1 illustrates his conceptualization.

The influence of traditional values on personal motives for work was also studied by Wollack, Goodale, Wijting, and Smith (1971) with industrial workers, government workers, and insurance company employees. For their purposes, the researchers developed the Survey of Work Values to measure the degree to which people's attitudes toward work are based on the Protestant work ethic. Examination of their two categories for their six subscales also reveals the potential conflict that could occur when "internal" locus of values is not commensurate with "external" locus of values:

Intrinsic Rewards	*Extrinsic Rewards*
Pride in Work	Attitudes toward Earnings
Job Involvement	Social Status of Job
Activity Preference	Upward Striving (Advancement)

The general sentiment of the culture is that work, or some kind of satisfying and productive activity, is both the means of achieving personal worth and also the means of maintaining or reaching the standard of living to

TABLE 7-1 Changing Values in Mainstream American Culture	
Traditional Values	*Emergent Values*
1. *Puritan morality*: Respectability, thrift, self-denial, and sexual restraint are prized.	1. *Relativistic moral attitudes*: Absolutes in right and wrong are questionable; morality is what the group thinks is right.
2. *Work-success ethic*: Successful people work hard to become successful; anyone can get to the top if he or she tries hard enough.	2. *Sociability*: One should like people and get along well with them.
3. *Individualism and independence*: The individual is sacred and always more important than the group.	3. *Conformity to the group*: Group harmony is the ultimate goal; everything is relative to the group.
4. *Achievement orientation*: Success is a constant goal; there is no resting on past glories.	4. *Consideration for others*: Everything one does should be done with regard for others and their feelings.
5. *Future-time orientation*: The future, not the past or even the present, is most important.	5. *"Hedonistic," present-time orientation*: No one can tell what the future will hold, therefore one should enjoy the present.

SOURCE: Adapted from *Education and Culture* by G. Spindler (Ed.) 1963, pp. 136–147.

which the society has become accustomed or for which it strives. Goodwin (1973), Gurin and Epps (1975), and Gurin, Gurin, Lao, and Beattie (1969) have noted that self-respect and personal satisfaction are usually identified with some aspect of a traditional work ethic, regardless of socioeconomic class status or racial identity. Brenner and Tomkiewicz (1982) found that Black college graduates in business attached more emphasis to many traditional mainstream work values than did their White counterparts.

▲ VARIATIONS IN ATTITUDES TOWARD A WORK ETHIC

Individually, of course, people do not all subscribe to the traditional work ethic to the same degree or in the same way.

> Voltaire acknowledged that "work alone makes life bearable, keeps away boredom, vice, and need."
> Chinese proverbs say, "work with the rising sun, rest with the setting sun"; "slow work produces fine goods."

Thomas Edison believed that "work is a better cure for wishing."

Henry Ford claimed that "life is work."

An African (Yoruba) proverb says, "work is the medicine for poverty."

Rolling Thunder said, "These days people want everything in a hurry and they want it without effort. They miss a lot of understanding because they don't want to work for it."

Einstein stated, "I do the thing which my own nature drives me to do."

Mark Twain felt that "work consists of whatever a body is *obliged* to do, and play consists of whatever a body is not obliged to do."

Variations in the meaning of work can be found among different communities, between rural and urban residents, and among people who live in different geographical regions of the country. Variations in meaning and emphasis can also be attributed to ethnic group membership. For example, the respect of Asian Americans and recently arrived Asians for learning and achievement is generally recognized in the United States. Asian-American students generally score above average in mathematics on the Scholastic Aptitude Test, and the college enrollment rate for Chinese and Japanese between the ages of 18 and 24 is higher than for other groups (Arbeiter, 1984). Quoted in *Time* magazine ("Confucian Work Ethic," 1983), sociologist William Liu says, "In the Confucian ethic which permeates the cultures of China, Japan, Viet Nam, and Korea, scholastic achievement is the only way of repaying the infinite debt to parents, of showing filial piety" (p. 52). According to Sue (1980, pp. 186–189), the behavior and achievement of sons and daughters are considered a reflection on the family. Parental expectations can create unbearable pressure, and failure to uphold them can lead to feelings of shame, guilt, and depression and a sense of having dishonored the family. Because the importance of education is so exalted in Asian culture, many American educators find Asian Americans to be willing students. But generalization about Asian students, risks oversimplification and may create stereotypes that become burdensome in the future.

People also differ in their attitudes toward the work ethic according to their occupational roles. Research suggests that people who prefer occupations dealing with concrete things and physical activity tend to support the Protestant ethic more than do people who have theoretical, artistic, and abstract interests (Mirels & Garrett, 1971). The results of a survey of graduate students in rehabilitation counseling (Thomas, Carter, & Britton, 1982) indicated that the students supported intrinsic values of the Protestant work ethic more than extrinsic values. An earlier study (Thomas, Britton, & Kravetz, 1974) suggested that practicing rehabilitation counselors strongly subscribed to most aspects of the Protestant work ethic.

▲ WORK AND CONTEMPORARY NEEDS

According to Maccoby and Terzi (1981), there are distinguishable work ethics that coincide generally with social and economic transitions in American culture:

- *Protestant ethic* (spiritual calling, hard work, moral obligation)
- *Craft ethic* (self-sufficiency and self-employment, pride in work, social obligation)
- *Entrepreneurial ethic* (self-initiative, getting ahead, taking opportunities and risks)
- *Career ethic* (planned success, ambition, upward mobility, financial reward, organizational loyalty)
- *Self-development ethic* (personal growth, self-fulfillment, and enjoyment of work as a total way of life)

Zunker (1990, p. 71) notes that emerging new values may be congruent with changes in the broader culture, but that managerial and organizational practices, often designed for a different era, may not be compatible with the emerging work ethic.

Winters (1972) has indicated that concepts underlying the work ethic need broadening for industrial workers who experience boredom and alienation in their repetitious work. Gartner and Riessman (1974) have emphasized the movement toward a new work ethic that would humanize the work of blue- and white-collar workers: "Efforts toward this end would include reducing the boredom, routinization, and fragmentation of the work process; modifying the traditional industrial discipline with its hierarchical organization and lack of autonomy for individual workers; and making work more meaningful in general" (p. 563). Deming (1986) and Wool (1976) have interpreted worker attitudes to show that the organization of work and the work institution itself are inadequate in meeting human needs, and that new criteria are needed to define the human quality in work. In this regard, the activity of *quality circles*—small groups of co-workers who meet regularly to identify, analyze, and solve work-related problems (Dewar, 1979; Pavilon, 1983)—has been found useful in mass-production industry for encouraging participative management and improving the quality of work.

A change in national priorities is also needed to increase the quantity of available work so that more Americans can participate in the movement toward quality of work. Quality of work (self-respect, personal fulfillment, individual recognition) for all Americans is possible only insofar as the society values and provides a structure for fair and equal access to the available work.

People today want more from their work and from life than they are getting (Kamerman & Kahn, 1987). Implications for career counseling can be found in the following examples of personal and social desires of most Americans:

- Improved socioeconomic status
- Elevated self-esteem
- Freedom to choose personal lifestyles
- Opportunity for significant relations with others
- Increased time for leisure
- Freedom of personal and geographic movement
- Development of a secure psychological identity

It is doubtful that a society would survive if all its people were totally selfish, or "self-regarding," in meeting only personal needs without providing for those of others. Neither would it be feasible if all the people were completely benevolent and altruistic, or "other-regarding." According to Brandt (1980), the moral or ethical system that works most beneficially and most practically for all people is one that will be supported by *both* self- and other-regarding people.

■ ECONOMIC SYSTEMS

All groups of people establish some organization, or system, to make their survival possible. This section surveys the importance of economies in cultures and the advent of complex economic systems.

▲ FUNCTION

The economic system of a nation structures the physical and social environment so that people can maintain themselves. It also provides the means whereby people can express themselves to one another through the work that they do. All people in all cultures throughout history have faced the same economic problems: how to choose what goods and services to make available for themselves. Survival would be impossible without some kind of meaningful organization for the distribution of resources. Choice and decision making are always necessary because what is wanted is scarce; the history of humanity is a struggle against scarcity and toward economizing what is available. The less complex societies, for example, often divide the food obtained from a hunt according to long-standing tradition. Other societies might provide a central authority that makes the decisions about what should be produced and for whom. No entire nation or group of people has enough resources or money to get or to buy everything they want; thus, all people must choose the best possible way to use their resources and money. It is a never-ending process in a free and productive society, for the range of existing opportunity allows for more choices and the potential to create something that becomes desirable in the culture. The range of human achievement and the available choices have steadily increased over hundreds of years due to human ingenuity, scientific and technological inventiveness, and the quality of life that people might desire. Figure 7-1 shows that in ancient times, when living was basically on a subsistence level, few choices were available in comparison with the present. The dips in the *potential* and *actual* lines show the decline in ingenuity and freedom for most people during the Middle Ages.

According to Barkley (1977), full economic potential may not be reached because

> society is inefficient and uses wasteful production processes. Or it may mean
> that society is in a recession and, because of a temporary failure of the

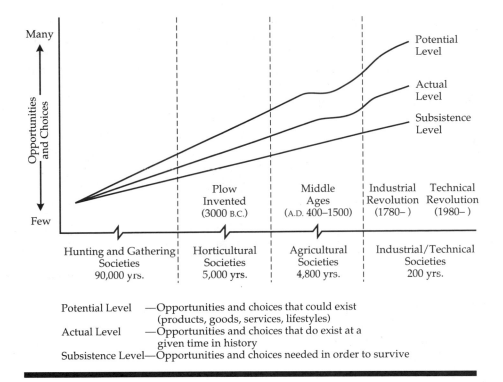

Potential Level   —Opportunities and choices that could exist
                     (products, goods, services, lifestyles)
Actual Level   —Opportunities and choices that do exist at a
                     given time in history
Subsistence Level—Opportunities and choices needed in order to survive

FIGURE 7-1   Opportunities and choices over 100,000 years of human existence.

SOURCE: Adapted from *Introduction to Macroeconomics* by Paul W. Barkley, p. 32. Copyright © 1977 by Harcourt Brace Jovanovich, Inc. Adapted by permission of the publisher.

economic system, has many unemployed resources. Another possible explanation is that society consciously chooses to operate at a slow pace, gaining leisure but sacrificing some opportunities that are potentially available. . . . Generally speaking, the world's developed nations have chosen to live close to the maximum attainable level of living. Individuals in these nations have a wide range of choice, and as science and technology have unfolded that range has increased. . . . The less developed countries have struggled to rise above the subsistence level, but even so the people of Bangladesh, Chad, Niger, and Burma have very few choices. They live much as their ancestors did—close to the level of bare subsistence. (pp. 32–33)

▲ INFLUENCE ON INDIVIDUAL CAREER DEVELOPMENT

The satisfaction of the needs and cultural wants of people is what sustains an economic system. The people in any culture must economize their scarce resources and provide a system for distributing those resources to ensure survival. Thus, an *economic system* is defined as the relationship among various components of an economy. The *components* include the consumers, the producers and service providers, and the government, all of which interact according to the society's framework of laws and customs. All these human and institutional components need or want something and compete to get what they need or want. Although the workings of the economic system might appear remote from the immediate realities of clients who have career decisions to make, they are interrelated. The relative freedom of choice to determine one's personal life career, as well as the limits and ranges of possible decisions about occupational work and life experience that will enhance one's development, both affects and is affected by the economic system of the nation.

▲ INFLUENCE ON INDIVIDUAL NEEDS AND WANTS

Modern society has created a psychologically new human being for whom work, employment, economic production, productivity, and product consumption in the marketplace have become the ends of life itself. Changes in cultural attitudes and outlook have occurred over hundreds of years concurrently with differentiation in the society (mass production, technological innovation, specialized work). People have always exchanged goods or services among themselves, but for many, profit, material accumulation, and material status are now objects for providing basic psychological security and personal self-fulfillment. Regarding material gain as a worthy pursuit has become a commonly accepted cultural attitude and behavior in U.S. society. Although possession of property or cash does not in itself equal quality of life, it is highly sought after and has become both a means and an end of life. The fact that acquisition of wealth generates the desire for more wealth is probably a consequence of cultural reinforcement; the process is continuous and thus has value in and of itself. The endless supply of material objects that can be gained with money is valued but produces progressively less satisfaction or only short-term usefulness and satisfaction for the possessor. Producing wealth, an abstraction, from nature has become a value object of the culture. The problems of human satisfaction are complex and related to basic human needs and acquired wants in interaction with what the culture has defined as important for security, status, and even self-esteem (Ferguson, 1980, pp. 323–360).

▲ THE FREE ENTERPRISE SYSTEM

The economic system established by a nation provides the means for allocating resources so that the people might get what they want. The process of choice is a part of the culture and the organization of the society, but it always takes place within limits. The economic system of North America and certain other areas of the world is the free enterprise system, or the market system: the interaction of the buyer and the seller in the marketplace determines what will be sold and at what price. The degree of influence of the government, or central authority, has always been controversial in the free economic system, but some governmental action is required to fill the void where the open system is lacking. Thus, the intervention of government is often necessary to relieve problems such as unemployment, unclean air and water, inadequate housing, inflation, recession, and depression, management of the money supply, and to provide for the common good by means such as police and fire protection, military forces and military hardware, recreational areas, health, and social welfare.

▲ THE DEVELOPMENT OF THE ECONOMIC SYSTEM IN THE UNITED STATES

Both the way society was organized and the people's way of life in Western Europe changed drastically during the Industrial Revolution in the eighteenth century. Huge mechanized, specialized factories increased output that was worth far more than the resources needed to run them. Specialization meant that people did only those things that they could do best and traded their products for the products of others. The economic system that emerged was characterized by a continuous flow of economic activity. Social lives were changed because families no longer needed to labor for food, clothing, and shelter. In a highly advanced industrial country the interdependence of the various parts of the economy and the high level of specialization are necessary for a smooth flow of trading. Choices in one place may yield bad results in another.

● INDUSTRIAL MASS PRODUCTION

When Henry Ford introduced the first assembly line in 1913, industrial production was again revolutionized. Less time and less skilled labor were needed to complete a product, and the result was greater profit for the manufacturer and less costly goods that became widely available to consumers. The great mass of industrial workers that was created needed less training, skill, and experience, since each worker contributed only a small portion to the finished product. Industrial management became identified with a smaller force of trained, better educated supervisors and white-collar workers. Prior to World War I, minority-group workers were more likely to be employed in agriculture and did not participate in the industrial system as did majority-group workers. Ninety percent of the African-American population at the time was located in the South and the great majority of Hispanics were in the Southwest. Until World Wars I and II brought labor shortages, they had minimal representation as mass production workers in the industrial workplace. In addition, minority-group involvement in labor and the industrial movement often met with resistance from majority-group workers (Meier & Rudwick, 1979).

● FROM INDUSTRY TO HIGH TECHNOLOGY

The pattern of industrial production has changed significantly during the past 30 years through what has generally been called the new technology and, most recently, "high technology." We are in the midst of the Technical Revolution. Sophisticated machinery has replaced simpler tools, and computerized systems and industrial robots are replacing manual labor; microelectronic devices and processes affect almost all aspects of society. The new technology and high technology have increased the need for more highly educated and specially trained workers, and mental power rather than machine power becomes more in demand. Mental power, or ordinary mental capabilities, may also be displaced at a slow pace by artificial intelligence. According to Leontief (1983), "Over the next 30–40 years many people will be displaced, creating massive problems of unemployment and dislocation" (p. 1). The changes created by high technology will also necessitate a reevaluation of the role of human labor. Work opportunity for more people may arise as a result of shorter work weeks, flexible working-time arrangements, and longer vacations, but cultural beliefs and morality associate reward and status with productivity and income. The most pessimistic outlook predicts a floating population of permanently unemployed. Social friction is likely unless government effort solves the problem of permanently dislocated labor and the fair distribution of income.

It is expected that the number of industrial mass-production workers will continue to drop in the 1990s, while the number of high-technology workers will increase. Included in this shift will be a greater demand for technicians who service high-technology products. One could visualize a future in which important equipment or appliances would be serviced before the trouble occurs. A medical apparatus, business computer, home furnace, or even a refrigerator, for example, might be programmed to signal a possible breakdown through sensors that detect the defect. This information could be relayed to a service center and the service technician (craftsperson) would appear at the place before anyone was even aware of the potential trouble.

The enormous increase in the range of information-collecting systems and public data networks will increase the need for people with the skills to use the systems. Communications skills will also be needed by service workers who must explain and interpret complex changes to others. These workers—information processors—will likely be necessary in diverse occupations and at different levels: for instance, computer programmers, bank customer service representatives who explain the multitude of money transaction systems, automobile service expeditors who tell customers about the technical trouble in their cars, and college career options counselors who advise students about the shifts occurring in a fast-changing society and in the curricula of college programs.

Careers of the future will show increased emphasis on quality of workers, replacing the notion of "hired hands" to perform menial tasks. The economic development of the *person* will have as much significance as the economic development of material resources (Deming, 1986). The increasing importance of the quality of human resources demands more education and training for specialized work and retraining for emerging occupations that replace obsolete ones. The heightened pace means that individuals can expect to develop new talents and to perform in a number of different occupational roles during a lifetime.

● TECHNICAL LITERACY

Computer and technical literacy as another "language system" in North America seems to be taking on importance as a possible factor in personal mobility and may be necessary for survival by the year 2000. The lack of financial resources among some school systems and some individuals may limit the use of computers to only certain groups.

The impact of computerized learning systems and computerized career development systems also has very real implications for the personal advancement of people. Technical changes have also influenced the work of counselors. Beginning with Tiedeman's Information System for Vocational Decisions (1967, 1968), many computer-based career information and instructional systems have emerged. According to Tiedeman (1984):

> These are now sufficiently numerous and diverse to appear as three distinct generations. However, at this moment, no operable system yet incorporates the reflexive principle of deciding and of simultaneously apprehending and accommodating one's personal decisional processes which Tiedeman . . . and colleagues prototypically devised as the not now operating Information System for Vocational Decisions. When interactive decisional systems advance to heuristic capability for illuminating one's informing process, one's formal inside procedure of accommodation, computer systems will have revolutionized counseling. Counselors will then have to go far beyond providing facts/data and urging decisions.

Counseling and learning through the use of computers is a challenge for counselors who seek to expand their services. Most everyone faces situations where important decisions must be made or self-understanding is needed and, as Tiedeman (1984) pointed out, decision-making and self-discovery will be greatly enhanced when computer technology is fully capable of evaluating the feedback of one's own thoughts and questions.

The fact that much of computer interaction is individually centered also leads to the possibility of "self-counseling." In this scenario, the counselor of the future might be a technician who provides clients with appropriate programmed material that translates the meanings from the broader society according to ways that are best understood and that can be used in the counseling interaction and in guidance programs (Rayman & Bowlsbey, 1977; Rayman, Bryson, & Bowlsbey, 1978). Again, the need exists for expertise in cross-cultural input—both for the *content* of programmed materials and the appropriate and sequential *format* through which it is presented. The direct intervention of a human service provider with the recipients of the service can be diminished, but it can never be entirely divorced from the process. The use of cross-cultural expertise for programming of authentic material that is suitable for culturally diverse clients seems analogous to what is now common practice in the use of teacher aides, counselor aides, peer facilitators, and linguistic interpreters. The impact of technology on career guidance services emphasizes the need for continuous planning to meet client needs. Two basic questions can be kept in mind: (1) What are the emerging trends? and (2) How might technology alter the counselor's work environment and client interventions (Cianni-Surridge, 1983)?

▲ ECONOMIC GROWTH AND OPPORTUNITIES

The human satisfaction and pleasure once gained from producing and seeing a complete, finished product are less possible in today's automated society than they once were. However, people can continue to get varying degrees of satisfaction through work itself if the economic rewards are equal, if progress and advancement are fair, and the activity gives personal satisfaction. Economists, sociologists, and others often point out that statistics collected only yesterday have little meaning for evaluating the economic and occupational situation of a society today. But a future picture of the North American economy and the economies of other developed nations of the world is often presented from one of two viewpoints:

1. The society is in a transition stage and the new potential is in a technology-driven industry. Like the Industrial Revolution that previously changed people's lives, the Technical Revolution will also produce radical changes. The traditional assumption is that the introduction of new and cheaper products—through automation and mass production—will bring about new types of job opportunities and increased spending; standard of living, as traditionally defined, is thus dependent on productivity. New manufacturing approaches that use computer systems and robots, however, have eliminated many employment opportunities and the need to train workers in assembly line skills. For example, "flexible manufacturing," in which different products are mass produced on the same assembly line, can be accomplished by adjusting the same devices to work on different products.

2. The President's Commission for a National Agenda for the Eighties (Horner, 1980) predicted that the optimal economic growth for the advanced U.S. industrial society would be much slower in the twenty-year period from 1980 to 2000. This "prediction" implied a shift toward *quality* of human living and away from *quantity* of product consumption as an indicator of standard of living. Although indicators of growth and productivity in the 1980s and into the 1990s have confirmed a widespread sense of uncertainty about the economic future, some measures of the quality of living, as reported by the U.S. Census Bureau (1991b), have not improved:

· The distribution of income has become more unequal over time, with the poor become poorer and the rich becoming richer. In 1989, the poorest fifth of all families shared 3.8% of the national income, while the richest fifth shared 46.8%.

· The 19.6% of all U.S. children under age 18 who live in poverty is the highest rate of any industrialized nation in the world.

· The number of persons below the poverty level has remained about the same from 1980 to 1990.

The equation of ever-higher standards of living with ever-higher levels of consumption was set many generations ago, when the economic system was created, and periods of rapid and sustained growth have led to improved conditions for the majority of Americans. The concept has produced both psychological and material rewards: immediate success, status, and pleasure are readily gained through plentiful work, access to higher education, home ownership, new cars, and other tangible and symbolic evidences of prosperity. However, patterns of expectations and values shift when a desired standard of living has been achieved, and people also desire more services. In addition, the increasing proportion of older citizens has resulted in demand for services over products. In 1900, three out of ten workers were employed in service occupations, whereas today the majority of the labor force are service workers (U.S. Department of Labor, 1980). The consumption of material goods has been partially replaced by a desire and concern for quality of life. Many Americans are now motivated toward health, meaningful self-development experiences, interpersonal relations, and communication with each other. The shift in the economy from an industrial production base to a service orientation also changes the consumption patterns and slows economic growth. The growing belief that there is a psychological limit to pleasure gained from material consumption will result in serious problems for those who are unemployed and frustration for many Americans in the multicultural society who have not yet experienced opportunity in the job market or the increase in standard of living that they had come to expect.

■ HOW ECONOMIC TRENDS AND CONDITIONS AFFECT WORK AND CAREER DEVELOPMENT

Economic realities and conditions created by fluctuations in the business cycle, trends in population growth, technological change, and governmental legislation and objectives all affect the whole cultural system in which people live and work. These macrolevel factors also affect the level and movement of personal accomplishment that is possible for an individual over a lifetime. Most counselors seem to be oriented primarily toward assisting their clients to comprehend and develop their inner resources, but the career development process is most complete when clients consider and anticipate the most visible macrolevel trends. Timely career information that includes knowledge of economic and societal conditions can be integrated with a client's personal incentives or potential goals. Among the trends and conditions that both counselors and clients need to consider and anticipate are these:

· The typical workers of today's generation will hold a greater number of *different jobs* than did the workers of preceding generations.

· The *rapid changes in demands* for specific skills in the job market in relation to the supply of workers often makes educational and occupational decisions difficult.

· The interaction among important components of the socioeconomic system causes *changes in the system.* Constant access to information and education is needed so that effective adjustments can be made to ensure continued personal satisfaction and security. One recurring interaction is the competition between military spending and social service spending, which affects when, how, and where huge sums of money are to be expended and what and where jobs will be available.

· *Accelerated technological and scientific developments* in a complex society have also decreased the period of time that workers have for adjusting to occupational changes. Rash decisions are often made by people thrown out of work because the jobs for which they were trained are no longer needed. Mass migrations of workers from the Frostbelt states to the Sunbelt states in the early 1980s, for example, cost many the resources that normally provide support, such as family, friends, and familiar surroundings.

· The *stress and insecurity* that accompany coping, constant changes, and adjustment intensify the need for new and better ways to maintain psychological, emotional, and physical well-being. Periods of economic inflation, recession, and depression all contribute to psychological problems (Amundson & Borgen, 1982). For example, personal self-doubt arising from severe competition for the limited number of desirable jobs and advancements that one has come to expect is amplified when the economy has slower growth. For many minority-group members, self-doubt, based on realistic views of disadvantages in competition for jobs and income, is an ever-present condition. Resentment and tension also build between socioeconomic classes of people when one person's gain is another's loss. Many middle-class employees, such as unionized blue-collar workers, technicians, clerical and retail sales workers, and professionals, have experienced disproportionate loss of earnings and jobs by comparison with their group as a whole. Brenner (1973, pp. 157–160) has pointed out that whenever the unemployment rate rises, so do the suicide rate, the number of admissions for mental health care, and the number of deaths from heart ailments. A more slowly growing economy also likely leads to income reversals for the poor. In addition, there is concern about whether the society can continue to maintain basic social welfare programs, such as aid to families and the educationally and economically disadvantaged, and entitlement programs, such as social security and health care for the aged. The emphasis on social issues in previous years (freedom of speech, right to vote, equal justice) appears to have shifted toward debate over economic issues in the 1980s and 1990s.

· An individual's *psychological view* of rapid changes in the society is potentially either positively or negatively oriented. When broad changes occur in the society, they offer the certain opportunity for new and different expression of individual potentialities and choices over a lifetime. As Sarason (1977, pp. 235–252) points out, career change can be attributed to positive reasons, such as desire for new challenges and stimulation; however, if the pattern of change is related to great frequency of job change, it may reflect personal dissatisfaction rather than self-challenge. Krantz (1977, pp. 165–188) has discussed the notion of "radical" career change as the search for a new life; it is one response to life situations that any of us might face. Thus, radical change in career pattern is not necessarily seen as the function of a "personal problem." The attitudes that a person assumes toward change can influence his or her career goals; they also have important implications for how counselors themselves conceptualize career development—whether from an adjustment viewpoint or from a growth viewpoint (Naisbitt, 1982; Naisbitt & Aburdene, 1990).

It is to be hoped that rapid change will not preclude the recognition of skills and personal qualities that people have acquired through work and life experiences and that continue to be valuable in diverse occupations. The identified skills and qualities that people bring to a prospective work situation can have as much value as past job titles or job descriptions. Demonstrating to a prospective employer that an applicant has integrity, is honest, dependable, conscientious, reliable, punctual, and cooperates with others—basic qualities that are important and transferable to most jobs—serves both the applicant and the employer. When individuals take the time to review their personal qualities in addition to their job skills, both to themselves and to prospective employers, the results help to strengthen self-esteem and confidence. The fact that rapid change has made some work outmoded does not have to mean that the human being is outmoded.

■ WORK AND CAREER DEVELOPMENT WITHIN CULTURAL DIVERSITY

A major aim of counselors who work with clients in the multicultural society is to understand the ever-changing conditions of the economy and work opportunities that generally influence the career development of all the people. In addition, they seek to understand—and develop a perspective that takes into consideration—cultural diversity in relation to employment and career development. What occupations do culturally diverse Americans engage in? Table 7-2 shows the distribution of employment by race/ethnic group and sex, as surveyed by the Equal Employment Opportunity Commission (1991).

TABLE 7-2 Employment in private industry by race/ethnic group/sex and by industry, United States, 1990.

Race/Ethnic Group/Sex[a]	Total	Officials and Managers	Professionals	Technicians	Sales Workers	Office and Clerical Workers	Craft Workers	Operatives	Laborers	Service Workers
				Participation Rate						
All employees	100.0%	100.0%	100.0%	100.0%	100.0%	100.0%	100.0%	100.0%	100.0%	100.0%
Male	53.9%	71.9%	52.0%	55.2%	42.9%	16.6%	89.4%	66.6%	65.6%	44.5%
Female	46.1%	28.1%	48.0%	44.8%	57.1%	83.4%	10.6%	33.4%	34.4%	55.5%
White	77.4%	89.9%	87.0%	81.0%	81.1%	76.9%	82.4%	71.1%	62.6%	60.2%
Male	42.4%	65.5%	45.9%	45.8%	35.5%	11.9%	74.6%	48.8%	41.1%	25.1%
Female	35.0%	24.4%	41.0%	35.2%	45.7%	64.9%	7.9%	22.3%	21.5%	35.1%
Minority	22.6%	10.1%	13.0%	19.0%	18.9%	23.1%	17.6%	28.9%	37.4%	39.8%
Male	11.5%	6.4%	6.1%	9.4%	7.4%	4.6%	14.8%	17.8%	24.4%	19.4%
Female	11.1%	3.7%	7.0%	9.6%	11.5%	18.5%	2.7%	11.1%	12.9%	20.4%
Black	12.7%	5.0%	5.2%	10.2%	10.7%	14.1%	9.2%	17.2%	19.6%	24.5%
Male	6.0%	2.9%	1.9%	4.1%	3.8%	2.5%	7.7%	10.4%	12.7%	10.9%
Female	6.7%	2.2%	3.3%	6.1%	6.9%	11.6%	1.6%	6.8%	6.9%	13.6%

TABLE 7-2 (*continued*)

Race/Ethnic Group/Sex[a]	Total	Officials and Managers	Professionals	Technicians	Sales Workers	Office and Clerical Workers	Craft Workers	Operatives	Laborers	Service Workers
Hispanic	6.7%	2.9%	2.5%	4.4%	5.9%	5.9%	6.3%	8.7%	14.8%	11.7%
Male	3.9%	2.0%	1.3%	2.7%	2.6%	1.3%	5.5%	5.8%	10.1%	6.8%
Female	2.8%	0.9%	1.2%	1.7%	3.3%	4.6%	0.8%	2.9%	4.7%	4.9%
Asian	2.8%	1.9%	5.1%	4.0%	1.9%	2.7%	1.5%	2.4%	2.3%	3.0%
Male	1.4%	1.3%	2.7%	2.3%	0.8%	0.7%	1.2%	1.3%	1.3%	1.5%
Female	1.3%	0.6%	2.3%	1.6%	1.1%	2.0%	0.3%	1.1%	1.0%	1.5%
Native American	0.5%	0.3%	0.3%	0.4%	0.4%	0.4%	0.6%	0.5%	0.6%	0.6%
Male	0.3%	0.2%	0.1%	0.3%	0.2%	0.1%	0.5%	0.3%	0.4%	0.3%
Female	0.2%	0.1%	0.1%	0.2%	0.2%	0.3%	0.1%	0.2%	0.2%	0.3%

SOURCE: Data from *1990 Report: Job Patterns for Minorities and Women in Private Industry*, by United States Equal Employment Opportunity Commission, 1991.
[a]Race/ethnic designations as used by the Equal Employment Opportunity Commission do not denote scientific definitions of anthropological origins; an employee may be included in the group to which he or she appears to belong, identifies with, or is regarded in the community as belonging.

▲ FACTORS AFFECTING EMPLOYMENT OF VARIOUS GROUPS

The under- and overrepresentation of minority groups in various occupational categories, as noted in Table 7-2, can be attributed to many factors present in the multicultural society. Some of the more obvious social conditions and personal issues that affect employment opportunities and occupational patterns are discussed in this section.

● EDUCATION

Many minority group members lack the education and skills essential for entry into certain occupations and necessary for occupational mobility and advancement. The quality and quantity of basic education that is received especially affects the range of occupational opportunity open to any individual. Deficiency in *basic* competencies (reading, writing, speaking, and computational skills) further impedes the acquisition of *advanced* education and skill training that are demanded by higher level occupations. One indicator of occupational potential is the percentage of baccalaureate degrees conferred by institutions of higher education to various groups, as shown in Table 7-3. Figures on recipients of doctorates are shown in Table 7-4.

Table 7-3, for example, shows some of the higher education trends for the sample that was studied at the time:

- Blacks tended to major *more* in education, business and management, and social sciences, and *less* in engineering and foreign languages.
- Hispanics tended to major *more* in education, foreign languages, and social sciences, and *less* in business and management and home economics.
- Asians tended to major *more* in biological sciences, business and management, and engineering, and *less* in education and public affairs and services.
- Native Americans tended to major *more* in education and social sciences, and *less* in business and management and foreign languages.

Among recipients of doctoral degrees, as shown in Table 7-4, women tended to be underrepresented in all fields, with the exception of education, but especially so in engineering, physical sciences, business and management, and life sciences. Most of the doctorates received by Native Americans were in education, and few were in business and management, engineering, and the professional fields (medicine, dentistry, and such). Asians received more of their doctorates in engineering, life sciences, and physical sciences. Most of the doctorates received by Blacks were in education and the social sciences, and few were in business and management and engineering. Most of the Hispanics, as a total group, received doctorates in education, life sciences, and social sciences, and fewer doctorates were in business and management, engineering, and professional fields.

● POVERTY

Access to education and employment opportunities is more difficult under poverty conditions. Developing a career can be expensive, and low-income people have fewer resources that might enable them to take advantage of available education, to commute to work, or to move to another geographical area where employment or occupational opportunities are more readily available.

Comparison of people's economic status is meaningful when it shows what financial resources can do *for* people and what the lack of resources can do *to* people. The middle-class family, through credit, delayed check cashing, preservation of capital, and interest accumulation, can continue to make purchases and enjoy other options with very little real cash. These advantages often produce a state of optimism and security, whether real or imagined. But sudden crises, such as might follow unemployment, can be extremely painful and traumatic for families not accustomed to financial hardships.

Overall, about 12.8% (31.5 million) of all persons in the United States were below the poverty level in 1989, but the poverty rates varied widely among subgroups and among classification categories. Generally, poverty has fallen over the last 30 years from the high of 22.2% (40 million persons) in 1960. Downward or upward fluctuations, such as the 15.2% (35.2 million) in 1983, do occur; these can be due to many problems such as recession, inflation, worldwide conditions, changes in government policies, and even changes in family composition. In 1989, the poverty rate for Whites was 10.0%, for Blacks it was 30.7%, and for Hispanics it was 26.2%. For Asians, the largest component of the remaining racial groups, the poverty rate was 14.1%. Even though the poverty rate for Whites was lower than that for the other groups, the *majority of all* poor persons in 1989 were White (65.5%); Blacks constituted 29.5%, and Hispanics constituted 17.2%.

Families and unrelated individuals are classified as being above or below the poverty level by using the *poverty index* adopted by a federal interagency committee in 1969. This index centers in the U.S. Department of Agriculture's Economy Food Plan and reflects the differing consumption requirements of families based on their size and composition, sex and age of the person maintaining the family, and farm/nonfarm residence. These poverty thresholds are updated every year in accordance with changes in the Consumer Price Index. The index is based solely on money income and does not reflect noncash benefits such as food stamps, Medicaid, and public housing. Basic statistics relating to poverty are shown in Table 7-5. Poverty rates in 1989 for persons and families with other selected characteristics are as follows:

2.9%—Families with householder who worked year-round, full-time
3.6%—Families with householder who has completed one or more years of college
5.6%—Married couple families
11.4%—Persons 65 years and over
20.7%—Families with householder who is not a high school graduate

TABLE 7-3 Baccalaureate degrees conferred in specific disciplines by selected institutes by race/ethnic group, United States, 1978–79.

Discipline	Black		Hispanic		Asian		Native American		Nonminority	
	Number	%	Number	%	Number	%	Number	%	Number	%
Agriculture and natural resources	312	0.6%	165	1.0%	277	2.2%	68	2.7%	14058	3.4%
Architecture and environmental design	250	0.5%	207	1.3%	196	1.6%	23	0.9%	5488	1.3%
Area studies	64	0.1%	70	0.4%	72	0.6%	2	0.1%	1249	0.3%
Biological sciences	2065	4.2%	852	5.3%	1172	9.5%	110	4.4%	22337	5.4%
Business and management	9412	19.2%	2549	15.9%	2606	21.0%	361	14.4%	76853	18.5%
Communications	1706	3.5%	356	2.2%	242	2.0%	56	2.2%	15737	3.8%
Computer and information sciences	444	0.9%	131	0.8%	213	1.7%	9	0.4%	4581	1.1%
Education	9870	20.1%	2537	15.8%	601	4.8%	513	20.5%	49848	12.0%
Engineering	1411	2.9%	930	5.8%	1536	12.4%	131	5.2%	32766	7.9%
Fine and applied arts	1362	2.8%	542	3.4%	538	4.3%	118	4.7%	18609	4.5%
Foreign languages	256	0.5%	786	4.9%	182	1.5%	18	0.7%	5062	1.2%
Health professions	2640	5.4%	780	4.9%	784	6.3%	133	5.3%	27157	6.5%
Home economics	1045	2.1%	141	0.9%	351	2.8%	66	2.6%	9899	2.4%
Letters	1673	3.4%	469	2.9%	334	2.7%	81	3.2%	18170	4.4%

TABLE 7-3 (continued)

Discipline	Black		Hispanic		Asian		Native American		Nonminority	
	Number	%	Number	%	Number	%	Number	%	Number	%
Library science	44	0.1%	2	—	2	—	2	0.1%	245	0.1%
Mathematics	550	1.1%	146	0.9%	238	1.9%	30	1.2%	4709	1.1%
Physical sciences	556	1.1%	240	1.5%	273	2.2%	44	1.8%	10188	2.5%
Psychology	2495	5.1%	986	6.2%	652	5.3%	137	5.5%	18826	4.5%
Public affairs and services	3704	7.5%	1025	6.4%	353	2.8%	144	5.8%	16797	4.0%
Social sciences	7166	14.6%	2382	14.9%	1288	10.4%	338	13.5%	47392	11.4%
Interdisciplinary studies	1997	4.1%	722	4.5%	478	3.9%	118	4.7%	15123	3.6%
All others	94	0.2%	19	0.1%	6	0.1%	2	0.1%	282	0.1%
Total	49116	100.0%	16037	100.0%	12394	100.0%	2504	100.0%	415376	100.0%

SOURCE: From "Minority Recruitment Data: A Preliminary Report," by Donald R. Deskins, Jr. *Rockham Reports*, 7 (1981), pp. 1–5. Reprinted by permission of the author.

NOTE: Data do not represent the number of degrees awarded by all the 1,658 institutions of higher education in the United States. Deskins selected 362 (21.8%) that were believed to represent good potential for minority professional schools and graduate school recruitment. To qualify for inclusion, the 362 schools had to meet a minimum threshold of 49 degrees conferred to any one of the minority groups, with the exception of Native Americans, with whom the minimum was dropped to 14 degrees. The 21.8% of the 1,658 institutions produced 81% of all minority degrees conferred in the country during the period from 1978 to 1979.

TABLE 7-4 Number of doctoral degrees conferred in specific disciplines by all institutions by sex and race/ethnic group, United States, 1989.

	Arts and Humanities	Business & Management	Education	Engineering	Life Sciences	Physical Sciences	Social Sciences	Professional Fields
Degrees conferred[a]	2,928	726[b]	5,357	2,218[b]	4,770	3,489[b]	4,413	845
Sex								
Male	54.5%	73.9%	42.5%	91.8%	61.8%	81.2%	54.8%	56.4%
Female	45.5%	26.1%	57.5%	8.2%	38.2%	18.8%	45.2%	43.6%
Racial/Ethnic Group[c]								
Native American	6	1	21	7	14	18	17	6
Asian	84	49	102	359	248	251	136	28
Black	82	16	429	31	100	45	185	54
Puerto Rican	23	1	54	7	29	24	35	4
Mexican American	23	2	48	13	24	14	43	5
Other Hispanics	61	7	64	27	48	45	66	11
White	2,582	635	4,591	1,718	4,212	3,001	3,861	729
Other or unknown	67	15	48	56	95	91	70	8

SOURCE: Data from the *Chronicle of Higher Education Almanac*, Aug. 28, 1991, p. 27. Courtesy, National Research Council.
[a]Figures cover only U.S. citizens and those with permanent visas.
[b]Foreign students in 1989 received 42.4% of the doctoral degrees in engineering, 28% in physical sciences, and 24.5% in business and management.
[c]Percentages cover U.S. citizens and those with permanent and temporary visas.

TABLE 7-5   Percentage of the total population in poverty, 1960–1990.

Year	All (millions)	All	White	Black	Hispanic	Poverty Level for Family of Four
1960	39.9	22.2%	17.8%	NA	NA	$ 3,022
1970	25.4	12.6	9.9	33.5%	NA	3,968
1975	25.9	12.3	9.7	31.3	26.9%	5,500
1980	29.3	13.0	10.2	32.5	25.7	8,414
1985	33.1	14.0	11.4	31.3	29.0	10,989
1989	31.5	12.8	10.0	30.7	26.2	12,675
1990	33.6	13.5	10.7	31.9	28.1	13,359

SOURCE: Data from *Characteristics of the Population Below the Poverty Level: 1980*, by U.S. Bureau of the Census, 1982; *Population Profile of the United States: 1991*, by U.S. Bureau of the Census, 1991. NA = Not available.

22.0%—Persons 65 years and over living alone
26.2%—Hispanic persons
30.7%—Black persons
32.2%—Families with female householder, no spouse present

● REGIONAL DIFFERENCES

Because businesses and industries are not always located in the densest population centers, the range of available work opportunities may be limited in any given locale. Migrant workers must follow the seasonal movement of agricultural employment.

● PREJUDICE AND SPECIAL INTEREST GROUPS

Individual, institutional, and cultural prejudice and discrimination against racial/ethnic groups and against women all influence the level and range of employability in the workplace. Preconceptions and stereotypes of minority group members often tend to underestimate actual potentialities and overlook strengths. Special interest groups in the society, such as craft unions, have often presented obstacles to entry into certain lines of work (Meier & Rudwick, 1979). Even governmental legislation can work inadvertently— or intentionally, according to some opinion—against minority groups. The late President Eisenhower often spoke of the dangers of the military-industrial-governmental complex that wielded strong influence over employment opportunity. Multitudes of laws, considered progressive at the time of enactment, quickly become outmoded and often actually prevent some people from getting into the job market. For example, the federal minimum wage law, originally enacted in 1938, was considered a revolutionary effort to assure workers a decent wage. In reality, many low-skilled workers were priced out of the labor market. Similarly, "self-help" projects having the assistance of federal money, such as community-based rehabilitation of buildings, have been abandoned when it was discovered that federal stipulation required the hiring of a certain number of higher-waged union workers for each apprentice worker.

● INDIVIDUAL AND GROUP PREFERENCES WITHIN CULTURAL DIVERSITY

Variations in the representation of racial/ethnic groups, women, and other groups are often attributed to *traditional* occupational interests and abilities that have been acquired through either choice or circumstance. Gottfredson (1978), for example, found that Black and White males, ages 36 to 65, differed on Holland's occupational interest categories:

Occupational Type	Black Males	White Males
Realistic	81.0%	53.8%
Investigative	2.3%	7.4%
Artistic	0.5%	1.6%
Social	6.3%	5.8%
Enterprising	5.4%	25.6%
Conventional	4.5%	5.8%

Holland's (1973) model claims that certain personality types search for environments and occupations that will permit them (1) to exercise their skills and abilities, (2) to express attitudes and values, and (3) to take on agreeable roles and to avoid disagreeable ones. The majority of Black males (81%) in Gottfredson's study were represented in the Realistic category, compared with 53.8% of the White males. The Realistic category consists of occupational environments that require concrete, physical tasks and limited interpersonal involvement. People having personality types compatible with that environment would possess manual skills and coordination and would prefer physical activities outdoors (for example, trade workers, craftspeople, farmers, truck drivers, forestry workers, mechanical engineers). The Enterprising category requires the ability to persuade and lead others in order to accomplish identified tasks (for example, retail salespersons, automobile salespersons, politicians, advertising representatives). Such a work environment requires association with people so that the job can be completed with efficiency and effectiveness. Women, in general, tend to be most represented in the Social (for example, teachers, social workers, nurses) and Conventional (for example, secretaries, bookkeepers, office workers, accountants) categories.

Other studies by Kimball, Sedlacek, and Brooks (1973) and Hager and Elton (1971) have shown that Blacks have high measured interest in social occupations. Though lower paying, social service work has attracted minority people out of altruistic motives and also because there is real opportunity for employment. Sue and Frank (1973) have noted the fact that Chinese and Japanese students tend to show interest patterns in science fields other than social, such as engineering, chemistry, biology, and physics, and that those patterns may be due to comparatively less cultural encouragement of self-expression or to discrimination in the society.

The impact of the family on career choice has been the major focus for other theorists (Bordin, Nachman, & Segal, 1963; Roe, 1972). Bratcher (1982) has proposed that understanding the family as a *system* will offer a way to conceptualize the influence on career choice. The implications that he sees are "the extent to which an individual can separate from the family . . . and the extent to which an individual can resist the system's tendency to impose its rules on the individual" (p. 89). In addition, he believes that needs within the family system tend to maintain certain values or traditions that exert strong pressures for conformity: "For example, it may seem unthinkable for a young person from a highly religious family with very strong rules about what demonstrates those values to consider some type of career outside of full-time religious work" (pp. 89–90). When generational differences exist, they are essentially a *relational* problem, not an *individual* problem, as encountered in the counseling process. Younger clients, especially, continue to need the emotional support that can be given only by parental and family association. The family needs emotional support, too. Providing the family with an opportunity to ventilate and clarify feelings, particularly regarding the expectations that each person has and the roles that each performs within the family, are major goals of conjoint family counseling. Emancipation of children is a general process for all families. It is best defined, planned, and discussed by the members of a family, with academic activities of the children remaining as consistent as possible while the potential for vocational goals is encouraged.

Implicit in much of the foregoing discussion is also the real need for providing career education and career guidance that include a variety of role models as evidence of opportunity for a wide range of occupational choices. McDavis (1980) has pointed out the lack of Blacks in fields or careers that are, for Blacks, nontraditional, such as medicine, dentistry, law, college teaching, engineering, pharmacy, architecture, and aeronautics. Furthermore, he believes, "Black students in school begin to perceive these and other such technical professions as career areas that Blacks do not enter when the only role models that they see in these areas are Whites" (p. 160).

▲ PERSONAL EXPECTATIONS

Ingrained attitudes that are reflected by the cultural totality—and generalized in the practice of traditional psychotherapy—tend to focus on intrapsychic motivations and desires as the primary source of achievement and accomplishment. Cultural attitudes also define the value that is placed on the objects of those desires. For example, most occupations are associated with a certain level of status. The work of trash collectors is usually assigned lower status in comparison to the work of school principals, though in reality each performs important functions that are necessary to the life of the other. The fact that similar social-status rankings are assigned to occupations across cultures, races, and sexes has persisted for decades and most likely exerts a strong influence on personal expectations of individuals (Brown, 1969; Harasymiw,

Horne, & Lewis, 1977; Isaacson, 1977; Kanzaki, 1976). The attribution of social status to oneself and to others, of course, also operates on a micro level, where status as defined in one's *immediate* work setting may differ from status as defined in the *general* social setting (Hatt, 1950). Thus, job activities and occupational titles are culturally bound and associated with individual worth and dignity. Mogull (1978) has postulated that discontent among many African Americans can be attributed to having to take "dead-end" jobs that are low-grade and offer little security.

According to cultural preconceptions, if individuals appear to lack strong desire to become better or do not seek some object of higher status, the cause is often assumed to be innate. Low personal drive toward an object of desire is generally conceptualized in mainstream culture as a problem of internal deficiency due to the absence of ambition or motivation (Stewart, 1972, pp. 29, 35). This cultural tendency belongs to the ethic of "rugged individualism," or the belief that all people can better themselves if they just try harder. Thus it follows that people are more valued if they possess, or demonstrate, the quality of ambition within their personalities.

● EFFECT ON CAREER DEVELOPMENT

Studies generally indicate that it is *not* low aspiration, or lack of motivation within the person, that impedes occupational movement and career development, but rather that *personal expectations* for success are often lowered by realistic perception of conditions. When severe competition for fewer jobs occurs—such as during periods of economic slumps—most people do not lose their aspirations, but their expectations for employment simply adjust under the realities of the unfavorable conditions. During periods of prosperity the expectation of opportunity realistically increases for most people. The level and reality of expectations can also be situation-specific, and for many minorities hastily organized "crash" vocational training programs are not generally viewed with optimism.

Parental expectations and family relations also influence the level and kind of support given to children in their career planning (Dole, 1973). Socioeconomic status, more than race and ability, can also restrict individual expectations for career potential (Antonovsky, 1967; Asbury, 1968; Cosby & Picou, 1971; Fuchs & Havighurst, 1973; Shaycroft, 1967; Thomas, 1976). When expectation manifests itself in self-doubt, it is more often based on a realistic view of the disadvantages or barriers in competing for jobs and income or other opportunities that might bring greater self-fulfillment. It corresponds to the notion that "knowledge follows experience" and has important implications for career counseling. Excessive labeling or lumping different cultural groups together as "minorities" can subtly engender focusing by both counselor and client on psychic-centered problems (internal weaknesses) and away from recognition of internal strengths and what might be situation-centered problems.

● **ISSUES FOR CAREER COUNSELING**

Personal change. It becomes difficult to implement *any* career plan when self-doubt—due to personal expectation—exists in the mind of the career developer. The goal of the counselor thus becomes one of helping the client to alter impressions that may be voiced as "Life has little to offer," "Everything is stacked against me," "I have nothing to offer," or "No one really cares." These states of mind are the manifestations of unrealistic or too pessimistic expectations. They are best controlled through helping clients learn more about the strengths and resources they possess, in balance with their points for improvement, and about the positive resources in the environment in balance with the shortcomings of the environment. Using this new knowledge needs to be a part of the process too. Narrowly focusing on the inner psychological dynamics—as expounded in many theories of psychotherapy and counseling—would generally be wasteful and nonproductive. Worse, the problem could be narrowly diagnosed, or conceptualized, as a form of personal deficiency. A person's expectations can become so depressed that the person loses perspective on life and a sense of his or her place in life. When this happens, a person who responds with indignation or outrage is in fact affirming higher expectations. That response is a legitimate first step toward fulfilling them.

Social change. Changes in the entire social system usually take longer than one person's lifetime. For most people, what matters is what happens during their own lives, and the importance of social change is its effect on themselves. What is a reasonable balance between personal expectations and what society can offer? Sinick (1977) warns that "raising clients' aspirations without an accompanying rise in appropriate occupational opportunities can simply raise anxieties and sometimes create emotional disturbances" (p. 246). Thus, counseling for personal expectations is a *relational* process that takes external factors into consideration so that real opportunities and desirable conditions can be sorted out from unreal opportunities and undesirable conditions.

■ RELATIONAL COUNSELING: EXPANDING PERSONAL DEFINITIONS AND EXPECTATIONS IN CAREER DEVELOPMENT

Helping clients to define personal expectations and goals in relation to who and what they are, in harmony with their own background of cultural experiences, is a significant part of the counseling interaction (London & Mone, 1987). Another is assisting clients to identify, develop, and use their special resources. Helping them to expand the opportunities and choices that they perceive as being available to them in the environment is a third goal in their career development. Counselors who use a relational approach with clients may consider the following examples of concepts, activities, and techniques.

▲ IDENTIFYING AND REINFORCING SELF-PERCEIVED QUALITIES AND SELF-MOVEMENT

It is often difficult for individuals to respond when asked, "What are some important qualities and skills that you have or that you admire in others?" Self-image is vague for many people because they have never really taken the time to conceptualize it as something that all people possess. Although mainstream cultural norms take pride in accentuating individualism, the self tends to be defined as what the self does. People are most likely to be recognized for what they have competitively achieved and disparaged for what they have not achieved (for instance, "A" students versus "D" students, or company managers versus common laborers). *Who's Who in America* lists titles, positions, degrees, accomplishments, achievements, honors, and organizational memberships for thousands of "notable" and "famous" people, but do we really know who they are? Triumphs and achievements seem to be the major references that people have for who they are. Lost in the conditioning process is a real feeling for and understanding of the self. Externalized achievement has become linked to a mechanized notion of internal motivation, which has gradually replaced the impression of an essential self that each person has and can know.

Asking clients to make a list of their personal strengths and abilities as they see them will help draw their attention to positive aspects and decrease the tendency to focus narrowly on personal shortcomings or on the traits others have assigned to them. Some clients might find it useful to keep in mind some short statements about what gives them a sense of satisfaction, or even to carry a few cards that list personally defined accomplishments and strengths for a quick reminder and self-reinforcement when things seem to be going wrong. For those who might need more awareness-raising of their self-progress through life, it is often helpful to chart chronologically the experiences and events that have been important or significant for their personal growth.

Yet another developmental strategy that some individuals have found helpful and purposeful is simply to compile a checklist of activities or experiences that one would like to accomplish sometime during one's life. Such individually created lists have included goals ranging from volunteering for a community project, visiting with senior citizens, and being a Big Brother or Big Sister, to canoeing through rapids, building a house, and writing a book. The idea underlying the setting of such individual goals is that risk is success, while fear is failure.

In group settings, such as classrooms or counseling groups, strength bombardment has been a useful technique for bolstering self-image. In small groups of about four or five, each person in turn hears the other state their observations about his or her positive behaviors and qualities. Someone other than the person being "bombarded" can keep a written list for the person to have at the end of the activity.

Helping clients to identify things that they would like to improve or strengthen within themselves or in their relations with others—and that can be accomplished as everyday, short-range goals—will also help reinforce the sense of well-being and personal movement. Borck and Fawcett (1982) emphasize the importance of helping clients to develop problem-solving skills through a basic three-step process: (1) identify and state the problem, (2) list alternatives to the problem that can be found in everyday experiences, and (3) determine the consequences of each alternative. They have also compiled a simplified index of everyday problems and possible "common sense" alternatives.

▲ BLOCKING NEGATIVE THOUGHTS

Negative ideas and unpleasant feelings that are related to low expectations of self may sometimes seem to override a client's ability to perceive other aspects of himself or herself. The overemphasis on concrete individual achievements—and the neglect of relatedness to others as similar beings—is reflected in group norms that are especially characteristic of U.S. middle-class culture. Low self-expectations in any task can serve as a defense against self-perceived vulnerability. Negative thoughts are reactions toward the self that are learned early in childhood. They can be perpetuated as lifetime themes unless challenged. Counseling clients toward a realistic perspective of themselves as imperfect human beings who do make mistakes will help reduce the need to rely on a defensive posture and increase their ability to take life for what it is, and what it isn't. In the process, they can learn to like themselves better and appreciate and include others in their lives. Encouraging clients to censor, or block out, those negative mental images that lower self-expectations and self-opinion will help reduce anxiety and improve many aspects of personal performance.

▲ PRACTICING POSITIVE VISUAL IMAGERY

Positive mental pictures and rehearsal to achieve success can be helpful to many clients. Encouraging clients to visualize (imagine) themselves practicing good performance before engaging in some situation or task will help boost morale and actual performance. For example, mental role playing of successful performance at a forthcoming job interview can help self-confidence and eventual performance. Sports psychologists have found that guided relaxation training in conjunction with the visual imagery technique is also helpful in improving athletic performance at sports events ("Sport Psychology Comes of Age," 1982). The scientific concepts underlying the phenomenon of interlocked self-regulating systems—the interaction between brain and body—are found in the fields of psychophysiology and psychocybernetics and in the techniques of biofeedback (Brown, 1977, 1980; Maltz, 1960). The philosophical approach and practice are holistic, and counselors who use the technique must perceive clients as *total persons*—with spirit, mind, and body interacting as a unit—rather than as persons with problems (Russell, 1981). The approach emphasizes the stimulation of expectations rather than the remediation or treatment of a problem as a single goal.

▲ VALIDATING SELF THROUGH IDENTIFICATION WITH OTHERS

Consensual validation (universalization) contains the logical argument that if others who are *similar* to yourself have achieved success—in spite of environmental obstacles—so can you. Appropriate career role models are an important part of this process and can be found in everyday examples. Overreliance on only exceptional people as examples, however, can lead to unrealistic expectations. To avoid the halo effect that might lead to overgeneralization of exceptional people, it is better for clients to concentrate on specific admirable behaviors in others, such as honesty, forthrightness, or persistence. Role models are best selected among individuals whom clients can observe in everyday life. Related to this process are the traditional career-development techniques of understanding work roles through reading biographies or autobiographies and through interviewing workers engaged in selected occupations. Interviews with workers aim for responses to four basic questions: (1) How did you get this job? (2) What do you like best or most about it? (3) What do you like least? (4) Who else do you know who has this job?

▲ LEARNING SELF-ASSERTION SKILLS

Teaching clients how to differentiate and use assertive communication, in contrast to behavior that communicates passiveness or aggression, will help increase respect for self in relation to respect for others (Minor, 1978). For example, if a worker believes he or she has been treated unfairly at work, it is important to face the appropriate person straightforwardly and directly with the request, complaint, or grievance—not attacking or criticizing the other person, but showing forthrightness. Learning and practicing how to be appropriately assertive also increases the ability to make decisions and to take personal risks (Siegelman, 1983). Related to self-assertion is the importance of helping clients to develop their decision-making potential in day-to-day living. Norman and Atlas (1978) point out how "enabling activities" that take into consideration both positive and negative consequences are involved in making choices. Direct confrontation by a client of his or her dissatisfying and unproductive behavior can also lead to better understanding and change of an impasse. Lopez (1983) has described the use of a *paradoxical* counseling approach in which vocational indecision can be overcome by instructing "the client to engage in the problem behavior instead of directly attempting to change it" (p. 410). In Lopez's example, the counselor composed a letter for the client to present to his domineering father, who was overinvolved in his son's life decisions, thus causing confusion for the son. The letter described the father's interventions and explained how the son's attempts to follow the many requests led to inaction and indecision. The father and son were not instructed to change their behavior, but the letter led them to recognize their unproductive interactions, and eventually the father decreased the frequency of interventions in his son's life decisions and the quality of the relationship improved. The father tempered his requests and advice, making them suggestions instead, and the son gained more freedom to think through his own decisions.

▲ UNDERSTANDING AND USING THE SYSTEM

Supporting clients and showing them how they might advantageously confront the imperfections and complexities of the system will help counteract impressions of powerlessness. Services and resources to which everyone is entitled are provided in the organized society. Many minority group members, especially of the older generation, have not had access to competent counseling services or are not aware of the help that counseling might offer them (McDavis, 1980, pp. 164–165). Others do not perceive the social system's resources as credible or trustworthy because they have had bad experiences with them (Sue & Sue, 1990, pp. 77–81). Counselors should encourage their clients to test the validity of these assumptions and assertively insist on getting good services; otherwise the potential value of counselors, affirmative action officers, legal aides, governmental representatives, mental and health care, and other legitimate resources that are provided in the society will go unnoticed and unused.

▲ ACQUIRING KNOWLEDGE AND INFORMATION THROUGH CAREER GUIDANCE AND EDUCATION

Providing reliable, relevant, realistic, and unbiased career information is essential in order for clients to expand their knowledge base for more effective decisions and to make possible a greater range of choices. Implicit in the process is the provision of experiences whereby clients can learn from workers about their work and find out how they accomplished or implemented their own careers. To ensure that career help is provided, some thoughtfully planned system of career guidance is important at all educational levels, in the transition from school to work, and in the transition from one career to another career or from one job to another job (Babcock & Kaufman, 1976; Harman & Dutt, 1974; Harris & Wallin, 1978; Hazel, 1976; Healy, 1974; Jepsen, 1972; Koch, 1972; Lipsett & Laidlaw, 1975; Perrone & Kyle, 1975; Thoni & Olsson, 1975; Thoresen & Hamilton, 1972; Woodcock & Herman, 1978). Furthermore,

Wernick (1982) points out that career education that chooses to take a "life-centered" approach must include "an individual's ethnic heritage and focus directly on ways each student and his/her family/culture background can be strengthened" (p. 172). A life-centered focus shifts the emphasis from personal success in the workplace to success motivation in social contexts—individual, family, culture, national, international.

■ TRADITIONAL CAREER THEORIES AND MODELS

Having some kind of conceptual process to understand individuals in their career planning and decision making is important. Without one, we would have to assume that a career over life is nothing other than a series of personal flounderings and unconnected events with no meaning. That condition of randomness does not seem to be the case in most societies, nor would it be desirable in highly developed societies, in which opportunity for the expression of individual potentialities is more likely and more varied.

▲ FACTORS IN CAREER DEVELOPMENT

Multiple factors influence work and career development. Generally, most traditional theories or models of career movement and development are psychologically oriented; thus, they tend to emphasize personality characteristics and functioning. How people think and feel about themselves and their environment and how self-expression is sequentially developed over time are matters given primary consideration in most psychological theories. All people are affected by biological factors, and the basis for any human functioning is inherited physical, emotional, and mental characteristics, as modified by experiences in the environment. The experiences that individuals have with occupations and the opportunity to make career choices are also determined by other factors in the culture:

· *Social factors.* Interpersonal influences on values, attitudes, relationships, and feelings derived from interaction in group living determine the career experience. Choices in work and quality of work life are influenced by family, friends, school, neighborhood, community. Choice and quality continue to be issues in adulthood in the interactions among employees and between employers and employees.

· *Economic factors.* Changes, development, and cycles in the life of the economy can all have an impact on individual career development. All people can be affected, but especially so are younger workers, older workers, and minority groups. Two basic types of unemployment, due to changes in the economy, affect career opportunity: (1) *cyclical* unemployment goes up and down with the overall economy and (2) *structural* unemployment is inflicted on workers who don't have the skills demanded in the current workplace.

· *Political factors.* Governmental legislation and pressures of special interest groups exert influence on the availability of occupational opportunities for members of certain groups. Current advances in high technology have increased the need for workers who possess high levels of mathematical and scientific knowledge and have resulted in governmental proposals that promote training programs for workers and teachers in those specialties. The counseling profession itself has lobbied to expand its own opportunities. The National Defense Education Act gave a boost to training and placement of counselors in the 1950s and early 1960s. Similar federal action was proposed in 1985 that dealt with the importance of mathematics, science, foreign languages, computer technology instruction, and vocational guidance, and encouraged school-age youth to pursue careers in those areas. Basically, such legislation aims to increase the productivity of the nation's economy and ensure an adequate number of high school graduates qualified to serve in the national defense.

· *Chance factors.* Events beyond the control of individuals, such as wartime, destructive weather conditions, timing, coincidence, and proximity to opportunities, are all elements of chance that influence advantage or disadvantage in career development. Traditionally, career counselors do not recognize chance factors and tend to downplay elements of "luck." Counselors are most likely to believe that opportunities probably come to those who seek them rather than to those who wait for them.

The complexity and changing nature of these four factors have discouraged theorists from moving toward some type of unification or integration with the individual psychological variables. Mitchell, Jones, and Krumboltz (1979) and others have sought to provide an empirical basis for environmental conditions and events. Krumboltz and Baker (1973) have applied learning theory to career-decision problems in which environmental alternatives and consequences are considered along with a client's goals. Krumboltz (1975) has also described a career decision-making approach that takes into account four factors influencing occupational choice: (1) genetic endowment, (2) environmental conditions and events, (3) learning experiences, and (4) the behavior skills and steps necessary for approaching decision-making tasks. Understanding the important existential process of making wise choices in an ever-changing environment (see, for example, Peatling & Tiedeman, 1977; Tiedeman, 1961; Tiedeman & O'Hara, 1963; Tiedeman & Miller-Tiedeman, 1975), may have more relevance for the counseling and guidance of people in their career movement than does the concept of uniform stages of development over the life span (for example, Ginzberg, 1972; Ginzberg, Ginzberg, Axelrad, & Herma, 1951; Roe, 1972; Super, 1957).

▲ CHARACTERISTICS OF CAREER DEVELOPMENT

Career is defined as the expression of one's self within the context of the environment and culture. Life work, life history, life themes, and lifestyle are all versions of self-expression. Career can also be conceived as the responses a person makes to experiences over a lifetime; thus, career development is the systematic changes in one's vocational behavior that can be observed over time. Helping clients to broaden their exposure to occupational experiences is a major function of career development counselors. Furthermore, career theories generally follow the notion of some type of underlying process. The lifelong process, as recognized in career and psychological development theories, suggests the following characteristics (the list is not intended to be all-inclusive):

· An orderly, patterned, predictable, generally irreversible movement from one time-bound stage to another
· The integration, through compromise or synthesis, of past experiences with present experiences in anticipation of the future
· The ongoing involvement in developing and expressing a self-concept
· The experience of developmental stages and the challenges and tasks that accompany each stage
· The presence of a hierarchy of basic needs related to vocational behavior

▲ CAREER DEVELOPMENT THEORIES AND CULTURAL DIVERSITY

There is some question of whether traditional theories, models, and paradigms—constructed to describe sequential and continuous career development—are adequate when applied in the context of the diverse populations of the United States (Asbury, 1968; Campbell, 1974; Ford & Ford, 1978; Ho, 1973; Jensen, Waler, & Chamberlain, 1978; LoCascio, 1967; Smith, 1975; Warnath, 1975). Most career development theories of the past 35 years have emerged out of mainstream cultural values and realities. Generalization, for the most part, is limited to middle-class and White male populations, since those are the groups that were most represented in many occupations and that had the most opportunity for career expression and development. Theories of psychological development, in general, have been based on phenomena that are most relevant to the cultural totality of the general population. To make the theories inclusive and to account for nonconforming individuals or nonconforming groups of individuals (nonconforming, that is, in comparison with the majority of the population), psychological theories have tended to explain exceptions on the basis of "abnormality," "deficiency," or "deprivation."

However, in many ways, the experiences of "culturally different" and "culturally distinct" groups have simply been ignored. Johnson (1981) has noted, in reference to ethnicity and psychotherapeutic interaction, that although consideration and study have been given to variables such as biological factors, sex, personality, and social class, there is a gap in the identification of developmental patterns that might be relevant to ethnic group membership. Very little parallel construction of developmental models that allow for cultural diversity, along with and in interaction with mainstream phenomena, has been attempted. Gottfredson (1981) has proposed a developmental theory of occupational aspirations in which she combines both developmental and social systems constructs about careers. She has assumed that all social groups share occupational ideas that are represented in "cognitive maps of occupations." She sees self-concept in relation to occupational preferences as developing in a series of four stages:

1. *Orientation to size and power* (ages 3 to 5 years): the child begins to grasp the concept of being an adult and has a fairly positive view of all occupations of which he or she is aware
2. *Orientation to sex roles* (approximately ages 6 to 8 years): the concept of a gender self is consolidated and occupations that are perceived to be inappropriate for the person's sex are eliminated from further consideration
3. *Orientation to social valuation* (around ages 9 to 13 years): abstract ideas related to social class and intelligence become important determinants of job-self compatibility; occupations perceived to have low status and occupations perceived to require effort greater than the person's image of his or her general ability level are ruled out
4. *Orientation to the internal, unique self* (beginning around age 14): making vocational choices based on personal feelings, interests, values, and self-capacities is recognized, but exploration of vocational alternatives is largely within those occupations that were deemed compatible with the person's sex, social class, and intelligence at earlier ages

Involved in the passage through the stages is the personal necessity for some type of compromise or synthesis when conflicting goals make choices difficult.

Sue and Sue (1990) and Atkinson, Morten, and Sue (1989) have also suggested models that they believe show the psychological development patterns of minority group members. Hypothetical constructs and descriptive statements are presented that seek to differentiate some patterns and sequences that might describe the psychosocial development of minority group members, or at least might describe those individuals who perceive their status to be that of minority and who thus act upon their own self-definitions. These models have potential value for clarifying phases in one's life that are possibly experienced as a reaction to, or as a result of, coexistence with the majority population. In this sense, the conceptualizations are as much minority adjustment-reaction models as they are minority identity development models. The models may be useful for defining critical components of any counselor-client interaction, in addition to those minority-majority dyadic mixes that produce relational discomfort. The hypothesized developmental process in the Atkinson, Morten, and Sue model contains the following general features:

1. *Conformity stage:* preference for dominant cultural values
2. *Dissonance stage:* cultural confusion and conflict toward dominant system
3. *Resistance and immersion stage:* active rejection of dominant society and

culture along with a strong desire to regain one's own primary cultural traditions and ways

4. *Introspection stage:* questioning of the influence of minority culture and dominant culture upon personal autonomy, perhaps incurring personal conflict

5. *Synergetic articulation and awareness stage:* acceptance of a cultural identity that is in harmony with personal identity along with an altruistic and realistic understanding of minority-majority group relationships and issues

Further refinement by Sue and Sue (1990) seeks to illustrate the psychological development of minorities in relation to majorities and has potential value in the counseling process for appropriate understanding of minority cultural identity, or states of perceived being. Sue and Sue propose that the conditions found in a client's locus of self-control (internal versus external) and perception of responsibility (internal versus external) will provide guidelines for determining an appropriate counseling process in relation to appropriate counseling goals.

■ EQUAL OPPORTUNITY/AFFIRMATIVE ACTION AND PRACTICES IN THE WORKPLACE

The actions, directions, and decisions of managers, supervisors, directors of personnel, human resources specialists, and personnel counselors have important consequences for diverse people who work in business, industry, education, government agencies, or any other organization. The central idea of management and supervision is to make every action or decision help achieve carefully chosen goals of the organization. The actions taken and decisions made critically influence the opportunity and possibility for career development of workers.

▲ HUMAN RESOURCES PRACTICES

Most organizational leaders who have competence, knowledge, or training in human resources concepts take into consideration the quality of employer-employee and employee-employee interactions (Cook, 1987). Successful achievement of organizational goals is related to important human ingredients, such as leadership style, interpersonal communication, motivation, and group dynamics and morale (Haimann & Hilgert, 1977, pp. 52–103, 265–303; Stuart-Kotze, 1980). Although most organizations apply some of the principles found in the psychology of human relations, personnel practices often lag behind the changes that take place in the broader cultural environment (Deming, 1986; Naisbitt & Aburdene, 1985). The reasons are often lack of knowledge and skill, fear of change, resistance, and cultural encapsulation. Weber (1975), in speaking of the contrasting managerial attitudes that can be found among different world nations, has pointed out: "Ordinarily we think and dream in terms of the norms and standards we have absorbed from the culture in which we have been reared. What our culture values, we value; what our culture abhors, we abhor. By education or experience, some become aware that there are other values and beliefs that also make sense—as much or more sense than our own. But we see them hazily, and all too often with age the awareness slips away. A few are able to overcome parochialism and see the world more objectively, but this is by no means desirable. We can feel alone and unsure if the comfortable values of our culture become irrelevant and are not replaced by a substitute" (p. 229).

▲ EQUAL EMPLOYMENT OPPORTUNITY LAWS

Since management works through people, it is important to recognize the interaction of the attitudes, assumptions, and practices of managers with the needs, wants, and aspirations of different groups of people. Some organizations—due to enlightened leaders who are perceptive of changes in the cultural environment—have applied human relations policies and practices to accommodate minorities effectively. Most organizations, however, have had to modify their policies and practices by necessity of law. Protection of the rights of diverse groups of employees in organizational structures is provided by various federal laws, such as:

- Title VII of the Civil Rights Act of 1964
- The Age Discrimination in Employment Act of 1967, and the 1978 and 1986 amendment disallowing mandatory retirement
- The Equal Pay Act of 1963, which prohibits sex discrimination in pay
- The Rehabilitation Act of 1973, amended in 1978 to include alcoholism as a handicap
- The Americans with Disabilities Act of 1990 (see Chapter 4)
- The Civil Rights Act of 1991 (see Chapter 4)
- State and local laws, some of which add protection for marital status and sexual orientation

● TITLE VII

This section of the landmark Civil Rights Act of 1964 prohibits discrimination in employment because of race, color, religion, sex, or national origin. All companies of 15 or more employees are affected. The federal government has set up the Equal Employment Opportunity Commission (EEOC) to investigate and, if necessary, prosecute any organization that might be implicated in a discrimination charge. Unfair practices claims can be filed by any individual, or his or her agent, if it is believed that discrimination exists in any of the following areas:

compensation	promotions
discharge	recruiting
hiring	training
job assignments	transfers

Race or color. The differential treatment of people on the basis of race or color has been extensively discussed throughout this book. It is easy to see that until recently few minorities received equal educational and employment opportunities. Most organizations do not openly refuse to hire or advance minorities, but the message is often somehow received that they are "not welcome." The *intent* of the organization may be innocent, but the *effect* could be discriminatory. The government is concerned with whether the *effect* is in violation of Title VII, and remedial action is necessary if such is the case. Under Executive Orders 11246 and 11375, the federal government can instigate action in companies of 50 or more employees where government grants and contracts total $50,000 or more. The Secretary of Labor or the contracting agency can also recommend that the EEOC or the Department of Justice institute proceedings under Title VII. Executive Order 11246 can also apply if the organization does not have in writing a plan of *action* or does not *affirmatively* seek out and employ minorities.

Religion. It is not always easy to define a person's religion or to say what are valid religious observances. Religion is the deepest belief of an individual. Unless, for example, a worker's absence from duty creates an *undue hardship* for the company, managers should make *reasonable* attempts to *accommodate* religious observances and needs.

Sex. In 1900, women 16 years of age and over constituted 19% of the civilian work force, 43% in 1970, 52% in 1980, and 58% in 1990. However, Hooks (1981, p. 18) has pointed out that women are especially underrepresented in crafts work (6%), managerial positions (23%), and nonretail sales positions (23%). Some of the conditions, issues, and situations that personnel managers and counselors must face in considering employment practices that might potentially abuse women include the following:

· The definition and practice of sexual harassment on the job
· Hiring and wages that reflect sexual stereotypes and different life patterns
· Unnecessary emphasis on marital status and the separation of marital status from the ability to perform a job
· Pregnancy and the related social issues surrounding abortion or the right of a woman to end a pregnancy before it has come to term

Discriminatory attitudes toward women are often conveyed, unknowingly or knowingly, through verbal and nonverbal communication in the workplace. Hogan (1975) has pointed out lessons that can be learned in corporate speech and action. The following excerpts are among her examples:

> · Mr. Z calls Sally Jones, one of the firm's account executives, into his office to congratulate her on landing an account the company has been pursuing for years. "Sally, you did a first-rate job on that Mercer account," he says. "You really surprised everyone. Don't get me wrong—it's not that we didn't think you could do the job. It's just : . . well, how did you manage to get old Mercer to sign? Never mind, we won't go into that," he says with a wink.
> · Six men and a lone woman attend a luncheon. The table conversation turns to capital gains, product diversification, and a new Management Information System (MIS) that will facilitate financial reporting for the large multinational corporation for which they work. Halfway through lunch, one of the men leans over and whispers to the woman, "Are we boring you?"
> · A male manager has recently transferred to head a new department. On the third day in his new assignment, he emerges from his office and asks a female standing near the Xerox machine to make four copies of a report and to get him a cup of coffee. The woman introduces herself; she is one of the production managers who report to him. (p. 34)
> SOURCE: From "A Woman Is Not A Girl And Other Lessons In Corporate Speech," by P. Hogan, *Business and Society Review,* Summer 1975, pp. 34–38. Reprinted by permission.

Perceiving people as representatives of a group rather than as individuals is one of the more serious obstacles to effective everyday conversations: "Nonsexist speaking habits can be acquired only by redirecting thinking patterns, discarding all the old assumptions and learning to interact on a one-to-one basis" (Hogan, 1975, p. 38).

The EEOC has set four basic guidelines to which counselors and workers can refer when they are unsure of what they should or should not do:

1. It is considered discriminatory to refuse to hire a woman because of sex on the basis of assumptions about comparative employment characteristics of women in general.
2. It is considered discriminatory to refuse to hire an individual based on stereotyped characterizations of the sexes.
3. It is considered discriminatory to refuse to hire an individual because of preferences of co-workers, employers, clients, or customers, except where sex is a bona fide occupational qualification. A bona fide qualification could, for example, be the employment of a female attendant in a women's restroom.
4. It is considered discriminatory to refuse to hire a woman because of state laws designed for the protection of women.

Schools, colleges, and other organizations are also affected by Title IX of the Education Amendments of 1972, which provides equal educational opportunity for female students. It is an important legal means for preventing discrimination against female students; furthermore, it provides funds for counseling programs to encourage female students to pursue careers in science and technology, to enroll in traditionally "male" courses, and to participate in athletic programs. Grants are also provided to study sex-role stereotyping in textbooks and other problems unique to female students. The rights of women to employment during and after a period of pregnancy have also been clarified in the Pregnancy Discrimination Act of 1978. In addition to the special needs of women as shown in federal law requirements and in conditions that exist in the working environment, Zunker (1990, pp. 382–387) has pointed out that complex problems in the following areas require attention:

- Need for counseling that will facilitate personal expectations in nontraditional career choices and career information that encourages women to consider a wide variety of careers
- conflict and stress from having to assume the dual roles of homemaker and worker
- older displaced homemakers whose lives no longer center on their husband's career and the raising of children and who are unprepared for entry into the workplace
- Younger divorced women who must work and also care for children
- Lack of appropriate role models and concerned mentors

National origin. Avoiding discrimination on the basis of national origin could be a very difficult and complex matter for organizational people who take their own culture too much for granted or who have limited knowledge of the cultures of others. Each worker must be seen for who and what he or she is. Insensitive supervisors, for example, might show discrimination by failing to explain a job clearly, or by explaining it too quickly or using unfamiliar terms. A company might have a policy that employees must be of a certain height or weight even though the actual job performance might not be related to those factors. The use of screening or placement tests in the English language could be considered discriminatory for jobs in which English language skill is not a requirement of the work to be performed.

● THE AGE DISCRIMINATION IN EMPLOYMENT ACT

The damaging effects of stereotyping and discrimination based on age have led to the establishment of protection for older workers. By the 1967 act, employers of 25 or more people are prohibited from discrimination in any area of employment against persons 40 to 65 years of age solely because of their age. The 1978 amendment extended the upper limit to age 70 and the 1986 amendment eliminated all references to mandatory retirement age. Age discrimination cases will become more common as the Baby Boom generation moves into the protected class of age 40 and over (the bulk of the Baby Boom generation will reach age 40 between 1990 and 2000). Older citizens in many societies are viewed as having experience and knowledge that can be valuable for younger citizens. But U.S. society in many ways views its older population like the consumable objects it mass-produces: once the object is used, is no longer desired, or is replaced by other products, it is discarded. Employment discrimination against persons who are approaching the prime of their life or who are facing mandatory retirement can be destructive to the self-esteem of people who take pride in their contribution. Age alone has nothing to do with a person's ability to work. Real advantages in hiring and promoting older workers have been established in research by the Department of Labor and other researchers:

· The ability to learn does not decline significantly with age. The ability to learn many tasks at ages 50 and 60 is about equal to that at age 16.
· There is minimal difference of output between older and younger workers.
· Older workers may be ill for longer periods of time, but the frequency of days off because of illness will be less than for younger workers.
· Older workers are highly motivated and tend to be more responsible and stable on the job.
· Older workers tend to stay on their selected jobs longer.

● THE EQUAL PAY ACT

Equal pay for racial/ethnic minorities and women performing work similar to that of others is the basis for the Equal Pay Act of 1963. The *gender gap*—the pay differential between full-time working men and women—is often pointed out as evidence of workplace inequities. Today, women earn 68 cents for every dollar earned by men. From 1960 until the early 1980s, the ratio hovered around 60%. In the 1980s, however, women's median earnings escalated much faster than men's, and the gap continues to narrow as the nature of the work force changes. In the 1970s, older women entering the labor market, mostly out of economic necessity, had less education and work experience and, as a result, lowered the income average for all women. Women who sought jobs in the 1980s had more education and larger work aspirations. Women's pay differential may be due less to discrimination than to the uneven division of family responsibilities, which may cut into the productivity of some women. The median weekly wages paid to fully employed workers in 1990 were:

Men	Women	White Women	Black Women	Hispanic Women
$485	$348	$355	$308	$280

Charges of unequal pay are evaluated on the basis of four criteria: skill, effort, responsibility, and working conditions. The Wage and Hour Division of the Department of Labor is generally responsible for investigating charges related to the Equal Pay Act. In such cases, the entire organization is investigated, and when the case goes to court, experience has shown that the employer usually loses. In the 1970s and 1980s, the issue for women was "equal pay for equal work." In the 1990s, it may be "comparable worth" (pay based on the social/economic value of work performed). The majority of women are in low-paying jobs and they have no place for advancement; thus, the demand for pay equity could induce organizations to review their pay classification systems for evidence of sex discrimination. A wage system based on the worth of work performed (versus open-market competition of supply and demand or negotiated labor agreements) is complex because it requires society to question its own values and to make value judgments about work. Hence, for example, why should dog-pound attendants be paid more than child-care center employees?

● **THE REHABILITATION ACT**

The 1973 Rehabilitation Act, along with Executive Order 11758 and several state laws, is intended to protect the handicapped from discrimination in the workplace. Affirmative action in employing and advancing qualified handicapped individuals is also called for. The determination of "physical handicap" must often be made by courts, but the nature of the handicap is always considered in relation to job performance and whether reasonable accommodation has been made to assure handicapped individuals the opportunity for employment and advancement. Examples of "reasonable accommodation" could include providing tutors, readers, or interpreters; making facilities accessible; restructuring jobs; and modifying work schedules. According to the law, a handicapped individual is defined as "any person who (1) has a physical or mental impairment that substantially limits one or more of such person's major life activities, (2) has a record of such impairment, or (3) is regarded as having such impairment." The implications of some handicaps, such as blindness, hearing loss, and orthopedic disability are obvious; but others, such as asthma, coronary attacks, cosmetic disfigurement, or emotional problems require sensitive, thoughtful, and fair attention to the worker's role in the work setting.

▲ OTHER CONSIDERATIONS FOR ORGANIZATIONS

Directors of personnel, work supervisors, recruiters, interviewers, training and development specialists, personnel counselors, and other organizational members all perform important roles in the development of human resources, and it is through their people-to-people efforts that actual changes can be made. The philosophy and mission of a company or organization also affect treatment of workers. Companies with progressive human resources policies have also taken into consideration the needs and rights of veterans of the Vietnam era and disabled veterans. More recently, as a result of a formal opinion by the United States attorney general, employee assistance programs have been promoted to help workers with personal and social handicaps. Some of the problems are related to alcohol or substance dependency. Assistance is provided by counselors within the organization or contracted with outside agencies. Again, sensitive, thoughtful, and fair attention to each worker's situation is called for (Busch, 1981; Dickman, Challenger, Emener, & Hutchison, 1988; Dickman & Emener, 1982; Forrest, 1983; Roman, 1981).

Other important issues facing employees *and* employers in the 1990s include: (1) rights of homosexual workers who were denied recourse under Title VII, (2) child day care now that so many women are working outside the home, and (3) unpaid family and medical leave for the birth or adoption of a child and to care for a seriously ill child, spouse, or aging parent.

■ SUMMARY

1. The reality of the conventional one-life/one-career pattern has changed over the past 30 years. Contemporary career development is now conceived more as a lifelong developmental process by which one seeks to express a self-concept within a complex, ever-changing society.

2. Work and career development are bound up with and influenced by attitudes and values of the dominant culture, as well as with those of the immediate culture with which a person most readily identifies.

3. Although the traditional meaning of the work ethic has changed, a work ethic continues to influence attitudes and values toward work, career development, choices, and lifestyles. People today want more personal satisfaction and growth out of work and life.

4. The functioning and characteristics of an economic system are important to the lives and the quality of life in the society and, over time, contribute to the shaping of the total culture.

5. Economic trends and conditions affect people in their opportunities for work choices and patterns of career development. Because of present trends, workers will hold more different jobs than ever before, rapid change will outdate skills, individuals will need greater knowledge and information to keep abreast of the changes, adjustment time will decrease in the face of occupational changes, and stress and insecurity will be accentuated; but rapid changes also increase the possibility of new opportunities and their challenges.

6. Different occupational employment patterns are evident for different racial/ethnic groups and for women and men.

7. Variations in employment opportunities and patterns for both majority and minority groups are affected by many factors and problems: education, poverty, regional differences, prejudice, individual and group preferences and traditions, and personal expectations for opportunity and self-movement.

8. The problem of raising personal expectations of clients was defined as a relational problem in which environmental factors outside the person must be given as much emphasis as psychological factors within the person.

9. Counseling to raise personal expectations can be approached from a relational framework: emphasis is placed on counseling the person in relation to his or her environmental situation. Examples of relational counseling strategies include identifying and reinforcing self-perceived qualities, decreasing inhibiting behavior, improving positive self-image, validating oneself through role models, learning self-assertion skills, using system resources, and acquiring realistic career knowledge and information.

10. Traditional career development theories do not fully address counseling needs within cultural diversity. Social, economic, political, and chance

factors also affect career development and work opportunity. There is need for better understanding of the psychological development process that might characterize cultural minorities. Gottfredson has proposed "cognitive maps of occupations" and Atkinson, Morten, and Sue have described a "minority identity development" model.

11. Many classes of individuals are protected by law from discrimination in employment. Included categories are race, color, religion, sex, national origins, age, and the handicapped.

12. Human relations practices that take into consideration the special needs of diverse people in the work environment are critical for the effective and fair treatment of all workers.

CHAPTER

SOCIAL AND PERSONAL GROWTH

Human development best occurs under environmental conditions that nurture the development. Three major environments of human development have been examined in previous chapters: the sociopolitical climate, educational institutions, and the workplace. This chapter examines the environment for social and personal growth. The topics included address both perennial and current issues confronting people who live in the United States. The multicultural counseling approach takes into consideration individual personality in interaction with environmental surroundings. Life in general is an ongoing process of adaptation and adjustment to environmental demands—a process of disintegration and reintegration, of tension and relaxation. The work of counselors involves assisting people in learning functional coping behaviors that lead to continuative personal adjustment and integration. The terms *social* and *personal* are used to convey the notion that issues of living involve relations with others and the society as well as relations with oneself. Topics of discussion include adjustment, maladjustment, and five experiences that affect the lives of many people today: (1) stress as a general condition in our culture, (2) marital and family concerns, (3) suicide, (4) substance abuse, and (5) aging and the aged.

■ ADJUSTMENT

Human nature is both social and personal. The effects of living in the physical environment, a social system, a group, and a family, and with oneself all influence the manner in which people adjust and adapt. Because the sources of influence are both inside and outside, one must adjust to oneself as well as to others and to various situations. Although group life and individual life are bound together in mutual interaction, social dynamics and individual dynamics are two distinctly separate things. Both aspects need consideration in the counseling process, the goal being to understand each factor as it might be instrumental in affecting adjustment and the eventual well-being of the client. Progress toward identified counseling goals is thus based on the assumption that both external social factors and internal psychological factors exert pressure on clients and thus need identification in the counseling process. Overemphasis on one factor without consideration of the other will lead to inappropriate client goals and counseling process. For example, drug misuse and abuse are a social problem that in some way affects most people in the general society, but how each person uses or copes with drugs in his or her own life and for what purpose is also a question of individual dynamics.

Although volumes have been written on the role that special experiences play in personality and adjustment, there are sharp contradictions in the findings, and serious cross-cultural study of important events and factors is also needed. Nine basic factors that influence the development of individual personality and patterns of adjustment are shown in Table 8-1, together with general examples of each.

▲ THE PROCESS OF ADJUSTMENT

Living involves a constant process of adaptation and adjustment to demands placed on the person by the environment. Individual personality, society, and culture can all be considered as adapting, adaptive, or adapted when viewed within the context of total human survival. The sources of disruption or threat are always partly internal (that is, self-imposed or due to personal limitations) and partly external (that is, other-imposed or due to situational limitations and constraints). Adaptation for the human group becomes increasingly dependent on learning. Unlike animal behavior (survival and reproduction), which is generally governed by instinct, human behavior beyond automatic reflexes is dependent on learning for survival. Skills and habits must be shared and learned from other members in the society and preserved for future generations. At the human level, learning increases the range of possible adaptive responses but also creates new problems for survival for which new adaptive responses are required. Threats to survival can originate in the geographical environment and in the distribution of members of the group by age, sex, and number; but threat can also arise in problems of social organization, social cohesion, and social integration in the culture. Density of population, for example, can increase interpersonal relationship problems.

Coping, accommodating, adjusting, and *adapting* are terms often used interchangeably when describing the process of human survival in the environment. Adaptation usually denotes changes that have biological

TABLE 8-1 Primary Factors That Influence Personality and Adjustment

Factor	Examples of Assumptions, Research Findings, and/or General Practices
Heredity	Genetic constitution plays a role in variations in intelligence level, physiological functioning, and bodily constitution. Temperament (moods, reactivity, energy level) conditions the person's susceptibility to emotional stimulation and is usually regarded as dependent on constitutional make-up.
Physical characteristics	A person's physical features or physical handicaps, when they affect others' reactions to the person, may account for differences in individual functioning. A relationship between body physique and personality traits has been supported by some research. Stereotypes and differential treatment of others as based on skin color and not as a result of personality correlates of skin color have also been shown.
Maturation and development	Intrinsic growth processes, as a type of regulatory mechanism, result in orderly changes in behavior over time. Although partly learned, the changes follow a sequential order and rate of appearance even within a wide range of environmental influences. Studies of individual personality variations due to the effects of hormonal differences versus differences due to social reactions (learned) are inconclusive. The magnitudes of personality differences are best discovered through individual appraisal and not through group norms such as might be based on sex differences or other groupings.
Early child-rearing practices	Shifting assumptions and practices have ranged between two extreme categories of beliefs: unconditional love and affection, intuitive understanding of needs, and cooperative discipline, on the one hand, versus conditional love and affection, strict feeding and other schedules, and uncompromising discipline, on the other.

(continued)

TABLE 8-1 (*continued*)	
Factor	*Examples of Assumptions, Research Findings, and/or General Practices*
Early parent-child relationships	Prolonged separation from the mother interferes with normal emotional and intellectual development, but stable substitute care by relatives or others can help develop self-confidence and less inhibition in the child. When substitute care involves frequently changing arrangements, results are often insecurity, anxiety, and dependence. On the other hand, constant care and overattention by the mother can potentially result in greater conformity and tendency toward guilt reactions.
Child rearing and birth order	Important obligations are assigned within family systems—in different ways by different cultures—to the relationships among brothers and sisters and between sons and daughters and parents. Generally, the firstborn tend to receive more attention, are likely to carry the family's ambitions, and are assigned a dominant role with respect to later children.
Sex-role typing	Children generally are encouraged by both parents, to different degrees in different cultures, to be and feel like the same-sex parent. Although attitudes are changing in North America, traits that seem to be persistently rewarded or encouraged for boys tend to be dominance and authority; for girls, warmth, nurturance, and supportiveness.

survival value. Any beneficial modification in behavior, or responses that are adjustive and appropriate, can be considered adaptive if it meets environmental demands. Adjustment and integration are the processes whereby an individual enters into a relationship of harmony or equilibrium with the environment and with himself or herself. It involves the ability to satisfy most of one's needs and meet most of the demands, both physical and social, that are put upon one, and it is also the condition of having attained such a relationship. Adjustment is a process; there is no finality, since the life process cannot reach a static position. Both the individual and the environment are in a state of constant change. Successful adjustment therefore is a process of ongoing learned adaptation.

TABLE 8-1 *(continued)*	
Factor	*Examples of Assumptions, Research Findings, and/or General Practices*
Socioeconomic class	The general assumption in our society is that the upbringing of children differs according to the socioeconomic class membership of the parents. Both working-class and middle-class parents are concerned with imparting standards for "good" behavior to their children. Generally, working-class parents *might* tend to emphasize external locus of control and middle-class parents *might* tend to emphasize internal locus of control. Generally, working-class parents may emphasize obedience, neatness, cleanliness, physical punishment or disciplinary techniques, and warnings to "stay out of trouble"; middle-class parents may emphasize self-control, curiosity, consideration for others, reasoning, discipline by disappointment or withdrawal of affection, self-control, inner standards, and verbal control in the form of shaming and sarcasm.
Cultural group membership	The range of possible long-term effects of group practices, or individual experience that might be related to membership and identity in cultural or community groups, becomes staggering when interaction of the events is brought into context of the broader society. In the multicultural United States, events and personality expression must be interpreted in the light of persistence of the values, norms, and practices that characterize communities and that preserve ethnic identities over many generations of residence in the country.

▲ THE PURPOSE OF ADJUSTMENT

Most people generally seek purpose, harmony, and health in their surroundings and for themselves. Individual adjustment is adequate, wholesome, or healthful to the extent that the person has established a harmonious relationship within himself or herself and with the conditions, situations, and other persons that constitute his or her physical and social environment. It is difficult to draw precise distinctions between individual adjustment and social adjustment; they overlap, both terms denoting the relationships of the individual to the multiple groups that form his or her social environment.

Though "health" is a loose concept, it is applied in practice over a wide area of human behavior. There is no well-defined or uniform mode of distinguishing health from other human conditions. Changing human knowledge and paradigm shifts in defining reality all prompt changing usage of the concept. Mental (and physical) health is often defined as the manner of adaptation to the physical and cultural environment and internal counterbalance. There are some environments in which the stresses and demands upon the individual distort the personality and may induce mental illness. "Similarly, the extent to which coping skills related to the management of the external and internal environments are developed influences greatly the ability of the individual to find satisfaction in daily living and to improve the quality of the environment" (President's Commission on Mental Health, 1978, p. 850). Although purpose, harmony, and health are all goals of adjustment, such formulations are not necessarily uniform in all spheres of life and may vary or have different priorities in such areas as work, family, education, and marriage. There are also differing standards of health and normality that mark differing societies and groups within those societies. Built-in judgments of value are often uncritically attributed to a particular localized set of conditions, and adjustment then slides over into conformity to those conditions, such as conformity to a work situation. Conformity can also be confused with adjustment when a person regarded as maladjusted is actively or passively persuaded to accept and embrace standards against which he or she may have revolted.

■ MALADJUSTMENT

Maladjustment is the antithesis of adjustment. The term denotes the absence of the adjustment process and/or the inability to attain such a condition. It signifies the failure of an individual to develop behavioral patterns necessary for personal and social success. Approaching individual idiosyncrasy as if it were maladjustment ignores the fact that no culture uses or emphasizes more than a small sector of its available values, motives, and incentives. To demand an uncritical level or form of adjustment may thus be to neglect and close a number of legitimate lines of conduct other than those that are, for the time being, conventionally esteemed in the society.

What is normal behavior (adjusted) and what is abnormal behavior (maladjusted) is difficult, if not impossible, to define in precise and acceptable terms. Conventionality and abnormality are especially ambiguous in a changing society. Theorists have attempted to use *statistical* models that define normal behavior as what is numerically typical of most people in a population, *criterion* models that establish a characterizing mark or trait as a standard by which a judgment or decision of abnormality may be based, *cultural* models that judge behavior in the context wherein it occurs, and *theoretical/scientific* models that portray ideal behavior as an index of normality, or fitness and efficiency; deviance is portrayed as departure from that theoretical absolute or ideal.

▲ THE CRITERION MODEL

Darley, Glucksberg, Kamin, and Kinchla (1981, p. 460), for example, have described abnormal behavior according to the following criteria:

- *Bizarreness and extremeness.* Hallucinations, delusions, and uncontrolled violence would be some common examples. Some "normal" behavior, such as compulsively checking many times to see that a door is locked, could also fall into this category.
- *Disturbance of others.* Social behavior that interferes with the well-being of others, such as drunken driving or child molestation, falls into this category.
- *Self-distress.* People may describe themselves as abnormal when they have troublesome inner feelings such as panic or deep depression.
- *Interference with daily functions.* Behavior may be considered abnormal if the person is unable to meet standards of daily functioning and interpersonal relationships.

▲ THE CULTURAL MODEL

According to the cultural model, a person can be considered normal to the extent to which he or she is socially adjusted to and in harmony with the ethical and cultural codes of the society. This point of view defines a normal person as one who is in harmony with self and environment. The definition emphasizes conformity with the cultural requirements, mores, and injunctions of the community. Thus, normality tends to be equated with what is conventional and abnormality with what is viewed as antisocial conduct and/or different behavior. The degree of cultural relativity in this concept of normality/abnormality requires the establishment and understanding of specific norms and social standards for each culture and each situation. Mental disorder is not seen as a condition in the person; rather, it depends on how the individual is seen by others. However, the applicability of cultural standards can be questioned if a society is maladjusted, such as one in which members display traits or follow practices that are harmful or encourage self-destruction. In a fast-changing environment it is especially necessary to work out standards by which to know when the culture or society is normal and when it is abnormal. Being sane in insane places was investigated by Rosenhan (1973) to show how diagnostic labels reinforce preexisting conceptions of patients in psychiatric hospitals. Szasz (1974) has attacked mental illness— pathological behavior—as a myth. Deviance from social norms has been discussed by Stone (1975) in three overlapping areas of behavior (normal, bad, mad):

1. *Normal:* acceptable behavior according to general social norms
   Normal/bad: trouble-provoking behavior (reckless driving, jealousy, sarcasm)
2. *Bad:* criminal behavior (robbery, murder)
   Bad/mad toward others: socially unacceptable behavior (spouse beating, child abuse, rape, arson, lynchings, murder)
   bad/mad toward self: self-destructive behavior (drug abuse, suicide)
3. *Mad:* irrational, crazy behavior (schizophrenia)

▲ THEORETICAL/SCIENTIFIC MODELS

● PSYCHOANALYTIC THEORY

Freud and other psychoanalytically oriented theorists have worked with the hypothesis of "continuity," which sets forth the notion that all human beings struggle with the same complexes (conflicting ideas and impulses having emotional meaning). The difference between a "normal" and an "abnormal" person lies mainly in the manner in which each handles conflict. For example, *real* anxiety is to be expected in times of threat or danger. A drastic change in the conditions of life can cause anxiety, which under the circumstances is a normal feeling. Real anxiety is objectively confined and rationally understandable in terms of the danger involved in the external situation. *Neurotic* anxiety is a pervasive, diffused, generalized, free-floating emotional state that has no apparent relation to a known or immediate threat or danger. According to psychoanalytic theory, normality connotes the dominance of conscious, rational determinants of behavior, while abnormality connotes a preponderance of unconscious, irrational determinants. Normal behavior facilitates adjustment to reality, both physical and social, whereas abnormality leads to maladjustment, such as might be observed in delusional behavior.

● THE MEDICAL MODEL

Psychiatrists and other health-care professionals have contended for many years that mental disorders and abnormalities are based on illness, whether organic or psychogenic. Mental illness is labeled *mental* because the symptoms are psychological, and the psychological symptoms are indicative of an underlying condition or cause. According to the medical model, abnormal psychological symptoms are regarded as a form of pathology. Mainline psychiatry does not "believe that social variables have primary (not secondary add-on) relevance to major psychiatric illness. Generally, the more serious the disturbance, the wider the belief that the patient's problems are primarily due to a biochemical, genetically based mechanism" (Benjamin, 1986, p. 600). Treating the psychological problem, or "cause," with psychoanalytically oriented therapy has been the traditional approach, but the trend now is toward the use of psychotherapeutic drugs that suppress or mask behavioral symptoms or that replace "depleted" brain chemicals. Four general types of psychotherapeutic drugs are prescribed in our society:

1. *Major tranquilizers.* Antipsychotic drugs that are used to suppress such psychotic symptoms as hallucinations and delusions.

2. *Minor tranquilizers.* Antianxiety drugs prescribed for a variety of symptoms, including anxiety, tension, nervousness, insomnia, stress, grief, and depression. They are also used to relax muscle spasms, to relieve convulsions, and to aid in the treatment of alcoholism.

3. *Barbiturates and sedative-hypnotics.* Barbiturates relieve anxiety and tension and produce calmness and muscular relaxation. Lithium carbonate, a sedative, is used for the treatment of hyperactivity in manic-depressive reaction. Sedative-hypnotics are sleep-inducing.

4. *Antidepressants.* Drugs used to treat "affective disorders," including severe and long-lasting depression in patients who are regressed and inactive.

● THE PSYCHIATRIC DIAGNOSTIC MODEL

The American Psychiatric Association has classified various mental disorders on the basis of symptoms, origin, course, and outcome. The latest revision of the third edition of the *Diagnostic and Statistical Manual of Mental Disorders* (DSM-III-R) (American Psychiatric Association, 1987) underwent lengthy field testing for appropriateness and adequacy (Goldman, 1988, pp. 241–251). DSM-III-R uses five axes as a composite for assessing an individual's problem. Axis I requires a statement of the specific clinical syndrome that an individual displays (for example, phobic disorders or depression); Axis II focuses on long-term personality and developmental disorders (for instance, compulsive personality); the third axis pertains to physical complaints or records of medical disorders. In Axis IV the diagnostician rates the severity of psychosocial stressors within the past year in order to assess pressures or disruptions in a client's life, as shown in Table 8-2. Axis V requires a rating of the individual's two-month period of highest functioning during the past year as well as his or her current status. Psychological, social, and occupational functioning on a hypothetical continuum of mental health and illness are considered, as shown in Table 8-3. Impairment in functioning due to physical or environmental limitations is not included.

DSM-III-R represents an effort to improve on the reliability and validity of classifications. Formerly vague and nonspecific categories (such as "neurosis") have been refined into more precise categories, such as anxiety disorders, somatoform disorders (psychosomatic), and dissociative disorders (for example, amnesia, multiple personality, depersonalization). Criticism of the clinical classification system itself has centered on both specific issues and general implications. The diagnostic categories, for example, have tended to maintain the medical model and psychoanalytic viewpoint related to normality/abnormality. Learning theorists in particular disagree with concepts of neurotic behavior defined in terms of anxiety, conflict, and defense mechanisms. Other arguments contend that DSM-III-R now includes many

TABLE 8-2 DSM-III-R, Axis IV: Rating scale for psychosocial stressors.

Severity	Examples
None	No psychosocial stressors are apparent.
Minimal	A minor violation of the law such as the temporary nonpayment of the bank loan or receiving a speeding ticket.
Mild	An argument with a casual friend or neighbor, reassignment to a different work shift.
Moderate	Taking a new job, death of a close friend, pregnancy, departure of a child leaving home for college.
Severe	Major or terminal illness in self or family member, mortgage foreclosure on a home, bankruptcy, marital separation, birth of a child.
Extreme	Death of a family member or close relative, divorce, jail or prison sentence.
Catastrophic	A natural disaster (flood, tornado) that causes devastation, a fire that destroys a home.
Unspecified	No information is available or the scale is not applicable.

SOURCE: American Psychiatric Association: *Diagnostic and Statistical Manual of Mental Disorders*, Third Edition, Revised. Washington, DC, American Psychiatric Association, 1987.

categories that are not within the province of psychiatry or clinical psychology. "Underachievement," for instance, should be viewed not as a psychiatric difficulty but as a learning difficulty. There is also the very important question of whether the rating system itself is reliable and consistent. Until clinicians are in agreement on terms and definitions, two different psychologists examining the same person could come up with two different diagnoses. Since many counselors probably make some use of DSM-III-R or work with psychiatrists and other clinicians who use it, it is important to be familiar with its categories (Downing & Paradise, 1989; Seligman, 1983) and its implications for clients in a multicultural society (Shea, 1988, pp. 363–368).

■ STRESS AS A GENERAL CONDITION IN OUR CULTURE

Stress is an uncomfortable, tense, anxious feeling, as if one were preparing for some kind of emergency. It can also be felt as disappointment, sadness, grief, sorrow, and passiveness and depression, as if one could no longer cope. It has been called the fight/flight mechanism and is believed to be the human defensive response to felt threat, self-perceived threat, or actual threat. Some levels of stress, of course, give motivation to pursue everyday challenges, and there are instances where traumatic stress events (for example, accidents) lead to unusual physical, emotional, and mental responses that are life-saving.

▲ INDICATORS AND EFFECTS OF STRESS

● PHYSIOLOGICAL RESPONSES

The human body adapts to stress or strain through changes in the autonomic nervous system. Bodily functions and conditions arising in response to threat include physical tension, blushing, fear, perspiration, and increase in blood pressure and volume, body temperature, and heart and pulse rates. The relation between stress and the occurrence and severity of ulcers,

TABLE 8-3 DSM-III-R, Axis V: Global Assessment of Functioning	
Code	*Level of Functioning*
90–81	Absent or minimal symptoms, such as mild anxiety before an examination or an occasional argument with family member; interested and involved in wide range of activities, socially effective, satisfied with life; everyday problems or concerns.
80–71	Transient symptoms and expectable reactions to psychosocial stressors, such as difficulty concentrating after family argument, slight impairment in social, occupational, or school functioning (for example, temporarily behind in schoolwork).
70–61	Mild symptoms, such as depressed mood and mild insomnia or some difficulty in social, occupational, or school functioning.
60–51	Moderate symptoms, such as few friends and conflicts with peers, little affect, occasional panic attacks or moderate difficulty in social, occupational, or school functioning.
50–41	Serious symptoms, such as no friends, inability to keep a job, suicidal thoughts, or serious impairment in social, occupational, or school functioning.
40–31	Some impairment in reality testing or communication, such as illogical, obscure, or irrelevant speech, or major impairment in several areas, such as work or school, family relations.
30–21	Delusions or hallucinations or serious impairment in communication or judgment, or inability to function in almost all areas.
20–11	Some danger of hurting self or others, or occasional failure to maintain minimal personal hygiene, or gross impairment in communication (for example, incoherent or mute).
10–1	Persistent danger of severely hurting self or others (for example, recurrent violence), or persistent inability to maintain minimal personal hygiene, or serious suicidal act.

SOURCE: American Psychiatric Association: *Diagnostic and Statistical Manual of Mental Disorders,* Third Edition, Revised. Washington, DC, American Psychiatric Association, 1987.

gastrointestinal problems, arthritis, hypertension, and other general health conditions has been studied. Consideration has been given to a link between cancer and a sense of loss or hopelessness caused by recent events; it is thought that stress inhibits the body's immune system—as measured by an abnormally low number of white blood cells—thus inviting vulnerability to diseases. If research is borne out, helping persons to master stress in childhood and adolescence could actually protect them from diseases later on.

● PSYCHOLOGICAL RESPONSES

Operational measures of stress include cognitive, emotional, and motivational functions and conditions. Anxiety, or personal anxiousness, is the most generally observed effect of stress and is characterized by either situation-specific or generalized feelings of fear, uneasiness, guilt, and/or role conflict. Psychological disturbances such as disorientation, hostility, and stammering are presumed to be stress effects, as are observable shifts or changes in attitudes toward self and others and in self-confidence, and excessive acts of blaming. Other indicators are impaired performance in ongoing psychological processes such as learning, short- and long-term memory, problem solving, reasoning, concentration, and the completion of tasks.

▲ STRESSFUL LIFE EVENTS AND ADJUSTMENT

Both unpleasant and pleasant experiences that are found in our culture can bring on stress. Getting fired from a job and getting a job promotion are both stressful, but the element common to both experiences is that some kind of adjustment or adaptation is required. Adjustment to stressful situations is most likely dependent on a person's level of personality integration and can be easily accomplished by some people at some *times,* whereas at other times they experience great difficulty. Reactions to certain *kinds* of stress can affect some people and not others; thus, individual sensitivity to stress also varies. The *methods* of coping may also vary from person to person and between groups of people. All people at one time or another experience stress and reactions to stress (Dohrenwend & Dohrenwend, 1982; Holmes & Rahe, 1967; Selye, 1980). Stress is a condition that occurs when people are faced with environmental demands that threaten them in certain ways, and the manner in which people cope with stress—beyond physiological reactions— encompasses many diverse social, personal, and/or physical demands and events (stressors) and reactions (stress responses) to those demands and events. Stressors can be physical or psychological. They can also be intrinsic to a situation (situation-based) or produced by a person's attribution of meanings to a situation that results in a stress response (response-based). Stressors can also be universal to most people or unique to one person's experience.

▲ CONTEMPORARY STRESS

Though the concept of human stress is pragmatic, research is in the early stages and does not yet offer definitive answers or solutions to human living. The value of the stress-adjustment conceptual paradigm rests more on gaining comprehensive understanding of a condition that, at certain levels, can inhibit ongoing social and personal development. Environmental stress, of course, always has been a part of human life; there are only different sources and kinds of stress today. Early studies of stress have concentrated on physical and physiological aspects in the areas of military combat, hazardous occupations, and space travel. Other research and study (McGrath, 1970, p. 3) has emphasized the effects of stress in relation to the following areas:

· Rapid technological and social change
· Social isolation
· Urban crowding
· Tasks that involve adapting to and coping with highly demanding and new situations
· Tasks that involve adapting to and coping with repetition, drudgery, and boredom
· Work and social situations that involve restricted interpersonal and role relations, especially in relation to authoritarianism and autocratic leadership modes
· Situations that involve ambiguous, unstructured, and conflicting role demands among people and between groups of people

▲ STRESSORS

Stress that requires adjustment to a situation or to oneself involves a relationship between the person and his or her environment. Stress occurs when there is an imbalance between the environmental requirements and the person's response capability, or between the subjective perception of demands and one's capability.

● PHYSICAL STRESSORS

Extreme noise, heat or cold, unfamiliar surroundings, and life-threatening situations all involve actual or anticipated physical injury, pain, or death. Some physical-stressor events are outside normal experiences and significant enough that almost anyone would have strong reactions to them. The DSM-III-R defines posttraumatic stress disorder as a type of stress reaction seen in individuals who have experienced an unexpected highly traumatic event. Included in this category would be such events as floods, tornadoes, military combat, assault, torture, earthquakes, airplane crashes, and other accidents resulting in serious injury or death. The stress response consists of an initial emotional outcry, followed by denial (for example, emotional numbing, avoidance of stressor ideas), an intrusive phase (that is, unbidden ideas and feelings), and a phase of working through and completion. The phases are not automatic, and early intervention is important to prevent a chronic disorder. The stress symptoms are related to the traumatic event and not necessarily a sign of other mental or emotional problems.

● THREAT TO SELF-ESTEEM

Actual or anticipated injury or pain to the psychological self is threatening to the ego. For example, negative self-evaluation due to task failure carries intense ego threat: the painful stress response of shame occurs, although there is no actual physical harm. The feeling of self-disparagement requires compensatory adjustment to the felt lowering of self-image. Failure to meet one's own expectations or ideals is especially stressful when it is unexpected.

● DISRUPTION OF SOCIAL RELATIONSHIPS

Interpersonal threat, or the actual or anticipated disruption of social relationships, is a stress-inducing condition. The loss or disruption of interpersonal relationships may represent a form of stress distinct from either physical threat or ego threat. It is based on the functions of *other* persons as sources of stimulation, demands, rewards, and definitions of reality (McGrath, 1970, p. 63). Stressful life events, particularly the disruption of attachment bonds (through, for example, death, marital discord, divorce, geographic movement, refugee status, end of child rearing, retirement), have been associated with the onset of clinical depression (Klerman & Weisman, 1986).

● RESTRICTED AND/OR IMPOVERISHED CONDITIONS

This is a compound form of stress. The restricted environment may involve deprivation of physical needs (such as sleep, movement, food), psychological needs (for example, varied stimulation), and/or interpersonal needs (such as interaction, affection, social affiliation). Restricted environments such as might be found in crowded living conditions, for example, contain elements of overstimulation leading to enforced intimacy with others or, conversely, offer less opportunity for individual self-expression.

● CONFLICT SITUATIONS

Another demand placed on people that results in stress is conflict. Conflict ensues when two or more incompatible responses take place simultaneously. A conflict of goals can occur when an inner need is incompatible with an external demand in the environment, when two external demands compete, or when two inner needs are in opposition. The conflicting situation, as originally studied and defined by Miller (1944), usually leads to either approach or avoidance behavior or a combination of the two.

· *Approach-approach conflict.* Two equally desirable goals conflict. Choosing one means giving up the other. Two good job offers, for example, would lead to agonizing over which one to take and the feeling of doubt after making the choice.

· *Approach-avoidance conflict.* Making a decision can have both positive and negative consequences. Entering into marriage is a happy occasion, but the anticipation of new responsibilities and the loss of individual freedom can also create apprehension.

· *Avoidance-avoidance conflict.* Making a decision between two equally undesirable goals is a stressful situation. People caught up in boring or unchallenging jobs during midlife often feel powerless and avoid making any change of career because the prospect of starting over again is too threatening or they fear that they will not be able to support their families.

· *Double approach-avoidance conflict.* Two different goals or desires may contain elements of both approach and avoidance. Deciding between a high-paying but boring job and a low-paying but stimulating job would be an example of this stressful situation.

● **FRUSTRATION**

Frustration is the obstruction of or interference with an ongoing action or thwarting of a felt need and the stressful feelings that result from such blocking. Any need can be obstructed, whether it involves the expression of an emotion, the desire to think of oneself or others in certain ways, or the striving for a specific goal or object. In a fast-paced and changing society, there are many sources of frustration:

· *Inaccessible material objects.* Consumption of goods and getting services have become necessary for many people as evidence of status and self-worth. People feel frustration when they cannot get the goods and services that they see advertised or others possessing.

· *Failure.* The likelihood of failure is increased in our society by our intense competitiveness. The value placed on individualism in the society also implies that each person is responsible for his or her own failure, and so the potential for frustration and the likelihood of blaming oneself are great.

· *Delays.* In a society that values time and emphasizes punctuality, any delay is frustrating. For example, missing the car pool to get to one's job in the city can be extremely frustrating and stressful.

· *Loss.* The death of a loved one, the breaking of friendships, the dissolution of a marriage, or movement to a different part of the country can cause sorrow, grief, and frustration. People feel helpless when they have no control over things that happen in their lives.

· *Meaninglessness.* Although living a more meaningful life is beginning to be recognized as an important value in our society, many people do not find opportunities in work or other areas of life that provide fulfillment. Growing out of the frustration is often the feeling that society is to blame and nothing can be done about it.

Fulfillment of needs can be completely or partly obstructed, and the interference can be external or internal, material or social, personal or impersonal. Frustration may be temporary or permanent; chronic frustration has been linked to gastric ulcers, lower back pains, and other illnesses that can be diagnosed as psychosomatic in nature. Because a person's response to frustration can become habitual, it is important for counselors to assist clients in developing frustration tolerance. It is especially important for clients to be aware of their frustration thresholds for different needs and needs-in-situations and to learn coping approaches that are most harmonious for them and in their relations with others.

▲ THEORIES ON COPING WITH STRESS

Coping is the means and process by which the person comes to terms with stresses; it is a way to prevent, alleviate, or respond to stress-inducing circumstances. *Wellness*, as a developmental-coping strategy, seeks optimal human functioning along six dimensions: emotional, physical, mental, social, occupational, and spiritual.

● PSYCHOANALYTIC THEORY

According to psychoanalytic theory, stress stems from intrapsychic conflict, and the defense mechanisms that are brought into play are automatic and unconscious reactions arising out of the conflict. Frustration can be dealt with through repression, displacement, projection, reaction formation, negation, intellectualization, regression, and sublimation (Mahl, 1971).

● PERSONALITY TYPES

Friedman (1969) and Glass (1977) have contended that people with certain personalities are more or less prone to stress. "Type A" personalities tend not to want to lose control and will struggle harder and become more aggressive, impatient, and competitive under stress. "Type B" personalities tend to take circumstances as they come and are more relaxed and easygoing. Type A personalities have been found to be more coronary-prone than Type B personalities. A great deal can be learned from the attitudes that Type B personalities have developed in facing life problems; part of the counseling endeavor is to help clients gain a realistic perspective of just what life is and how best to live it. There are always many sides to a predicament—positive as well as negative. Gaining a realistic perspective on oneself in life is a major goal, along with learning how to relax, pursuing interesting ventures, maintaining physical health, and balancing physical activity and exercise in relation to mental activity and work.

● LEARNED HELPLESSNESS

Learned helplessness is a response to finding that one can exert no influence over an outcome. The feeling is one of helplessness, being out of control, or depression. According to some researchers (Hiroto & Seligman, 1975; Seligman, 1975), this is a learned attitude. According to others, the condition may actually help to reduce stress (Gatchel & Proctor, 1976). Because life is full of stresses, almost everyone suffers occasionally from low spirits and a sense of helplessness. However, a client who has multiple occurrences of these feelings that cause negative changes within his or her life, or whose feelings of depression last for more than six to eight weeks, needs help to overcome the condition. Helping clients to see the whole picture rather than dwelling on specifics, and the future rather than the past, is especially crucial in the multicultural counseling approach.

■ MARITAL AND FAMILY CONCERNS

Though customs concerning marriage and family differ in societies around the world, no society is without the family. It is the basic unit in society, having as its nucleus two or more adults living together and cooperating in the care and rearing of their own or adopted children. The family is important for (1) providing satisfactions, patterning, and control of affectional needs (intimacy and social-sexual relations), (2) care and rearing of the young, (3) economic cooperation, and (4) enculturation into the society. Marriage and family, thus, provide opportunities for important social and personal interaction that can foster social and personal growth.

▲ CONTEMPORARY LIVING PATTERNS

Since 1790, our federal government has asked Americans to report where they live and with whom. The people living in a house (or an apartment, or a room) are known collectively as a *household*. In 1990, 245.8 million persons—out of a total population of 249 million—belonged to some form of household unit (the remainder were in institutions or other kinds of group living arrangements) (U.S. Bureau of the Census, 1991b).

The 93.4 million households in our country exist in a wide variety of types and sizes (average size is 2.63 persons per household), but just two basic categories of households are identified: family and nonfamily. A *family household* consists of at least two persons, the householder and one or more additional family members related to the householder through marriage, birth, or adoption. Three major subtypes of family households are further distinguished: married-couple, female householder (no husband present), and male householder (no wife present). A *nonfamily household* consists of a householder who either lives alone or exclusively with persons who are not related to the householder. The 1990 census reported 66 million family households among the 93.4 million households (71%) (U.S. Bureau of the Census, 1991b).

● TRADITIONAL NUCLEAR FAMILIES

Nuclear families are those composed of husband, wife, and their own or adopted children. The nuclear family is universal in all known human groups, past and present. The historical background of the nuclear family in the United States is based on the traditional family structure of Europe as modified in this country. However, traditional family structure and function have changed in response to a changing ethic of the family in Western culture. Burgess and Locke (1953, p. vii) in the early 1950s noted the transition of the family in the United States from "institution" to "companionship"—that is, a unity of interacting persons. Today, studies and popular opinion reveal that the traditional nuclear family model, once considered the ideal family institution, may be less possible in today's fast-changing society. Attainment of the nuclear family ideals has become more difficult as a result of the rise in divorces, dual-career marriages, and economic necessity forcing both adults to be employed.

In 1990 almost 80% (52.3 million) of the 66 million families in the United States were married couples, and almost half (37%) of those families had children of their own under age 18. Significant changes in the traditional American family have taken place since 1970. Average family size declined from 3.58 members in 1970 to 3.17 in 1990, and the percentage of married-couple families without children rose from 44% in 1970 to 51% in 1990. Although married-couple families without children present in the home have consistently accounted for about 30% of all households since 1970, the proportion accounted for by two-parent families *with* children has declined dramatically. Only 26% of all households were two-parent families in 1990, down substantially from their 40% of the total in 1970, while the number of single-parent families more than doubled between 1970 and 1990, from 3.8 million to 9.7 million (8.4 million of these were maintained by women).

Special issues. The nuclear family is generally thought to be a better structure for coping with the stresses of a technical society, while the extended family structure is generally thought to be more effective, or at least more characteristic, in rural, agricultural societies (Ruiz, 1981, p. 193). However, major psychological dilemmas confront the nuclear family in the United States:

- Frustration and guilt felt by working mothers (64% of all families with children under age 18 had an employed mother in 1990) who cannot devote attention to their children and home
- Conflict or neglect between husband and wife in assuming shared household duties
- Desire of the wife for creative self-expression, challenge, and a career outside the home
- Pressures on both husband and wife from a mixture of nuclear family idealism and desired standards of parenting practices for children
- In closely knit families whose emotional needs are met through ongoing personal interactions, painful separation anxiety when children leave for college, work, or military service, or to establish their own families

In addition, the members of a traditional nuclear family also have certain legal responsibilities toward one another. The laws of most countries require that a husband and wife must live together and not physically or mentally harm each other. Laws also require parents to support their children and not neglect or abuse them. The society further expects each member of the family to respect and help the other members. Most families, of whatever form, find ways to solve their daily living problems, even when other problems require the support of relatives, friends, or professional help. Additional stresses on the family unit include insufficient financial resources, quarrels between parents, rebellion of children, and infertility.

Some ethnic-cultural groups are often singled out for their absence of serious family conflict. The low rate of divorce for Chinese and other Asian Americans, for example, is often attributed to the characteristics of their family system and their segregated position in the general society, which insulates them from the pressures of modern life. It is also believed that whatever deviance might be present is taken care of by the ethnic community itself. However, Berk and Hirata (1973) have pointed out that these generalities may be more myth than fact, and Kim (1978) has postulated: "There is in fact a whole collection of culturally-based Asian-American behavior patterns which ought to lead—if we are to accept the tenets of Western psychiatry—to wholesale mental disorders. Subordination of self to family, disapproval of emotional expression, enforced deference to the vertical authority structure of the family, and disapproval of self-assertion or expression of desires presumably do not lead to mental disorders in the Asian societies of which they are integral and essential cultural elements. To the Asian American, however, they may well be not only sources of psychological stress, but may also serve as impediments to seeking professional help" (p. 24).

Dissolution of a marriage. Evidence for the decline in the traditional American nuclear family is seen in the annual rate of marriages and divorces; in 1990, there were 2.4 million marriages and 1.2 million divorces. Also frequently cited is the ratio of divorced persons to 1000 married persons. For example, between 1970 and 1990, the proportion tripled from 47 in 1970 to 142 in 1990. For Black Americans, the rise was even greater, going from 83 per 1000 to 282 per 1000 in the same period. For White Americans, the ratio was 44 per 1000 in 1970 and 133 per 1000 in 1990, and for Hispanic Americans, the ratio was 61 per 1000 in 1970 and 129 per 1000 in 1990. The highest divorce ratio overall with regard to race, sex, or age was for Black women: 358 divorced in 1990 per 1000 married and living with their husbands. Various explanations are given for our high divorce rates:

· The stress of demands from living in a rapidly changing society
· Individually centered desires and options for self-expression and freedom

Long-term trends toward later marriage—after age 25—point to the possibility of marital stability in the future.

Generally, there is more concern about the aftermath of divorce than about distressed intact families. Services for troubled families should be available before family life deteriorates to the point where a divorce is imminent or children must be placed in care outside the family. Family counseling and support programs should be available at the time when parents are first becoming distressed, are considering divorce, or file for legal separation, and not only after the divorce has occurred. Family counseling is also important even when dissolution is seen as a solution and not as the problem. Dissolution of intolerable marriages may, for example, allow women to leave their alcoholic or violent husbands, ending detrimental situations that would otherwise entrap family members.

Children's responses to dissolution of a marriage. Children suffer especially painful experiences in the period during or following parental and family turmoil, separation, and divorce (Furman, 1974; Gardner, 1970, 1976, 1977; Kelly & Wallerstein, 1976; Loewenstein, 1979; Logan, 1980; Tessman, 1978; Wallerstein, 1977). Very young children show increased anxiety, fearfulness, insecurity, temper tantrums, fantasy withdrawal, and regression. Older children express sorrow, sadness, and helplessness. Many children also wish for reconciliation, feel guilt and take personal responsibility for the breakup, feel abandoned, or attempt to act as parental surrogates. Children are most likely to adjust to the changes in their lives "if parents make a satisfactory adjustment and maintain adequate relationships with their children" (Logan, 1980, p. 28; Wallerstein & Blakeslee, 1989; Wallerstein & Kelly, 1990). Throughout the history of the human experience, a large proportion of children have experienced loss of a parent sometime during childhood through death, divorce, or desertion. Formerly, many children were sent to live in orphanages, in foster homes, or with relatives. Today, many more children with single parents live with their mothers (or fathers) in an independent household. Because of this change the number of children in single-parent families has been rising gradually in the past two decades.

● SINGLE-PARENT FAMILIES

Single-parent families consist of either father or mother and his or her children. These heads of families include divorced, never-married, separated, and widowed women or men. Besides marital discord, spouses may be missing due to military service or employment elsewhere, or otherwise away from home involuntarily. The number of single-parent situations rose from 3.8 million in 1970 to 6.9 million in 1980 and 9.7 million in 1990. The majority of single-parent families are headed by the mother. Mother-child families represented 6% of all families in the United States in 1970, 9% in 1980, and 10% in 1990.

All three of the largest racial/ethnic population groups—White, Black, and Hispanic—have shown an increase in one-parent families with children under age 18 corresponding to the decline of two-parent families. Changes in the family compositions of the three population groups have generally followed the same pattern, although the proportions and shifts in proportions have been much greater for Black Americans, as shown in Table 8-4.

Children in single-parent families. An increasing proportion of children are in one-parent families. The high incidence of divorce means that there is an increased likelihood that children will not be living in a home with both parents present. Seventy-three percent of the 64 million children under

TABLE 8-4   Changes in composition of families, 1970–1990.

	White			Black			Hispanic[a]	
	1970	1980	1990	1970	1980	1990	1980	1990
Two-parent family	90%	83%	77%	64%	48%	40%	74%	67%
One-parent family:								
Mother-child	9%	15%	19%	33%	49%	56%	24%	29%
Father-child	1%	2%	4%	3%	3%	4%	2%	4%

SOURCE: Data from *Population Profile of the U.S. 1991*, U.S. Bureau of the Census, 1991.
NOTE: Numbers are rounded.
[a]1970 data not available.

18 years old in 1990 were living with *two* parents, as compared with 77% in 1980 and 85% in 1970. These two parents are not always the natural parents of the child; they may include stepparents and parents by adoption. About 15% of children living with two parents are stepchildren. The proportion living with only *one* parent increased from 12% in 1970 to 20% in 1980 and 25% in 1990. While the vast majority of children in a one-parent situation live with their mothers, the proportion living with their fathers rose from 9% in 1970 to 13% in 1990. Of the 15.9 million children who lived with one parent in 1990, 39% lived with a divorced parent, 31% with a never-married parent, 20% with a separated parent, 7% with a widowed parent, and 3% with a married parent whose spouse was absent for some reason other than separation due to marital discord. Fifty-five percent of Black children under 18 years old, 30% of Hispanic children, and 19% of White children lived with one parent in 1990 (U.S. Bureau of the Census, 1991b).

Special issues. All types of families have some problems and need some support. Many of the issues in single-parent families are similar to those in other family systems, such as traditional nuclear families or those in which both parents are employed. The most pressing concern for single-parent families is economic—providing and maintaining an adequate standard of living. A personal experience for the single parent is loneliness and a sense of isolation. These feelings are often associated with lack of social contact with other adults, feelings of being locked into a child's world, and having no one to consult or help with personal, economic, and child-rearing problems. The difficulty is compounded by fatigue and task overload, since many single parents have to fulfill the work role as well as the roles of homemaker and parent. Kimmel (1980) adds, "There is also some degree of social stigma about being a single parent that may involve a kind of 'second-class-citizenship' in settings where two parents are the norm or where single persons without children are more easily accepted"(p. 210).

Clinical depression can become a major mental condition for single parents. It is related to anger and resentment or a feeling of failure and low self-esteem as a result of the disrupted marriage (Weissman, 1977). In the case of a deceased spouse, the single parent may have to carry the burden of grief and mourning. Social-sexual life is also of concern for single fathers and single mothers. Studies have noted that divorced fathers with children felt that living together with a woman was not acceptable as a lifestyle and most did not feel comfortable about revealing their social-sexual life to their children (Orthner, Brown, & Ferguson, 1976; Rosenthal & Keshet, 1978). Children of single-parent families have also been observed to have more than usual behavioral and achievement problems in school.

Most of the foregoing conditions are not unique to single-parent families. They are also reported in nuclear families in which one parent is uninvolved, frequently absent, or otherwise unavailable.

● BLENDED FAMILIES

Blended families are families reconstituted by the remarriage of a divorced man and/or divorced woman. They could include his or her children, or both children, from the former marriage. Because the majority of divorced couples tend to remarry, this family form will probably increase in the future. Men are more likely than women to remarry and do so more quickly after a divorce. Special issues include readjustment to parent and child roles, acceptance of other siblings, cohesion of a family unit, and the development of role-appropriate and emotionally mature sex-role relations between the new parent and half-children and between stepbrothers and stepsisters.

● EXTENDED FAMILIES

Extended families, or joint families, include other relatives or in-laws who share the household with the nuclear family. Several generations of related families may live in the same household or in nearby neighborhoods. In many cases, the oldest male is in charge. Extended families could also include a single, abandoned, legally separated, divorced, or widowed mother or father living with his or her own children, plus other relatives. Economic conditions often compel young families to live with more stable relatives until they can make it on their own. Ethnic group traditions also foster extended-family living.

The extended family, with its kinship relations, is traditional to Mexican Americans and other Hispanic groups: "Close relationships are not limited to the nuclear family, but include aunts and uncles, grandparents, cousins, inlaws, and even *compadres* (godparents). Hence, those on whom one can rely for support form a numerically large group" (Alvirez & Bean, 1976, p. 277). Though familial idealism can hinder mobility when attachment to people, places, and things is overemphasized, the support and sustenance given by an extended family is valuable in helping each member attain goals that might be individually difficult, or impossible, to achieve. Caring for the aged within the household is one example that characterizes some extended-family living.

Although the tribal groupings of Native Americans do not fall within the strict definition of the extended family, the feeling of never being alone has dimensions similar to those of an extended family. For example, adoption between kin is easy and widespread among the Eskimos of North Alaska (Chance, 1966). In the case of the Pueblo culture, "men join their wives' households and economically support them but retain ritual, leadership, and disciplinary roles in their natal households. Thus, they discipline their sisters' children and play a passive role in their wife's household" (Price, 1976, p. 261).

● AUGMENTED FAMILIES

Augmented families include nonrelatives who share the household with the nuclear family and other related family members. They may be roomers, boarders, lodgers, friends, transients, or other long-term guests. Although not related, these persons often serve as surrogate parental models and may exercise major influence on the group living pattern (Billingsley, 1968).

● SHARED LIVING BY UNMARRIED COUPLES

A nonfamily shared household is defined as consisting of two or more unrelated persons of the same or opposite sex living together in the same housing unit. Because the arrangement meets many personal and social needs, it can be considered as a family variation.

The number of single persons of the opposite sex living together (cohabitation) has increased. In 1970 there were 523,000 unmarried-couple households, in 1980 there were 1.6 million, and in 1990 there were nearly 2.9 million. Of the 5.7 million partners who were in unmarried-couple households in 1990, the largest proportion was 25 to 34 years of age (41%), followed by partners under 25 years (23%). Thirty-one percent of the unmarried households contained children under age 15. Despite the spectacular nature of the increase in nonfamily households, the fact remains that the majority of Americans live in some kind of family situation. However, this does not deny that the structure and size of the family has undergone major changes in recent decades, only that its strength as a basic social unit has withstood powerful forces for change. Nonetheless, unmarried couples have many of the same relationship concerns, and problems that need managing, as married couples do:

- Need for the relationship to continue evolving and growing, or to salvage or end a relationship
- Lifetime expectations of each other
- Need to be flexible
- Lack of someone to talk to
- Need for handling conflict and emotions
- Need for communication and negotiation and compromise skills
- Responsibilities of child rearing; relationships with children from previous marriage
- Sexual compatibility with partner
- Balancing two careers, different religions, and divergent family backgrounds
- Being shadowed by one's divorce, or that of parents
- Biological deadlines for having children

● NONFAMILY HOUSEHOLDERS LIVING ALONE

In 1990, 23 million adults lived alone. These persons accounted for 12% of all adults in 1990, compared with 7% in 1970. The majority of persons living alone are women (61%), although the rate of increase is faster for men. Women living alone tend to be older than their male counterparts. Women, on average, live longer than men, and women are more likely to be widowed. In 1990, more than half of the women living alone were 65 years or older, compared to 21% of men living alone. However, among women living alone, the proportion aged 25 to 44 doubled between 1970 and 1990 (from 9% to 21%). The largest proportion of men who lived alone in 1990 were 25 to 44 (47%), a considerably higher proportion than in 1970 (26%).

Living alone, either by choice or circumstance, implies the need for acceptance and understanding of a single's lifestyle. Living alone has a number of benefits, including greater independence, freedom, and time for one's self. According to Andre (1991), because people living alone tend to develop feelings of loneliness, it is crucial for them to differentiate loneliness from aloneness; one does not have to equal the other.

● HOMELESS PERSONS

Homelessness has become a chronic condition for an increasing number of Americans. During the 1980s, there was a threefold increase in the number of shelter beds and shelter occupancy (Burt, 1992). Estimates of the total number of homeless persons throughout the country on a given night range from 250,000 to 3 million. The first census count of homeless people was in 1990, when for two nights between 6 P.M. and 4 A.M., a total of 228,621 persons—178,828 in emergency shelters and 49,793 at street locations—were counted, although the estimate was considered to be low. The number of homeless differs from city to city and from state to state. New York City has the highest reported number (33,830), followed by Los Angeles (7,706), Chicago (6,764), and San Francisco (5,569). According to a 1991 study by the U.S. Conference of Mayors, the composition of the homeless population in cities was:

50% single men	48% Black
35% members of families	34% White
12% single women	15% Hispanic
3% unaccompanied youth	3% others

A 1988 Institute of Medicine review of data found three patterns of homelessness: temporary, episodic, and chronic. Various explanations for the increase of homeless people have been proposed:

· The shift in the nation's economy away from manufacturing to service, resulting in unemployment and underemployment
· Lack of affordable housing
· Reduced government funding for assistance programs
· Increase in other social and personal problems, such as substance abuse,

poverty, domestic violence, and inattention to the needs of deinstitu-tionalized mentally ill persons.

Local, state, and federal programs for the homeless include emergency shelters, food, health care, mental health care, housing, educational programs, job training, and other community services.

● INTERGROUP MARRIAGES

Mixed or interracial marriage—marriage outside one's own racial group—continues to be the exception in the United States. As recently as 1967, when the Supreme Court declared unconstitutional laws prohibiting mixed marriages, such marriages were illegal in 18 states. Since then, marriages between Whites and Blacks and between members of other groups have increased dramatically—a 92% increase between 1970 and 1977, although the total 421,000 mixed marriages represented only 0.2% of the 48 million marriages in the United States that year. At that time, 125,000 of the 421,000 mixed marriages were between Blacks and Whites; the incidence of Asian/out-of-group marriages is higher. In 1980, 166,000 Black-White married couples were reported (Sherman, 1983). The "exchange theory" suggests that each partner in a mixed marriage exchanges a benefit that he or she has in society; taken together, these benefits elevate each partner in one sort of status or another.

Marital homogamy, a union of husband and wife who possess similar social and psychological attributes and characteristics, appears to be the prevailing American mate-selection pattern: "Most people marry others like themselves in age, residence, racial and ethnic group membership, religion, education, and social class. And in all of these matters, marriage arrangement, in the sense of family influence, may have considerable influence. Only in the matter of the psychological characteristics of the mate is there evidence of heterogamy in American mate-selection patterns" (McGee, 1977, p. 376).

Special issues. The rule of confining relations to one's own group is prescribed by both majority and minority groups, and informal sanctions or ostracism are frequently invoked when the rule is broken. However, according to Manuel (1982), the endogamous nature of social relations in the multiculture also has the effect of strengthening group identity: "Obviously, restriction of a large proportion of one's social relations to the group, especially in mate selection, strengthens the sense of peoplehood, accentuates the distinctive characteristics, and possibly reinforces the special ethnic qualities of the group" (p. 22). The major social issue facing members of mixed marriages, or individuals contemplating cross-racial or cross-ethnic marriage, is the attitude or existing social group norm held by various groups in the society. Many American ethnic groups retain strong values about marrying only within their own group; according to McGee (1977), "It is probably accurate to say that in general persons defining themselves as ethnic marry others of the same ethnicity more often than they do other people" (p. 377). It is especially painful to the participants in cross-group marriages when parents and friends reject them or fail to give them support. According to Porterfield (1978), young Black women in particular are hostile to the practice of interracial dating and marriage. Black women outnumber Black men in the United States, and to many Black women, according to Porterfield, intermarriage is seen as siphoning off of the most eligible Black males. They see it also as personal rejection, and Black men who marry Whites, they believe, are accepting the dominant White society's concept of beauty.

Children of intergroup marriages. Children of mixed marriages also suffer emotional consequences, especially during the period of adolescence. When they are young, they seem to have less problem adjusting than they will later. It can be assumed that young children are aware of different shades of skin color, but they have not learned the racial significance society attaches to them. When parents help their children to identify with both their heritages, the problem of cultural-racial-ethnic "limbo" can be minimized.

Children of American military servicemen and Korean, Japanese, Vietnamese, Laotian, and Cambodian women also suffer emotional consequences in foreign countries. No one knows how many Amerasian children there are, but estimates begin at 30,000 and run to five times that number. In Vietnam, the children's plight seems more one of neglect and avoidance—they are not recognized as people. Unlike in Korea and Japan, where the children of American servicemen often suffer overt discrimination, racism is not a strong factor in Vietnamese life. Most Vietnamese Amerasian children are not orphans, but live with their mother and/or grandmother. Many of the children and mothers correspond with the father and other relatives in the United States, and most of the children are the products of long-term, stable relationships. All the Amerasian children who are being accepted under current immigration law have been adopted (Allman, 1982; "Amerasians, Vets Bond," 1990).

▲ VIOLENCE IN FAMILIES

Although there has been great public concern and fear about violence in general, it is only recently that violence within the family has received attention. The concept of family is normally cherished as the source of love and nurturance, but the family is also the most frequent setting for all kinds of violence, including homicide. According to surveys, violence in some form or another is believed to occur in 50% of American families (Gelles, 1974, 1979; Gelles & Straus, 1975; Straus, Gelles, & Steinmetz, 1980). Marital violence also has greater acceptance among those with higher educational levels; although the highest reported incidence of spouse abuse is found among the poor, it is believed that poor people are more likely to come to the attention of public agencies, while middle- and upper-class women have their privacy protected (Levinger, 1966; Martin, 1976; Steinmetz & Straus, 1974).

● **WHAT IS VIOLENCE?**

In interviews with more than 2,000 married couples (Straus, Gelles, & Steinmetz, 1980), the following incidents were reported:

16% said one spouse had thrown something at the other, and 10% had used an object to hit a spouse

18% had experienced slapping

24% had pushed or shoved a spouse

6% had beaten up a spouse

4% had used a knife or gun to threaten a spouse

Fifty-three percent of children had seriously beaten up a brother or sister, making "extreme" violence more frequent between siblings than between parent and child or husband and wife. In violence toward children between 3 and 17 years old, 71% of parents had slapped or spanked them, 46% had pushed or shoved them, 20% had hit them with an object, and 8% had kicked, punched, or beat them.

● **WHAT CAUSES VIOLENCE?**

Women are especially vulnerable to violence in our society, and violence toward women cuts across ethnic group lines, lifestyles, economic status, educational levels, marital status, and age ranges (Green, 1980; Lieberknecht, 1978).

Myths and attitudes that harm women. According to Lieberknecht (1978) and Heppner (1978), to understand the battered woman it is necessary to understand her situation and her needs and to recognize and deal with common misconceptions, such as:

· A woman who is beaten must like it, otherwise she would leave. Her endurance of abuse is falsely attributed to masochistic enjoyment.

· If the woman were a better wife or loved the man more he would not beat her. According to this misconception, the woman "caused" the attack and she must try harder. Women are sometimes beaten for insignificant reasons, such as a coffee cup left sitting on the kitchen counter, or for no reason.

· It is a man's right, prerogative, or duty as head of the family in his home to do whatever is necessary, including striking his wife and children. "The idea that the man should have all the responsibility and power in the family has been common. However, people are becoming increasingly aware that every person in a family needs to have autonomy and an equal share in family matters. No matter how responsibility is divided in the family, beatings are never justified"(Lieberknecht, 1978, p. 654).

The fact that violence toward women and children generally seems to have underlying moral and socially condoned reasons for it has serious implications for the entire culture (Greven, 1991). "Spare the rod and spoil the child" has long been a favorite saying, and surveys show that violence may be a cultural norm: 16% to 32% of American adults approve of husband- and wife-hitting (Martin, 1976; Stark & McEvoy, 1970).

Other factors related to violence. Alcoholism is related to the triggering of many cases of family violence, but it is commonly viewed as a symptom of deeper underlying problems. It is also common for women to be abused while pregnant. Battered women do not have personality characteristics dissimilar to those of other women, men who batter do not necessarily have observable personality characteristics that differ from those of other men, and the family that experiences violence may appear normal to outsiders. External stresses such as unemployment are also related to violence in the family. Even rising temperature and humidity make tempers flare. The commonsense view, as evidenced by police reports and occurrences of collective violence such as riots, shows that aggressive behavior in general increases as the temperature rises to about 85 or 90 degrees.

Sexual abuse—forced sex without consent and with children—may be considered a form of violence. Family sexual abuse occurs in all social classes and in urban as well as rural environments (Finkelhor, 1977). The overwhelming majority of child victims are girls, who can carry the psychological effects to later years. Liss (1980) has noted in her study of adult women prostitutes that the mean age of the first sexual experience for the prostitute group was 14.6 years, in contrast to 16.8 years for the nonprostitute group. Nearly 23% of the prostitute group had experienced a forced first sexual situation, while 12.5% of the nonprostitute group had experienced a forced situation. It is believed that incestuous abuse usually begins when the child is between 6 and 11 years old (Browning & Boatman, 1977), though many younger children are also molested and cases involving infants have been reported. Physical force is rarely used, but the child is often exploited by her natural trust and desire for affection.

● COUNSELING CONSIDERATIONS

Prevention and awareness of the scope of violence are major goals for counselors. People in the society need to realize the extent of violence in families, of what people do to each other, and how powerless people feel. Counselors need to help those who have been abused in working through their feelings of fear, shame, sense of helplessness, and grief over the loss of a relationship and self-respect. Rebuilding self-confidence and self-belief is the ultimate goal. Intervention is often called for and placement of the abused person away from the abuser may be necessary (Flanzer, 1982).

■ SUICIDE

Suicide is another serious concern in American society. Two distinctions can be made: (1) *suicide* as a fatal act and (2) *suicidal attempt* as a declaration of intent to commit self-injury with the aim of self-destruction.

More than 30,000 Americans kill themselves each year. In 1988, the suicide rate for all ages was 12.7 suicides per 100,000 population; 79% of the suicides were committed by men and 21% by women. Twenty-one percent of all suicides are committed by people over 65 years of age. Suicide is apparently the highest cause of death of youth ages 15 to 24, and the rate for this age group has nearly tripled since 1950; in 1977, the suicide rate for this age group reached a peak of nearly 14 suicides per 100,000 population and in 1988 was 13 per 100,000 (U.S. Department of Health and Human Services, 1990). Resnick (1980) reports increased risk in association with the absence of a spouse. Single, never-married persons show double the suicide rate of 11 per 100,000 for married persons, while divorced women show 18, widowed individuals show 24, and divorced men show a startling rate of 69 per 100,000. It is also probable that many deaths such as accidents and murders actually are suicides, raising the rate even higher. Society generally finds suicide repugnant, and it can be contended that physicians, coroners, hospitals, families, and insurance companies intentionally or unintentionally deny or conceal suicides. Suicide attempts have been recorded in children under 5—some attempt to jump out of windows, refuse to eat, or threaten to run in front of cars, and others have bitten themselves. Other marginal suicide attempts could include driving while intoxicated, riding motorcycles without protective gear, repeated car accidents, and anorexia nervosa (severe loss of appetite).

▲ THEORIES OF SUICIDE

The act of intentionally taking one's life or threatening to take one's life defies uniform sociological and psychological explanation or agreement. Various social problems and conditions are often blamed for suicide or attempted suicide: unemployment, economic deprivation, broken love affairs, increased divorce rate, single-parent families, widespread drug abuse, permissiveness, loss of traditional social and psychological support structures, and others. Suicide occurs in different proportions in all societies—both primitive and technologically advanced—and no period of history is without records of suicide. There are probably few individuals to whom the idea of suicide has never occurred at some time(Hendin, 1982).

● SUICIDE AS A SOCIAL CONDITION
Early theorists in sociology and other related fields, such as Durkheim (1951), Cavan (1928), Gibbs and Martin (1958), Henry and Short (1954), and Sainsbury (1955) viewed suicide and/or attempted suicide as the product of collective social problems that faced certain kinds of societies or certain disorganized areas within a society. General explanations provided by these writers, respectively, were: (1) diminished social integration, such as might be noted in the loss of a family following divorce; (2) urban plight; (3) the powerful influence of social class status, or status integration; (4) external and internal social restraints related to one's socioeconomic class; and (5) the interaction of constant residential movement with social isolation and loneliness. Social integration, or disintegration, theories look to external causal

agents and have generally precluded individual determinants to explain suicide.

● SUICIDE AS A PSYCHOLOGICAL CONDITION

Very little in the sociological literature deals with the question of anticipating or preventing suicide. Intervention with suicidal acts, as well as prevention of suicide, is what counselors and other helping professionals consider important. Psychological, psychiatric, and interdisciplinary literature offers a few key formulations and factors that are frequently used to explain personal circumstances of the suicidal person (Farber, 1968; Farberow, 1975, 1980; Farberow & Schneidman, 1961; Giovacchini, 1978; Jacobs, 1971; Roberts, 1975; Stengel, 1970).

Suicide as an irrational act. The thought or idea of taking one's life or the actual killing of oneself is theorized in psychoanalytic principles as an impulsive act that is unconsciously motivated. Freud wrote of the unconscious life/death wish and the love/hate (affection/aggression) dichotomy. Early childhood experiences such as might occur in a disrupted or broken home are believed to contribute to suicide. The suicide-prone person who gives up life has given up hope of being loved. It is also believed that frustration leads to aggression; in the frustration-aggression model, aggression is turned inward (suicide) or outward (homicide). Alfred Adler believed that the urge to inflict pain on relatives or other significant people constituted a significant motive in suicide. A psychological state of depression is also thought to be a prelude to suicide. The psychoanalytic approach defines suicide and suicide intentions as acts of disordered thinking and constitutional irrationality within the individual's personality. Experimental psychologists have shown how groups of rats when inflicted with pain (electric shock) first will attack each other in escape reactions and finally will attack themselves in moments of escape from the stress frustration. Although the experiments are based on behavioral theory, they also appear proximal to psychoanalytic concepts of the turning inward or outward of aggression .

Suicide as process and circumstance. According to this model there is a suicide process that is associated with circumstances in the person's life. The individual and his or her motives and morals (religious and personal concepts of life and death) must all be taken into consideration. Jacobs (1971) believes that suicides and suicide attempters have in common some or all of the following factors:

- A long-standing history of problems from early childhood to the onset of adolescence
- An escalation of problems since the onset of adolescence beyond those normally associated with that stage of development
- Failure to find the adaptive techniques needed to cope with the increasing problems and progressive isolation from meaningful social relationships

· Dissolution of any meaningful relationship in the time preceding the attempt

Jacobs also postulates that adolescents, adults, and individuals from all socioeconomic classes and statuses are subject to the same process. The suicidal person, in this model, believes that he or she has ups and downs in life, but in addition is convinced that life is always down and the future contains the same. Such a vulnerable person, when faced with an unexpected stressful or unsolvable problem, does not view it as simply a part of life, but perceives it within the context of a long history of such situations and the expectation of future ones for which death may be the only answer. Social isolation further compounds the situation, as does rationalizing—justifying away—internalized views that suicide is irrational or immoral (for example, "I'm a worthless person anyway, so it doesn't make any difference if I end my life").

● SUICIDE AS A PSYCHOCULTURAL CONDITION

The psychocultural approach to understanding suicide examines the people and the culture and how the suicidal act has been institutionalized in the group or society. One of the first to take this approach was Firth (1961), who described how on Tikopia, a small Polynesian island, a person who has been insulted will paddle a canoe or swim far out into the Pacific. When his or her absence is noted, a search party will be sent out, and if it is successful, the rescued person regains self-esteem and is sympathetically welcomed back and reintegrated with the society. Farber (1968) has pointed out, "There is the test: 'if they care for me enough, they will come and find me; if they don't, I want to die'" (p. 8).

This approach uses case histories, interviews, questionnaires, and statistics compiled on suicide rates in various cultures and countries as reflections of suicide-producing forces and/or as reflections of the structure of suicide-prone personalities. Although all countries and all cultures face low and high periods of suicide that are related to social changes such as war, economic depressions, and value shifts, there are also suicide rates that tend to be fairly stable over many years. For example, though both Denmark and Norway belong to the same cultural area, Farber reported in 1968 that "Denmark has a very high suicide rate whereas Norway has a low rate (approximately 20 per 100,000 versus 7 per 100,000)" (Farber, 1968, p. 6). The World Health Organization reported in 1989 that the ratio was approximately 27 to 15 (U.S. Bureau of the Census, 1991c). Suicide rates in traditional Jewish populations, such as in Israel, are generally low. According to Headley (1975), in Israel "the largest group of suicides came from Eastern European families, particularly Polish and Rumanian" (p. 220). Headley also contends in his study that "collective identity of the Jews seems to lead to apprehensiveness about personal maintenance of the group ideal. Failure reflects not only on individual self-esteem but on the status of the group as a whole" (p. 227). He also points out a coping mechanism whereby "verbalization is frequent, and it is expected that others will share in the contemplation of the problem"

(p. 228). He continues: "Humor, particularly wry and self-deprecatory, is a means of anticipating pain from the world and blunting its impact, or taking the sting out of suffering. Jewish humor is seldom aggressive toward non-Jews, rather the aggression is turned back on oneself" (Headley, 1975, p. 229). LeVine and Padilla (1980) have also pointed out that "one severe and acute depression reaction among Puerto Ricans is called 'suicide fit.' In a state of intense emotional excitement, the person attempts suicide. The suicidal fit is generally precipitated by disrupted interpersonal relationships" (p. 124); in these cases, disappointment and anger are turned inward against the self rather than outward against significant others.

Cultural stress and suicide. General stress that can be found in most cultures is often seen as leading to suicide: physical illness, emotional exhaustion, loss of loved ones, loss of a job or means of livelihood, and congestive environments are all examples of factors that contribute to stress. Farberow and Simon (1975), in a cross-cultural study of suicide in Los Angeles and Vienna, found that those persons "in Los Angeles were more often in strained or broken interpersonal relationships and under great social and occupational pressures. . . . Alcohol was a serious problem for at least one-third of the decedents in both groups. Those in Los Angeles were occupationally and residentially more mobile than the Viennese" (pp. 201–202). No significant differences were shown for age, sex, and marital status. One major weakness of international studies is the different methods and degrees of accuracy of reporting suicides or attempted suicides by agencies of different governments.

Ethnic group "personality" and suicide. Though overgeneralization must be guarded against, there is some basis for the impression that ethnic group membership may be associated with suicide rates. For example, cultural attitudes of Anglo-Saxons may deny expression of pain, but Italians freely express their feelings both verbally and nonverbally. Americans, especially White males, are oriented to cultural attitudes such as the importance of individual success, the significance of achievement, concern about masculine role, and feelings about dependency relationships. Because Americans are conditioned by their culture to believe they are failures or to feel guilty for not achieving certain standards of conduct, they become frustrated and are vulnerable to suicide. In 1986, the suicide rate for all Americans was 12.7 per 100,000 population. The rate for White males was 22.3, and 11.1 for Black males; it was 5.9 for White females and 2.3 for Black females. Except for the important fact that the suicide rates for White males and females are much higher at most age categories than those of their Black counterparts, the *pattern* of suicide by age categories is similar for White and Black males and White and Black females (for example, the rate rises for all males around adolescence and again after age 65). Reynolds, Kalish, and Farberow (1975) note that in their study of cross-ethnic suicide attitudes, the majority of Black Americans (89%) perceived White Americans as more likely to commit suicide than members of other ethnicities. These researchers also collected information for ethnic groups in Los Angeles County and found that the suicide rate for Japanese Americans in 1970 was 12.0 per 100,000 and for Mexican Americans was 5.0 per 100,000. On the basis of their other findings in general for the ethnic groups studied, the authors concluded:

- "Black Americans are likely to see suicidal persons as crazy . . . and do not see suicide as being a major concern of their ethnic group."
- Japanese Americans are "very likely to see the suicidal person as functioning under extreme stress." They also seem to have less patience with the idea of suicide and the suicide attempter and believe the person is "demanding unreasonable amounts of attention and concern."
- Mexican Americans "see the suicidal person as mentally ill" and "feel that the potential suicide should receive professional help, perhaps the counsel of a priest."
- White Americans "perceive suicide as the outcome of extreme stress, and they respond to it by turning to mental health professionals rather than friends or relatives" (p. 49).

Thus, Black Americans and Mexican Americans tend to see suicide as an act of a mentally ill person, whereas White Americans and Asian Americans tend to see it as a reaction to stress. Both the White American group and the Mexican American group think the person should get help from others.

Suicide in Native American tribes. Native Americans are singled out because of the existence of misconceptions regarding their suicide rate. Traditionally, the phenomenon of suicide has been believed to occur at a higher rate among Native Americans than in any other ethnic group in the United States, but an overall comparison of Native American suicide with that of other groups indicates about the same rate except for some age groups and sex. Fuchs and Havighurst (1973) point out: "First, Indian women show only half the rate of suicide of other American women. Second, Indian males between the ages of fifteen and forty-four show a much higher suicide rate than other American males. Third, after the age of forty-five, Indian suicide rates are substantially lower than the general American rates" (p. 152). The Native American population is numerically small and it is also youthful. The generalization of rates of suicide to whole ethnic groups, such as Native Americans, can be misleading when localized conditions contribute to higher rates and/or contagious (epidemic) suicide occurs. Webb and Willard (1975) contend that "many of the current studies of American Indian suicide are examples of the mistake of viewing American Indian cultures as disturbed forms of Euro-American culture, and therefore to be treated within the same framework as that used for disturbed Euro-Americans" (p. 17). Fuchs and Havighurst (1973) also believe that "if two or three suicides take place on or near a given Indian reservation, this fact is given lurid headlines in the newspapers and the inference is drawn, explicitly or implicitly, that the Indian group suffers from poor mental health" (p. 150).

Regardless of how it is defined or explained, suicide among Native Americans is a problem. Review of the literature by Webb and Willard (1975) has shown different cultural patterns of suicide. These are some of their findings for particular tribal groups:

· *Shoshone*—The often quoted overall suicide rate of 100 per 100,000 Native Americans (approximately ten times the national average) apparently has been misleadingly derived only on Shoshone reservations. The approximately 5,000 Shoshones on reservations in Idaho, Wyoming, and Nevada live a marginal existence with few employment opportunities and "a high level of family disorganization with deaths of significant members." The tragic problem is especially characterized by a high suicide rate "among adolescent males who have been found to have many problems in school, have often dropped out of school, have experienced difficulties with the law, and have records of abusing alcohol and sniffing solvent" (p. 21).

· *Pueblo tribes*—There are diverse Pueblo tribes; some have acculturated to the dominant culture and some continue traditional ways. Overall, Pueblo tribes show no consistent suicide patterns, although the rate has generally been lower than average over extended periods of time.

· *Plains tribes (Dakota and Cheyenne)*—The Dakota and Cheyenne do not seem to have suicide as such, but they do place themselves in high-risk situations, such as driving on the wrong side of the road, so the actual suicide rate may be masked.

· *Uto-Aztecan*—The Pima, Papago, and Yaqui Indians, former desert farmers, have experienced an increase in attempted suicides and some completed suicides. "Acculturational stresses seem to be involved in these groups where suicide until recently was a rarity" (p. 30).

· *White Mountain Apache and Navajo*—Apache and Navajo "suicide patterns seem relatively unchanged over the years. . . . self-inflicted death is, and always has been, intended to influence the behavior of someone in a close kinship or marital relationship" (p. 30). The rate of suicide among the Navajo is low; in 1971, only 8 per 100,000 were reported.

There is no one pattern of suicide among Native Americans. Counselors who work with Native Americans need to take into consideration each client's circumstantial situation, motives, and intentions, in addition to cultural concepts of suicide and death and whether an institutional pattern of suicide is present.

▲ HIGH-RISK CONDITIONS

Can suicide potential be determined? Suicide is one of the most serious yet least understood problems in human communities. A great many myths about suicide tend to lull relatives, friends, and even professional care-providers into a false sense of security about a person's likelihood of committing suicide and recognizing when appropriate crisis intervention is called for (Golan, 1978;

Rueveri, 1979). Because counselors are concerned with helping clients preserve and develop their lives, the question of some kind of "lethality" scale is often foremost in their minds. There are many symptoms that often suggest the conscious intention or possibility of self-destruction: for example, states of depression, loss of appetite or overeating, or talking about suicide and the means to suicide. Metour and Metour (1979) and Slaby, Lieb, and Tancredi (1981), in a comprehensive review of the literature, have compiled a list of high-risk conditions. The various conditions, when grouped into major categories, include the following:

● **INDIVIDUAL FACTORS**
- *Sex.* Women attempt suicide with greater frequency, but only 30% of the attempts are fatal, whereas the fatality rate for men is 70%.
- *Age.* The highest rate of suicide is in the 75 and over age group, second highest is in the 55-to-74 age group, and third highest rate is in the 25-to-34 age group.
- *Occupation.* Professional persons are high risks; this category especially includes business executives and physicians. Physicians over 65 years old and divorced physicians have high rates of suicide.
- *Marital status.* Divorced and widowed individuals have rates four to five times greater than married persons. The first year of widowhood is an especially critical time for suicide.
- *Sexual orientation.* Homosexuals have an increased risk, but especially so if they are subject to depression, are older, or are alcoholic.
- *Living alone.* A person living alone is at increased risk.
- *Education.* Students at prestigious colleges have a higher suicide rate.

● **PSYCHOLOGICAL CONDITIONS AND FACTORS**
- *Depression.* The likelihood of suicide increases 500 times when the person is deeply depressed; insomnia and loss of appetite are often associated with a depressed mood. Suicide is not as frequently associated with depression in young people.
- *Meaninglessness in life.* Suicide-prone persons may have no plans for the future and talk of what people will do when they are gone. When the person feels and demonstrates helplessness or threatens self-destruction—and it goes unnoticed—the risk of suicide is increased.
- *Positive tension.* The person's desire to reduce internal tension can be a motivator for referral. If the person is able to consider alternatives to self-destruction, such as commitment to therapy, the suicide risk is reduced.
- *Hypochondriasis.* Morbid concern with health or delusions of physical diseases increase suicide risk.
- *Schizophrenia.* Males who have combined depressed moods and reality distortion are especially vulnerable to suicide. Hallucinations in which the person believes he or she is being commanded to kill himself or herself increase the risk of suicide.

● BEHAVIORAL SYMPTOMS AND PATTERNS

· *Substance abuse.* Chemicals that alter the person's moods and awareness may amplify self-directed or other-directed violence. Alcohol is involved with 90% of all suicide attempts. The combination of barbiturates with alcohol is especially lethal and can cause either intended or accidental death. Overdose of tricyclic antidepressants is lethal.
· *Giving away personal property.* A person who gives away cherished items is at increased risk.
· *Previous attempts at suicide.* Fifty to 80% of those who ultimately commit suicide have previously attempted it.
· *Lethality of attempt.* The more violent and painful the method used—gunshot or hanging, for example—the greater the suicide risk.
· *Accident-proneness.* Persons who subject themselves to accidents or life-threatening situations or who experience a series of accidents constitute a high-risk category whose behavior may be due to an unconscious death wish.

● STRESSFUL EVENTS AND CRISES

· *Recent loss.* Grief occasioned by a loss such as death or separation increases the risk of suicide.
· *Recent surgery or childbirth.* The trauma of surgery and postbirth depression are associated with increased risk.
· *Unemployment or financial difficulty.* Economic worries and problems are high stress factors.
· *Physical illness.* Formerly robust, active, healthy persons are especially vulnerable when physical illness debilitates or limits them.
· *Family history.* Though suicide does not run in families, the risk increases if there has been a suicide in the immediate family, especially suicide of the same-sex parent.
· *Time.* Spring and fall are the seasonal times for highest rates of suicide. Christmas holidays have a high depression rate, but not as high as during the spring and fall.

● CULTURAL/ETHNIC/GEOGRAPHIC FACTORS

· *Religion/race/ethnic background.* Catholics commit suicide much less frequently than Protestants or Jews. The highest rate of suicide is found in the White male population. Foreign-born have a higher rate than native-born and it tends to correlate with the suicide rate of the country of origin.
· *Urban versus rural.* Socioeconomic status is a more critical factor than geographic locale. For example, upper-class White males react more strongly to fluctuations in the business cycle than do lower-class non-Whites. However, the suicide rate for farmers in 1988 was 48 per 100,000 farmers and ranchers.
· *Geographic location.* Nevada, New Mexico, and Arizona have the highest rates. New Jersey and New York have the lowest rates.

▲ SUICIDE COUNSELING CONSIDERATIONS

The previous list of indicators may at first glance seem overwhelming to a counselor, but the contents can serve as a general guideline to understanding and assessing suicide potential. Counselors must also bear in mind the fact that increasing numbers of people now consider that a person has the right to end his or her life if the person has an incurable disease.

When counselors sense that they may be working with a possibly suicidal client, it is extremely important that they establish and maintain a relationship of acceptance, trust, confidence, and optimism and sincerely care about the client's situation in order to get the full story. A second step is helping the client to recognize and place in order the central and secondary problems out of what may be seen and felt as a profound sense of confusion, disorganization, and chaos. Clients who are in psychological crisis or who are trying to cope under heavy stress are often unclear about specific problems and become lost in details. As an objective outsider the counselor can move the exploration toward concreteness and specificity and eventually help provide other alternatives for the client's predicament.

■ SUBSTANCE ABUSE

Throughout history, people have sought ways to find relief from life stresses or to improve their human condition. Religious, social, and recreational activities and medical practices are all cultural ways to satisfy some inner urge, to change conscious awareness, to relieve tension, to gain peace and harmony, to reduce pain, or otherwise to feel better and more secure. Of the many substances available, alcohol has historically been most commonly used for many of these purposes by most cultures. Hallucinogenic mushrooms, cactus, seeds, and other herbs have also been used by Aztecs and members of the Native American church and other groups to enhance spiritual communication "in order to gain inner peace, inspiration, or prophecy" (Engs, 1979, p. 8).

Our U.S. society today is a drug-oriented society. We have pills, capsules, liquids, powders, salves, herbs, and other forms of natural and chemically synthesized substances to put us to sleep or wake us, to relax us, to stimulate us, to mask pain, to stop sneezing, to inhibit infection, and to relieve or cure countless other physical and psychological conditions. Drugs are also used for personal recreation and to promote social interactions and in religious ceremonies. They are often intentionally used to create desirable individual states of being that are missing in one's life, and the perceived feeling of euphoria, stimulation, or well-being that can be gained from some drugs can easily lead to physical and/or psychological dependence on the drug. The abuse of drugs in the United States is estimated to cost about $100 billion per year; the expenditure of $10 billion to $16 billion stems from the effect of drug abusers on the health care system, the law enforcement and judicial systems, the employment market, and general welfare and social service systems. Another $70 billion to $80 billion is estimated to be the cost of vandalism, accidents, violent crimes, and other drug-related circumstances (U.S. Department of Health and Human Services, 1983).

Because ours is a drug-oriented society, a major role for counselors is to help clients develop self-responsibility in the use of any drug. A second key role is to assist clients in the treatment process to overcome drug dependence. In both prevention and treatment, the counseling process works toward the following client goals:

- Acquiring accurate drug information
- Clarifying personal attitudes and values toward drug use
- Making careful and thoughtful decisions
- Accepting responsibility for actions

The question of just what is responsible behavior arises when self-responsibility is accepted as an ultimate goal. Responsible versus irresponsible use of drugs is illustrated in Table 8-5. The same concept of responsible behavior versus irresponsible behavior might also be applied with clients who engage in compulsive and addictive behavior other than drug use, such as watching television, eating food, gambling, sexual activity, political movements, weight-lifting, jogging, and numerous other activities.

▲ HOW CAN DRUGS HARM?

A drug is any substance that can alter the chemical function of the body, affecting the person in such a way as to bring about physiological, emotional, mental, and/or behavioral change. By this definition even food and water, which alter bodily functions, are drugs. Drugs do not harm; it is how drugs are used that can be harmful. According to some authors (Engs, 1979, p. 21; Girdano & Girdano, 1976, p. 2; Peele, 1979), the physical and psychological purposes for using drugs can be categorized on three levels: drug use, drug misuse, and drug abuse.

● DRUG USE
The conventional use of drugs is to take them for the pharmacological and psychological purposes for which they were intended. Eating food in response to hunger signals and using prescribed tranquilizers according to the directions are examples of responsible drug use. Drinking alcoholic beverages with others at a party is within the social norms of the culture; smoking marijuana with others at a party is also within some norms of the culture, although it is an illegal substance. Using an antacid occasionally for an upset stomach can also be considered responsible use. Thus, drug use can be defined as the responsible use of any substance for its intended purpose. It can include drugs that are used to sustain the life process, drugs that are used medically to prevent, cure, or alleviate a disease or a disability, and drugs that are used recreationally in social settings.

TABLE 8-5	Behaviors and Attitudes That Constitute Responsible Versus Irresponsible Use of Drugs	
Area of Life Affected	*Responsible Use*	*Irresponsible Use*
Relationship to self	Promotes a search for accurate information about drug effects.	Neglects information about drug effects.
	Enhances self-respect.	Destroys or detracts from self-respect.
	Helps personal creativity and efficiency.	Interferes with personal creativity and efficiency.
	Drugs are used when necessary; nondrug alternatives and solutions are sought to eradicate pain, tension, anxiety, and the problems that bring on those things.	Drugs are depended on to eradicate awareness of pain, tension, anxiety, and the problems that bring on those things.
Relationship to others	Increases trust among people.	Decreases trust among people.
	Improves other involvement.	Destroys other involvement.
	Dissolves interpersonal barriers (friends, family, work).	Creates interpersonal barriers (friends, family, work).
Relationship to society	Responsibility is assumed for both positive and negative consequences of personal actions.	Responsibility is not assumed for either positive or negative consequences of personal actions.
Relationship to nature	Improves or satisfies (provides for) bodily functions and health; is pleasurable and gratifying.	Endangers bodily functions and health; is not pleasurable and gratifying.

● DRUG MISUSE

Using drugs for purposes other than those for which they were intended or the short-term overuse of drugs solely for the high or down effect is the misuse of drugs. Not following prescribed instructions for medications, using another person's prescription, and giving one's prescription to another person are examples of drug misuse. Using tobacco, coffee, or marijuana to bolster self-confidence or enhance behavioral skills in social situations or under high-stress conditions is another common example. Although some drugs seem temporarily to resolve personal problems, drugs cannot pharmacologically fulfill a need. The misuse of legally prescribed steroids—a chemical compound found in the male hormone testosterone—to increase muscle fiber or body mass has been reported with some weight lifters and other athletes participating in the Olympics. Long-term effects of steroids are unknown, but possible temporary side effects can include increased virilism (facial hair, deepness of voice), impaired liver function, diminished libido, testicular atrophy, and hypertension (Cohen, 1981, p. 355). Amphetamines and, less frequently, cocaine are also sometimes used by athletes to stimulate motor performance, but drugs cannot make a person intrinsically a better athlete, nor can marijuana and alcohol make a person socially skillful. Interruption of one's daily activities is the most common result of misuse. "Drug misuse occurs because of ignorance of a drug's effects or refusal to accept one's true motives for taking a drug" (Girdano & Girdano, 1976, p. 2).

● DRUG ABUSE

Drug abuse is long-term, excessive, and repeated use of a substance to escape a condition or to produce a condition. While the words *drug addiction* and *drug addict* have historically been used most often "to describe a person who has become deeply involved with one of the narcotic analgesics such as morphine or heroin" (Liska, 1986, p. 6), the term *drug dependence* is currently applied in all situations in which the user has developed chronic dependence on a chemical substance. Jaffe (1975) describes heavy involvement with drugs as "a behavioral pattern of compulsive drug use, characterized by an overwhelming involvement with the use of a drug, the securing of its supply, and a high tendency to relapse after withdrawal" (p. 285). Compulsive dependence—psychological habituation and/or physical dependence—on sedatives or narcotics to feel relaxed, on amphetamines and cocaine to gain stimulation, or on marijuana and alcohol to escape life's responsibilities and realities is drug abuse. The compulsive and excessive use of coffee, soft drinks, or a laxative or other over-the-counter drugs could also be considered drug abuse. For counseling purposes, Lewis, Dana, and Blevins (1988, p. 3) define a client's problem as related to substance abuse if continuous use of a drug is affecting his or her social or occupational functioning.

Since many substances that produce a perceived state of euphoria and well-being are illicit, socially unconventional, and/or dangerous to health, drug abuse can also lead to deviance from society's laws, social norms, and health practices. According to some points of view (Fort, 1981; Hughes & Brewin, 1979), the oversedation of mental patients without other forms of psychological assistance can also be considered a form of drug abuse imposed by physicians on their patients. Likewise, the elderly, children, and others in the general public are believed to be overexposed to both prescription and over-the-counter drugs.

Drugs that are often abused can be generally classified in one of three categories:

1. *Depressants* (alcohol, barbiturates, methaqualone, minor tranquilizers, and narcotics including opium, morphine, codeine, and heroin)
2. *Stimulants* (amphetamines, cocaine, nicotine, and caffeine)
3. *Hallucinogens* (marijuana, LSD, peyote cactus, hallucinogenic mushrooms, PCP, and inhalants)

▲ WHY ARE DRUGS MISUSED OR ABUSED?

Rapid and continuous technological and social changes in the general American culture seem to have impinged on the movement toward a quality of life that many individuals desire and think possible. The compulsive use of drugs and other forms of addiction as reaction to the stresses that are inherent in modern life have led to the formulation of diverse theories that seek to explain underlying causes, motivations, and patterns. Of primary concern is the upsurge of drug taking in younger age groups and in the general population since the 1960s and early 1970s and the degree to which the welfare of the culture is threatened. Problems often related to preoccupation with drugs or abuse of drugs include absenteeism, accidents, insurance claims, leaving work early or arriving late, money spent on illicit drugs, stealing and embezzling and other drug-related crimes in order to pay for drugs, association with criminal elements in the drug subculture, and homicide and suicide.

There is rarely a single cause for substance abuse. Similar-appearing people do not all abuse drugs, and similar drugs are not all abused by all people, although nicotine, caffeine, marijuana, and alcohol are—in general—the most widely used or abused substances. Theory and research that seek to explain drug abuse generally consider the availability of drugs and psychological, sociocultural, and biomedical factors. Though single factors may predominate for some individual users, general patterns of drug use normally involve the interplay of multiple factors (Byrd, 1970; Engs, 1979; Girdano & Girdano, 1976; National Institute on Drug Abuse, 1980; Weil & Rosen, 1983; Wilson & Wilson, 1975). Helping clients assess their experience with drugs and their motivation for drug use is a crucial step in the counseling process.

● AVAILABILITY OF DRUGS

Ease of access to drugs is probably the most obvious factor related to degree of drug abuse and is the factor that most directs the work of the law enforcement sector of the society. Populous environments ranging from urban areas to middle-class suburbs and the presence of illicit drug trading in any location contribute to availability and ease of access. Epidemics of drug abuse have even occurred in some communities when one or a small number of chronic users have moved in, and drug abuse can be spread within a group of close friends if one shares a supply of drugs (Cohen, 1981, p. 78). It also seems that the more the society presents desirable norms in inflexible, demanding, or moralizing ways, the greater may be the reaction of young users to rebel and experiment with drugs. This principle is especially the case when discrepancies exist between what adults say should be proper drug use and their actual use of drugs in their own lives.

● SOCIOCULTURAL PATTERNS AND FACTORS

Attitudes toward drug use and conditions within family, cultural, subcultural, racial, ethnic, and social-class milieus is a second important predisposing factor. Living within a culture with considerable pressure to use drugs—regardless of the underlying personal or social motives—influences the manner of use and proneness to use (Peele, 1982).

Population patterns. According to the National Institute on Drug Abuse (1977, p. vii), prior to the 1950s narcotic use was essentially a problem of Whites, but during the 1950s the trend reversed (as measured by drug arrest statistics) and narcotic use became a problem of the Black community. Finally, the 1960s and 1970s have seen the trend reverse again and Whites make up the bulk of drug arrests. Since 1967 Whites have been at least as likely as Blacks and other minorities to be multiple drug users and to use all drugs, except heroin and cocaine (Callan & Patterson, 1973; O'Donnell, Voss, Clayton, Slatin, & Room, 1976; Petersen, 1974). While older Blacks appear somewhat more likely than Whites to try heroin and cocaine, among the generation born in the early 1950s, racial differences in cocaine and heroin use seem to be diminishing (O'Donnell et al., 1976). Moreover, among persons ever trying heroin, cocaine, or opiates, only relatively small racial differences in regular drug use exist. It has been found (Robins, 1976) that among Vietnam veterans, Blacks were more likely than Whites to try heroin; but among heroin users, Whites were more likely than Blacks to become addicted.

In studies having sizable numbers of Native Americans, it has been found that this group was more likely to use drugs than Whites or Blacks (Cockerham, Forslund, & Raboin, 1976; Porter, Vieira, Kaplan, Heesch, & Colyar, 1973). Despite the fact that different tribes may have different rates of heavy alcohol use, studies have found that rates are higher among male and female Native American youth than among their White counterparts (Donovan & Jessor, 1978; May, 1982). However, Whittaker (1982) has found a higher number of abstainers among Native Americans than in the general population; he attributed this finding in part to the fact that a higher percentage of Native American men over the age of 40 were recovered alcoholics. Twenty-one percent of the deaths of Native Americans have been attributed to accidents, and 75% of those accidents have been determined to be alcohol-related (Cohen, 1983, p. 131).

According to LeVine and Padilla (1980), "Findings suggest that the problem of drug addiction has reached epidemic proportions [in the United States] among Hispanics," and "Alcoholism ranks third among causes of admission to state and county mental health hospitals for Hispanics and second for Anglos and Blacks" (pp. 125–126). Alcoholism has been estimated to affect 25 to 35% of the Los Angeles gay community (Fifield, 1975).

Social motivations and the use of alcohol. Some international cultural populations, such as the French, American, and Irish, have traditionally had high rates of alcoholism, and others, such as the Italians, Chinese, and Jews, apparently have low levels. The motives underlying the use of alcohol may have different meanings or purposes for different groups. For some group cultures, drinking may represent a display of manliness, group identification and socialization, or an acceptable way to release inhibitions. Young urban men in the United States, for example, are often considered a high alcohol-risk group.

Some of the motives have historical and cultural antecedents. It has been speculated that Native Americans adapted their drinking practices from the rapid and heavy drinking style, often followed by violent behavior, of frontiersmen and cowboys; other speculation holds that the intoxicated state meshed with a spiritual quest for "out-of-body" and visionary experiences (as reported by Cohen, 1983, p. 130). Though Native Americans had used peyote and other natural hallucinogenic substances in religious ceremonies prior to the settling of the New World, alcohol was probably introduced by early European settlers in order to exploit the native peoples and negotiate trading agreements.

Whatever the reasons—"loss of self-respect, homelands, or the ancient spiritual solidarity" (Cohen, 1983, p. 130)—Native Americans have had to cope with alcohol-related problems. As early as 1883 various problems were experienced, and laws were passed prohibiting the sale of alcoholic beverages on reservations. Two-thirds of all Native American reservations still have laws prohibiting the sale of alcohol (National Institute on Alcohol Abuse and Alcoholism, 1980). In effect, the historic restrictions increased bootlegging and the compulsion to drink rapidly, which denied the opportunity "to learn how to drink moderately or to develop social taboos against drunken comportment" (Cohen, 1983, p. 131). Nonetheless, Anderson and Ellis (1980) have noted that the typical alcoholism syndrome of drinking continuously and in isolation "is considerably rare among reservation Indians although its incidence increases dramatically as the Indian becomes isolated from the tribe" (p. 120). Among Native Americans, who may consider personal reserve a component of self-worth, the style of drinking is more often a group social event that serves as a "social facilitator." A person declining to share a beer, for example, would be regarded as saying that he or she is better than the others. Similar sociocultural patterns are also noted for Mexican Americans and other Hispanic cultural groups, and for the Irish, whose social life often centers in a pub and the ethic of learning to "drink like a man." Sociability and consumption of alcohol are also strongly interrelated in the gay community, where bars may be the only place to make social contacts. Marshall (1980) has pointed out that the diversity of cultural traditions that persist beneath a common American culture have often been ignored in counseling and treatment programs aimed at alcohol abuse:

One important means many of these groups use to express their unique style is in the choice of alcoholic beverages they consume. The contexts in which these drinks are taken and the expected behavior that follows, not to mention the meanings given to these acts, vary from group to group. For example, an Irish wake differs from a Jewish wedding, and a Chinese New Year's celebration is distinct from a Greek birthday party. Historically in the United States, failure to acknowledge these important cultural differences in drinking heritages has produced misunderstanding, stereotyping, and occasionally, repression. By learning to tailor counseling and treatment programs to the client's background we can undoubtedly increase the effectiveness of our efforts to reduce alcohol abuse and its sequelae. (p. 6)

Cultural identity conflict. Loss of personal identity based on one's primary culture is another factor that may influence alcohol and drug abuse (Graves, 1967; Pedigo, 1983). Marginal persons are those who have lost their traditional cultural identity or otherwise are unable to relate to either their own traditional culture or the modern specialized culture. A person who is unable to gain social and personal support and relations from other group members and who must cope with frustration associated with high rates of unemployment and low income, inferior education, and prejudice and discrimination in the general society often finds a sense of well-being and self-esteem in alcohol or other drugs.

Social scapegoatism. Minority groups are often vulnerable to stereotypes that make them scapegoats for social problems. Group stereotypes, like self-fulfilling prophecies, may be a factor in proneness to alcohol and other drug misuse and abuse. According to Dawkins (1980), "The stereotype of the skid row alcoholic is probably less widespread than the stereotype of the Black alcohol abuser, who is viewed as the product of a broken home evidencing early problems of delinquency and other symptoms of Black pathology . . . and the negative social label which is attached to alcohol abusers in general is compounded for Blacks by the stereotypic image of the Black alcohol user"(p. 101). More research is needed to determine the extent to which a self-fulfilling prophecy may contribute to drug abuse by *both* majority and minority group members.

● PSYCHOLOGICAL FACTORS

The level at which most counselors work involves the third most crucial predisposing factor—developmental and/or idiosyncratic personality variables for which drugs have adjustive value. For example, the sporadic misuse and abuse of drugs by adolescents with relatively normal personality structure can be considered to be due to *developmental* experiences rather than basic personality inadequacy.

Adolescent developmental stage. One peak period for drug experimentation, misuse, or abuse is within the 15-to-25-year age range. This is an especially stressful period of life for many young persons in our society, one in which drug use is often perceived as a ritual entry to adulthood and in which many developmental tasks are faced. Parent-child relationship conflicts, gaining sexual identity, feeling self-confident, developing the capacity for intimacy, being accepted by peers, and choosing life's work all typically confront persons in this age group.

Personal motivations. According to reviews by Girdano and Girdano of surveys by others (1976, pp. 5–8), various motivations for drug use (except for alcohol and tobacco) coincide with the frequency of use:

- *Curiosity* motivates drug use one or two times and accounts for 55% of the drug-using population.
- *Boredom, pleasure, spiritual search, peer influence, and social alienation* motivate drug use ranging in frequency from once a month to once a week and account for 40% of the drug-using population.
- *Psychological alienation, lack of self-identity, and apathy* motivate drug use once a day and account for 5% of the drug-using population.

Inadequate coping mechanisms. There is probably no one single personality type that predisposes people to abuse drugs, but some people are more susceptible than others under certain conditions. Those who are tense, easily frustrated, fearful, or dependent, or feel guilt, shame, low self-esteem, or inferiority may have greater difficulty coping with ordinary life conditions or conditions of constant pressure and may resort to drugs to relieve tension and anxiety.

Role modeling. Although the family is traditionally believed to be the setting in which drug use habits are formed, peer-group practice also makes a significant contribution. Overidentification with the behavior of others obviously makes it difficult to arrive at individual choices for individual behavior, but it can also result in a reaction formation against all drug use. The least desirable situation for learning responsible drug use is one in which role modeling is totally absent, ambiguous, or overrestrictive.

● BIOMEDICAL FACTORS AND THEORIES

Genetic factors. Because alcoholism appears to run in families, the genetic hypothesis assumes that an individual would enter life with a certain level of genetically influenced biological predisposition toward alcoholism or drug abuse. There is little, or inconclusive, evidence to support this theory: "At most it would speak for an inherited vulnerability to become an excessive drinker, perhaps on the basis of a diminished capacity to tolerate stress. It is therefore not inevitable that a son will follow his father's drinking pattern, especially if he is aware of the predisposition" (Cohen, 1981, p. 190).

Biochemical abnormalities. Defects in metabolism, causing alcohol to be compounded in the brain to form a morphine-like structure, are theorized to produce an addictive state (Myers & Melchior, 1977).

Biochemical deficiency. Inherited defects or dysfunctions of metabolism cause the nutritional needs of people to differ. It is postulated that excessive use of alcohol becomes associated with the craving for unusual amounts of essential vitamins; however, nutritional deficiencies may be the result of improper diet related to drinking practices rather than the cause. Endocrine theory also suggests a dysfunction of the endocrine system. According to Cohen (1981), "Alcoholic cirrhosis is found in an unusual number of men with scanty body hair," and "Cirrhosis of the liver interferes with the metabolic breakdown of sex hormones, particularly estrogens" (p. 191).

Pleasure as a biological preference system. One theory suggests a type of "chemical love." It postulates the reinforcement of psychological behavior by a natural drive aimed at a specific pleasure or the avoidance of a specific discomfort (Bejerot, 1980). Psychological symptom-substitution could also be attributed to excessive drug use.

Chronobiological variables. Hochhauser (1980) speculates that drug effects may be particularly sensitive to changes in biological rhythms, which might occur over one's lifetime or at certain points in life, such as during adolescence, during old age, or during periods of depression.

▲ PROGRAMS AIMED AT SUBSTANCE ABUSE

Many programs or strategies for coping with substance misuse and abuse have evolved from the culture. They fall into two major categories: prevention and treatment.

● PREVENTION

The prevention approach provides accurate and realistic *information* for responsible drug use and *education* for a meaningful life. Schools, parent groups, community groups, and the mass media are becoming more involved in information and education about drug use, and town meetings are being organized to increase awareness of and concern about the problem of chemical dependence.

Community organizations provide support and assistance in prevention, recovery, and crisis situations; they include Alcoholics Anonymous, Al-Anon, Alateen, Narcotics Anonymous, Synanon, crisis telephone lines, and youth centers. *Self-help and self-development movements* are a kind of spontaneous growth among people in our society. They encourage each person to assume responsibility for his or her own health, proper nutrition, and diet, physical activity and exercise, and relaxation, and emphasize avoidance of stress, concern for the welfare of others, and awareness of values and behaviors that give the most meaningful and enjoyable lifestyle. Informal identification with others who seek the same thing gives a group identity. *Social and economic programs* to relieve problems that might contribute to stress and drug use are an ongoing responsibility for public agencies in the areas of housing, jobs, and family and welfare assistance. *Laws* that provide drug-control schedules, punishment, and incarceration are found necessary in many societies. Such has become the role of the government in the United States and elsewhere, but laws will not cure a problem as complex as drug abuse. Laws, of course, are also meant to protect the public, as in the case of prescription drugs and untested and questionable drugs that can easily be purchased over the counter.

● TREATMENT AND REHABILITATION

Treatment and rehabilitation programs take the following forms:

· Individual and group counseling and psychotherapy for drug dependence
· Family interaction therapy
· Crisis intervention centers and procedures for drug overdose
· Drug therapy and medication, using one drug to counteract another drug or substitute for another drug
· Detoxification and medical intervention for the physical and psychological pain of withdrawal
· Hospital treatment programs
· Residential programs and drug-free therapeutic communities
· Encounter-group therapy, confrontation groups, self-help groups

▲ SUBSTANCE ABUSE COUNSELING

When counselors counsel clients with possible drug dependence or drug misuse problems, it is important for them to understand the totality of the client's experience. A drug experience always includes the following components:

· *Dose.* What is the chemistry of the abused drug, what are the effects, and how long do they last? Is it a drug that is often commonly adulterated when sold on the street? The individual person's biochemical predisposition to the drug may also govern his or her reaction to it.
· *Psychological set.* Basic personality characteristics of the user may be amplified by the use of a drug. For example, an aggressive person may become hostile during an alcohol spree. Moods and feelings at the time of use will also influence the drug experience.
· *Environmental setting.* Where, when, and with whom the drug is used will contribute to the drug's effect. The solitary use of drugs also has different psychological implications from use when with others. One symptom of alcoholism is solitary drinking. The risk of lethal overdose is also increased for a person who uses drugs in isolation from others.

● COUNSELING PROCESS AND OTHER CONSIDERATIONS

Counselors may take into consideration the following framework as a guide for substance abuse counseling:

· Establish and maintain a client-counselor *relationship* of trust that will encourage exploration of the experiences the client is having.

· If necessary, *consult* with medical resources to help determine if referral for detoxification is needed. Withdrawal from some drugs can be safely accomplished only in a medical setting.

· Counseling and *assessment* of the client's drug-taking history and exploration and determination of personal needs for using drugs are a critical step. Both social motivations and personal motivations should be explored.

· Counseling and *intervention* strategies and *alternatives* to drug dependency can be considered at this stage. Helping and supporting the client to act on what is needed—environmental adjustments to be made, relationships to be improved, self-confidence to be built, or other important steps—is the major goal here.

· The establishment and use of *support networks* by the client—whether it be a group such as Alcoholics Anonymous, or friends, or family—are especially important. During times of stress or when old problems seem to reappear, relapse back to drug use is always a possibility. The drug that was formerly used may also be replaced by another drug—excessive cigarette smoking during recovery from alcoholism, for example. Some substance abuse counselors believe that a person who has had an experience of drug dependence never fully recovers, but is always in a state of recovery. For the person to believe otherwise—that he or she has recovered—may lead to another drug dependence experience, and total abstinence may be the only guideline to prevent relapse.

● SELF-MOTIVATION

Self-motivation is probably one of the most important considerations in drug abuse counseling. Overcoming chemical dependence may be largely a matter of will power and self-determination, to judge by the fact that some heroin and alcohol abusers have quit on their own, as have tobacco users and compulsive food eaters. Others—family, friends, or organized groups—can give support, and counselors can help in the clarification of motivational needs and in the planning of alternative strategies, but users ultimately have to quit on their own. The key factor is whether the person can take control of his or her own problem. Self-mastery, self-efficacy, and free will all contain the same basic elements: (1) the urge or strong desire to quit, (2) the attitude or belief that it can be done, and (3) the emotional realization of the fact that the person must quit—no one else can do it for him or her. This approach to self-cure, as adapted from aspects of Frankl's existential logotherapy (Frankl, 1960, 1963, 1967) and Perls's Gestalt therapy (Perls, 1969; Perls, Hefferline, & Goodman, 1951), follows a pattern or cycle of events:

· *Unhappiness.* There is enough unhappiness with the drug-dependent life that the user cannot rationalize or deny it away. Heroin addicts, for example, may be tired of the constant hassle and hustling that is present in the drug subculture and the ever-present threat of imprisonment. Tobacco users may become weary of alienating nonsmoking colleagues and friends who do not want to be around them when they smoke.

· *Sudden insight.* The sudden realization of the truth occurs—namely that what they see in themselves is not something they want. For some, the experience may come when a close friend or relative dies from cancer or when they experience a dangerous, life-threatening situation such as a car accident or an overdose of drugs. For others, it takes the form of a realization and acceptance of the fact that they have been playing a game of denying and rationalizing away the problem (Steiner, 1971). The counseling process can be helpful at this point by facilitating self-confrontation of defense mechanisms.

· *Change in environmental living pattern.* People who cure themselves make some active changes in their living environments. They may move away from the drug subculture, occupy themselves with new avocations, take renewed interest in their work, or become more involved in their physical health, activity, and exercise.

· *New self-identity.* Self-changers become new people with new lives when the attraction of drug use is weakened. They like themselves better, feel better, get along with other people better, and have more fun.

· *Handling relapses.* Ex-users who have successfully modified their personal habits and living styles are able to recognize the possibility of slipping and can control it when they see it. One viewpoint inherent in biological theories of addiction is the imminent, ever-present possibility of relapse. However, this perceived danger can also work against the sense of self-mastery and self-control and, for the self-curing person, may actually impede progress.

● INFLUENCE OF THE PATHOLOGY MODEL

It has already been pointed out that the use of chemicals as readily available solutions to personal problems and the stresses of modern life seems to have become incorporated in the culture, along with its ramifications. Many approaches and strategies to deal with the condition have been tried. The treatment for alcoholism and narcotic dependence has been especially influenced by the pathology model and its extension into the medical model as a treatment modality. The pathology model views drug abuse as an overt symptom of an underlying condition that has a certain course and outcome. The disease or pathology could be either somatogenic (organic) or psychogenic (psychological) or some of both. The medical model in particular assumes that the underlying pathology is organic in origin, course, and outcome and is thus best understood and best treated only through medical and psychiatric concepts and personnel. However, there seems to be limited value in the application of a strict pathological or medical model to those youthful abusers who may be experiencing environmental demands and stresses or who are exploring and experimenting with who they are and their relations with others—these are social and personal issues, not pathological diseases.

The culture has especially adopted the view of alcoholism as a pathological condition, and at this time those users who have become encultured within that closed system may be more amenable to treatment. However, any single-model approach that is restrictive and works against other possibilities and approaches risks the danger of creating a new dependent state for the person with problems, and in some ways it can be considered an infringement on his or her personal development. Ultimately, in many cases, the person must realize that he or she has the problem and can take charge of it—that it does not have to be a lifelong condition.

■ AGING AND THE AGED

The social and personal needs and concerns of citizens in the last half of the life span have been gaining recognition because this group is increasing in number. Today's 31.7 million persons over 65 years of age constitute 12.6% of the total population, according to the 1990 census. By 2030, as members of the Baby Boom generation finally become senior citizens, it is estimated that 21% of the population will be 65 years old or older. By comparison, in 1950, the over-65 population totaled only 8.1% of all Americans. The age group 45 to 64 constituted 18.7% of the population in 1990 and is projected to reach 22.9% by 2000.

There are also age differences between generational groups and among cultural groups. In 1820, the median age of the U.S. population was 16.7 years, and two hundred years later, in 2020, it is projected that the median age will be 40.2. The median age in 1990 for all Americans was approximately 33 years, up from 30 years in 1980. White Americans were the oldest in 1989–90 with a median age of 33.6, followed by Asian Americans (29 years), Black Americans (27.7 years), and Hispanic Americans (26 years). In 1980, the median age for Native Americans was 23 years.

▲ THE LIFE CYCLE

Ancient views proposed that substances in the human being are eventually depleted or destroyed through wear and tear or that the human being is programmed genetically for an allotted life span. Little is known with certainty about the aging process itself, but it has always concerned people. Gerontologists (Walford, 1983) have even predicted that human life will be extended to 150 years some time in the future. Others (Pearson & Shaw, 1982) believe that life can be extended by certain diets and exercises. Findings from the study of communities containing people who have lived to great age (Leaf, 1973) have suggested that unusual longevity might be attributed to (1) a diet low in calories and fats, (2) physical activity, and (3) psychological and cultural factors that influence the elderly to continue to participate in activities of the society as productive members, that afford status and dignity, and that demonstrate respect for their accumulated life experiences and wisdom. Scientific studies seem to show that some of the human genes involved in aging are controlled by hormones; when the hormones are depleted, aging sets in (for example, the likelihood of cancer, atherosclerosis, strokes, arthritis, hypertension, and such, increases).

Important events in the life cycle that are observed and given attention by all societies are birth, maturity, marriage, and death. All mark transition from one kind of life experience to another and all require adjustments to stressful situations and new relationships. The cultural status of the aged in primitive societies was first studied by Simmons (1945), who showed, for example, that aged women tend to keep property rights more readily than men in simple hunting, fishing, and gathering societies, whereas it is aged men who retain the greatest advantage in farming and herding societies. His findings also suggested that in most societies the aged possess prestige, but only until they are no longer able to care for themselves. More recent research (Maxwell & Silverman, 1970, p. 381) has shown that esteem for the aged is related to the amount of control they have over key information that might be useful to the young. T. R. Williams (1972, p. 155) has also reported that the role of older people as cultural guides within families declines with industrialization of the society.

The study of aging in the United States and elsewhere seems to concentrate on the undesirable roles, conditions and status and the unfair treatment of the aged. The aging process is often portrayed as a disabling process characterized by illness, loneliness, regression and dependency, out-group status, and dying. The aging process has also been studied as a *normal* development of life. McCoy (1977) has speculated that there is a type of normal psychological cycle that characterizes adult life: "While the content of one's life may vary because of unique heredity, special environment, and personal interaction with the environment, everyone's development consists of the same stages, encountered at about the same time, and resolved in a manner similar to that of most other human beings in the world" (p. 14). Various social scientists generally agree that there is some kind of life span that characterizes adults living in modern specialized societies (Erikson, 1963; Gould, 1972; Havighurst, 1953; Levinson, 1978; Neugarten, 1968; Sheehy, 1976; Vaillant & McArthur, 1972). McCoy (1977) has reviewed and elaborated upon a topography of adulthood that includes the following age phases:

16–22: leaving the family
23–28: reaching out; becoming an adult
29–34: questioning life
35–43: midlife reexamination
44–55: restabilization to realities of life
56–64: preparation for retirement
65– : retirement

Though psychological life cycle theory may offer heuristic insight, especially into developmental patterns and special problems faced by middle-class men, it has not been verified by rigorous research as fully describing the complex social and psychological process of adult life. In any event, counselors must be wary of stereotypes that can emerge from trying to place clients in rigid categories. According to McCoy (1977), "Few minority group members, women, and working-class men have been studied" (p. 15). Different life cycles might also be found for persons engaged in different occupations, and one study of career changers has indicated that internal motivational needs, such as autonomy, may be more important than chronological age-related variables (E. Axelson, 1983).

▲ EXPERIENCES OF MIDDLE AGE

Although studies of middle age might tend to emphasize weaknesses or even pathology, there is a growing focus that may lean toward the glorification of middle and old age (for example, Maclay, 1977; "The Myths of Middle Age," 1983). Whereas our culture has always been apprehensive of what the young might become, it may be inclined to accept, or even ignore, older citizens as having already developed for better or worse. Until recently, aging has not been a popular topic in the United States and was considered an unhealthy and morbid preoccupation. Concepts of personality as influenced by psychoanalytic theory have also long tended to view one's development as fixed and closed early in life. Barnouw (1973) believes that despite a carry-over from early life experiences, personality may change over time and the adult is a different person from the child. As in a culture, there is also both consistency and change in personality, and reality dictates that the socialization process does not end in childhood. The adult group faces as many adjustment issues in normal life events as does almost any other age group. The major events taking place during the period of middle age (46 to 66) are having children leave home, the peak years of economic well-being, grandparenthood, retirement, onset of chronic illness, widowhood, and the care of infirm parents. Because the general society values youthfulness and success, two potential self-adjustment dilemmas confront those in the midlife period.

● ACHIEVING SELF-ACCEPTANCE

The desire to be forever young is pronounced in the general culture. Although people say, "Age means nothing; you're only as old as you feel," many middle-aged and older persons privately regard physical change as a terrifying experience. There also appears to be a double standard for the sexes. Gray hair may be fine on a man, perhaps even suave and sexy, but for a woman the culture encourages the opposite with dyes and cosmetics meant to restore a youthful appearance. According to Melamed (1983), both the media and the medical community might contribute to what the culture reflects in "symbolic annihilation." Ageism and sexism seem to go hand in hand in portraying women especially unsympathetically and unrealistically. The effects can be seen, for example, in a woman who feels complimented when others tell her she does not look her age, in the tendency of physicians to attribute physical complaints to menopause and dismiss them as normal female behavior, or in husbands who leave their wives for younger women. Ambivalence about aging is found in many older persons and the feelings of being trapped in a changing body, a divided person, can create self-doubt and identity conflict (Weibel, 1977).

● ACHIEVING LIFE GOALS

Frustration and the feeling that there is not enough time remaining in life to accomplish one's goals is especially found in a complex, technical society that stresses competition and successful upward mobility as signs of personal worth. The need for security, which is often related to the accumulation of material property and the sense of power it brings, puts pressure on many persons at midlife. Self-imposed attitudes toward success in career, parental roles, and socioeconomic status must be faced. Unresolved past personal issues often reappear that contribute to stress and adjustment at this time.

▲ EXPERIENCES OF THE ELDERLY

The manner of adjustment to environmental changes and physical and psychological changes within the person generally follows the pattern by which the person has faced other stressful times throughout life. Although the adult is not the child, many personality habits and former coping strategies are simply amplified when stress is encountered in older age.

● DISCRIMINATION AND STEREOTYPING

The nation doesn't seem ready for the gray-haired world, and many older citizens must cope with prejudice and acts of discrimination in the society because of age. According to Riker (1980), "By means of discrimination, younger persons place older persons in a category of inferiority and describe older persons as different from themselves. This kind of discrimination enables younger persons to deny the possibility of their own aging. The irony of this situation is that these younger persons eventually find themselves the victims of their own prejudice" (p. 205). A related condition that may occur for many older persons is a self-fulfilling prophecy causing them to believe and act upon the stereotypes of inferiority and weakness that are applied to them (Butler, 1975). Riker (1980, pp. 205–209) has compiled a list of common misleading stereotypes of older persons, some of which are abbreviated in Table 8-6.

● PHYSICAL AILMENTS AND LIMITATIONS

Physical aging is a reality: the organs do decline with age. Visual impairments, arthritis, diseases of the heart, cerebrovascular diseases, malignancies, brittleness of the bones, and other physical conditions are debilitating and can create fearsome situations for many elderly persons. Accident-proneness is another problem. Many elderly persons experience sudden falls that break bones, inability to move quickly away from a dangerous situation, or inability to see an obstacle.

TABLE 8-6 Common Stereotypes of Older Persons	
Stereotypes	*Facts or Assumptions*
Unproductiveness and decline in learning	Mandatory retirement requirements and "enforced idleness" have probably contributed to this myth. Although jobs requiring "rapid response" or "prolonged periods of physical stamina" may be more difficult for older persons, they have been found to be "dependable, maintain excellent attendance and safety records, and require minimum supervision after job requirements are learned" (Riker, 1980, p. 206). Reduced learning speed may be more related to lack of environmental stimulation and interest than to age; some aspects of memory decline with age, but verbal ability is retained if normally practiced. Many examples show that older people have completed college degrees or have successfully entered new career areas.
Withdrawal from life and others	Some older persons do preoccupy themselves with memories of past days and interact less with others, but many are also engaged in community and other activities. The pattern of older age is most likely a continuation of interaction styles that have been generally followed throughout the life span.
Inflexibility	Physically healthy older persons continue to adjust to their world in the way that has been their lifelong pattern. Some personality traits may be amplified during periods of stress.

● HELPLESSNESS AND POWERLESSNESS

Older persons often feel vulnerable when they are less able to take care of themselves and must depend on others. Reduced income and rising costs of living further compound the feeling of powerlessness. Some feel lonely and abandoned when they cannot maintain social and physical contact with the significant people in their lives. And many others must constantly fight depression and recurring periods of down moods. People who want to care for their elderly relatives or friends but whose circumstances work against their desires feel frustration and agony. Often the last resort is to place the elderly in nursing homes, something that is usually dreaded by all parties.

TABLE 8-6 *(continued)*	
Stereotypes	*Facts or Assumptions*
Senility and other physical conditions	Research often attributes permanent brain damage, arteriosclerosis, and other physical conditions only to "old age." According to Farb (1978, p. 444), a 75-year-old person compared to a 30-year-old person does have less heart output, hand grip, oxygen intake during exercise, and taste buds. Although many physical conditions are irreversible, the attribution to the aged lends itself to a prejudice of uselessness. Old age does not have to mean sitting down and dying.
Lessened sexual activity	The belief that sexual relations are properly meant only for the young or that older persons are not capable of sexual activity can contribute to problems of sexual dysfunction for the elderly. Sex therapists can provide psychological counseling and educational approaches to enable continued social-sexual life for the elderly.
Contentment	The image of happy grandparents rocking in a chair or delightedly helping their grown sons or daughters and caring for their grandchildren is often presented in the media and popular literature (Cohler & Grunebaum, 1981). However, older persons have their own lives to lead and face daily problems the same as any other age group.

SOURCE: Major categorical areas are adapted from "Older Persons" by H.C. Riker, in N. A. Vacc and J. P. Wittmer (Eds.), *Let Me Be Me*, 1980; pp. 205-209. Adapted by permission.

● CRIME AND ABUSE

The aged are often targets for robbery, swindles, false promises, faulty products, and other exploitation. Some are also physically assaulted within and outside their homes. It is estimated that approximately 2% of the population in the over-65 age group may be subject to family violence. The abuse may be touched off by stresses that are involved in caring for a helpless, sick, irrational old person. The typical victim is often a woman over age 80 who is extremely dependent on others because of physical and/or mental disability ("A New Look at Abuse of Old People," 1983).

● DEATH AND DYING

People in all societies display great mourning over a death, and most emphasize in one way or another that death is not final. Because of the reality of ongoing life demands, most quickly turn to new interactions that replace those with people who have died. Like other life experiences, the experiences of aging, dying, and death are not homogeneous phenomena. Philosophic beliefs and coping strategies associated with death and dying can be expected to be culturally bound. The care given to the elderly and the notions of death itself and life after death are intertwined with individual identity and cultural group ways.

Glaser and Strauss (1968) and Kübler-Ross (1969) have proposed that awareness and acceptance of dying and death are a gradual process. Typical stages in facing death are thought to include denial, anger, bargaining, depression, and acceptance. However, in a multicultural society there are many factual circumstances related to death and there are many sociocultural-religious concepts of life, dying, and death. Serious comparative cross-group research is missing in the general counseling literature or remains as fugitive material in special collections. For example, the fact that Black Americans have higher death rates may mean that their dying and death experience is different from others or that their coping strategies are different. Does death seem to be philosophically accepted as a caring and meaningful part of life that is best resolved during a period of bereavement and deep mourning? Is it so to Catholics? to Hispanics? to White ethnic Americans? to most people? It is believed that to most people a process of grieving is essential for personal adaptation to loss. Grief can be both anticipatory—mourning before death—and subsequent to death. Kavanaugh (1974) has outlined the process of mourning as shock, disorganization, volatile emotions, guilt, loss and loneliness, relief, and reestablishment.

Are death and dying resisted as a personal part of life? The general cultural emphasis on the extension of vital life-signs through medical/mechanical means seems to be eroding toward an acceptance of death as part of life. This change may be due partly to the fact that more people are living to older age, that prolonged periods of time of dying are experienced due to the shift in causes of death from acute and sudden illness to chronic or multiple conditions, or that reevaluation of lifestyles and values is taking place in the general society. The 1991 federal Patient Self-Determination Act has increased the importance of the role that counselors and bioethicists will have in helping persons decide when to let life end.

In the Navajo Nation, modern ideas and economic resources have been incorporated into the traditional culture, but the belief in ghosts is still strong. Insensitive psychiatric diagnosis could inadvertently label hallucinations experienced under the stress of death as a psychotic symptom rather than a part of the pattern of symptoms associated with unresolved grief. As Harper (1982, p. 132) has described in a case example, participation in tribal ritual and ceremonies that have evolved over thousands of years could more readily resolve grief and facilitate the return to reality than psychiatric treatment. And what is the psychological pattern for the closely knit Asian family, or how have coping strategies been affected for those Asian Americans whose practice of ancestral worship has been interrupted by migrations to the United States?

Even though few assumptions about various cultural practices have been left unquestioned in recent years, many questions regarding cross-cultural views of death and dying remain unanswered, awaiting future research. Counselors need to relate harmoniously with diverse clients and to recognize cultural specificity related to suffering, loss, and the entire life process.

▲ CULTURAL DIVERSITY AND THE ELDERLY

Although it is generally agreed that the aged have many problems in common, such as income, health, housing, employment, fear of crime, loneliness, and alienation from others, some cross-group differences can be noted for elderly persons.

● SOCIOECONOMIC CLASS STATUS

Adjustment to aging by minority group members is frequently compounded by their minority status, which can affect education, income, employment, housing, political power, and oppression. Very little longitudinal information or good cross-sectional data is available about aging minorities. According to Jackson (1980), however, it is generally theorized that (1) "minority status determines social and psychological aging and indirectly affects biological aging" and (2) "social class, and not race, is the major determinant" (p. 10). Analysis by Jackson of the 1974 Harris Survey of Aging indicates that Black and White elderly persons with higher levels of income and education were less likely to regard a given problem as a personal problem; however, low-income aged Blacks "were substantially more likely to report personal problems with insufficient clothing, job opportunities, housing, medical care, education, and monies" than were low-income Whites (Jackson, 1980, p. 203). Sauer (1977) also found no differences in overall levels of life satisfaction between elderly Blacks and Whites when socioeconomic levels were controlled. Schaie, Orchowsky, and Parham (1982) have reported that life satisfaction for a group of Whites, 30 to 73 years of age, during the period of 1973 to 1977 remained stable, but increased for the group of elderly Blacks over the same period studied, when controlled for health and income. Their findings suggest that sociocultural changes that occur during one's lifetime also need to be considered in order to understand fully the impact of aging.

● FAMILY RELATIONS

Structured interpersonal relations vary with cultural heritage and traditions and have been shown to influence behavior between children and their parents in diverse ethnic families. The family is a major source of emotional and financial support for elderly parents in ethnic groups such as Italian, Mexican, Polish, and Jewish Americans. Irish and Black Americans depend on friendship for part of their daily lives, and others, such as Scandinavians, rely on social organizations (Woehrer, 1978). Manuel and Reid (1982), in their comparative study of minority and nonminority aged, concluded that whereas the extended family household is probably typical of "neither the minority nor the nonminority elderly, substantially more of the minority elderly do live in extended households" (p. 50). McAdoo (1978) has noted extensive kin involvement among three generations of upwardly mobile Black families. Greeley (1969, pp. 51–53), in his review of a 1967 study of urban neighbor-hoods, has pointed out differences in the proportion of ethnic Americans who saw their parents weekly. Among Catholics, 79% of Italian Americans in urban neighborhoods saw their parents weekly; 65% of Polish Americans, 61% of French Americans, 49% of Irish Americans, and 48% of German Americans did also. Among Protestants in urban neighborhoods, 44% of German Americans and 39% of those from England and Scandinavia saw their parents weekly. Among Jews, 58% saw their parents weekly.

Forty percent of the Italian group were also found to live in the same neighborhood as their parents. When controlled for socioeconomic class and physical proximity, it was found that Italians were still the most likely to visit parents, and Jews were in second place. Greeley (1969) further speculates: "It would seem that the stereotypes of the tight Italian family, the dominating Jewish parent and the clannish Irish sib group are, at least to some extent, backed up by hard statistics" (p. 52). Other studies have also supported the importance of ethnic family ties, often extending into the third generation (Cohler & Grunebaum, 1981). But LeVine and Padilla (1980, p. 118) question whether a view of the traditional role of the extended Hispanic family as a support system for family members may be fallacious. They cite evidence (Bachrach, 1975) that more than twice as many Hispanics as Whites over the age of 65 are admitted to state mental hospitals (278 per 100,000 admissions versus 127 per 100,000 admissions). The condition of poverty probably accounts in part for the higher rate of admissions of elderly Hispanics to *state* hospitals.

In her study of elderly Black women, Taylor (1982) identified two basic kinds of coping strategies: (1) the operation of a personal support network consisting of kin, friends, and service providers, and (2) a "mind set" that emphasized religious faith, family, a strong belief in the American work ethic, self-help, and independence, and pride in getting through tough times (p. 97).

● DIFFERENTIAL MORTALITY AND LIFE EXPECTANCY

Culture is not static, and changes or improvements in health, nutrition, medical care, sanitation, and other living conditions affect the experiences of aging for one generation, or one age group (cohort), over another. Such historical effects have contributed to the gradual increase in life expectancy for the total population, but cohort differences still exist. For example, the life expectancy of a White male born in 1930 was 59 years, and for a Black male, 48 years; for those born in 1980, it was 71.4 years for a White male, 64.8 years for a Black male, and 71.9 years for a Hispanic male. For females born in 1930, the life expectancy was 63 years for a White female and 50 years for a Black female; for those born in 1980, it was 78.7 years for a White female, 73.8 years for a Black female, and 79.1 years for a Hispanic female. Different rates of death are also evident for different population groups. Among males, the number of deaths is greater and the death rates are higher (9.22 per 1,000 population in 1990) than for females (8.16 per 1,000), with Black males having significantly higher numbers and rates than White males. Hispanic Americans, Asian Americans, and Native Americans have lower death rates than the population as a whole, primarily due to their comparatively youthful age distribution.

White/non-White mortality crossover. In the later years, "remaining life expectancy is greater for blacks and other nonwhites than for whites" (Jackson, 1980, p. 89). Both non-White males and females start at birth with a mortality disadvantage in comparison with Whites, but at advanced ages (75 to 80) a racial crossover occurs and the probabilities of life expectancy and the proportion surviving are greater for non-Whites. For example, by age 80, the mortality rate for non-White males is 12% lower than that for White males, and the decline continues to age 100. A similar pattern is also shown for non-White females (Manton, 1982, p. 64). Assuming that census enumerations are correct, several explanations have been proposed to explain the differences in later age (Jackson, 1980; Manton, 1982):

- Status (social, economic, family) of the non-White elderly improves with age.
- Status (social, economic, family) of the White elderly decreases with age.
- Non-White and White population groups have different aging mechanisms, rates of aging, or aging experiences.
- "Mortality selection" operates where individual variation in longevity exists in the population; variation could be due to intrinsic factors (for example, susceptibility to diseases) and/or environmental influences (such as medical care and nutrition). The most susceptible individuals die at a faster rate, ensuring survival of the most "robust" or "fittest."

Common causes of death. Better nutrition, improved medical care, and family planning education for low-income Black mothers since the 1960s have greatly reduced deaths of Black infants under 1 year old and consequently have increased Black life expectancy, although infant mortality (17.1 per 1,000 live births in 1988) is still twice that of White (8.3) and Hispanic (8.1) population groups. The lower mortality rate for Hispanic infants may be attributable to better diets for mothers, fewer single mothers, lower smoking rates, and help from strong extended families.

There are other causes for mortality rates that reflect population group differences. Table 8-7 shows some of the leading causes of death for Americans of all ages. Deaths caused by accidents, homicide, and hypertension were higher for minority Americans, while the death rates for heart diseases, cancer, cirrhosis of the liver, and suicide were higher for White Americans. Homicide is the leading cause of death for Black males under the age of 35. The acquired immune deficiency syndrome (AIDS) epidemic is expected to increase the differences between males and females for life expectancy in the future because males are much more likely to die of AIDS, and AIDS victims are

TABLE 8-7 Causes of death in the United States, 1975 and 1989.

Cause	Death Rate Per 100,000 Population		
	White (1975)	Non-White (1975)	All (1989)
Heart diseases	350.0	244.1	296.3
Malignant neoplasms	175.8	144.0	200.3
Influenza and pneumonia	26.4	24.6	30.3
Accidents	25.9	33.1	38.2
Motor vehicle accidents	21.5	21.4	18.9
Cirrhosis of the liver	14.2	10.0	10.6
Suicide	13.6	6.8	12.6
Homicide	5.9	37.1	9.3
Hypertensive heart	2.8	5.4	—
AIDS	—	—	8.6

SOURCE: Data from *Vital Statistics of the United States: Mortality, Part A, 1960, 1969, 1975 (Vol. 2), National Center for Health Statistics, 1978; Monthly Vital Statistics Report*, National Center for Health Statistics, August 1990.

concentrated in the young adult ages, so that mortality will have a larger-than-expected impact on life expectancy. The gap between Blacks and Whites in life expectancy will increase, as AIDS has affected Black Americans more than White Americans.

● PSYCHOLOGICAL AGING

Little is known about the psychological adaptation styles and stages of aging of different groups of people. Many men and women suffer trauma near or at retirement because work has been a meaningful portion of life for them. It is also likely that both men and women experience a void in their lives after child-rearing responsibilities diminish. The emotional boredom and feeling of meaninglessness are especially vexing if the person has not had the opportunity to develop—or in any case did not develop—some life-satisfying activities that could be used to fill the void (Havighurst, Munnichs, Neugarten, & Thomas, 1969).

The capacity to adapt throughout life to changes in self and environment is probably characterized by individual coping styles that have been established early in life and modified over the life span. Aging persons in particular find themselves having to adapt increasingly to loss, generational differences, and the possibility of reduced physical activity and the ability to maintain themselves. Thus, there is an interaction between reality conditions (sociodynamics) and self-imposed factors (psychodynamics) that affects the continuing development of the aging person. Studies (Bengtson, Kasschau, & Ragen, 1977; Reynolds & Kalish, 1974) of equivalent age groups of Blacks, Whites, Mexican Americans, and Asian Americans in Southern California have shown that Whites are likely to see themselves as "old" at about 70 years of age; Blacks at about 65; and Mexican Americans at about 60 years of age. However, Blacks believed that they would live longer than did Whites, and Mexican Americans expected fewer remaining years than did either Blacks or Whites. Jackson (1980, p. 108) has cited the dangers for the elderly of accepting, or having imposed on them, a self-perceived "functional" definition of aging, saying that a chronological definition may be more realistic. Nevertheless, *psychological* death is most serious for any elderly person. It occurs when he or she becomes isolated from meaningful personal contacts, or is not shown respect, or has no motivating activities or sense of usefulness.

● COUNSELING CONSIDERATIONS

Relatively few counselors have been specially trained to understand and work with the problems of aging and the aged within the context of a multicultural society. Working against inaccurate stereotypes that prevail for both the elderly in general and the elderly within identified cultural groups is a major task for the professional counselor. Furthermore, it is important for counselors to approach elderly persons with the view that they may be socially integrated and adjusted within the context of their own cultural value system and expectations, as Coles (1973) has so genuinely described in his personal study of elderly, "old line" Spanish Americans living in New Mexico. Personal patterns of involvement in the social environment can best be understood by taking into consideration the uniqueness of each person and each family within the context of their current sociocultural time-generation, their ethnic traditions, and their socioeconomic, educational, and rural or urban background. Thus, the purpose of counseling is doing what is in the best interest of your client.

■ SUMMARY

1. Adjustment and adaptation to the social environment and to oneself are viewed as an integrating process. Adjustment is a learned human process, a lifelong process, an incentive for social and personal goals, and a measure of mental health.

2. Maladjustment denotes the absence of the adjustment process. The definition or description of maladjustment is generally found in statistical models, criterion models, cultural models, and theoretical/scientific models. Three theoretical/scientific models were reviewed that have especially influenced definitions of maladjustment in the general culture: psychoanalytic, medical, and the psychiatric diagnostic model as exemplified in DSM-III-R.

3. Five areas of social and personal issues that currently affect many, or all, people in one way or another are stress, marital and family concerns, suicide, substance abuse, and aging and the aged.

4. Stress is seen as an experience that in some ways affects all people in our society. The implications of stress can be observed in physical and

psychological effects. Individual adjustment to stress will vary according to the person's current level of personality integration. Reactions to certain kinds of stress are individually based, and methods of coping vary for individuals and identified groups of individuals. Stress can be intrinsic to a situation or can be self-imposed. Stressors can be universal to most people or unique to one person. Common stressors are physical stressors, threats to self-esteem, disrupted relationships, restricted and/or impoverished conditions, conflict, and frustration. Coping with stress was viewed from three theoretical models: psychoanalytic theory, which emphasizes the operation of psychological defense mechanisms; personality theory, which contends that people with certain personality characteristics are more prone to stress effects; and learning theory, which describes how helplessness is learned in response to stress.

5. Marital and family concerns are viewed within the context of a changing society and changing lifestyles. Some type of family unit is found in all societies and is important for meeting basic emotional, psychological, and economic needs of individuals and for transmission of cultural ways. Wide variation exists in the current structure of families in the United States. Family structures in today's society include traditional nuclear families, single-parent families, blended families, extended families, augmented families, and unmarried couples living together. Many persons—the divorced, elderly, and young adults who have postponed marriage—live alone. Each family unit or living arrangement has its own features. Special problems for both adults and children within different family structures were indicated and issues related to intergroup marriages were pointed out. Violence in the family was presented as a serious problem; women and children are especially vulnerable to abuse. Homelessness was discussed as a chronic condition for many Americans.

6. Suicide, as a fatal act or attempted nonfatal act, is especially serious for elderly and adolescent populations. Suicide has existed in various proportions in all societies throughout history. Theories have attempted to explain it as a social problem, as a psychological problem, and as a psychocultural problem. Attitudes toward suicide or attempted suicide are culturally bound. The high suicide rate for White males was pointed out. Conditions that constitute high-risk potential for suicide were identified in five major categories: (1) individual factors, (2) psychological conditions and factors, (3) behavioral symptoms and patterns, (4) stressful events and crises, and (5) cultural/ethnic/geographic factors.

7. Substance abuse is viewed within the context of a drug-oriented society. The behaviors and attitudes that characterize responsible versus irresponsible use of drugs were presented, and distinction was made between drug use, misuse, and abuse. Commonly abused drugs are categorized as depressants, stimulants, and hallucinogens. No single factor can be associated with how drugs are used. The use, misuse, or abuse of drugs is explained by availability, sociocultural patterns, psychological factors, and biomedical factors. Programs aimed at substance abuse generally focus on prevention or treatment and rehabilitation. Basic counseling steps for approaching drug abuse were proposed.

8. Aging and the aged are receiving more attention because the size of the older population is increasing and attitudes toward lifestyles and life values during the second half of the life cycle are undergoing examination. The life cycle is marked by transition from one kind of life experience to another; birth, maturity, marriage, and death are given special attention in all societies. A normal adult cycle for the general population has been studied and is believed to include successive stages of identified experiences. The aging experience places stress on the need for self-acceptance and the achievement of life goals. Earlier patterns of adjustment and coping are amplified during the later years. Issues and experiences for elderly persons include discrimination and stereotyping, physical ailments and limitations, helplessness and powerlessness, crime and abuse, death and dying. The experience of death and dying is conceptualized in different ways by different groups of people; the existence of diversity of views is in need of better understanding. The experiences of aging and the elderly are influenced by cultural diversity. Factors that can contribute to different experiences include socioeconomic status, family relations, differential mortality and life expectancy, causes of death, and psychological aging. Counseling considerations emphasize knowing and helping elderly clients as unique persons within the context of their cultural milieu.

PART

TODAY'S COUNSELING PRACTICES

■ Traditional Approaches to Counseling and Psychotherapy

■ Eclectic and Synergetic Approaches to Counseling and Psychotherapy

■ The Interaction of Counselor and Client

CHAPTER

TRADITIONAL APPROACHES TO COUNSELING AND PSYCHOTHERAPY

This chapter has two major purposes. First, it describes the cultural context within which the helping process is conducted. The discussion focuses on the historical view of human problems, the helping function, and concepts of human nature in interaction with the socialization process and psychological reality. Second, this chapter summarizes the basic constructs of traditional counseling and psychotherapy approaches. "Traditional" approaches are designated as those theoretical models that historically and/or currently are most widely used or are best known in the professions of counseling and psychotherapy. The theories so selected for review, of course, do not include all the many schools or systems, but only those that, in the author's judgment, best reflect changes and events in our culture and have influenced or potentially could influence what is psychological reality for our culture. The theories fall into three major categories: the psychodynamic, existential-humanistic, and behavioral models.

■ CULTURAL HISTORY OF THERAPY

This section examines the dynamic interplay between cultural changes and human problems. It shows how systems of helping follow as well as shape the culture and ultimately what is defined as a problem and how it is best treated.

▲ PROBLEMS OF HUMAN EXISTENCE

The view of life as a series of problems and the search for solutions takes the same path as modern science, which focuses thinking on cause and effect in order to gain the feeling of mastery over human nature and environment.

Views that might be labeled "prescientific" or "nonscientific" most likely accept and flow with human nature and the cultural environment by taking life philosophically as it comes, both fearing and respecting the forces, and in general living as creatively as possible under the existent conditions and definitions of life. Historic problems of human existence and problems of modern life—at least such as might be found in a technical society—are similar in that people experience and focus attention on rapid social changes, the breakdown of many traditional forms of society, and conflicts between old and new values. In fact, all societies experience cycles of conflict between traditional and new ways as the culture is transformed or built on what preceded it. Thus ways that are considered modern in today's world will become the traditional ways of tomorrow's world. One difference between Old World culture and New World culture is that change has been more rapid in the New World, or at least might seem that way within the microscopic dimensions of one lifetime.

● TRADITIONAL VERSUS MODERN CULTURE

Traditional society emphasizes direction and regulation through the bonds and mutual understandings found in family, kinship, friends, religion, and custom. The security, strength, and status afforded by this arrangement give meaning to social relationships, self-identity, and a sense of belonging. Traditional societies create and sustain families and communities in which people feel a sense of belonging, purpose, and meaning; modern societies tend to weaken the bonds of family and community, reducing the individual or separating the person from the group. In modern societies, members of the same family tend not to work together at the same activity. Because people have specialized jobs, their interests become channeled and they find it hard to establish relationships with others, to exchange ideas, to understand what others do, and to focus on problems that affect all of them. Life becomes fast paced, time- and work-oriented, and bureaucratized, and commitment to family, community, and others declines. On the plus side, the modern system affords freedom for improvement and individual development without the restraints of group and family attachment and loyalty. People in modern society believe that a person has the opportunity to make choices on the basis of thoughtful consideration of his or her ability rather than on the basis of customs or traditions to which the person is born (McLemore, 1980, pp. 12–13). In reality, this belief has become the new tradition and also the source of problems in modern society.

Discontent in today's American society about the deteriorating quality of life goes beyond the cultural shocks of rapid and uncomfortable change or an understandable yearning for the simple value systems. It comes from serious anxieties about disintegrating and stressed-out families, inability to protect children and youth from drugs and violence, high rates of homicide and suicide, disappearing moral values, and a multitude of family issues: broken marriages, fatherless children, child abuse and neglect, problems of single-parent homes, and lack of quality family time. Our presently conceptualized and constructed mental health delivery system can't come close to dealing with the problems resulting from the great cultural and social forces that have been undermining the social environment in the last two decades. However, these "contemporary" problems began years ago in the Industrial Revolution with the displacement of traditional European values (that is, respect for tradition and ritual, sacred belief in the origins of the universe, and family/group identity) by our modern beliefs (that is, secularism, individualism, egalitarianism).

● "OLD" VERSUS "NEW" COUNSELING THEORIES

Theoretical approaches to therapy, in general, address the problems of modern Western society over the past 75 years. The fact that theories originate from the experiences of the theorists in the culture and in the society allows for a compatible arrangement between the conceptualization of the problem and the theories. Whether theories of counseling and therapy follow shifts from old to new ways, or precede and influence the changes, depends on the impact that generalization of any one or more theories has on the culture. Freudian concepts, for example, have influenced most aspects of psychological reality in Western society, as have behavioral and existential-humanistic concepts. Rogerian principles of human relations have been generalized into the society at large, and Glasser's reality therapy and Adler's individual psychology have found useful application in education. However, theory-building and treatment systems that comprehensively address human problems within a culturally pluralistic environment are conspicuously absent. Most traditional theory systems pay slight attention to environmental factors, giving the impression that the larger cultural environment within which the client lives either is a static condition or has little influence on behavior.

▲ HUMAN RELATING AND THE HELPING FUNCTION

The fact that human needs are met in the social environment emphasizes the point that human relations are the primary avenue by which personal development and adjustment can be reached. Nonverbal expression of inner emotions and gestures of meaning have probably always existed on some level as a means of human communication (Darwin, 1872/1965). Furthermore, with evolution of the human capacity to communicate and the development of language have come increased opportunity for self-reflection and the exchange of self-reflection with others. Spoken communication between or among two or more individuals has long been known to have desirable effects on the thinking, feeling, and actions of individuals. However, the difference between "general" talk that might seek to influence attitudes and actions and the special sort of talk that is counseling or therapy rests in the agreement between counselor and client that the purpose or goal for both parties in the experience is to help the client's thoughts, feelings, and actions become more desirable to him or her and to others.

Designated individuals who provide some form of help to others in facing problems of daily living have probably always existed in most civilizations throughout history. The designated persons most likely based their "theories" and "approaches" on the spiritual, religious, philosophical, or world view of reality to which they were privy or that prevailed in the culture at the time. Guidance in life can also be considered a community endeavor when group norms serve as functional principles for proper personal conduct and contribute to successful movement through life. Thus, when a community of people is cohesive or in general agreement on what is "healthy" conduct for a "good" life, there are more likely to be present many mutual or informal sources of help and assistance. Maslow (1970) believes that the "complementary" fulfillment of needs between individuals at different self-actualization levels may explain why people are helped by persons who are self-actualized (informal helpers) but who are untrained in counseling theory or techniques. The emergence of *formal* helpers—technically trained specialists—as exemplified in the professions of psychiatry, social work, psychology, counseling, and other human services is a function of modern society. In many ways the basic incentive behind the counselor's role may not differ from what has existed for formal and informal helpers throughout history and in different cultures. As Draguns (1981) has noted, "On the most general plane, the functions of psychotherapy and counseling are probably universal: to alleviate distress, to reintegrate the client into the culture, and to enable him or her to respond to cultural roles and to meet cultural expectations" (p. 4).

Although formal systems of helping may have functional similarity, there are vast differences in (1) the philosophical and psychological views of human nature and social nature, (2) the counseling relationship and goals stemming from those views, and (3) the system of techniques and action to carry out the goals. The most basic aim of modern human services providers may be similar to that of helpers in other societies and cultures of the past, but the helping theories and procedures of the current era coincide with how human problems are interpreted within the context and culture of the modern industrial and technical society. The theories in which counselors are trained are all based on Western world thought, adapted or modified to meet the problems and conditions of the changing mainstream U.S. culture. Culture also determines options for women and men. Most major theories contain assumptions regarding gender roles in the socialization process, and contemporary understanding of therapy systems in relation to women has been accentuated by the women's movement and advances in the psychology of women. In this regard, some of the areas of attention and/or reformulation include: (1) conceptual survey and implications (Adler, 1991; Gilligan, 1982; Lott, 1987; Miller, 1986; Mitchell, 1974; Penfold & Walker, 1983), (2) counseling and psychotherapy theory (Burstow, 1992; Dutton-Douglas & Walker, 1988; Sturdivant, 1980), and (3) application and practice (Robbins, 1990).

▲ CONCEPTS OF HUMAN NATURE, THE SOCIALIZATION PROCESS, AND PSYCHOLOGICAL REALITY

Questions about interaction in the social world and how it governs actions, motives, thoughts, and emotions have always existed. Treatment of mental illness or deviations in human behavior has taken many forms: the ancient practice of chipping holes in the skull (trephining) in order to release demons or evil spirits contained within the person; exorcism through prayer, making the person's body an undesirable place for evil spirits or the devil; confession and death or imprisonment for the practice of witchcraft; and hospital treatment for mental illness. More recently, many professional helpers are paying less attention to the discrepancies between normal and abnormal functioning in the belief that people who need help do not have to be confined to hospitals or institutions but that both informal and formal sources of help are available within the community and that proper use of these resources can be accomplished. There is also the prevailing theme in our society that development comes from strengthening personal resources within the individual.

Views of human nature and the process of socialization have changed as cultures and societies have changed. At least until recently, changes in the culture were barely perceptible during the lifetime of an individual, whereas changes related to social, economic, educational, and political events are probably always more keenly felt in the course of a life. The belief systems that prevail in the psychotherapies are those that have emerged from the minds of theorists and practitioners in the course of a life. The belief systems that prevail in the psychotherapies are those that have emerged from the minds of theorists and practitioners in the course of their experiences in the context of the culture and have eventually become formally organized. The process is, of course, reciprocal: if the belief system becomes accepted as a part of the culture, it then is taken for reality.

● HUMAN NATURE

The expression *human nature* implies what is believed to be intrinsic to all humans. Modern psychology has largely avoided a simple explanation of human nature as one's will and favored a concept of human nature as a mechanistic interactive process. Aristotelian logic interprets will as a natural striving toward or away from an exciting course that is pleasurable or painful, thus making personal development dependent on forces external to the person. Theoretically and philosophically, the problem or question of free will continues. Believers in free will maintain that thought and volition are or may be directed by individuals themselves, regardless of external influences and (according to some proponents) regardless of physical or mental constitution. In contrast, the determinism of orthodox psychoanalytic or genetic-behavioral theories, for example, provides little room for freedom of will in any sense.

Human nature is whatever is assumed to exist at birth and includes the dynamic potential and powers of development. In the most basic sense it is the ability to communicate on the symbolic level or conceptual level. Not already formed at birth, personality and/or character are acquired in the course of socialization, whereby the fundamental nature of human beings is developed and expressed in face-to-face groups. One feature is not possible without the other: the elements of original nature are necessary but not sufficient conditions of personality. Without the process of socialization, the inborn elements will remain unrealized potentialities. The nature of the socialization process within a culture can be defined, in one sense, as whatever nurtures the dynamic elements of human nature, enabling a person to grow and mature. The elements that are developed are ideas, concepts, thoughts, feelings, values, attitudes, norms, behavior, and other elements that constitute the individual's personality in the social world. Thus nature and nurture complement and influence each other. All approaches to counseling and therapy contain philosophical/theoretical presumptions regarding the relationship between nature and nurture: good nature and bad nurture, bad nature and good nurture, or a potential for both good and bad in both nature and nurture.

The organization of whatever exists in the world of the mind (that is, intrapsyche) has been the primary goal of most psychotherapy approaches. The process of reflecting on one's own self is probably not an event of everyday life; most people think about themselves only when they become aware of uncomfortable feelings or difficulties around them. Thinking about problems and having to solve problems is not pleasant or easy because it threatens the feeling of security. From another perspective, the problems of the modern Western world may in fact seem especially difficult and threatening because consciousness (self-awareness) has become more open to systematic and scientific examination, which has brought the realization that there is no final or ultimate reality except what is created by each person. What may be thought to be reality dissolves and must be re-sorted and worked into another reality as the world changes around the person. The process can be exciting and challenging, but also fearsome and disrupting. The psychodynamic approach to reconstruction of the basic personality is very stressful, and when environmental problems related to living are of foremost importance, having to cope with past psychological experiences in addition may only contribute to current maladjustment.

● SUDDEN SHIFTS IN CONCEPTS OF PSYCHOLOGICAL REALITY

Science, as a feature of the modern culture and society, is notable for sudden or periodic changes in thought and practice. It is generally believed that maturity in scientific disciplines does not occur by the linear and orderly accumulation of concepts, principles, facts, and hypotheses but that it comes about through revolutions in thought that change the conceptual foundations of the discipline. The major contributions of Darwin, Einstein, and Marx caused such shifts, and likewise the impact of the belief system contained in Freud's psychoanalysis revolutionized all subsequent concepts of what human beings are like, how they become what they are, and how they can be helped in the life experience. To some writers, Freudian thought represents the freeing of the human mind from the history and culture of "European medieval bondage." Although undesirable images and rejection of "mentally ill" persons continue to linger in our society, the psychoanalytic era in Western conceptualization of human nature and the socialization process represents a positive transition away from viewing mentally ill persons as subhuman. Some also believed that psychoanalysis finally brought "order out of chaos," whereas actually one view of reality had simply been substituted for another in the evolving picture of human nature. The mystical view of reality in the orderliness of nature was transformed into a scientific view with its own definition of orderliness. Thus, world views that once were believed to give direction to human affairs have been replaced, or superseded, by psychoanalysis, which in turn has been followed by many other competing views of psychological reality.

● WHY STUDY THE CULTURAL HISTORY OF THERAPY?

The counselor draws on what has emerged from the wisdom of the culture. Acceptance of the tentativeness of what can be done to help clients is a professional choice that is guided by one's beliefs about human nature, knowledge of each theoretical system, and ethical responsibilities. The next section reviews the major helping options that are available to counselors and therapists. Like any other consumer, the beginning counselor needs to know the primary features of the many choices that are available. This brief review is meant only as a general introduction. Further in-depth study and supervised practical experience are, of course, necessary for professional competence.

The ultimate question to ask of each theoretical approach is: What does it teach about human nature and the socialization process? Does it make sense, does it fit with what you believe or have experienced? Is it the type of philosophy and theory that you would like to identify with? Is its proposed treatment of people something that you yourself would want to experience? Might it meet the varying needs of all people with real problems and developmental concerns? If not, for whose needs and problems might it be most helpful?

■ MAJOR THEORETICAL APPROACHES TO COUNSELING AND THERAPY

Three major movements have emerged from European and U.S. cultures since the beginning of the 20th century. These movements, described as "forces" by Goble (1970), have influenced much of the direction in mainstream psychology and in the formulation of theories of counseling and psychotherapy. The three movements—psychoanalysis, behaviorism, and existential-humanistic psychology—represent divergent pictures of what human nature might be and what modes of helping might best coincide with those pictures. Freud's psychoanalytic theory attributes human nature solely to intrapsychic monitoring of the conflict between genetic, instinctual drives and the requirements demanded by the socialization process and society. Behaviorism defines "human nature" as learned responses, acquired by living in the environment, which can be modified or replaced by more adaptive responses—those that bring ever greater reward and satisfaction to the person or that avoid punishing conditions. Freud's theory was derived from his clinical work with mental patients, whereas the behaviorists concentrated on the objective "scientific" approach. The existential-humanistic movement, unwilling to accept the strict psychoanalytic view of human nature "trapped" within its own psychodynamic functioning or the behaviorist's mechanistic assumptions about the individual's conditioning by external forces, contends that human nature is neither caught up in itself nor controlled by the environment. The existential-humanistic viewpoint proposes that human nature contains the potential for unlimited development through the process of self-awareness and personal change. When one accepts this challenge, one will have the freedom to make fundamental choices that shape one's life and to become the person one chooses to become.

Each movement has a different view of human nature, different goals and actions stemming from those views, and a system of approaches or techniques to carry out the goals or actions. The term *psychodynamic* is used to designate those approaches that include Freudian psychoanalysis, the neopsychoanalytic theories, and other extensions or adaptations of psychoanalysis. In addition to the three major categories treated here, two other approaches are discussed in Chapter 10: the eclectic, the merging of different approaches, and the synergetic, the merging of approaches in harmony with the changing nature of the culture. Table 9-1 charts the major categories of counseling and therapy and some of the theoretical systems that are included in those categories.

■ PSYCHODYNAMIC APPROACHES

Psychodynamic approaches to counseling and psychotherapy seek to explain or interpret mental and emotional forces or processes within the person, especially those developing in early childhood, and their effects on behavioral and mental states in the personality. Most important, psychodynamic approaches emphasize working with the motivational forces that act at the unconscious level. Whereas traditional *Freudian psychoanalysis* stresses bringing to conscious awareness an objective interpretation of motivational forces acting on the client's unconscious level, psychoanalytic *psychotherapy* places greater emphasis on adjustment to life problems and the external reality of the client's unconscious that emerges in the relationship between client and therapist (transference and countertransference). Thus approaches that are identified as psychoanalytic psychotherapy could involve infinite varieties of client-therapist situations and countless varieties of approaches. But whatever modifications might be made in the therapeutic approach used by each therapist with each client, the unifying system that underlies all psychoanalytic psychotherapy is grounded in the basic concepts of psychoanalysis.

TABLE 9-1 Approaches to Counseling and Psychotherapy

Traditional Approaches	Eclectic Approaches	Synergetic Approaches
1. *Psychodynamic* Freudian psycho- analysis Psychoanalytic psychotherapy *Neopsychoanalytic* Jung Adler Horney Fromm Sullivan	1. *Counselor-* *centered* Integration of parts of theo- ries that fit counselor's personality and setting	1. *Selected exam-* *ples of early* *transitional* *models* Nonracist com- munication Accountable action Systemic Transcendent Culturally spe-
2. *Existential-humanistic* Frankl (logotherapy) May (existential therapy) Rogers (person- centered) Perls (Gestalt therapy) Assagioli (psychosyn- thesis) Transpersonal psychology	2. *Process-centered* *communication* *skills model* Egan (skilled helper) Carkhuff (hu- man resource development) Ivey (micro- counseling)	cific 2. *Cross-cultural* *analysis* 3. *Person-* *environment* *analysis* 4. *Multicultural* *development*
3. *Behavioral* *Conditioned responses* Wolpe (systematic desensitization) Relaxation training Biofeedback Implosive therapy Aversive therapy *Social learning* Social modeling Behavior rehearsal Behavior contracts Assertiveness training *Cognitive behavior* Ellis (rational-emotive therapy) Glasser (reality therapy)		

Neopsychoanalytic approaches are further extensions and adaptations of psychoanalytic theory. The realization of the neo-Freudian theorists—the ego analysts—was that the ego must undergo changes or strengthening in order to handle painful repressed material brought up in the "free association" atmosphere of the therapeutic relationship. Strong reactions against the predeterministic power and influence of unconscious instinctual drives and the deterministic flavor of the psychosexual developmental stages gave way to concern for the ego and its failures, especially as manifested through anxiety. Thus a psychology of control and power of the id was expanded to a psychology of the ego, the conscious self. Furthermore, forces that are found outside the person and that are inherent in social drives acquired in the social and cultural environment were given greater importance. Although there is overlap in conceptual systems and variations in emphasis, the theories of Jung, Adler, Horney, Fromm, and Sullivan are presented as representative examples that deviate from traditional Freudian psychoanalysis. Their general view of human nature is that the person (ego) has the power for reconciliation of relations with self and with others. Both are contributory factors to life's problems, as well as the sources of adjustment and growth. Thus, the neopsychoanalysts give consideration to both psychodynamics and sociodynamics. Within this classification, Jung and Adler stress the person in interaction with others, while Horney, Fromm, and Sullivan may be regarded as emphasizing people in interaction with social systems. All psychodynamic approaches share the same belief that intrapsychic conflict is the source of human problems and that personal *insight* is essential for improvement.

▲ FREUDIAN PSYCHOANALYSIS

The first psychotherapy system was created by Sigmund Freud in his psychoanalysis procedure. The initial transition toward a more organized and comprehensive examination of human dynamics in contemporary times can be attributed to Freud's theory of psychoanalysis. His comprehensive theory of human nature, the socialization process, and treatment procedures continue to have influence in the general American culture, and many basic concepts that are accepted in general psychology today as universal "truths" can be traced to the frame of reference that was initially constructed by psychoanalysis. Freud's concepts grew out of the Victorian era, the second half of the 19th century, a period in which human fulfillment was defined as harmony with the tastes, personal standards of conduct, moral values, and growth of the industrial economy of the time. Moral harmony was seen as victory in the struggle to control one's base drives. In today's culture, the Victorian concept of human nature is generally viewed as narrowly restrictive of free expression and hypocritical, in the sense that psychosocial sexual relations are hidden from view, although in reality they influence human behavior. The fears aroused by facing the nature of human nature are related to the belief system that is derived from the culture, and Freud's special interest in the sex drive and its relation to human nature was especially controversial in the post-Victorian era. Historic cultural concepts of the energy found in psychosocial sexual drives include a belief in the existence of demons that seek to control the human personality; a battle between evil (aggression) and good (love) forces in human nature; the mechanistic concept of the brain as an extension of the genital glands; and effective sexual expression as merely a behavioral function that depends on learned techniques and skills. A thread that runs throughout is the fear that aggression is contained in the sexual drive or that aggression or harm can result from the drive. The implication—at least for many people and many cultures—is that the energy in those drives, or that part of the person represented by them, has not been fully developed in ways that might afford a balance in living.

The detailed attention given here to psychoanalytic theory is not meant to imply that this is the most relevant, valid, or important approach to counseling, but that present-day theories have their roots in what is often termed the first comprehensive mapping of human dynamics. Psychoanalysis itself provides the theoretical approach, or points of belief, and "psychic therapy"—the moral therapy of the second half of the 19th century—became "psychotherapy," or the process of using the concepts of psychoanalysis with persons having a wide range of *intrapsychic* problems, as seen in their behavioral symptoms. Freud's psychoanalysis and therapy process and subsequent neopsychoanalytic theories are no longer the single form of psychotherapy, but they continue to influence or play an important role in defining human nature and psychological reality, both in the culture and in the theories and practices of the helping professions.

● CENTRAL THEME: COMPETING INTRAPSYCHIC FORCES

The central hypothesis of psychoanalysis is that human nature is found in the phenomena of intrapsychic experiences and that human behavior is determined in large part by unconscious motives in this "world in the mind." Human motives and behavior can best be understood and helped through the revelation and reconstruction of past experiences that have been repressed—driven out of consciousness and into the unconscious—but that continue unconsciously to impinge on the human desire for homeostatic balance within the psyche, the person. The ideal balance is the harmony, or psychic integration, that can be gained among the three structural processes—three different reaction patterns—of the personality; achieving it is an ongoing lifetime endeavor.

Id. The id is the completely unconscious source of psychic energy that is derived from the unity of inherited instinctual needs and drives. It is the power for psychological functioning and is governed by the pleasure principle (avoidance and reduction of tension). Stating it another way, human behavior is directed toward the immediate satisfaction of important life-affirming instinctual drives and immediate relief from life-threatening pain or discomfort. Thus, the energy of the id can be viewed as the urge for human survival, in that the need for water, food, development and growth, and reproduction of one's own kind are essential for the life process. Nourishment, warmth, affection, and love are the underlying psychological needs that are intrinsic to the sexual drive. The death instinct, also assumed by Freud, is the human drive found in aggression and destruction and in hostility toward one another. Thus the sex drive is creative and life-giving, while the death drive is destructive and life-threatening. Love and hate can be directed inward to the self or outward toward others.

Ego. To allow for appropriate transactions with the outside world, the ego develops the capacity to select what it will respond to in the environment and which needs will be satisfied and in what order. It is the organized conscious mediator between the person and reality, and it functions in both perception of and adaptation to reality. Whereas the id can produce only irrational fantasies or wishes for what is desired or needed, the ego provides the means by which—through reality testing—the discharge of tension is possible when an object that is appropriate for satisfaction is discovered.

The psychological self and esteem for self are also necessary for living. Ego defense mechanisms maintain one's sense of personal worth. In psychoanalysis these protective fictions are the unconscious attempts by the ego to dispose of the unwelcome anxiety (tension) created by instinctual drives. Anxiety has an important purpose in life functioning, since it alerts one to dangers from within and without; otherwise, one would be left at the mercy of instinctual impulses or unknown external dangers. Because the sensation of anxiety is generally blended into life experiences, the person is often not consciously aware of the *source* of anxiety. One obvious source of anxiety is something that is *real*—external to the individual—and present in the situation or environment, such as direct physical threat, trauma, and dangerous predicaments. A second source of anxiety is internal, *neurotic* anxiety. To Freud, it represents the feelings and instincts that break free from ego inhibitions. We become anxious about being overwhelmed by an uncontrollable urge to commit some act or think some thought that the ego defines as harmful. It is not the fear of the instincts themselves that alarms us, so much as fear of punishment for following them. Neurotic anxiety can take three forms: (1) *free-floating anxiety,* which is pervasive, vague, and general and represents a fear of punishment and authority, (2) *phobic anxiety,* which is object-specific and irrational and derived from unconscious fear of instinctual forces, and (3) *panic,* which is the sensation that id impulses are about to break through controls; the impulses may be acted out in ways such as expressing anger or getting drunk. A third source of anxiety is *moral,* which is essentially going against the conscience, thus creating fear and guilt. "Punishment" by conscience results from doing or thinking something that is contrary to one's moral standards. Whatever the source of anxiety, when the anxiety becomes excessive the ego will defend itself by forcing the matter out of consciousness and into the unconscious (repression), attributing the anxiety felt by the person to something else in the environment (projection), or consciously replacing the feeling that produces the anxiety by its opposite feeling (reaction formation). Habitual overuse of defense mechanisms can work against or inhibit the full development of personality; sublimation is the creative use of anxious energy.

Superego. The superego, only partly conscious, represents internalization of parental authority (conscience) and the rules and mores of society. It functions to reward and punish through a system of moral attitudes, conscience, and a sense of guilt. Thus conscience punishes when we go against our ideal values, and our ego ideal (aspirations) gives rewards when we act in accordance with our values or when we reach a compromise with our values.

● DEVELOPING A BALANCE AMONG INTRAPSYCHIC FORCES

Serious imbalance among the three divisions of the personality structure or defects in a division are considered as indicators of disorder. The most serious disorder is *psychosis,* which is characterized by defective or lost contact with reality (ego functioning). Reality becomes a world of fantasy in which various serious mental symptoms may occur, such as delusions, hallucinations, obsessions and compulsions, and morbid fears. *Neurosis* is considered a functional disorder that hinders efficiency in personal everyday living or disrupts interpersonal relations. Current distinctions among symptoms of neurosis generally group them into three categories: anxiety disorders, somatoform disorders, and dissociative disorders.

From his experiences in psychotherapy, Peck (1978, p. 35) believes that most people who see a psychiatrist suffer from either a neurosis or a character disorder. "Character" in Freudian conceptualization basically implies the development of ego functioning in the job of moderating the personality divisions. Thus an adult may be chronologically mature but psychologically immature in his or her psychosocial development. A neurotic person, according to Peck, assumes all the blame for what goes wrong in his or her life. This person's self-image finds verbal expression in phrases such as "I ought," "I must," "I should," "I shouldn't." In contrast, the person with a character disorder does not take enough responsibility for his or her conflicts with the world and assumes that the world is at fault. This person uses expressions such as "I can't," "I couldn't," "I hate to," and "I had to." His or her self-image is that of a being who has no power of choice and whose behavior is completely directed by external forces beyond his or her control. A combination of both neurosis and character disorder—character neurosis—can also be found in persons who assume some responsibility that is really not theirs, while in other areas failing to take realistic responsibility for their lives. Thus the many of us who suffer the pains of neurosis tend to make ourselves miserable with guilt, and those of us who experience disorders in character make everyone else miserable.

● PSYCHOSEXUAL STAGES

Coping with each stage of psychological development is anxiety-arousing as the ego works to achieve balance between needs and social demands. If each stage is not successfully handled, through anxiety reduction, the personality is oriented through life toward meeting the unfulfilled needs related to that stage. Though space does not permit in-depth explanation of each stage, it should be noted that fixation at any stage implies a carry-over of unresolved anxiety into adult years. Thus the developmental experiences found in life stages set in motion the themes that are carried out in life and from which future conflict can emerge. Although most modern theorists do not adhere to a notion of the deterministic nature of each stage, Corey (1986, p. 17) defines the general areas of personal and social development that occur during the first five years of life as (1) love and trust, (2) dealing with negative feelings, and (3) developing a positive acceptance of sexuality. The final stage of character development is the achievement of balance and harmony in the structural divisions of personality, enabling the person to achieve complete satisfaction of the sexual drive, to become free of self-centeredness, and to give and receive affection. At this stage a person has resolved internal conflicts from earlier stages of development and can focus on adult tasks (Corey, 1986, p. 25).

● PSYCHOTHERAPY

The general goal of Freudian psychotherapy is to discover unconscious motivations and eventually to reconstruct and balance the elements in psychodynamic functioning. This is accomplished through insight, analysis, and interpretation. The corrective emotional experience in the relationship between client and therapist is seen as most important: the client's sharing of emotions with the therapist gives strength to the ego to handle repressed materials.

▲ NEOPSYCHOANALYTIC THEORIES

Neopsychoanalytic theories represent an extension and adaptation of Freudian psychoanalytic theory. All give less emphasis than does Freudian theory to the biological side of human nature, the power of the unconscious, and the deterministic view of psychosexual stages of development. They place importance on the development of the individual self and the influences of sociocultural factors in personality development. References to these theories may be found in Corey (1986), Schultz (1981), and Hall and Lindzey (1978).

● CARL GUSTAV JUNG AND ANALYTICAL PSYCHOLOGY

Although Jung adopted many of Freud's concepts, he, like Adler, was mainly interested in the purposive and goal-striving behavior of individuals. However, unlike Adler, he additionally sought to understand unconscious *collective* life purposes that influence behavior. Thus he was concerned with both direction of movement (teleology) of human beings and past experiences (causality). He placed primary emphasis on mapping unconscious human behavior.

Personal unconscious. At one level the direction of movement of human behavior is seen in the personal unconscious that adjoins the ego. This contains the complex of experiences organized around significant persons (for example, mother and father) and objects (such as money) and also provides a place to discard unwanted or threatening items and simply forgotten experiences. Unconscious material may "congeal" into a complex (group of experiences) that acts as a pull on current related experiences. For example, a person of strict moral upbringing might repress thoughts or tendencies that would conflict with his or her code; thus the personal unconscious is what it is because the conscious personality is what it is. If a certain complex is powerful enough it can even act as a separate personality. The psychological reaction or conflict in awareness is felt as emotional fears and anxiety, which can eventually disrupt individual functioning.

Collective unconscious. Jung theorized another unconscious zone deeper than the personal unconscious, one that could *not* have been acquired from personal experiences. This he called the *collective unconscious.* Its images resemble experiences, thoughts, or emotions of primitive people. This inherited collective unconscious is what Jung believed to be composed of the residual imprints of ancestral experiences. It is the common heritage possessed by all human beings and represents what has been repeated, experienced, over the life of the human species. These unconscious predispositions for thinking, feeling, perceiving, and acting are those forms that have survived over thousands of generations (and are carried in the genes) and are therefore already in the mind. In essence the fears that we all have today are no different from those our ancestors had. Whether these predispositions emerge depends on one's current experiences in the environment and the role any predisposition will play in one's life.

Components of the collective unconscious. The components of the collective unconscious are termed *archetypes.* They are the original images or forms that have always been experienced and that underlie all manifestations produced by cultures. There are probably as many archetypes as there are repeated experiences in the history of human beings; they are represented in the content of evolutionary history, mythological figures, symbols, and religious and instinctual behavior. The complex patterns formed by these experiences are manifested in dreams, fantasies, delusions, and eventually in myths, literature, art, and other creative expression. The daily movement of the sun, for example, has its imprint in the collective unconscious as a type of supreme god. Other common symbolic themes of human existence are expressed in archetypes such as water (a void or sinking down experience), animals (givers of life), and the wise old man (revealer of meaning). Yet other forms are birth, death, power, the child, the mother, and the hero.

There may be culture-specific expressions of the same archetypal forms. Thus the English may tend to portray the hero as controlled, courteous, reluctant to show emotions, honest, and straightforward, whereas a Greek hero might be portrayed as being clever—a trickster who would use guile to defeat enemies—and showing emotion when the situation warranted it. The Christian culture represents Christ in the hero-rescuer archetypal image, seeing him devoured by the monster (death) but appearing again in a miraculous way to overcome the monster. The universal mold is not seen until a culture fills it with a myth, which defines it but which itself is not definable (Storr, 1973, pp. 33–34). The separation of the positive and negative dimensions of human nature, both of which are basic to human psychodynamics, plays a central role in how mental health problems are defined by modern society. Perhaps the Christian emphasis on moral living and the general denunciation of other forms of expression such as those found in myths and folklore have contributed to this split. Denial of forms belonging to the collective unconscious may be denial of energy for creative living; or equating the past with satanic forces may have resulted in misunderstanding or confusion of the life insight contained in the messages transmitted by past generations.

The archetypes that have evolved into systems may be considered as having existence clearly separate from the rest of the psyche. Those that are most directly related to personality development and that may be experienced as conflicts between the conscious and unconscious realms include the following four archetypes:

1. *Persona.* The persona is the superficial public mask that a person presents in response to others in social relationships. It has evolved as a self-protective way to impress others or to hide one's actual feelings and thoughts. In one sense, it could imply the tendency toward conformity that enables us to get along well with numerous people, whether at work, at home, or in social situations. Domination of the "real" personality by the facade can result in artificiality and dullness, a condition in which the person has lost touch with the rest of what he or she is.

2. *Anima and animus.* The anima is the feminine aspect of men and the animus is the masculine side of women. It is the inward face, as opposed to the persona, which is the outward face. Through living and interacting with the opposite sex over generations, each sex has acquired some of the characteristics of the other, enabling each to understand and relate to the other. Development of the inner self, the personality, is found in the expression of its opposite side in consciousness and behavior. The part that has been learned from the opposite sex can be used to complement and balance one's own basic masculinity or femininity.

3. *The shadow.* The shadow represents one's own sex and relationship with someone of the same sex. It can be composed of what one thinks is undesirable or evil and is met when one criticizes the other person for what one could not criticize in oneself. The shadow also contains our basic animal nature no longer consciously recognized in modern humankind. Although perhaps frightening, it is also the spontaneous, impulsive aspect that can urge us into creativity and satisfying activities. When the wisdom of a person's instinctual nature and the ego work together, the person feels more alive mentally and physically.

4. *The self.* A state of selfhood emerges or is achieved when the archetypes have been developed and are harmonized and integrated in a uniting of the personality (persona and anima or animus), giving a sense of oneness. Self-realization comes from unity, wholeness, and completeness and is seen as the central purpose or goal for striving in life. The self is the organizing principle of the personality and is the central archetype in the collective unconscious. The impression or image of individuation that is experienced is thought to occur through knowledge of oneself and making conscious that

which is unconscious, allowing one to live in greater harmony with one's own nature. The archetypical form of wholeness is sometimes seen in cultural representations that take the form of a mandala, a circular figure, which symbolizes integration.

The ego. Self-concept is the integrator of the conscious and unconscious processes. Developing the aware part of the self (who one is) is a lifetime pursuit that brings the person closer to wholeness, or the desired experience of the self.

Psychotherapy. A client's neurosis is seen as a part of a larger whole. By achieving philosophical calmness and detachment, the client is prepared to contact and transcend his or her own unconscious. Free-association and word-association devices may be used to reveal and compare one's unconscious values with one's conscious values as an assessment of ego strength (level of integration). Both objective interpretation by the therapist and subjective interpretation by the client are used to relate symbols to aspects of the client's psychic self. The media can be verbal description, active fantasizing, and creative expression such as painting or drawing symbols. As recurring symbols or themes emerge from the unconscious, they may be related to the universal archetypes experienced by all people (consensual validation). Reconciliation, or resolving conflicts in the person to gain wholeness, is an important part of the therapeutic process. When one pole works against the functioning of the other (as between masculinity and femininity) or dominates the personality, it works against selfhood. Application to real life in the environment is often left up to the client, since the goal of Jungian analysis, similar to that of psychoanalysis, is self-insight.

● ALFRED ADLER AND INDIVIDUAL PSYCHOLOGY

Adler's psychology is a study of the subjective perceptions of the creative self—the person who can be understood only as a social being in interaction and cooperation with other social beings *(social interest)*. Thus the indivisible personality is a unified whole (holistic). All parts function cooperatively to serve the person, and actions can be seen as having *purpose* in the same sense as they might in a society of people. It is more important to understand how the unique person interprets the facts or details of his or her life or circumstance than to know the facts themselves. The personal self-system interprets and makes meaning out of life by searching for experiences or creating experiences that help fulfill the individual's special and unique style of life (teleology). Thus people are primarily social beings rather than the sexual beings of Freud's belief.

Style of life. Style of life is whatever is exhibited in the distinctive and unique actions of each person. One's lifestyle determines what a person learns, how a person behaves, thinks, and feels, and what experiences will be incorporated into the personality. Thus life is goal-directed, the goals being those developed and established by the creative self early in childhood (by the age of 4 or 5). The family culture, the first social interaction experience, sets the basic structure of the lifestyle and, unless challenged, is consistent throughout life. A child's life plan does not grow out of a certain peculiarity in the psyche or out of isolated experiences in life stages, but out of expectations for the future. Future expectations, real or imagined, exercise a profound influence on a person's discouragement or encouragement in life. The striving for superiority—the perfection of one's own development— is inherent in all human beings, and it is in striving that individual character traits are formed and individual lifestyles are developed. To be fully human is to feel the inferiority that arises from a sense of imperfection or incompletion. The ultimate compensation for individual inferiorities—those things that cannot be perfected in the person—is found in making contribu- tions to society in order to make it more perfect, subordinating private gain to the general welfare in such ways as cooperation, sharing, showing interest in others, and understanding others. Thus mental health is not seen in isolated beings, but in socially interactive beings who are developing higher levels of social interest. What is good for the individual is what is good for a group, and vice versa.

Seeking significance, through achieving self-identity (purposes) and belongingness (social interest), is influenced by individually chosen goals (lifestyle). Normal inferiority feelings are what give incentive to solving problems successfully, whereas the inferiority complex produces the convic- tion that one is unable to improve what is wrong. The inferiority complex develops from pampering, spoiling, or neglect in the early years. Its roots can be found in the power positions that children hold in relation to other children in the family *(family constellation)*. Individuals with mistaken opinions (attitudes) of themselves and the world—that is, with misdirected goals or purposes and mistaken lifestyles—will resort to various abnormal behaviors aimed at safeguarding their opinions of self when confronted with situations that they feel they cannot meet successfully. The neurotic person is anxious and looks for power in destructive, unrealistic means (obstinacy, cruelty, domination, diffidence, submission, conceit, greed, envy, or intolerance, for example), whereas the normal self-confident person chooses socially useful attitudes and actions (cooperation, goodwill, pride, love, and so forth).

Counseling and psychotherapy. The development of social feelings is a major aim in Adlerian counseling and therapy. The client is considered disturbed (not mentally ill, as in the Freudian sense) as a result of concealed hostility to others arising from his or her need for significance and superiority. The client's underlying belief is that he or she is powerless to accept responsibility. The counselor has four tasks: (1) to establish contact with the client, (2) to disclose the error in the client's lifestyle, (3) to encourage the client, and (4) to develop the client's social interest. The client's confidence must be maintained, and cheerfulness, a sense of humor, and an optimistic attitude are important for the counselor. The client is led gradually and indirectly to recognize his or her goal, lifestyle, and erroneous view of life. The ultimate aim is "reorientation" in such a manner that the client connects himself or herself with others on an equal and cooperative footing.

● KAREN HORNEY AND SOCIAL PERSONALITY

Horney rejected instinctual theory and structural dimensions of the intrapsyche (id, ego, superego). In her system, the need for security is each person's major motivation, and when the person fails to find it in relation to parents and other significant persons, he or she views the world as a hostile place (basic anxiety). The strategies that are developed to cope with this feeling of alienation and helplessness become dynamic personality needs (idealized self-image) and are irrational ways to find a solution to disrupted human relationships. Horney lists ten neurotic needs basically grouped under three categories: (1) moving *toward* people: a dependent and compliant self that says "take care of me," (2) moving *away* from people: a detached self that says "leave me alone," and (3) moving *against* people: an aggressive self that says "see how powerful I am." The "adjusted" or "normal" person is able to achieve some degree of balance or integration among these basic movements.

Helping the person confront and deal with the unrealistic or idealized self-image and the neurotic needs that fuel the social image is the major goal of counseling and psychotherapy. Realistic acceptance by the client of his or her idealized self as it is actually functioning will allow for emergence of the real self—the self that does not need to depend on the ten needs or to be obstructed by them. The person is not neurotic; it is the false needs that are neurotic. Thus getting rid of false needs as they influence the present living situation will allow for integration of personality.

● ERICH FROMM AND SOCIAL CHARACTER

Forces in the individual psyche are interrelated with the society in which one lives. Social character is "the nucleus of the character structure which is shared by most members of the same culture." The development of self-fulfillment—social character—is thus also bound up with how people can influence or shape their society. People will lead lonely and individuated lives if they do not exercise the freedom that society offers to experience mutual respect and love. Nonproductivity is found in the security of constrictive conformity to irrational authority.

Fromm does not prescribe a system of counseling or psychotherapy, but the implication of his theory is that people have been separated from meaningful relations with others and with nature. Fromm believed that lives in Western nations are empty because people have (1) passively accepted authority for direction and security (dependency-receptivity), (2) used others for their own gain (exploitation), (3) held onto or accumulated material objects, feelings, and thoughts (hoarding orientation), or (4) relinquished themselves to fleeting, current fads (market orientation). He proposes that health can be achieved through the development of a productive orientation, which is defined as the actualization of human potentialities that are reciprocally creative and loving toward both the self and society.

● HARRY STACK SULLIVAN AND INTERPERSONAL RELATIONS

Sullivan may be considered one of the first theorists to construct a social "systems" approach to understanding individual human behavior. Like other modern systems theory, Sullivan's focuses on the organization of whole systems. The approach represents a basic shift in thinking from the mechanistic Galilean-Newtonian linear and one-way cause-and-effect principles of relationship to the characteristics of whole systems of interpersonal interaction among people. Thus, rather than reducing behavior to the sum of basic parts, Sullivan's theoretical approach looks at the characteristics of the total living system. Mechanistic cause-and-effect principles are seen as only one part of a vital larger system that has some purpose or direction (teleology). All individual behavior is interpersonal, and understanding can be found in interactions among people. Thus Sullivan's viewpoint is most concerned with the interpersonal situation and not the intrapsyche of the person. Except for the human dynamics in unconscious motivation and defense mechanisms, this approach abandons traditional Freudian concepts, terminology, and principles.

Dynamism and the self-system. Dynamism (power) is the basic characteristic of a person. Like a habit or trait, it is the same for all people, but is individually expressed in different ways. Thus dynamism is the whole emerging self and its component systems. The form that emerges—self-dynamism—determines one's perceptions and serves as a guide for making important value decisions at any point in life. Dynamism involved in interpersonal relations serves to satisfy two basic and interactive human goals (needs): (1) biological satisfaction: rest, sleep, sexual fulfillment, clothing, shelter, food and drink, physical closeness to others, and (2) social security: psychological well-being, belongingness, acceptance. Expression of the two goals is lifelong. Although the society may interfere or conflict with biological satisfaction, most problems arise out of one's pursuit of security. The release of energy that security triggers is dependent on the person's ability to understand and communicate with the social environment. When good feelings about oneself (respect, worth, love) are threatened or falter, the euphoric feeling is lost; the resulting anxiety can be best understood in the dynamics of the self-system.

The *self-system* is the use of energy to defend an imperfectly perceived self. Self-defined ways are used to distort interpersonal relations (parataxic distortion) that are threatening to one's security and thus anxiety-producing. The process of socialization through interpersonal relations involves incorporation of the values and attitudes that bring security; thus "correct" behavior is what brings security to the self-system and conforms to the "good-me" self. Personification—personalizing a relationship—is the image that an individual has of himself or herself or another person and is related to the anxiety (level of security) that a person feels toward self or others. The "good-me" is organized around security experiences and the "bad-me" is organized around anxiety states. Though the self-system serves the purpose of protecting the person, it can also interfere with one's ability to live

constructively with others. Self-defensiveness uses energy that might otherwise work for self-development and the "actual self falls far short of the real
self." In addition, the more irrational the society (that is, the system of
interpersonal relations), the more likely the person is to learn irrational
attitudes and feel anxious—things that he or she would not otherwise do.
When a number of people share the same personification, it becomes a
stereotype.

Counseling and psychotherapy. One becomes what one is in relation to
others, and development, motivation, adjustment, and maladjustment can be
understood only in terms of one's interpersonal relations. Life itself can be a
corrective experience when one takes the opportunity to compare one's
thoughts and feelings with those of others (consensual validation), but many
people need the help of someone else to correct their errors. The energy
expended in defending oneself in relation to others can be used for personality development by a client who believes that perceptual distortion is
not a necessary condition for security. This belief is accomplished by realizing that anxieties and anger in reaction to earlier experiences are understandable conditions often found in the lives of most human beings (consensual validation) who want fulfillment in self-respect and the feeling of
worthwhileness. More rational and realistic concepts are needed to replace
the experience of anxiety in childhood, which has served to give a highly
distorted picture of self and relationships with others as a means of avoiding
anxiety. Concentration on the distortions that have been produced by and
serve to perpetuate anxiety is a goal. Open communication between counselor
and client is important; there is a two-way flow of thoughts and feelings, with
the counselor playing the dual role of participant and observer. Because
defensive distortion is a result of interpersonal relations, the relationship that
emerges between counselor and client can be used as a dimension to explore
in counseling, and the counselor should be alert to anything in his or her own
attitudes and means of communication that might hinder the communication
flow. The ultimate goal is for the client to learn something about interpersonal
communication.

■ EXISTENTIAL-HUMANISTIC APPROACHES

Existential-humanistic theories have chosen, as have the neopsychoanalytic
theories, to emphasize the important role that the self plays in meeting the
problems of living. However, the most common emphasis for the existential-
humanists is on personality as the expression of a whole self, as opposed to
personality as an aggregate of behaviors. Thus, the crucial—almost
grandiose—role of personal power is set radically against both biological and
environmental determinism (nature and nurture). The central issue is one's

need and ability to make choices and to achieve the personal responsibility that choice implies. One's own personal experience is the most important factor in understanding life, and what the experience means to the individual forms the key to human personality and behavior. New experiences will also help provide new perceptions and meanings in life. Thus, to understand the behavior of any client in counseling means to understand the way the client constructs his or her subjective world. Counseling, as an experience in and of itself, will allow for new ways of looking at old problems.

The existential and humanistic movements are both European and contemporary American trends that value direct experience and the actualization of humankind. *Progress, perfectibility, limitlessness, full capacity, potential, freedom, energy, fulfillment, positive growth,* and *congruity* are among the terms that convey the optimistic values contained in their concept of human nature. The existential-humanistic viewpoint, unlike that of the psychoanalytic theories, tends to be concerned less with abnormal or psychopathic behavior or classic neurosis and more with ordinary human conditions of unhappiness, alienation, and the failure to reach or strive toward one's full potential. Thus "abnormal functioning" is the failure to be oneself or to fulfill oneself.

Although each approach included in the existential-humanistic category has its own distinctive techniques and modes, the main goal they share is to get in touch with the real self and to make deliberate choices in line with the real self and its wants, rather than permitting outside persons or events to determine behavior. Personal elements and movements that are stressed in counseling and life include conscious perceptual changes, spontaneity, genuine self-expression, emotional honesty, and ideal personal happiness in the present (here and now).

▲ EXISTENTIAL ANALYSIS

Existentialism (Frankl, 1963; Jourard, 1971; May, 1953; Yalom, 1981) is the philosophic analysis of existence and of the way people find themselves existing in the world. Since existential analysis involves the total experience of human existence, individuals are not exhaustively describable or understandable in scientific terms. Whatever is reality (existence) is what is seen in one's experiences; thus *being* is whatever is experienced. There is no human existence apart from the world. The world and the individual are therefore a oneness—neither can exist without the other and this mutual dependence is what the human condition is. What the world is to an individual can only be found in the individual, and only individuals can disclose the world. As an empirical science, existentialism seeks to describe phenomena in terms of space and time. The degree of closeness or apartness between oneself and others measures the degree of one's being-in-the-world and can be sensed in loneliness and alienation. Disclosure of the world is found in the unfolding of the person's totality of experience, which is contained in the past, the present, and future possibilities. There is no limit to disclosing the world and the possibilities.

Because the individual has both the *freedom* and the *responsibility* to exercise options, the choices are ultimately up to the individual. *Nonbeing,* or nothingness, is not using the possibilities that one has the freedom and responsibility to use. Not to take the freedom to realize all possibilities—not to become what one is fully able to become—causes a sense of guilt (existential anxiety). Acceptance of ultimate death as part of existence gives the present experience a greater significance in the progression toward achieving one's actual potential. Being is the ongoing process of becoming human, which is to actualize or fulfill all the possibilities that are available in human existence. The way one defines his or her life determines what and who one is. Understanding of what and who one is can come only from each person's existential experience.

▲ CARL ROGERS AND THE PERSON-CENTERED APPROACH

Like Jung and Adler, Rogers emphasizes conscious awareness and the role of the self. The self is wholeness, as opposed to a collection of fragmented subparts. It is also optimistic, growth oriented, rational, realistic, and forward moving. In therapy, Rogers focuses on the positive self-perception: when this core of good self-feeling is brought out, the negative unworthy perceptions that are distortions of the real self will be counteracted. Rogers's theory is notably American value-centered psychology and is the approach most followed by human services specialists, counselors, counseling psychologists, and many psychotherapists. It can also be described as the conceptual approach that has elevated counseling, traditionally a subprofession, to equal status with psychotherapy. Unlike most of the therapists, who in therapy are working with disturbed patients, Rogers worked out his approach in an academic environment. There, his clients were primarily college students, although his approach has been studied in use with psychotic clients. His belief that the helping process can be found in most effective human relations places an emphasis on normality rather than abnormality.

● PHENOMENAL FIELD

The phenomenal field of the person—the person's total experience at a given moment—is known only by the person. This is the source with which therapists work. How a person interprets or perceives his or her total experience is the basis for therapy. Elements of a person's experience may be misrepresented or not represented when a portion is distorted or denied. Related to perceptual accuracy or inaccuracy are self-image and self-concept. One's view of oneself (condition of worth) is in terms of the worthy or unworthy actions, feelings, and values for which one has been rewarded or punished; thus portions of oneself may be denied full experience and could become perceptual problems at some time in life. People find it difficult to perceive themselves accurately and feel the positive self-regard that everyone needs; the condition is most likely related to evaluative and threatening experiences that they had in childhood. They develop a perceptual life that is based on defensive self-distortion—the selective perceiving of events and behavior that are consistent with self-image. When self-perceptions are not compatible with an actual experience—that is, they are *incongruent*— movement toward self-actualization is less likely. *Congruence* is the state in which one's experiences are accurately symbolized in the self-concept. For example, a college student delivering a presentation before his classmates perceives that they are uninterested in his topic and that he is doing a poor job; in actuality his presentation is excellent, but he distorts the experience to conform to his low self-image.

● SELF-ACTUALIZATION

Self-actualization in the process of maturation is learning to trust one's own experiences and evaluations, rather than those of others. Integrally related to this is the existential belief that people have the freedom to choose the actions they take, along with the possibility of actions that might limit their lives. Choosing is their responsibility and can be observed by the counselor as clients learn to make choices.

● BASIC THERAPEUTIC ATTITUDES

Rogers's theory is oriented toward positive growth and consequently the viewpoint in and of itself is therapeutic. However, certain basic attitudes must be actively conveyed by the therapist, undergoing the same process as the client. The therapist's own *congruence* is honesty in what he or she is experiencing and communicating to the client. Seeing the counselor or therapist as a genuine person and not just a role or title is the essential attitude. Expressing what the client is experiencing through *accurate empathy* and the demonstration of *unconditional positive regard* for the client are other important attitudes. The therapist-person's accurate reflection of the client's own thoughts and feelings, conveyed with positive esteem, creates an experience for the client that promotes growth.

● CONCEPTUAL DEVELOPMENT

Rogers's theory as identified in his writings has evolved through four general stages or phases of conceptual development wherein certain dimensions of the therapeutic process were emphasized and applied. Hart and Tomlinson (1970) have outlined the theoretical movement in the first three phases as (1) nondirective psychotherapy, (2) reflective psychotherapy, and (3) experiential therapy. The fourth stage of conceptual development has become known as the person-centered approach for its wide application to a variety of fields.

1. *Nondirective therapy* (1940–50). During the first stage in the evolution of Rogers's approach (Rogers, 1942) the counselor or therapist was basically an accepting and permissive observer who primarily encouraged clients to clarify

their own thoughts. The procedure was very contrary to the traditional directive approaches, which emphasized therapist-centered advice, direction, persuasion, and diagnosis and interpretation. The nondirective approach presupposed that clients had the capacity for their own internal directions and that by the therapist's not intervening or directly interacting, clients would learn to trust their own cognitive insights into themselves and their situation. The therapist was essentially seen as a detached, neutral monitor who helped to clarify the client's thoughts.

2. *Client-centered reflective therapy* (1950–57). This phase represents the development of Rogers's theory of personality and the therapeutic process (Rogers, 1951), in which attention was given to the establishment of a threat-free environment through the therapist's careful listening for feelings behind the client's words. Thus the therapeutic relationship was centered on the client's expression of feelings, made possible by the therapist's sensitive and accepting responses to those feelings. Listening and reflection of feelings in reflective therapy by a nonjudgmental therapist was nonthreatening because feelings were accepted as they were expressed and simply mirrored back. Perceptual distortion as a self-protection against threat was less likely, and clients were able to develop or accept greater congruence (honesty) between what they perceived or experienced themselves to be (self-concept) and what they desired to be (ideal self-concept). In this benign atmosphere they had the opportunity to have their feelings accepted by another person, to accept their own feelings as legitimate parts of themselves, and finally to reorganize their self-concepts in ways that would be more true to their desired or real selves. The therapist was essentially a facilitator of feelings.

3. *Experiential therapy* (1957–70). Whereas the first phase of conceptualization emphasized acceptance and clarification of the topical content of clients' expressions and the second phase the reflection of clients' feelings, the third stage centered on the therapist's attitudes toward the movement of clients in the therapeutic process. Effective facilitation of the client's progress in therapy was observed when the conditions of genuineness (congruence), unconditional positive regard and acceptance, and empathic understanding were demonstrated in the therapist-client relationship (Rogers, 1957, 1961). Releasing the potential for growth was most possible when the client experienced and could immediately use the therapist's own expressions of what he or she was genuinely experiencing at the moment. Thus these attitudes of the counselor are the elements that form the "necessary and sufficient" conditions for personality change and growth. The emphasis in this third phase shifted to the experience between client and therapist and allowed the therapist greater opportunity to participate in the relationship. It also emphasized within the therapeutic experience some of the characteristics of a fully functioning person.

4. *The person-centered approach* (1970–present). The ways of becoming a more fully actualized person have been generalized into sectors outside the therapeutic setting, and thus the current phase of Rogers's theory may be considered as having cultural value for the society (Rogers, 1969, 1970, 1972,

1977, 1980). The "person-centered" approach has application for therapy, counseling, human relations, marriage, education, and industry, and simply as a way that enables the responsible person to direct his or her own life.

● LIMITATIONS OF THE APPROACH

Since the problems that many Americans and others have are related to self-regard, the desire to feel better about themselves, and self-confidence, the approach has wide use. When life's stresses bring out feelings of inferiority or self-defeat in achieving one's goals, the person-centered approach may be the most effective in motivating the person. However, the usefulness of the approach is questionable when environmental situations are overwhelming and more direct action is needed, when behavioral social skills need improvement, or when unconscious disturbances motivate the person.

▲ FREDERICK PERLS AND GESTALT THERAPY

Frederick Perls (1969) has been the most notable contributor to Gestalt therapy. According to the Gestaltists, the *natural* integrity and wholeness of human thinking, feeling, and acting become fragmented in the course of contact with the culture. Anxiety is basically the sensing of the person in working toward the construction of meaningful and organized wholes (gestalts). When a need is met, the gestalt has become complete and no longer influences the person, so attention can be directed toward other needs. In Gestalt psychology the relationship between figure and ground is the basic underlying principle. Whatever we perceive—an emotion, a situation, a thought—we ordinarily tend to pay attention to only part of the whole experience. Usually we concentrate first on the figure that is in the foreground and ignore the background. For example, if we were told at a meeting with our job supervisor that our work was not satisfactory, we would most likely concentrate on defending our behavior (foreground) during the conversation and be only partially aware of the anger and frustration we felt during the conversation (background). Unfulfilled needs, such as a repressed emotion that was not expressed in the past (unfinished business) or a feeling that is not recognized at the experiencing moment, continue as incomplete gestalten and will block the formation of new gestalten. Taking responsibility for one's own life (maturation) is an ongoing process that involves gaining awareness of and paying attention to the dissonance in one's own thinking, feeling, and acting at the moment of experience. The ultimate goal of Gestalt therapy is integration of a person's existence. Perls, in his recognition of the integrality of human nature, helped to resolve the mind-body split. In this regard his approach can be considered similar to Reich's organismic-functional theory. Wilhelm Reich (Boadella, 1973), who can be categorized as a neopsychoanalytic theorist, conceptualized repressed emotional energy as manifested in the character of bodily expression and observable in posture, facial expression, muscular tension, and the like. Other therapies such as the bioenergetic approach, primal therapy, and Rolfing are also oriented to working with the body and have been influenced by Reichian concepts. Like Reich, Perls worked with body messages.

● COUNSELING AND THERAPY

"To lose your mind and come to your senses" might be one way to state the principle of Gestalt therapy. Perls's approach to learning about one's total self focuses not so much on words or thoughts as on the feeling and awareness that are communicated through the body's nonverbal messages. Thus the basic goal of the approach is to catalyze awareness of *how* and *what* the body is communicating and to use this information to achieve unification and wholeness. Though Gestalt therapy is most commonly used in group encounter experiences, excellent and practical application of the concepts and techniques to a wide range of individual counseling predicaments has been made by Passons (1975) and other writers. Gestalt techniques can be useful for getting in touch with emotions that might block action or that interfere with seeing the whole picture of a problem. Techniques include role reversal, in which the client takes on the role of another person; role playing the indecisive parts of the self, as in top dog versus underdog; imagining dialogue with an empty chair that represents another person with whom the client has unfinished business; and concentrated use of "I" statements instead of "you," "others," or "we" to encourage awareness of and responsibility for one's own thoughts and feelings.

● LIMITATIONS

Like the other existential-humanistic approaches, Gestalt therapy emphasizes improvement of the inner psychological functioning of the person. If the client has a special problem or an environmental condition with which to cope, this approach will not afford the comprehensive knowledge of the client that would give immediate assistance. In addition, the emotional demands that it makes upon clients might only aggravate and confuse their condition.

▲ ROBERTO ASSAGIOLI AND THE PSYCHOSYNTHESIS APPROACH

Assagioli's psychosynthesis (Assagioli, 1965; Crampton, 1977; Firman & Vargiu, 1980) is a psychological/educational approach that can be associated with the transpersonal movement. Assagioli recognizes the will as a positive, purpose-oriented side of personality that can be used to sublimate counterproductive energies. This approach is an incorporation of traditions from East and West, from Europe and North America, into an emphasis on both the spiritual and the psychological personality of a being. Through the will of the personal self comes freedom of choice, power of decision over actions, and the potential to regulate and direct the functions of the subpersonalities within oneself. Being "centered"—increasing contact with self—is being able to choose a direction that is in accordance with what is best within the person. To do centering, the individual needs a sense of values and a good functioning of the will. This "superconscious" acts as a felt source of inner *strength* and *guidance.*

● TRANSPERSONAL PSYCHOLOGY

Psychosynthesis is an inspiring and intriguing approach. Though space does not allow responsible treatment here of the theoretical details and training methods of Assagioli's approach, a related orientation is noted in the emerging *transpersonal* paradigm (Astor, 1972, 1975; Boorstein, 1980; Sutich, 1969). The transpersonal focus goes beyond understanding the self as it is traditionally conceived and views the self that is possible by transcending what is presently known or accepted in formal knowledge. The search for human nature and how to live life is turned ever inward. The ultimate states from which understanding and direction might be gained are sought in spiritual paths, becoming, common needs and synergy of humankind and nature, ultimate values, compassion, mystical experience, ultimate meaning, essence, wonder, oneness, spirit, cosmic awareness, meditation, and the eventual transcendence of self to an awareness of a personal meaning of human existence. Although transpersonal psychology has yet to be organized as a discipline, the following three components contain examples of the varied subjects that it might encompass:

1. *Therapeutic body knowledge and self-development:* aikido, t'ai chi, yoga, Rolfing, dance, relaxation and biofeedback techniques, anatomy and physiology, nutrition, massage.
2. *Group knowledge and self-development* to transcend inter- and intragroup and cultural differences: human relations, Gestalt techniques, conjoint family therapy, transactional analysis, psychodrama.
3. *Intellectual knowledge and self-development:* understanding philosophical and spiritual meanings and religions of all faiths in order to clarify personal goals, values, and ideals; intuition, imagery, fantasy, extrasensory perception, centering.

● LIMITATIONS

Adding fuel to the self through transpersonal approaches would be especially inspirational, insightful, and helpful to the person who is seeking higher purposes in life or is perhaps alienated from or bored with everyday realities, but it is difficult to discern what it has to offer the person who must cope in his or her immediate environmental situation. Furthermore, if environmental constraints are present, concentration only on self-responsibilities can lead to self-blame or preoccupation with the self rather than the focus on action related to the person in the situation. As a general and extended psychoeducational approach (Hendricks & Weinhold, 1982) it has merits for developing a more open and accepting person who is in possession of an inner source of guidance and strength. Also, the possibility of a new paradigm for the psychology of the self, or the disciplined study of the self, that takes into consideration the wisdom found in the human knowledge and practices of other cultures and forms is a worthwhile goal toward the greater unity and wholeness of humans across groups and cultures.

▲ CONTRIBUTION TO EVOLUTION OF COUNSELING PSYCHOLOGY

Psychodynamic and existential-humanistic approaches represent two stages in the cultural evolution toward defining human nature and the human experience. Orthodox Freudian psychoanalytic theory has stressed the unconscious intrapsychic force driven by biological instincts (id) and rational attempts by the person (ego) to gain a balance between the needs of that inherited force, on the one hand, and the demands placed on the person by the realities of the external environment (superego), on the other. Needs that have not been fulfilled in past interactions with parents and other significant people during the stages of psychosexual development have become repressed as painful or conflicting memories in the unconscious but continue to have a life of their own and clamor for recognition and resolution. The modern neopsychoanalytic theorists have, for various reasons, shifted the focus of therapeutic help to faith in the power of the ego and in strengthening the ego. Some became alarmed about the pain and suffering of the ego that was apparent during therapy; others appraised personal conflict as related more to the influence of the punishing sociocultural environment than to biological drives. Still others desired to focus on a special, greater intrinsic purpose in the person, as a human being rather than as an animal.

The value judgment of whether human nature is "good" or "bad" has generally been discarded as an unproductive or moot philosophical question, but the subtle bias either way continues to be found in the theories of helping professions and the society at large. The serious implication that underlies the belief that human nature is intrinsically bad is that people should be punished for their "bad" acts; this belief also frees those who punish from responsibility, allowing them to be cruel and punitive. The conviction that human nature is "good" initiates the fretful, never-ending search for an essence of self and the intensive press of responsibility to fully become that "good" person—to be self-actualized at one's highest possible level; otherwise the punishment of guilt will take its toll.

The existential-humanistic theorists have continued the search for how the inner self can best be developed. Reality is whatever is in the experiences and perceptions of the self, and the resolution of self-conflict is the major goal of the existential-humanists. Facilitation of free expression of the self and giving strength to the personal self in deciphering the meaning of life and dealing with life problems are the general therapeutic avenues. This unfolding process parallels a continuum for counselor role and function that ranges from intervention and guidance of the client toward self-awareness and realization to full personal participation in the experiencing process as a helper who works cooperatively with the client in a mutual endeavor.

■ BEHAVIORAL APPROACHES

The behaviorists are basically not concerned with human nature because they believe that individuals are what they are on account of their own learning, which is externally determined by environmental factors. Both human nature and environment might be considered "neutral," and whatever the individual might be is a matter of what has been learned. Learning theorists—among them Pavlov, Thorndike, Dollard and Miller, and Skinner—have conducted studies of lower-order species such as rats and pigeons and from their findings have derived principles of learning to analyze the nature of human personality. They contend that personality is a collection of learned behavior that is overt and observable; differences in individual personalities can be attributed to differences in stimulus patterns, reinforcement contingencies, and punishment patterns.

The simplest kind of learning is *classical conditioning*. Any environmental stimulus could potentially evoke, or *elicit*, a response from the respondent. Instinctively we will pull our hand away from a hot object or identify the smell of food. Classical conditioning explains how we have been conditioned so that stimuli evoke responses from us simply because they have been paired with unconditioned stimuli and reinforced. Many of our learned patterns of behavior—anxiety and irrational fears, for example—can be attributed to classical conditioning. Childhood includes many experiences in which conditioning of fears takes place. A child may be startled by a playful dog and become fearful of other similar dogs; thus anxiety is conditioned as a cue for fear responses that were initially produced by the startle experience. The traumatic conditioning or the series of experiences that originally took place is not the major concern of behavior therapists, but rather how the connection between stimulus and fear or other undesirable behaviors can be extinguished. The problem is in the individual's behavior, not its origins.

Goal-seeking, or *emitted*, behavior such as in Skinner's *operant conditioning* takes place when emitted behavior is reinforced (rewarded), thus making repetition more likely. The more pleasurable the effects of behavior, the more likely is the behavior to be repeated. Through stimulus generalization and discrimination of stimuli the individual learns to respond to what is rewarding and to avoid what is nonrewarding or punishing. Drug addiction, for example, can be explained by simple operant conditioning when the effect of drug use is pleasurable or reduces anxiety.

Other behaviorists (Bandura, 1977, 1978) believe, in addition to the conditioned response theories, that people learn through simply observing and imitating others without being reinforced themselves or seeing others being reinforced for the response. In *social learning* theory, conditioned emotional fears and anxieties are explained as due to observation and vicarious learning of the conditioned fears and anxieties of others, not as a result of the individual's own experience of anxiety. Cognitive social learning theory also contends that individuals learn self-standards from others. From those standards come satisfaction and pleasure when goals are reached and dissatisfaction and displeasure when goals are not reached.

Most individuals can learn to extinguish ineffective, uncomfortable, or undesirable behavior, and all individuals have some level of capacity to learn new or more effective behavior. Thus the planned and orderly modification of observationally defined client behavior according to scientific principles of learning, by a trained behavior therapist or counselor, constitutes the important goal of behavioral approaches.

▲ BEHAVIORAL THERAPY APPROACHES BASED ON CONDITIONING

The following approaches generally aim to *weaken* maladaptive behavior.

● SYSTEMATIC DESENSITIZATION

Joseph Wolpe (1958) developed the procedure of systematic desensitization for "unlearning" irrational fears (phobias) by displacing anxiety with relaxation. The basic idea is to block or inhibit the original conditioning by counterconditioning. The stimuli that evoked the fear are connected to a new response (muscular relaxation) that is incompatible with fear and eventually will replace it. The client is taught how to relax when incremental units of fearful situations or events that approximate the original fear are presented in the imagination. Once the anxiety hierarchy is completed without the client's experiencing the undesirable level of muscular tension (anxiety), the fear has been counterconditioned and the anxiety-producing situation is met with relaxation. Variations of Wolpe's procedure carry out the counterconditioning in real situations that evoke anxiety. Overcoming the fear of heights or of ascending or descending a steep flight of stairs, for example, may be practiced in conjunction with a relaxed state, actually trying out a step at a time until the entire staircase can be surmounted without experiencing fear.

● RELAXATION TRAINING

Although Jacobson's (1938) method of progressive muscle relaxation was initially developed as a systematic procedure to reduce anxiety, it has been applied to a wide variety of problems such as high blood pressure, migraine headaches, insomnia, and asthma. Relaxation training has been demonstrated to be very helpful as a method to help people cope with tension from the general stresses and anxieties of modern living. It is also valuable in general counseling as a technique that enables an anxious client to become more relaxed and thus more amenable to the counseling process. The basic principle involves alternately contracting and relaxing muscles.

● BIOFEEDBACK TRAINING

Biofeedback training, autogenic training, and meditation are similar methods that aim to countercondition anxiety and tension through achieving a relaxed state of mind. Biofeedback involves training an individual to control his or her own physiological processes. The self-control of internal functions (heart rate, blood pressure, muscle tension level, skin temperature, brain-wave rhythms) is achieved by getting in touch with one's ongoing physiological processes. "Information" is instantaneously presented (feedback) by visual or auditory electrophysiological devices, the goal being to monitor and adjust one's own body signals, such as the following:

- Skin temperature: carded finger thermometer, wrist thermometer, or electronic temperature trainer
- Muscle tension: electromyogram (EMG)
- Brain states: electroencephalogram (EEG)
- Heartbeat and pulse: electrocardiogram (EKG)
- Emotional skin-reflex reactions: galvanic skin response (GSR), electroderm response (EDR)

● IMPLOSIVE THERAPY

Implosive therapy is also known as "flooding" or the use of paradoxical intention. It is based on the idea that having a fear or anxiety works toward making its object come true, while *intending* to have the object of a fear or anxiety makes it impossible. Thus the client is instructed to intend that which is feared until he or she sees how ridiculous the unrealistic fear really is. The potential danger in this technique, if it doesn't work, is that it could reinforce the fear, making it greater than it was.

● AVERSIVE THERAPY

Associating negative feelings with stimulus situations that are pleasurable to the client, but that both therapist and client agree are undesirable, is the basic idea of aversive therapy. Use of the drug Antabuse to counteract alcoholism is one example; Antabuse produces nausea when paired with alcohol; in fact, for some, even the use of after-shave lotion will cause the reaction. A simple trick like snapping a rubber band on one's wrist when reaching for a cigarette has been found helpful for some clients who desire to stop smoking. The question raised by aversive conditioning is whether it actually continues to produce the desired effect once treatment is stopped.

▲ BEHAVIORAL COUNSELING APPROACHES BASED ON SOCIAL LEARNING

Whereas the behavioral approaches already described seek to weaken maladaptive behavior, social learning approaches generally aim to *strengthen* adaptive behavior such as how to assert oneself without being overly aggressive, how to approach a job interview, and how to communicate with another person.

● SOCIAL MODELING

The client learns a response or behavior by observing and imitating a model's performance. The model can be a live model, filmed or taped models, or a constructed self-model. Bibliotherapy involves asking the client to identify with a preselected character in a novel, play, or story and to project himself or herself into the story. This experience and its related feelings are also used to assist the client to gain insight. Related to modeling is the counselor's technique of acting as a model or as a verbal (for example, praise-giving) and nonverbal (for example, smiling) reinforcer. A reinforcer might be given after the client makes statements that indicate movement toward the counseling goals.

● BEHAVIOR REHEARSAL

Behavior rehearsal is practicing behaviors that one wants to learn. *Role playing* is the basic technique. It involves the client in acting out social roles of others or trying out new roles for himself or herself with the counselor during counseling sessions. *Role shift* is the encouragement of a role opposite to a maladjustive one and is aimed at reducing conflict between the client and other people. Role plays and role shifts are basically simulations that provide opportunity to practice behaviors safely in the privacy of counseling under conditions that approach reality.

● BEHAVIOR CONTRACTS

Behavior contracts can be used in a variety of settings for a variety of problems. A written or oral contract is negotiated between the person and the other significant person(s) (spouse, parents, brothers and sisters, teachers, counselor, ward attendant). The specific behavior that the client desires to change is regulated by the reward consequences when the contract is fulfilled.

● ASSERTIVENESS TRAINING

Assertiveness training usually involves the use of modeling and role playing to teach the client the differences among aggressive, passive, passive-aggressive, and assertive behaviors. The assertive behavior that is learned allows the client to engage in more spontaneous, genuine, desirable, and outgoing behavior that promotes respect for self and others.

▲ BEHAVIORAL COUNSELING AND THERAPY APPROACHES BASED ON COGNITIVE BEHAVIOR

The conditioned-response approaches are based on problems related to the evoking stimuli or to overt, undesirable behavior, and the social learning approaches are based on problems related to the need to learn new and more adaptive overt responses. In contrast, cognitive approaches are based on the covert thinking process of individuals. Their underlying assumption holds that cognitive mediation—the content of one's thoughts—is the major cause of behavioral problems. Cognition includes whatever can be known by the person, as explained through perception, judgment, reasoning and remembering, thinking, and imagining. Beck's cognitive therapy (1976), for example, which is often applied to problems of depression, emphasizes a *direct* approach to the client's thinking process and content with the intent of replacing irrational beliefs and attitudes that cause emotional distress by a more appropriate mode of thinking that is in accord with reality. Other cognitive behavior techniques such as thought transference, also termed "thought suppression" or "thought stopping," are sometimes applied to block negative, self-defeating assumptions. The client is asked to imagine a situation in which he or she has negative thoughts; the counselor commands the client to stop the negative scene and substitute a more positive thought. For example, if the client imagines embarrassment in a social situation or lack of control and feelings of frustration due to missing a plane, he or she is instructed to think of something positive to block the negative thoughts. This approach is also helpful when concentrated attention on some task is urgent and suppression of other preoccupations is needed.

The alignment of cognitive theories with behavioral approaches is based on regarding thought patterns as a form of behavior. These approaches are related to the covert knowledge (cognitions) that an individual acquires and the *behavior* or *expectations* to which the knowledge leads, whereas the other behavioral approaches are related to instrumental learning—the weakening or strengthening of overt response tendencies.

● ALBERT ELLIS AND RATIONAL-EMOTIVE THERAPY

Rational-emotive therapy (RET) (Ellis, 1973) is one of the most widely practiced forms of cognitive counseling and psychotherapy. It has been found useful with clients classified as neurotic, who may tend to hold many irrational beliefs, such as "I must be loved or approved of by virtually every significant other person around me" or "I must be thoroughly competent, adequate, and achieving in all possible respects or I can't consider myself worthwhile."

Approach. These thoughts and many others are what cause self-blame and anxiety; by replacing these unrealistic and self-defeating demands with more realistic, reasonable, and rational expectations, the individual becomes more self-accepting and less anxious. It is a direct approach aimed not at depth of insight but at the development of a thinking process that is logical, scientific, and objectively sound. The approach makes use of a wide variety of techniques whereby the unreason that underlies fears and problems is exposed and attacked by reasonable logic. Such techniques might include challenging and disputing unreasonable thoughts, confronting inappropriate thoughts and behaviors, showing the responses one gets through saying illogical versus logical sentences to oneself, direct instruction that teaches logical thought processes, role playing effective behaviors in session, and trying out new thoughts and behaviors in homework assignments.

Limitations. RET is highly oriented to the thought processes to the exclusion of real emotional pain the client could be feeling. The useful understanding that might potentially come from experiencing those feelings as part of the human person is given less priority, though Ellis certainly views "reasonable" emotions as a component of human beings. In addition, the client could be overwhelmed by the steady barrage of disputations and confrontations imposed by this therapist-centered process. The client may tend to take on the role of a passive listener and observer awaiting the commands of the therapist or counselor.

● WILLIAM GLASSER AND REALITY THERAPY

Reality therapy (Glasser, 1965, 1969, 1972, 1976) and "behavior control of perception" (BCP) psychology is based on two fundamental human needs: (1) the need to be loved and to love; (2) the need to feel that one is worthwhile to oneself and others.

Approach. People who come to therapy, whatever the problem, are unable to fulfill their needs for love and a sense of self-worth; however, their condition is the result not of a mental disease but of irresponsible behavior the person has chosen. Responsible behavior fulfills needs for love and self-worth and leads to the formation of a *success identity*, which is defined as that of an involved person who is self-disciplined, self-accepting, and rational and who looks forward to something in life. Irresponsible behavior does not fulfill the two fundamental needs and leads to the formation of a *failure identity*, which is defined as that of a lonely person who is undisciplined, self-critical, and irrational and who has little or nothing to look forward to. Self-worth comes from knowledge and ability to think and learn how to solve problems and self-confidence to give and receive love. If an individual has self-worth (success identity), he or she can tolerate rejection when trying to love. Love gives motivation to succeed and self-worth; thus the interaction between needs and behavior is a circular developmental process, with each influencing the other.

A key concept is the important involvement with other people in the present; the past is over and not considered important in order to change the present. Feelings and attitudes related to past experiences are not unimportant, but therapy focuses on present behavior and autonomy to govern oneself without environmental support. Blaming social problems for one's own problems only removes personal responsibility and works against learning responsible behavior. Responsible behavior also means fulfilling one's needs in a way that does not deprive others of the ability to fulfill their needs.

The teaching and training approach consists of a series of sequential and well-defined steps or phases aimed at eliminating irresponsible behavior and learning responsible behavior:

1. A personal relationship and *involvement* with the client and concern for the client in his or her environmental setting (school, family, work, and so forth) are established.

2. *Current* behavior is examined and the question asked is "What are you doing?" not "What did you do?" This directed focus draws attention to conscious awareness of present behavior and plans for the future, not the irresponsibilities of the past.

3. The client is encouraged to critically *judge* his or her own behavior to determine if it is good for him or her and good for the other people in the client's life or situation. The counselor does not make the value judgment, but leads the client to evaluate his or her own behavior by bringing the behavior out into the open.

4. Learning how to be *responsible* to oneself and others is the fourth step. Teaching the client how to choose behaviors that fulfill needs in a way that does not deprive others of the ability to fulfill their needs is the major goal. The client is guided to formulate a realistic plan to carry out the value judgments.

5. *Commitment* by the client to the plan and executing the plan are seen by Glasser as an experience in itself that will help maturity and self-worth.

6. *No excuses* are accepted if the commitment to a specific course of action is not fulfilled. Either the value judgments or the plan itself, or both, may need reconsideration or reformulation. Going along with failure only reinforces a failure identity.

7. *No punishment* occurs. Sarcasm, disappointment, pity, hostility, or other form of psychological pain inflicted for not fulfilling a plan destroys the chances for involvement and contributes to the client's failure identity. Allowing the client to experience the natural consequences of his or her behavior is part of the process of learning responsible behavior.

Limitations. Although the therapist might be viewed as a tough and controlling person, he or she is also an interested and sensitive human being who understands and accepts behavior uncritically, but who never agrees with the client's irresponsibility. Being more concerned with behavior than with attitudes, the therapy is not intended to make someone happy, but to make someone responsible. Deeper problems that exist may go unnoticed when the emphasis is on control of future behavior and advice giving. Another major concern involves responsible behavior and social reality. Learning how to satisfy personal needs responsibly could be inconsistent with learning at the same time to face the demands of society, which is viewed as reality or as the therapist's interpretation of reality. Would a woman who deserts her abusive husband be considered unrealistic and irresponsible? Would she be guilty of inappropriate behavior? Would a person who escapes from the military draft because he or she believes a war is unjust be considered irresponsible?

■ SUMMARY

1. The cultural context for the helping function was described in this chapter. Modern science has emphasized the application of scientific principles to controlling or solving the problems of human existence, whereas

traditional society has generally accepted life as a given situation in which cooperation with others and flowing with the conditions are the rule. Helping approaches have come out of the culture and in turn have influenced cultural beliefs and practices. Helping has probably always existed in some form; however, modern formal helpers are seen as technicians who follow specific theoretical and/or scientific procedures. The goals of all helpers are similar in that they seek to alleviate distress and reintegrate the person in order to help him or her to meet cultural roles and expectations. A definition of human nature and how best to work with and develop it are presumed in all theoretical formulations. Important questions that the counselor should ask of each approach were also presented.

2. Three major theoretical movements have evolved in Western psychology: psychoanalysis, behaviorism, and existential-humanistic psychology. The constructs of various counseling and psychotherapy approaches were reviewed as representatives of these three movements.

3. The psychodynamic model describes and explains human behavior in terms of specific motivations within the individual as he or she copes with the frustrating social world. Traditional Freudian psychoanalysis emphasizes the development of human personality and its relationship to independent intrapsychic dynamics of the personality system. Extensions and adaptations of psychoanalysis by the neopsychoanalytic theorists have assigned a much more determinative and constructive role in the shaping of personality to special relations in the social environment and in the functioning of the ego.

4. Existential-humanistic models seek to understand the person as behaving according to his or her perceptions. The individual is seen as acting toward others in the ways that he or she perceives as most adaptive for an organism in his or her environment. These self-created perceptions are largely influenced or determined by the attitudes or behaviors of others who form the social environment of the person. The influence of the self or self-concept is the major factor that governs behavior. Other theoretical extensions and adaptations from self-theories and from psychodynamic theories have given extraordinary power to the self, conceptualizing the person as transcending his or her own consciousness and becoming aware of his or her own awareness and that of others.

5. The behavioral model defines the individual as driven by various needs to confront an environment that may gratify or frustrate. Directly observable expressions of human behavior are stressed, as opposed to imputed subjective elements. Individual behavior is determined by the association that is formed between a stimulus and a response. Classical conditioning was described as a theoretical learning process in which a particular stimulus in the environment consistently elicits a response. Through generalization and reinforcement, a new stimulus comes to elicit the response. This response is the conditioned response, and the process may be termed respondent conditioning. In contrast, Skinner's scientific analysis of conditioning contends that most behavior is conditioned by the stimulus reinforcement that follows the response. Thus behavior is gradually drawn and shaped, and this process is termed operant conditioning. Various approaches based on conditioning

principles were described. Social learning, as another behavioral model, was pointed out and examples of its application were given. Cognitive-behavioral theories have also been included among the behavioral approaches. These theories emphasize individual ability to regulate self-behavior through cognitive mediation within oneself and with environmental events and experiences.

CHAPTER 10

ECLECTIC AND SYNERGETIC APPROACHES TO COUNSELING AND PSYCHOTHERAPY

The preceding chapter outlined and described what were designated as traditional approaches to counseling and psychotherapy. This chapter continues the presentation of approaches by pointing out other models and conceptualizations that are emerging from the culture and the profession and that are believed to contain new direction and emphasis for counseling and psychotherapy.

■ ECLECTIC APPROACHES

Eclecticism in counseling and psychotherapy basically means integrating or unifying ideas from a diversity of sources. An eclectic counselor or psychotherapist selects what appears to be best in various theories and practices to compose an approach. All counselors and psychotherapists are probably eclectic to some degree. Even for the original theorists or the puristic practitioners, beliefs and practices evolve over time—a natural consequence of variation in individual clients and change in the world. Thus counselors who are doing only what they initially learned in their basic training programs are living in the Stone Age while the rest of the world has long since shifted into high technology.

▲ TWO TYPES OF ECLECTICISM

There are two basic types of eclecticism: counselor- or therapist-centered and process-centered.

1. *Counselor/therapist-centered eclecticism* holds that counselors will be more effective when they do what is true to their own personalities. The eclectics establish their own personal counseling systems that seem to work for them with the clients in their settings. The advantage in the development of a sound, personal eclectic rationale is best summed up by Corey (1986): "Beginning students of counseling, by familiarizing themselves with the current major approaches to therapeutic practice, can acquire a basis for a counseling style tailored to their own personalities. Thus, I recommend a personal synthesis as a framework for the professional education of counselors. The danger in presenting one model that all students are expected to advocate to the exclusion of other fruitful approaches is that the beginning counselor will unduly limit his or her effectiveness with different clients. Valuable dimensions of human behavior can be overlooked if the counselor is restricted to a single theory" (p. 2). The wide array of theories and techniques and the difficulty of becoming acquainted with and proficient in all the various ways of changing behavior have led other eclectics to select and integrate two or three complete approaches. Palmer (1980), for example, has integrated psychodynamic and behavioral theories in interaction with the client's social experience and social value systems.

2. *Process-centered eclecticism* holds that there are certain underlying factors common to all therapeutic endeavors. It focuses primarily on the behavioral repertoire of the helping person rather than the principles of the theories; what counts is what the counselor does that gets results. The principal movement in process-centered eclecticism is found in the communication skills approaches. These approaches generally use the scientific method of goal identification and goal meeting but may borrow principles and techniques from whatever seems to work and is philosophically and conceptually compatible. Their most intensive borrowing has been from the person-centered approach, and their emphasis is on important counselor attitudes and actions.

▲ COMMUNICATION SKILLS APPROACHES

Moving beyond the established and traditional psychological systems of counseling and psychotherapy has been an expanding array of programs using psychoeducational and social skills training methods. These approaches generally stem from or are based on client-centered facilitative conditions of empathy, genuineness, and unconditional positive regard (Rogers, 1957) as the core of good interpersonal relationships in general (Rogers, 1961). During the 1960s the shortage of mental health personnel led to the training of professionals, paraprofessionals, and lay helpers in these facilitative conditions to enhance their own interpersonal functioning with clients and others (Guerney, 1969; Traux & Carkhuff, 1967). From this movement the facilitative conditions became known as skills, a development that led to the emergence of systematic skills-training programs (Carkhuff, 1969).

Robert Carkhuff, one of the original pioneers of the skills-training approach, has emphasized the *responsive* dimensions of empathy, respect, and genuineness and the *initiative* dimensions of self-disclosure, confrontation, and immediacy. Other skills approaches have further operationalized the qualitative levels of the responsive dimensions. Egan (1982), for example, makes a distinction between "primary-level" accurate empathy and "advanced" accurate empathy: "Helpers are accurately empathic if they can (1) get inside their client's world, get a feeling for what this world is like, and look at the outer world through their client's perspective or frame of reference and can (2) communicate this understanding in a way that shows they have some understanding of their client's feelings and the experiences and behaviors to which these feelings relate" (p. 86). Primary-level accurate empathy is communicating understanding of the client's feelings and the experiences and behaviors underlying these feelings. Advanced empathy, in addition to what the client clearly states, gets at what the client implies or only half expresses. D'Augelli, D'Augelli, and Danish (1981) seek to clarify application of the core conditions through specific verbal *continuing* responses, *leading* responses, and *self-referent* responses. Gazda, Asbury, Balzer, Childers, and Walters (1984) have an excellent human relations development model that school counselors and other personnel should find very helpful in the educational setting. In this model, *perceiving* and *responding* behaviors are both taken into consideration for each of the eight facilitative dimensions (empathy, respect, warmth; concreteness, genuineness, self-disclosure; confrontation, immediacy).

● GERARD EGAN AND THE SKILLED HELPER APPROACH

Egan (1982) has proposed "a flexible, humanistic, broader based *problem-solving* model or framework" that he believes will assist "the counselor [to] organize and make sense of the vast helping literature" (p. 7). His three-stage model for problem solving or problem management generally focuses on the following basic skills:

Stage 1: *Initial problem clarification*
primary-level accurate empathy
respect
genuineness

Stage 2: *Setting goals based on dynamic understanding*
challenging skills
information sharing
advanced accurate empathy
confrontation
self-disclosure (sharing by counselor)

Stage 3: *Facilitating action*
program development (means to goals)
facilitating action (preparation, challenging, supporting)
evaluation

● ROBERT CARKHUFF AND
THE HUMAN RESOURCE DEVELOPMENT MODEL

Carkhuff's human resource development (HRD) model (1981; Carkhuff & Berenson, 1977) likewise has proposed levels of goals, but they emphasize an ongoing process rather than an end state. The uniqueness in Carkhuff's approach is the concept that what is good for the client is also good for the counselor. The counselor is also a person striving for full development and as such is the model representing what he or she is helping the client to achieve. However, Carkhuff also indicates that one person cannot be the other. The client cannot simply imitate the counselor; the process is self-directed from within. Carkhuff defines his levels of goals thus:

Level 1:   *Process goals*
            exploration (where client is in relation to wants or needs)
            understanding (where client wants to be; goal defining)
            action (getting from where client is to where client wants
            to be)
Level 2:   *Intermediate goals*
            skills result from achieving process goals:
            physical skills (exercise, diet, and other functional habits)
            interpersonal skills (attending, listening, responding, ini-
            tiating)
            cognitive skills (analyzing, synthesizing, interpreting)
Level 3:   *Ultimate goals*
            self-actualizing through high levels of responsiveness and
            initiative in the human experience

● ALLEN IVEY AND THE MICROCOUNSELING SKILLS APPROACH

One of the first skills-training programs to be operationally developed and applied to counseling is that of Allen Ivey and Jerry Authier (1978)—namely, microcounseling. In their training and research endeavors, Ivey and Authier eliminated traditional conceptual frameworks and theoretical constructs in favor of a method that when applied would show results. From those practical results they believed a theoretical principle would emerge. Like the communication skills approaches already described, microcounseling pursues ideal and practical goals that will allow the individual client "to create new and unique responses." However, microcounseling research is also committed to the broader concepts of counselor *cultural expertise* and a framework within which to compare the *alternative* forms of counseling and psychotherapy that are currently practiced in the American culture. The complex matter of determining just how culture fits into the practices of the helping professions and how awareness of cultural issues and cultural constraints might be incorporated into a theoretical helping framework is yet to come, though it is a primary focus of interest and vitality for the microcounseling approach.

Though space here does not permit full elaboration of microcounseling skills, the following quantitative and qualitative skills are included in the Ivey Taxonomy:

A. Basic attending and self-expression skills (verbal and nonverbal)
B. Microtraining skills (helping leads)
   Attending skills (giving attention to the client)
   closed questions
   open questions
   minimal encouragement
   paraphrase
   reflection of feeling
   summarizing
   Influencing skills (leading the client)
   directives
   expression of content
   influencing summary
   interpretation
C. *Focus dimensions* (who or what is the center or target of discussion content)
   client
   others
   topic
   helper
   direct mutual communication
   cultural-environmental context
D. *Qualitative dimensions* (process facilitators that underlie the attending skill)
   concreteness
   immediacy
   respect
   confrontation
   genuineness
   positive regard

● SUMMARY OF THE COMMUNICATION SKILLS APPROACH

This new professional field is in many ways revealing psychology to the public and may be considered as representing a shift from a medical model to an educational model as the foundation for the practice of counseling. Whereas the traditional medical model emphasizes a physicianlike role for the counselor or psychotherapist in diagnosing and prescribing treatment that is in line with a hypothesis, the communication skills approach uses training or education for treating "normal" human problems. The medical model emphasizes psychological malfunctions or abnormalities and impairments or deficits in psychological and interpersonal skills, while the skills approach conceptualizes or views human problems as learning problems for which new knowledge and effective skills are needed in order to mobilize resources. The training of counselors and the procedural application with clients most often focus on the dyadic relationship and interaction between the helper and client, the basic premise being that a helper trained in communication skills will be most effective with the widest range of clients. The proliferation of communication models is reminiscent of the movement stemming from Freudian psychology: not clones of the first model, they are nonetheless offshoots of the same root. As most adherents to any theory will claim, communication skills technologists believe that the skills they have selected and defined and the sequential scientific process within which the skills are applied are universal constructs.

The communication skills approach emphasizes the helper's mechanistic, overt behaviors to the exclusion of in-depth analysis of human nature. To reduce the counselor and client to a bundle of skills or a pattern of overt responses seems artificial and lacking in any other meaning for existence. The emphasis on "getting the job done" and meeting goals could allow deeper, internal disturbances to go unnoticed. The communication skills approach is not a panacea, but considering that the culture is fast-paced and constantly changing, the approach is expedient in the "real" world. It also offers something systematic and orderly for counselors and helpers, especially less trained helpers, to hang their hats on. If helping professionals can be raised to higher levels of effective communication through competent application of the skills, there will be less labeling, stereotyping, and dominating of clients and more opportunity for fair, equitable, and relevant helping.

■ SYNERGETIC APPROACHES

Synergetic is the most apt term for describing the synthesis of helping approaches with cultural/environmental factors. Synergism is the principle that responses or ideas result from the combination of coordinated factors working together. In general, it emphasizes a workable unity of therapeutic theory and practice with the person *and* environmental factors. *Environmental* factors are defined as clients' past or present experiences in the environment that have influenced their personalities and view of reality and thus give special meaning to them and their development. Social, economic, and political changes in the movement toward equality, for instance, have affected the lives and personalities of all people in different ways. It is the background out of which the figure (meaning) emerges. These cultural changes form the context in which the helping process is applied and can be especially noted in the following counseling-process dimensions: (1) topic content, (2) problems presented, and (3) expectations for the helping relationship and the helping process. The changing role of women, for example, has increased or changed the meaning of life for many women. It has also caused confusion and conflict for many women: in moving toward what they want to be, they must change or withstand changes in other aspects of their lives. They are also subjected to greater environmental obstacles, such as prejudice and discrimination, than they had felt or noticed before. Women in transition and seeking help would expect knowledge, awareness, and sensitivity from the helper and ultimately real assistance from the helping process in doing something about themselves in the situation. A synergetic approach aims for a synthesis of theories and procedures in harmony with a synthesis of the client and his or her environment.

▲ SYNERGISM AND CULTURAL CHANGE

Synergetic counseling contains features of eclecticism and the communication skills approaches but goes beyond eclecticism; like the many theoretical counseling approaches that have preceded it, it evolves from developments in the culture and thus may be presumed to reflect the culture. If this presumption is correct, the focus of synergistic counseling parallels the special needs that are becoming identified in our society, which is currently believed to be in a culturally pluralistic phase of evolution.

Syntality, as originally used by Cattell (1950), is to a group what personality is to a person. The term recognizes that a group can have a character; thus a culture or a nation has its own particular traits. The syntality of a group is shaped originally at the family-group level; but synergism involves shaping within the total cultural/environmental context. From a practical viewpoint, the major feature inherent or implied in the synergetic model is that of the counselor and client working and cooperating together through the process that is most effective for them and toward the goals that are most important for or relevant to the client in his or her cultural environment.

▲ PRELIMINARY ASSUMPTIONS IN SYNERGETIC APPROACHES

A synergetic approach provides the initial framework for approaching the diversity of the multicultural society and the complex counseling problems it presents. To use the approach, counselors may have to consider or reconsider their own positions with respect to two assumptions: (1) the general system of counseling and psychotherapy, as we now know it, is incomplete; (2) the role that environment and culture play in the helping process needs greater understanding and emphasis.

● ARE COUNSELING AND PSYCHOTHERAPY SYSTEMS INCOMPLETE?

The first step in answering the question of whether counseling and psychotherapy systems are incomplete is to understand and decide whether, how, and where the general system of counseling and psychotherapy is incomplete. Monumental efforts over the last 50 years have contributed to understanding the human personality, developing the psychology of counseling and therapy, and finding ways of helping people. Development of theory and practice has, in one sense, followed political, economic, and social events of the society; that is, the theory reflects where the society is. But theory has also contributed to the culture through providing rationales that afford some meaning and purpose in secular life and offer methods of coping with the frustrations of living.

The counseling and therapy profession, however, is not without its critics. One obvious criticism holds that the profession has lagged far behind the social, political, and economic changes started in the 1960s. Therapy, and to a lesser degree also counseling, was developed to best fit the needs of the great number of members of middle-class society. The society was organized for many years as a fairly well-regulated system of values and institutions through which people could move through life and achieve socioeconomic success. The system of therapy and the system of the society interact mutually. The particular activities of the middle class are the activities and goals that are often emphasized in counseling and therapy theories: language orientation, optimism, comfort orientation, conformity, future-directedness, success and achievement orientation, self-assurance, competitiveness with others, punctuality and time-orientation, self-mastery, restraint of tactless behavior, and industriousness, hard work, and productivity. This list is not meant to devalue the activities, values, and ethics of middle-class life or to suggest that other classes or groups of people do not subscribe to similar goals; it is intended simply to accentuate the fact that most theory building has grown out of clinical experiences with disturbed middle-class clientele and thus especially reflects the special problems, topics, frustrations, situations, and other experiences of that group.

The fact that all the theorists and the great majority of professionally trained counselors and therapists are or have become members of the general middle class suggests that their social system might be reflected in their ideas, concepts, and practices in interaction with the events and experiences of their times. In the 1960s, one researcher (Schofield, 1964) even described the preferences of therapists for YAVIS clients—young, attractive, verbal, intelligent, and successful—and their consequent tendency to deny attention or efficiency of service to others. It is generally known that some school or college counselors, using test scores or personal stereotypes, have "guided" lower-class students to trade occupations or common labor jobs that require little or no training or have discouraged them from seeking higher education.

Other radical viewpoints see the general mental health and therapy system as a type of political suppression that has unknowingly or knowingly emerged out of the culture to diffuse, control, or otherwise direct the emotional energy of people unhappy with the way the society is going, as experienced in the prejudice, discrimination, alienation, stress, pressure, and competitiveness of modern life (Kovel, 1976; Ryan, 1971). Thus "adjusted" or "therapeutized" personalities have no reason to form protest groups against environmental conditions; their rehabilitation allows the present societal system to continue. The adjustment of personalities also implies that mental and emotional disturbance is to be found only in the person, not the environment. Along the same lines, Szasz (1970, 1974) and Laing (1967, 1969) see the mental health system as a type of social institution that has evolved from the culture to protect the members of the society from the madness and insanity it contains, with the mental health system being a partner to the madness.

● ENVIRONMENT AS A DIMENSION

Mental health systems, and the counseling and therapy processes and procedures within them, need to continue to focus on developing and strengthening the client, but they also need to develop insight into how the cultural environment might be given more weight in the helping process. In one sense such a broadened perspective could encourage the helping professionals to serve as environmental "change agents" on behalf of their clientele (as did one short-lived movement in the counseling profession). But in another sense—here, the principal one—it means gaining a basic conceptual understanding of environmental factors on an equal footing with individual personality dynamics and behaviors and discovering how that understanding might eventually be used in the traditional counseling and therapy process.

● PROBLEM-CENTERED APPROACHES

An emerging class of human services counselors constitutes an exception to traditional practice (McGrath, 1989). They are the ones who are most involved in helping clients with their daily problems in the environment. These "problem solvers" view the problem situations and the people in them from multiple practical approaches that may include single-session therapy, time-limited counseling, brief therapeutic contacts, crisis intervention, direct confrontation, problem-solving strategies, education and teaching, outreach, resource linking, and any other practical modes that work toward reintegration of the person and reintegration into the culture. In many respects their theory and problem-oriented strategies are based on the lessons of experience and common sense. Thus, rather than letting therapy theory trickle down into practice, these practitioners build theory out of what works in practice and for each problem situation. Rarely, however, do such theories trickle upward to the theoreticians whose feedback could have implications for systematic modification of traditional theories. The person-problem orientation is most useful when the application of traditional models or forms of long-term therapy may not be effective or appropriate, such as in cases of alcoholism and drug addiction, suicide prevention, and the personal crises found in terminal illness, death, hunger, unemployment, desertion by a spouse, sexual anxieties, or abuse of some sort, and in the aftermath following environmental disasters such as floods, accidents, and other catastrophes. In these cases, or when there are large numbers of clients to be served, brief therapy characterized by intervention between the situation and the personal life of the individual is what is most expedient and helpful. Dramatic changes in attitudes and perceptions can occur during these moments of emotional opening and crisis counseling.

▲ ENVIRONMENTAL FACTORS

This section considers how the environment and culture influence the client in the helping process. Balancing the strict psychological viewpoint with the reality of the environment is a major goal. The goal of balancing simply implies that all problems, behaviors, and concerns and the nature of the helping function cannot be attributed solely to the client's inner psychodynamics, to the perceived self, or to behavioral skills; culture-environmental dimensions must also be taken into account.

Environment is defined as consisting of all *external* sources and factors to which a person or group of persons is actually or potentially responsive. Thus counselors who take into consideration environmental factors will examine all the possible external things that influence or could influence the behavior of clients and how or whether they are debilitating or growth-producing for each unique client. The factors in the counseling or therapy environment itself are also considered. An environment can be further broken down into *physical, social,* and *cultural* elements.

● PHYSICAL FACTORS

Any physical object, structure, instrument, or thing is a means to an end. At the most basic level are the things we all need for physical security—food, clothing, shelter. In a technical and highly developed society the tangible means to personal security become especially complex and most often involve the ability to use or develop adequate coping skills and strategies.

Tangible factors. Changes in the environment, such as unemployment, are highly stressful and disrupting life events. Reactions are highly individual and depend on how strongly a person identifies with his or her job. If a person's major source of identity is work, it will be difficult for that person to feel good about himself or herself after losing a job. Obviously the person in this case needs to regain self-esteem, but the major problem source is in the environment and often beyond the control of individuals. It thus requires directed and planned strategies beyond "feeling good about oneself." Breakdowns in public transportation, inadequate or unaffordable housing, poor nutrition, inadequate medical care, crowded urban areas, and desolate rural areas are other factors that can have direct effects on life, manifested in psychological behavior or "symptoms." A father who becomes hysterical, angry, or depressed when his family is evicted from its housing is reacting to a loss of shelter and first needs assistance in remediating or coping with the environmental problem.

A client in counseling complained of frequent headaches that occurred when he arrived at home and seemingly had to cope with all the domestic problems his family had experienced during the day. What seemed to be a psychosomatic symptom that could best be treated by psychodynamic or behavioral approaches was actually traced to the client's place of employment, where he was exposed to noxious fumes. Major problems for migrant agricultural workers in some areas of the country can still be observed in substandard housing and exposure to herbicides, insecticides, and carbon monoxide in their working environment. Unforeseen dangers to people continuously emerge in a fast-changing technical society. "Computer phobia" is a phenomenon that has captured the attention of some writers, but to others the effect on physical, mental, emotional, and attitudinal behavior is of greater importance. Dehumanization that occurs in assembly line work has long been studied and is well known.

External versus internal locus of problem. Distinguishing what is *external* to the person, which may primarily require environmental adjustment or improvement of environmental coping strategies, from what is *internal*, which may primarily require intrapsychic or behavioral adjustment, is essential if environmental factors are to be used as a meaningful part of the helping function. Possession of a means of transportation or knowing how to cope with discrimination in employment, for example, could be critical in actually meeting one's physical security needs. In that instance, what is actually external to the person—what lies outside the person—is a problem source. To another person, external events such as earning all "A" grades in a program of studies or caring for an aging parent may become symbolic, representing a need or attachment that the person believes and feels to be an essential part of his or her life. In this case, the external event may center primarily in the self and become a symbol for one's own personal worth. What is external to the person has become incorporated into the person, and the result is basically an internal problem.

The helping environment. In addition to assessing the balance between external factors and internal factors that bear on clients, counselors and therapists can also examine what perhaps is taken for granted or as traditional in their own helping environments and helping process. Two factors are discussed as examples: (1) the setting structure and (2) the time structure.

The physical environment of a counseling setting itself could constitute a potential or transitory influence on clients, but it is also the factor most readily modified. The color of the walls, the decorations, the type and placement of furniture, the lighting, the presence of a clock, and the attire of the counselor are all distinguishable elements in the physical environment. The physical setting can potentially convey to clients what to expect initially from the helping process, as well as making them comfortable or ill at ease. An inner-city storefront counseling setting furnished in the decor of an orthodox Freudian psychiatrist's office, for example, with couch and portrait of Sigmund Freud, would most likely set a strange and perhaps frightening tone. The sterile or aseptic quality found in some community mental health centers or in the psychiatric units of hospitals conveys other images, as does the word *mental*, which might be boldly listed on the sign. The trend for most counseling settings is generally toward realistic moderation and, where possible, a private, comfortable, secure atmosphere. Obstructions such as a desk between client and counselor are usually assumed to impede the value of counseling as an endeavor where people work cooperatively and closely together at the task. In other settings a desk and physical separation might be used to emphasize the greater authority of the counselor or therapist and the businesslike qualities of the service. All the aforementioned physical "props" most likely do have influence or suggest certain first-impression images. It could be worthwhile for counselors to evaluate what their settings might symbolically suggest as an extension of themselves and the nature of their services. Another physical dimension that should be considered is the availability and accessibility of services. Are the hours such that clients can only have problems between 9:00 A.M. and 4:00 P.M., with one hour off for lunch? Do, or can, counselors and therapists conduct their work in the client's home or other environments, if such were seen as important to the client's personal dynamics and particular problem?

The traditional pattern of therapy involves 50-minute sessions, and, on the basis of most theoretical rationale, treatment terminates when the psychological condition is resolved. Psychoanalysis, for example, may require years for a client to meet his or her expectations. Criticism of Rogers's person-centered therapeutic process says that it takes forever to observe client change or movement. Like the speeded-up, fast-paced society, the helping profession is also under pressure to deliver more in less time, and most professionals are also interested in providing better services. Some of the pressure toward "efficiency" is of course based on the economics of reduced human services budgets, waiting lists of clients, and the inability of many people to pay for lengthy treatment. Most impoverished people have never received adequate mental health services, many do not expect to be served, and others do not have confidence in therapy or are too much in need of immediate help to relate to what might seem like aimless or non-action-centered help. There is enough evidence in the general literature to suggest that Black Americans and other minority group members tend to drop out of traditional therapy after a few sessions, prior to mutual agreement with the counselor or therapist. Fifty percent of Black-American, Asian-American, Mexican-American, and Native American clients, as compared with 30% of White clients, have been reported as terminating after the first interview (Sue, 1977; Sue & McKinney, 1975; Sue, McKinney, Allen, & Hall, 1974).

Studies are emerging of changes that might be made in the time-dimension rationale of traditional therapy (Gelso & Johnson, 1983; Mann, 1973). The basic question asked is whether effective counseling or therapy really needs to be equated with a lengthy or open-ended experience. Brief therapy, or time-limited therapy (TLT), has been defined as therapy having a specific number of sessions; the duration of therapy for clients is limited and indicated at or prior to the initial contact. Duration may vary but typically is established as 8, 12, or 16 sessions. Anything beyond 20 or 25 sessions is considered time-unlimited therapy (TUT), or an experience that is of open duration. The structured process is guided by the counselor or therapist and has a clear beginning, middle, and end phase. Important to TLT is whether the client is suitable for the procedure. Research reported by Gelso and Johnson (1983) with college counseling-center clients notes that a client's "self-perception of chronic problems or maladjustment are critical selection factors for TLT. Effective TLT can be done with the clients who perceive themselves as more acutely and moderately disturbed, whereas TUT may be a better choice for clients who perceive themselves as more chronically and seriously troubled" (p. 198). Thus an appropriate client for TLT would want help with feelings or behaviors that are bothersome or troublesome and are of recent onset. Although the internal experience is painful and the presenting problem is real to the person, his or her external behavior does not appear disturbing to others. Generally, the person has a good self-concept, is able to form a relationship, and sees the problem as something that can be changed.

The most significant factor for the counselor's role was reported as the ability to form a quick and positive relationship, as indicated by the "expected enjoyment of working with the client; if a client and counselor seemed to 'click' well together from the beginning, a positive outcome could be predicted with more assurance than that based on any counselor factors" (p. 203). General theoretical orientation and experience of the counselor were found not to be related to TLT effectiveness, whereas close personal relationships such as might be demonstrated in deeper levels of counselor self-disclosure were more related to client-rated outcomes in TUT. Counselors following a TLT procedure will be more effective when personality reorganization is not emphasized, but TLT must go beyond the role of a counselor who provides only psychological support and move toward actual behavioral change. The time restriction of TLT is also used as an *in vivo* experience in coping with reality. Insight in the presenting problem is a goal, but not to the exclusion of behavior change. Follow-up after termination is further seen as an endeavor important to a sense of completeness for both counselor and client.

TLT appears to attempt to synthesize "psychological" time with "clock" time. In general, a different type of counselor-client relationship is needed: one that is characterized by cooperative and mutual working together to accomplish a task. In TUT, resistance to formation of a deeply personal relationship must be worked out between counselor and client. Considering the psychological and social separation between multiple cultural groups in the United States society, the nature of the TLT *relationship* and *procedure* may be more appropriate than traditional methods in the helping process, at least with clients whose general problems and issues of daily living constitute the major concern (Griswold, 1986; Sperry, 1989).

● SOCIAL SITUATION FACTORS

The term *social situation* denotes the total field of other persons and groups of people to which the client is oriented. The social situation can be defined as that part of the external world that means something to the client. The object of orientation is other people, most likely those in present or past family relationships and peer relations. A philosophical/theoretical issue that is sometimes raised is whether the person (client) is an object to himself or herself and takes the role of others (that is, through imitation), which becomes a part of the person in or out of the social situation, or whether the situation is completely external to the person and acts as a stimulus to the person to produce distinguishing behavior only in that situation. It seems most probable that it is both: parts of the personality will be carried (generalized) out of one social situation to other situations. Important personality elements such as motivations, attitudes, feelings, and behaviors will most likely be demonstrated in the social situation where they were originally acquired (learned), but aspects will also be generalized to other social situations (Padilla, 1985).

This principle is important in the counseling experience itself because clients will demonstrate who they are in relation to what they learned in other social situations. This principle of generalization is important in two ways: (1) in the exhibition of positive or negative *feelings* toward the counselor, as noted in the traditional description of the transference phenomenon, and (2) in the content of the client's *topics* that are associated with relationships in important primary social situations. For example, a Chinese college student who had recently emigrated from Vietnam with her family experienced no difficulty in openly discussing with a non-Chinese counselor her need to learn how to drive and to get a job in order to support her education. There was little stimulus for transference of deep feelings that might affect the helping relationship, since the counselor and client initially approached the "problem" from realistic aspects of the environmental situation. The trust thus built led the client from that point to further disclosure and counseling for the conflict between her and her father, involving his resistance to her movements toward independence and her own guilt at failing to meet the social situation that demanded respect for the wishes of her family. A primary consideration related to trust and confidentiality in this counseling example was the client's impressing on the counselor—and the counselor's accepting—the fact that to the others in her social situation her "real problem" was to get a good education, along with financial and job-related concerns. Thus personal weaknesses were not the reason for seeing a counselor and she was able to save face.

A second example illustrates the rigid application of a behavioral technique at the expense of the client's total social situation. A woman has developed an unrealistic fear of her neighbor, who has angrily rebuked her many times for not promptly taking in her empty trash cans from the curb. The client also complains that her husband does not give her enough attention and is critical of how she carries out her domestic activities. However, the therapist discounts these topics as practical problems that the client and her husband will have to work out and proceeds to treat her phobia through systematic desensitization.

How might the foregoing discussion and two counseling examples be summarized? First, the social situation of the client's environment may be as important an element as what is going on within the client's psychodynamics, the client's self-perceptions, or what might be observed in the client's behavior. Second, when the counselor or therapist expects a problem to originate only in the mind, the self, or behavior of the client, other elements that could be related to the social environment will be missed and the treatment will be incomplete. Third, how the role of the counselor or therapist is perceived by outside others or the actual attitude of the counselor or therapist in the counseling environment itself can potentially generate negative impressions in the client (the transference phenomenon). When the counselor or therapist expects or presumes chronic problems to originate only with intrinsic weaknesses in the client, and subtly or otherwise conveys the attitude, the client will resist the defined helping process as a self-protective strategy. Transference of negative emotions is less likely to occur when the counselor or therapist views and accepts the client as a person in a situation. Person and situation are interrelated, and both may need attention. Fourth, the collaboration of counselor and client, with both taking responsibility, eventually becomes most important in determining appropriate goals, although in the beginning phases the counselor's initiative in orienting and setting the direction for mutuality may call for an approach that uses logical and rational structuring rather than ambiguous and personal reflective listening.

● GROUP CULTURE FACTORS

For present purposes, group culture is defined as the background of a group of people. It consists of what the group has derived and selected from its historic experiences and thus is considered traditional. The *ideas* or *beliefs* of a group and their attached *values* are the most obvious elements that can be identified in any culture. Another element is the set of patterns of and for *behavior* that might stem from the ideas, beliefs, and values. Traditional patterns of behavior or modes of action for a particular group of people also generally show a stylized *preference* for one path to a goal when two or more are equally open and functionally effective.

Culture as action preference. The third cultural element—action preference—is especially important for counselors and therapists in cross-cultural situations and calls for creative sensitivity to how a client's learned modes of action can best be used in the movement toward agreed-upon counseling goals. The awareness that various groups may prefer different ways to reach goals is necessary for effective counseling. For example, the results of some studies (Atkinson, Maruyama, & Matsui, 1978; Peoples & Dell, 1975) that used taped recordings of counseling sessions indicated that Black Americans and Asian Americans seem to perceive counselors who use direct counseling approaches, as opposed to nondirective approaches, as more credible. If this is correct in the *actual* counseling experience, the implication is that these study subjects are culture-bound. If the nondirective counselor were also culture-bound to only one theoretical approach, the result would be an impasse. Nevertheless, to conclude that all Black Americans or all Asian Americans are best approached through culture-bound counseling that is logical, rational, and structured seems oversimplified and misleading. A sensitive counselor who is flexible and knowledgeable in a number of approaches would most likely and logically use the action preference mode that the client has most at hand in his or her own personality and in his or her cultural background.

Culture as problem-solving techniques. A counselor can use the client's cultural background as an asset rather than letting it form a barrier in the helping process. Cultural differences should not be accepted as a block to counseling. The cultural core of any group is primarily a set of techniques for satisfying needs, for solving problems, and for adjusting to the external environment and to each other. Thus, from the psychological viewpoint of adjustment, culture is the traditional way of solving problems—it is simply the responses that have been accepted because they have met with success. The manner in which counselor and client can use these adjustments in the helping process could be very valuable and depends on the ingenuity of the counselor with each client in any single experience. One counselor had an Asian-American client who was submissive, shy, and overly willing to please the counselor. Shyness was his main problem in facing a business course that required high social interactions and initiative in applied laboratory sessions of the course. The nature of the client's reserved manner in waiting for authority-centered direction was used as a strength in the counseling sessions: through active direction by the counselor and a few role-playing experiences, the client contrasted the rewards of his quiet, shy demeanor in one sphere of cultural life with its hindrance of his achieving desired educational goals in another sphere of his life. Behavioral practice in assertiveness both in and out of counseling sessions, along with the counselor's psychological support, encouragement, and good humor to relieve tension, enabled the client to pass the laboratory sessions without losing either cultural values or face. Thus a therapeutic procedure is most effective when there is *synergism* with a client's background and situation (Tainsri & Axelson, 1990).

Judicious use of cultural meanings. There is meaning in the culture of the clients, and any insight that might be gained into underlying factors—the beliefs, the attached values, the behavioral patterns, the action preferences—will contribute to a more relevant counseling approach. However, a danger exists in the zealous pursuit of a "group character." There is obviously individual variation of world view and behavioral styles within any cultural group, and trying to fit a group cultural style to any single individual is tenuous at best. Furthermore, it runs the risk of stereotyping. Attribution of cultural distinctiveness to any single client is only meant to increase the counselor's level of sensitivity to human variability. Expected differences, for example, could simply be used only as *tentative* hypotheses, which should be discarded when the evidence does not support them.

Too little awareness of cultural patterns can also impair a counselor's effectiveness. Lack of knowledge and objective understanding of cultural influences can potentially lead the uninformed counselor to misidentify a certain client behavior as symptomatic of personal conflict when it might be more accurately defined as a cultural habit, as culturally related, or simply as an individual idiosyncrasy. For example, to label an Asian-American client as dependency-prone because he or she desires more advice and guidelines, or to label a Hispanic client as self-evasive because he or she wants to know more about *your* personal life, or to label a client as an anal personality fixated at a psychosexual development stage because he or she stubbornly accentuates his or her vocabulary with the word *shit*, is an obvious misapplication of personality theories at the expense of the client's actual referential source.

Yet another important goal is to understand what might truly be signs of serious personal conflict, expressed through culturally unique behavior. One example, perhaps not encountered in the usual counseling experience and that might be threatening to counselors, is the experience of culturally related hallucinations. Basically any hallucination is conjured out of what is or has been within the experience of the client, but it seems to have no basis in externally constructed reality. The case in point involves a Japanese client who feared and agonized that she had let her family down and expressed to the counselor that she had had a vision of Buddha beckoning to her, that it was time to leave the earth, and that Buddha would take care of her family for her. The counselor, trained in both cross-cultural counseling and substance abuse counseling, determined that the client had mistakenly taken an overdose of an antianxiety drug. She accepted the client's hallucination as a culturally based experience and stayed with her until the drug's effect wore off. Since she was in the client's home during the crisis, she also was able to reassure the family members that the hallucination was caused by the drug and that if the family stayed close to her and accepted her, she would be all right. The client's physician did indeed confirm the counselor's speculation that an overdose could produce hallucinations. The counselor, by accepting the content of the client's drug-induced hallucination as a culturally meaningful expression, was able to maintain an effective relationship and to offer constructive help. Later counseling sessions were oriented toward guiding the client's understanding of her family relationships, enabling her to see how she could best communicate with others and still accept herself as a responsible person without feeling guilty that she was going against their wishes.

● SUMMARY OF ENVIRONMENTAL FACTORS

Elements of three environmental factors—physical/material, social situation, and group culture—have been illustrated, showing how they can work against individual development or can be reflected in a client's behavior. There are, of course, elements in the same factors that promote, give strength to, or can be used as resources for individual development and problem resolution. Thus the interaction of the environmental milieu with the lives of clients is an important consideration in comprehending clients' *expectations*, realistically *assessing* clients, establishing desired client *goals*, and determining an appropriate therapeutic *process*. The purpose of this section has been to introduce the reader to how environmental factors can be meaningfully and realistically applied in a synergetic approach to multicultural counseling. The next section discusses other specific models or proposals that take into consideration cultural/environmental factors.

▲ SYNERGETIC CULTURAL/ENVIRONMENTAL MODELS

Some of the earliest writers who addressed environmental factors as worthwhile considerations in the counseling and guidance function include Lawrence H. Stewart and Charles F. Warnath (1965) and Esther M. Lloyd-Jones and Norah Rosenau (1968). Theodora M. Abel and Rhoda Métraux (1974) and Georgene H. Seward (1972) have similarly addressed cultural issues for the role of psychotherapy. All have emphasized the bridge between the social/cultural sciences and the practice of counseling or psychotherapy and have shown how the social system and its ways and values have been too long taken for granted in these professions. Those writings were attuned to the social changes beginning in the late 1950s and running through the 1970s and thus may be considered as initial transitions in the movement for greater wholeness and completeness in counseling and therapy approaches. Table 10-1 shows early and recent transitional examples of counseling approaches that contain synergetic features at various levels. Elements of the eight approaches listed in Table 10-1 are discussed at greater length in the following pages.

● NONRACIST COMMUNICATION APPROACH

Patterson (1973) has clarified prejudicial bias that can distort perception and communication when counseling disadvantaged Black clients. Effective communication is seen as a function of differences in cultural background of counselor and client. The basic dimension emphasized is the attitude that underlies the counselor's perception of the client in the counseling process. Effective communication and assistance are related to a nonracist attitude, whereas a racist-based attitude works against the helping process. A facilitative attitude could thus be defined as a nonbiased view of others, as operationally shown in Figure 10-1.

● ACCOUNTABLE ACTION APPROACH

Tucker (1973) believes that traditional counseling services are inappropriate for low-income disadvantaged students, because the services involve "the necessity for self-referral, social class differences, sedentary talk, and the verbal requirements of the dyadic encounter," all of which "serve to vitiate the counselor's effectiveness with culturally different clients" (p. 35). His problem-solving model of counseling aims for "specificity of goals and aggressive commitment on the part of the counselor to maximize emotional involvement of the client through the arousal of his (her) expectancy and hope" (p. 36).

The following components or steps are basically managed or directed by the counselor:

1. *Outreach.* Counselor makes contact and establishes relationship with client.
2. *Trust.* Counselor communicates both verbal and nonverbal acceptance.
3. *Problems/goals.* Counselor and client explore areas that are important to client.
4. *Long-term objectives.* Client's statements of desirable outcomes for the future are clarified and made more concrete (for example, "Become an engineer").
5. *Current conditions.* Counselor and client examine and determine the probability of accomplishment of each long-term objective (for example, grades in classes important for engineering).
6. *Needs assessment.* Client's current conditions are related to long-term objectives, and a list of needs is compiled (for example, need to get higher grades in algebra).

TABLE 10-1 Examples of Counseling Models That Contain Synergetic Features

Model	Author	Major Emphases
Nonracist communication	Patterson (1973)	Counselor's nonbiased attitude versus biased attitude
Accountable action	Tucker (1973)	Counselor's use of problem-solving skills with low-income disadvantaged students
Systemic	Gunnings and Simpkins (1972)	Client's environmental systems
Transcendent	Harper and Stone (1974)	Counselor's personal being and professional skills to assist client in satisfaction of basic needs, modification of lifestyle, and transcendence of negative environmental influences
Culturally specific	Stikes (1972)	Counselor's proficiency in cultural knowledge in harmony with client's background in order to activate client's self-understanding in the context of social realities
Cross-cultural differences analysis	Sue and Sue (1990)	Differences between dominant-culture counselors and minority-culture clients and the process and skills related to counseling of racial/ethnic minorities
Person-environment analysis	Ivey (1981)	Analysis of counseling theories, microskills, and counselor-client interpersonal environment
Multicultural development	Ramirez (1991)	Synthesis of a pluralistic world view, a psychology of individual and cultural differentness, and eclectic counseling processes

7. *Priority of needs.* Client's immediate needs are arranged in a priority list, with other needs deferred for later action.
8. *Short-term objective.* Counselor and client decide on one objective that can be successfully achieved and that will reduce or eliminate one of the priority needs (for example, get higher unit-test scores in algebra).

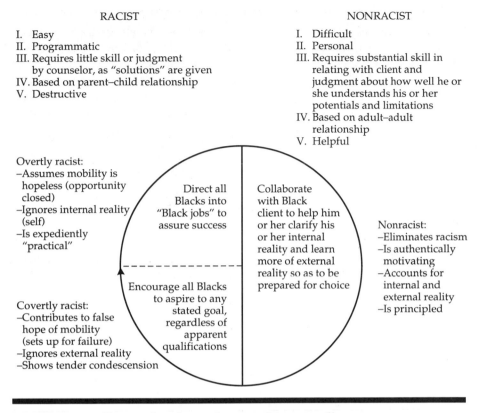

RACIST

I.   Easy
II. Programmatic
III. Requires little skill or judgment
     by counselor, as "solutions" are given
IV. Based on parent–child relationship
V.   Destructive

NONRACIST

I.   Difficult
II. Personal
III. Requires substantial skill in
     relating with client and
     judgment about how well he or
     she understands his or her
     potentials and limitations
IV. Based on adult–adult
     relationship
V.   Helpful

Overtly racist:
–Assumes mobility is
 hopeless (opportunity
 closed)
–Ignores internal reality
 (self)
–Is expediently
 "practical"

Direct all
Blacks into
"Black jobs" to
assure success

Collaborate
with Black
client to help him
or her clarify his
or her internal
reality and learn
more of external
reality so as to be
prepared for choice

Nonracist:
–Eliminates racism
–Is authentically
 motivating
–Accounts for
 internal and
 external reality
–Is principled

Covertly racist:
–Contributes to false
 hope of mobility
 (sets up for failure)
–Ignores external reality
–Shows tender condescension

Encourage all Blacks
to aspire to any
stated goal,
regardless of
apparent
qualifications

FIGURE 10-1   Bases of racist and nonracist counseling.

SOURCE: Reprinted from "The Strange Verbal World," by L. E. Patterson, *Journal of Non-White Concerns*, 1973, 1(2), p. 99. Copyright © ACA. Reprinted with permission. No further reproduction authorized without written permission of American Counseling Association.

9. *Solution strategy.* Counselor decides best action to take from a variety of alternatives in order to achieve short-term objective. All possible resources are considered in determining the feasibility of the strategy (for example, tutoring, learning test-taking cues, talking with algebra instructor).

10. *Implementation of the strategy.* Initial success on the first short-term objective is important, as is the emotional involvement of the client (hope, expectancy, suggestibility). The results of the strategy are reviewed (for example, test score) and evaluated.

● SYSTEMIC APPROACH

Gunnings and Simpkins (1972; Gunnings, 1973) view traditional counseling as teaching clients how to cope with or adjust to themselves, family, or environment. However, they see these not as the basic causes of most problems but as the symptoms. The societal system in which we live elicits deviant behavior and thus the system must be counseled (Tucker & Gunnings, 1974). Possible symptoms of a defective system are seen in (1) feelings of being locked out of society, frustration, noninvolvement, aloneness; (2) little opportunity for input of a person's cultural patterns and resultant feelings of inferiority or inability for full self-expression; and (3) hostile, deviant behavior and disruption. The systemic approach is based on the assumption that clients' problems are in actuality the system's problems and that effective interaction is needed between the client and the system to effect change. Treating the system for its problems will help bring about changed individuals. Thus the systemic approach is problem oriented rather than client oriented, emphasizes causation rather than symptoms, and works with both the system and the client as opposed to just the individual.

Components of systemic counseling might include the following steps for counselors:

1. Activate feelings and concerns.
2. Gain understanding with client of how the system might be contributing to personal feelings and concerns. Any situation could be potentially oppressive or stressful and contain obstacles to the opportunity for full development and self-expression.
3. Become an advocate of the client; present yourself as a friend, helper, and as insurance of fair treatment.
4. Provide a bridge between the client and others in his or her life. These others may not really understand the client's background or pattern of behavior or even care to understand it. Thus the critical role of the counselor is as an agent or consultant who seeks to promote understanding and to change behavior and perceptions of others.

In essence, the counselor's role in the systemic approach is that of a system changer more than an individual changer. The major function of the systemic counselor is as an establisher of effective relationships.

● TRANSCENDENT APPROACH

The basic proposition in the transcendent approach (Harper & Stone, 1974; Stone, 1973) is that counseling should center in helping clients to satisfy their basic needs, to develop new lifestyles, and to transcend the undesirable environmental conditions of U.S. society that work against positive growth and mental health. The fact that we are all born into a predetermined culture means that those who find the insight and willpower to transcend culture will escape the socialization that works against full development.

Effective counseling with Black clients, and, by implication, for other culturally diverse clients, is a function of the counselor's being, techniques used, and the specific process employed. The effective counselor is an integrated, mentally healthy person who can demonstrate the basic facilitative conditions in the helping relationship as defined by Rogers and Carkhuff. The counselor is also knowledgeable of the forces at work in the society and is sensitive to special needs of culturally diverse clients. Critical techniques that lead to "awareness and action" include the following:

General Techniques	Specific Techniques
supportiveness	accepting, assuring
directiveness	advising, approving, persuading, probing
information giving	informing

"Slow" therapies, such as client-centered and psychoanalytic, and the techniques of reflection, interpretation, and "personal illustration" are used only with caution, whereas approaches such as rational-emotive therapy, reality therapy, and the behavioral models are thought to be more acceptable. The counseling process emphasizes the responsibility of both counselor and client and basically follows the sequential steps of *assessment, prescription, counselor's action,* and *client's action.* These process goals are aimed at the satisfaction of basic needs (such as affiliation) , modification of lifestyle and behavior (such as time management), and transcendence of negative environmental influences (such as hostility toward White peers or White institutions).

● CULTURALLY SPECIFIC APPROACH

Stikes (1972) has proposed that a complete counseling theory will take into consideration the problems and backgrounds of the many culturally different groups that constitute U.S. society: "Because of the hostility of the environment and because of their cultural heritages, these (visible) minorities have maintained behaviors and values different from those of the dominant society" (p. 15). Counseling is viewed as "a growth-inducing experience designed to change behavior"; thus the theoretical perspective of a counselor using the approach would be humanistic and behavioral and would "reflect the values, attitudes, and expectations of the persons it purports to help" (p. 15). It is optimistic, positive, and oriented to the motivational pride that comes from cultural identity.

To take a culturally specific approach, the counselor needs knowledge and skill in certain areas. Though these areas coincide with the problems of the poor Black client, they can probably be generalized to other groups of clients:

- Familiarity with the group's cultural heritage (behavior and mannerisms, orientation to space and time, language, values)
- Recognition of the group's adjustive behaviors to oppression (for example, matriarchal family structure)
- Acknowledgement of the group's perceptions of society (for example, negative orientation toward society as a normal response to frustration)
- Ability to view personal problems within their environmental context (for example, numerous assumed personality "fronts" in order to cope with various social situations; regional differences in expression of feeling; self-disclosure related to level of trust; stress management)

The counseling process emphasizes active self-understanding and ways of constructively energizing one's feelings in relation to one's perceptions of social realities. Sessions may be brief, frequent, informal, spontaneous, and centered in the present. Appropriate implementation of the process can be assisted by a number of techniques:

support and confirmation
environmental manipulation
advocacy
advising
modeling and simulation
verbal reinforcement
setting limits and commitments
relationship review (counselor and
    client)

active analysis and summary by
    counselor
genuineness and sincerity of
    counselor
recognition of discrepancies
    between client's feelings and
    behavior

● CROSS-CULTURAL DIFFERENCES APPROACH

A cross-cultural approach generally tends to emphasize *differences*, usually those points of difference that might be found in the nature of the relationship between the majority cultural group and minority groups. Thus the model may be especially valuable in aiding understanding between a counselor and a client who are of different cultural backgrounds. In another sense, when a more general definition of culture is applied, all counseling may be considered cross-cultural. If a counseling theory purports to be cross-cultural according to this definition, it should be fairly inclusive, or seek to explain most of the phenomena that might be observed in the general helping relationship and process.

The cross-cultural approach (Marsella & Pedersen, 1981; Pedersen, Draguns, Lonner, & Trimble, 1981; Sue & Sue, 1990), like the culturally specific approach, emphasizes a framework for examining important social and personal factors and issues related to the counselor's role and function, the counseling process, and cultural diversity. Sue and Sue (1990) and other representations of the cross-cultural approach are discussed in this section. Four general topics are seen as important in cross-cultural counseling, and in other approaches as well: (1) barriers, (2) relationship factors, (3) cultural identity, and (4) the conditions for a culturally skilled counselor. These four areas generally emphasize major differences that might be observed between counselors and clients who are culturally different and that could be cause for conflict or obstacles in counseling.

Barriers. Obvious differences in *cultural values, class values, nonverbal communication,* and *language* could create communicative misinterpretations. These four potential blocks to counseling are prior conditions and, as such, constitute basic factors that may be encountered in any cross-cultural situation.

Although Sue and Sue (1990) offer no solutions and there seem to be no ready-made techniques for dealing with these conditions, sensitive and creative adjustment to them obviously depends on the counselor's breadth of societal understanding in general, regardless of whether the counselor's background is similar or dissimilar to that of the client. The counselor should avoid viewing barriers only as weaknesses without considering their potential as strengths. Constant review of the communicative accuracy between counselor and client in any cross-cultural situation will be helpful, as well as open admission by the counselor of his or her own cultural encapsulation. When blocks seemingly cannot be resolved, the situation may best be handled by consultation with or referral to more appropriate counseling resources (for example, counselor of same cultural background, priest or minister or rabbi, women's center, gay liberation personnel, AA, or storefront counseling center, depending on the circumstances).

Relationship and rapport factors. According to Sue and Sue (1990), for counseling to be a real service to the client and for clients to be most attracted to the counselor and his or her services, there must be the potential for a credible relationship and positive rapport. A *credible* relationship depends on the client's perception of the counselor as having *expertness* and *trustworthiness*, and rapport is the emotional climate that is felt by both client and counselor. Expertness is the counselor's ability, as perceived by the client, to handle a counseling situation as an informed and knowledgeable person. Trustworthiness relates to the counselor's underlying motivations, as perceived by the client, for wanting to help; it might be presumed on the basis of the title of "counselor" itself or inferred from the counselor's actual demonstrations of honesty and nondefensiveness in the counseling relationship. Testing of the counselor's expertness and trustworthiness is most likely to be found in clients who doubt the counselor's intent. Although there are many variables that could influence or stress the credibility of a relationship in a cross-cultural encounter, three are given special emphasis here: (1) expectations, (2) counselor-client similarity, and (3) developmental experiences.

The *expectation* that the client and the counselor bring to the early stages of interaction is what the client expects or wants and what the counselor can or does actually deliver. For example, the client may expect to receive reliable information in order to solve a problem; to be treated consistently with how he or she sees the world; to be able to relate to or identify with a counselor as he or she might be accustomed to doing with significant others; to use the counselor as an important source of authority in order to gain reward, praise, or power. The last mind set probably works most against a credible relationship.

The *similarity* of background between client and counselor is believed to influence the important elements of credibility and congruity that are needed for rapport. The traditional dogma of cross-cultural counseling research is oriented toward ferreting out differences that are assumed might exist between or among groups of people and counseling environments. Depending on prior assumptions, people are classified and studied by properties such as skin pigmentation, language, nationality, ethnicity, religion, sociopolitical status (for example, minority/majority, oppressed/oppressor), and elusive subtleties such as personal temperament, racial attitudes, world view, and ritualized proxemics (human/social needs for space, time, order). Since the 1970s, cross-culturalists have focused on the appropriateness of White middle-class counselors counseling non-White racial minority clients. Little attention has been paid to client groups characterized by sex orientation, gender, age, or urban/rural location. The similarity (or differences) question basically centers on the issue of whether the counselor and client must be of the same ethnic or racial background. The research on whether or not a counselor to be most effective must be of the same race, ethnicity, sex, age, or socioeconomic class as the client is generally inconclusive. This issue, which often appears in cross-cultural research, is an oversimplification of the complex nature of any two-person interaction, reduces minority group membership to a homogeneous stereotype, is divisive, and generally works against helpful assistance that could result from cross-cultural endeavors.

However, this is not to say that such research is without value. The insights that might be derived from research on cross-cultural counseling situations can be very valuable for determining just what adjustments the counselor might make and, if possible, how, in order to facilitate and accommodate the helping process with those clients who have different cultural experiences (Ross, 1984). First, adjustment is affected by the degree to which both counselor and client are culture-bound, or ethnocentric. Second, extreme ethnocentricity should not imply total failure in the relationship, but success most likely depends on the ego strength and security possessed by both counselor and client in their desires and their pursuit of the goals each has for the helping process.

Lacking conclusive evidence to show that White counselors and minority clients are unable to work together in a counseling environment, cross-culturalists are now turning their attention to the influence that a racist society might have on the psychological development of personality. According to Sue and Sue (1990) and others, there are stages or phases of *psychological identity development* that are believed to be applicable to racial/cultural minority group members who must cope with racial oppression in U.S. society. Similarly, it is postulated, the counseling relationship and counseling effectiveness will be influenced by the stage of personal development at which the culturally different client might be. Stages or phases are speculated during which tasks are faced and obstacles must be overcome before ascending to the next level of desirable accomplishment, in a kind of psychological upward mobility. The Minority (Racial/Cultural) Identity Development model (Sue & Sue, 1990), which was described in Chapter 7, consists of these stages:

1. Conformity
2. Dissonance
3. Resistance and immersion
4. Introspection
5. Integrative awareness

Sue and Sue (1990) and others (Corvin & Wiggins, 1989; Helms, 1989; Ponterotto, 1988) contend that equal consideration should be given to the development of racial attitudes in White persons, since the majority of counselors are White. Sue and Sue (1990) postulate a White Identity

Development model that uses the same stages as their Minority Identity Development model. Their conceptualized model essentially exploits three sociological judgments (social stereotypes): (1) all aspects of life in the United States are racist; (2) all light-skinned people are inherently racist; (3) White identity is an aberration that has a predictable developmental sequence. Movement through the various stages of development is described as a kind of moral struggle against one's attitudes of racial superiority. The person who is fortunate enough to mature is absolved in stage 5 and comes to terms finally with his or her racist proclivities.

The Minority Identity Development model and the White Identity Development model are both interesting ideas, but biological populations (races) are confused with a sociological phenomenon (racism). Biologically, a race is a breeding population that displays a number of hereditary attributes more frequently than in other breeding populations. Most scientific attempts to identify races have focused on the adaptation of skin color (melanogenesis) and other physical features in interaction with the environment; thus the association of race with color (white, black, brown, and so on) and/or geographical location (Europe, Africa, Asia, and so on). However, since all humankind shares the same basic collection of genes, there are no pure races. The genetic difference *within* a geographical population group is nearly as great as the genetic difference *between* two geographical population groups. The pejorative subdivision of human beings into races perpetuates barriers among people and influences the operation of psychological mechanisms that contribute to the notion of racism (see Chapter 5). Biologists do not make generalizations about the superiority or inferiority of different races; however, the phenomenon of racism defines entire groups psychologically and culturally on the basis of purely biological characteristics and eventually as sociologically superior or inferior. Under certain conditions, any population group may be susceptible to racism. Romans, Greeks, Muslims, Chinese, Japanese, Brazilians, Asian Indians, Native Americans, Germans, Anglo-Saxons, and many other groups have held, or hold, prejudices against others who are considered different. The assumption of superiority by light-skinned Europeans (and the influence this has on U.S. society) is a recent historical development that is largely due to the colonial adventures of the industrialized nations.

Why the two models were not constructed as comparable entities is not known; a *majority* identity development model, or *intergroup* relations model, in place of the White Identity Development model would make more sense. Sue and Sue (1990) do not state whether they believe that under certain conditions racism is likely to be found in *any* population group of humans. Their extensive referrals to White racism throughout their writing implies that they believe the condition is specifically a problem limited to White, North American people. If so, this could work against sincerely understanding multicultural counseling interaction. Worse yet, it seems to be a throwback to the rhetoric of Black-White encounter groups during the late 1960s and early 1970s wherein the participants would verbally attack each other and, feeling satisfied, go their separate ways.

Cultural identity and world views. One's cultural identity is the frame of reference through which the world and relationships therein are viewed. The frame of reference through which one person views the world may be different in some ways from that of another person. It is the cultural baggage that one carries and through which one derives meaning in life.

People tend to perceive life as generally being either *internally* or *externally* controlled. A person characterized with high internality would believe: "I have maximum control and influence in the world." A person characterized with high externality would believe: "The world has maximum control and influence over me." High internality is believed to typify the values of mainstream culture and most likely constitutes the core feature of most counseling approaches and definitions of good mental health. Internal-external discrepancies can influence both the counselor and the counseling relationship, process, and goals. A disparity, for example, could exist in an African-American client who has ideologically adopted the general cultural beliefs about internal control but finds that they cannot always be applied to her personal life situations when she encounters unemployment and discrimination. The important implication here is that the counselor cannot assume that internality is the only gauge for mental health when reality and experience may demonstrate otherwise. The fact that the society has built-in laws that support fairness and that can be used in the environment must also be reinforced in the client to counteract the self-defeating notion that the world and life are all dependent on outside things over which the person has no control.

The question of responsibility is also raised in cultural identity. Who or what is responsible for adjustment and mental health? The person or society? Focusing exclusively on either extreme produces an incomplete picture; it is unproductive either to blame the person for his or her shortcomings and imperfections or to blame the situation or system. The two factors are interactive, and it is important for the counselor to make a rational assessment of both client dimensions (and self-assessment of the counselor's own psychological viewpoint as well).

The four basic types of world views that can result from the various combinations of internal-external locus of control and internal-external locus of responsibility can be summarized in the following descriptions:

Type 1. The "pride-in-identity" person who believes in society
Type 2. The marginal person
Type 3. The "give-up" person who gives up on society
Type 4. The "pride-in-identity" person who is realistic about the imperfections of society

I also believe the cultural identity quadrants can be explained from a transactional analysis approach, as shown in Figure 10-2.

Cultural skills. Today's counselor needs the skills to transcend multitudinous changes in the society and the complexities of cultural diversity. Gladding (1992) emphasizes that counseling is a comprehensive profession

I. (Assertive/Passive)	IV. (Assertive/Assertive)
I'm OK and have control over myself.	I'm OK and have control but need a chance.
Society is OK and I can make it in the system.	Society is not OK and I know what's wrong and seek to change it.
II. (Marginal/Passive)	III. (Passive/Aggressive)
I'm OK but my control comes best when I define myself according to the dominant culture.	I'm not OK and don't have much control; might as well give up or please everyone.
Society is OK the way it is; it's up to me.	Society is not OK and is the reason for my plight; the bad system is all to blame.

FIGURE 10-2 Transactional analysis of cultural identity quadrants

covering a variety of specializations and serving a wide range of people. Effective counseling is more than a collection of skills; it is an art, a personalized endeavor. Thus, professional ethical standards are especially important for the protection of both counselor and client. The need for culture-based skills should not be used as a convenient way to promote political manifestos nor to patronize racial groups. The purpose of any proposed set of skills should be to advance the effectiveness of counselors and counseling. Sue and Sue (1990) propose three general categories of skills needed by White counselors when counseling non-White clients: (1) self-awareness; (2) understanding of the world view of racial/cultural minority clients; (3) development of appropriate intervention strategies and techniques.

● PERSON-ENVIRONMENT "METHATHEORY" APPROACH

The major purpose of Allen E. Ivey's person-environment perspective (Ivey, 1981) is a search for greater insight into the interplay of counselor, client, and environment. It is basically an extension of the conceptual goals of the microcounseling skills approach already described in this chapter. Microcounseling (Ivey & Autheir, 1978; Ivey & Galvin, 1984; Ivey, Ivey, & Simek-Downing, 1987) is a systematic training procedure for effective interpersonal communication skills. The person-environment perspective departs from "traditional" models of counseling and psychotherapy in that a major goal is to discover basic underlying constructs and principles; in this respect it may be considered a metamodel or a metatheory—a theory about theories. A "person-environment" approach is applied because it is most central to a metatheory of counseling and psychotherapy. The perspective proposes (1) basic conceptual dimensions, and (2) a training procedure. It also provides

(3) a framework upon which traditional or alternative forms of counseling and psychotherapy may be examined, and (4) implications for the generalization of microcounseling skills to cross-cultural counseling situations and the application of the microskills in a variety of alternative settings, including business, medicine, and education.

Basic person-environment dimensions. The concept of "environment" as used here has a special definition. The individual environment consists of the transactions that individuals have with themselves. Each person is an interactive environment to himself or herself. An individual influences his or her environment and is in turn influenced by that environment; thus transactions take place through a mutual and continuous back-and-forth process or circular feedback loop. Environments are the transactions that people have with other people. The counseling or psychotherapy situation contains two environments—the counselor and the client. Each person (counselor and client) in the counseling dyad is the other person's environment, and each participant experiences the other as environment. Since both counselor and client have distinctive transactions in their personal environments, all counseling is literally cross-environmental, or cross-cultural, if you will.

Counseling is a process of interpersonal influence in which the counselor's selected response will lead, or influence, the client to various thoughts, feelings, and directions. The ability of the counselor to generate and select responses is dependent on the counselor's world view, which consists of the counselor's own *personal* frame of reference and his or her *theoretical* orientation. It is desirable for a counselor to have an integrated and unified world view; thus it is important to discover any inconsistencies between one's own perception of human nature and the picture of human nature that is presented by various counseling theories. All theories contain special world views, and it is best for counselors to develop their own general theory, from which will come typical patterns of responding to clients. One way to grasp the major constructs of various counseling approaches (for example, self-actualization and empathy, genuineness, and positive regard, as in the Rogerian model) would be to review the summaries of the approaches set forth in this chapter and Chapter 9. In addition, when possible, observing actual interviews or reading transcripts will help to clarify the basic theoretical themes and patterns of counselor responses that characterize different approaches. Developing one's own general theory, however, is more than sheer eclecticism, for the counselor must take a *reasoned* approach to the selection of parts of many theories, a process that implies that there is a best *response* for a specific *client* at certain *times* and under certain *conditions*. From this implication, the first important dimension—namely, intentionality—is drawn.

1. *Intentionality.* The view of human nature underlying the micro-counseling/educational approach is that most problems not traced to bio-chemical causes are psychosocial. Thus normal human development and the

emotional need for self-determination and self-esteem are related to and influenced by imperfect environmental/cultural/social systems. Self-direction and
self-control belong to a continuous process of self-improvement, with the goal
being the development of one's intentionality. The effective person is the
intentional person, and when the counselor works toward being a more intentional person he or she is more able to respond to the client in order to assist the
client's movement toward intentionality. Like fully functioning counselors,
fully intentional counselors can perceive what their intentions are, what they
intend to do, and how they will do it. An intentional counselor and an intentional client both work toward acquiring a repertoire of responses to meet a
variety of situations. According to microcounseling proponents, this objective
is behaviorally accomplished by the counselor's ability to generate voluntarily
an array of responses to a client's statements. The external reference for responses is found in the microskills of attending and influencing. Reasoned use
of microskills is the major goal of intentional counseling, and critically related
to this is the judicious assessment of the client's environment.

2. *Assessment.* In order to select counseling responses that are most likely
to facilitate a client's growth and development, the counselor takes into
consideration the client as a unique human being who experiences and acts in
the world according to his or her environmental-cultural background. Thus
the *focus* is on person-environment transactions and the cultural issues, topics,
and problems within them that might be important. Fundamental questions
that Kelly (1955) says are important have been outlined by Ivey, Ivey, and
Simek-Downing (1987, pp. 170–171). The questions that the counselor might
ask himself or herself about the client and that could serve as a map to guide
the intentional process include the following: What is the problem? What are
the client's constructs for viewing the world? What is the client's situation and
environmental context? What are the counselor's basic theories and constructs? What is to be done?

3. *The decision-making process.* Decision making is a dynamic process of
interaction between the counselor and the client that extends to other
significant people and events in the client's life. In this process, all factors that
are relevant in the life experiences of the client to the making of decisions can
be subjected to a systematic empirical examination. It is a process that relates
all knowledge that can be derived from both counselor and client and
emphasizes not only the elements of rational choice but also the limits. The
systematic decision-making model includes the following components:
(a) define the problem; (b) determine alternatives; (c) select one alternative and
implement it.

4. *Process skills.* Intentional human interaction generally can be seen to
follow a pattern; counselor responses appear in sequence at different phases
of counseling. For example, open questions that encourage the client to explore
concerns are usually followed by closed questions aimed at assessment or
diagnosis and are found especially in the beginning phases of counseling. The
single dimensions of encouraging, paraphrasing, reflecting meaning and
feeling, and summarizing are also related to the counseling phase focusing on
definition of the problem. These basic attending/observing and listening

skills are followed or complemented by other higher-level quantitative and qualitative skills, such as the ability to focus on specific aspects of the interview, to influence, to confront, and eventually to use appropriate sequencing of skills in order to structure stages of the interview. The highest level of intentional counseling will be found when the counselor is able to integrate, discriminate, relate, and use microskills in conjunction with the following aspects or conditions: (a) *individual experiences and situations* that are presented or encountered by the client in the various phases of counseling and that require specific patterns of skill usage by the counselor; (b) *cultural experiences and situations* that might give cause for specific patterns of skill usage with clients who are members of various cultural groups; and (c) various *theoretical counseling approaches,* such as psychodynamic, existential-humanistic, and behavioral, that accentuate specific patterns of skill usage, and in different settings, such as business, educational, medical, and correctional, that emphasize different patterns of skill usage.

Application of person-environment concepts and the microskills to other aspects or conditions. The endeavor by the proponents of microcounseling to integrate the communication concepts and skills with special client situations, cultural groups, and other theoretical counseling approaches is both novel and intriguing. I have observed that school counselors, for example, seem to emphasize the use of influencing skills such as directives, advice/information, explanation/instruction, and logical consequences and to make less use of the basic attending and listening skills. If this is true, the implication could be that either the school environment-culture context is less appropriate for certain skills and more appropriate for other skills or that some school counselors may not be using the full range of skill responses of which they could or should be capable.

The appropriate application and sequencing of microcounseling skills with different populations is not precisely known. However, the proponents emphasized that some single skills may be more effective than others, especially in the use of questions and nonverbal communication (Ivey & Galvin, 1984, p. 214). The usefulness of specific microskills with culturally diverse populations must be determined by each counselor with each client in each situation. The personal and cultural background of the counselor could add further influences, especially if the client's own background is distinctly different from that of the counselor. The fact that clients may tend to track (that is, follow or learn) the counselor's helping mode may be especially important in the beginning phases in order to mobilize the client and to allow the counselor some structure and relevancy in dealing with the client, but continued indoctrination into the counselor's environment will work against the client's full development of intentionality (generating a wider range of responses). However, the importance of the counselor's tracking the client's language (that is, mode of responses in the context of the client's own culture) is stressed. The more varied are the helping responses that the counselor has at hand, the more likely it is that the client can be helped. For example, some believe that an active and directive style for some Black clients is more in accord with their linguistic frame of reference, whereas some White clients may be more amenable to a listening style. Basically it is a question of giving clients the power to determine their own environment for counseling. When clients are empowered (can fully participate) in their own diagnoses and treatment processes, the counseling will be most complete and most effective.

It is important for the counselor to know that he or she could have many alternative environments at his or her disposal, depending on the theoretical approaches that he or she might or could potentially take with the client. Language communication is the primary mode of helping for most counseling and interviewing approaches, the major goal being to increase the proportion of verbalizations of the client that are in line with the particular theoretical approach used. Thus it can be assumed that if the client indeed does seem to track the language of the counselor, the therapeutic helping environment is compatible with the environment of the client. An important consideration in employing microskills and other microcounseling dimensions is which skills might be most characteristically used with various theoretical approaches and also which skills might be most characteristically used in various settings. This relationship has been proposed as shown in Figure 10-3. The basic counselor-training format, aimed at an integration of microskills and the various counseling approaches, follows a sequence of activities based on social learning principles:

1. Understand the core constructs of a theory.
2. Determine the sequencing of skills by observing an interview or reading a transcript that illustrates the theoretical counseling approach.
3. Practice the theoretical counseling role and microskills as observed, using videotapes and/or audiotapes of performances for feedback.

● MULTICULTURAL COUNSELING AND DEVELOPMENT

Revival of the psychology of individual differences (respect for human diversity) combined with an optimistic sociology of pluralism (cooperation among people) is the focus for Manuel Ramirez's (1991) model of psychotherapy and counseling based on a multicultural perspective. The general objectives inherent in the approach are (1) to present a theoretical framework for the psychosocial issues and problems faced conjointly by all people living in multicultural societies in the Americas; (2) to provide a culturally compatible treatment modality and eclectic strategies that will facilitate personal development of the client (and counselor) toward a more culturally congruent, flexible state of being; and (3) in the final phase of (community) therapy, for the client to restore good relations with important others in his or her social environment and to participate with others as "ambassadors" in the development of a multicultural society.

Background. Although scientific knowledge is assumed to have universal application, Ramirez (1983) believes that psychology in the Western Hemisphere has been excessively slanted by the European outlook on life, society,

MICROSKILL LEAD	Nondirective	Modern Rogerian encounter	Behavioral	Psychodynamic	Gestalt	Trait and factor	Tavistock group	Vocational group (such as life planning)	Business problem solving	Medical diagnostic interview	Correctional interrogation	Traditional teaching	Student-centered teaching	Eclectic
ATTENDING SKILLS														
Open question	○	○	◐	◐	●	●	○	◐	◐	◐	●	◐	●	◐
Closed question	○	○	●	○	◐	◐	○	◐	◐	◐	●	●	◐	◐
Encouragement	◐	◐	◐	○	◐	◐	○	◐	◐	◐	◐	○	◐	◐
Paraphrasing	●	●	◐	○	◐	◐	○	◐	◐	◐	◐	○	●	◐
Reflection of feeling	●	●	○	◐	◐	○	◐	◐	○	○	○	○	●	◐
Reflection of meaning	◐	●	○	◐	○	○	◐	○	○	○	○	○	◐	◐
Summarization	◐	◐	◐	○	◐	◐	○	◐	◐	◐	◐	○	●	◐
INFLUENCING SKILLS														
Feedback	○	●	○	○	◐	○	○	◐	○	○	○	○	●	◐
Advice/information/ and others	○	○	◐	○	○	●	○	●	●	◐	◐	●	●	◐
Self-disclosure	○	●	○	○	◐	○	○	◐	◐	○	○	○	◐	◐
Interpretation	○	○	○	●	●	○	●	◐	◐	◐	◐	○	◐	◐
Logical consequences	○	○	◐	○	○	◐	○	◐	◐	◐	●	●	◐	◐
Direction	○	○	●	○	●	◐	○	◐	◐	●	●	◐	◐	◐
Influ. summary	○	○	◐	○	○	◐	○	●	●	◐	○	◐	◐	◐
CONFRONTATION (Combined Skill)	◐	◐	◐	◐	●	◐	●	◐	◐	◐	●	◐	◐	◐
FOCUS														
Client	●	●	●	●	●	●	○	●	●	●	●	○	●	◐
Counselor, interviewer	○	◐	○	○	○	○	○	○	○	○	○	○	◐	◐
Mutual/group/"We"	○	◐	○	○	○	○	●	◐	○	○	○	○	◐	◐
Other people	○	○	◐	◐	◐	◐	○	◐	◐	○	◐	○	◐	◐
Topic or problem	○	○	◐	◐	○	●	○	●	●	●	●	●	●	◐
Cultural/ environmental context	○	○	◐	○	○	◐	○	◐	◐	○	○	○	◐	◐
ISSUE OF MEANING (Topics, key words likely to be attended to and reinforced)	Feelings	Relationship	Behavior problem solving	Unconscious motivation	Here-and-now behavior	Problem solving	Authority, responsibility	Future plans	Problem solving	Diagnosis of illness	Information about crime	Information/ facts	Student ideas/ info./facts	Varies
AMOUNT OF INTERVIEWER TALK-TIME	Low	Medium	High	Low	High	High	Low	High	High	High	Medium	High	Medium	Varies

Legend

● Frequent use of skill

◐ Common use of skill

○ Occasional use of skill

FIGURE 10-3 Examples of microskill leads used by interviewers from differing theoretical orientations or in differing settings.

SOURCE: From *Intentional Interviewing and Counseling* (2nd ed.) by A. E. Ivey. Copyright © 1988 by Wadsworth, Inc. Reprinted by permission of the publisher, Brooks/Cole Publishing Company, Pacific Grove, California.

and institutions. According to his review and interpretations of relevant literature, powerful sociopolitical and economic events in history shaped the European world view, which ultimately influenced the framework of psychology. However, he also believes there is an emerging mestizo—amalgamation of European and Native American—point of view in psychology that is compatible with people of the Americas and contemporary melting pot/multicultural ideology. Furthermore, a psychology of the Americas can provide innovation for a therapeutic/counseling process that is more appropriate to American societies.

1. *Influences on the European world view.* Three historical events helped to shape the European world view and the direction of psychology: the Industrial Revolution, colonialism, and the separation of science and religion.

The *Industrial Revolution,* which initiated the industrialized society in Great Britain between 1760 and 1880 and was followed by similar revolutions in other countries, displaced the traditional cultural belief systems in Europe (stressing family and ethnic group belonging, sacred origins of the universe, tradition and ritual) with a modern system (emphasizing individualism, secularism, egalitarianism). Traditional views were seen as incompatible with the modern technology and modern progress that had become identified with European ways. Traditional culture and values—and traditional individuals and traditional groups—were assumed to be dysfunctional and needing Western psychology and psychiatry; hence, the level of psychological development of a people became equated with the level of technological development of their country.

Colonization programs by European nations—an outgrowth of the Industrial Revolution—exploited the natural resources of less-developed countries, but the colonizers also sought to move these "traditional" countries into the "modern" era. The colonizers' attitude of benevolent superiority gave incentive for the development of a cross-cultural psychology that was applied to explain groups of people whose cultures differed from the colonizers'. Psychological points of view toward individual differences and cultural diversity, for example, were shaped by interest in and study of cross-group comparisons such as "dependency needs of the colonized versus the individualism of the colonizers" and "personality traits of tribal people versus personality traits of civilized people."

The *separation of science and religion* into dual entities, with religion and spiritualism playing little or no role in psychology and psychiatry, influenced the belief that scientific knowledge and methods (that is, technical language) are superior to other sources of knowledge and methods. It was only in the process of secularization that psychology became detached from religion. Culture is secular when its acceptance is based on rational and utilitarian considerations rather than on reverence and veneration. Thus, science has become the dominant way to understand human action, to predict and control human behavior, to solve problems of value and value-implementation in human life, and ultimately to determine human destiny.

2. *Influences on the American world view.* Since cultures and people have development of their own, it should not be assumed that only European world

views are frozen into the American character. Historical circumstances and experiences unique to living and surviving in the New World have also shaped an American (mestizo) perspective. Since all people in the Americas are transplants from other geographical areas, "the key to survival was cooperation—collaboration among peoples of different backgrounds in order to learn skills and life styles that ensured success in the new environment" (Ramirez, 1983, p. 7). Thus, elements of cooperation, collaboration, adjustment, and survival are present in the American experience.

Intermarriage and amalgamation of different world views was a common practice between European settlers and the native North and South Americans. The fact that Americans are of different cultures lends itself to compatibility with a multicultural orientation to life.

Revolution against European domination in the Western Hemisphere created the identity of being an American and the realization of being different from Europeans, while *also* feeling pride for old value systems and ways of life. The people who persevered in the new environment had to develop a feeling for or a consciousness about diversity and about pluralistic identities.

3. *A confluence of world views?* In the European view, two cultures cannot coexist without conflict of identity. In the mestizo perspective, adoption of both European and non-European cultures and lifestyles is viewed as a process of cultural change; a pluralistic identity represents a synthesis of different cultures. Ramirez's multicultural prototype takes the mestizo world view that has evolved from "the synthesis or amalgamation of native American and European people, cultures, and life styles. . . . All people in the Americas (regardless of race, nationality, or ethnic group) are considered to be psychological mestizos because they have been socialized in mestizo environments" (Ramirez, 1983, p. xiii). This includes a predisposition to develop certain traits and coping styles in a specific geographic area. Thus, there is a pattern of cultural development that is available, and it is characterized by flexibility, adaptability, openness, diversity in orientation, pluralistic identities, heterogeneity, and other attributes and states of being. These, and other pluralistic-transcendent identities, are components of *multicultural personality;* it is not an accumulation of static characteristics, skills, or cultural sensitivities, but a personal-interpersonal transactional process within the context of many cultural realities.

Basic concepts. The multicultural psychotherapy/counseling approach is based on (1) the psychology of individual and cultural differentness, and (2) a cultural and cognitive dual theory of personality. Psychological adjustment and development are seen as functions of personality flexibility and a multicultural orientation toward life.

1. *Psychology of differentness.* People wanting to fit in, people feeling alone and different from those around them, people who feel they don't belong or are not accepted—these are typical themes expressed by many members of minority groups. Ramirez (1991) defines a minority group as "any group that

is in some way different from the societal ideal" (p. 2). Differentness is a condition that is likely to prevail in a multicultural society in which members of diverse groups maintain an autonomous participation within the confines of a common civilization that stresses adherence or conformity from its members to certain ideals and patterns. Individual differences that make a person unique can also contribute to one's feelings of being mismatched to important others and to the environment. According to Ramirez (1991), the *mismatch syndrome* can be noted in a number of clinical symptoms: self-rejection, depression, emphasis on the negative, rigidity of thinking and problem solving, and attempts to escape reality.

Defining problems of maladjustment as degrees of match/mismatch between people and their environments follows a *person-environment fit* paradigm in which human problems are not located solely in the person or solely in the culture, so that causation cannot be focused on only one dimension. The pressure to conform, to give up individuality, affects more than minority-group members. Any individual difference (gender, lifestyle, value system, physical characteristic, and so on) is subject to the pressure to conform.

2. *Personality: cultural styles and cognitive styles.* Marginality (mismatch syndrome) is characterized by the incorporation of values and habits from two divergent cultures and by incomplete assimilation in either. Ramirez (1991) contends that two styles (modes) of personality are related to coping effectiveness in problems of marginality: cultural and cognitive.

Cultural styles can be classified as *traditional* or *modern* in regard to a number of domains: gender role definition, family identity, sense of community, time orientation, age status, tradition, deference to authority and convention, spirituality and religion. A client's cultural orientation can be observed in the context of the counseling/therapy session, as Ramirez (1991, p. 154) notes:

Traditional	Modern
Behaves deferentially toward therapist	Seeks to establish equal status with therapist
Expects therapist to do most of the talking	Does most of the talking
Appears shy and self-controlling	Appears assertive and self-confident
Is observant of social environment	Seems to ignore social environment
Focuses on important others in relating reason(s) for seeking therapy	Focuses on self in relating reason(s) for seeking therapy

Cognitive styles are classified as *field sensitive* and *field independent.* Cognitive styles are the learning modes in which a person organizes and classifies his or her perceptions of the environment. Although most individuals use a combination of both cognitive styles depending on the demands of a situation, each person has a preference for one of the styles. Cognitive styles are reflected in person-to-person communication, interpersonal relationships, motivational responses to rewards, and in specific role relationships like that between student and teacher or client and counselor. According to Ramirez (1991, p. 155), characteristics of client cognitive styles that can be observed in the context of counseling or therapy are as follows:

Field Sensitive	*Field Independent*
Self-disclosing	Depersonalizes problems
Shows interest in personalizing relationship with therapist	Relationship with therapist secondary to focus on problems to be addressed in therapy
Indicates that social rewards from therapist will be important to progress	Indicates that increase in personal well-being will be important to progress
Global focus and deductive (global-to-specific) learning style	Detail-focused and inductive (specific-to-global) learning style

Therapeutic process. Psychological adjustment is a matter of the degrees of cultural and cognitive match and mismatch between a person and his or her environments. The objectives of multicultural counseling and therapy are to help people who feel different and alienated to understand and accept their own uniqueness and to develop cultural values and cognitive flexibility in the direction of a multicultural personality. The increasingly diverse nature of American societies emphasizes the importance of personality flexibility; thus diversity is an incentive for more complete development of personality.

The theory and strategies of multicultural counseling and psychotherapy are based on an eclecticism drawn from psychodynamic approaches, humanistic perspectives, and cognitive and behavioral approaches and theories. Initial analysis of the client's cultural and cognitive mismatch is conducted by assessment and study of the client's life history, introduction of the cultural/cognitive flex theory, development of insight, and identification of mismatch goals. Cognitive-behavioral strategies include setting behavioral goals, learning stress reduction, completing homework assignments, and practicing new behaviors. Phenomenology and the humanistic perspective give special attention to the freedom of self-expression and acceptance of the unique self. The counselor or therapist seeks to develop his or her own multicultural personality and is alert to his or her own behaviors that might interfere with the client's development of flexibility.

The final phase of multicultural counseling seeks to work against the fear that counseling and psychotherapy are tools of conformity. Clients are encouraged to extend to others in the broader environment the insights and flexibilities they acquired during the course of their therapy. The societal ideal is cooperation, harmony, and sensitivity toward cultural and individual differences.

■ SUMMARY

1. This chapter has included representative examples of what are designated as eclectic and synergetic approaches to counseling and psychotherapy.

2. Eclecticism in counseling and psychotherapy was defined as the inclusion of ideas from a variety of theories to form a single approach. Two types of eclecticism were described. One is counselor/therapist-centered eclecticism, in which the counselor or therapist integrates parts of theories to develop the approach that best fits his or her personality and that seems appropriate for the setting in which the person works. The second type was defined as process-centered eclecticism, in which the counselor or therapist develops proficiency in using and combining certain behavior skills and in the appropriate sequencing of the various skills at different phases of the counseling process. Various communication skills models were identified for this type of eclecticism. Most communication skills approaches have borrowed and expanded on the concepts of empathy, genuineness, and positive regard as basic counselor conditions. Definitions of behavior skills have been developed for these dimensions, and other important behavior skills have been added to facilitate the helping communication process in counseling, therapy, and other interpersonal situations. The skills approach conceptualizes or views human problems as learning problems for which new knowledge and effective skills are needed in order to mobilize resources. The scientific method of goal identification and goal meeting and the decision-making process are generally used as action-oriented steps.

3. *Synergetic* is the term given those approaches that endeavor to synthesize helping approaches with cultural-environmental factors. They give the events, conditions, and experiences in the client's life situation the same importance and attention as the client's intrapsyche, self-concept, or behaviors. Thus both the person and the environment are seen as important considerations for effective counseling and psychotherapy. Environment is seen as the background that gives greater clarity to the client in counseling and that suggests how the counselor might provide the best helping format. The interaction of the client and his or her environment can be noted in the topic content, problems presented, and expectations for the helping relation and helping process. A synergetic approach presumes that present theoretical models are incomplete and that the influence of environment as a determinative factor needs greater consideration. Environment was defined and discussed as comprising physical factors, social situation factors, and group culture factors. The judicious use of cultural meanings was also pointed out. Various transitional synergetic models were described, including the nonracist communication approach, the accountable action approach, the systemic approach, the transcendent approach, and the culturally specific approach.

4. The cross-cultural differences approach of Derald Sue and David Sue was outlined and the four topics they see as important in cross-cultural

counseling were discussed: (a) barriers, (b) relationship factors, (c) cultural identity, and (d) the conditions for a culturally skilled counselor.

5. Allen Ivey's person-environment "metatheory" approach was also outlined. The concept of person-environment was discussed and four important dimensions of microcounseling were described: (a) intentionality, (b) assessment, (c) the decision-making process, and (d) process skills. Application of person-environment concepts and the microskills to various cultures and to different theoretical counseling approaches and various settings was also noted.

6. The basic concepts and synergetic features of Manuel Ramirez's multicultural model of psychotherapy and counseling were outlined and discussed. These included: (a) the confluence of the cultures of Europe and the Western Hemisphere, (b) a psychology of differentness, (c) styles of personality: cultural and cognitive, (d) psychological adjustment as the reconciliation of cultural and cognitive mismatch, and (e) a therapeutic/counseling process based on eclectic principles and the development of multicultural personality.

CHAPTER

THE INTERACTION OF
COUNSELOR AND CLIENT

Part 1 contained material describing the people in our multicultural society and Part 2 emphasized four major categories of issues and situations experienced by the people. Part 3 has thus far summarized the counseling and psychotherapy approaches that are commonly available or practiced in today's society.

This chapter gives excerpts from counseling interviews to illustrate some of the details, ideas, and dimensions treated in Parts 1, 2, and 3. These excerpts do not come from the annals of the theoreticians. They have been collected from the experiences of counselors who have from one to ten years of experience in a variety of settings and at various levels of graduate and postgraduate training. Though their counseling styles may appear at times to lean toward certain theoretical orientations, these counselors could most likely be categorized as eclectic. It is safe to assume that each counselor used the strategy that he or she considered most appropriate at the moment. The main premise in the presentation of these excerpts is that counselors and psychotherapists can learn from the comparison of their own strengths and points for improvement with those of others. The problems and situations of the clients also illustrate the experiences that any general population of clients and counselors might have in our multicultural society. At the conclusion of each excerpt is a discussion of the immediate counseling problem and the counseling relationship, followed by suggested counseling goals , and, where appropriate, supplementary information. Although they do overlap, the 11 counseling excerpts are categorized according to general themes and issues:

Sociopolitical Issues
1. Dennis
2. Jessie
3. Juan

■ COUNSELING EXCERPTS: SOCIOPOLITICAL ISSUES

▲ COUNSELING EXCERPT 1: DENNIS

A Native American client desires to resolve personal conflict through self-confirmation of his own cultural values. The counselor is non-Indian.

Client: Where can I start? Take religion, for instance. OK? I have a strong, traditional Indian background . . . and I try to cope with whatever is good in the non-Indian society. But, coming from the Indian way of life, I feel that how I can relate myself to the way of praying to nature is not the same as saying I got to be good and go to church on Sunday and pray to a certain god. How can I relate myself to that way? *(States a concern)*

Counselor: You're saying that you are religious, that you don't find that the White religion is in harmony with what you are; you find a conflict in some practices of the White religion. *(Emphasizes White religion over Native American religion)*

Client: I'm not sure that you understood.

Counselor: Would you try to explain to me again?

Client: I know that I feel there is something around me that is good. I can take a piece of rock and say that it was formed from something that I believe in. I can take a tree branch and say that I pray to this tree and feel good. I feel the obligation that is imposing on me to make me go to church; and I don't want to do that. *(Expresses deep feeling for Native American religion over "church" religion)*

Counselor: You feel an obligation to go to church and somehow you want to resist the obligation. You're caught in the middle in giving in to it and fighting against it. You'd rather fight against it than do it; somehow you're not quite free to do that. *(Pause)*

(Counselor emphasizes value of "church" religion)

Client: Do you think I should? . . . go to church? *(Pause)*

Counselor: I'm wondering if going to church would help you, like anybody else, since you feel so reluctant. It just doesn't seem to be you.

(Emphasizes client's nonattendance)

Client: Eh . . . they tell me I *should* go to church.

Counselor: Who are "they?"

Client: The people who taught me about their religion. The Catholic church.

Counselor: You don't want to do this. Somehow I'm puzzled because you don't want to do it; in other words, you feel an obligation to go to church because they told you to. And yet you don't feel a real need inside yourself to go. *(Pause)*

(He is puzzled because he does not fully comprehend the value of the Native American religion to the client)

Client: I think. . . . *(Pause)* . . . I think the need is there.

Counselor: The need to go to church on Sunday?

(Counselor continues from same frame of reference)

Client: Eh . . . I think the need is there because . . . I don't know . . . I don't know what to say. It's kind of confusing now.

(Client feels misunderstood)

Counselor: You sound like you don't understand yourself. It's almost like someone sneaked up and put this need in you.

(Counselor implies doubt of client's credibility)

Client: I think I know what is good and I know that there is something there that is good. You know, why should I go to church on Sunday when I know that there is the same thing outside the church?

(Client again tries to express his personal experience and feelings)

Counselor: One thing. You see yourself as a good man. Is that right? And, as a good man, you can recognize good within this Catholic religion and that gives a. . .

(Counselor continues to convince himself that the client, in order to feel good, wants to see the good in the Catholic religion)

Client: I don't know what's good within the Catholic religion.

Counselor: You feel some kind of obligation or attraction to the good that you see there, but not enough obligation to make you feel that you want to go to church, or go to that church. That you can be good by praying before the stone or tree branch. Or by doing whatever you do on Sunday besides going to church.

(Counselor ignores client's strong expression of opinion)

Client: What do you think I should do?

Counselor: *(Sighs)* . . . What do you want to do?
(Pause)

Counselor: What do you think a good man would do in your situation?
(Pause)

Client: I'm confused. I don't want to talk about it.

(Client gives up)

● IMMEDIATE COUNSELING PROBLEM

The counselor's lack of understanding of and feeling for the client's valuing of his traditional religion has created a serious relationship problem in the counseling process. In spite of the client's being raised in the Catholic religion (attending Catholic missionary schools, in this case), the Native American religion is a crucial part of his essence and innermost being. This is a classic example of dissonance between counselor and client due to cultural differences as well as miscommunication. The counselor is unable to separate his own frame of reference from the client's situation and thus cannot fully appreciate or offer an active challenge to the client to accept that integral part of himself. The counselor overemphasizes passive and inaccurate reflection of content, with little direct attention to the underlying sentiments, experiences, meanings, and intuition expressed by the client. Supportive responses and the seeking of understanding by the counselor, such as, "Sometimes you have to trust your own feelings," or "Your own religion is really what is the most important to you," or, "Check me out on what I just heard you say," might have been helpful in assisting the client to face what seems on the surface to be ambivalence. If the counselor feels that he isn't really comprehending what the client is saying, it would be more effective to ask the client directly to explain the situation.

Although an initial impression of trust and rapport is usually fostered when counselor and client are of the same cultural background or ethnicity, the communication style used by any counselor is also crucial. In working with Native Americans, overuse of a nondirective client facilitation style seems to impede the clients' perceptions that progress is being made. Considering that Native American styles of speaking and Native American sensitivity to how words are interpreted have persisted through generations, a more directive or "cultural/experimental" style may be more effective (Dauphinais, Dauphinais, & Rowe, 1981). Thus awareness of Native American cultural values, and the mutual clarification of verbal communication meanings between counselor and client in order to avoid semantic misunderstanding, will probably lead to greater collaboration and less dissonance between non–Native American counselors and Native American clients.

● COUNSELING GOALS

In a postsession review, the client himself said: "I was looking for more of a direction to take. I think I was using him [the counselor] as someone who knows, you know, knows something. I wanted him to say this is good for you. I wish he would have taken this route. I wanted him to say that my way of knowing that I know, that praying in what I believe in is OK. I wanted a feeling of support in what I believed in. I think that I had already made the decision because I know my way of life, but being caught in with the Catholic way of religion . . . I was sort of saying, you know, I don't like to go that route. I'd rather stay in the Indian way of life, which is good for me." When asked, "If you knew this before, why did you go to a counselor?" he answered, "Because I wanted someone to tell me or help me whether I'm making the right decision; to tell me, 'If you feel this way, don't go to church.' I didn't feel that the real questions that I had were faced . . . that knowing that I was brought up in the Indian religion and straying away from that and learning the Catholic religion and reverting back to what I thought was good. I found that the Catholic way is not too good for me; I want to go back, but then society says that you can't have two religions at the same time, or the Catholic church says that."

Identity conflicts in cases such as this may be attributed to the education of Native Americans in the formal structures of the society and their subsequent failure to fit in or find acceptance by the larger social system. Rejection of primary culture is likely to lead to the confusion and self-doubt that is found in a marginal existence. Counselors who seek to assist in the resolution of a state of marginality need to understand the client's psychodynamics, the two cultures, and a process that will facilitate movement toward desired goals. Contemporary Native Americans maintain cultural and tribal identities that are different from those of most other Americans, and many of their rituals, beliefs, or kinship differences are not clearly understood by non-Native Americans. Anderson and Ellis (1980, p. 113) suggest that human services counselors who intend to work with Native Americans must take at least the following preparatory steps:

1. *Recognize* that Indians approach life with a different set of expectations, values, and interpretations of events and that their approach can be as satisfying and as rich to them as any other culture is to any other person.
2. Become *familiar* with those cultural values so that one can begin to understand and appreciate the pressures being faced by Indian clients.
3. *Resist* the temptation to interpret a particular behavior or problem as if it were caused by the same kinds of pressures that may cause that problem in a non-Indian middle-class society.
4. *Converse* with Indians with an attitude of respect rather than paternalism.

▲ COUNSELING EXCERPT 2: JESSIE

A Black client blames the system to avoid taking responsibility for himself. The counselor is White.

Client: Well, you're the one who wanted to talk, so talk. *(Defensive)*

Counselor: Yes, the absence list showed you weren't in school for three days. Didn't we have an agreement that when things weren't going right for you, we'd talk, rather than you cutting out? *(Confronts discrepancy in behavior)*

Client: All this same White counselor talk. You Whites always coming down on us and jiving us. *(Avoids the immediate issue)*

Counselor: Jessie, I thought we were going to talk about what happened during the three days of absence. *(Confronts the avoidance)*

Client: This whole damn system of yours—it's hooked us all into money. *(Avoids the immediate issue)*

Counselor: Would you cut out all that crap about the system and talk about what's been going on with you the last few days? You know we can talk about what you can do for you, but that other thing is out there and not in here. *(Shows feelings, confronts, and indicates willingness to help)*

Client: Uh? Yeah, tell me more, ha! *(Relaxes defenses)*

Counselor: Jessie, I know you believe unfair things happen to you, but I want you to talk about what's been happening to you the last few days and try to forget that other for now. *(Recognizes where he's coming from)*

Client: Uh? Well, uh, see, our check didn't come in and we had the bills and I had to get us some quick bread and . . . *(Willing to discuss his situation)*

● IMMEDIATE COUNSELING PROBLEM

In his anger and frustration, Jessie is defensively attributing his situation solely to an external, imperfect, and unfair social system and generalizing it to the counseling relationship.

● COUNSELING GOALS

The displacement of the client's frustration onto the counselor can be helped through the counselor's understanding and acceptance of where the client is coming from. It is necessary for Jessie to recognize and confront his reliance on avoidance and excuse making, along with his development of coping mechanisms that will help him face the situation instead of running away from it. The counselor's demonstration of a high level of trust in Jessie is essential, as is Jessie's gaining a feeling of control over his life. In reality, he is confronting, not avoiding, the economic needs of his family as first priority, but in the process he isn't making full use of the helpful resources that a skilled counselor can provide for his personal (psychodynamic) and situational (sociodynamic) dilemma. Black male clients in particular may on the basis of first impressions stereotype all White male counselors as having racist attitudes. The situation is a complex one that stimulates extreme masculine competitive urges, which are behaviorally manifested in suspiciousness and distrust of the underlying intent of the White male counselor. The more negative personal experiences the client has had in the environment, the greater is the chance for generalization of the distrust. A counselor who has integrated his or her own personal experiences will be able to indicate honestly what prejudice he or she has or has had. It is also important for the counselor to be free to help the client dispute his or her own stereotypes, whether directed toward the counselor or all "those others." Since some of the conflict in minority-majority relations is based on sex in addition to group identity, women face similar cross-cultural problems, but as a result of different psychological dynamics. Some of the dynamics may be attributed to competition for male relationships. Many Black men and women also entertain deep fears of racial and cultural genocide—fears that may be perpetuated by the relational situation in which Blacks and Whites find themselves.

▲ COUNSELING EXCERPT 3: JUAN

A Mexican-American client and a White counselor collaborate using both mainstream ways and ways that are indigenous to the cultural group.

Counselor: Juan, workers' employment compensation will pay for your lost time, but the health insurance will pay only for the authorized medical treatment that you received for the accident you had at work.

Client: My eyes still don't work so I can see the assembly charts. I get so darn shaky whenever I think about all my money problems, bills, if I can do the work, what's going to happen to my children. . .

Counselor: Yeah, I know, it seems like everything is hitting you all at once.

(Recognizes the situation as Juan is experiencing it)

Client: Ha! You know, maybe it sounds crazy or something, but there's this woman in my neighborhood who has some things that she gives me and advises me how to feel better. It really helps.

(Checks the counselor out to gain affirmation of his actions)

Counselor: I can't really advise you on what type of treatment you should receive. If it helps and you feel better, why not use it? You're also getting the medical help for your visual problem. You're doing the most you can for yourself at this time, Juan.

(Counselor is straightforward and supportive)

● IMMEDIATE COUNSELING PROBLEMS

A potential conflict between the personnel counselor and Juan is avoided by the counselor's acceptance of Juan's belief in the value of receiving treatment through his own cultural ways (Kiev, 1968). It is also balanced by the counselor's encouraging Juan to continue the scientific medical treatment for his visual impairment.

● COUNSELING GOALS

Concerned follow-up of Juan's situation, in the form of support, helping him with his fears and lack of confidence, and checking on his medical progress, is important. It is also essential that he receive assistance with the complexities of his legal and financial rights, as well as the help he is receiving from the health care professionals.

In working with Chicano clients, the counselor must be knowledgeable of Chicano lifestyle and religion. Some Chicano families have some beliefs that to a White person would appear to be superstition. Axelson and Jimenez (1977, pp. 3–4) state:

> The counselor should be aware of such beliefs as *mal de susto*, which is a behavioral condition of nervousness caused by a bad fright, and *mal de ojo*, the evil eye, which is thought of as a hex causing a physical illness with no apparent medical findings. In the Chicano culture, extensive use is made of home remedies and herbs in treatment of medical illness. The *curandero* (community medic) and the *brujo* (community healer) play an important and respected role in many Chicano families. The counselor who comes into a Chicano family and finds, for instance, a family member being treated with herbs, covered with hot cloths soaked in boiled tomatoes, and surrounded by neighbors, should be cautious in making his or her skepticism evident. At this time, maintaining close contact with the family and establishing communi-

cation with the father or dominant figure in the family will assist the counselor with the intervention of professional services.

■ COUNSELING EXCERPTS: EDUCATION AND ACHIEVEMENT

▲ COUNSELING EXCERPT 4: MARCIA

A Black female high school senior has overcome shyness and feelings of personal inadequacy but now faces new doubts and perceptions of personal discrimination.

Client: I was so shy, I couldn't believe it. At one point I was so scared, I couldn't speak. I could feel myself getting so nervous whenever I had to give an oral report. I was criticized a lot as a child and I cared what people who were important to me would say.   *(Speaks of her self-image in the past).*

Counselor: What criticisms have you had?   *(Tries to help her be more concrete)*

Client: I don't think I was a slow learner, but when my mother hollered at me to spell words correctly, I couldn't think straight. I really believed I was stupid. My grandparents were always nice to me, though, and I don't remember them ever saying anything bad to me. *(Pause)*

Client: I don't know, I guess I wouldn't have gotten this far if I was stupid. That part was hard for me . . . my hair was kinky, my teeth were buck, until I got braces. I guess I used to think I was ugly. I used to stay in my room to avoid everybody.   *(Actually, by most standards, Marcia would be considered a very attractive person).*

Counselor: But don't most children evaluate themselves harshly at times?   *(The counselor attempts through consensual validation to help her accept that part of her past as something many preadolescents and adolescents experience)*

Client: A lot of people would cut me down, but when I got older I was able to come back. I guess if I wasn't a strong person within myself, I'd probably have broke . . . and believe I had a low self-concept and no motivation.

Counselor: That's a positive point of view, to see how, in growing up, you saw the things that hurt you and . . .

(Attempts verbal reinforcement)

Client: I used to go to my room and just want to be alone. . .

(Old feelings of wanting to get away from the pain)

Counselor: Are you the only child?

(This shift in direction seems to draw on Adlerian theory to demonstrate something to Marcia)

Client: No, there's five of us, but I was the middle child and . . .

(Counselor doesn't seem to really know Marcia's family background, in spite of the fact that she is a senior in the school)

Counselor: Sometimes a middle child is caught in the crunch.

Client: Oh, I can blame it on a lot of things, parents, family environment, but I have to start looking on it as my mistake. I try so hard to look back and see how I overcame my shyness. I think it had a lot to do with being poor and my color.

(She doesn't seem to relate to the idea of an unmet need for a recognized "place" in her family)

Counselor: Oh?

(Counselor expresses surprise)

Client: I kept entering beauty pageants, plays, and things. I didn't think I was convincing enough. I always sounded shy and scared, so I kept entering pageants. I won one in my sophomore year. I don't know how, but I did. That was giving me what I needed. I got fourth place in the county contest last summer. Something in

(She has worked hard on her desire for achievement and recognition)

me told me I should have won first. The thing that hurt me the most was they didn't even put me in the newspaper.

Counselor: I wonder why that was?

Client: I think I was just lucky that year . . . things were going more for Blacks then . . . a Black had never won any place before.

Counselor: You know, I'm real surprised that you would think that was the reason.

Client: Since I won, they don't have the county pageant anymore and various people say it's because you're Black. It's something they have to deal with here in this city . . . no matter how great you are, or beautiful, or how well you can speak, or anything else.

(Perceives discrimination against Blacks in her community)

Counselor: Do you really believe it was stopped because of your race? I just don't have that impression.

Client: Oh . . . I just feel when I graduate I'll have to get out of this town to get anywhere—or any other small town like this one. I really don't want to stay here and go to [the community college]. If I can get the money, I want to go away to [state university]. I also thought about attending a Black college.

(Doesn't really accept the counselor's response)

● IMMEDIATE COUNSELING PROBLEM

What has started out as a fairly productive and insightful session seems to vacillate between what the counselor perceived as Marcia's "real" inner expression and what is currently on Marcia's mind. The dynamics of her family constellation pattern is superseded by, but interwoven into, her conditioned experiences of discrimination in the culture. Her intense sense of injustice works against her seeing deeper implications of how she, as an individual personality, interacts in the culture, but it also gives her strength and determination to do something with her life, even if it means moving away from her family and the town where she has lived all her life. The counselor should have accepted her feelings of injustice as a Black person and helped her express it as a legitimate feeling that she has, regardless of what is or is not the "real" situation. Movement to reality testing from that point would have helped her put it into perspective for her own self in the situation. Perceived discrimination can be both a crutch to avoid facing one's inadequacies and a stimulus to motivate self-determination and personal assertiveness. If there is a link between Marcia's shyness and her stereotypical impressions of racial identity, it should be expressed and put into perspective for what it means and what it does not mean.

● COUNSELING GOALS

Breaking old patterns of life through seeking other experiences and places that might offer new opportunities seems to Marcia a way to gain self-improvement. An important question for her is, does she always tend to move away from obstacles or problems as a first line of defense? Her former pattern of retreating to her room when faced with hurtful times is not unusual for teenagers. "Alone time" can permit a person to think and to deal with what's happening to him or her. Marcia displays determination and a "fighting" attitude by actively working on her shyness and fears and forcing herself to become a public figure. According to Adlerian theory, middle children will tend to compete in areas in which the older children are not proficient, and thus may be good or may strive to be good in an area where the older ones aren't skilled. This is the case with Marcia. Middle children also tend to be more sociable—which is an important goal for Marcia. Finally, middle children are often especially sensitive to injustices and unfairness and to having no place in the group. Middle children are "dethroned" when younger siblings are born into the family.

Marcia wants to get out of her town and attend the predominantly White state university, or a Black college, even though it would cause financial hardship. What are the implications of attending an institution of higher education that consists primarily of students who are of the same minority cultural background?

Black colleges. For about 100 years, beginning in the middle of the 1800s, Black institutions of higher education traditionally gave Blacks just about the only education they could get beyond high school. In 1964, 51% of all African-American students, 120,000 out of 234,000, were enrolled in Black colleges (Crossland, 1971, p. 38). In 1970, the percentage had dropped to 34%, or 160,000 out of 470,000, and in 1980, to approximately 22%, or 220,000 out of one million. Between 1980 and 1990, total enrollment at the approximately 104 predominantly Black colleges grew by 7.6%, according to the American Council on Education. Still, during the same period, African-American enrollment at colleges that aren't traditionally Black also grew by 8%. Black colleges have played a significant role in the education of Blacks, as evidenced by the 62% of Black officers in America's armed forces, 80% of all Black elected officials, 85% of all Black medical doctors, 81% of all Blacks with doctoral degrees, and 76% of all Black lawyers who received their education in traditionally Black institutions (Jarrett, 1982).

Although many private colleges are facing financial trouble in the 1990s, Black private institutions are especially stressed and many face extinction. They are generally less well endowed and receive a lower percentage of their revenues from tuition than do other private colleges. The United Negro College Fund has been especially instrumental in fund-raising drives for the small private institutions. Many African-American students have chosen traditionally Black colleges because they see them as more comfortable and nurturing places than predominantly White institutions.

Which college to attend? The reasons for attending a traditionally Black institution involve factors such as Black pride, self-identity, racial interest, and family tradition. Another significant issue is personal transition in life: What point has the client reached in his or her own personal development? What would the Black college provide that would help the client's self-expression and accomplishment? The decision also involves practical issues such as availability, accessibility, and cost.

Marcia is also considering attending the predominantly White state university. To assist minority students in their choices, high school counselors should make themselves aware of the admissions policies and practices of colleges that relate to minority access and admissibility. Bailey and Hafner (1978) and Willie (1981) have discussed at length the policy issues that have been historically involved in the fair treatment of minority students. Personal issues are also at stake. What feelings and environmental influences might affect Black students in predominantly White colleges? Black students who attend primarily White colleges often report typical feelings of culture shock that include loneliness, isolation, alienation, excessive self-consciousness, insecurity, and hypersensitivity. Situational factors that sometimes stress Black students in a predominantly White institution include the following:

· Isolation or rejection from many campus activities, with feelings of "nothing to do"
· White social life and relations to which they are unaccustomed
· Conflicts in dormitory life and with roommates
· Academic pressures for which many are not prepared
· Perceived prejudice and acts of discrimination

The experience of marginal existence, due to living in two distinct cultures, is a phenomenon that many African-American students must face in a mostly White institution. Daniel (1976) has pointed out how joining Black fraternities and sororities and other organizations represents one adaptation to marginality, even though it may also indicate a withdrawal from the marginal situation. Smith (1981), in her case study of "Elaine Thomas," has described how a young Black woman adjusted to her experiences through the help of a realistic, honest, and caring counseling relationship. Elaine's background of cultural experiences seemed to work against what she found in her college life and made her feel less confident, angry, and untactful in her interpersonal relations. The counselor assisted her in understanding her self-dynamics as well as the cultural contradictions she was facing at college. "The counselor suggested that she talk with the few other Black students in the program to see if they could form a support group for each other and share ideas regarding how to meet the academic requirements and deal effectively with their professors" (p. 179). Nelson (1989) has shown the importance of planned interventions—such as personal support groups and peer counselors—in the retention of African-American students at predominantly White institutions .

Native Americans and higher education. Many Native Americans face similar issues in deciding on a college. College education is being brought closer to Native Americans through classes offered on a number of reservations by state institutions of higher education. At least six colleges, in North Dakota, South Dakota, Arizona, Nebraska, and Kansas, now have an almost total enrollment of Native Americans, and in California one college, D-Q University at Davis, serves predominantly Native Americans and Americans of Mexican descent. D-Q University, a community college, is the only independent indigenous institution of higher education that is controlled by Native American peoples. Ayres (1977, p. 26) points out some of the questions and issues that Native Americans might have in deciding on a college to attend:

> American Indian students seeking higher education may wish to consider the proportion of Indian students in an institution. A school with a high proportion of Indian students is more likely to have Indian cultural courses, counseling, and classes targeted toward their special needs. Such a college may be particularly good preparation for the Native Americans who wish to contribute to the Indian community after graduation. On the other hand, one American Indian, a graduate of an eastern Ivy League school attended by few Indians and now a successful professional, has this to say: "I'd advise an Indian against taking Indian cultural courses and against enrolling in a college with a large Indian population. If he wishes to compete in the larger society with non-Indians, courses other than Indian cultural courses and competition with non-Indians in school will be of the greatest value to him. And Indians in colleges with a large minority enrollment frequently feel the backlash of discrimination that can come when there is a concentration of a minority population."

▲ COUNSELING EXCERPT 5: LUIS

A Puerto Rican youth has the desire to achieve in school and wants to feel good about himself, but he fears his domineering father and can't seem to please him.

(Luis and his father were requested to see the high school counselor after the father had reported to the school to reinstate Luis, who had been suspended for many unexcused absences. The father tells Luis in Spanish to wait in the hallway while he talks with the counselor.)

Counselor: I'm sure you must feel relieved now that Luis has been admitted back to school.

Father: Señora, Luis gonna give no trouble. Plez, lemma know. Es obstinado, no respecto! No worry. Luis es OK.

(The interaction, although brief, superficial, and hindered by the language barrier between the counselor and father, seems at least a basis for understanding. Besides, the counselor has five students and another parent waiting to see her. Two weeks later, Luis again shows his usual pattern of truancy.)

Counselor: Luis, I just don't understand you. You've done so well in school before, but you've cut all these classes. And yet you still say you didn't. Can you bring me up to date on what's going on? Are you getting along with your teachers? And what was that fight about that you and Carlos had?

(Takes a "shotgun" approach in trying to understand his situation; excessive absence seems to be only a symptom of what is happening in Luis's life, but the confrontation of symptoms is a first step)

Client: I *was* in my classes!

Counselor: Now look, you know that's not true. Why do you continue to say that? Even your father knows that when he came in with you after the last suspension. . . .

(In the United States, it is unusual for the father to take responsibility for the children's education, whether due to cultural tradition or inability to take off work or absence of the father; by default or by tradition, the mother often assumes the major responsibility)

Client: Hey, get off my case. I can't do everything perfect. And please leave my father out of this.

Counselor: What do you mean by "everything"?

(Seeks concreteness in Luis's statement)

Client: I've got to please teachers, Mr.— [assistant principal in charge of attendance], the whole school, my father, and now you.

Counselor: How is that? It sounds like you believe nothing is going right.

Client: No, I'm all right. I'm jes not sure. . . . Hey, didn't you respect your father when you were my age? No, I guess a woman wouldn't understand that. A man protects his honor and his family.

Counselor: Why don't you test me, Luis? If you would talk about it, you could do something about what's bugging you. How is *respect* getting blocked?   *(Doesn't let his sex-role attitude get to her; seeks to establish in his mind the confidence and optimism for a solution)*

After a number of sessions with Luis, two emotional home visits by the family priest, and a counseling session with Luis and his parents, rapport and an understanding of the complexity of the situation are established. It is natural for any family unit to be protective of its members from outside intrusions or threats to the status quo. Often, the family props up a single member who has personal inadequacies that are being met through the family structure. This is the situation for Luis's family, in which the father harshly dominates the children and his submissive wife by taking every opportunity to prove his masculinity.

● IMMEDIATE COUNSELING PROBLEM

The immediate problem for Luis is to acknowledge the fact that he is unhappy with himself and his truancy problem. It is also important for him to see that he isn't abandoning respect and loyalty to his family because he is exploring possible changes in what seems to him to be one big, endless conflict with no solution. Getting a feeling of control over himself and responsibility for his life is essential. Another problem for the counselor, as it is for many school counselors, is to separate herself from being perceived as a judgmental arm of the administration and to let Luis see her as someone who can be a source of help. Absenteeism and class-cutting are a major issue for many urban and suburban schools and can often be attributed to social, psychological, and even physical abuse problems. Taking a positive approach to the problem is especially important and necessary when many of the students are poor. Reducing absenteeism, class-cutting, and behavior problems is best accomplished through counseling of students and parents. Also important are visits to parents' homes for counseling and discussing solutions for things such as baby sitting, work, and parent-child relations that might keep students out of school. The cooperation of parents with school personnel is essential in monitoring their children's progress. Providing nutritious meals, proper rest, and a quiet place to study are also important responsibilities of parents that should be discussed. Some schools have inaugurated a behavior contract approach with parents for their children, stating specific outcomes that can be successfully achieved (Brown, 1982).

● COUNSELING GOALS

Puerto Ricans are often divided into at least three groups: older immigrants, recent immigrants, and those born and reared on the mainland. Each has a different generational frame of reference and espousal of traditions. Painful role reversals and changes in male-female and parent-child relations, which are often experienced in the process of cultural assimilation, can contribute to family tension or even family disorganization if not reconciled in some manner.

Luis's father speaks little English, keeps to himself at his place of employment, which employs Spanish-speaking Puerto Ricans, and displays a strong machismo attitude in most aspects of his life. His security in his family seems to depend on his need to be an aggressive and superior figure. The fact that neither the father nor mother speaks much English after having lived on the mainland for 20 years, while Luis has become increasingly bilingual and bicultural, seems to have pushed the father into fits of rage directed toward Luis. Luis's mother is a passive spectator in the family dynamics, but she usually takes a moderator role in family arguments. Although members of any cultural group adapt and do change according to contemporary demands (Ruiz, 1981, pp. 191–192), Luis's father and mother adhere rather strongly to the traditional sex-role relations that might be found in many families in Puerto Rico. In this case, the father's sense of masculinity is expressed through excessive physical and psychological dominance, while the mother assumes a submissive and nurturant role. Machismo, as an aspect of personality, is an exaggerated assertion of masculinity and is the way that one faces challenges.

Guiding the father and mother to use their learned roles in ways that are more adaptable for contemporary times and more helpful for Luis are major counseling goals. The father will be invited to visit the school to become familiar with the curriculum and to meet Luis's teachers, encouraged to participate in community action groups, and counseled to relate to himself as a man in new ways that are more realistic and flattering for him, his family, and his relations with Luis. His cultural traditions and his desire for a strong, close-knit family are respected and viewed as strengths that will continue to be important and valued.

■ COUNSELING EXCERPTS: WORK AND CAREER DEVELOPMENT

▲ COUNSELING EXCERPT 6: DIANE

Diane is anxious but excited about her prospects for a job as first level clerical supervisor, and the employment interview seems to be going well. (Although not considered a counseling interview, this dialogue has implications for the work of counselors.)

Interviewer: Tell me about yourself, Diane.

(Wants to know about her qualifications)

Diane: I completed my associate degree in personnel and office procedures a year ago. I really enjoyed the program and feel that it gave me good preparation in supervisory approaches, office organization, and the use of business machines. I had a really well-rounded and thorough six-month internship at—— Company, where I was able to get experience in just about every segment of the office routine. My supervisors were very competent and so interested in giving their ideas on how to do the work the best way possible.

(Concisely and briefly describes her education and some of her practical experiences)

Interviewer: Sounds like a good training experience for you. Is there any reason why you wouldn't have wanted to be employed there?

(This question has the potential for arousing defensive behavior; interviewer may be wondering why she didn't stay there)

Diane: Well, you see, as part of the training purpose, future employment was understood not to be part of the internship contract.

(Straightforward answer)

Interviewer: Oh, I see. Tell me about the other work experience you have had.

Diane: Since graduation, I have been employed at —— Company, where I am responsible for the major part of the word processing operation. The assigned work basically involves the preparation of promotional material that is mailed out to certain target populations. I've had the opportunity to participate in the complete process from entering the original material into the computer to enveloping and preparing it for mail-out.

Interviewer: What did you like most and what did you like least about the work?

(This is a motive question intended to determine if she enjoys doing the job)

Diane: I really enjoy being able to see the whole job through from the beginning to the end. It gives me a sense of accomplishment. Of course, we never really get to see how effective the promotional materials are. At times, I feel there are excessive pressures to meet deadlines, and sometimes if someone doesn't get their part completed, I don't have as much control over my part. I don't enjoy taking home the feeling of not getting a job done.

Interviewer: I see. What kind of a clerical supervisor would you want to be? I noticed that you're married. Do you have children or do you plan to have children?

(This starts off as a person- ality question to determine if she has the qualities being sought, but gets entangled with a possible stereotype re- lated to her marital and family status and could be in violation of statutes related to sex discrimi- nation)

Diane: Ah . . . well, in answer to your first question, I believe that it's important for the members of an office unit to fully understand and cooperate with the orga- nized plan for the work. As a supervisor, I would want to have good communication and be consistent and fair as much as possible. For your second question, my husband and I, like many young married couples, want children to complement our family. It's an important thing in our lives, but I'm having trouble seeing how that might be related to the job as it's been described or how it might affect my performance on the job. Is there something else about the work that I'm not aware of?

(She wants to make it clear that she is handling his statement as two separate questions; Gives asser- tive and straightforward, honest answer as she sees her situation, with- out trying to make the inter- viewer feel that he asked something wrong)

Interviewer: Oh, ah, ha, ha . . . ah, I can empathize with your desire that you previously stated in not wanting to

(Regains his composure, per-

carry job problems home with you. The work that's involved is really calculated so that it can be accomplished in the normal working day. What salary do you expect?

haps realizing that he had asked some questions irrelevant to potential job performance)

Diane: I'm presently earning $ —— , and although I expect an increase, I don't know enough about the opportunity as yet.

(She is negotiating from a position of strength and avoids answering this question until the job is offered)

● IMMEDIATE INTERVIEW SITUATION

Until the interviewer asks Diane whether she has or is going to have children, the job interview proceeds in fairly routine fashion. Both participants are communicating and performing well in their given roles. As a technical matter, the question per se is probably not illegal. But the interviewer is treading a thin line. If the interviewer had said that the employer only wanted someone unmarried, or married, or someone with or without children, it would have indicated a discriminatory intention and Diane could file a complaint. The worst thing that Diane could do when the interviewer asks her about having children is to become defensive, elusive, or antagonistic. These are nonaffirming responses, and her application would be sure to be dropped. She recognizes that it is a critical situation: if she answers as she truly believes and feels, she may lose the job because of the employer's possible prejudice; if she protests, she risks being labeled a troublemaker and an unsuitable job applicant. She recognizes the question as possibly discriminatory and she doesn't want her response to hurt her chances of getting the job, but she also doesn't want the interviewer to get away with asking the question and possibly confusing the issue, which is what her competencies actually are. Her affirmative manner of handling the question doesn't hurt the interviewer and probably causes the interviewer to think, "Now, that was a dumb question to ask her."

Some interviewers may try to hide their biased intentions and say that they are not going to use the information, but that they need to know it for filling out insurance forms once the applicant is hired or in order to give her information about company benefits. Filling out forms can be done after the hiring decision has been made, and company benefits can be explained without asking personal questions. Some questions that are seemingly discriminatory may be legitimate, depending on the situation. For example, interviewers may ask about child-care arrangements if they are concerned that applicants may be away from work often if their children become ill or perhaps (as Diane's interviewer may have thought) when a young infant needs special care. Applicants can point out that there won't be a problem because they can make arrangements for someone to take care of the children. If child care seems to be an issue, applicants can also show that their absenteeism has been only a certain percent in their current job, despite family responsibilities. By keeping the issues clear, the individual can focus on actual qualifications for employment and keep away from stereotypes. Sometimes it helps to foresee awkward questions that may arise, and it may be best to bring them up as soon as the interview begins. By explaining a situation, one can often handle what could be a potential negative as a positive.

● COUNSELING GOALS

Counselors can help their clients to become better job interviewees by pointing out situations such as the one Diane had to face and showing them how to recognize the differences between fair and unfair questions and the differences between appropriate and inappropriate answers. Some areas of questioning that are faced by applicants may be clearly discriminatory; for example:

applicant's mother tongue
applicant's birthplace or nationality
whether applicant's name has been changed
applicant's marital status and dependents
applicant's handicaps
applicant's religious affiliation
applicant's draft classification
date and conditions of military discharge
number and kind of applicant's arrests
applicant's age or date of birth

In most states an applicant may be asked how many times he or she has been convicted of felonies and the types of felonies, but how the information is used may be discriminatory. Some racial and ethnic minorities, according to national statistics, are arrested more often than others, and a company that has a policy of not hiring those who have been arrested can be discriminatory. A fair interviewer will look at the type of conviction, how long ago it occurred, and whether there have been any infractions since. The offense may be relevant only if it applied to the particular job in question. Obviously an applicant who has been convicted of theft may be a questionable candidate for a cashier's job. In addition to specific qualifications, interviewers are usually interested during an interview in answering for themselves the following two basic questions: (1) What is this person telling me about himself or herself? (2) What kind of person is he or she?

To get at answers to these questions, interviewers often assess the following personality characteristics:

Interviewee's Personal Characteristics	Interviewer's Possible Questions
Attitude	"Ever lose in competition? Feelings? " "What duties did you like most in your last job? Least?"
Motivation	"How will this job get you what you want?"
Initiative	"How did you get into this line of work?" "When have you felt like giving up on a task? Tell me about it."
Stability	"How do you get along with people you dislike?" "What things disturb you the most?" "What have been your most pleasant work experiences?"
Planning	"Where do you want to be five years from now?"
Insight	"Tell me about your strengths/weaknesses."
Social skills	"What do you like to do in your spare time?" "How would you go about making friends?"

Other areas that affect employment opportunity are the responsibility of employers themselves and must be carefully monitored in order to ensure fair treatment. The verbal and nonverbal behavior toward applicants by company personnel, ranging from the guard at the gate to the receptionist, can subtly convey that a person is not desired. If screening tests are given to applicants, the content must be sufficient and accurate. Questions on application forms must relate strictly to job performance, and objective care must be taken in how the raw data is used. For example, rejection of a large percentage of applicants who live in a particular neighborhood or area may be evidence of discrimination or lack of an affirmative action effort. Basing a hiring decision on an individual's credit rating, or whether he or she has had wage garnishment, would be a questionable practice. Since a high percentage of racial/ethnic minorities are still found in low-paying jobs, their wages are garnished more often than those of nonminorities. The following guidelines are recommended by the Equal Employment Opportunity Commission when reviewing application forms:

- Do questions tend to have a disproportionate effect in screening out minorities or females?
- Is the information necessary for judging an individual's competence to perform a particular job?
- Are there alternative, nondiscriminatory ways to secure necessary information?

▲ COUNSELING EXCERPT 7: CHUYEN

A Vietnamese refugee family needs help in the transition to work and life in the United States. Family members are as follows:

wife: Chuyen, age 25
husband: Kien, age 27
children: Kim, age 7; Van, age 6
Chuyen's sister Lan, age 16
Kien's mother, age 60

(The following excerpt is an interview with Chuyen by a counselor who works for the Comprehensive Employment and Training Act program. Because of Chuyen's lack of fluency in English, the excerpt has been edited so that the content and scope of the issues and problems faced by Chuyen and her family can be better understood.)

Counselor: How are things going now that you and your family have settled into your new apartment?

Client: Yes. *(Smiles and glances down)*

Counselor: Sometimes moving into a strange neighborhood and new home brings problems.

Client: Many things for Kien fix up, work hard . . . need stove, one [burner] only work, but cos' so much. Friends [sponsors] help get good price, and get TV.

Counselor: A TV?

(Seems startled at the request for a TV)

Client: Yes *(glances up at counselor)*, TV help learn American way, American words.

Counselor: Oh, I see. Yes, that will help. And how is school going for Kim, Van, and Lan?

Client: Yes, they get good education, get better life. Can no teach English Kim and Van, school help . . . *(Pauses)* . . . worry abou' Lan. Change so much, go far from Vietnamese way. She have American boyfriend. Want be like American. *(Smiles, and becomes very quiet, looks at floor, seems embarrassed by what she has said)*

Counselor: You seem sad.

Client: *(Grins and laughs)* My father tell me take care of Lan. My brothers all made dead by soldiers . . . only me left to watch Lan . . . *(Pauses)* . . . our boat ge' Thai pirates. Lan and me make face black, hide in boat . . . no see us! *(Laughs and begins to sob quietly)* Oh, excuse me.

Counselor: That's OK. I know it's difficult to talk about those past days and the things that hurt you. And it's a big responsibility to look out for Lan. It's all right to show me how you feel. I won't take it as being impolite to me and I'll try to help you in any way I can—

including listening and caring for how you feel about something that hurts or makes you sad or angry. It's my job to help you with things that are difficult for you.

Client: Oh *(Faint smile)* so many problems, wan' to please father, help Kien . . .

Counselor: Yes, that's all important to you. How is Kien's job training going for him?

Client: Kien in Vietnam, big navy officer . . . now nothing- . . . feel bad, but training good . . . become computer-electronic man. That good for him, get job, more money, feel better.

Counselor: Yes, that's a good thing for your family.   *(Recognizes strength of the family as a unit)*

Client: Thank you.   *(Polite forms of expression are used only with great care and sincerity)*

Counselor: Let's talk now about the work that you want. You said before that you like to sew. That's a skill that you have that you can use right now to add to the family income.

Client: Yes, make clothes for children, mend Kien's shirt.

Counselor: I know. You showed me some of the good work you have done. There's a job that I'd like to see you try at the — — store. It will be to alter clothes that customers buy.

Client: Oh . . . speak little English, so har' for me, make   *(Afraid, but others feel bad . . . no way go store . . . can't find seems willing . . . where bus?   to take the risk)*

● IMMEDIATE COUNSELING PROBLEM

Chuyen faces a constellation of practical questions and personal issues. One immediate problem is coping with the frightening prospect of the job at the clothing store. She is fearful that she will not be able to communicate adequately and might embarrass her employer or others. Actually, except for the basic instructions for alteration for each piece of clothing, the job would involve little ongoing reliance on English language skills and would be done in relative isolation from the rest of the social activity in the store. In fact, the situation could discourage her desire to continue her classes in English as a second language (ESL). The counselor should keep this possibility in mind, while encouraging her attendance in the ESL classes. ESL classes will help her develop a command of language skills and also provide her with assistance in the social conventions for functioning in the culture and adapting to the community. A well-planned ESL class will provide simulated life experiences that are related to social functioning in the American culture.

Chuyen needs a lot of personal and emotional support to help raise her self-expectations and confidence in facing her fear of the unknown situation. The store is willing to take her on, under the CETA program plan for partial reimbursement of her wages. The counselor's cooperation with the work supervisor in the form of suggestions for communication with Chuyen and occasional follow-up phone calls will be helpful to all parties. The practical questions of transportation and location of the store can be readily resolved by explaining bus schedules and cost. The counselor should go with Chuyen on the first day of work, with the expectation that Chuyen will gain self-sufficiency in these practical everyday matters. Chuyen's desire to contribute to the family income is an incentive, and the development of independent employment functioning is the ultimate goal.

● COMMUNICATION PATTERNS

Attention to Chuyen's social behavior during the counseling session reveals a communication style that might be unexpected or puzzling to non-Asian counselors. These are some of the more obvious features of her communication pattern.

Humility. Many traditional Indochinese women and men have learned to value politeness, humility, and modesty as important social graces that give harmony and balance to interpersonal relations. Humility might be interpreted by non-Asians as shyness or passiveness; however, expressions of humility are intended to show reserve toward a person one does not know well. It is also polite to show respect and obedience for elders, superiors, and authorities. Not to disagree openly in order to maintain harmony in a social situation is important. *Traditionally,* children are taught to conceal antisocial emotions, such as anger and hostility, as a stoic way to preserve the peace and harmony and as a way to save face of others in interpersonal relations. Restraint of personal feelings and unwillingness to disclose personal problems or to reveal emotions will work against traditional counseling goals of self-disclosure. Therefore, openness as a basis of understanding and talking out problems in a traditional counseling process will not be possible to the same degree as with most culturally assimilated Americans. Group therapy and group counseling will not be as effective as it otherwise might because of their reluctance to verbalize feelings and confront others (Tran, 1981, p. 7).

"Yes." Not to disagree is a component of humility. "Yes" may be merely a polite acknowledgment of something the counselor has said. It does not necessarily mean understanding or agreement, but simply that the client is listening and paying attention. Many will answer "yes" if they believe that it is the desired answer or fear that a negative reply would be rude; thus, a "yes"

may also mean "no" or "maybe." The counselor can gain some clarity of understanding by ignoring the initial "yes" and concentrating on the statement that follows the "yes."

Smiling. Smiling in the American culture usually means happiness, agreement, affirmation, assent, acquiescence, or simple acknowledgment. It may signify the same thing to Asians, but smiling can also indicate confusion, fear, embarrassment, disappointment, rejection, bitterness, or even anger and hostility. Smiling that is inconsistent with underlying emotional states and feelings may seem inappropriate to most Americans, but it is a polite and stoic way to hide undesirable impulses and is admired by Asians.

Eye contact and physical touching. Pattern of eye contact is often interpreted in counseling theory as related to the psychological impact of the content of the client's message. Evasion of eye contact, for example, may indicate anxiety about the topic being discussed. However, traditional Vietnamese people have been brought up to respect and accept orders and directions from elders, superiors, and authorities. Directing the gaze downward, or glancing up only occasionally, can also be interpreted as polite deference to the counselor. "Eye avoidance is especially noticeable in girls and in the lower class," writes Tran nhu Chuong (1981, p. 7). Being quiet and sitting quietly are part of the respect that comes from listening to the guidance of elders and superiors. "Touching a young person on the head is offensive to them. Also, social touching of the opposite sex is usually not done in the Vietnamese culture except [with] family members" (Tran, 1981, p. 7).

Status and hierarchical roles. Deference to age, profession, and marital status is acceptable to traditional Vietnamese culture. A counselor in a society that emphasizes equality and freedom can experience a conflict of values in facing what might seem to him or her to be differential or preferential treatment of clients based on sex, age, or occupational status. The counselor must remember, first, that objective perception of the client's situation and background is basic to counseling ethics. Also basic is assisting clients toward individual expression that is most developmental for them. Any counseling approach takes into consideration where the client is in his or her life, and each situation must be faced in ways that are best for the individuals as they define and redefine the meaning that life has for them. For example, an alert counselor should be sensitive to Confucian customs and, if deemed appropriate, talk to the husband before talking to the wife to make the husband feel that he is head of his family. The same principle holds true in showing respect through communication with Vietnamese elders. If group activities are conducted by counselors for presenting information or other such purposes, and if some level of verbal exchange or discussion is desirable among the participants, consideration should be given to organizing the groups either by self-choice or by age and profession. Placing husband and wife in different groups is especially recommended in a classroom situation, where, in deference to her spouse, a wife may be hesitant "so as not to overshadow the progress and ability of her husband" (Intercultural Development Research Association, 1976, p. 34).

● COUNSELING GOALS

Chuyen is also troubled by a number of personal issues and concerns that involve her cultural identity and sense of responsibility. The counselor should pay attention to them if the counseling sessions are to continue. The heavy burden of guardianship of Lan, placed on Chuyen by her father, needs exploration and adjustment to a kind of responsibility that is more in line with the present situation for both Chuyen and Lan. Chuyen's submissive role in the patriarchal family relationship may also have potential for conflict when she moves into full employment if she cannot continue her traditional role of wife and mother, as her husband may expect, or if she desires modification of her role. Kien's mother can be a possible harmonizing resource in care of the children, although elderly Vietnamese who are used to traditional language and ways often find themselves alone and alienated when the children and grandchildren become oriented to the American language and culture. To most elderly Asian Americans, the real world is the old world. In the old world, "the elderly are considered important, integral members of the family" (Montero, 1979, p. 31). The United States culture, in many ways, tends to treat the aged as second-class citizens who are expected to behave in a helpless, even childlike way. Finally, the potential for identity confusion *or* identity growth could be experienced by Chuyen in contemporary U.S. culture if she encounters feminist ire toward patriarchy. Sensitive understanding of what it means to be caught between two cultures is important, and helping the client decide how best to resolve the dilemmas is called for.

● TRADITIONAL VIETNAMESE CULTURE

Knowing the cultural background of Vietnamese and other Indochinese people is important in order for effective counseling to take place. Under Chinese domination for hundreds of years, until 939 A.D., the Vietnamese culture and that of other Indochinese countries is based on Confucian teachings. Confucian doctrine guides the national rulers, who guide the religious leaders and teachers, who in turn instruct the people. Likewise, the father guides the son and the husband guides the wife. Traditional Asian women are obedient to the father, and to their elder brothers if they have any, to the husband when married, and to the oldest son when widowed. Under their belief system, women are responsible and loyal to men and their self-identity is always relative to men (daughter, sister, wife, mother). For Chuyen, who abides by traditional ways, her major identity is as wife and mother.

Other belief forms—Buddhism, Taoism and, in rural areas, animism— have also influenced Indochinese people. French domination from 1876 to 1945 also infused Western concepts of equality and freedom into the culture of Indochinese countries, especially in urban centers, as did the U.S. presence in South Vietnam. During the war years, from 1945 to 1975, Vietnamese women had to play major leadership roles in the family and many became more involved in the society. Briefly, the contributions of the various belief forms that shape the complex mosaic of cultural personality are as follows:

· Confucianism—Patriarchal ideas are embraced and a formal relationship system emphasizes humility, politeness, and respect.

· Buddhism—Self-improvement can be found through doing good work and study and through the control of undesirable emotions; optimism, inner calmness, and harmony are valued.

· Taoism—Ancestor worship provides guidance and advice for present living. Refugees have lost the opportunity for ancestor worship, a circumstance that for many may produce a sense of loneliness and the feeling that they are incapable of making decisions without ancestral advice. Traditionally, followers of Taoism are attached to burial sites (location) of ancestors, where they can go to pray, meditate, and pay respects before the graves of the ancestors. The annual visit to the burial site is also viewed as a moment of celebration and an opportunity for social interaction with relatives; "After the ceremony, the family usually enjoys a pleasant picnic at the grave site" (Crane, 1967, p. 23).

· Westernism—Teaches the importance of equality, freedom, and individual direction.

Rural dwellers tend to adhere to traditional cultural ways more than do urban dwellers. The Hmong and Mien refugee people are special examples in whom cultural conflict may be inevitable. Consisting largely of illiterate farmers who migrated from Mongolian China to the mountains of Laos and Thailand in the 19th century, they were conscripted by the United States as guerrilla fighters during the Vietnam War. Estimates are that almost two-thirds of their clan were exterminated by the Vietnamese. Their special problems in American culture include coping with electrical conveniences, indoor sanitation, "strange" processed foods, urban jobs, mass transit systems, medical and health approaches, and the fast pace of city life. According to Baldwin (1981), "Their animist religious background instills in them the belief that all living things have spirits, and that illness, or a sick spirit, can be removed by a sacrifice of a chicken or pig" (in the home) (p. 138).

The degree of exposure to Western culture, French and American, will also influence the world view of Indochinese people. In addition, the father's former occupation will give some indication of possible adjustment problems in the current situation. Consideration of each condition can provide counselors with basic cues indicating a method for working with each client.

■ COUNSELING EXCERPTS: SOCIAL AND PERSONAL GROWTH

▲ COUNSELING EXCERPT 8: RUBEN

A transfer student to a large university expresses feelings of alienation and explores some critical family experiences.

Counselor gives a brief orientation to various aspects of the counseling process, including confidentiality, mutual responsibilities, and decision making.)

Counselor: Well, Ruben, what brings you here today?

Client: I'm in this psychology class on personal development and mental health . . . and I've been doing a lot of thinking about myself lately . . . it's become sort of a project with me and the instructor suggested I work on it with a counselor. *(Quietly laughs to himself)*

(Indicates motivation to work on "something"; instructor's relationship with client seems to have played some role)

Counselor: Ha! I guess that's one way to look at yourself and life—as a project! You might as well be practical about it. Just how do you think counseling might help?

(Tries to clarify client's motivation through how he perceives counseling might help him)

Client: I'm a transfer student from —— Community College.

(Doesn't respond to counselor's statement)

Counselor: Oh, yes, I used to live near there. Tell me about yourself.

Client: OK. I'm 26, come from a big family—seven of us kids. I'm the youngest. I was born and raised in Mexico for 11 years and we moved to California for 2 years and then came to Michigan, where my father got a better job and where we've lived ever since. While going to the community college I worked part-time with mentally handicapped people in a home.

(Wants counselor to know about him by detailing his experiences)

Counselor: How did you get started in that experience?

Client: Well, I worked in a restaurant for seven years and a friend had told me about the job. It didn't appeal to me at first, but I got so tired of working in the same restaurant . . . and found that working with the handicapped people gave me a rewarding feeling to help them with things like combing their hair and helping them eat. They seemed to be so friendly and warm— something I haven't seen from other people in the outside world . . . ha, ha.

(Shows that getting and giving affection is an important need for him; Wants close relationships, but can't seem to get them)

Counselor: The restaurant work was really just a job to earn money?

(Doesn't pick up on the client's most recent statement)

Client: I'm a hard-working person, but that wasn't my idea of a job for me—cleaning, washing dishes, et cetera.

Counselor: Did it seem demeaning?

(Shows a value judgment of client's work)

Client: No, I wouldn't say demeaning; to some people, they like cooking and that's fine. Not only that, but—if I can explain it—I couldn't really get to know the people there. But I didn't have any other skills. I want to get into a biology/nutrition major if I can keep my grade-point average up. I got into the whole physical fitness thing back at the community college.

(Corrects counselor's perception)

Counselor: It sounds like you might enjoy that kind of career, and also that you enjoy working with the mentally handicapped. How does that fit in?

(Counselor tries to "fit" client's statement into a work/career development frame of reference)

Client: Maybe as something to fall back on. I'm really too shy and withdrawn to be a teacher or something like that.

(Client seems convinced that he is more of an inward person than an outward person)

Counselor: No, I don't think so—perhaps you just feel more comfortable in relating one-on-one. Do you relate to the type of work that your father does?

(Counselor doesn't seem to want to relate to this aspect of the client, but apparently wants to make some association between client's career interests and the father's occupation)

Client: Well . . . my father was a factory worker until he got laid off, then he worked in a laundry.

Counselor: Does your mother work?

(A "stab in the dark"; counselor has lost direction in the relationship with client)

Client: No, she's never worked . . . my father wouldn't allow it.

Counselor: Oh, I guess there are many people like that.

(Counselor's attention has shifted to an issue that seems unrelated to where client is at)

Client: *(Becomes silent, as if he's thinking about something)* It seems like everybody is in their own little world in my classes . . . and . . . basically, maybe it's just me. . . . I'll say hello or smile, but people here think you're trying to do something against them—and look the other way or avoid looking at you.

(Redirects the topic content to his personal self; feels human contact is missing)

Counselor: Ha, ha, maybe they're all freshmen. All the streets are like that, aren't they? What did you expect?

(Counselor continues to depersonalize the client's expressions of his experience)

Client: I'd like more friendly feelings in return. I'm shy, but I'll make the first move. I always thought it was good to move out to others.

(Ignores the counselor's overgeneralizations and asserts his desire to make contact with others)

Counselor: You say you're shy, but in greeting others you're not shy.

(Counselor doesn't seem to accept client's perception of his shyness and tries a confrontation strategy)

Client: I think I can explain that, uh ... I can't get my thoughts together now ...
(Long pause)

(Client is thrown by sudden confrontation because the counselor has neglected to facilitate basic exploration and understanding of the meaning that experiences have had for the client; action without some meaning is usually unproductive)

Counselor: Well, it seems like one-on-one is OK like we're doing now, but group relating is a different proposition. Has it always been this way for you?

(Counselor's interpretations are presented as "closed" statements, but at least there is some movement toward facilitating understanding of what's going on in the client's perceptions)

Client: I guess so. ... I'd say family environment has something to do with it. My dad, ah ...

Counselor: Can you expand a bit on your family?

(Finally, seems to support what client wants)

Client: I'd say ... let's see ... how can I describe it? There was always tension between my dad and my brothers and sisters. My dad wanted each of us to study real hard. We didn't come here for nothing. He couldn't get an education in Mexico ... couldn't make it on his job in Mexico to provide for us. Even his job washing dishes in California was better; he came over first and was alone in this country for about three years. When he was gone my brothers became independent. See ... my dad was very domineering and strict—they resented it—you know, be home early, always study. My sisters weren't allowed to date or go out alone. Being the youngest, I saw all this. My mother is very loving, my dad unloving. There was so much pain and suffering—with my mother crying and everybody fighting. . . .

Counselor: Ruben, I've noticed that you've been using "was" when you talk about your father. . . .

Client: Oh ... I guess I forgot to tell you. My dad is dead.

Counselor: I see. How long has it been?

Client: Well, ah ... three years ... that was a real hard time for me.

Counselor: Oh, yeah, I guess so. It must have been.   *(Genuinely shows his feelings for the death experience)*

Client: Like I told you, he was strict. Most of us never got close to him, like we did with my mother. I was the only one at home when he had a stroke. It was a scary thing. . . . I can still remember the moment when he died. That same day we had a discussion that we didn't like each other. I was holding him face to face and he said "Let me go, let me go," but I had to hold him because the doctor was injecting something into him. When your dad is dying and at the same time you want him to die, and at the same time you are so guilty, so guilty because you are, you know, not supposed to wish your dad's death ... I've not really accepted him, see.

● IMMEDIATE COUNSELING PROBLEM

A counselor-client relationship discrepancy has permeated most of this excerpt. It is only toward the end that the counselor finally starts to listen and hear what Ruben is trying to say: that he sees himself as unassertive, perceives others as being unresponsive to him, and cannot accept the father side of himself. He wants to share these things in a personal way with the counselor. His persistence and patience in sharing his personal side in spite of the counselor's insensitivity is a strength. It also shows that he has issues that he wants to do something about. If the counselor can overcome his own resistance to accepting a more personal relationship with Ruben and assist him with his thoughts and feelings, movement in the counseling process can occur.

● COUNSELING GOALS

To feel alienated in a new or different environment is not an unusual predicament for many people, and most establish friendship ties and adjust after a period of time. Ruben seems to have strong needs to establish some kind of meaningful human contacts. Family experiences that have influenced Ruben's thoughts and feelings are touched upon during the interview. Continued exploration of these experiences, how they affect his view of himself and others, and what it was that he might have learned would be one goal. Developing awareness of both the reasonable (realistic) and unreasonable (unrealistic) demands (expectations) that he places on himself and others would constitute an important step toward this goal and would also help control the stress and anxiety, which could be caused by his self-imposed fear of the possibility of not being recognized or even of being rejected. It would also help him to accept simple disappointments. Working on reducing unrealistic expectations of himself and others and emphasizing reasonable expectations would be an important part of this step. Finally, the practice of skills aimed toward enhancing his social contacts and getting desired responses from others in everyday situations of interpersonal relating would help him to overcome his shyness and allow him to become more confident. It would provide him with immediate feedback that would give reinforcement and/or cues for continued shaping of his own behavior in order to get what he wants or needs. Determining how much exploration for self-understanding, changing of attitudes, and real-life practice he needs or wants is Ruben's prerogative at this time in his life. He is motivated by a desire to get responses from others, to have his presence recognized, and to be known for who he is; but he is also cautious about negative experiences that can result from relationships. Personal encouragement and support by the counselor for achieving what he wants are an ongoing part of the counseling process.

A more complex issue for Ruben is the unfinished business with his father and the circumstances surrounding his father's death. It is an emotional release for him just to share the relationship that he experienced with his father, but most likely additional working through of unwanted feelings and perceptions will be necessary. The conflict between disliking his father and a guilty feeling that he should respect or like him needs perceptual adjustment. Perhaps the dichotomy can be resolved through an integration of both positives and negatives. Learning new meanings for the old experience will help put it into the past and bring Ruben into the present.

▲ COUNSELING EXCERPT 9: NICK

At the insistence of his wife, a 27-year-old man sees a counselor; he has drinking and family problems.

Client: I'd like some information about drinking. My wife seems to think I have a problem.

Counselor: She thinks you have a problem? What is the problem?

Client: I guess so. She thinks I drink too often.

Counselor: What do you think?

(Seeks the client's perceptions)

Client: I don't believe there's a problem, but she thinks there is. I do drink alcoholic beverages, but I can hold my own pretty well.

Counselor: Uh? How do you mean that?

(Seeks clarification and concreteness)

Client: Well, see, I've been drinking since I was a teenager and I know how to handle it. I've always been careful not to drive or anything like that if I think I had too much. I will admit that I did some heavy drinking during the time I was in the service.

Counselor: Oh, yeah, can you fill me in?

Client: You probably know how military service is if you've served time. On weekends there's nothing to do except go out, get drunk, and look for girls. I was young then and really inexperienced. I guess I enlisted partly because I didn't know what I wanted in life and I was having some problems at home.

(Perceives his drinking pattern as caused by external events)

Counselor: It was kind of a hassle for you at that time, eh? What kind of problems were you having at home?

(Accepts client's feeling of stress, but seeks concreteness)

Client: Oh, my parents were constantly on me to go to college or some kind of vocational training. I just couldn't take the constant yelling.

Counselor: That seemed to put some heavy pressure on you at that time, eh?

(Accepts his feeling of stress)

Client: Yeah . . . but the army wasn't a total flop. I did learn auto mechanics.

Counselor: Is that your present work?

Client: Yeah, I'm really good at what I do, too. I wish my wife would see more of that in me, instead of complaining about my drinking.

(Feels his personal worth goes unrecognized)

Counselor: You think she's only seeing the drinking part of you?

(Recognizes his view and encourages further exploration)

Client: I guess you could put it that way. She's always worrying, or nagging, or complaining, or whatever you'd call it about my not making more money and not having more education. She really bugs me when she compares me with some of the other guys in our neighborhood. I provide for our family but she thinks we're just making ends meet.

(Perceives his wife as "hitting" on him rather than as communicating personal needs)

Counselor: What do you think?

(A kind of challenge to get him to think through his own perceptions)

Client: You know how it is, there's always more things a family could have, or want. I'm satisfied with our standard of living. If she'd just pay more attention to her family responsibilities instead of getting on my case all the time, things would be better.

Counselor: What especially bugs you?

(Aims for concreteness)

Client: Ha, ha . . . well, for one she's always running around to some community group or carting the kids to some activity. I come home and there's a note that says my supper is in the fridge. Who'd like that!

Counselor: Sort of like being left out in the cold, eh?

(Recognizes his feelings)

Client: Hell, yes! Well, kinda . . . *(Becomes quiet)*
(Pause)

Counselor: What do you do when you find yourself alone at those times?

(Counselor might have asked him what was on his mind at that moment)

Client: Well, I'll tell you . . . I'm usually so tired, or grouchy I guess, when I come home that it helps me to have a couple of drinks or beers, watch TV, and fall asleep.

Counselor: Do you sometimes drink before coming home?

(Wants to know more about his drinking pattern)

Client: That's probably one thing that bugs her. Yeah, the guys from the shop will have a few after work— you know, we talk about things at work and just socialize.

Counselor: And how do you usually feel when you get home?

Client: Uh? Well . . . it depends—sometimes I feel pissed.

Counselor: What are you pissed at? How do you show it?

(Aims for clarification and concreteness)

Client: Hey, the first thing I have to face is her nagging or something about what the kids did. Yeah, I can get physical sometimes, like slap the kids for misbehaving or making too much noise, but I really feel awful afterward.

(Admits that he does things that he regrets)

Counselor: You really don't like to do that, do you?

(Recognizes his predicament)

Client: No, but they usually deserve it. I suppose I could cut down on hitting the bars after work . . . one thing happened to me that really scared me . . . *(Pauses)*

(Tries to justify his actions and resolve his guilt)

Counselor: What was that? Do you want to fill me in?

(Encourages exploration)

Client: Well, this one time I was feeling lousy after work and was really hitting the bars when I met this old friend who I hadn't seen since high school days—an old drinking buddy, ha, ha. The next thing I remember is waking up in this motel the next day in —— [about 50 miles away]. I was really hung over and my friend was gone. My wife really blew her stack over that one and the guys at work kidded me for the whole week. That's something I don't want to happen again.

Counselor: Yeah, I can see how that blackout and not knowing what might happen to you is something that you should be very concerned about. Let's review some of the things that you've talked about so far in order to identify the areas that are important to you, your wife and family, and what possible alternatives there are.

(Realistic and straightforward show of concern for the seriousness of the situation; moves toward what was garnered from the counseling exploration)

● IMMEDIATE COUNSELING PROBLEM

A relationship of trust between the client and the counselor seems to have developed. The counselor accepts Nick's statements of his life experiences and does not impose values or judgments regarding his drinking "problem." Warning him of the health and social hazards of drinking would only skirt the issues and make him feel that he was being patronized. Reminding him that he is ruining his life and that of his wife and children would probably only make him feel more guilty and aggravate his drinking problem. Suggesting a divorce without consideration of other alternatives would be inappropriate.

Drinking sprees can be considered a symptom of alcoholism. His "blackout" was a frightening experience and is used by the counselor to express a moment of concern for his welfare. Using it as a scare tactic would have been inappropriate, and softening it as something that everybody experiences once in a while would also have been inappropriate. Nick does have a problem to worry about, and if the counselor did not reinforce this fact, the client would lose confidence in the counselor's ability to help.

Assuming that the counseling relationship continues and that upsurges in Nick's defenses (denial, rationalization, and so on) can be handled with patience and tact by the counselor, additional exploration and assessment of what he thinks about his drinking pattern are necessary in order for him to comprehend what is actually happening to him. Many problem drinkers often simply accept their experience as a kind of reality and are unable to detach themselves from their self-imposed reality in order to view it objectively from the "outside." It is important for Nick, through his own insight, eventually to acknowledge his drinking practices and link them with consequences to himself and others. Reinforcement of the belief that his drinking self and his real self are not the same is also important. What he does or gets under the influence of drinking is not something that he necessarily wants or needs in order to gain self-respect. A basic source of personal recognition is the family unit; if it cannot be obtained there, it will be sought elsewhere. Nick does not do the same things sober that he does drunk, and the use of alcohol seems to amplify certain motives in his personality and in relationships with himself and others. Two general hypothetical assumptions regarding his self-concept can be explored in the counseling process: what is his self-image in relation to expectations and behavior of his parents, and what is his self-image in relation to expectations and behavior of his wife and family?

● COUNSELING GOALS

Participating in Alcoholics Anonymous would probably not be effective unless Nick can admit that he has a drinking problem and take responsibility for it. If he can accept that he is worried about drinking too much and that he would like to stop, perhaps hospitalization and treatment would be a possibility. Because his present problems are related to experiences with his wife and family, family counseling would be a good approach. Whether the current counselor does the counseling or makes a referral to a family counselor depends on the counselor's level of competency and commitment. Nick's drinking pattern in relation to his own motives and how he expresses his motives through drinking need exploration. Family therapy would involve both the husband and wife, and perhaps even the children and parents of the husband and wife, but would concern itself primarily with resolving marital difficulties. What is the background of the marital relationship and what is the current relationship? What does each need or want from the other? What is the wife's attitude? Does she in some way fulfill, or enable, his drinking pattern to continue? Is she considering a divorce, and will that threat help Nick to get over denial of a drinking problem? Family counseling is a long and strenuous procedure, but the results for a family can also be very productive and strengthening. When the family is counseled as a unit, as conceptualized in family systems theory, changes in one family member will affect another member, or all the members, where need-meeting is interrelated. The counselor should be alert to emotional needs that are stirred up, especially when their arousal could stress the alcoholic or substance-abusing family member. The pain and confusion that often result from recognizing unresolved family issues can be relieved by attempting to end each session on an "up note," with each member of the family, or the family as a unit, feeling some optimism. Keeping lines of communication open to the substance-abusing member is especially important, as is resolving the hidden agendas of each member.

Counselors should accept the fact that traditional counseling approaches are useless at the time when a client is spaced out on drugs. Counseling is basically a mediational process, and just how verbal and nonverbal exchange might be best used when the client's moods and perceptions have been chemically altered becomes a simple trial-and-error situation. The opportune time for the counseling process comes when the client has withdrawn from a drug, or is working toward recovery, responsible use, or abstinence. Preventive/educational strategies and counseling aimed toward awareness of personal motives are also important when clients seem to be exploring the use of drugs or are coping with drug use at the predependent stage. Finally, drug abuse and misuse are not seen as related to any one factor or membership in any one group, but cut across socioeconomic and ethnocultural group lines.

▲ COUNSELING EXCERPT 10: PRESTON

A Black college student feels pressured by many stresses in his life and has attempted suicide.

Counselor: Now that you're about to graduate and face the working world, what are you seeing?

Client: I know the water's cold, but after coming to the university here I know I got serious instruction in my major—photography and art with a minor in business. Of course, it's going to require a lot of footwork to get a job and I just have to face that with the way the economy is.

Counselor: OK. This is a time when you have to be diligent in your job-search approach. Do you think you're pretty good in art? *(Moves toward career development as a possible area of exploration)*

Client: I'm pretty good, judging by others' reactions. I'm realistic. I've got a long way to go. I've got my own standards. I'm slow, but I get it done—maybe I'm lazy. *(Has ideas about own goals, but some doubts)*

Counselor: Is it lazy or procrastination? *(Aims for concreteness)*

Client: I have my moods—sometimes I can get my work done, other times I have to do the drawing over and over until it becomes like me. You know, good images. Sometimes I just want to sit back and relax. I've got so many incomplete grades, but I'll finish them. *(Perceives gaps in his performance)*

Counselor: What seems to distract you?

Client: That's the problem! There aren't any distractions here. No new things happen except what are organized or set up. That's something I haven't come to grips with, and procrastination. *(Wants more control over his life; things seem static)*

Counselor: How do you fill in your time, or procrastinate? *(Aims for concreteness)*

Client: A lot of thinking. There are times when I wish I wasn't here, but I don't wish I was at home. I think of real experiences where I'd like to be, not places. But that's how I waste my time . . . like when I have a new problem . . . I have a lot of fear, or frustration, then. I got so many things in my mind that don't even apply to this school and so they affect me and my motivations.

Counselor: Yes, I imagine especially in the art field where your emotions and moods are pulled. *(Counselor seems to assume there is something basic to his personality)*

Client: Uh, uh. I have to feel my way into something.

Counselor: What else seems to get in the way?

Client: Sometimes my whole train of thought . . . I think a lot about . . . ah . . . outside stuff.

Counselor: I was going to say, what are those outside things coming in? *(Aims for concreteness)*

Client: Just like, I have a girl out there who I'm engaged to and who screwed me up. And, ah . . . I have a son who is almost two years old. I mean this stuff goes back to high school. And, ah, you know I've gone through so many changes. I know I really love her, otherwise she wouldn't stay on my mind. But it's a no-win situation for me.

(Past events, over which he sees no control, are frustrating him)

Counselor: How so?

(Aims for concreteness)

Client: We started out all wrong. I was in a turmoil. I didn't know if I wanted a girlfriend—or any certain girl. I liked her off and on. I was never sure until I went away to college. I mean a commitment. She wouldn't go to the same college, which made me wonder. All the emotions were up and down. I was really lonely and didn't know where I stood. When she told me she was pregnant, I wasn't shocked but was really positive. I felt good about myself, you know, a good relationship, a bright future. Then she wanted to get married right away before the baby was born. I wasn't prepared for it—I hadn't graduated, no job. My mother said to do what was most important to me . . . my girlfriend turned cold toward me after the birth of the baby and I've really gotten pessimistic since then.

(Perceives the past as imperfect and something that he couldn't control)

Counselor: Do others see that in you?

(Wants to know about his support system)

Client: I know I was rotten, or had my rotten times . . . people think I can take it. I get tired—see, she was terrible to me, but I don't judge her on that. I judge her by how I feel toward her from my heart. But people don't do that to me in return.

(Self-deprecating; no one seems to see his side)

Counselor: You do seem to have a confident appearance. I wonder if people don't know you by how you really feel?

Client: I think it has something to do with putting up a good front.

(Guarding himself)

Counselor: Uh, huh.

Client: See, a lot of that treatment is guilt by association. People always knew where I was. I never really went anyplace and had only a few close friends. I don't know . . . I put up a good front—a strong front. *(Cries)*

(No one really knows him as he sees himself—but he

wishes they could)

Counselor: Do you believe you do this not to release emotions?

Client: Yeah, a defense mechanism—you know, to be cool is better, not hyper. I didn't cry at my father's funeral for him. I didn't hate him.

Counselor: It's kind of hard to let it out, isn't it?

(Relates to his difficulty in emotional expression)

Client: You know, none of my brothers are working—only my sisters and mother. What kind of male model is that? What do I want to be? I have a fantasy to be famous and be known.

(Self-deprecating)

Counselor: You want this to happen?

Client: Something . . . I don't want to sit around in a housing project or have to worry about my mother and little sisters living in a high-crime area. I'm going to make it . . . the pressures are terrible. I don't know what I'll do when my mother dies. Everybody's going to freak out. *(Cries)*

(Deep sense of obligation to help family, but also needs mother's support)

Counselor: It's going to be hard to hold it together.

Client: *(Cries)* I hate it because they don't even see it—when she's gone, all we're going to have is each other—that's all—you can't do it by yourself all the time. My family makes me sick. We all struggle so hard to get it and then we're all selfish as hell. *(Sobs)* I just wish I can make it. Everybody just treats you like shit.

(Anticipates the loss of some of his most important resources— people whom he believes ought to give support and understand him)

Counselor: That's a lot of pressure to put on yourself.

Client: I try to take care of myself—think of myself first. But people notice and work against it—unless it's just in my mind. I'm just sapped. If I was a braver, or weaker, person I'd just finish myself.

Counselor: What's stirring in you?

(Encourages clarity and awareness of his feelings)

Client: All I see is depression and death.

Counselor: You're depressed?

Client: At one time, I thought it was really bad and ah *(Sobs)*, I ran into the kitchen and got a knife and put it right there . . . I wanted to do it. I said, wait a minute. All I wanted to do was make somebody care . . .

● IMMEDIATE COUNSELING PROBLEM

The counselor could assist Preston with the many current issues that he faces or help him develop new perspectives on the past experiences that he has internalized as part of his self-image. But the area that needs the most immediate attention is the emotional pain he is currently experiencing from the accumulation of varied external (situation-imposed) and internal (self-imposed) stresses. Like many other men, he tends to be cool and stoic and carries his emotions and thoughts inside. He needs plenty of opportunity to have his emotions recognized and accepted for what they are or for what they might mean to him. His suicide gesture should not be taken lightly. As he says, "All I wanted to do was make somebody care." His preoccupation with death and dying—with the loss of relationship with his girlfriend, his father's funeral, the imagination of what it would be like if his mother died, the estrangement from his brothers and sisters, and his aloneness—all reflect his internal "down mood." Helping him to talk away his mood of depression and strategies to control its recurrence are major present goals. Heading off depression before it occurs could be encouraged by instructing Preston to isolate and discard the bad feelings he tends to get during an unpleasant situation or memory (anger, sorrow, emptiness, or any other negative emotion). Making a list of all the ways he makes himself feel bad and then a second list of the ways he can deal with that emotion to get back to feeling better or happy could be helpful to him. The second list can be used whenever he needs it. Follow-up and keeping in touch with him are also important.

● COUNSELING GOALS

Preston is having to cope with many situational stresses at this time in his life. Keeping up with his academic course work in order to finish his college degree is an ongoing demand on him, and facing the job market is potentially an anxiety-provoking endeavor for him. As he notes, "When I have a new problem, I have a lot of fear, or frustration." He is also bothered by the loss of relationship with his girlfriend. He is emotionally attached to her but sees the experience as having come at a time when he wasn't ready for it. Feelings toward his son and concern for his son's welfare are not expressed. This may be an area in which he experiences anxiety and which could be explored, but it could also stir up additional stress for him that would add to an already stressful situation.

Preston has other internal stresses as well. As a young person, he wants to develop competence in his work specialty and gain recognition and mobility in his career. He has set his own standards and is working toward them. There seems to be a balance in that area of his life. But he has internalized the impression that except perhaps for his mother, no one really knows or cares about him and the burdens he has to carry. In short, he feels neglected. When he talks about taking care of himself first—his struggles to be somebody famous and his aspirations—he sees no one really giving him any recognition. Because he believes he has no support from members of his family or others for his hard work, he may also be experiencing guilt that he hasn't done the right thing in regard to his girlfriend and the child. Whatever the assumptions that could guide the counseling exploration, there are internal conflicts that need to be worked through and followed by learning other alternatives on which to base his feelings, thoughts, and actions in relation to both himself and others.

▲ COUNSELING EXCERPT 11: JANICE

A young White woman has low self-esteem and feelings of guilt and is unable to communicate with her authoritarian mother.

Client: She [mother] never agreed with me on my views of morality and what I thought was right or wrong, but just once couldn't she just listen and accept me? She starts in, "I failed in bringing up all my daughters. I can't trust any of them—Jean, Donna—going out with those niggers. Oh, they'll come home with them." She never says anything about her son. She feels so sorry for herself. "How could you do this to me?" she says. She doesn't like Polish people, Black people, Jews, doesn't particularly care for Spanish or Italians. That leaves French, Germans, Dutch, English or maybe Irish—which is permissible to her. I know this real nice Jewish kid and this neat Italian guy. Oh, if she only knew, she'd die. *(Minorities are used as scapegoats by the mother for the displacement of her own personal problems)*

Counselor: So your mother is very intolerant of others, has all kinds of faults, she's irrational, right? *(Recognizes mother's personal rigidity)*

Client: That's what I said and, of course, I'm perfect, ha, ha. That's what it just sounded like when you said that. *(Discredits herself)*

Counselor: You still want approval from your mother, though, don't you? *(Confronts her conflict)*

Client: I think basically I do.

Counselor: You still want her to love you.

Client: I don't know, I just want her to accept me. I want to stop worrying about what Mom thinks. If . . . I still feel guilty. Oh, if she knew that I smoked, or that New Year's Eve party I went to—oh, she'd die.

Counselor: It sounds like you're never going to meet with her on common ground, and yet you go back and try to . . . to communicate and win her respect . . . to make her listen to you. *(Confronts her behavior)*

Client: Why?

Counselor: I don't know. Do you need your mother more than you think you do? Do you want her love? Is there something you think you should have had that you didn't get? *(Probes her motives)*

Client: I just don't know. Sometimes I get to the point where I don't want to make another decision. I don't want to do anything on my own. I want someone to do it for me. I just can't take it, I feel like crying and running to someone to make up my mind.

Counselor: You feel like a little girl? *(Reflects)*

Client: I really do. . . . I don't know what I'm looking for.

Counselor: A mother to tell you what to do, and what's right and what's wrong, or at least what's wrong. *(Confronts and challenges)*

Client: I just can't accept myself feeling the way I do.

Counselor: Is mother saying that Janice is nothing, that Janice is incapable, that Janice can't? You sound like you want to prove to yourself that you are an individual and that you're capable to do things by yourself without your mother—was this a way of possibly asserting yourself?

Client: Just to myself. No one else knew or cared. I just accept me the way it is now and what I can do. *(Feels abandoned)*

Counselor: About your mother, you mean?

Client: My mother will never, never, never agree. If she knew I drank, had premarital sex, smoked, danced.

Counselor: But yet, there's something there that attracts yourself to your mother. Do you believe when you become a mother you will have total agreement with your child?

Client: I'm not sure I ever want to be a mother. I don't want the chance of raising kids like I was raised. *(Self-fulfilling prophecy?)*

Counselor: Janice, many children have strained relations with their parents. Possibly more so in the last 20 years than in previous times. Times have changed so much and so fast that your parents think much differently about things. Ideologically and philosophically they're *(Consensual validation of her experiences with that of others)* going to be miles apart in some cases. So there's always going to be a strain on the relationship because they don't think alike. Perhaps, periodic short visits can only result in toleration, but not close the gap.

Client: So what's for me? *(Cries)* How do I start getting over my guilt and just accept me as I am . . . ?

● IMMEDIATE COUNSELING PROBLEM

Janice is unable to accept herself fully without feeling guilty that her mother will disapprove of everything she does. She is warring with the deep feeling that she can be an acceptable person only as her mother has so defined her. However, the mother has defined for Janice only what Janice could *not* be, not what she could be. Emphasis on weaknesses, not strengths, has left Janice unable to please her mother in order to gain approval and recognition. The counselor is having difficulty in helping Janice bring her feelings to full awareness, as well as asking too many indirect questions concerning her psychological dynamics. He vacillates between probing her deeper underlying motives, which seem to be unclear to her or which she is not yet ready to accept, and confronting her real life.

● COUNSELING GOALS

The mother, unable to accept herself, has projected her own inadequacies onto Janice, and Janice has taken her negativism seriously, believing that everything she does is bad. A major goal for the counselor is to help Janice see that her mother's personality has nothing to do with Janice's own personal self-doubts and that she can accept herself without her mother's approval or the rigid thoughts that have been projected onto Janice. Separating her personality from that of the mother through helping her to disprove the thoughts that she has of herself as a "bad object" and concentrating on her actual accomplishments as proof of her "goodness" would increase her self-acceptance and self-esteem. She will be more of herself when she unlearns what she has learned through past personal experiences in which only others have defined who and what she is.

■ SUMMARY

1. Excerpts from 11 counseling interviews were presented. Although each excerpt has distinctive features not found in any of the others, together they suggest a number of fundamentals for counselors working in a multicultural society. These fundamentals are basic to accurately perceiving clients, forming a cooperative working environment, and making the counseling process effective.

2. *For the counselor,* essential ingredients are (a) self-awareness and comprehension of one's own cultural group history and experiences; (b) self-

awareness and comprehension of one's own environmental experiences in mainstream culture; (c) perceptual sensitivity toward one's own personal beliefs and values.

3. *For understanding the client,* essential traits are (a) awareness and comprehension of the history and experiences of the cultural group with which the client might identify or that the client is encountering; (b) perceptual awareness and comprehension of the environmental experiences in mainstream culture with which the client might identify or that the client is encountering; (c) perceptual sensitivity toward the client's personal beliefs and values.

4. *For the counselor in the counseling process,* essential skills are (a) careful and active listening, not casual attention; (b) demonstration of a broad repertoire of genuine verbal and nonverbal responses that show the client you understand what he or she is communicating; (c) caring about the client and his or her situation in the same way that you would care about yourself if you were in that situation; (d) encouragement of optimism in seeking a realistic solution; (e) asking for clarification when you don't understand; (f) being patient, optimistic, and mentally alert.

REFERENCES

ABEL, T. M. (1973). *Psychological testing in cultural contexts.* New Haven, CT: College & University Press.

ABEL, T. M., & MÉTRAUX, R. (1974). *Culture and psychotherapy.* New Haven, CT: College & University Press.

ABRAMSON, H. J. (1970). *Ethnic pluralism in the central city.* Storrs, CT: Institute of Urban Research, University of Connecticut.

ACKERMAN, N. W., & JAHODA, M. (1950). *Antisemitism and emotional disorder: A psychoanalytic interpretation.* New York: Harper & Row.

ADLER, L. L. (ED.). (1991). *Women in cross-cultural perspective.* New York: Praeger.

ADORNO, T. W., FRENKEL-BRUNSWIK, E., LEVINSON, D. J., & SANFORD, R. N. (1950). *The authoritarian personality.* New York: Harper & Row.

ALCÁNTARA, R. R. (1981). *Sakada: Filipino adaptation in Hawaii.* Lanham, MD: University Press of America.

ALLMAN, T. D. (1982, September 28). Our children of the Vietnam war. *Chicago Tribune,* Sec. 1, p. 11.

ALLPORT, G. W. (1954). *The nature of prejudice.* Boston: Beacon Press.

ALVIREZ, D., & BEAN, F. D. (1976). The Mexican American family. In C. H. Mindel & R. W. Habenstein (Eds.), *Ethnic families in America: Patterns and variations.* New York: Elsevier.

AMERASIANS, VETS BOND. (1990, April 9). *Newsweek,* p. 65.

AMERICAN ASSOCIATION FOR COUNSELING AND DEVELOPMENT. (1988). *Ethical standards.* Alexandria, VA: Author.

AMERICAN ASSOCIATION FOR COUNSELING AND DEVELOPMENT. (1991, Sept. 12). Personal communication.

AMERICAN PERSONNEL AND GUIDANCE ASSOCIATION, ASSOCIATION FOR COUNSELOR EDUCATION AND SUPERVISION, COMMISSION ON STANDARDS AND ACCREDITATION (1977). Standards for the preparation of counselors and other personnel service specialists. *Personnel and Guidance Journal, 55,* 596–601.

AMERICAN PSYCHIATRIC ASSOCIATION. (1987). *Diagnostic and statistical manual of mental disorders* (3rd ed. revised). Washington, DC: Author.

AMERICAN PSYCHOLOGICAL ASSOCIATION. (1981). *Ethical principles of psychologists* (rev. ed.). Washington, DC: Author.

AMERICAN PSYCHOLOGICAL ASSOCIATION CONFERENCE FOLLOW-UP COMMITTEE. (1973, September). National conference on levels and patterns of training in professional psychology. Report from the meeting of the American Psychological Association, Vail, Colo.

AMERICAN PSYCHOLOGICAL ASSOCIATION EDUCATION AND TRAINING COMMITTEE OF DIVISION 17. (1980, September). *Cross-cultural counseling competencies, a position-paper.* Paper presented at the meeting of the American Psychological Association, Montreal, Canada.

AMERICAN SCHOOL COUNSELOR ASSOCIATION. (1984). *Ethical standards.* Alexandria, VA: Author.

AMUNDSON, N. E., & BORGEN, W. A. (1982). The dynamics of unemployment: Job loss and job search. *Personnel and Guidance Journal, 60,* 562–564.

ANDERSON, C. H. (1970). *White Protestant Americans.* Englewood Cliffs, NJ: Prentice-Hall.

ANDERSON, E. (1938). *We Americans.* Cambridge, MA: Harvard University Press.

ANDERSON, E. (1990). *Streetwise: Race, class, and change in an urban community.* Chicago: University of Chicago Press.

ANDERSON, M. J., & ELLIS, R. H. (1980). Indian American: The reservation client. In N. A. Vacc & J. P. Wittmer (Eds.), *Let me be me.* Muncie, IN: Accelerated Development.

ANDRE, R. (1991). *Positive solitude: A practical program for mastering loneliness and achieving self-fulfillment.* New York: Harper Collins.

ANNUAL REPORT OF THE COMMISSIONER GENERAL OF IMMIGRATION. (1929). Washington, DC: U.S. Government Printing Office.

ANTEL, W. (1978). The education of American Indians: Critical problems and alternative solutions. In *Beyond desegregation: Urgent issues in the education of minorities.* New York: College Entrance Examination Board.

ANTONOVSKY, A. (1967). Aspirations, class, and racial-ethnic membership. *Journal of Negro Education, 36,* 385–393.

ARBEITER, S. (1984). *Profiles, college-bound seniors.* New York: College Entrance Examination Board.

ARREDONDO, P. (1984). *Bilingual counselor training project.* Unpublished manuscript, Boston University, School of Education.

ASBURY, F. A. (1968). Vocational development of rural disadvantaged eighth-grade boys. *The Vocational Guidance Quarterly, 17,* 109–113.

ASHE, A. (1988). *A hard road to glory: The history of the African-American athlete since 1946,* Vol. III. New York: Warner Books.

ASHMORE, H. (1982). *Hearts and minds: The anatomy of racism from Roosevelt to Reagan.* New York: McGraw-Hill.

ASSAGIOLI, R. A. (1965). *Psychosynthesis.* New York: Viking.

ASTOR, M. (1972). Transpersonal approaches to counseling. *Personnel and Guidance Journal, 50,* 801–808.

ASTOR, M. (1975, February). Transpersonal counseling as a form of transcendental education. *Counseling and Values,* 75–81.

ATKINSON, D. R. (1981). Selection and training for human rights counseling. *Counselor Education and Supervision, 21,* 101–108.

ATKINSON, D. R., MARUYAMA, M., & MATSUI, S. (1978). Effects of counselor race and counseling approach on Asian Americans' perceptions of counselor credibility and utility. *Journal of Counseling Psychology, 25,* 76–83.

ATKINSON, D. R., MORTEN, G., & SUE, D. W. (1989). *Counseling American minorities: A cross-cultural perspective* (3rd ed.). Dubuque, IA: William C. Brown.

AXELSON, E. (1983). *Adult career development: A comparison of career changers and career maintainers among male secondary public school teachers.* Unpublished doctoral dissertation, Northern Illinois University.

AXELSON, J. A., & JIMENEZ, G. (1977). *Counseling with Chicanos.* Unpublished manuscript.

AYRES, M. E. (1977, Spring). Counseling the American Indian. *Occupational Outlook Quarterly, 23–29.*

BABCOCK, R. J., & KAUFMAN, M. A. (1976). Effectiveness of a career course. *The Vocational Guidance Quarterly, 24,* 261–266.

BACHRACH, L. L. (1975, June). *Utilization of state and county mental health hospitals by Spanish Americans in 1972* (Statistical Note 116). Rockville, MD: National Institute of Mental Health, Division of Biometry.

BAGLEY, C., VERNIA, G., MALLICK, K., & YOUNG, L. (1979). *Personality, self-esteem, and prejudice.* Lexington, MA: Gower.

BAILEY, R. L., & HAFNER, A. L. (1978). *Minority admissions.* Lexington, MA: Lexington Books.

BAKER, N. (1981, May). U.S. programs for Indochinese unaccompanied minors. *Helping Indochinese families in transition conference* (compiled proceedings). Lincoln: University of Nebraska.

BALDWIN, J. (1981, May). Community outreach and health education classes with Hmong and Mien in Northeast Portland. *Helping Indochinese families in transition conference* (compiled proceedings). Lincoln: University of Nebraska.

BANDURA, A. (1977). Self-efficacy: Toward a unifying theory of behavior change. *Psychological Review, 84,* 191–215.

BANDURA, A. (1978). The self system in reciprocal determinism. *American Psychologist, 33,* 344–358.

BANKS, J. A., & GRAMBS, J. D. (EDS.). (1972). *Black self-concept.* New York: McGraw-Hill.

BANKS, W. C. (1976). White preference in Blacks: A paradigm in search of a phenomenon. *Psychological Bulletin, 83,* 1179–1186.

BARKLEY, P. W. (1977). *Introduction to macroeconomics.* New York: Harcourt Brace Jovanovich.

BARNOUW, V. (1973). *Culture and personality* (rev. ed.). Pacific Grove, CA: Brooks/Cole.

BARRETT, D. (ED.). (1982). *World Christian encyclopedia.* New York: Oxford University Press.

BECK, A. T. (1976). *Cognitive therapy and emotional disorders.* New York: International Universities Press.

BEJEROT, N. (1980). Addiction to pleasure: A biological and social-psychological theory of addiction. *Theories on drug abuse: Selected contemporary perspectives* (Research Monograph Series 30). Rockville, MD: National Institute on Drug Abuse.

BENGSTON, V. L., KASSCHAU, P. L., & RAGEN, P. K. (1977). The impact of social structure on aging individuals. In J. E. Birren & K. W. Schaie (Eds.), *Handbook of the psychology of aging.* New York: Van Nostrand Reinhold.

BENJAMIN, L. S. (1986). Adding social and intrapsychic descriptors to Axis I of DSM-III. In T. Millon & G. L. Klerman (Eds.), *Contemporary directions in psychopathology.* New York: Guilford Press.

BERK, B. B., & HIRATA, L. C. (1973). Mental illness among the Chinese: Myth or reality? *Journal of Social Issues, 29,* 151.

BILLINGSLEY, A. (1968). *Black families in White America.* Englewood Cliffs, NJ: Prentice-Hall.

BIRNBAUM, N. (1959). The Zwinglian reformation in Zurich. *Past and Present, 27–47.*

BLASSINGAME, J. (ED.). (1972). *The slave community: Plantation life in the antebellum south.* New York: Oxford University Press.

BLAUNER, R. (1969). Internal colonialism and ghetto revolt. *Social Problems, 16*, 393–408.

BOADELLA, D. (1973). *Wilhelm Reich: The evolution of his work.* London: Vision.

BOORSTEIN, S. (ED.). (1980). *Transpersonal psychotherapy.* Palo Alto, CA: Science and Behavior Books.

BORCK, L. E., & FAWCETT, S. B. (1982). *Learning counseling and problem-solving skills.* New York: Haworth Press.

BORDIN, E. S., NACHMAN, B., & SEGAL, S. J. (1963). An articulated framework for vocational development. *Journal of Counseling Psychology, 10*, 107–117.

BOROW, H. (1973). Shifting postures toward work: A tracing. *American Vocational Journal, 48*, 28–29, 108.

BOYD, D. (1974). *Rolling Thunder.* New York: Random House.

BOYER, L. R. (1981). *United States Indians: A brief history.* Reynoldsburg, OH: Advocate Publishing Group.

BRANCH, T. (1988). *Parting the waters: America in the King years, 1954–1963.* New York: Simon & Schuster.

BRANDT, R.(1979). *A theory of the good and the right.* New York: Oxford University Press.

BRATCHER, W. E. (1982). The influence of the family on career selection: A family systems perspective. *Personnel and Guidance Journal, 61*, 87–94.

BRENNER, M. H. (1973). *Mental illness and the economy.* Cambridge, MA: Harvard University Press.

BRENNER, O. C., & TOMKIEWICZ, J. (1982). Job orientation of Black and White college graduates in business. *Personnel Psychology, 35*, 89–103.

BRISLIN, R. W., LONNER, W. J., & THORNDIKE, R. M. (1973). *Cross-cultural research methods.* New York: Wiley.

BROOKHISER, R. (1991). *The way of the WASP: How it made America, and how it can save it, so to speak.* New York: Free Press.

BROWN, B. (1977). *Stress and the art of biofeedback.* New York: Bantam Books.

BROWN, B. (1980). *Super mind.* New York: Harper & Row.

BROWN, J. (1982, December 6). Farragut has far to go, but "it has been done." *Chicago Tribune,* Sec. 1, p. 1.

BROWN, R. (1969). Occupational prestige and the Ethiopian student. *Personnel and Guidance Journal, 48*, 222–228.

BROWNING, D., & BOATMAN, B. (1977). Incest: Children at risk. *American Journal of Psychiatry, 134*, 69–72.

BRYDE, J. F. (1971). *Modern Indian psychology* (rev. ed.). Vermillion, SD: Institute of Indian Studies, University of South Dakota.

BURGESS, E. W., & LOCKE, H. J. (1953). *The family* (2nd ed.). New York: American Book.

BURLAND, C. (1965). *North American Indian mythology.* London: Hamlyn Publishing Group.

BURSTOW, B. (1992). *Radical feminist therapy.* Newbury Park, CA: Sage.

BURT, M. (1992). *Over the edge.* New York: Russell Sage Foundation.

BUSCH, E. J., JR. (1981). Developing an employee assistance program. *Personnel Journal, 60*, 708–711.

BUTLER, R. (1975). *Why survive? Being old in America.* New York: Harper & Row.

BUTLER, R. O. (1992). *A good scent from a strange mountain.* New York: Holt, Rinehart & Winston.

BUTTINGER, J. (1977). *Vietnam: The unforgettable tragedy.* New York: Horizon Press.

BUZAN, T. (1976). *Use both sides of your brain.* New York: Dutton.

BYRD, O. E. (1970). *Medical readings on drug abuse.* Reading, MA: Addison-Wesley.

CALLAN, J. P., & PATTERSON, C. B. (1973). Patterns of drug abuse among military inductees. *American Journal of Psychiatry, 130*, 260–264.

CALLOWAY, N. O., & HARRIS, O. N. (1977). *Biological and medical aspects of race*. Madison, WI: American Publishing.

CAMPBELL, R. E. (1974). Career guidance transcending the present. *The Vocational Guidance Quarterly, 22*, 292–300.

CANNON, M. S., & LOCKE, B. Z. (1977). Being Black is detrimental to one's mental health: Myth or reality? *Phylon*, 408.

CARKHUFF, R. R. (1969). *Helping and human relations* (Vols. 1 & 2). New York: Holt, Rinehart & Winston.

CARKHUFF, R. R. (1981). *Toward actualizing human potential*. Amherst, MA: Human Resource Development Press.

CARKHUFF, R. R., & BERENSON, B. G. (1977). *Beyond counseling and therapy* (2nd ed.). New York: Holt, Rinehart & Winston.

CARMICHAEL, S., & HAMILTON, C. V. (1967). *Black power: The politics of liberation in America*. New York: Vintage Books.

CARTER, T. P., & SEGURA, R. D. (1979). *Mexican Americans in school: A decade of change*. New York: College Entrance Examination Board.

CATTELL, R. B. (1950). *Personality: A systematic, theoretical, and factual study*. New York: McGraw-Hill.

CAUDILL, H. (1963). *Night comes to the Cumberlands*. Boston: Little, Brown.

CAVAN, R. S. (1928). *Suicide*. Chicago: University of Chicago Press.

CHANCE, N. A. (1966). *The Eskimos of North Alaska*. New York: Holt, Rinehart & Winston.

CHAVEZ, L. (1991). *Out of the barrio: Toward a new politics of Hispanic assimilation*. New York: Basic Books.

CHILDE, V. G. (1951). *Social evolution*. New York: H. Schuman.

CHIN, F., CHAN, J. P., INADA, L. F., & WONG, S. H. (EDS.). (1974). *Aiiieeeee! An anthology of Asian-American writers*. Washington, DC: Howard University Press.

CHRONICLE OF HIGHER EDUCATION ALMANAC. (1991, Aug. 28).

CIANNI-SURRIDGE, M. (1983). Technology and work: Future issues for career guidance. *Personnel and Guidance Journal, 61*, 413–416.

CIVIL RIGHTS PROGRESS REPORT 1970. (1970). Washington, DC: Congressional Quarterly.

CLARK, K. B. (1963). *Prejudice and your child* (2nd ed.). Boston: Beacon Press.

CLARK, K. B. (1965). *Dark ghetto*. New York: Harper & Row.

COAKLEY, M. (1982, February 21). Castro's "gifts" filling New York jails. *Chicago Tribune*, Sec. 1, p. 5.

COBBS, P. M. (1972). Ethnotherapy in groups. In L. N. Solomon & B. Berzon (Eds.), *New perspectives on encounter groups*. San Francisco: Jossey-Bass.

COCKERHAM, W. C., FORSLUND, M. A., & RABOIN, R. M. (1976). Drug use among White and American Indian high school youth. *International Journal of the Addictions, 11*, 209–220.

COHEN, S. (1981). *The substance abuse problems*. New York: Haworth Press.

COHEN, S. (1983). *The alcoholism problems: Selected issues*. New York: Haworth Press.

COHLER, B. J., & GRUNEBAUM, H. U. (1981). *Mothers, grandmothers and daughters: Personality and socialization within three generation families*. New York: Wiley-Interscience.

COLES, R. (1973). *The old ones of New Mexico*. Albuquerque: University of New Mexico Press.

CONFUCIAN WORK ETHIC: ASIAN-BORN STUDENTS HEAD FOR THE HEAD OF THE CLASS. (1983, March 28). *Time*, p. 52.

COOK, MARY F. (1987). *New directions in human resources*. Englewood Cliffs, NJ: Prentice-Hall.

COOPER, G. (1974, Spring/Summer). Black dialect: Its place in the reading program of Black children. *Illinois Schools Journal*, pp. 3–10.

COPELAND, E. J. (1982). Minority populations and traditional counseling programs: Some alternatives. *Counselor Education and Supervision, 21,* 187–193.

COREY, G. (1986). *Theory and practice of counseling and psychotherapy* (3rd ed.). Pacific Grove, CA: Brooks/Cole.

CORNELIUS, J. D. (1991). *When I can read my title clear: Literacy, slavery, and religion in the antebellum South.* Chapel Hill: University of South Carolina Press.

CORPUS, S. F. (1938). *An analysis of the racial adjustment activities and problems of the Filipino-American Christian Fellowship in Los Angeles.* Unpublished thesis, University of Southern California. Printed in 1975 by R and E Research Associates, San Francisco.

CORVIN, S., & WIGGINS, F. (1989). An antiracism training model for white professionals. *Journal of Multicultural Counseling and Development, 17,* 105–114.

COSBY, A., & PICOU, J. S. (1971). Race, residence, class and the vocational aspirations of adolescents in four deep-South states. *The Vocational Guidance Quarterly, 19,* 171–182.

CRAMPTON, M. (1977). *Psychosynthesis: Some key aspects of theory and practice.* Montreal: Canadian Institute of Psychosynthesis.

CRANE, P. S. (1967). *Korean patterns.* Seoul: Hollym Corporation.

CRESS WELSING, F. (1974, May). The Cress theory of color-confrontation. *Black Scholar,* 32–40.

CROSSLAND, F. E. (1971). *Minority access to college.* New York: Schocken Books.

CUBBERLEY, E. P. (1909). *Changing conceptions of education.* New York: Riverside Educational Mimeographs.

DANIEL, J. H. (1976). A study of Black sororities at a university with marginal integration. *Journal of Non-White Concerns, 4,* 191–201.

DANIELS, R. (1962). *The politics of prejudice: The anti-Japanese movement in California, and the struggle for Japanese exclusion.* Berkeley: University of California Press.

DARLEY, J. M., GLUCKSBERG, S., KAMIN, L. J., & KINCHLA, R. A. (1981). *Psychology.* Englewood Cliffs, NJ: Prentice-Hall.

DARWIN, C. (1965). *The expression of the emotions in man and animals.* Chicago: University of Chicago Press. (Original work published 1872)

D'AUGELLI, A. R., D'AUGELLI, J. F., & DANISH, S. J. (1981). *Helping others.* Pacific Grove, CA: Brooks/Cole.

DAUPHINAIS, P., DAUPHINAIS, L., & ROWE, W. (1981). Effects of race and communication style on Indian perceptions of counselor effectiveness. *Counselor Education and Supervision, 21,* 72–80.

DAWKINS, M. P. (1980). *Alcohol and the Black community: Exploration studies of selected issues.* Saratoga, CA: Century Twenty-One Publishing.

DECECCO, J. P., & RICHARDS, A. K. (1974). *Growing pains: Uses of school conflict.* New York: Aberdeen Press.

DELORIA, V., JR. (1969). *Custer died for your sins.* New York: Avon.

DELORIA, V., JR. (1973). *God is red.* New York: Grosset & Dunlap.

DEMING, E. D. (1986). *Out of the crisis.* Cambridge, MA: Massachusetts Institute of Technology Center for Advanced Engineering Study.

DESKINS, D. R., JR. (1981, Fall). Minority recruitment data: A preliminary report. *Rackham Reports, 7,* 1–5. Ann Arbor: University of Michigan.

DEWAR, D. L. (1979). *Quality circles.* Red Bluff, CA: Quality Circle Institute.

DIALECT OF THE BLACK AMERICAN [Cassette recording]. (1970). Recording and booklet developed under the guidance of Kenneth Johnson, University of Chicago, and William Stewart, Education Study Center of Washington, DC.

DICKMAN, F., CHALLENGER, B. R., EMENER, W. G., & HUTCHISON, W. S., JR. (EDS.). (1988). *Employee assistance programs.* Springfield, IL: Charles C Thomas.

DICKMAN, F., & EMENER, W. G. (1982). Employee assistance programs: Basic concepts, attributes and an evaluation. *Personnel Administration, 27,* 55–62.

DILLARD, J. L. (1972). *Black English: Its history and usage in the United States.* New York: Random House.

DOHRENWEND, B. S., & DOHRENWEND, B. P. (EDS.) (1982). *Stressful life events and their contexts.* New York: Neale Watson Academic Publications.

DOLE, A. A. (1973). Aspirations of Blacks and Whites for their children. *The Vocational Guidance Quarterly, 22,* 24–31.

DONDERO, A. (1973). *Los Angeles County mental health services to the Chicano population.* Unpublished doctoral dissertation, California School of Professional Psychology.

DONOVAN, J. E., & JESSOR, R. (1978). Adolescent problem drinking: Psychosocial correlates in a national sample study. *Journal of Studies on Alcohol, 39,* 1506–1524.

DOWNING, H. D., & PARADISE, L. V. (1989). Using the DSM-III-R in counseling. *Journal of Counseling & Development, 68,* 226–227.

DRAGUNS, J. G. (1981). Cross-cultural counseling and psychotherapy: History, issues, current status. In A. J. Marsella & P. B. Pedersen (Eds.), *Cross-cultural counseling and psychotherapy.* New York: Pergamon Press.

D'SOUZA, D. (1991). *Illiberal education: The politics of race and sex on campus.* New York: Free Press.

DURKHEIM, E. (1933). *The division of labor in society* (G. Simpson, Trans.). New York: Cromwell-Collier & Macmillan.

DURKHEIM, E. (1951). *Suicide.* New York: Free Press.

DUTTON-DOUGLAS, M. A., & WALKER, L. E. (EDS.). (1988). *Feminist psychotherapies: Integration of therapeutic and feminist systems.* Norwood, NJ: Ablex Publishing.

EGAN, G. (1982). *The skilled helper* (2nd ed.). Pacific Grove, CA: Brooks/Cole.

ELLIS, A. (1973). *Humanistic psychotherapy: The rational-emotive approach.* New York: Julian Press.

ELLISON, N. M. (1978). Differential career counseling for minority students as partial compensation for their backgrounds. In *Beyond desegregation: Urgent issues in the education of minorities.* New York: College Entrance Examination Board.

ELASSER, G. (1982, June 20). Wider demands for illegal aliens seen. *Chicago Tribune,* Sec. 1, p. 5.

ENGS, R. C. (1979). *Responsible drug and alcohol use.* New York: Macmillan.

ERIKSON, E. (1963). *Childhood and society* (2nd ed.). New York: Norton.

FAIRCHILD, H. P. (1926). *The melting pot mistake.* Boston: Little, Brown.

FARB, P. (1978). *Humankind.* Boston: Houghton Mifflin.

FARBER, M. L. (1968). *Theory of suicide.* New York: Funk & Wagnalls.

FARBEROW, N. L. (ED.). (1975). *Suicide in different cultures.* Baltimore, MD: University Park Press.

FARBEROW, N. L. (ED.). (1980). *The many faces of suicide.* New York: McGraw-Hill.

FARBEROW, N. L., & SCHNEIDMAN, E. S. (EDS.). (1961). *The cry for help.* New York: McGraw-Hill.

FARBEROW, N. L., & SIMON, M. D. (1975). Suicide in Los Angeles and Vienna. In N. L. Farberow (Ed.), *Suicide in different cultures.* Baltimore, MD: University Park Press.

FARMER, J. (1985). *Lay bare the heart: An autobiography of the civil rights movement.* New York: Arbor House.

FAST, H. M. (1977). *The immigrants.* Boston: Houghton Mifflin.

FAST, H. M. (1978). *Second generation.* Boston: Houghton Mifflin.

FERGUSON, M. (1980). *The Aquarian Conspiracy: Personal and social transformation in the 1980s.* Los Angeles: J. P. Tarcher.

FERNANDAZ, J. (1981). *Racism and sexism in corporate life.* Lexington, MA: Lexington Books.

FESTINGER, L. (1954). A theory of social comparison process. *Human Relations, 7,* 117–140.

FIFIELD, L. (1975, July 11). *On my way to nowhere: An analysis of gay alcohol abuse and an evaluation of alcoholism rehabilitation services of the Los Angeles gay community.* County of Los Angeles, Contract no. 25125.

FINKELHOR, D. (1977). *The sexual abuse of children in their families: How much?* Unpublished manuscript, University of New Hampshire.

FIRMAN, J., & VARGIU, J. (1980). The perspective of psychosynthesis. In S. Boorstein (Ed.), *Transpersonal psychotherapy.* Palo Alto, CA: Science and Behavior Books.

FIRTH, R. (1961). Suicide and risk-taking in Tikopia society. *Psychiatry, 24,* 1–17.

FISCHOFF, E. (1944). The Protestant Ethic and the spirit of capitalism. *Social Research, 2,* 53–77.

FITZPATRICK, J. P. (1971). *Puerto Rican Americans: The meaning of migration to the mainland.* Englewood Cliffs, NJ: Prentice-Hall.

FLANZER, J. P. (ED.). (1982). *The many faces of family violence.* Springfield, IL: Charles C Thomas.

FOGEL, R. W., & ENGERMAN, S. L. (1974). *Time on the cross.* Boston: Little, Brown.

FORD, C., & FORD, D. J. (1978). Is career counseling for Black people? *Journal of Non-White Concerns, 6,* 53–62.

FORREST, D. V. (1983). Employee assistance programs in the 1980s: Expanding career options for counselors. *Personnel and Guidance Journal, 62,* 105–107.

FORT, J. (1981). *The addicted society.* New York: Grove Press.

FRANKL, V. (1960). Paradoxical intention. *American Journal of Psychotherapy, 14,* 520–525.

FRANKL, V. (1963). *Man's search for meaning.* New York: Washington Square Press.

FRANKL, V. (1967). *Psychotherapy and existentialism: Selected papers on logotherapy.* New York: Simon & Schuster.

FRAZIER, E. F. (1932). *The free Negro family.* Nashville, TN: Fisk University Press.

FREDRICKSON, R. H. (1982). *Career information.* Englewood Cliffs, NJ: Prentice-Hall.

FRENKEL-BRUNSWIK, E. (1949). Intolerance of ambiguity as an emotional and perceptual personality variable. *Journal of Personality, 18,* 108–143.

FRIEDMAN, M. (1969). *Pathogenesis of coronary artery disease.* New York: McGraw-Hill.

FUCHS, E., & HAVIGHURST, R. J. (1973). *To live on this earth: American Indian education.* Garden City, NY: Anchor Books.

FURMAN, E. (1974). *A child's parent dies: Studies in childhood bereavement.* New Haven, CT: Yale University Press.

FUTILE RAIDS ON ILLEGAL ALIENS. (1982, May 1). *Chicago Tribune,* Sec. 1, p. 10.

GAMIO, M. (1971). *Mexican immigration to the United States: A study of human migration and adjustment.* New York: Dover. (Original work published 1930)

GANS, H. H. (1962). *The urban villagers.* New York: Free Press.

GAPP, P. (1982, April 14). Architects and public housing. *Chicago Tribune,* p. 11.

GARDNER, R. A. (1970). *The boys' and girls' book about divorce.* New York: Aronson.

GARDNER, R. A. (1976). *Psychotherapy with children of divorce.* New York: Aronson.

GARDNER, R. A. (1977). *The parents' book about divorce.* Garden City, NY: Doubleday.

GARRETT, S. V. (1976). Putting our whole brain to use: A fresh look at the creative process. *Journal of Creative Behavior, 10,* 239–249.

GARTNER, A., & RIESSMAN, F. (1974). Is there a new work ethic? *American Journal of Orthopsychiatry, 44,* 563–567.

GATCHEL, R., & PROCTOR, J. D. (1976). Physiological correlates of learned helplessness in man. *Journal of Abnormal Psychology, 85,* 27–34.

GAZDA, G. M., ASBURY, F. S., BALZER, F. J., CHILDERS, W. C., & WALTERS, R. P. (1984). *Human relations development: A manual for educators* (3rd ed.). Boston: Allyn & Bacon.

GELLES, R. J. (1974). *The violent home: A study of physical aggression between husbands and wives.* Newbury Park, CA: Sage.

GELLES, R. J. (1979). *Family violence.* Newbury Park, CA: Sage Library of Social Research, Vol. 84.

GELLES, R. J., & STRAUS, M. A. (1975). Family experience and public support of the death penalty. *American Journal of Orthopsychiatry, 45,* 596–613.

GELSO, C. J., & JOHNSON, D. H. (1983). *Explorations in time-limited counseling and psychotherapy.* New York: Columbia University, Teachers College.

GIBBS, J. P., & MARTIN, W. T. (1958). A theory of status integration and its relation to suicide. *American Sociological Review, 23,* 140–147.

GILLIGAN, C. (1982). *In a different voice: Psychological theory and women's development.* Cambridge, MA: Harvard University Press.

GINZBERG, E. (1972). Toward a theory of occupational choice: A restatement. *The Vocational Guidance Quarterly, 20,* 169–176.

GINZBERG, E., GINZBERG, S. W., AXELRAD, S., & HERMA, J. L. (1951). *Occupational choice: An approach to a general theory.* New York: Columbia University Press.

GIOVACCHINI, P. (1978). *The urge to die.* New York: Free Press.

GIRDANO, D. D., & GIRDANO, D. A. (1976). *Drugs: A factual account* (2nd ed.). Reading, MA: Addison-Wesley.

GLADDING, S. T. (1992). *Counseling: A comprehensive profession* (2nd ed.). Columbus: Merrill.

GLASER, B. C., & STRAUSS, A. L. (1968). *Time for dying.* Chicago: Aldine-Atherton.

GLASS, D. (1977). *Behavior patterns: Stress and coronary disease.* Hillsdale, NJ: Erlbaum.

GLASSER, W. (1965). *Reality therapy: A new approach to psychiatry.* New York: Harper & Row.

GLASSER, W. (1969). *Schools without failure.* New York: Harper & Row.

GLASSER, W. (1972). *The identity society.* New York: Harper & Row.

GLASSER, W. (1976). *Positive addiction.* New York: Harper & Row.

GLAZER, N., & MOYNIHAN, D. (1970). *Beyond the melting pot* (2nd ed.). Cambridge, MA: MIT Press.

GOBLE, F. (1970). *The third force.* New York: Grossman.

GOLAN, N. (1978). *Treatment in crisis situations.* New York: Free Press.

GOLDMAN, H. H. (Ed.). (1988). *Review of general psychiatry* (2nd ed.). Norwalk, CT: Appleton & Lange.

GOMEZ, R. (ED.). (1972). *The changing Mexican-American.* El Paso: University of Texas, El Paso.

GOODWIN, L. (1973). Poor people and public policy. *The Vocational Guidance Quarterly, 21,* 191–198.

GORDON, M. M. (1964). *Assimilation in American life.* New York: Oxford University Press.

GOTTFREDSON, L. S. (1978). Providing Black youth more access to enterprising work. *The Vocational Guidance Quarterly, 27,* 114–123.

GOTTFREDSON, L. S. (1981). Circumscription and compromise: A developmental theory of occupational aspirations. *Journal of Counseling Psychology Monograph, 28,* 545–579.

GOULD, J., & KOLB, W. L. (EDS.). (1964). *A dictionary of the social sciences.* New York: Free Press.

GOULD, R. L. (1972). The phases of adult life: A study in developmental psychology. *American Journal of Psychiatry, 129,* 521–531.

GRAVES, T. R. (1967). Acculturation, access, and alcohol in a tri-ethnic community. *American Anthropologist, 69,* 306–321.

GREELEY, A. M. (1969). *Why can't they be like us?* New York: Institute of Human Relations Press, The American Jewish Committee.

GREELEY, A. M. (1974). *Ethnicity in the United States: A preliminary reconnaissance.* New York: Wiley.

GREELEY, A. M. (1977). *The American Catholic: A social portrait.* New York: Basic Books.

GREEN, M. R. (ED.). (1980). *Violence and the family.* Boulder, CO: Westview Press.

GREEN, R. L., SMITH, G. S., GUNNINGS, T. S., & MCMILLAN, J. H. (1974). Black athletes: Educational, economic, and political considerations. *Journal of Non-White Concerns, 3,* 6–38.

GREVEN, P. (1991). *Spare the child: The religious roots of punishment and the psychological impact of physical abuse.* New York: Random House.

GRISWOLD, K. W. (1986). *Brief therapy: A review and analysis.* Unpublished doctoral dissertation, Northern Illinois University.

GROF, S. (1976). *Realms of the human unconscious: Observations from LSD research.* New York: Viking Press.

GROF, S., & HALIFAX, J. (1977). *The human encounter with death.* New York: Dutton.

GROSSMAN, J. (1989). *Land of hope: Chicago, Black Southerners, and the great migration.* Chicago: University of Chicago Press.

GUERNEY, B. G. (ED.). (1969). *Psychotherapeutic agents: New roles for nonprofessionals, parents, and teachers.* New York: Holt, Rinehart & Winston.

GUNNINGS, T. S. (1973). Systemic counseling: An effective approach to counseling minority students. *Proceedings: First national conference on counseling minorities and disadvantaged,* pp. 18–19. East Lansing, MI: Michigan State University, College of Urban Development.

GUNNINGS, T. S., & SIMPKINS, G. (1972). A systemic approach to counseling disadvantaged youth. *Journal of Non-White Concerns, 1,* 4–8.

GURIN, P., & EPPS, E. G. (1975). *Black consciousness, identity, and achievement.* New York: Wiley.

GURIN, P., GURIN, G., LAO, R., & BEATTIE, M. (1969). Internal-external control in the motivational dynamics of Negro youth. *Journal of Social Issues, 25,* 29–54.

HAGER, P. C., & ELTON, C. F. (1971). The vocational interests of Black males. *Journal of Vocational Behavior, 1,* 153–158.

HAIMANN, T., & HILGERT, R. L. (1977). *Supervision: Concepts and practices of management.* Cincinnati, OH: South-Western.

HALL, C. S., & LINDZEY, G. (1978). *Theories of personality* (3rd ed.). New York: Wiley.

HALL, E. T. (1976). *Beyond culture.* Garden City, NY: Doubleday.

HALL, M. (1968). The Black perspective. In J. Axelson (Ed.), *Guiding youth who are disadvantaged.* Moline, IL: Quad-City Merit Employment Council.

HALLINAN, M. T. (1982). Classroom racial composition and children's friendships. *Social Forces, 61,* 56–72.

HANSEN, M. L. (1938). *The problem of the third generation immigrant.* Rock Island, IL: Augustana Historical Society.

HARASYMIW, S. J., HORNE, M. D., & LEWIS, S. C. (1977). Occupational attitudes in population subgroups. *The Vocational Guidance Quarterly, 26,* 147–156.

HARMAN, R. L., & DUTT, L. G. (1974). Career counseling workshop: A new approach for undecided college students. *The Vocational Guidance Quarterly, 23,* 68–70.

HARPER, B. C. (1982). Some snapshots of death and dying among ethnic minorities. In R. C. Manuel (Ed.), *Minority aging.* Westport, CT: Greenwood Press.

HARPER, F. D., & STONE, W. O. (1974). Toward a theory of transcendent counseling with Blacks. *Journal of Non-White Concerns, 2,* 191–196.

HARRIS, T. L., & WALLIN, J. S. (1978). Influencing career choices of seventh-grade students. *The Vocational Guidance Quarterly, 27,* 50–53.

HART, J., & TOMLINSON, T. (1970). *New directions in client-centered therapy.* New York: Houghton Mifflin.

HATT, P. K. (1950). Occupations and social stratification. *American Journal of Sociology, 55,* 533–543.

HAVIGHURST, R. J. (1953). *Human development and education.* New York: Longmans, Green.

HAVIGHURST, R. J., MUNNICHS, J., NEUGARTEN, B., & THOMAS, H. (EDS.). (1969). *Adjustment to retirement: A cross-national study.* Assen, The Netherlands: Van Gorcum.

HAYAKAWA, S. I. (1979). *Through the communication barrier: On speaking, listening, and understanding.* New York: Harper & Row.

HAZEL, E. R. (1976). Group counseling for occupational choice. *Personnel and Guidance Journal, 54,* 437–438.

HEADLEY, L. (1975). Jewish suicide in Israel. In N. L. Farberow (Ed.), *Suicide in different cultures.* Baltimore: University Park Press.

HEALY, C. C. (1974). Evaluation of a replicable group career counseling procedure. *The Vocational Guidance Quarterly, 23,* 34–40.

HELMS, J. E. (1989). Considering some methodological issues in racial identity research. *The Counseling Psychologist, 17,* 227–252.

HENDIN, H. (1982). *Suicide in America.* New York: W. W. Norton.

HENDRICKS, G., & WEINHOLD, B. (1982). *Transpersonal approaches to counseling and psychotherapy.* Denver, CO: Love Publishing.

HENRY, A. F., & SHORT, J. F., JR. (1954). *Suicide and homicide.* Glencoe, IL: Free Press.

HEPPNER, M. J. (1978). Counseling the battered wife: Myths, facts, and decisions. *Personnel and Guidance Journal, 56,* 522–525.

HERNTON, C. C. (1965). *Sex and racism in America.* New York: Doubleday.

HIGGINBOTHAM, H. N., & TANAKA-MATSUMI, J. (1981). Behavioral approaches to counseling across cultures. In P. B. Pedersen, J. G. Draguns, W. J. Lonner, & J. E. Trimble (Eds.), *Counseling across cultures* (rev. ed.). Honolulu: University Press of Hawaii.

HIROTO, D. S., & SELIGMAN, M. E. (1975). Generality of learned helplessness in man. *Journal of Personality and Social Psychology, 31,* 311–327.

HO, MAN KEUNG (1973). Cross-cultural career counseling. *The Vocational Guidance Quarterly, 21,* 186–190.

HOCHHAUSER, M. (1980). A chronobiological control theory. *Theories on drug abuse: Selected contemporary perspectives* (Research Monograph Series 30). Rockville, MD: National Institute on Drug Abuse.

HOGAN, P. (1975, Summer). A woman is not a girl and other lessons in corporate speech. *Business and Society Review,* 34–38.

HOLLAND, J. L. (1973). *Making vocational choice: A theory of careers.* Englewood Cliffs, NJ: Prentice-Hall.

HOLLIS, J. W., & WANTZ, R. A. (1983). *Counselor preparation 1983–85: Programs, personnel, trends* (5th ed.). Muncie, IN: Accelerated Development.

HOLLIS, J. W., & WANTZ, R. A. (1990). *Counselor preparation 1990–92: Programs, personnel, trends* (7th ed.). Muncie, IN: Accelerated Development.

HOLMES, T. H., & RAHE, R. H. (1967). The social readjustment rating scale. *Journal of Psychosomatic Research, 11,* 213–218.

HOOKS, B. L. (1981). *Government and the advancement of social justice, health, education, and civil rights in the eighties.* Englewood Cliffs, NJ: Prentice-Hall.

HORNER, M. S. (1980). *The quality of American life in the eighties.* Englewood Cliffs, NJ: Prentice-Hall.

HSU, F.L.K. (1961). Kinship and ways of life: An exploration. In F.L.K. Hsu (Ed.), *Psychological anthropology.* Belmont, CA: Wadsworth.

HSU, F.L.K. (1970). *Americans and Chinese.* Garden City, NY: Doubleday.

HSU, F.L.K. (1971). Psychosocial homeostasis and *jen:* Conceptual tools for advancing psychological anthropology. *American Anthropologist, 73,* 23–44.

HSU, F.L.K. (ED.). (1972). *Psychological anthropology.* Cambridge, MA: Schenkman.

HUANG, L. J. (1976). The Chinese American family. In C. Mindel & R. W. Habenstein (Eds.), *Ethnic families in America: Patterns and variations.* New York: Elsevier.

HUBER, J. (ED.). (1973). *Changing women in a changing society.* Chicago: University of Chicago Press.

HUDSON, W. (1961). *American Protestantism.* Chicago: University of Chicago Press.

HUGHES, R., & BREWIN, R. (1979). *The tranquilizing of America.* New York: Harcourt Brace Jovanovich.

INSTITUTE OF MEDICINE (U.S.). (1988). *Homelessness, health, and human needs.* Washington, DC: National Academy Press.

INTERCULTURAL DEVELOPMENT RESEARCH ASSOCIATION. (1976). *Handbook for teachers of Vietnamese students.* San Antonio, TX: Author.

ISAACSON, L. E. (1977). *Career information in counseling and teaching* (3rd ed.). Boston: Allyn & Bacon.

IVEY, A. E. (1981). Counseling and psychotherapy: Toward a new perspective. In A. J. Marsella & P. B. Pedersen (Eds.), *Cross-cultural counseling and psychotherapy.* New York: Pergamon Press.

IVEY, A. E. (1988). *Intentional interviewing and counseling* (2nd ed.). Pacific Grove, CA: Brooks/Cole.

IVEY, A. E., & AUTHIER, J. (1978). *Microcounseling* (2nd ed.). Springfield, IL: Charles C Thomas.

IVEY, A. E., & GALVIN, M. (1984). Microcounseling: A metamodel for counseling, therapy, business, and medical interviews. In D. Larson (Ed.), *Teaching psychological skills: Models for giving psychology away.* Pacific Grove, CA: Brooks/Cole.

IVEY, A. E., IVEY, M.B., & SIMEK-DOWNING, L. (1987). *Counseling and psychotherapy* (2nd ed.) . Englewood Cliffs, NJ: Prentice-Hall.

JACKSON, J. J. (1980). *Minorities and aging.* Belmont, CA: Wadsworth.

JACOBS, J. (1971). *Adolescent suicide.* New York: Wiley.

JACOBSON, E. (1938). *Progressive relaxation.* Chicago: University of Chicago Press.

JAFFE, J. H. (1975). Drug addiction and drug abuse. In L. Goodman & A. Gilman (Eds.), *The pharmacological basis of therapeutics* (5th ed.). New York: Macmillan.

JARRETT, V. (1982, December 5). Black colleges fight for their lives. *Chicago Tribune.*

JENSEN, A. R. (1969). How much can we boost IQ and scholastic achievement? *Harvard Educational Review, 39,* 1–23.

JENSEN, A. R. (1972). *Genetics and education.* New York: Harper & Row.

JENSEN, A. R. (1973). *Educational differences.* London: Methuen.

JENSEN, J. L., WALER, L. R., & CHAMBERLAIN, J. M. (1978). *The effects of group counseling on locus of control and self-esteem of disadvantaged youth.* Unpublished manuscript, Brigham Young University.

JEPSEN, D. A. (1972). The impact of videotaped occupational field trips on occupational knowledge. *The Vocational Guidance Quarterly, 21,* 54–62.

JOHNSON, F. A. (1981). Ethnicity and interactional rules in counseling and psychotherapy: Some basic considerations. In A. J. Marsella & P. B. Pedersen (Eds.), *Cross-cultural counseling and psychotherapy.* New York: Pergamon Press.

JONES, J. M. (1972). *Prejudice and racism.* Reading, MA: Addison-Wesley.

JOURARD, S. (1971). *The transparent self* (rev. ed.). New York: Van Nostrand Reinhold.

JUNG, C. G. (1933a). *Psychological types.* New York: Harcourt Brace Jovanovich.

JUNG, C. G. (1933b). *Modern man in search of a soul.* New York: Harcourt Brace Jovanovich.

JUNG, C. G. (1964). *Man and his symbols.* Garden City, NY: Doubleday.

KALLEN, H. M. (1956). *Cultural pluralism and the American idea.* Philadelphia: University of Philadelphia Press.

KAMERMAN, S. B., & KAHN, A. J. (1987). *The responsive workplace: Employers and a changing labor force.* New York: Columbia University Press.

KANTROWITZ, N. (1973). *Ethnic and racial segregation in the New York metropolis.* New York: Praeger.

KANZAKI, G. A. (1976). Fifty years (1925–1975) of stability in the social status of occupations. *The Vocational Guidance Quarterly, 25,* 101–105.

KATZ, J. H. (1978). *White awareness: Handbook for anti-racism training.* Norman, OK: University of Oklahoma Press.

KAVANAUGH, R. E. (1974). *Facing death.* New York: Penguin.

KELLER, S. I. (1953). *The social origins and career lines of three generations of American business leaders.* Unpublished doctoral dissertation, Columbia University.

KELLY, G. A. (1955). *The psychology of personal constructs: Vol. 1. A theory of personality. Vol. 2. Clinical diagnosis and psychotherapy.* New York: Norton.

KELLY, J. B., & WALLERSTEIN, J. S. (1976). The effects of parental divorce: Experiences of the child in early latency. *American Journal of Orthopsychiatry, 46,* 20–32.

KHAN, J. A., & CROSS, D. G. (1980). Counseling-orientation preferences: American and Australian comparative data. *Counselor Education and Supervision, 20,* 92–100.

KIEV, A. (1968). *Curanderismo: Mexican-American folk psychiatry.* New York: Free Press.

KIKUMURA, A., & KITANO, H.H.L. (1973). Interracial marriage: A picture of the Japanese-American. *Journal of Social Issues, 29,* 1–9.

KIM, B. C. (1978). *The Asian Americans: Changing patterns, changing needs.* Urbana, IL: AKCS/Publication Services.

KIM, I. (1981). *New urban immigrants: The Korean community in New York.* Princeton, NJ: Princeton University Press.

KIMBALL, R. L., SEDLACEK, W. E., & BROOKS, G. C., JR. (1973). Black and White vocational interests in Holland's Self-Directed Search (SDS). *Journal of Negro Education, 42,* 1–4.

KIMMEL, D. C. (1980). *Adulthood and aging* (2nd ed.). New York: Wiley.

KINDER, M. (1990). *Going nowhere fast: Stepping off life's treadmills and finding peace of mind.* Englewood Cliffs, NJ: Prentice-Hall.

KING, R. G. (1974). I am somebody. *Social Change, 4,* 3–5.

KITAGAWA, D. (1967). *Issei and nisei: The internment years.* New York: Seabury Press.

KITANO, H.H.L. (1969). *Japanese-Americans: The evolution of a subculture.* Englewood Cliffs, NJ: Prentice-Hall.

KITANO, H.H.L., & KIKUMURA, A. (1976). The Japanese American family. In C. H. Mindel & R. W. Habenstein (Eds.), *Ethnic families in America: Patterns and variations.* New York: Elsevier.

KITANO, H.H.L., & MATSUSHIMA, N. (1981). Counseling Asian Americans. In P. B. Pedersen, J. G. Draguns, W. J. Lonner, & J. E. Trimble (Eds.), *Counseling across cultures* (rev. ed.). Honolulu: University Press of Hawaii.

KLERMAN, G. L., & WEISMAN, M. M. (1986). The interpersonal approach to understanding depression. In T. Millon & G. L. Klerman (Eds.), *Contemporary directions in psychopathology.* New York: Guilford Press.

KLUCKHOHN, C., & MURRAY, H. A. (EDS.). (1948). *Personality in nature, society, and culture.* New York: Knopf.

KNOWLES, L., & PREWITT, K. (EDS.). (1969). *Institutional racism in America.* Englewood Cliffs, NJ: Prentice-Hall.

KOCH, J. H. (1972). An applied systems approach to career exploration. *The Vocational Guidance Quarterly, 20,* 229–232.

KOCHMAN, T. (1981). *Black and White styles in conflict.* Chicago: University of Chicago Press.

KOVEL, J. (1970). *White racism: A psychohistory.* New York: Pantheon.

KOVEL, J. (1976). *A complete guide to therapy.* New York: Pantheon.

KRANTZ, D. L. (1977). The Santa Fe experience. In S. B. Sarason (Ed.), *Work, aging, and social change.* New York: Free Press.

KRECH, D., CRUTCHFIELD, R. S., & LIVSON, N. (1974). *Elements of psychology* (3rd ed.). New York: Knopf.

KRUG, M. (1976). *The melting of the ethnics.* Bloomington, IN: Phi Delta Kappa Educational Foundation.

KRUMBOLTZ, J. D. (1975, September). Presidential address, Division 17. Delivered at the American Psychological Association Convention, Chicago.

KRUMBOLTZ, J. D., & BAKER, R. D. (1973). Behavioral counseling for vocational decisions. In H. Borow (Ed.), *Career guidance for a new age.* Boston: Houghton Mifflin.

KUBLER-ROSS, E. (1969). *On death and dying.* New York: Macmillan.

KUBLER-ROSS, E. (1975). *Death, the final stage of growth.* Englewood Cliffs, NJ: Prentice-Hall.

KUBLER-ROSS, E. (1981). *Living with death and dying.* New York: Macmillan.

LAING, R. D. (1967). *The divided self.* New York: Pantheon.

LAING, R. D. (1969). *The politics of experience.* New York: Pantheon.

LANG, J. J. (1975). Scientism and parapsychology. *Counseling and Values, 19,* 91–97.

LASCH, C. (1983). *The culture of narcissism.* New York: Norton.

LASCH, C. (1984). *The minimal self: Psychic survival in troubled times.* New York: Norton.

LASCH, C. (1991). *The true and only heaven: Progress and its critics.* New York: Norton.

LASKER, B. (1969). *Filipino immigration.* New York: Arno Press.

LEAF, A. (1973). Getting old. *Scientific American, 229,* 45–62.

LEE, B. M., & SCHMIDT, W. H. (1969). Toward more authentic interpersonal relations between Blacks and Whites. *Human Relations Training News, 13,* 4–5.

LEMANN, N. (1991). *Promised land: The great black migration and how it changed America.* New York: Random House.

LEONTIEF, W. (1983). The new age that's coming is already here. *Bottom Line, 4,* 1–3.

LEVINE, E. S., & PADILLA, A. M. (1980). *Crossing cultures in therapy: Pluralistic counseling for the Hispanic.* Pacific Grove, CA: Brooks/Cole.

LEVINGER, G. (1966). Sources of marital dissatisfaction among applicants for divorce. *American Journal of Orthopsychiatry, 36,* 803–807.

LEVINSON, D. (1978). *The seasons of a man's life.* New York: Knopf.

LEWIS, H. (1979, September 24). Trained professionals and mountaineers: Cross-cultural contrasts. (Presentation given at Northern Illinois University by Ms. Lewis, of the Highlander Research and Education Center, Monteagle, TN.)

LEWIS, J. A., DANA, R. Q., & BLEVINS, G. A. (1988). *Substance abuse counseling: An individualized approach.* Pacific Grove, CA: Brooks/Cole.

LEWIS, R. G., & HO, M. K. (1975). Social work with Native Americans. *Social Work, 20,* 379–382.

LIEBERKNECHT, K. (1978, April). Helping the battered wife. *American Journal of Nursing,* pp. 654–656.

LINDSEY, P., & LINDSEY, O. (1974). *Breaking the bonds of racism.* Homewood, IL: ETC Publications.

LIPSETT, L., & LAIDLAW, W. J. (1975). Career exploration for college credit. *Personnel and Guidance Journal, 54,* 108–110.

LISKA, K. (1986). *Drugs and the human body: With implications for society* (2nd ed.). New York: Macmillan.

LISS, M. (1980). *Prostitution in perspective: A comparison of prostitutes and other working women.* Unpublished doctoral dissertation, Northern Illinois University.

LIU, W. T., & YU, E.S.H. (1985). Ethnicity and mental health. In J. Moore & L. Maldonado (Eds.), *Urban ethnicity.* Newbury Park, CA: Sage.

LLOYD-JONES, E. M., & ROSENAU, N. (EDS.). (1968). *Social and cultural foundations of guidance.* New York: Holt, Rinehart & Winston.

LOCASCIO, R. (1967). Continuity and discontinuity in vocational development theory. *Personnel and Guidance Journal, 46,* 32–36.

LOESCH, L. C., & MCDAVIS, R. J. (1978). A scale for assessing counseling-orientation preferences. *Counselor Education and Supervision, 17,* 262–271.

LOEWENSTEIN, S. F. (1979). Helping family members cope with divorce. In S. Eisenberg & L. E. Patterson (Eds.), *Helping clients with special concerns.* Chicago: Rand McNally.

LOGAN, N. (1980). The single parent. In N. A. Vacc & J. P. Wittmer (Eds.), *Let me be me.* Muncie, IN: Accelerated Development.

LONDON, M., & MONE, E. M. (1987). *Career management and survival in the workplace.* San Francisco: Jossey-Bass.

LONGSHORE, D. (1982). Race composition and White hostility: A research note on the problem of control in desegregated schools. *Social Forces, 61,* 73–78.

LOPATA, H. Z. (1976). The Polish American family. In C. H. Mindel & R. W. Habenstein (Eds.), *Ethnic families in America: Patterns and variations.* New York: Elsevier.

LOPEZ, F. G. (1983). A paradoxical approach to vocational indecision. *Personnel and Guidance Journal, 61,* 410–412.

LOPREATO, J. (1970). *Italian Americans.* New York: Random House.

LOTT, B. (1987). *Women's lives: Themes and variations in gender learning.* Pacific Grove, CA: Brooks/Cole.

LOWENTHAL, D. (1972). *West Indian societies.* New York: Oxford University Press.

LYMAN, S. M. (1974). *Chinese Americans.* New York: Random House.

MACCOBY, M., & TERZI, K. A. (1981). What happened to the work ethic? In J. O'Toole, J. L. Scheiber, & L. C. Wood (Eds.), *Working changes and choices.* Sacramento: The Regents of the University of California.

MACLAY, E. (1977). *Green winter: Celebration of old age.* New York: McGraw-Hill/Reader's Digest Press.

MAHAN, J. M., & CRIGER, M. K. (1977). Culturally oriented instruction for Native American students. *Integrated Education, 15,* 9–13.

MAHL, G. F. (1971). *Psychological conflict and defense.* New York: Harcourt Brace Jovanovich.

MALAMUD, B. (1963). *Idiots first.* New York: Farrar, Straus & Giroux.

MALCOLM X (as told to Alex Haley). (1964). *The autobiography of Malcolm X.* New York: Ballantine Books.

MALDONADO, B. M., & CROSS, W. C. (1977). Today's Chicano refutes the stereotype. *College Student Journal, 11,* 146–152.

MALTZ, M. (1960). *Psycho-cybernetics.* Englewood Cliffs, NJ: Prentice-Hall.

MANN, J. (1973). *Time-limited psychotherapy.* Cambridge, MA: Harvard University Press.

MANTON, K. G. (1982). Differential life expectancy: Possible explanations during the later ages. In R. C. Manuel (Ed.), *Minority aging.* Westport, CT: Greenwood Press.

MANUEL, R. C. (1982). The minority aged: Providing a conceptual perspective. In R. C. Manuel (Ed.), *Minority aging.* Westport, CT: Greenwood Press.

MANUEL, R. C., & REID, J. (1982). A comparative demographic profile of the minority and nonminority aged. In R. C. Manuel (Ed.), *Minority aging.* Westport, CT: Greenwood Press.

MARQUIS, A. (1974). *A guide to America's Indians*. Norman, OK: University of Oklahoma Press.

MARSELLA, A. J., & PEDERSEN, P. B. (EDS.). (1981). *Cross-cultural counseling and psychotherapy*. New York: Pergamon Press.

MARSHALL, M. (1980, Summer). Alcohol and culture: A review. *Alcohol Health and Research World, 4*, 2–7.

MARTIN, D. (1976). *Battered wives*. San Francisco: Glide Publications.

MASLOW, A. H. (1970). *Motivation and personality* (2nd ed.). New York: Harper & Row.

MATTHEWS, E. (1982). *Culture clash*. Chicago: Intercultural Press.

MAXWELL, R. J., & SILVERMAN, P. (1970). Information and esteem: Cultural considerations in the treatment of the aged. *Aging and Human Development, 1*, 361–392.

MAY, P. A. (1982). Substance abuse and American Indians: Prevalence and susceptibility. *The International Journal of the Addictions, 17*, 1185–1209.

MAY, R.(1953). *Man's search for himself*. New York: Dell.

MAY, R. (1972). *Power and innocence: A search for the sources of violence*. New York: Norton.

MAY, R. (1981). *Freedom and destiny*. New York: Norton.

MAYNARD, E. S. (1972). *Endogamy among Barbadian immigrants to New York City*. Unpublished doctoral dissertation, New York University.

MCADOO, H. P. (1977). The development of self-concept and race attitudes in Black children: A longitudinal study. In W. E. Cross, Jr. (Ed.), *Proceedings: The third annual conference on empirical research in Black Psychology*. Washington, DC: U.S. Department of Health, Education and Welfare, National Institute of Education.

MCADOO, H. P. (1978). Factors related to stability in upwardly mobile Black families. *Journal of Marriage and the Family, 40*, 761–776.

MCCARTHY, J. D., & YANCEY, W. L. (1971). Uncle Tom and Mr. Charlie: Metaphysical pathos in the study of racism and personal disorganization. *American Journal of Sociology, 76*, 648–672.

MCCOY, V. R. (1977). Adult life cycle change. *Lifelong Learning: The Adult Years, 1*, 14–18.

MCDAVIS, R. J. (1980). The Black client. In N. A. Vacc & J. P. Wittmer (Eds.), *Let me be me*. Muncie, IN: Accelerated Development.

MCGEE, R. (ED.). (1977). *Sociology*. Hinsdale, IL: Dryden Press.

MCGRATH, J. E. (ED.). (1970). *Social and psychological factors in stress*. New York: Holt, Rinehart, & Winston.

MCGRATH, P. R. (1989). *Human service education: State of the discipline—A survey of faculty members of the National Organization for Human Service Education*. Unpublished doctoral dissertation, Northern Illinois University.

MCGUIGAN, F. J. (1981). *Calm down*. Englewood Cliffs, NJ: Prentice-Hall.

MCGUIRE, W. J., MCGUIRE, C. V., CHILD, P., & FUJIOKA, T. (1978). Salience of ethnicity in the spontaneous self-concept as a function of one's ethnic distinctiveness in the social environment. *Journal of Personality and Social Psychology, 36*, 511–520.

MCLEMORE, S. D. (1980). *Racial and ethnic relations in America*. Boston: Allyn & Bacon.

MCWILLIAMS, C. (1964). *Brothers under the skin* (rev. ed.). Boston: Little, Brown.

MEIER, A., & RUDWICK, E. (1979). *Black Detroit and the rise of the UAW*. New York: Oxford University Press.

MELAMED, E. (1983). *Mirror, mirror: The terror of not being young*. New York: Linden Press.

METOUR, C., & METOUR, G. E. (1979). Suicide. *Women in treatment II*. Rockville, MD: National Institute on Drug Abuse.

MILLER, J. B. (1986). *Toward a new psychology of women* (2nd ed.). Boston, MA: Beacon Press.

MILLER, N. E. (1944). Experimental studies of conflict. In J. M. Hunt (Ed.), *Personality and the behavior disorders*. New York: Ronald Press.

MINOR, B. J. (1978). A perspective for assertiveness training for Blacks. *Journal of Non-White Concerns, 6,* 63–70.

MINTZBERG, H. (1967, July-August). Planning on the left side and managing on the right. *Harvard Business Review,* 49–58.

MIRELS, H. P., & GARRETT, J. B. (1971). The Protestant work ethic as a personality variable. *Journal of Consulting and Clinical Psychology, 36,* 40–41.

MITCHELL, A. M., JONES, G. B., & KRUMBOLTZ, J. D. (EDS.). (1979). *Social learning and career decision making.* Cranston, RI: Carrol Press.

MITCHELL, J. (1974). *Psychoanalysis and feminism.* New York: Pantheon Books.

MOGULL, R. (1978). Dissatisfaction and habits of Black workers. *Personnel and Guidance Journal, 56,* 567–570.

MONTAGU, A. (1974). *Man's most dangerous myth: The fallacy of race* (5th ed.). New York: Oxford University Press.

MONTERO, D. (1979). *Vietnamese Americans: Patterns of resettlement and socioeconomic adaptation in the United States.* Boulder, CO: Westview Press.

MOODY, R. (1976). *Life after death.* New York: Bantam Books.

MOORE, J. W. (1970). Colonialism: The case of the Mexican Americans. *Social Problems, 17,* 463–472.

MORACCO, J. C., & MCFADDEN, H. (1982). The counselor's role in reducing teacher stress. *Personnel and Guidance Journal, 60,* 549–552.

MYERS, R. D., & MELCHIOR, C. L. (1977). Alcohol drinking: Abnormal intake caused by tetrahydropapaveroline in brain. *Science, 196,* 554–555.

MYRDAL, G. (1944). *An American dilemma: The Negro problem and modern democracy.* New York: Harper & Row.

THE MYTHS OF MIDDLE AGE. (1983, February 14). *Newsweek,* pp. 73–75.

NAISBITT, J. (1982). *Megatrends.* New York: Warner Books.

NAISBITT, J., & ABURDENE, P. (1985). *Re-inventing the corporation.* New York: Warner Books.

NAISBITT, J., & ABURDENE, P. (1990). *Megatrends 2000.* New York: Morrow.

NAKANE, C. (1970). *Japanese society.* Berkeley, CA: McCutchan.

NATIONAL CENTER FOR HEALTH STATISTICS. (1978). *Vital statistics of the United States: Mortality, Part A, 1960, 1969, 1975* (Vol. 2). Washington, DC: U.S. Government Printing Office.

NATIONAL CENTER FOR HEALTH STATISTICS. (1990, August 30). *Monthly vital statistics report.* Washington, DC: U.S. Government Printing Office.

NATIONAL INSTITUTE ON ALCOHOL ABUSE AND ALCOHOLISM. (1980, August). *In Brief.*

NATIONAL INSTITUTE ON DRUG ABUSE. (1977, December). Drugs and minorities. *Research Issues, 21.*

NATIONAL INSTITUTE ON DRUG ABUSE. (1980, March). *Theories on drug abuse* (Research Monograph Series 30). Rockville, MD: Author.

NEIMEYER, G. J., & FUKUYAMA, M. (1984). Exploring the content and structure of cross-cultural attitudes. *Counselor Education and Supervision, 23,* 214–224.

NELSON, W. L. (1989). *Retention of entering Black students at Northern Illinois University through facilitation of nonacademic needs to enhance personal development.* Unpublished doctoral dissertation, Northern Illinois University.

NEUGARTEN, B. L. (1968). Adult personality: Toward a psychology of the life cycle. In B. L. Neugarten (Ed.), *Middle age and aging.* Chicago: University of Chicago Press.

NEVAS, S. R. (1977, Fall). Factors in desegregation and integration. *Equal Opportunity Review.* New York: Institute for Urban and Minority Education, Teachers College, Columbia University.

A NEW LOOK AT ABUSE OF OLD PEOPLE. (1983, July 12). *Chicago Tribune,* Sec. 1, p. 6.

NORMAN, D., & ATLAS, J. W. (1978). Decision-making skills: Minority group preparation for the future. *Journal of Non-White Concerns, 6,* 78–86.

NOVAK, M. (1971). *The rise of the unmeltable ethnics.* New York: Macmillan.

O'DONNELL, J. A., VOSS, H., CLAYTON, R., SLATIN, G., & ROOM, R. (1976, February). *Young men and drugs: A nationwide survey* (Research Monograph Series 5). Rockville, MD: National Institute on Drug Abuse.

OLDENQUIST, A. (1986). *The non-suicidal society.* Bloomington: Indiana University Press.

ORNSTEIN, R. E. (1972). *The psychology of consciousness.* San Francisco: W. H. Freeman.

ORTHNER, D. K., BROWN, T., & FERGUSON, D. (1976). Single-parent fatherhood: An emerging life style. *Family Coordinator, 40,* 679–688.

PADILLA, F. M. (1985). *Latino ethnic consciousness.* Notre Dame, IN: University of Notre Dame Press.

PALEY, V. G. (1979). *White teacher.* Cambridge, MA: Harvard University Press.

PALMER, J. O. (1980). *A primer of eclectic psychotherapy.* Pacific Grove, CA: Brooks/Cole.

PARADIS, F. E. (1981). Themes in the training of culturally effective psychotherapists. *Counselor Education and Supervision, 21,* 136–151.

PASSONS, W. R. (1975). *Gestalt approaches in counseling.* New York: Holt, Rinehart & Winston.

PATTERSON, L. E. (1973). The strange verbal world. *Journal of Non-White Concerns, 1,* 95–101.

PAVILON, M. D. (1983, April). *Quality circles: The latest fad in industrial psychology or here to stay?* Presentation at the meeting of the Chicago Psychological Association.

PEARSON, D., & SHAW, S. (1982). *Life extension: A practical scientific approach adding years to your life and life to your years.* New York: Warner Books.

PEATLING, J. H., & TIEDEMAN, D. V. (1977). *Career development: Designing self.* Muncie, IN: Accelerated Development.

PECK, M. S. (1978). *The road less traveled.* New York: Touchstone.

PEDERSEN, P. B., DRAGUNS, J. G., LONNER, W. J., & TRIMBLE, J. E. (EDS.). (1981). *Counseling across cultures* (rev. ed.). Honolulu: University Press of Hawaii.

PEDIGO, J. (1983). Finding the "meaning" of Native American substance abuse: Implications for community prevention. *Personnel and Guidance Journal, 61,* 273–277.

PEELE, S. (1979). Redefining addiction. *Journal of Psychedelic Drugs, 2,* 289–297.

PEELE, S. (1982). Love, sex, drugs and other magical solutions to life. *Journal of Psychoactive Drugs, 14,* 125–131.

PEÑARANDA, O., SYQUIA, S., & TAGATAC, S. (1974). An introduction to Filipino-American literature. In F. Chin, J. P. Chan, L. F. Inada, & S. H. Wong (Eds.), *Aiiieeeee! An anthology of Asian-American writers.* Washington, DC: Howard University Press.

PENFOLD, P. S., & WALKER, G. A. (1983). *Women and the psychiatric paradox.* Montreal, Can.: Eden Press.

PEOPLES, V. Y., & DELL, D. M. (1975). Black and White student preferences for counselor roles. *Journal of Counseling Psychology, 22,* 529–534.

PERLS, F. (1969). *Gestalt therapy verbatim.* Lafayette, CA: Real People Press.

PERLS, F., HEFFERLINE, R., & GOODMAN, P. (1951). *Gestalt therapy: Excitement and growth in the human personality.* New York: Julian Press.

PERRONE, P. A., & KYLE, G. W. (1975). Evaluating the effectiveness of a grade 7–9 career development program. *The Vocational Guidance Quarterly, 23,* 317–323.

PETERSEN, D. M. (1974). Acute drug reactions (overdoses) among females: A race comparison. *Addictive Diseases, 1,* 223–233.

PETERSEN, W. (1978). Chinese Americans and Japanese Americans. In T. Sowell (Ed.), *American ethnic groups.* Washington, DC: Urban Institute Press.

PETRONI, F. A., HIRSCH, E. A., & PETRONI, C. L. (1970). *2, 4, 6, 8, when you gonna integrate?* New York: Behavioral Publications.

PETTIGREW, T. F. (ED.). (1980). *The sociology of race relations.* New York: Free Press.

PHILIPS, S. U. (1983). *The invisible culture.* New York: Longman.

PONTEROTTO, J. G. (1988). Racial consciousness development among white counselor trainees: A stage model. *Journal of Multicultural Counseling and Development, 16,* 146–156.

PORTER, J.D.R. (1971). *Black child, White child: The development of racial attitude.* Cambridge, MA: Harvard University Press.

PORTER, M. R., VIEIRA, T. A., KAPLAN, G. J., HEESCH, J. R., & COLYAR, A. B. (1973). Drug use in Anchorage, Alaska: A survey of 15,634 students in grades 6 through 12—1971. *Journal of the American Medical Association, 223,* 657–664.

PORTERFIELD, E. (1978). *Black and White mixed marriages: An ethnographic study of Black–White families.* Chicago: Nelson-Hall.

POWELL-HOPSON, D., & HOPSON, D. (1990). *Different and wonderful: Raising black children in a race-conscious society.* Englewood Cliffs, NJ: Prentice-Hall.

POWLEDGE, F. (1991). *Free at last? The civil rights movement and the people who made it.* Boston: Little, Brown.

PRATSON, F. J. (1970). *Land of the four directions.* Riverside, CT: Chatham Press.

PRESIDENT'S COMMISSION ON MENTAL HEALTH. (1978). *Task panel reports,* Vol. 3, Appendix. Washington, DC: U.S. Government Printing Office.

PRIBRAM, K. H. (ED.). (1969). *Perception and action.* Baltimore, MD: Penguin Books.

PRICE, J. A. (1976). North American Indian families. In C. H. Mindel & R. W. Habenstein (Eds.), *Ethnic families in America: Patterns and variations.* New York: Elsevier.

RACIST MAY ESCAPE CHARGES. (1982, August 19). *Quad City Times,* p. 26.

RAHE, R. H., LOONEY, J. G., WARD, H. W., TRAN, M. T., & LIU, W. T. (1978). Psychiatric consultation in a Vietnamese refugee camp. *American Journal of Psychiatry, 135,* 185–190.

RAMIREZ, M. (1983). *Psychology of the Americas: Mestizo perspectives on personality and mental health.* New York: Pergamon Press.

RAMIREZ, M. (1991). *Psychotherapy and counseling with minorities: A cognitive approach to individual and cultural differences.* New York: Pergamon Press.

RAYMAN, J. R., & BOWLSBEY, J. H. (1977). Discover: A model for a systematic career guidance program. *The Vocational Guidance Quarterly, 26,* 3–12.

RAYMAN, J. R., BRYSON, D. L., & BOWLSBEY, J. H. (1978). The field trial of Discover: A new computerized interactive guidance system. *The Vocational Guidance Quarterly, 26,* 349–360.

REDFIELD, R. (1941). *The folk culture of Yucatan.* Chicago: University of Chicago Press.

REID, I. (1939). *The Negro immigrant.* New York: Columbia University Press.

RESNICK, H. L. (1980). Suicide. In H. I. Kaplan, A. M. Freedman, & B. J. Sadock (Eds.), *The comprehensive textbook of psychiatry* (3rd ed.). Baltimore: Williams & Wilkins.

REY, K. H. (1970). *The Haitian family.* New York: Community Service Society.

REYNOLDS, D. K., & KALISH, R. A. (1974). Anticipation of futurity as a function of ethnicity and age. *Journal of Gerontology, 29,* 224–231.

REYNOLDS, D. K., KALISH, R. A., & FARBEROW, N. L. (1975). A cross-ethnic study of suicide attitudes and expectations in the United States. In N. L. Farberow (Ed.), *Suicide in different cultures.* Baltimore: University Park Press.

RICHARDS, B., & OXEREOK, C. (1978). Counseling Alaskan natives. In G. R. Walz & L. Benjamin (Eds.), *Transcultural counseling: Needs, programs and techniques.* New York: Human Sciences Press.

RICHARDSON, E. H. (1981). Cultural and historical perspectives in counseling American Indians. In D. W. Sue, *Counseling the culturally different.* New York: Wiley.

RIESMAN, D. (1950). *The lonely crowd*. New Haven, CT: Yale University Press.

RIKER, H. C. (1980). Older persons. In N. A. Vacc & J. P. Wittmer (Eds.), *Let me be me*. Muncie, IN: Accelerated Development.

ROBBINS, J. H. (1990). Knowing yourself: Women tell their stories in psychotherapy. New York: Plenum Press.

ROBERTS, A. R. (1975). *Self-destructive behavior*. Springfield, IL: Charles C Thomas.

ROBINS, L. N. (1976). Estimating addiction rates and locating target populations: How decomposition into three steps helps. In J. D. Rittenhouse (Ed.), *The epidemiology of heroin and other narcotic drugs*. Rockville, MD: The National Clearinghouse on Drug Abuse.

ROE, A. (1972). Perspectives on vocational development. In J. M. Whiteley & A. Resnikoff (Eds.), *Perspectives on vocational development*. Washington, DC: American Personnel and Guidance Association.

ROGERS, C. (1942). *Counseling and psychotherapy*. Boston: Houghton Mifflin.

ROGERS, C. (1951). *Client-centered therapy*. Boston: Houghton Mifflin.

ROGERS, C. (1957). The necessary and sufficient conditions of therapeutic personality change. *Journal of Consulting Psychology, 21*, 95–103.

ROGERS, C. (1961). *On becoming a person*. Boston: Houghton Mifflin.

ROGERS, C. (1969). *Freedom to learn*. Columbus, OH: Charles E. Merrill.

ROGERS, C. (1970). *Carl Rogers on encounter groups*. New York: Harper & Row.

ROGERS, C. (1972). *Becoming partners*. New York: Dell.

ROGERS, C. (1977). *Carl Rogers on personal power: Inner strength and its revolutionary impact*. New York: Delacorte.

ROGERS, C. (1980). *A way of being*. Palo Alto, CA: Houghton Mifflin.

ROKEACH, M. (1960). *The open and closed mind: Investigation into the nature of belief systems and personality systems*. New York: Basic Books.

ROLLE, A. F. (1972). *The American Italians: Their history and culture*. Belmont, CA: Wadsworth.

ROLLE, A. F. (1980). *The Italian-Americans: Troubled roots*. New York: Free Press.

ROMAN, P. (1981). From employee alcoholism to employer assistance. *Journal of Alcohol Studies, 47*, 165–173.

ROSENHAN, D. L. (1973). On being sane in insane places. *Science*, pp. 250–258.

ROSENTHAL, K. M., & KESHET, H. F. (1978). The not-quite stepmother. *Psychology Today, 12*, pp. 82–86, 100–101.

ROSENTHAL, R., & JACOBSON, L. (1968). *Pygmalion in the classroom*. New York: Holt.

ROSENTHAL, V. (ED.). (1971). *Illinois Psychological Association Directory of Professional Services, 1971–1972*. Chicago: Illinois Psychological Association.

ROSS, D. B. (1984). A cross-cultural comparison of adult development. *Personnel and Guidance Journal, 62*, 418–421.

ROWAN, C. T. (1990). *Breaking barriers: A memoir*. New York: Little, Brown.

RUEVERI, U. (1979). *Networking families in crisis*. New York: Human Sciences Press.

RUIZ, A. S. (1975). Chicano group catalysts. *Personnel and Guidance Journal, 53*, 462–466.

RUIZ, R. A. (1981). Cultural and historical perspectives in counseling Hispanics. In D. W. Sue, *Counseling the culturally different*. New York: Wiley.

RUIZ, R. A., & PADILLA, A. M. (1977). Counseling Latinos. *Personnel and Guidance Journal, 55*, 401–408.

RUSSELL, R. D. (ED.) (1981). Education in the 80s. *Health Education*. Washington, DC: National Education Association

RYAN, W. (1971). *Blaming the victim*. New York: Pantheon.

SAINSBURY, P. (1955). *Suicide in London*. London: The Institute of Psychiatry.

SAMPLES, B. (1975, February). Learning with the whole brain. *Human Behavior*, pp. 17–23.

SARASON, S. B. (1977). *Work, aging, and social change*. New York: Free Press.

SAUER, W. (1977). Morale of the urban aged: A regression analysis by race. *Journal of Gerontology, 32,* 600–608.

SCHAIE, K. W., ORCHOWSKY, S., & PARHAM, I. A. (1982). Measuring age and sociocultural change: The case of race and life satisfaction. In R. C. Manuel (Ed.), *Minority aging*. Westport, CT: Greenwood Press.

SCHIAVO, G. E. (1975). *The Italians in Chicago: A study of Americanization*. New York: Arno Press.

SCHLESINGER, A. M., JR. (1991). *The disuniting of America: Reflections on a multicultural society*. Knoxville, TN: Whittle Direct Books.

SCHMIDHAUSER, J. R. (1959). The justices of the Supreme Court: A collective portrait. *Midwest Journal of Political Science, 3,* 1–57.

SCHOFIELD, W. (1964). *Psychotherapy: The purchase of friendship*. Englewood Cliffs, NJ: Prentice-Hall.

THE SCHOOLING OF ILLEGAL IMMIGRANTS. (1982, June 18). *Chicago Tribune*, Sec. 1, p. 8.

SCHULTZ, D. (1981). *Theories of personality* (2nd ed.). Pacific Grove, CA: Brooks/Cole.

SCHWARTZ, S. (1951). Mate-selection among New York City's Chinese males, 1931–38. *American Journal of Sociology, 56,* 562–568.

SELIGMAN, L. (1977). Haitians: A neglected minority. *Personnel and Guidance Journal, 55,* 409–411.

SELIGMAN, L. (1983). An introduction to the new DSM-III. *Personnel and Guidance Journal, 61,* 601–605.

SELIGMAN, M.S.P. (1975). *Helplessness: On depression, development, and death*. San Francisco: W. H. Freeman.

SELYE, H. (ED.). (1980). *Selye's guide to stress research*, Vol. 1. New York: Van Nostrand Reinhold.

SERVICE, E. (1962). *Primitive social organization*. New York: Random House.

SETON, E. T. (1936). *The gospel of the red man*. New York: Doubleday.

SEVERINSEN, K. N. (1979). Should career education be founded in the Protestant Ethic? *Personnel and Guidance Journal, 58,* 111–114.

SEWARD, G. H. (1972). *Psychotherapy and culture conflict* (2nd ed.). New York: Ronald Press.

SEWARD, G. H., & WILLIAMSON, R. (EDS.). (1970). *Sex roles in a changing society*. New York: Random House.

SHADE, B. J. (1978). Social-psychological characteristics of achieving Black children. *Negro Educational Review, 29,* 80–86.

SHAYCROFT, M. (1967). *Project Talent—The high school years: Growth in cognitive skills*. Pittsburgh, PA: American Institute for Research, School of Education, University of Pittsburgh.

SHEA, S. C. (1988). *Psychiatric interviewing*. Philadelphia: W.B. Saunders Co.

SHEEHY, G. (1976). *Passages: Predictable crises of adult life*. New York: Dutton.

SHERMAN, J. (1983, July 10). 166,000 couples are giving Black-White marriages a new look—normality. *Chicago Tribune*, Sec. 15, D, p. 8.

SIEGELMAN, E. Y. (1983). *Personal risk*. New York: Harper & Row.

SIMMONS, L. W. (1945). *The role of the aged in primitive society*. New Haven, CT: Yale University Press.

SINICK, D. (1977). Can vocational counselors change society? *The Vocational Guidance Quarterly, 25,* 245–251.

SLABY, A. E., LIEB, J., & TANCREDI, L. R. (1981). *Handbook of psychiatric emergencies*. Garden City, NY: Medical Examination Publishing Co.

SLOCUM, W. L. (1974). *Occupational careers*. Chicago: Aldine-Atherton.

SMITH, D. (1982). Trends in counseling and psychotherapy. *American Psychologist, 37,* 802–809.

SMITH, E. J. (1975). Profile of the Black individual in vocational literature. *Journal of Vocational Behavior, 6,* 41–59.

SMITH, E. J. (1981). Cultural and historical perspectives in counseling Blacks. In D. W. Sue (Ed.), *Counseling the culturally different.* New York: Wiley.

SMITH, W. D., BURLEW, A. R., MOSLEY, M. H., & WHITNEY, W. M.(1978). *Minority issues in mental health.* Reading, MA: Addison-Wesley.

SOLOMON, B. M. (1965). *Ancestors and immigrants.* New York: Wiley.

SOME RADICAL IDEAS FROM THE RIGHT. (1982, September 12). *Chicago Tribune,* Sec. 2, p. 4.

SOWELL, T. (1974, Spring). Black excellence: The case of Dunbar High School. *The Public Interest,* pp. 5–7, 10–12.

SOWELL, T. (1978). Three Black histories. In T. Sowell (Ed.), *American ethnic groups* (pp. 7–64). Washington, DC: The Urban Institute.

SOWELL, T. (1982). *Weber* and *Bakke,* and the presuppositions of "affirmative action." In W. E. Block & M. A. Walker (Eds.), *Discrimination, affirmative action, and equal opportunity.* Vancouver, British Columbia, Canada: The Fraser Institute.

SPENCER, M. H. (1980). *Contemporary microeconomics* (4th ed.). New York: Worth.

SPERRY, L. (1989). Contemporary approaches to brief therapy: A comparative analysis. *Individual Psychology, 45,* 3–25.

SPERRY, R. W. (1975, August 9). Left-brain, right-brain. *Saturday Review,* pp. 30–33.

SPINDLER, G. (ED.). (1963). *Education and culture.* New York: Holt, Rinehart & Winston.

SPORT PSYCHOLOGY COMES OF AGE IN THE '80S. (1982, September). *APA Monitor,* p. 1.

STAPLES, R. (1976). The Black American family. In C. H. Mindel & R. W. Habenstein (Eds.), *Ethnic families in America: Patterns and variations.* New York: Elsevier.

STARK, S., & MCEVOY J., III. (1970, November). Middle-class violence. *Psychology Today,* pp. 52–54, 110–112.

STEELE, S. (1990). *The content of our character: A new vision of race in America.* New York: St. Martin's Press.

STEINER, C. M. (1971). *Games alcoholics play: The analysis of life scripts.* New York: Grove Press.

STEINMETZ, S. K., & STRAUS, M. A. (EDS.). (1974). *Violence in the family.* New York: Harper & Row.

STENGEL, E. (1970). *Suicide and attempted suicide* (rev. ed.). Middlesex, England: Penguin Books.

STEWARD, J. H. (1955). *Theory of culture change.* Urbana, IL: University of Illinois Press.

STEWART, E. C. (1972). *American cultural patterns: A cross-cultural perspective.* Pittsburgh, PA: University of Pittsburgh, Society for Intercultural Education, Training and Research.

STEWART, E. C. (1981). Cultural sensitivities in counseling. In P. B. Pedersen, J. G. Draguns, W. J. Lonner, & J. E. Trimble (Eds.), *Counseling across cultures* (rev. ed.). Honolulu: University Press of Hawaii.

STEWART, L. H., & WARNATH, C. F. (1965). *The counselor and society: A cultural approach.* Boston: Houghton Mifflin.

STIKES, C. S. (1972). Culturally specific counseling: The Black client. *Journal of Non-White Concerns, 1,* 4–8.

STONE, A. (1975). *Mental health and law: A system in transition.* No. 75176. Washington, DC: U.S. Department of Health, Education and Welfare.

STONE, W. O. (1973). *Transcendent counseling for Blacks: A modular-conceptual theory.* Paper presented at the second annual Region V, TRIO conference, Fontanna, WI.

STORR, A. (1973). *C. G. Jung.* New York: Viking Press.

STRAUS, M. A., GELLES, R. J., & STEINMETZ, S. K. (1980). *Behind closed doors: Violence in the American family.* Garden City, NY: Anchor Press/Doubleday.

STUART-KOTZE, R. (1980). *Introduction to organizational behavior.* Reston, VA: Reston.

STURDIVANT, S. (1980). *Therapy with women.* New York: Springer.

SUE, D. (1980). Asian-Americans. In N. A. Vacc & J. P. Wittmer (Eds.), *Let me be me.* Muncie, IN: Accelerated Development.

SUE, D. W. (1977). Counseling the culturally different: A conceptual analysis. *Personnel and Guidance Journal, 55,* 422–425.

SUE, D. W., & FRANK, A. C. (1973). Chinese and Japanese American college males. *Journal of Social Issues, 29,* 129–148.

SUE, D. W., & SUE, D. (1990). *Counseling the culturally different: Theory and practice* (2nd ed.). New York: Wiley.

SUE, S., & CHIN. (1976, July 29–August 1). Report of the National Asian American Psychology Training Conference, Long Beach, CA.

SUE, S., & MCKINNEY, H. (1975). Asian Americans in the community mental health care system. *American Journal of Orthopsychiatry, 45,* 111–118.

SUE, S., MCKINNEY, H., ALLEN, D., & HALL, J. (1974). Mental health delivery of community services to Black and White clients. *Journal of Consulting and Clinical Psychology, 42,* 794–801.

SUNDBERG, N. (1977). *Assessment of persons.* Englewood Cliffs, NJ: Prentice-Hall.

SUNG, B. L. (1990). *Chinese American intermarriage.* Staten Island, NY: Center for Migration Studies.

SUPER, D. E. (1957). *The psychology of careers.* New York: Harper & Row.

SUTICH, A. J. (1969). Some basic considerations regarding transpersonal psychology. *Journal of Transpersonal Psychology, 1,* 11–20.

SZASZ, T. S. (1970). The crime of commitment. *Readings in clinical psychology today.* Del Mar, CA: CRM Books.

SZASZ, T. S. (1974). *The myth of mental illness: Foundations of a theory of personal conduct* (rev. ed.). New York: Harper & Row.

TAINSRI, R., & AXELSON, J. A. (1990). Group sensitivity training with Thai workers and managers as a process to promote inter- and intrapersonal relations, and work performance. *International Journal for the Advancement of Counselling, 13,* 219–226.

TAWNEY, R. H. (1926). *Religion and the rise of capitalism.* London: John Murray.

TAYLOR, S. P. (1982). Mental health and successful coping among aged Black women. In R. C. Manuel (Ed.), *Minority aging.* Westport, CT: Greenwood Press.

TERRY, R. W. (1970). *For Whites only.* Grand Rapids, MI: Eerdmans.

TESSMAN, L. H. (1978). *Children of parting parents.* New York: Aronson.

THOMAS, J. J. (1976). Realism and socioeconomic status (SES) of occupational plans of low SES Black and White male adolescents. *Journal of Counseling Psychology, 23,* 46–49.

THOMAS, K. R., BRITTON, J. O., & KRAVETZ, S. (1974). Vocational rehabilitation counselors view the Judeo-Christian work ethic. *Rehabilitation Counseling Bulletin, 18,* 105–111.

THOMAS, K. R., CARTER, S. A., & BRITTON, J. O. (1982). The Protestant work ethic, disability, and the rehabilitation student. *Counselor Education and Supervision, 21,* 269–273.

THONI, R. J., & OLSSON, P. M. (1975). A systematic career development program in a liberal arts college. *Personnel and Guidance Journal, 53,* 672–675.

THORESEN, C. E., & HAMILTON, J. A. (1972). Peer social modeling in promoting career behaviors. *The Vocational Guidance Quarterly, 20,* 210–216.

TIEDEMAN, D. V. (1961). Decision and vocational development: A paradigm and its implications. *Personnel and Guidance Journal, 40,* 15–21.

TIEDEMAN, D. V. (1984, May 10). Personal communication.

TIEDEMAN, D. V., ET AL. (1967). *Information system for vocational decisions: Annual report, 1966–67.* Cambridge, MA: Harvard Graduate School of Education.

TIEDEMAN, D. V., ET AL. (1968). *Information system for vocational decisions: Annual report, 1967–68.* Cambridge, MA: Harvard Graduate School of Education.

TIEDEMAN, D. V., & MILLER-TIEDEMAN, A. (1975). *A choice and decision process and careers.* DeKalb, IL: ERIC Clearinghouse on Career Education.

TIEDEMAN, D. V., & O'HARA, R. P. (1963). *Career development: Choice and adjustment.* New York: College Entrance Examination Board.

TIGER, R. L. (1978). *The Filipino community in Los Angeles: A summary of attitudes and activities.* Unpublished doctoral dissertation, University of California–Los Angeles.

TOONIES, F. (1957). *Community and society: Gemeinschaft and Gesellschaft* (C. P. Loomis, Ed. & Trans.). New York: Harper & Row.

TRAN, N. C. (1981, May 11–12). Counseling Vietnamese women in transition. *Helping Indochinese families in transition conference* [Compiled proceedings]. Lincoln: University of Nebraska.

TRAN, T. N. (1976). Vietnamese refugees: The trauma of exile. *Civil Rights Digest, 9,* 59–62.

TREVOR-ROPER, H. R. (1963). Religion, the Reformation and social change. *Historical Studies, 4,* 18–44.

TRIMBLE, J. E. (1981). Value differentials and their importance in counseling Indians. In P. B. Pedersen, J. G. Draguns, W. J. Lonner, & J. E. Trimble (Eds.), *Counseling across cultures.* Honolulu: University Press of Hawaii.

TRUAX, C. B., & CARKHUFF, R. R. (1967). *Toward effective counseling and psychotherapy: Training and practice.* Chicago: Aldine-Atherton.

TUCKER, R. N., & GUNNINGS, T. S. (1974). Counseling Black youth: A quest for legitimacy. *Journal of Non-White Concerns, 2,* 208–216.

TUCKER, S. J. (1973). Action counseling: An accountability procedure for counseling the oppressed. *Journal of Non-White Concerns, 2,* 35–41.

TURNER, J. H., & SINGLETON, R., JR. (1978). A theory of ethnic oppression: Toward a reintegration of cultural and structural concepts in ethnic relations theory. *Social Forces, 56,* 1001–1018.

TYLER, G. (ED.). (1975). *Mexican-Americans tomorrow: Educational and economic perspectives.* Albuquerque: University of New Mexico Press.

TYLER, S. L. (1973). *A history of Indian policy.* Washington, DC: U.S. Department of the Interior, Bureau of Indian Affairs.

UNIVERSAL ALMANAC, 1991. (1990). John W. Wright (Ed.). Kansas City, MO: Andrews & McMeel.

U.S. BUREAU OF THE CENSUS. (1981, May). *Supplementary reports* (PC80-S1-1). Washington, DC: U.S. Government Printing Office.

U.S. BUREAU OF THE CENSUS. (1981, June). *Population profile of the United States: 1980* (Current Population Reports, Series P-20, No. 363). Washington, DC: U.S. Government Printing Office.

U.S. BUREAU OF THE CENSUS. (1982a, March). *Ancestry and language in the United States,* (Current Population Reports, Series P-23, No. 116). Washington, DC: U.S. Government Printing Office.

U.S. BUREAU OF THE CENSUS. (1982b). *Characteristics of the population below the poverty level: 1980* (Current Population Reports, Series P-60, No. 133). Washington, DC: U.S. Government Printing Office.

U.S. BUREAU OF THE CENSUS. (1990a). *Household and family characteristics: March 1990 and 1989.* (Current Population Reports, Series P-20, No. 447). Washington, DC: U.S. Government Printing Office.

U.S. BUREAU OF THE CENSUS. (1990b). *Marital status and living arrangements: March 1990.* (Current Population Reports, Series P-20, No. 450). Washington, DC: U.S. Government Printing Office.

U.S. BUREAU OF THE CENSUS. (1991a). *Educational attainment in the United States: March 1989 and 1988.* (Current Population Reports, Series P-20, No. 451). Washington, DC: U.S. Government Printing Office.

U.S. BUREAU OF THE CENSUS. (1991b). *Population profile of the United States: 1991.* (Current Population Reports, Series P-23, No. 173). Washington, DC: U.S. Government Printing Office.

U.S. BUREAU OF THE CENSUS. (1991c). *Statistical abstract of the United States: 1991.* Washington, DC: U.S. Government Printing Office.

U.S. COMMISSION ON CIVIL DISORDERS. (1968). *Report of the U.S. Commission on Civil Rights.* Washington, DC: U.S. Government Printing Office.

U.S. CONFERENCE OF MAYORS. (1991). Washington, DC: Author.

U.S. DEPARTMENT OF COMMERCE. (1991, March 11). Bureau of the Census *News*, CB 91-100. Washington, DC: U.S. Department of Commerce.

U.S. DEPARTMENT OF EDUCATION. (1990). *Digest of education statistics,* (National Center for Education Statistics). Washington, DC: U.S. Government Printing Office.

U.S. DEPARTMENT OF HEALTH AND HUMAN SERVICES. (1983, December). *Fifth special report to the U.S. Congress on alcohol and health* (National Institute on Alcohol Abuse and Alcoholism). Washington, DC: U.S. Government Printing Office.

U.S. DEPARTMENT OF HEALTH AND HUMAN SERVICES. (1990, November). *Monthly Vital Statistics Report.* National Center for Health Statistics. Washington, DC: U.S. Government Printing Office.

U.S. DEPARTMENT OF LABOR, BUREAU OF LABOR STATISTICS. (1980, November). *Employment and earnings.* Washington, DC: U.S. Government Printing Office.

U.S. DEPARTMENT OF LABOR, BUREAU OF LABOR STATISTICS. (1990, April). *Occupational projections and training data* (Bulletin 2351). Washington, DC: U.S. Government Printing Office.

U.S. EQUAL EMPLOYMENT OPPORTUNITY COMMISSION. (1991). *1990 Report: Job Patterns for Minorities and Women in Private Industry.* Washington, DC: U.S. Government Printing Office.

VAILLANT, G., & MCARTHUR, C. (1972, November). Natural history of male psychological health: I. The adult life cycle from 18–50. *Seminars in Psychiatry, 4.*

VAN DEN BERGHE, P. L. (1958). The dynamics of racial prejudice: An ideal-type dichotomy. *Social Forces, 31,* 138–141.

VAN DEN BERGHE, P. L. (ED.). (1972). *Intergroup relations.* New York: Basic Books.

VOCI, F. (1982, February 4). *Multicultural education: A global awareness.* Presentation given at Northern Illinois University, by Dr. Voci, Coordinator, Midwest National Origin Desegregation Assistance Center, University of Wisconsin–Milwaukee.

VONTRESS, C. E. (1976). Counseling the racial and ethnic minorities. In G. S. Belkin (Ed.), *Counseling: Directions in theory and practice.* Dubuque, IA: Kendall/Hunt.

WADE, R. C. (1967). *Slavery in the cities.* New York: Oxford University Press.

WALFORD, R. L. (1983). *Maximum life span.* New York: Norton.

WALLECHINSKY, D., & WALLACE, I. (EDS.). (1975). *The people's almanac.* Garden City, NY: Doubleday.

WALLERSTEIN, J. S. (1977). Responses of the preschool child in divorce: Those who cope. In M. F. McMillan & S. Henao (Eds.), *Child psychiatry: Treatment and research.* New York: Brunner/Mazel.

WALLERSTEIN, J., & BLAKESLEE, S. (1989). *Second chances: Men, women and children a decade after divorce.* New York: Basic Books.

WALLERSTEIN, J., & KELLY, J. B. (1990). *Surviving the breakup: How children and parents cope with divorce.* New York: Basic Books.

WARNATH, C. F. (1975). Vocational theories: Directions to nowhere. *Personnel and Guidance Journal, 53,* 422–428.

WEBB, J. P., & WILLARD, W. (1975). Six American Indian patterns of suicide. In N. L. Farberow (Ed.), *Suicide in different cultures.* Baltimore: University Park Press.

WEBER, M. (1930). *The Protestant Ethic and the spirit of capitalism* (T. Parsons, Trans.). New York: Scribner's. (Original work published 1904–1905)

WEBER, R. A. (1975). *Management.* Homewood, IL: Richard D. Irwin.

WEBSTER, S. W. (ED.). (1972). [Interview with Stanford M. Lyman]. *Ethnic minority groups.* Scranton, PA: Intext Educational Publishers.

WEIBEL, K. (1977). *Mirror, mirror: Images of women reflected in popular culture.* Garden City, NY: Anchor Books.

WEIL, A., & ROSEN, W. (1983). *Chocolate to morphine: Understanding mind-active drugs.* Boston: Houghton Mifflin.

WEINGARTEN, P. (1982, April 18). The not-me generation: Can you get to the top of the corporate ladder if you only climb from 9 to 5? *Chicago Tribune Magazine,* p. 20.

WEISSMAN, M. M. (1977). *Depressive disorders.* Working paper prepared for the President's Commission on Mental Health, Yale University.

WERNICK, W. (1982). The ethnic imprint of career options. *Journal of Career Education, 8,* 169–172.

WHITE, A. (1983). A factor analysis of the Counseling-Orientation Preference Scale (COS). *Counselor Education and Supervision, 23,* 142–148.

WHITE, L. A. (1959a). *The evolution of culture.* New York: McGraw-Hill.

WHITE, L. A. (1959b). The concept of culture. *American Anthropologist, 61,* 227–251.

WHITTAKER, J. O. (1982). Alcohol and the Standing Rock Sioux tribe. *Journal of Studies on Alcohol, 43,* 191–199.

WHYTE, W. F. (1956). *The organization man.* New York: Simon & Schuster.

WILLIAMS, J. E., & MORELAND, J. K. (1976). *Race, color, and the young child.* Chapel Hill, NC: University of North Carolina Press.

WILLIAMS, R. L. (1972). On Black intelligence. *Journal of Non-White Concerns, 1,* 9–14.

WILLIAMS, R. L. (1975). Developing cultural specific assessment devices: An empirical rationale. In R. L. Williams (Ed.), *Ebonics: The true language of Black folks.* St. Louis: Institute of Black Studies.

WILLIAMS, T. R. (1972). *Human culture transmitted: An introduction to the study of the socialization process.* St. Louis: C. V. Mosby.

WILLIE, C. V. (1981). *The ivory and ebony towers.* Lexington, MA: Lexington Books.

WILSON, M., & WILSON, S. (EDS.). (1975). *Drugs in American life.* New York: H. W. Wilson.

WINERIP, M. (1981, December 31). Gentle victims: Haitian refugees fenced in by fear. *Chicago Tribune,* Sec. 1, p. 13.

WINTERS, R. A. (1972). Another view of the American work ethic. *The Vocational Guidance Quarterly, 21,* 31–35.

WIRTH, L. (1928). *The ghetto.* Chicago: University of Chicago Press.

WOEHRER, C. A. (1978). Cultural pluralism in American families: The influence of ethnicity on social aspects of the aged. *The Family Coordinator, 27,* 329–340.

WOLLACK, S., GOODALE, J. G., WIJTING, J. P., & SMITH, P. C. (1971). Development of the survey of work values. *Journal of Applied Psychology, 55,* 331–338.

WOLPE, J. (1958). *Psychotherapy by reciprocal inhibition.* Stanford, CA: Stanford University Press.

WOODCOCK, P. R., & HERMAN, A. (1978). Fostering career awareness in tenth-grade girls. *The School Counselor, 25,* 256–264.

WOODSON, C. G. (1919). *The education of the Negro prior to 1861*. Washington, DC: The Associated Publishers.

WOOL, H. (1976). What's wrong with work in America? A review essay. *The Vocational Guidance Quarterly, 24*, 159–164.

YALOM, I. (1981). *Existential psychotherapy*. New York: Basic Books.

YANG, K., & BOND, M. (1980). Ethnic affirmation by Chinese bilinguals. *Journal of Cross-Cultural Psychology, 2*, 411–425.

YANKELOVICH, D. (1981). *New rules: Searching for self-fulfillment in a world turned upside down*. New York: Random House.

ZANGWILL, I. (1910). *The melting pot*. New York: Macmillan.

ZUNIN, L., & ZUNIN, N. (1972). *Contact: The first four minutes*. New York: Ballantine.

ZUNKER, V. G. (1990). *Career counseling: Applied concepts of life planning*. Pacific Grove, CA: Brooks/Cole.

ZYCHOWICZ, M. J. (1975). *American Indian teachings as a philosophical base for counseling and psychotherapy*. Unpublished doctoral dissertation, Northern Illinois University.

NAME
INDEX